THE FREEDMAN IN THE ROMAN WORLD

Freedmen occupied a complex and often problematic place in Roman society between slaves on the one hand and freeborn citizens on the other. Playing an extremely important role in the economic life of the Roman world, they were also a key instrument for replenishing and even increasing the size of the citizen body. This book presents an original synthesis, for the first time covering both republic and empire in a single volume. While providing up-to-date discussions of most significant aspects of the phenomenon, the book also offers a new understanding of the practice of manumission, and its role in the organisation of slave labour and the Roman economy, as well as the deep-seated ideological concerns to which it gave rise. It locates the freedman in a broader social and economic context, explaining the remarkable popularity of manumission in the Roman world.

HENRIK MOURITSEN is Professor of Roman History at King's College London. He has published widely on Roman history, including local politics, Pompeii and Ostia, freedmen, Latin epigraphy, Roman Italy, and republican politics. His other books include *Elections, Magistrates and Municipal Elite: Studies in Pompeian Epigraphy* (1988), *Italian Unification: A Study in Ancient and Modern Historiography* (1998), and *Plebs and Politics in the Late Roman Republic* (2001).

THE FREEDMAN IN THE ROMAN WORLD

HENRIK MOURITSEN

CAMBRIDGE
UNIVERSITY PRESS

CAMBRIDGE UNIVERSITY PRESS
Cambridge, New York, Melbourne, Madrid, Cape Town, Singapore,
São Paulo, Delhi, Dubai, Tokyo, Mexico City

Cambridge University Press
The Edinburgh Building, Cambridge CB2 8RU, UK

Published in the United States of America by Cambridge University Press, New York

www.cambridge.org
Information on this title: www.cambridge.org/9780521856133

First published 2011

Printed in the United Kingdom at the University Press, Cambridge

A catalogue record for this publication is available from the British Library

Library of Congress Cataloguing in Publication data
Mouritsen, Henrik.
The freedman in the Roman world / Henrik Mouritsen.
p.   cm.
Includes bibliographical references and index.
ISBN 978-0-521-85613-3 (hardback)
1. Freedmen – Rome – History.   2. Slaves – Emancipation – Rome.   I. Title.
HT731.M68   2011
306.3′620937 – dc22   2010038875

ISBN 978-0-521-85613-3 Hardback

Contents

Acknowledgements

This study of Roman manumission was made possible through the generous grant of a Major Research Fellowship by the Leverhulme Trust which allowed me to devote three years to the project. During my work on the freedmen I have received valuable help and advice from many scholars, among them Jens Barschdorf, Simon Corcoran, Sophie Lunn-Rockliffe, Roland Mayer, Elizabeth Meyer, April Pudsey, Dominic Rathbone, Walter Scheidel, and Michael Trapp. Claire Holleran, Margaret Robb, and Jane Webster read the whole manuscript, offering important feedback and pointing out mistakes. Margaret Robb also provided invaluable assistance with the index. Wilfried Nippel and the Humboldt University kindly provided me with hospitality and a visiting fellowship during my stay in Berlin in May 2008. Papers related to the project were presented at seminars and conferences at the universities of Hamburg, St Andrews, Newcastle, Mannheim, Stanford, and McMaster, to whose organisers and audiences I would like to express my thanks. I would also like to thank two of the three anonymous readers for Cambridge University Press, as well as my editor Michael Sharp and his helpful staff. My greatest thanks go to Peter Garnsey for his unfailing support throughout the process and his sharp eye for any weakness of argument which has done much to improve the final result. Finally, I would like to thank my family for their strong support and interest in my work.

CHAPTER I

Introduction
Approaching Roman freedmen

Adding another volume to the ever-expanding mass of scholarly literature on the ancient world requires some justification. But in the case of the Roman freedman[1] there does seem to be a surprising gap; for although most works on Roman history or culture make passing references to freedmen in some context or other, few of them have tried to grasp the nature of Roman manumission and its wider function within Roman society. Attempts to deal comprehensively with the question of Roman manumission are relatively rare, a notable exception being Keith Hopkins' chapter in *Conquerors and Slaves*.[2] Moreover a general synthesis of the Roman freedman, covering both republic and empire, has never been ventured, and the last book-length treatment of the imperial period was Duff's problematic work of 1928. By contrast, the republic is much better served with Treggiari's fundamental monograph (1969) and Fabre's detailed study of the patron–freedman relationship (1981). Most dedicated studies have dealt with specific, often highly technical aspects of manumission, particularly the legal ones, or with individual groups of freedmen, above all those of the emperor.[3]

The apparent reluctance to tackle the phenomenon as a whole merits closer consideration. For once the reason cannot be lack of evidence, since few groups in Roman society are more fully documented or covered by such a diverse range of sources, legal, literary, epigraphic, and documentary. In fact, the sheer scale of the evidence may have militated against a synthetic approach, not least in the current age of increasing academic specialisation.

---

[1] Throughout this study 'freedmen' will be used as convenient shorthand for both men and women, and unless otherwise stated it covers freed persons of either gender.

[2] Hopkins (1978). Valuable syntheses were outlined by Bradley (1984a) 81–112; Andreau (1993); Los (1995), all anticipated by Strack's perceptive article from 1914.

[3] The essential studies of Roman slave law remain Buckland (1908) and Watson (1987). For the imperial freedmen see Chantraine (1967); Boulvert (1970), (1974); Weaver (1972). Much scholarly attention has also been paid to the *Augustales*, for which see chapter 7.

But part of the explanation may also be sought in the one factor which also makes a reassessment of the subject so much more urgent, namely the ambivalence about freedmen still discernible in much of the modern scholarship. Since the first serious studies of slavery and manumission appeared in the nineteenth century, the freed slaves have been approached with a certain unease, which might explain some of the neglect they have suffered.

The modern image of the Roman freedman has rarely been a flattering one. In the nineteenth century Wallon presented a thoroughly negative vision of manumission, and Mommsen associated the freedmen with the corruption of the Roman plebs.[4] To Warde Fowler manumission led to 'the introduction into the Roman State of a poisonous element of terrible volume and power'.[5] The most notorious denunciation, however, remains Duff's still widely used monograph whose main thesis is the contention that race-mixture, following large-scale manumission of slaves, diluted the old Roman stock and eventually caused the fall of the Roman empire. His work is littered with racial, ethnic, and social stereotypes,[6] and while his contemporaries may have queried the nature of the freedman's negative influence, they tended to agree on the end result. Thus, Gordon argued the damage done to Roman society from manumission was moral rather than racial.[7] She declared that even 'Deserving slaves would not have been free from the vulgarity of outlook which was one of the worst evils of the empire, and the canker of slavery would have remained.' 'They were not responsible for the evils of Roman civilisation, however much they may have helped to intensify them.'[8] Importantly, her disparaging comments on freedmen contrast with a positive view of Roman slaves, typically regarded with much greater sympathy.

This position might seem contradictory but already in 1847 Wallon had provided the key to reconciling them. As a staunch abolitionist and

---

[4] Wallon (1847) 2.385–438; Mommsen (1875) 3.511–12.   [5] Warde Fowler (1908) 232.

[6] Duff's racism was far from unique, cf. e.g. Meyer (1913) 6, who referred to 'der dem Orientalen eigenen Gerissenheit und Skrupellosigkeit', and 'orientalischer Geriebenheit und Frechheit', 59. Barrow (1928) 208–29, 215, described Rome falling 'victim to the insidious poison of Oriental languor, which rouses itself only to domineer'. Last (1934) 429, 464, used expressions such as 'uncontrolled contamination' and 'infiltration of foreign blood'. See also Frank (1916).

[7] Gordon (1927) 182: 'The inferiority of the servile element did not lie in its racial character.' She later took issue with 'vulgar prejudices' against Orientals, referring to saints Paul and John as exceptions to the stereotype: (1931) 77. Her disavowal of racism was not entirely consistent, however, since she also assumed that freeborn aristocrats naturally had more dignified features than the vulgar-looking freedmen: (1927) 181; cf. Mouritsen (1996) 140.

[8] Gordon (1931) 77, also speaking of the 'moral handicap of servile origin', and the 'moral taint which would cling about the descendants of freedmen': (1927) 182.

opponent of contemporary slavery in the New World, Wallon denounced ancient slavery as inherently evil, but precisely for that reason he also saw it as degrading to those subjected to it.[9] The paradoxical result was that although enslavement was unjust, releasing people from it posed a danger to society because of its corrupting effect on those who had endured it. This logic was, as I shall argue, directly inspired by the Romans' own perception of freedom and virtue and has informed the views of scholars such as Mommsen, Warde Fowler, and Gordon who condemned both slavery and its victims.[10] Thus, Gordon declared that, on the one hand, the descendants of slaves were 'the victims of an ancient and cruel wrong', but on the other hand slavery 'must have too often tended to debase and vulgarise' the character of the slave. 'These evil influences affected the family life of his offspring', and through manumission they would seep into free society. The notion of the 'damaged' freedman recurs in more recent works on Roman social history, e.g. in references to their 'unprincipled energies', which supposedly stemmed from the corrupting influence of masters and patrons.[11] Therefore, although the blame may have shifted, the freedman is still seen as a dangerous figure whose impact on society is accepted as a legitimate source of concern.

This approach would explain the language often used to describe manumission. Thus, even sober accounts like that of Treggiari could refer to the 'infiltration of the Roman population by foreigners' and the 'libertine blood in the veins of the Roman people'.[12] Other scholars have written in similar terms about the corrosive effects of manumission.[13] Apparent in this approach is also a tendency to identify with the viewpoint of the master/patron rather than the freedman – in sharp contrast to most slavery studies where it is the slave who provides the emotional and analytical focus. When dealing with freedmen many scholars have slipped into the mindset of Roman slave owners, as illustrated by the casual references to 'deserving' and 'undeserving' slaves, and to 'trivial' grounds for manumission. Some even operate with 'excessive', 'indiscriminate', and 'reckless' manumission

[9] Wallon (1847) 2.426–7, described the corrupted freedman as 'Jeté au sein d'une société viciée elle-même par le mélange de l'esclavage, il y devint plus librement mauvais, plus dangereusement encore.' On his abolitionist stance see e.g. Davis (1966) 32–4. Meyer (1913) 55, noted that the freedmen at Trimalchio's dinner 'bleiben rohen Sklavenseelen'.
[10] Mommsen (1875) 3.511, referred to 'die von der Unfreiheit unzertrennliche Demoralisation'. Warde Fowler (1908) 230; Gordon (1931) 77; cf. Gordon (1927) 182.
[11] MacMullen (1974) 103.
[12] Treggiari (1969a) 231–2, 214. In an echo of Duff she referred to the 'racial purity of Rome', 215.
[13] Ebersbach (1995) 202, referred to the 'zersetzenden Wirkungen der Freigelassenenwirtschaft', in contrast to Strack's positive image of the freedman as 'die frische aufstrebende Schicht': (1914) 28.

of 'unsuitable' slaves as valid historical concepts.[14] The remarkable implication of such distinctions is of course that some slaves ideally should be kept in servitude.

There has been a notable willingness to accept at face value the negative image of the freedman which pervades much of the ancient record. In some cases we may suspect specific political agendas, in others simply conventional snobbery and disdain for upstarts. But whatever the specific motives the result has been a convergence between ancient stereotypes and modern prejudices, which has made the Roman freedman an obvious candidate for a less biased reassessment. Indeed, few social categories would seem more deserving of rescue from what E. P. Thompson famously called the 'enormous condescension of posterity' than the reviled Roman freedman. Despite the general shift in political outlook that has taken place among historians over the last generation, this has not yet happened, for while interest in ancient slavery has increased, the freedman has been only marginally affected by modern concerns for the 'victims of history'. A number of possible reasons may be ventured.

Firstly, historians have been understandably reluctant to appear as apologists for slavery. Putting too much stress on manumission might seem to be introducing a mitigating factor, in effect reducing servitude to a mere phase in the lives of most slaves. This could be seen as playing into the hands of the 'apologetic' school of slavery studies, for which there is a longstanding tradition among ancient historians. Already Meyer insisted on the steady improvement of the treatment of slaves and found that Roman manumission represented a 'generosity . . . that keeps causing astonishment and admiration'.[15] Later Carcopino presented an equally sunny picture, declaring that, 'With few exceptions, slavery in Rome was neither eternal nor, while it lasted, intolerable', since 'The practical good sense of the Romans, no less than the fundamental humanity instinctive to their peasant hearts, had always kept them from showing cruelty toward the *servi*.'[16] Vogt expanded on this view of Roman slavery, although – for specific ideological reasons – he did not pay much attention to manumission.[17]

---

[14] E.g. Last (1934) 432; Jones (1970) 133; Sherwin-White (1973) 327. Ebersbach (1995) 201–2, thought freedom was given 'oft aus so läppischen Gründen'. Further examples in the discussion of Augustan manumission laws, below pp. 80–2.

[15] Meyer (1924) 186: 'Liberalität . . . die immer aufs neue Staunen und Bewunderung hervorruft.' Also, Behrends (1980) 54, mentioned 'ausserordentlich grosszügig gehandhabten Freilassungen'.

[16] Carcopino (1941) 56–61, 56.

[17] Vogt (1975). The limited attention paid to manumission might seem surprising given the overall tenor of his work, but is explicable in terms of Vogt's immediate concern which was to offer a response to Marxist attempts to present the conflict between masters and slaves as the driving

Alföldy, however, offered the most sustained argument for near universal manumission.[18] Finley famously distanced himself from any attempt to 'humanise' ancient slavery, and this view has since been followed by most scholars – at least outside the German-speaking world.[19] In line with the focus on the suffering of the slave and the inhumanity of slavery, the limitations of manumission are often emphasised as well as the self-interest of owners.[20]

Secondly, the negative image of the freedmen and their evident lack of 'class' solidarity with those left behind in slavery may have made them less obvious candidates for a revisionist history 'from below'. Most often they would have owned slaves themselves, and the fact that they were the lucky ones who escaped slavery and apparently embraced materialist values wholeheartedly has made it difficult to write an 'emancipatory' history of the freedman. In this context it is perhaps symptomatic that the most extensive recent study of freedmen, the work of Fabre, presents the position of the republican freedman as little better than that of a slave, thereby restoring the 'victim status' to the freedman, despite his escape from slavery.[21]

The growing focus on the suffering of slaves and the inhumanity of slavery may therefore have led to a certain lack of interest in manumission. As a result there have been few serious challenges to the conventional view of the freedman. This study is partly an attempt to formulate such an alternative, but the aim goes beyond a mere 'rehabilitation'. The primary ambition is to explore the wider historical implications of such a revision for our understanding of Roman manumission and the freedmen's place in society.

---

force behind the transformation of ancient society. Vogt therefore put particular emphasis on the humanitarian aspects of the master–slave relationship, which he claimed could be both friendly and affectionate; cf. an unpublished paper delivered by Heinz Heinen at a seminar at the University of Edinburgh, 2007. Viewed from that perspective, manumission was less relevant, since it terminated the owner's *potestas*; indeed it might carry the inconvenient implication that slaves were happy to leave their master's authority. Later studies following in Vogt's footsteps include Waldstein (1986), (2001); Kudlien (1991); Gamauf (2001); Wacke (2001); Knoch (2005). On the apologetic tradition see Horsley (1998) 20–1.

[18] Alföldy (1986a), also showing awareness of the wider implications for Roman slavery, 289.

[19] Finley (1998); Bradley (1984a), (1994); Shaw (1998).

[20] Bradley (1994) 154–65, queried the overall impact of manumission, and Hopkins (1978), followed by Wiedemann (1985) and Hezser (2005) 304–6, stressed that manumission was self-interested rather than charitable, a view anticipated by Strack (1914). Wiedemann (1985) 163, also suggested manumission merely made slavery more acceptable and helped owners sleep with a better conscience.

[21] Fabre (1981). For a critique of this thesis, e.g. D'Arms (1984); Rawson (1993) 231 n. 39. Interestingly, the recent work by Zelnick-Abramovitz (2005) on Greek manumission offers a vision of the freedman's limited freedom and tied status very similar to that of Fabre.

This also involves reconsidering what remains the central legacy of the conventional approach, namely its view of the freedman as an inherently problematic category and potential source of social, cultural, economic, and even racial conflict. This perception has coloured almost all studies of manumission irrespective of their ideological leanings. Indeed the notion has become so entrenched that Vittinghoff could refer to the 'Freigelassenenproblem' as an objective fact, and a standard reference work described the 'slave and freedman-phenomenon' as 'a case history in the problem of incorporating the essential, but unwelcome, new arrival'.[22] Moreover, the freedman does not simply pose a problem but constituted a peculiarly modern one. Economically and socially he is presented as an outsider, trying to force his way into society. A prominent section are seen as 'self-made' men, active in trade and commerce, mobile and entrepreneurial, even forming that most modern of social strata, the aspiring 'middle class', which paved the way for further ascent by their children. As such the freedman emerges as a strangely familiar figure and the world historians have constructed around the stereotypical Roman *libertus* is a recognisably modern one, full of social tension, economic dynamism, and status anxiety. Freedmen have in that respect become the defining figures of the Roman empire, its society and economy.[23]

This vision of Roman society reminds us that the freedman also poses a conceptual problem. It has often been remarked that the former slave entering free society has no modern parallel.[24] To make sense of the figure, modern scholars have therefore typically fallen back on the long-established image of the parvenu, who also happened to be particularly prominent in the age of industrialisation when the first modern syntheses were produced. By shifting the emphasis away from their unique background as slaves onto their position as new citizens and social risers, they have become assimilated to the archetypal category of the 'arriviste'. Manumission could thus be classified under the reassuringly familiar heading of 'social mobility', which also explained the animosity they encountered.

---

[22] Vittinghoff (1990) 169; Purcell (1994) 654. Strack (1914) on the other hand presented a remarkably positive image of the freedmen and their contribution to Roman society.

[23] The peculiar element of 'modernity' they lend Roman society has gone largely unquestioned. For example, in the debate about the nature of the Roman economy their status as a commercial 'middle class' was taken as proof of the essential modernity of economic structures and practices. Perhaps more surprisingly, later 'primitivist' historians, troubled by the apparent anachronism of this reconstruction, did not query the freedmen's role as a commercial class but chose to focus on their social isolation, which indicated the overall marginality of trade in the ancient economy, e.g. Veyne (1961); Jongman (1988).

[24] E.g. Andreau (1993) 176; Los (1995).

But there is a risk in that we familiarise a phenomenon that was in fact profoundly alien. In order to reconstruct a more authentic – or at least less anachronistic – picture we will have to return to the basic fact that first and foremost they were ex-slaves. It was their servile past that set them apart and defined their place in society. Not simply a person of humble origin, the former slave constituted a category *sui generis*. And it is the concerns caused by the entry of ex-slaves into free society that provide the key to understanding the place of freedmen in Roman society and the reactions they provoked.

The modern parvenu stereotype of the freedman is firmly rooted in an ancient tradition, above all Petronius' *Satyricon*, which presented a very similar image of the former slave. Some of the sentiments about freedmen expressed here are echoed in other sources, e.g. Horace, Martial, and Juvenal, but the ancient record is more diverse than that. The focus on the freedman as upstart has obscured the existence of another, far more positive strand of Roman opinion, represented for example by the younger Pliny. These sources have had relatively little impact on modern perceptions and as a result we are now faced with a fundamental paradox, since the freedman was not a naturally occurring element of Roman society but the product of specific social practices. As a category freedmen were continuously replenished by slave owners who could have chosen not to do so. The apparent litany of problems caused by freedmen becomes incomprehensible when the practice could simply have been curbed or even discontinued. That did of course never happen and throughout the period for which we have any evidence the Romans continued to free large numbers of slaves, irrespective of any publicly stated misgivings, which would indicate that individual slave owners found it personally beneficial. Therefore, given the undiminished popularity of manumission it is not surprising to find Roman authors expressing appreciation for individual freedmen and for the practice in general.

Nevertheless, a prominent section of Roman public opinion remained critical of freedmen, which is puzzling given the consistently high level of manumission. Manumission was, it seems, not just remarkably common but also highly controversial. How do we explain this contradiction? One way to proceed is to look at what might be called the 'discourse' on freedmen and analyse it on its own terms. As many studies have demonstrated, there are fundamental risks involved in using moralising, normative texts to reconstruct the practice of manumission. While the 'discourse' and the 'reality' of course influenced each other in oblique and complex ways, they were by no means identical. Methodologically the two questions should be separated, not least because any blurring would make it impossible to explain the paradox just outlined, i.e. why the Romans – at least in some contexts – complained bitterly about an institution they could simply have abolished.

For that reason a study of freedmen might logically begin at the same point as the freedman's own personal journey – that is, with slavery and the past which would define him throughout his life. Here we may consider first what it meant to be a former slave, and hence why their entry into free society triggered the reactions it did. It will be argued that the concerns about manumission were essentially moral and ideological rather than socio-economic. And from these particular concerns stemmed the need to define the freedman as a specific type of person, one who was in vital respects inferior to freeborn citizens. Roman *liberti* were in more than one sense 'made', and this 'construction' of the freedman, ideologically, legally, and socially, is the theme explored in the first three chapters of this book, which deal with the 'stain of slavery', the freedman's relationship with his former owner, and his status as a Roman citizen and the particular concerns about rank and authority that gave rise to.

Chapter 5 turns from the 'discourse' to the practice of manumission. Here the aim is first to establish a quantitative framework for understanding the phenomenon, its scale and frequency, which forms the basis for a discussion of the motivation behind the owners' willingness to free what appears to be a very substantial proportion of their slave holdings. In this context it is important to remember that manumission is not specific to Rome but a feature of most slave societies.[25] Comparative studies suggest that manumission was a perfectly normal practice, especially in advanced slave systems where unfree labour was put in positions of trust and required to work independently. In that situation incentives are needed and the most powerful spur is always the prospect of freedom. However, the Romans appear to have freed more frequently than most other slave societies, which might be explained in terms of the anticipated outcome, since in Rome the freedman as a rule remained bound to the patron through a web of moral, social, and economic ties. In effect therefore the owner's authority was redefined rather than discontinued. This also affected the modalities of manumission, particularly the question of payment and testamentary

---

[25] While in many respects illuminating, comparative evidence presents both opportunities and pitfalls and should be used with caution. Above all it is important to avoid 'homogenising' comparisons, which fill the gaps in our knowledge with reference to 'typical' patterns observed elsewhere. In fact, comparative material frequently highlights what was uniquely Roman rather than revealing universal patterns.

manumission, which will be considered in the following chapters. Finally an attempt will be made to view the practice within the context of slavery as a whole, including the question of sustainability and economic 'rationality'.

Chapters 6 and 7 looks at the place of freedmen in Roman society, beginning with their economic roles particularly in the urban context. This also involves a critical assessment of the common notion that they constituted a kind of commercial 'middle class'. This discussion takes us directly to the question of their public roles and the significance of the *seviri Augustales*, which have been interpreted as a formalisation of this 'middle class'. While the freedman was himself barred from any position of public authority, that did not apply to his son, and the relative success of this group has been seen as a reflection of the social and economic importance of their parents. Finally in chapter 8, as a form of epilogue, an attempt will be made to grasp the identity and experience of being a Roman freedman.

Chronologically the main focus will be on the central period to which most of our sources belong, i.e. between the second Punic War and the early third century CE. The approach will be mostly synchronic, which may raise some eyebrows given the length of the time span covered. However, as will become clear, I believe there were some fundamental constants which allow us to treat the period as a single whole. Thus, I have found no compelling evidence to suggest any major changes to the practice of manumission or the attitudes towards it. Geographically the emphasis is – mostly for reasons of evidence – on the city of Rome and Italy, although material from other parts of the empire will be considered where relevant. Finally it must be stressed that this study is an attempt at producing an interpretation rather than an encyclopaedia of Roman manumission. An exhaustive analysis of all aspects would go far beyond the scope of a single volume. A large number of – not least juridical – issues will therefore have to be treated in less detail and depth than some readers might have wished, while others are mentioned only cursorily. That is inevitable, however, and hopefully the new synthesis will compensate for some of these shortcomings.

CHAPTER 2

Macula servitutis

Slavery, freedom, and manumission

The crossing of basic boundaries is a source of considerable anxiety in most societies, and in the Roman world few distinctions were more fundamental and sharply drawn than that between free and unfree. The jurists divided the whole of humanity into these two basic categories. As Gaius stated, 'all people are either free or slaves', and *libertas* and *servitus* were defined as the direct negation of each other.[1] Moreover, freedom was, like servitude, conceptualised as a natural state. Thus, it was in principle, if not quite in practice, impossible to surrender one's freedom, except in very special cases.[2] As one Roman orator declared, 'What nature gave to the freeborn cannot be snatched away by any injury of fortune.'[3] Roman law thus considered free status inalienable, as illustrated by the prescriptions concerning self-sale. In principle no one could sell himself or herself into slavery, and formal loss of freedom only happened if the buyer believed the person to be unfree, and the person sold himself in order to gain from the sale.[4] This was clearly a muddled compromise between the principle of inalienability and the reality of Roman society, where self-sale might be an attractive option under certain circumstances.[5] Ordinary people, ignorant of the law, may have tried to gain a better life, but the jurists insisted on the essential difference between slave and free, a distinction which an open recognition of self-enslavement would have

---

[1] Gaius *Inst.* 1.9: 'omnes homines aut liberi sunt aut servi'; cf. D. 1.5.3; 1.5.4 pr. (Florentinus). Also in everyday life this appears to have been a fundamental distinction. For example, in curse tablets asking for divine justice a standard definition of the perpetrator is 'whether woman or man, whether slave or free', e.g. Gager (1992) nos. 95, 96.

[2] Wieling (1999); Söllner (2000); Herrmann-Otto (2001); (2005) 73–4. Enslavement was increasingly used as a punishment under the empire; cf. Millar (1984), who discusses the condemnation to hard labour, *ad metallum*.

[3] Ps.-Quint. *Decl.Min.* 311.4: 'Id quidem quod ingenuis natura dedit, nulla fortunae iniuria eripi potest.' Interestingly, a slave without a master, e.g. through abandonment, did not become free but a *servus sine domino*; cf. Affolter (1913).

[4] Wieling (1999) 15–16, 25–6.

[5] Cf. Ramin and Veyne (1981). Glancy (2002) 80–5, rightly questions the scale of this practice.

undermined. Throughout Rome's history the basic division appears to have remained intact, despite modern attempts to show that the distinction between slaves and poor freeborn became increasingly blurred during the empire.[6]

Within this construction of slavery and freedom manumission posed a problem. It meant the transition from one supposedly natural category to its direct opposite, and the very possibility of such movement automatically called into question the given character of both statuses. In order to neutralise this risk, the transition process had to be carefully managed and regulated. On a formal level this was achieved by a set of procedures designed to negate that any transition had taken place at all.[7] Early on in Roman history three different procedures were developed which would transform the slave into a free person – *manumissio vindicta, censu,* and *testamento*.[8]

Manumissio vindicta took the form of a mock trial by which the owner of the slave appeared before a magistrate with *imperium* together with a Roman citizen. The latter would act as *adsertor libertatis* and declare the free status of the slave. This claim was left uncontested by the owner, and the *adsertor* would then touch the slave with the rod, *festuca* or *vindicta*, while pronouncing the standard formula: 'hunc ego hominem liberum esse aio ex iure Quiritium'.[9] The magistrate then confirmed the slave's freedom. The procedure implied that the person had been wrongly enslaved and was restored to his or her rightful status through the trial.

The two other forms of manumission may seem less overtly fictional, but at least one of them also lends itself to this interpretation. Thus, the *manumissio censu* involved the entry of the slave into the census record. In effect this act also represented an uncontested claim that the person was really a free citizen. As Buckland noted: 'it is a fictitious renewal of an entry, and the Censor is recording the fact that the man is a *civis*, not making him

---

[6] E.g. Thebert (1993) who referred to the deepening divide between *honestiores* and *humiliores* as evidence of this development. But although the legal position of the free poor undoubtedly deteriorated in that period, their status was still regarded as fundamentally different from that of slaves. Thus, Aubert (2002) argued that 'servile' punishments maintained their distinct character, even when occasionally applied to free citizens.

[7] Watson (1967) 190–4; Treggiari (1969a) 21–5.

[8] Cf. Cic. *Top.* 2.10; Gaius *Inst.* 1.17, 35, 138; Ulp. *Reg.* 1.6–9; *Frg.Dosith.* 5. The relative date of these three forms has been much debated. Most likely, however, they all went back to the earliest historical periods, cf. Fabre (1981) 5–7.

[9] Watson (1967) 220. Fabre (1981) 20–1, interpreted the procedure as a 'rite de passage' but the logic of the ritual seems to have been restoration rather than transition. As Ville (1963) demonstrated, the famous Mariemont relief does not, as previously thought, represent *manumissio vindicta*, cf. Wacke (1982a); *pace* Pack (1980). For the symbolic aspects of the procedure see also Tondo (1967).

one'.[10] Testamentary manumission would seem to differ in that respect, since the formula commonly used, 'Stichus servus meus liber esto' ('My slave Stichus shall be free'), involves an explicit change of status.[11] The point was that the master's intentions had to be clear and the phraseology unambiguous, not least because a statement of the slave's free status could be taken as an admission of wrongful enslavement and lead to demands for *restitutio natalium* rather than manumission.[12]

These formal arrangements are significant as indicators of the sensitive nature of manumission. They served to uphold the illusion of stable, ideally immutable categories, between which no movement in principle was possible. In reality, of course, it would have been obvious to any observer that the slave had crossed a fundamental boundary, changed his personal status, and joined the class of his master. The question is therefore how this transition was negotiated and conceptualised and to answer that we must first consider the nature of the categories which were called into question by the slave's transformation. This means asking what it was that made a slave a slave in the eyes of the Romans. Here the legal definition of the slave and the formal relationship between the slave and the freedman might form the logical starting point for the discussion.

Despite the 'essentialist' approach to personal status found in the legal sources, the jurists did of course recognise the reality of status change. The fact that slaves could become free therefore inspired the jurists to add a further distinction to the basic division already mentioned. Free people, Gaius declared, may be subdivided into two categories, freeborn and freed.[13] This distinction implied that those who had at some point been unfree remained separate from those who had never experienced servitude. In other words, freed slaves carried a trace of their former status, which set them apart from *ingenui*. This trace could also be defined as the *macula servitutis*, the 'stain of slavery' which never left the freedman and entailed a number of legal and social disabilities.[14] The nature of this 'stain' needs to be investigated before we can understand Roman manumission. As we

---

[10] Buckland (1908) 441; *contra* Daube (1948). Watson (1967) 184–5, discussed whether manumission happened immediately when the name was entered on the list or when it was published. This problem is immaterial to this point, however, which focuses on the formal procedure. Fabre (1981) 10–16, noted that the slave of course was registered 'iussu domini'.

[11] Fabre (1981) 26–7, who notes the alternative form: 'Stichum servum meum liberum esse iubeo.'

[12] Buckland (1908) 443, had already noted that testamentary manumission was the only form which was not based on fiction, and inferred from this that it might be a later invention which did not originally lead to complete freedom. But see Watson (1987) 25.

[13] *Inst.* 1.10; cf. D. 1.5.5 (Marcian); *Frg.Dosith.* 4. D. 1.1.4 (Ulpian) distinguishes between 'tria genera', free, slaves, and freed, 'id est hi qui desierant esse servi'.

[14] D. 40.11.5 (Modestinus); *Cod.Iust.* 7.16.9; 10.32.2.

shall see, the nature of the stigma was closely bound up with the Roman definition of slaves as such.

In strictly legal terms a slave was defined as property, subject to *ius mancipii* similar to land and livestock. This entitled owners to exercise unlimited property rights over their slaves, who could be sold, punished, or even killed. The slave enjoyed no legal protection of his or her person, no right to own property, no formal marriage, and no authority over his own children. Some improvements may have been introduced under the empire, but they seem to have been of limited practical consequence, merely granting the slave the most basic right to life.[15]

The legal definition of the slave as property does, of course, not imply that the Romans failed to recognise the humanity of their slaves. Varro may have categorised rural slaves as 'instrumenti genus vocale', 'speaking tools', but that does not entail that he – or any other Roman – regarded them as inert objects. This particular definition was part of an attempt to conceptualise the various elements of farming and was unconcerned with slavery as such. Moreover, the category of 'speaking tools' also covered free labourers employed at the farm.[16] In addition, Latin literature is full of statements which illustrate the Romans' appreciation of their slaves as fellow human beings. The younger Pliny, for example, notes that illness was the same for free men and for slaves, while Juvenal has a character believing that 'the souls and bodies of slaves consist of the same stuff and elements as our own'.[17]

The definition of the slave proposed by Orlando Patterson may therefore have been closer to Roman practice and ideology. He argued forcefully that legal or theoretical definitions are of little help when trying to understand how the Romans regarded their slaves. The split in the Roman view of slaves, argued by Finley for example, between objects and human beings becomes a red herring.[18] As an alternative to the 'slave as object', Patterson proposed a definition of slavery as 'social death', meaning that the person has no social existence, rights, or ties.[19] The slave becomes a person who

<hr/>

[15] Gaius, *Inst.* 1.52–3. Bradley 1984a; (1987 edn) 123–8. A detailed discussion in Knoch (2005), who tends to over-estimate their impact; for a more balanced view see Watson (1983).

[16] Varr. *Rust.* 1.17.1. For the inclusion of free labour e.g. 1.17.2: 'Omnes agri coluntur hominibus servis aut liberis aut utrisque'; cf. Perl (1977) 424; Roller (2001) 225. The passage has frequently been over-interpreted, e.g. McCarthy (2000) 22, 170.

[17] Plin. *Ep.* 8.24; Juv. 14.16–17: 'utque animas servorum et corpora nostra materia constare putet paribusque elementis'.

[18] Finley (1998) 139–43; Watson (1987) 46–66. Kaser (1971) 285, noted that while the slave legally was 'persona' and 'res', outside Roman private law the slave was always regarded as a person.

[19] Patterson (1982) 1–13, 35–76, followed by e.g. Zelnick-Abramovitz (2005) 25–7.

would otherwise have died but has been spared and kept in servitude. Despite being alive, he or she was 'dead' as a social being. This definition has major advantages and seems to be better in line with Roman perceptions of slavery. For example, the legal sources derived the term 'servus' from 'servare', 'to preserve'.[20]

None of these definitions, however, brings us much closer to understanding the *macula servitutis*. Was the 'stain' derived from a perception of slaves as qualitatively different on a basic biological level? The notion that some people were naturally suited for slavery takes us to Aristotle's much-debated theory of slavery, which argued that some slaves were slaves 'by nature'. The model was practically unworkable and Aristotle himself accepted some of its shortcomings, which other Greek writers also seem to have noted.[21] Certainly, the idea of 'natural slavery' appears to have found little resonance in Rome, where the jurists explicitly rejected it. Florentinus, for example, stated unequivocally that it was 'against nature'.[22]

Many Roman writers, some under the influence of Stoic thought, went even further, stressing not just the common humanity of all people but also the role of chance in deciding one's place in the world. Thus, in his *Paradoxa Stoicorum* Cicero implied that slaves were not inferior by nature and that their servitude was determined by external circumstances, while he also referred to the unhappy lot of slaves as 'infima condicio et fortuna'.[23] According to one of Publilius Syrus' proverbs, slavery is honest when brought on by fate – but he was of course a freedman himself.[24] However, Caesar also noted in passing that all men naturally long for freedom and despise the state of slavery.[25] Likewise, Seneca Maior declared: 'no one is naturally free or slave. These are titles imposed later on individuals by fortune.'[26] The idea was most fully developed in the works of the

---

[20] D. 1.5.4.2 (Florentinus); 50.17.209 (Ulpian): 'Servitutem mortalitati fere comparamus'; 35.1.59.2 (Ulpian): 'servitus morti adsimulatur'; 49.15.18 (Ulpian). Cf. Herrmann-Otto (2001) 25–8; (2005) 64; Wieling (1999) 4–8. Rix (1994) 54–87, has argued that the etymology is unlikely, but that is immaterial to the point made here.

[21] Arist. *Pol.* 1.2.1254b; *contra* e.g. Euripides' *Ion* 854–6. Cambiano (1987); Garnsey (1996) 107–27; Papadis (2001) with further literature.

[22] D. 1.5.4: 'contra naturam'; cf. D. 1.1.4 (Ulpian) and 50.17.32: 'quod ius naturale attinet, omnes homines aequales sunt', 'as far as concerns the natural law all men are equal'; cf. *Inst.Iust.* 1.2.2; 1.3.2.

[23] *Par. Stoic.* 5.33–4; *Off.* 1.41. Treggiari (1969b) 195, therefore believed Cicero's prejudices against slaves were merely for public display, not reflecting his private views. As we shall see, that is unlikely to be the case.

[24] H17, 219: 'Honeste servit, qui succumbit tempori.'

[25] *BG* 3.10: 'omnes autem homines natura libertati studere et condicionem servitutis odisse'.

[26] *Contr.* 7.6.18: 'dixit neminem natura liberum esse, neminem servum; haec postea nomina singulis inposuisse Fortunam'. Cf. Petr. *Sat.* 71.1, on slavery brought on by 'malus fatus'.

younger Seneca. In the *De Beneficiis* he stressed the fundamental equality of mankind, who, no matter what their place in society might be, all spring from the same source and share the same origin.[27] Similar sentiments were voiced by Greek writers in Rome. Thus Dionysius of Halicarnassus, despite his apparent hostility to freedmen, included a speech attributed to Servius Tullius which took to task those who thought that free men differed from slaves by their very nature rather than by their condition. According to the Roman king, slaves were created by fortune, which in principle could strike anyone: all people should therefore be judged on their character and merit.[28]

The rejection of 'natural slavery' does not mean, however, that the Romans did not discriminate between rightful and wrongful enslavement. Indeed this distinction was crucially important to them, as shown by numerous historical instances. For instance in 172 BCE the senate decided that the surrendered Ligurian Statellates had been unjustly enslaved and should be restored to liberty. If that did not happen, officials should investigate and punish those 'by whose malice they had become slaves'.[29] Two years later the senate decided that those from the town of Abdera who had been captured and enslaved should be released, and shortly afterwards a similar action was taken concerning the free persons from Chalcis who had been wrongly enslaved.[30] When taking these decisions the Roman authorities were not concerned with the character or general behaviour of the defeated peoples. It was entirely a question of the circumstances under which they had been enslaved. In each case the war had been declared *iniustum* which meant that the enslavement was illegal and had to be reversed.

[27] 3.28.1: 'Eadem omnibus principia eademque origo.' Likewise he described the common soul of all people irrespective of status and the irrelevance of status. *Ep.* 31.11: 'Hic animus tam in equitem Romanum quam in libertinum, quam in servum potest cadere. Quid est enim eques Romanus aut libertinus aut servus? Nomina ex ambitione aut iniuria nata.' It is worth remembering in this context that it was theoretical discourse, and as we shall see probably detached from conventional thinking. Moreover, Seneca's main focus was not the status of slaves but the morals of their owners, cf. Griffin (1976) 256–85; Roller (2001) 272–86; Garnsey (1996); Bradley (2008).

[28] 4.23.1–2. Klees (2002) 97–111, nevertheless argued that among Greeks of the early empire the notion of 'natural slaves' was still alive. There are also occasional references to 'true' and 'false' slaves, e.g. in Statius' *Silv.* 6, where the poet wonders whether his recently deceased favourite was really a slave or Fortune's mistake (cf. Thebert (1993) 169). Horace speculated that a slave girl might be of royal descent, and the victim of hostile gods, 'penatis iniquos', who have turned against her, *Odes* 2.4. Such instances may suggest a distinction between 'true' and 'false' slaves at a more personal level, but they remain isolated and – perhaps not surprisingly – they are found only in poetic texts. Q. Cicero's comment that Tiro was too good to be a slave – 'indignum illa fortuna' – was presumably a conventional figure of speech, implying that Tiro was now ready for manumission, *Fam.* 16.16.1.

[29] Livy 42.21.5: 'cuius dolo malo is in servitutem venisset'. Pittenger (2008) 231–44.

[30] Livy 43.4.13; 43.8.7.

In this context it is worth remembering that the Roman concept of the 'just war' was highly formalistic and largely determined by observance of proper procedure.[31] Consequently the enslavement of defeated peoples was justified less by moral arguments than by formality.[32]

Roman jurists justified slavery by reference to the fact that it was a commonly accepted institution among all peoples.[33] As such it was founded on *ius gentium*, i.e. 'the law which natural reason has established among all human beings', and therefore required no specific justification.[34] What this law did require, however, was a clear set of rules which defined the precise circumstances and situations in which people could be properly enslaved. Laying down the correct procedure for enslavement, *iusta servitus*, was a concern, precisely because these rules provided the only bulwark against arbitrary enslavement.[35] Since slavery and freedom ultimately were governed by chance, it was paramount that the field over which fortune was allowed to rule be carefully delineated in order to minimise the degree of uncertainty experienced by the individual.[36]

The two most important forms of enslavement were capture and slave birth. The victor's right to deal with the defeated foe as he pleased was commonly accepted in antiquity, and that also included the right to enslave them, in principle as an alternative to execution. In the same way, breeding of slaves could be justified according to the *ius gentium* since among all ancient peoples the child took the status of the mother.[37] There were borderline cases, however, which attracted considerable legal attention, such as exposed children and self-sale.[38] Wrongly enslaved people could regain their freedom and even *ingenuitas* through a process of 'vindicatio

[31] Harris (1979) 166–75.
[32] Watson (1967) 159. Likewise, Plutarch, *Luc.* 19.7, mentions that the enslavement of the captured grammarian Tyrannio was deemed unjustified because of his learning but he also stresses the significance of his freeborn status; cf. Yarrow (2006) 39–40. Cic. *Cluent.* 162, includes a case where a woman wrongly enslaved was automatically given her freedom.
[33] Gaius *Inst.* 1.52, cf. D. 1.6.1.1; D. 1.1.4 (Ulpian); 1.5.4.1 (Florentinus); 1.5.5.1 (Marcian). See full discussion with references in Wieling (1999).
[34] Gaius *Inst.* 1.1: 'quod vero naturalis ratio inter omnes homines constituit'; cf. D. 1.1.9.
[35] Herrmann-Otto (2005) 66–74.
[36] Dio Chrysostom, *Or.* 15, discusses the permanent risk to the status of Roman citizens. Plautus' *Captivi* evolves around this uncertainty and the vagaries of Fortune: 'fortuna humana fingit artatque ut lubet: me, qui liber fueram, servom fecit, e summo infimum', 304f. Cf. the discussion in Leigh (2004) 57–97, which also concludes that 'Nothing in the *Captivi* validates any concept of the slave by nature', 96.
[37] D. 1.5.5.1–2 (Marcian); 7.1.68 (Ulpian); Cic. *Fin.* 1.12. See in general Herrmann-Otto (1997); (2005) 69–74.
[38] E.g. Suet. *Gramm.* 21; Paul.Sent. 5.1.1; *Cod.Iust.* 7.16.1. Watson (1967) 171.

in libertatem', which did not leave them with libertine status afterwards.[39] In principle it was impossible for freeborn to forfeit their *ingenuitas*.

The Roman justification of slavery was, in short, based on formalism rather than essentialism. External circumstances – fate and bad luck – made people slaves, not nature. Watson therefore rightly observed that: 'To be a slave is a misfortune for the individual, assuredly a grave one, but it is not inevitable, natural, or necessarily permanent.'[40] But Watson then drew the conclusion that since the Romans based slavery entirely on formal criteria – ultimately ruled by fate – slaves were not regarded as intrinsically different from free people: 'Except financially or socially, the slave need not be thought inferior to his master – indeed, there is no necessary obstacle to the notion that the slave may often be superior, morally, intellectually, and even in education.'[41]

This might seem a logical inference but it still raises a number of questions. Could any slave society really function on the simple premise that slavery was accepted and universal? Would 'bad luck' have been sufficient rationale for keeping large numbers of people in a permanent state of 'social death'? We might expect the extreme treatment meted out to these people to be accompanied by the attribution of certain characteristics which justified their misfortune. Moreover, by reducing slavery purely to the work of fortune the 'macula servitutis' of the freed population is left unexplained. If there were no intrinsic difference between free or slave, why were former slaves stigmatised and made to suffer for a past for which they bore no personal responsibility or blame?

Even a brief glance at the literary evidence shows that the notion of servitude as a source of stigma was not confined to the legal discourse. In fact, Watson's claim seems to fly in the face of a remarkably consistent Roman tradition which insisted on the slave's innate inferiority to all free men. One of the most striking expressions of this view comes from Horace's fourth *Epode* which delivers a stinging attack on an anonymous freedman,

---

[39] Watson (1967) 218–22. For example, Vespasian's wife Flavia Domitilla regained her *ingenuitas* at a trial before the *recuperatores*, Suet. *Vesp.* 3; *Epit. de Caes.* 10.1; 11.1. She may have been freeborn but exposed/sold and then freed informally. Although formally restored to freeborn status, she received remarkably few honours by her husband or sons, cf. Barrett (2005). Presumably some 'taint' still remained in the eyes of society because of the reality of servitude, however unjustified. Interestingly, in Roman Greece *threptoi*, children exposed and reared as slaves, could become free through a 'causa liberalis' but not gain *ingenuitas*, Plin. *Ep.* 10.66; cf. Buckland (1908) 653–75; Sherwin-White (1966) 654.

[40] Watson (1987) 3; followed by e.g. Harrill (1995) 26–7.

[41] Watson (1987) 3, further stated that: 'However lowly the economic and social position of a slave might be, the slave was not necessarily and in all ways regarded as inferior as a human being simply because he was a slave.'

who had done well for himself and liked to advertise his success, thereby overstepping the boundaries laid down for *liberti*.[42] Horace reminds him in no uncertain terms that manumission and good fortune do not change who he is; it does not affect his 'genus', 'kind'.[43] There is, Horace insists, a natural enmity between them as profound as that between the lamb and the wolf. The passage is remarkable not just for the degree of hostility it shows towards the freedman, but also for its suggestion that slaves belonged to a distinct category of humanity with inherent characteristics, which remained resistant to any change of status.

While Horace's tirade may be extreme, the notion that a servile past makes a person inferior seems to have been commonplace. Roman literature is full of casual references to the characteristics of slaves, who were instinctively associated with a range of negative qualities.[44] The term 'servilis' was thus typically combined with words like 'humilis', 'inbecillus', 'caducus' – 'lowly', 'weak', and 'perishable' – just as 'serviliter' occurred alongside 'abiecte', 'timide', 'ignave', 'muliebriter' – 'despondent', 'cowardly', 'slothful', and 'womanish'.[45] Likewise, Quintilian could describe a gesture which conveyed 'humiliation and servility, and almost hypocrisy'.[46]

These negative associations were primarily focused on the mind and character of the slave, and it was commonly assumed that slaves possessed a distinct nature. Sallust noted, for example, that Spartacus' army had a 'servile ingenium',[47] and the notion of a 'servilis animus' also appears regularly in the sources.[48] Likewise, Cicero ascribed servile qualities to

---

[42] Ancient commentators speculated as to the identity of the freedman, suggesting Menas/Menodorus, Sex. Pompey's admiral, who defected to Octavian, Ps.-Acron and Porphyr. *praef.* on Hor. *Epod.* 4. This idea has since been rejected, and P. Vedius Rufus, the father of Vedius Pollio, now seems a more likely candidate, cf. Kirbihler (2007).

[43] The Loeb edition translates it as 'breeding', while Treggiari (1996) 881, prefers the direct opposite, namely 'birth', as does Watson (2003) 156. The readings seem equally questionable, and the latter fails on the simple grounds that the freedman might not have been slave-born. The *genus* of slaves recurs in Statius' *Silvae* 3.3.45, which refers to the parents of Claudius Etruscus' freed father with the phrase 'genus culpamque parentum', and in Suet. *Aug.* 44.1: 'libertini generis'.

[44] On the negative stereotypes of slaves see Bradley (1984a; 1987 edn) 26–31. The moral construction of freedom and slavery was also reflected in the terminology used about freeborn, since the term *ingenuus* denoted not just civic status but also moral nobility. *TLL* s.v. *ingenuus* II.

[45] Sen. *Vit.Beat.* 7.3; Cic. *Tusc.* 2.55.

[46] *Inst.Or.* 11.3.83: 'humilem atque servilem et quasi fraudulum'.

[47] *Hist.* 3.98 (Maurenbrecher), 3.66 (McGushin). In Tac. *Ann.* 14.43, Cassius expressed his suspicion of the 'ingenia servorum', even of the closest *vernae*. Commenting on the difficulty the emperor had finding out what people really thought, Tacitus mentioned the problem posed by his 'freedmen's servile minds', 'libertorum servilia ingenia', *Ann.* 2.12.3; cf. *Hist.* 5.9.3, on the imperial freedman Felix's 'servili ingenio'.

[48] Val. Max. 3.3 ext. 7. In Tac. *Ann.* 15.54.4, a freedman driven by his 'servilis animus' betrays his patron. Conversely, a slave who acted bravely did so 'non servili animo', *Ann.* 2.39.

Verres and his followers, contrasting free and servile minds and bodies.[49] Cicero could approvingly quote Aristotle's dismissal of those who enjoyed frivolous entertainment as 'children, silly women, slaves and free men with a mind similar to that of slaves'.[50] In his outline of the qualities required of the bailiff Columella suggested that he should not just be skilled in farming but also, as far as his 'servile ingenium' allowed, possess a certain natural authority over his fellow slaves on the farm.[51]

The servility of slaves expressed itself primarily in their judgement and moral faculties, rather than in their general intellectual ability. Thus, the stereotypical slave could display both cunning and a certain amount of cleverness, but he could not act according to moral principles. The slave's nature was routinely associated with treachery, cruelty, mendacity, greed, cowardice, and criminality.[52] It is therefore not surprising that Cicero in a philosophical context could compare the rule of the master to that of the soul over the baser instincts, which the slave embodied.[53]

Slavery and bravery were generally considered incompatible, as illustrated by Plutarch's account of the battle of Chaeroneia. The enemy had freed 15,000 slaves and put them in the front line, to which a Roman centurion remarked that he had never heard of slaves behaving like free men except at Saturnalia. However, the ex-slaves stood firm and showed great valour, which Plutarch observed was quite uncharacteristic of the slave nature.[54] Likewise, in his *Panegyric* the younger Pliny mentioned entertainment which inspired the spectators to contempt of death and injury, and *even* in slaves and criminals a desire for glory and victory.[55]

Loyalty and self-sacrifice were seen as anomalous in slaves, as underlined by Seneca's discussion in the *De Beneficiis*, which suggests that an 'exemplum virtutis' performed by a slave was even greater because of its rarity.[56] This prejudice also underlies Valerius Maximus' section 'De fide servorum', 6.8, on outstanding acts of moral courage performed by slaves during the

---

[49] *Verr.* 2.4.126; cf. 2.3.62; 2.4.112.
[50] *Off.* 2.57: 'pueris et mulierculis et servis et servorum simillimis liberis'.
[51] 1.8.10: 'animi, quantum servile patitur ingenium, virtutibus instructus'.
[52] Hopkins (1978) 121, suggested that: 'It seems reasonable to suppose that the stereotype was based in reality; many slaves' characters were moulded by their overt powerlessness', but that may take the notion of slavery as dehumanising a step too far.
[53] *Rep.* 3.37. Cf. Marcus Aurelius 5.30; Garnsey (1996) 38–43, 124, 145–50. The social model that the lower things are made for the sake of the higher and that each element has been given its proper place can also be found in Galen, cf. Schlange-Schöningen (2003) 259.
[54] *Sulla* 18.5–6, referring to the 'unnatural courage with which they held their ground', 'παρὰ φύσιν μένειν τολμῶντας'.
[55] *Pan.* 33.1.   [56] 3.19.4.

proscriptions, which confounded common expectations so much that they could serve as *exempla*. Thus, Tacitus also praised the freedwoman Epicharis who showed bravery under torture, and said she provided a shining example at a time when freeborn men, knights, and senators were busy denouncing each other.[57]

Mind and body were not clearly separated in antiquity and in some contexts the bodies of slaves could also be described as servile and affected by the 'macula servitutis'. According to Gellius, Favorinus of Arles believed children were influenced by the milk they were fed and advised mothers to breastfeed their own children, since it would be damaging to use a wet nurse who was slave or freed and of a barbarous nation.[58] The implication of this advice is that the negative characteristics of the slave could be passed on physically through the milk. Similarly, a declamation evolved around a case of a freeborn child who was presumed dead but in fact had been enslaved; when he was later rescued, it was argued that 'his face itself pleaded the cause of his free birth'.[59]

The bodies of slaves could even be seen as causing different degrees of pollution after death. The *lex libitinaria* from Puteoli which regulated burial practices gave detailed prescriptions concerning the removal of bodies from the city. Generally bodies were to be dealt with in the order the deaths were reported. Slaves, however, had to be removed within two hours of daylight, suggesting that the pollution caused by the death of a slave was considered more serious than that of a freeborn. In fact they were second only to suicides, who had to be removed within an hour of being reported.[60]

---

[57] *Ann.* 15.57. The slave character Tyndarus in Plautus' *Captivi* is the most noble and virtuous of all Plautus' slaves, but as Spranger (1961) 27–8, noted, he was not really the exceptional slave he appeared to be since he later turned out to be freeborn. The playwright instinctively divided free and slave 'als ob zwischen den beiden Welten eine unüberbrückbare Kluft bestände'; cf. McCarthy (2000) 169–70, whose analysis of servility assumed a good slave could overcome the stigma and dishonour of slavery, which seems doubtful. Propertius' poem 3.6 to a great extent evolves around the question of a slave's (lack of) reliability, also using the expression 'servo teste', 20, to underline the point. Bradley (1984a; 1987 edn) 26–31, stressed the assumption of thieving and criminality; cf. Brunt (1988) 287–9.

[58] *NA* 12.1.17.

[59] Ps.-Quint. *Decl.Min.* 388.7: 'ipse vultus causam ingenuitatis suae ageret'. The notion of distinct slave and freeborn features reappears in Juv. 11.154, on a slave with features suitable for freeborn boys, and Petr. *Sat.* 107.6, where 'vultus ingenuos' are hidden under a servile disguise (in this case fake facial tattoos). It is worth noting, however, that 'race' generally did not play a part in this construction. The appearance of slaves was often indistinguishable from that of their masters, and house-born slaves, especially urban ones, would have been fully acculturated into their masters' culture, language, and lifestyle. Weiler (2002) argued slaves were associated with ugliness, but the pretty slave was also a stereotypical figure. George (2002) showed that distinct slave dress did not exist in Rome.

[60] 11.22–3. Panciera (2004) 50.

There are indications that the Romans believed that these negative traits somehow could 'rub off' on freeborn who got too close to slaves or former slaves. According to Dio, the emperor Claudius had been brought up by women and freedmen, and therefore acquired none of the qualities of a free man but had himself become a slave, implying that when freedmen dominate others these may themselves become slavish.[61] Verres is also described as having been corrupted by his freedmen and contaminated by their servile nature.[62] This concern would explain the taboo against adulterous relations between freedmen and *ingenuae*. Augustus made an example of his favourite freedman Polus, whom he forced to commit suicide after he had been convicted of adultery with *matronae*, married freeborn women.[63] Valerius Maximus also tells the story of a senator who divorced his wife after she had engaged in private conversation with a common freedwoman in public.[64] The element of shame associated with such relations is reflected in Augustus' decision never to socialise with former slaves, and although he occasionally allowed freedmen to serve in the army he confined them to separate, inferior units.[65] Augustus also passed legislation banning senators and their descendants from marrying freedwomen, actresses, or *infames*, whose taint apparently was considered to be of a similar nature. Again the ban reflected a perceived need to prevent 'contamination' of the citizen body in general and of the highest order in particular.[66]

It may have been the same logic which informed the *Senatus Consultum Claudianum* from 52 CE, which dealt with sexual relationships between free women and male slaves belonging to other owners.[67] A major concern of the edict seems to have been the fate of the children produced by these unions; contrary to common practice for illegitimate births – in Rome as elsewhere in the ancient world – the children would not follow the status of the mother but become the slaves of their father's owner. As Crook plausibly suggested, this might have been particularly relevant in cases where a slave woman had been freed with Latin status while her *contubernalis* remained

---

[61] 60/61.2.5.   [62] E.g. 2.3.158; cf. below p. 103.
[63] Suet. *Aug.* 67.2; cf. *Caes.* 48.   [64] Val. Max. 6.3.11: 'libertina vulgari'.
[65] Suet. *Aug.* 74; cf. Maecenas who also refused to dine with freedmen, Hor. *Sat.* 1.6.8. Martial 10.27, on senators disgracefully accepting dinner invitations from a rich freedman. On the drafting of freedmen, Suet. *Aug.* 25.2: 'sub priore vexillo habuit, neque aut commixtos cum ingenuis aut eodem modo armatos'. Welwei (1988) 20, plausibly suggests reading 'sub peiore vexillo', indicating different equipment and separate units.
[66] Gardner (1993) 123–5. McGinn (2002) plausibly suggests the ban was of little practical consequence, since few senators married women so far below their own status.
[67] *Cod.Iust.* 7.24.1; Gaius *Inst.* 1.84, 89, 91, 160; Tac. *Ann.* 12.53. Crook (1967a) 62; Gardner (1986) 141–2; Sirks (1994), (2002), (2005).

a slave.[68] In these situations the owner would have lost his claim to any offspring which was produced by such a 'mixed' couple.

Apart from regulating the status of the children, the *Senatus Consultum* also contained provisions concerning the status of the women themselves. If her partner's owner disapproved of the union and gave the woman three formal warnings, which went unheeded, she would become his slave. Alternatively, if he did approve, her status would be reduced to that of a freedwoman.[69] This last provision is remarkable, since it represents the only instance in Roman law where somebody could gain libertine status without ever having been a slave.[70] Freed status would in this instance have been acquired not through slavery but through association with a slave. The implication seems to be that interaction with slaves under certain circumstances – as in this case where the contact was deemed particularly shameful – could make the free person take on servile characteristics.

In sum, slaves were generally associated with a number of specifically 'servile' traits in character, mentality, and occasionally even body. They carried a 'taint' against which free people, and particularly those of the higher orders, had to guard themselves. This conclusion brings us back to Watson's suggestion that the Romans saw no qualitative difference between slaves and free. Not only does this claim seems difficult to reconcile to the literary and legal evidence; there is also a flaw in the underlying logic, since the rejection of natural slavery does not per se imply that slaves were not regarded as inferior. The argument overlooks a crucial factor, which is the possibility that slavery itself may change the person subjected to it. Fortune may have been responsible for the enslavement, but having done so it would then turn the person into a different kind of human being, a slave. The rule of fortune did therefore not create an essential equality between all human beings, since a change in status might also transform the person.

[68] Crook (1967b). Weaver (1972) 162–9, followed by Evans-Grubbs (1993) 128, (1995) 263, 267, thought it was about maintaining *vernae* for the *familia Caesaris*; *contra* D'Arms (1975) 337; Storchi Marino (1999) 415. See also pp. 44, 194 n.33.

[69] Tac. *Ann.* 12.53: 'pro libertis haberentur'. Sirks (2002) 176–7, (2005); cf. Sirks (1994), argued the measure was not about punishing the women, but maintaining the master's authority over the slave, who might become impertinent from living with a free woman. The argument is based on *Paul. Sent.* 2.21.11, which prescribes that a freedwoman who forms a union with a slave belonging to her patron, but against his wishes, is exempt from enslavement and remains his *liberta*. However, the degradation to freed status does suggest a punitive aspect, as stressed by several sources. Herrmann-Otto (1997) 28–33; (2005) 72–3, believed the *Senatus Consultum* was concerned with slave reproduction not punishment.

[70] It was of course also less shameful for a *liberta* to live with a slave than it was for an *ingenua*, so the demotion to freed status would paradoxically help restore her honour by bringing the two parties closer to each other in status.

The Romans treasured the ideal of the free, unfettered mind, which alone could make morally informed decisions and act according to the highest principles. Any form of dependency, psychological as well as material, reduced the person's honour and moral standing.[71] Slavery represented the ultimate state of dependency and lack of self-control, and the slave's total subjection to the will of another inevitably shaped his or her personality. As Longinus noted, slaves were unable to produce oratory, since servitude acted as a 'cage of the soul'. The slave could not develop the degree of rationality and moral maturity required for oratory, because he was not master of his own life.[72] Plutarch also declared in his treatise on the education of children that 'Free birth is the honourable treasure chest of free speech.'[73]

In his panegyric for Claudius Etruscus' father, a prominent imperial freedman, Statius made a curious attempt to minimise the stigma of servitude. Following the observation that the freedman had served an emperor whom the whole world obeys, Statius argued that all things are subjects and rule in their turn; even gods have their laws.[74] The argument smacks of special pleading and sophistry, but it is revealing in its implication that the only effective way of eulogising a freedman was to play down the dishonour normally associated with subservience.

Paradoxically it was slavery itself which produced the 'servile' slave, the distinct features they carried being the product of their condition rather than any natural disposition. Given the apparent tautology inherent in this model it obviously fails as a justification of slavery as such, and we might therefore dismiss it as little more than a set of conventional prejudices. Still, its importance in everyday life should not be underestimated, since it served as a means of separating masters from their slaves. The stereotype of the slave turned a formal hierarchy of status into a qualitative differentiation

---

[71] Hence the common use of slavery as a metaphor for all kinds of dependencies; Garnsey (1996) 220–35; Fitzgerald (2000). Propertius, for example, could refer to *amor* as *servitium*, 1.12.18, cf. Tibullus 2.4.1–5. See also Edwards (2003) on honour and morality in Roman political discourse.

[72] 44.4–5. Longinus' comments invoke Hom. *Od.* 17.322–3, on slaves losing half their soul when they were enslaved; cf. Pl. *Leg.* 776d–778a. The linking of oratory and freedom can also be found in Cic. *Fam.* 7.32.2, on a certain Selius who proves himself free(born?) by his oratory, implying that a slave could not make proper speeches. A similar point was made by Quintilian, *Inst. Or.* 2.11.7; 2.17.6; cf. Bradley (1994) 143.

[73] *De lib. educ.* 1B(1): 'καλὸς οὖν παρρησίας θησαυρὸς εὐγένεια'. Cf. the detailed discussion of Bloomer (2006), who summarised Plutarch's view as: 'The freeborn will not suffer the inequality of status or resources that requires the subordinate to keep silent. Free birth is a freedom from physical and material constraint and, importantly, from doing the bidding of another', 82. Later he also notes that: 'The circularity of the argument is clear: the free body is the vessel of free speech, free speech marks the worthy body and person', 95.

[74] *Silv.* 3.3.46–58.

based on personal characteristics, with the further implication that slaves were unable to control their own lives and their best interest lay in willing submission to the guidance of paternalistic masters.

The Roman construction of the slave as morally deficient and dishonoured was in no sense original, but can be found in most slave societies. It may reflect a common, perhaps even universal, tendency of rulers and masters to despise their subjects for their very servility and submission.[75] Thus, the same logic by which the powerless are dishonoured through their very capitulation could be used politically and applied to entire peoples.[76] Cicero, for example, referred to Jews and Syrians, long subjected to autocratic rule, as 'nations born to slavery', 'nationibus natis servituti'.[77] Likewise, Livy ascribed to Quinctius the view that Syrians are better fitted to be slaves than warriors because of their 'servilia ingenia', presumably acquired through prolonged experience of despotism.[78]

Turning the argument on its head, Cicero could complain about the slavishness of the provincials in Asia, a trait they had attained through 'diuturna servitute'.[79] In a similar vein Tacitus dismissed Rome's Gallic subjects as soft and degenerated through their very submission, contrasting them with Rome's opponents across the Channel who still maintained their fighting spirit; for the Gauls, Tacitus claimed, 'courage and liberty have been lost together'.[80] Subjection to Rome is frequently presented as akin to slavery, bringing with it a slow decline and moral degeneration.[81] Tacitus' apparent critique of the Roman empire should of course not be taken at face value, since it formed part of a broader exploration of the relationship between freedom, slavery, and honour. According to Tacitus the lack of political freedom in Rome was comparable to slavery, and like slavery the tyranny of bad emperors weakened the moral fibre of the people.[82] It was therefore Rome's internal decline which corroded the virtue of her empire, making it tyrannical and degrading for her subjects. On rare occasions Tacitus offers a slightly less bleak vision of the effects of oppression. Thus, his biography of his father-in-law Iulius Agricola can be seen as a plea for the possibility of maintaining honour even under a tyranny – albeit

---

[75] Greek constructions of the slave are well documented; e.g. Schlaifer (1960).
[76] Isaac (2004) 187–93.
[77] *Prov.Cons.* 5.10; a view echoed in Lucan, *BC* 7.442–5; Tac. *Hist.* 4.17: 'Servirent Syria Asiaque et suetus regibus Oriens'; Philostr. *Vit.Apol.* 8.7.37, and 7.14.9, on the moral corruption of tyranny.
[78] 35.49.8.   [79] *Q.fr.* 1.1.16.   [80] *Agr.* 11.4 : 'amissa virtute pariter ac libertate'.
[81] Cf. Tac. *Ann.* 12.34; 14.26, 31–5; *Agr.* 21, 24.3, 30.   [82] E.g. *Hist.* 2.71; *Ann.* 1.7; 3.65.

in the face of almost insurmountable obstacles.[83] Still, men like Agricola remained the exception and their example therefore illustrates the normal link between submission, dishonour and moral corruption.

Precisely how the Romans envisaged the enslaved became 'servile' is not entirely clear, and since we are dealing with conventional, barely rationalised prejudices we should not expect to find a consistent model.[84] Nevertheless, some patterns may be gleaned from the evidence. At one level enslavement represented an instant blow which irreversibly destroyed a person's honour; in that respect the 'social death' he or she experienced could never fully be overcome. All slaves appear to have suffered the same stigma irrespective of their background. It did not matter whether they had once known freedom or not; *servi nati* and *servi facti* were equally stigmatised and no distinction was made according to the duration of their servitude either. Apparently even those freeborns who had sold themselves into slavery were considered as 'servile' as any other slave. Thus, Claudius' freedman Pallas was an *ingenuus* who had entered into slavery to become an *actor*, but later was no less vilified for his servile past.[85] Likewise in the *Satyricon* a plea for the humanity of slaves is put into the mouth of a character at Trimalchio's dinner who claimed he had been born free and sold himself into slavery.[86]

On the other hand, it is also clear that such undifferentiated notions of 'servility' do not tell the whole story. It stretches belief to assume that the Romans thought that enslavement at a stroke deprived a man of his moral faculties, and it seems that the individual experience of slavery was recognised as a factor in the creation of the 'servile' personality. Although a slave was formally defined by his subjection to the authority of another, the practice of slavery obviously mattered too. While the slave's 'social death' left him permanently dishonoured, it may have been the treatment he received that was held primarily responsible for his 'servile' mind and

---

[83] Most explicitly at *Agr.* 42.

[84] The self-serving nature of this construction is also underlined by the 'exemptions' accorded Romans who had been enslaved abroad. They were allowed to return and regain their former status, including their *ingenuitas*, which remained undiminished, Hermann-Otto (2005) 67–9. Likewise, the rule that a freedman 'who had been restored to this birthright is treated as if he had been born free and not been besmirched by slavery (*macula servitutis*) in the intervening time', D. 40.11.5 (Modestinus). This inconsistency highlights the fact that the 'servility' of slaves was a social construct which served a specific function in maintaining a system that arbitrarily kept people in servitude.

[85] Tac. *Ann.* 12.53; cf. Oost (1958).

[86] *Sat.* 57.4–5. The freedman's claim is inconsistent with the biography he presents which implies that he arrived in Italy as a boy and received his education there.

body.[87] This point is brought out very clearly when we compare the position
of sons and slaves; for adult sons *in potestate* were in principle subjected to
a paternal authority which was not dissimilar to that exercised by masters
over slaves. But in their case no stigma was attached to their formal lack
of autonomy. The crucial difference lay in the application of the *pater
familias'* authority, which was tempered by conventions and a social code
that, for example, limited the relevance of the *pater familias'* power over
life and death ('potestas vitae necisque') to the early stages of childhood.[88]
The *pater familias* was also required to convene a 'family court' or *consilium*
before condemning any members of his family.[89] Physical punishment of
adult sons was generally considered unacceptable, precisely because that
put them on a level with slaves.[90] Thus, Plutarch warned against whipping
children, because that 'would make them servile and dishonour them'.[91]
Quintilian also advised against beating pupils because it was disgraceful and
'fit only for slaves'.[92] As Saller rightly observed, there was 'a fundamental
polarity in Roman civic values between *libertas*, represented as freedom
from the whip, and *servitus*, especially subjection to the whip'.[93]

In sharp contrast to sons 'in potestate', there were no restrictions – formal
or informal – on the power of the master over his slaves.[94] The authority
exercised over sons was therefore clearly distinguished from a master's power
over his slaves. Cicero made the difference quite explicit when he stressed
the need for masters to use force against their slaves, 'coercet et frangit',
'restrain and break'.[95] The mutilated and scarred body of the slave was
therefore a commonplace.[96] For example, when Dio Chrysostom explored

---

[87] As Watson (1987) 39, noted, the Roman sources reveal 'a strong suspicion that slavery was detrimental
to the slave's character'.
[88] Cf. Thomas (1984); Harris (1986); Roller (2001) 237ff.
[89] Kunkel (1966); Thomas (1990).   [90] Cf. Dumont (1990); Saller (1991), (1996).
[91] *De lib. educ.* 8F(12); cf. Saller (1996) 127; Bloomer (2006) 95–6.
[92] 1.3.14: beating of children being 'deforme atque servile'.   [93] Saller (1996) 127.
[94] Watson (1987) 115–33. Some restrictions were introduced under the empire, 120–8. Knoch's suggestion (2005) 45–6, based on Dion. Hal. 20.13.3, that the censors would regulate the behaviour of slave
owners under the republic seems implausible; cf. Watson (1983) 53–6, who also showed, 60–1, that
Antoninus Pius' 'humanitarian' measures were concerned with damage to property affecting heirs.
The growing care for slaves, often claimed for the later empire, may be a modern fiction, cf. Watson
(1983); Bradley (1984a) 126–9; (1994) 165–73; Ligt (2002); Bruggisser (2005). Knoch's attempt to
demonstrate the practical limitations to the *dominica potestas* seems to ignore the recurring stress
in the ancient sources on violence as an accepted means of controlling slaves. The idealised picture
of self-imposed limitations to the masters' power (e.g. 87) is heavily reliant on a moral discourse
advocating moderation and self-restraint, which might have been very far from the reality.
[95] *Rep.* 3.37, cf. Saller (1996). On cruelty to slaves see e.g. Hopkins (1978) 118–23.
[96] See Schlange-Schöningen (2003) 276–83, for references to beatings and torture of slaves in the works
of Galen and other ancient authors. On the ways in which the beating of slaves – and the immunity
of the free – occupied the literary imagination see Fitzgerald (2000) 32–50.

the problem of determining who is really a slave, the physical markers of servitude – fetters, tattoos, and branding – featured prominently, along with hard physical labour.[97]

The slave's body did not enjoy any protection from violence or other kinds of physical abuse, which might also include sexual exploitation. The Roman sources reveal a general expectation that slaves might be abused sexually by their masters.[98] This is illustrated, for example, by the legal principle that freedwomen could not be victims of *stuprum* committed by their patron, suggesting that even former slaves did not regain full physical integrity.[99] Likewise, Seneca Maior famously referred to a saying by Haterius, who was defending a freedman charged with being his patron's *concubinus*, 'Losing one's virtue is a crime in the freeborn, a necessity in a slave, a duty (*officium*) for the freedman.' The statement is obviously frivolous, since sexual services could never be part of formalised *officia*, but it nevertheless underlines the natural expectation that a slave – and perhaps also a freed person – would be sexually available.[100]

The violability of the slave's body was central to the creation of the servile person. The legal sources were aware that physical abuse affected the whole person. Thus, a jurist discussed a situation where a slave had been pledged by his master, who then put him in chains for a trivial offence; this was found to have reduced the market value of the slave.[101] The logic behind the opinion was that a degraded body leads to a degraded person, and this perceived link also underlies Quintilian's warning against the use of physical force against pupils because their characters would suffer along with their bodies.[102] Scars – along with branding marks and tattoos – were therefore not just physical signs of servitude but visual markers of a servile mind and recall Horace's attack on the anonymous freedman, mentioned above.[103] Horace emphasised the essential difference between the freed

---

[97] *Or.* 14 and 15, esp. 14.18–19. Likewise, as the elder Seneca observed, the sign of an experienced slave – even a metaphorical slave as, in this case, Cicero – is that he has 'a worn neck' from carrying the yoke, *Suas.* 6.12: 'Iam collum tritum habet'; cf. Roller (2001) 215–16. Tertullian used the terms 'perverbustos' and 'flagra rumpentium' to describe slaves – 'loaded with floggings' and 'whip-spoilers', *Pallio* 4.8.4; *Apol.* 6.3.
[98] Cf. e.g. Fabre (1981) 258–61; McGinn (1991) 353; (2002) 65; Williams (1999) 99–100; Pollini (2003).
[99] D. 25.7.1 (Ulpian); 34.9.16.1 (Papinian).
[100] *Contr.* 4 pr. 10: 'impudicitia in ingenuo crimen est, in servo necessitas, in liberto officium'; cf. D. 38.1.38 pr. (Callistratus); Petr. *Sat.* 63.3; 69.2–3; 75.11.
[101] D. 20.1.27 (Marcellus). Watson (1983) 55–6; (1987) 118.
[102] *Inst. Or.* 1.3.13–7. Callistratus, D. 50.2.12, found it 'inhonestum' if people who had been flogged by the aediles were admitted to the *ordo*, although he conceded it was not illegal. The central concern seems to be the personal dishonour they had incurred.
[103] For the visual marks of slavery see Jones (1987).

and the freeborn, and central to his argument were the physical scars the freedman still carried from the whip and the shackles. As we saw, Horace implied that the freedman's submission had shaped him both physically and mentally to such an extent that he now belonged to a different *genus* from that of freeborn Romans.[104]

This construction of the slave was self-reinforcing; the mental and moral deficiencies ascribed to slaves meant that they would have to be 'educated' corporeally through force according to the rationale that the lower instincts are reached through the body, not the mind. As Demosthenes had already stated, free men and slaves are different in that a slave is 'answerable with his body for all offences'.[105] Special slave penalties were therefore also invented to fit their separate nature.[106] This logic was entirely circular and reached its natural conclusion in the systematic use of torture against slaves. In all criminal and civil court cases the testimony of slaves was deemed admissible only when made under duress. The Roman state therefore employed torturers, as did the local authorities, and their work was regulated by public decree.[107] The routine nature of public torture is chillingly illustrated in Cicero's *Pro Cluentio* and other ancient sources.[108] Under the empire some modifications were introduced to limit the use of torture in some instances, but the basic principle remained that slaves had to be tortured if their evidence was to be accepted in a court of law.[109] The reliance on torture was not rooted in a belief in its universal efficacy, and the jurists were aware of the difficulties in getting to the truth through torture, noting that some people could resist it while others would confess to anything.[110] The use of torture was therefore rooted in the social construction of the slave as a natural stranger to the truth – which therefore had to be extracted through the application of physical force.

In everyday life this stereotype would often have been self-confirming since it allowed any resistance or intransigence on the part of slaves to be construed as an expression of their criminal nature and moral deficiency,

---

[104] Juvenal, 7.14–6, revealed a similar concern with the physical marks of servitude when he mentioned the 'knights from Asia', who were betrayed when they showed a bare ankle – with the marks of the fetters. Martial, 2.29, suggested that a person sitting in the front rows with an eye patch might be covering up the marks of slavery, i.e. tattoos or branding.
[105] 22.55. Cf. Finley (1998) 161.
[106] E.g. D. 2.9.5 (Ulpian); cf. Garnsey (1970) 122–31, 158–72.
[107] *Lex lib.* 11.8–14; cf. Brunt (1980); Bradley (1994) 165–73.
[108] *Cluent.* 176–7. Cf. e.g. Livy 26.27.9, on the 'examination' of slaves 'foro medio'; Val. Max. 6.8.1; D. 2.1.7.3 (Ulpian).
[109] For this development see e.g. Knoch (2005) 213–18.
[110] D. 48.18.1.23–5 (Ulpian). Likewise *Rhet. ad Her.* 2.10; Cic. *Sulla* 78; *Mil.* 60; Sen. *Ep.* 47.5; cf. Watson (1983) 59; Bradley (1994) 167.

which in turn demanded further use of violence and oppression. The resulting cycle of degradation deepened the gulf between masters and slaves whose mutual relationship – unsurprisingly – often is described as dominated by fear and loathing; as the old saying went: 'tot servi, quot hostes', 'as many slaves, so many enemies'.[111]

The servile stereotype performed a vital function in maintaining the slave system by setting slaves apart from free and reinforcing the notion of stable, ostensibly natural hierarchies of authority.[112] But precisely that construction of the slave also raised fundamental problems whenever a master decided to free a slave, since the 'essentialising' approach to slavery and freedom worked on the ideal premise that people remain within their categories. The construction of the slave as carrier of specific 'servile' traits, designed to entrench the basic boundary between free and unfree, was compromised by the practice of manumission which meant that people invested with distinct personal deficiencies were admitted into the free population – even the Roman citizen body. Procedurally the Romans may have pretended that no change took place, but this fiction did of course not obscure the fact that real transitions occurred. Thus, while the 'invention' of the slave helped in stabilising slavery as an institution, it made manumission more problematic.

The paradox of the 'servile' free lay at the core of the Roman preoccupation with freedmen and manumission, which may be understood as an attempt at negotiating this particular conundrum. The problem how to reconcile the notion of personal 'servility' with a – fairly widespread – practice of manumission was not unique; manumission existed in most slave systems, the majority of which also constructed slaves as qualitatively different. But there were factors which made the issue more pressing in Rome, particularly concerned with the civic status given to the former slave. In Greece freedmen were kept separate from the citizen body and granted a status as metics, resident aliens, reflecting their collective inferiority to the freeborn citizens.[113] In the early modern world in the Americas,

---

[111] Festus 314L; Sen. *Ep.* 47.5; Macr. *Sat.* 1.11.13; cf. Hopkins (1978) 119. The consul C. Cassius advocated terror as a means of controlling slaves, Tac. *Ann.* 14.44, and Propertius, 3.6.6, observed that 'timens servus habere fidem'. Hor. *Sat.* 1.1.77–8, on the fear of slaves stealing or running away. In general on Roman fear of their slaves, Gamauf (2007). On slave resistance see Bradley (1994) 107–31.

[112] As Boulvert and Morabito (1982) 111, observed: 'La reconnaissance d'une macule servile est nécessaire au maintien du système, au clivage bien net entre libres et non libres.'

[113] On Greek manumission see Garlan (1988) 73–84; Fisher (1993) 67–71; Weiler (2003) 180–9; Zelnick-Abramovitz (2005). Kamen (2009) discusses the anxieties the crossing of these boundaries caused in Athens and the opposition to manumission it engendered. It is probably not incidental that Polybius denounced the practice of manumission altogether, implying that slaves were made to serve and only became insolent when freed, e.g. 38.15.10; cf. Texier (1979) 121–33.

slavery generally had a 'racial' element to it, which distinguished the freedman from his former master. Typically they were also given a lesser civic
status which barred them from political influence, while in North America
manumission was extremely rare, and effectively banned in some states.[114]

By contrast, the Romans had traditionally enfranchised their freedmen,
in principle making them equal to their masters, which gave the universal
problem of manumission a different edge in Rome. It meant that strategies
had to be developed that would neutralise the problem of 'servile' citizens,
and these strategies, informal and *ad hoc* as they were, exploited the inherent
inconsistencies in the 'construction' of the slave, which seemed at the same
time to operate with an absolute and a relative concept of 'servility'. On
the one hand, all slaves carried the same permanent stigma and dishonour,
while, on the other hand, it was also recognised that not all slaves were
equally degraded by their experiences. By linking the degree of 'servility'
to the treatment the slaves had suffered at the hands of their owners, it
became possible for the Romans to distinguish between those slaves who
were beyond redemption and those who were not. It was the latter, less
'damaged' slaves who might properly be considered for manumission.

The connection between a slave's treatment and his moral development
is drawn in several sources. Cicero, in an uncharacteristically charitable
passage of his fourth Catilinarian speech, praises the urban lower classes,
saying that even freedmen feel more patriotic than some Roman nobles do.
He then adds that 'There is no slave, *none at least who is the better treated*,
who does not abhor the audacity of such citizens' and hope and work
for the safety of the Roman state.[115] A similar distinction can be traced
in Roman comedy. For example, in Terence's *Andria* Sosia is a virtuous
character and we are told that he was well treated and, as Rawson noted,
'spared corrupting experiences as a slave'.[116] Conversely, Valerius Maximus
mentions a slave who had been put in chains and branded but nevertheless
saved his master during the triumviral proscriptions, a remarkable act not
just because it confounded expectations but also because a person so deeply
degraded generally was thought incapable of displaying such virtue.[117]

While the Roman construction of 'safe' manumission relied on the
notion of 'servility' as relative rather than absolute, it was also assisted by

---

[114] For a broad comparison of manumission practices see Patterson (1982) chs. 8–10, and below
pp. 141–80.
[115] *Cat.* 4.16: 'Servus est nemo, qui modo tolerabili condicione sit servitutis, qui non audaciam civium
perhorrescat, qui non haec stare cupiat, qui non quantum audet et quantum potest conferat ad
salutem voluntatis.'
[116] *Andr.* 35–9. Rawson (1993) 220. The same applies to Tyndarus in Plautus' *Captivi*.
[117] 6.8.7; cf. Dio 47.10.

the image of the slave as a kind of perpetual child, which entailed the possibility of personal growth. A common feature of most slave societies is the designation of slaves as children irrespective of their age. Thus, 'pais' was used in Greece, 'boy' in America, and 'puer' in Rome.[118] The first definition of 'puer' offered by the jurist Paul was slave – 'cum omnes servos pueros appellaremus' – and it even became part of Roman slave names such as Marcipor and Gaipor, i.e. the boy of Marcus and the boy of Gaius.[119] This perception of the slave is also reflected in pictorial representations, where adult slaves are typically shown as roughly half the size of free people.[120] The visual effect produced by this convention of 'hierarchical scaling' is slightly surreal but corresponds to the notion of grown men answering to the name of 'boy'.

The infantilisation of slaves provided a means of explaining manumission as the recognition of a maturing process, which had gradually raised them above the level of other slaves. The servile character was considered neither fixed nor absolute – such rigidity would have been impractical and stifled the otherwise profitable institution of manumission. For that reason the social 'construction' of the slave had to allow for the possibility of personal improvement, if not complete recovery. In line with this model Cicero referred to *liberti* as 'men who have won the advantages of our citizenship on their own merit', suggesting their *virtus* had brought them out of slavery.[121] Likewise, Seneca described the education which might lead to manumission, indicating that, despite the stoic belief in their common humanity, slaves could not immediately and without preparation receive their freedom. The strategy Seneca followed was to 'promote a slave to such a position that he will, in many respects, be a free man'.[122] In his speech for the actor Roscius, Cicero also emphasised the crucial role of training, claiming that the worth of a slave was not innate but came entirely from

---

[118] Wiedemann (1989) 27, defined slaves as 'in a sense children who had not been allowed to grow up', but that is obviously applicable only to *servi nati*. In the case of adult enslavement the person is at a stroke reduced to a childlike status. Golden (1985) suggested that the double use of 'pais' refers to the similar status of children and slaves, rather than the attribution of childlike features to slaves. But one might argue that adults kept in a position similar to that of children are themselves infantilised. Maurin (1975) offered a complex analysis of the Latin word pair *liber* and *puer*, their respective meanings and social significance.

[119] D. 50.16.204. According to Pliny, *NH* 33.26, this naming practice reflected the small households in earlier times. See now the critical discussion of this tradition in Cheesman (2009).

[120] See e.g. D'Ambra (1995) fig. 1; Schumacher (2001b) figs. 30–9 (pp. 80–8); Roller (2006) 28 fig. 2; 32–3 figs. 3–4; 150 fig. 17, plates IV–VI.

[121] *Cat.* 4.16: 'sua virtute fortunam huius civitatis consecuti'.

[122] *Ben.* 3.19.2: 'eo perducam servum, ut in multa liber sit', cf. 2.21.2. Garnsey (1996) 90, F7. Sosia in Terence's *Andria* had been freed because he served his master 'liberaliter', 38, that is, like a free man.

the teaching he had received.[123] The distinction between slaves that might qualify for freedom and those that did not seems to have been drawn almost instinctively by the Romans, as indicated by Cicero's rhetorical question, 'For what free citizen – indeed, what slave worthy of freedom – did not have my safety at heart?'[124] The criterion applied here was clearly a moral one, with the implication that within the body of slaves two sub-categories could be discerned, the 'deserving' and the 'undeserving', only one of which might be properly considered for manumission.

This strategy may have helped address the problem of the 'servile citizen' but it did not solve it altogether. While it opened up an avenue for ideologically 'safe' manumission, it became crucial that the process be seen as selective and discriminating. If the divide between free and unfree could be crossed by any slave at any time, both categories would be called into question and society threatened by an influx of the 'undeserving'. Only those who had been allowed to reach a level of personal maturity that qualified them for freedom ought to be considered.

These fundamental concerns are key to understanding much of the overt hostility towards manumission we find in the sources as well as the measures taken to regulate the practice. One of the most famous tirades against manumission is that of Dionysius of Halicarnassus.[125] After a spirited defence of Servius Tullius' enfranchisement of freedmen, Dionysius launches a sustained attack on contemporary manumission practices. Prominent among his complaints is the freeing of criminal slaves, who finance their freedom through robbery, burglary, or prostitution. Others, he claims, are freed in order to benefit from the grain dole and other forms of public largesse. Others again – sometimes entire *familiae*, including criminals! – are given their freedom testamentarily by self-indulgent masters concerned with posthumous popularity and grand funerary processions attended by grateful freedmen. Faced with these iniquities, Dionysius proposes that censors or consuls oversee the manumission process and make inquiries into those who are freed and the reasons why. They should also decide

---

[123] *Rosc. Com.* 27–30. This passage is well analysed in Thebert (1993) 152.

[124] *Leg.* 3.25: 'quis enim non modo liber, sed servus libertate dignus fuit, cui nostra salus cara non esset?' A practical differentiation between the quality of slaves can also be found in the *Digest*, where Ulpian, 47.10.15.44, notes that the severity of insults and defamation against slaves depends on the standing of the slave: 'for it is highly relevant what sort of slave he is, whether he is honest, an *ordinarius*, a steward or only a common slave, a drudge or whatever. And what if he be in fetters, branded, and of the deepest notoriety?'; 'etenim multum interest, qualis servus est, bonae frugi, ordinarius, dispensator, an vero vulgaris vel mediastinus an qualisqualis. Et quid si compenditus vel male notus vel notae extremae?'

[125] 4.24.4–8.

whether the freedman should be inscribed in *tribus*, i.e. enfranchised, or perhaps be expelled from the city. The whole outburst is informed by the conviction that indiscriminate manumission poses a real danger to society; admitting unworthy slaves to the citizen body, he claims, will inevitably lead to contamination.

The shrill tone of the passage might suggest a conventional piece of moralising, but Dionysius' concerns seem to have found a direct response in the Augustan legislation that dealt with freedmen and manumission. These laws sought to enforce proper discrimination in one form or another and particularly revealing are the prescriptions concerning the so-called *dediticii*, laid down in the *lex Aelia Sentia* of 4 CE. According to Gaius, those slaves who had been chained by their owners as a punishment, branded, publicly interrogated under torture and found guilty, or used to fight in the arena or sent to a gladiatorial school or imprisoned would not become citizens upon manumission, but instead receive the status of *peregrini dediticii*, defeated and surrendered foreigners.[126] In addition they were banned from living in the city of Rome, having to remain beyond the hundredth milestone.[127] Most scholars have seen this as an attempt to keep 'criminal' slaves out of the citizen body,[128] and the criteria used to define those excluded may broadly have signalled 'trouble-makers' to the Roman public. Still, the guilt of the slave is only mentioned in the context of public trials, and while it may have been implicit in the list of punishments administered by masters it is not the same as proven criminality.[129]

What seems to unite all the experiences which disqualified slaves from becoming citizens was their degrading effect; indeed the jurist Gaius defined those affected by the law as 'huius . . . turpitudinis servos', that is, 'slaves who have been disgraced in the manner mentioned'.[130] The stress on the demeaning treatment of the slave would suggest that the disgrace

---

[126] *Inst.* 1.13–6; cf. Ulp. *Reg.* 1.11. On the complex legal issues involved in defining 'vinctus' see Wenger (1941) 356–60.

[127] Gaius *Inst.* 1.27. Gardner (1993) 40. This particular provision must also be seen in context of the perceived risk of 'contamination' from close contact with the 'servile' population.

[128] Thus, Treggiari (1969a) 237, believed it was a measure against 'rash manumission' especially of 'criminal slaves'; cf. Klees (2002) 116. Sherwin-White (1973) 334, described those who became *dediticii* as the 'vicious slave', despite the fact that they were defined entirely by their owners' decision to punish them.

[129] Buckland (1908) 544–6. Watson (1987) 30, (1995) 48, observed, however, that the state generally did not come between owner and slave, so any punishment could be accepted as indicative of guilt.

[130] *Inst.* 1.15. Trans. Zulueta (1946) 5. The slaves affected by the law were those 'in nulla tali turpitudine', 1.16. Revealingly, the term 'turpitudo' is translated by Gordon and Robinson (1988) 25, as 'wickedness', which, in line with the modern stress on the slave's criminality, shifts the emphasis away from the treatment on to the slave. Isid. *Etym.* 9.4.50, explained that they were excluded from citizenship because of the 'marks of punishment that they had manifestly experienced'. In the

it entailed was as important as any potential guilt.[131] The measure there-fore seems to have had a broader scope than simply keeping delinquent slaves away from citizenship. It barred from that status all those who had been so profoundly debased that they would never be able to recover. In doing so the legislators reinforced a common prejudice, as expressed by, for example, Horace whose scarred freedman of the fourth *Epode* would never have become a citizen after the passing of the *lex Aelia Sentia*. In a broader perspective the law also excluded all those slaves who did not enjoy the kind of support and encouragement from their masters which the Romans deemed necessary for their personal development and the attainment of freedom. Slaves who had suffered the kind of treatment described by Gaius were those who were out of favour with their masters – or perhaps in many cases just out of his sight – and they could never reach a level of maturity that would qualify them for citizenship.

Later under the empire the issue of proper discrimination resurfaces in Tacitus' debate about the re-enslavement of *liberti ingrati*.[132] The answer to the problem was a careful vetting in advance of manumission, granting each slave the status he or she deserved and using the tools of distinction with which Augustus had provided slave owners. The *lex Aelia Sentia* thus defined a 'minimum threshold' for slaves who were about to enter the Roman citizen body. A basic age requirement was set at 30, below which they would not become full Roman citizens but receive a new status as *Latini Iuniani* (already introduced by the *lex Iunia*). The *lex Aelia Sentia* also required manumitters to be of sound mind and at least 20 years of age. According to Dio, the aim was to prevent owners freeing slaves 'indiscriminately', specifically using the term ἀκρίτως.[133]

Another Augustan law, the *lex Fufia Caninia* from 2 BCE, gave very detailed prescriptions concerning testamentary manumission.[134] It devised a graded scale which indicated the proportion of slaves in a given household that might be manumitted in this way. In households containing between two and ten slaves half might be freed; from ten to thirty a third, from

---

epitome of Gaius, 1.1.3, specific mention is made of those 'in quorum facie vel corpore quaecumque indicia aut igne aut ferro impressa sunt, ut deleri non possint'.

[131] Thus, Watson noted that in cases where the slave has been shackled or branded by his owner the question of guilt was irrelevant: (1983) 55, (1987) 118. It is striking too that although the owner's decision to free a slave he had previously punished would seem to indicate improved behaviour and rehabilitation, the law took no account of that. The fact that the slave at some point had been physically mistreated was sufficient to bar him from citizenship indefinitely. Similarly, D. 40.5.43 (Paul) stated that fideicommissary manumission of a slave who had later been chained by his master no longer applied.

[132] *Ann.* 13.26–7.   [133] 55.13.7.   [134] Gaius *Inst.* 1.42–6; Ulp. *Reg.* 1.24f; *Paul.Sent.* 4.14.

thirty to a hundred a quarter, and between one hundred and five hundred a fifth of the slaves might be freed. The upper limit of one hundred also applied to households that were even larger. The law further required that each slave manumitted by will be mentioned by name in order to prevent *en bloc* manumissions of entire sections of a household.[135] The objective was to force owners to consider each case individually before taking a decision of such importance.

All these regulations illustrate the perceived need for manumission to be selective and reflect a careful assessment by their master. The aim was to shore up the moral construction of manumission as the reward for individual slaves who had managed to 'grow up' and mature into responsible human beings. The laws therefore set basic qualifications for both master and slave and identified those slaves degraded beyond redemption and masters incapable of performing their task. In practice the most important consequence was probably the minimum age of 30 for slaves to acquire Roman citizenship, which reflected the ideal of slaves receiving freedom after a long record of devoted service. More broadly it tied in with the conceptualisation of manumission as the recognition of a maturing process, which sat uneasily with the freeing of young slaves. It did not bar owners from freeing younger slaves – that would have infringed their basic property rights – but introduced a multi-tiered system of status for freedmen. The measures ensured that manumission appeared to be judicious and selective, thereby making the practice ideologically 'safe', and they were so effective that they remained in place throughout the imperial period with no serious attempt to regulate manumission further. However, while they successfully addressed the central concern about discrimination, two issues remained which would continue to preoccupy the Roman authorities: firstly, the freedman's need for continued 'guidance' by his former owner, and, secondly, the possibility that a freedman might usurp a status in society that was considered incompatible with his perceived disabilities. These two issues will be dealt with in the following chapters.

---

[135] Gaius *Inst.* 2.239.

CHAPTER 3

Freedmen and their patrons

The act of manumission did not transform the slave as a human being. In the eyes of society he still carried many of the moral and mental deficiencies associated with servitude. For example, even if he was adopted by a free-born, the jurists insisted that legally he remained a freedman, a condition regarded as innate to his person; despite the change to his formal status he was in essence still a former slave.[1] Naturally therefore a freedman could never become entirely equal to an *ingenuus*, and when he entered society as a free man he needed help and supervision. Logically this guidance would be provided by the former master, whose support – at least in theory – had enabled him to reach a level of personal development that qualified him for freedom. Manumission was therefore not supposed to terminate the relationship between the freedman and his former owner. Also after freedom had been granted the two were expected to be closely involved, and in many respects manumission merely redefined their relationship rather than bringing an end to it. The previous ownership was replaced by a new bond based on debt and gratitude for the 'beneficium' of freedom.[2]

The new relationship between the freedman and his former master was constructed socially and legally through a combination of elements derived from different spheres of Roman life. The terminology is important in this context. While the freed slave became a *libertus* or *libertinus*, i.e. a person who had received *libertas*,[3] the former owner gained the title of *patronus*.

---

[1] Gell. *NA* 5.19.11–14; D. 1.5.27 (Ulpian); cf. 1.7.46; 23.2.32 (Marcellus). Fabre (1981) 37–9; Gardner (1993) 16; (1998) 187–90; Lindsay (2009) 123–37.

[2] D. 38.2.1 pr. (Ulpian): 'tam grande beneficium'; cf. D. 1.1.4 (Ulpian): 'beneficium manumissionis'. Cicero commented on a freedman who helped his patron 'a quo summum beneficium acceperat', *Verr.* 2.1.124.

[3] It is commonly assumed (e.g. *TLL* s.v. 'libertinus', 2.a, and Fabre (1981) 125 n. 1) that 'libertus' indicated the freedman's position in relation to his patron and 'libertinus' his public status, and there are some traces of this distinction in Plautus, e.g. *Poen.* 832; *Curc.* 413, 547. Most later writers, however, seem to use the terms interchangeably (cf. *TLL ibid.*), although Suet. *Claud.* 25.1 and Sen. *Contr.* 7.6.19, may echo the old distinction.

This particular designation is significant, since it associated the freedman with two different social institutions – that of *clientela* and that of the Roman household, the *familia*. As far back as we can trace, the term carried a double meaning, denoting both a person who had freed a slave and the senior partner in a *clientela* relationship. The word *patronus* was derived from *pater* in the same way as *matrona* was derived from *mater*.[4] The use of the paternal model in both contexts is important given the exceptional position of authority held by the *pater familias* within the Roman household. Thus, Isidor of Seville explained the title *patronus* by reference to the fact that a patron ruled his clients like a father.[5] As far as we know, that is factually inaccurate, but the father–son relationship functioned as a moral template for the relationship that ought to exist between a client and his protector and between a freedman and his former owner.

In the case of the freedman the paternal element went beyond the purely symbolic. For, unlike clients, the former slave's position did in many respects come close to that of a quasi-son, just as the position of the former master commonly was associated with that of the father.[6] Most explicitly this ideal was expressed in Publilius Syrus' famous dictum 'Probus libertus sine natura est filius', 'the good freedman is a son without nature', implying that he behaves like a son although they were not blood-related.[7] The same connection is made in Terence, where a freedman exclaims: 'All our hope lies in you, Hegio. You're the only person we have, our patron, our father.'[8] This construction of their relationship was facilitated by the ancient convention according to which slaves had no relatives. In Roman law the slave, being socially 'dead', had no recognised parents or children. In the same way they had no civic persona, so they were also deprived of any familial identity, formally not being the child of their parents or parents of their children. This convention was more than a legal fiction, and can be traced in popular perceptions of the freedman, who was frequently taunted for his lack of parentage. As Martial said, Zoilus is welcome to the *ius trium liberorum*, as long as 'nobody gives you a mother or a father', and Cicero

---

[4] *TLL* s.v. 'patronus', 10.1 781–2. In legal sources 'patronus' was used synonymously with manumitter.

[5] *Orig.* 10.P (205). The relationship between the two meanings of the word, patron of a client and manumitter of a slave, is further complicated by the double meaning of 'pater' itself which can refer to both a father and a patrician.

[6] Cf. Fabre (1981) 125–7.

[7] P 1 (450). The direct parallel between sons and freedmen is also drawn in e.g. D. 37.15.9 (Ulpian): 'Liberto et filio semper honesta et sancta persona patris ac patroni videri debet.'

[8] *Adel.* 455–6: 'In te spes omnis, Hegio, nobis sitast. Te solum habemus, tu's patronus, tu pater.' A similar connection, albeit inverted for comical purposes, is found in Plaut. *Rud.* 1265–6.

quoted a line warning those who have neither mother nor father from over-confidence.[9]

Manumission could therefore be conceptualised as a 'birth', through which the master became a quasi father who gave life and social existence to the slave. Thus, Martial could claim that although a certain Diodorus received senators and knights at his table, nobody thought he was born, implying he was a former slave.[10] Moreover, his repeated reference to people being treated 'as if they had not been born' suggests this may have been a common Roman expression relating to the freedman's fatherless condition.[11]

It was commonly assumed that somebody who had saved your life became like a father to you. Cicero mentions the reluctance of soldiers to grant the *corona civica* to those who rescued them, because of the 'burden of being under the same obligation to a stranger that they owe a parent'.[12] Polybius also said that it was Roman custom that a man who had been saved in battle must treat his saviour like a father throughout his life.[13] Given the construction of the slave as 'socially dead', lacking both family and parentage, it was entirely natural that the former master who had created the new person would fill this crucial gap in the freedman's identity.[14] Thus, at census registrations citizens were asked to give 'their *nomina*, their *praenomina*, their fathers or patrons, their tribes, their *cognomina*'.[15] And in one of Horace's *Epistles* a stranger's identity is ascertained by asking 'where he came from, who he was, what his standing was, who his father or patron was'.[16] The patron's role as a 'substitute father' was formalised in the freedman's new name. Thus, instead of the standard filiation, e.g. 'Marci filius', the freedman received a pseudo-filiation (also

---

[9] 11.12; *De Or.* 2.257. Cf. Stat. *Silv.* 3.3.44, on the freed father of Claudius Etruscus, whose good fortune made up for his missing 'stemma', family tree.

[10] 10.27.4: 'nemo tamen natum te, Diodore, putat'.

[11] 4.83.4; 8.64.18; cf. Plaut. *Capt.* 574; *Paul.Sent.* 4.10.2. Tacitus' reference to a slave's 'paternal estate', *Ann.* 14.43.4, seems to be an ironic play on the same convention, cf. Koestermann (1963–68) 4.109.

[12] *Planc.* 72: 'sed onus beneficii reformidant, quod permagnum est alieno debere idem quod parenti'.

[13] 6.39.6–7; cf. Roller (2001) 188.

[14] This correlation of the role of the patron with that of a father was not completely unique to Rome. Also in medieval and early modern Islam, freedmen, especially those of the Caliph, were seen as the 'creatures' of their master, and the freeing of a slave was compared to the birth of a son. As in Rome, the manumission created a lasting bond, which also involved the patron's right to inherit from the freedman, Forand (1971). Marmon (1999) 15, also stresses the 'artificial kinship created by manumission' in the Mamluk empire, as well as the frequent comparisons with a father/son relationship.

[15] *Tabula Heracleensis*, *CIL* 1^2.593 line 146; *Roman Statutes* 368: 'eorumque nomina praenomina patres aut patronos tribus cognomina'.

[16] 'unde domo, quis, cuius fortunae, quo sit patre quove patrono', 1.7.53–4.

known as 'libertinisation'), which indicated who his patron was, i.e. 'Marci libertus'.[17]

Moreover, while a slave carried just a single name given to him by the master, the freedman's new civic identity required a full Roman name. Like a son he therefore received the gentilicial *nomen* of the patron,[18] and during the republic it also became common practice to give him the patron's *praenomen*, in the same way as sons increasingly received that of their fathers.[19] There are wide implications of the Roman naming practice.[20] Not only did the patron take the place otherwise reserved for the natural parent, but the freedman also came to share the patron's family name which traditionally embodied the honour and social standing of the lineage. In that way he came to perpetuate the name, which, as Saller has argued, might have been as important as the actual bloodline.[21] In many testamentary provisions the shared *nomen* was also singled out as the defining bond between the testator and the beneficiaries.[22] For example, A. Plautius Euhodus stipulated that access to his tomb was restricted to his children and freedmen 'and their descendants who are called Plautius'.[23]

---

[17] Since women could own and free slaves but had no *praenomina*, the practice of pseudo-filiation led to the introduction of a pseudo-*praenomen*, Gaia, which represented women generically and in inscriptions is given as an inverted C to distinguish it from Gaius.

[18] Cf. Kunst (1999) 159. However, despite receiving the *nomen gentilicium* of their patron, the freedmen did not become part of their *gens*, cf. Cic. *Top.* 29; Smith (2006) 15.

[19] Fabre (1981) 108–14; Salomies (1987) 229ff, showed it had become the norm in the first century BCE. A freedman might be given a name different from the manumitter's. Thus, shortly after his own adoption, Atticus named a freedman T. Caecilius Eutychides, mixing his old *praenomen* with his new *nomen*, *Att.* 4.15.1. Atticus also gave his freedman Dionysius the *praenomen* Marcus in homage of his friend Cicero, *ibid.*

[20] Eighteenth-century Jamaica forms an interesting contrast to Rome, since there former slaves did not take the master's family name, neither did they emulate the common practice of multiple names. Many of them even adopted new personal names for themselves, thereby completely abandoning their slave past, Burnand (2001) 339–41. This pattern has also been observed in Bermuda; Handler and Jacoby (1996).

[21] Saller (1994) 79–80.

[22] Saller (1994) 169. Champlin (1991) 133, noted that *liberti* and *libertae* 'in a very important sense . . . carried on the family'.

[23] 10.3750: 'posterisque eorum is qui Plauti vocitabuntur'. No fewer than forty-four urban inscriptions refer to the *nomen* as a criterion for tomb use, with the formulation 'ne de nomine meo exeat', *vel sim.*, 6.1825, 3472, 7457, 8589, 9485, 10026, 10243, 10246, 10701, 11781, 13195, 13203, 13785, 15221, 16177, 17549, 17618, 18435, 19319, 19844, 19915, 21925, 22208, 22303, 22348, 22421, 22518, 23319, 25771, 25961, 26340, 26940, 27883, 28318, 29240, 29726, 29909; 29912, 29931, 29939, 30556,29, 30566,2, 36693, 38164. Variations of this stipulation, restricting use to carriers of the *nomen*, also occur in: 6. 6193, 7394a, 7788, 7803, 8456, 8480=33728, 9485, 10219, 10239, 10848, 10915, 11137, 13040, 13387, 15053, 20061, 29383, 29919, 35595, 36262. Likewise in Ostia, e.g. 14.1452: 'libertis libertabus posterisque eorum ex familia nominis mei'; 14.766: 'externum nomen inferri non licet'; Portus: Thylander (1952) B 51.

The position of the freedman as 'filius sine natura' is strikingly illustrated by the fact that according to the *lex Pompeia* (55/52 BCE) a *libertus* who killed his patron was liable for parricide, which was regarded as a particularly heinous crime.[24] The inclusion of freedmen carried considerable symbolic weight. Because the patron had given the freedman 'life' the freedman owed him the same reverence as a biological child and would suffer the same punishment if he committed the ultimate crime against his patron.[25]

The Roman jurists were generally keen to protect the bond between patron and freedman, which also meant shielding it from damaging legal disputes. The *lex coloniae genitivae* stipulated that no one could be forced to give evidence against a son-in-law, father-in-law, stepfather, stepson, patron or freedman, or cousin.[26] Likewise, the *lex Iulia de vi* on criminal proceedings listed all those who were not allowed to give evidence in court against each other, including freedmen or patrons.[27] Roman law also endowed the bond between the patrons and the freedmen with an element of reciprocity, since both parties were obliged to assist the other in times of need, including providing economic support.[28]

The close bond between patrons and freedmen meant that the latter could be used as pledges of good faith and even exchanged as hostages. Thus, Plancus wrote to Cicero that Lepidus as a hostage of his good faith – 'obside fidei illius' – had sent him a certain Apella, presumably a trusted freedman of Lepidus.[29] Freedmen were also barred from acting as witnesses in divorce cases of their patrons. Apparently they were not considered to be reliable witnesses because of their dependent status.[30] The assumption of close links between patron and freedman may also explain the provisions made for the foundation of a colony at Carteia (171 BCE) for the descendants of Roman soldiers and native women. Livy reports that the senate decreed they should register themselves and any slaves they might

---

[24] D. 48.9.1 (Marcian). Treggiari (1969a) 80; Fabre (1981) 217–19.

[25] It is interesting too that a freedman who informed on his patron could be crucified, *Cod. Th.* 4.10.2 (320–23). In other words, when he acted against his patron 'servilis ingenii', he was punished as if he were still a slave; as indeed happened to Vitellius' freedman Asiaticus, Tac. *Hist.* 4.11.

[26] 95.15–19. *Roman Statutes* 407, 426.

[27] D. 22.5.4 (Paul); cf. 2.4.4.1; 2.7.1.2 (Ulpian). Fabre (1981) 219–21.

[28] D. 38.2.33 (Modestinus), on the obligation of patrons stipulated in the *lex Aelia Sentia* to support freedmen in need. If failing to do so, they could lose the right to any services as well as a share of the freedman's estate. Cf. D. 25.3.6 pr. (Modestinus); 38.1.18 (Paul); 38.2.33 (Modestinus). D. 37.14.5.1 (Marcellus) reports a Severan ruling on the loss of *ius patroni*, 'si patronus libertum suum non aluerit'. Waldstein (1986) 284.

[29] Cic. *Fam.* 10.17.3; cf. Treggiari (1969a) 187.   [30] D. 24.2.9 (Paul); cf. Noy (1988).

set free, '[nomina] eorumque, si quos manumisissent', in effect placing them on the same footing as children.[31]

The pseudo-filial construction of their relationship offered economic advantages to the patron, who could make claims on the freedman's estate. Already in the Twelve Tables it was prescribed that if a freedman died intestate with no *sui heredes*, the patron or his descendants in the male line would inherit.[32] This was entirely logical since they represented the agnates of a freedman who had no legally recognised ancestry of his own.[33] The patron's pseudo-parental role established a basic entitlement which later legislators could develop further – to the detriment of the freedman. Thus, between 118 and 74 BCE a praetorian rule was introduced entitling a patron to half of the freedman's property in case he had no natural heirs, allowing the patron to succeed if there was no will and take half even when there was.[34] Later under Augustus the *lex Papia Poppaea* (9 CE) entitled the patron to a share of the property, also when there were natural heirs. It required three children to eliminate the patron's share.[35]

The definition of the freedman as a quasi-son created an asymmetric claim, since the patron was a statutory heir of the freedman but not vice versa. The patron's claim to a share in the freedman's estate was considered so central to the Roman conception of their relationship that it was carefully preserved even in the most anomalous situations. For example, when Claudius granted freedom and Iunian status to sick slaves who had been abandoned by their masters on the Tiber Island, he took specific steps to protect the former masters' property rights over these freedmen's estates.[36] And Trajan was singled out for particular praise by Martial, 10.34, when he restored the rights of exiles to their freedmen. Even patrons of

---

[31] 43.3.1–4. The passage is much debated, cf. below p. 265 n.68.

[32] V.8. *Inst.Iust.* 3.7.1; Ulp. *Reg.* 29.1; Gaius *Inst.* 3.40; D. 50.16.195.1 (Ulpian); *Frg.Vat.* 308, cf. *Roman Statutes* 646–8. If the freedman left no heirs, he could apparently still dispose over parts of his estate; cf. Watson (1975) 109; *pace* Fabre (1981) 302–4.

[33] Cf. Gardner (1998) 16, 18.

[34] Gaius *Inst.* 3.41. Treggiari (1969a) 79, 81; Watson (1967) 231–6 (before 74 BCE); Sherwin-White (1973) 326 ('age of Sulla'); Fabre (1981) 310–11 (77–74 BCE); Gardner (1993) 21–3; Andreau (1993) 183 ('late second century').

[35] Gardner (1998) 60–1. A patron could also pass on this claim to a relative. Claudius allowed a patron to designate a child or grandchild as patron and statutory heir of his freedman, D. 38.4.1 (Ulpian); *Inst.Iust.* 3.8.3, cf. 23.2.48 (Terent. Clem.). He also established the order of succession for Latini Iuniani, again securing the interests of patrons who would be entitled to the entire estate, Gaius *Inst.* 3.56–7, 63–5; *Inst.Iust* 3.7.4. Levick (1990) 124.

[36] Suet. *Claud.* 25.2; Dio 60.29.7; D. 40.8.2 (Modestinus); *Cod.Iust.* 7.6.3; cf. Poma (1982) 161; Faro (1996); Major (1994).

freedmen who had received the attributes of freeborn status through the so-called *ius anulorum* retained the claim to their estates.[37]

Defining the patron's role in parental terms was a means of neutralising the problem of the 'servile' citizen, mentioned above, and considering the immense symbolic and practical power invested in the Roman *pater familias* the significance of this construction can hardly be overestimated. Assimilating the patron–freedman relationship to that between father and child reminded the freedman that he did not become a fully independent agent; in a sense the authority of the master had merely been redefined. The Roman perception of the freedman as legally free but morally dependent gave him a position fundamentally different from that known in other slave societies. And more than simply addressing the ideological issues raised by manumission, it also expanded the range of practical uses that could be made of them. The pseudo-filial status meant the freedman became a 'born' member of the patron's *familia*, as also underlined by their shared family name.[38] Discussing the illness of a favourite freedman, Zosimus, the younger Pliny presented him as a natural part of his *familia* – one of his 'mei', and Cicero noted that there is no large *familia* without a bad slave or freedman – clearly counting the latter as part of the household.[39]

In spite of his humble status, the freedman was fully integrated into a social environment where the stigma of his origins hardly counted at all. It is one of the paradoxes of Roman manumission that between patron and freedman the conventional shame associated with close intimacy with social inferiors did not exist. Inside the *familia* different rules applied, and relations that would have been shameful with other people's freedmen appear to have been perfectly acceptable with your own. This disparity is most strikingly illustrated by the lack of opprobrium attached to sexual

---

[37] D. 38.2.3 pr. (Ulpian); 40.10.5 (Paul).

[38] Artemidorus' *Oneirocritica* 1.47, offers a striking illustration of the freedman's position, comparing the household to a human body, where the slaves represent the feet, while the freedmen correspond to the knees, thus forming part of the same organic whole. On slavery in Artemidorus see Pomeroy (1991) 72–4.

[39] *Ep.* 5.19.1–2; *Rosc. Am.* 22. Legal definitions of the *familia* depend on the context, some only including the slaves, others covering both *servi et liberti*, cf. D. 7.8.2.1; 50.16.195.1 (Ulpian); 40.4.48 (Papinian); cf. Flory (1978) 78; Bürge (1988) 317–18. Epitaphs often use the phrase 'liberti et familia', e.g. 6.8413, 5420, 9323, 6068, 16451, 21418, 9573, 11183, 35132, 7395, 38711, 26033. But we also find expressions such as 'libertis libertabusque utriusque sexus qui ex familia mei erunt', 6.8456, and 'libertorum et decurionum famil(iae) P. Licini Silvani', 6.10258. The inscription published in Calza (1939) also includes *liberti* in the *familia*. Similarly inscriptions may refer to the *nomen* of the *familia*, 6.1825, 22208, 13203, 22348, implying freedmen were included. Cf. Fabre (1981) 151. The difference is often stylistic, while in some contexts it might have made sense to distinguish between the free and the unfree members of the *familia*.

relations between patrons and freedwomen. There was never any attempt to regulate or limit patrons' intimacy with their *libertae*; marriage and concubinage were generally considered acceptable, although, as we shall see, there were important social distinctions particularly affecting senators. Thus, the Roman jurists drew a distinction between concubinage with *liberta sua* and *liberta aliena*. As McGinn has shown, only the former received explicit mention in the Augustan marriage law, which granted it protection from accusations of *stuprum*.[40] Later some jurists recognised only that particular form of concubinage. Thus, Ulpian thought that only *concubinae* who were also *libertae suae* should be regarded as quasi-wives.[41] Certainly, concubinage with a *liberta aliena* was never considered as respectable as with a *liberta sua*.

Marriage to *libertae suae* was actively promoted in the Augustan legislation, which counted an owner's wish to marry a slave as valid grounds for exemption from the manumission regulations of the *lex Aelia Sentia*.[42] Moreover, the *lex Iulia et Papia* stipulated that the freedwoman had no right to refuse marriage to her patron or to divorce him, implying – quite exceptionally – that mutual consent was not required for this type of marriage. [43] Marriages between *ingenui* and *libertae alienae* had probably always been legal, but socially unacceptable.[44] Despite their formal legality, such unions were probably, as McGinn suggests, 'socially despised and liable to punishment by the censors'.[45] Augustus took steps to remove some of the stigma as part of his policy of promoting marriage and childbirth. Aiming to remove any obstacles to marriage, the *lex Iulia et Papia* explicitly stated that unions with *libertae alienae* were indeed fully legal.[46]

The Augustan reforms reflected the common notion that relations with your own slaves – or former slaves – were largely devoid of stigma, that is, as long as they conformed to the 'natural' hierarchy of male and female. Unions between free women and male slaves were far more troubling to the Roman mind than vice versa, and while marriage between patrons

---

[40] McGinn (1991) 347ff.   [41] D. 48.5.14 pr. McGinn (1991) 347ff; Treggiari (1991) 281.

[42] Gaius *Inst.* 1.18–19.   [43] D. 23.2.45 pr.; 24.2.11 pr. (Ulpian).

[44] Most scholars now doubt the existence of a bar on marriage between *ingenui* and *liberti* suggested by Mommsen (1887) 3.429; e.g. Watson (1967) 32–8; Kaser (1971) 315; *contra* Treggiari (1991) 64, 62; Fabre (1981) 185–6.

[45] McGinn (1991) 346; (2004) 201 n.9. Cf. Livy 39.19.5, on the special permission granted the freedwoman Faecenia Hispala to marry an *ingenuus*, without 'fraudi ignominiaeve'.

[46] D. 23.2.23 (Celsus): 'Lege Papia cavetur omnibus ingenuis praeter senatores eorumque liberos libertinam uxorem habere licere.' Dio, 54.16.2, tells us that, 'because there were far more upper-class males than females, he gave permission to marry freedwomen to those who wished to do so, except senators, having laid down that their offspring would be legitimate'. For the exclusion of senators and their descendants see D. 23.2.44 pr. (Paul); Treggiari (1996) 888.

and *libertae suae* was actively encouraged by Roman legislators, *patronae* marrying their freedmen were frowned upon and regarded as adulterous.[47] In late antiquity such unions were even outlawed, and severe punishments, including confiscation of property, deportation, and the enslavement of children, were prescribed.[48] But also in the case of women we can detect a fundamental difference between intimacy with people under your authority and people under the control of others. Thus, the *Senatus Consultum Claudianum*, mentioned above, only applied to women who formed unions with other people's slaves, not with *servi sui*, which was controversial but not illegal. The decree can be seen as an attempt to neutralise the conflict between gender and status by bringing the two parties closer to each other in status. In doing so it addressed a clash between different hierarchies; for while the male was seen as dominating the female, free status automatically outranked unfree, and freeborn the freed.

The fundamental difference between your own and others' freedmen is illustrated by Augustus' relationships with both categories. According to Valerius Messala, he never invited a freedman to dinner with the exception of Sex. Pompey's defected admiral Menas/Menodorus, and that only after he had been formally enrolled among the *ingenui*.[49] On the other hand, with his own freedmen Augustus showed no fear of social intimacy. Suetonius tells us that he held many of his freedmen 'in honore et usu maximo', and this closeness is illustrated by his habit of watching the circus from the *cenaculi* of either friends or freedmen, in whose suburban houses he would also seek peace and quiet.[50]

Examples such as these suggest that it was acceptable to be close, even physically intimate, with people of much lower status than yourself as long as they remained subject to your authority.[51] This explains the remarkably

[47] D. 23.2.13 (Ulpian); *Cod.Iust.* 5.4.3. Weber (2008) thought the practice might have been more common than the jurists imply, but the evidence is largely absent, cf. Huttunen (1974) 151.

[48] *Cod.Th.* 4.12.1 (314 CE); *Novellae Anthemiae* 1.3 (468 CE). The harsh provisions were later abolished; Watson (1987) 14–15; Evans-Grubbs (1993); (1995) 96, 261–316.

[49] Suet. *Aug.* 74. Leading aristocrats also dined with their freedmen and those of their noble guests and absent friends, cf. Cic. *Att.* 13.52.2; *Fam.* 10.25.3; Plin. *Ep.* 2.6.2.

[50] *Aug.* 67.1; 45; 72.2.

[51] Bernstein's discussion of Statius' *Silvae* 2.1 (2005) misses this vital distinction and interprets the poet's lament for Atedius Melior's deceased 'alumnus et libertus', Glaucias, as an attempt to avert the social opprobrium normally attached to the advancement of freedmen. However, it was perfectly acceptable for patrons to be close to their freedmen and promote them economically and socially, as long as they did not overstep conventional boundaries, which there is no suggestion Melior did. Thus, Bernstein's suggestion that Glaucias had been his (sole) heir is speculative, 261, and his attempt to interpret the poem as a negotiation of 'status dissonance' carries little conviction, since there was no 'dissonance' in the relationship between Melior and Glaucias; indeed, fosterage can be seen as the logical continuation of the freedman's pseudo-filial status.

intimate relationship between patrons and freedmen we encounter in the letters of Cicero, which offer a rare insider's view of the Roman household. They reveal a world where freedmen are not only ubiquitous but also deeply involved in all aspects of their patrons' affairs. The fullest information naturally comes from Cicero's own *familia*, where the role played by his secretary Tiro is particularly well documented.

Modern observers have been struck by the intimacy which characterises their relationship.[52] A series of letters demonstrate the genuine affection felt by Cicero and the rest of his family for their favourite slave/freedman.[53] Even before his manumission in 53 Tiro's poor health was a source of great concern to Cicero.[54] And later, when Tiro lay bedridden in Greece in 50/49, Cicero again wrote a series of letters full of worries and hopes for the freedman's recovery, a pattern which recurred in 46/45.[55] Some of these letters were sent on behalf of the whole family, and Cicero frequently shared his concerns for Tiro with his friend Atticus.[56]

When Tiro was freed in 53, the happy event was celebrated by the entire family. Cicero's brother Quintus wrote to congratulate and famously said that Tiro now became a friend instead of a slave.[57] Quintus' letters to Tiro are strikingly intimate in tone. On one occasion he jokingly complained about not having received any letters from Tiro, while on another he finishes with an affectionate postscript, calling him the apple of his eye and promising to kiss him the next time they meet.[58] Tiro's closeness to the Cicerones is further illustrated by the letters sent to him by the younger Marcus, who addressed him as 'Tironi suo dulcissimo'. This letter is highly personal, also referring to Tiro's *humanitas*, and expressing gratitude for his 'studium et consilium'. The younger Cicero also congratulated Tiro on his newly purchased house, which he apparently intended to share with the Cicerones.[59]

---

[52] So much so that some scholars even have speculated – without any foundation – that Tiro might have been Cicero's natural son; McDermott (1972) 265, 270–1.

[53] Pliny, *Ep.* 7.4.3–6, refers to an epigram, supposedly written by Cicero to Tiro, that seems to imply a sexual relationship between Cicero and Tiro. While the authenticity of the epigram is much disputed, it might suggest that later imperial observers found the idea plausible. For an attempt to save Cicero's virtue see McDermott (1972) 272–5.

[54] *Fam.* 16.10, 13, 14, 15.   [55] *Fam.* 16.1-9; 16.11; 16.12.6; 16.22.1; 16.17.2; 16.18.1; 16.20.

[56] *Fam.* 16.1, 3–7, 9, 11; *Att.* 6.7.2; 7.2.3; 7.3.12; 7.5.2; 9.17.2; 10.4.12; 12.10.

[57] *Fam.* 16.16.1: 'nobis amicum quam servum esse maluisti'. For the date of Tiro's manumission see Treggiari (1977).

[58] *Fam.* 16.26, 27.2: 'tuosque oculos, etiam si te veniens in medio foro videro, dissaviabor', cf. 16.8.

[59] *Fam.* 16.21. In 16.25 Cicero *iunior* asks Tiro for more letters.

Tiro may have been remarkably close to his patron and his family but we have no reason to believe their relationship was exceptional. Cicero's brother Quintus had his own favourite freedman, Statius, who appears to have been very closely involved in all his political and personal affairs, even getting drawn into his divorce proceedings.[60] Likewise, Cicero's friend Atticus was distraught when a certain Athamas died, presumably a trusted household slave or freedman, and his *familia* also included a direct counterpart to Tiro, 'imaginem Tironis', Alexis, whose health caused his patron similar concerns.[61]

The Roman elite were not just surprisingly close to their freedmen, they also invested a remarkable degree of confidence in them. Freedmen appear as advisors and confidants of the rulers of the empire, seemingly enjoying the complete trust of their patrons. Cicero lists Tiro's services as being 'in my home and in the forum, in Rome and abroad, in private affairs and public, in studies and in my literary work', in effect covering all aspects of his activities, public as well as private.[62] In 44 Cicero wrote to Tiro asking for full reports on the political situation, also wanting to hear what Tiro thought might happen: 'quid futurum putes'. And in the other direction Cicero wrote to Tiro with summaries of the political situation in 49.[63] Cicero's brother also shared personal observations on current affairs with Tiro, noting that 'Your letters always tell me things most true and agreeable.'[64]

There are no signs in the surviving literary sources that a patron's close relationship with his former slaves could be seen as undignified or shameful. On the contrary, it appears that patrons were expected to have no secrets from their freedmen. Thus, Cicero jokingly warned his friend M. Fabius Gallus not to spread his private advice, adding 'keep it to yourself – not even a word to your freedman Apella'.[65] Conversely, there was an expectation that freedmen always acted with their patron's knowledge and consent. Thus, Cicero was at pains in his defence of Sex. Roscius to dissociate his appointed villain, Sulla's freedman Chrysogonus, from his blameless patron, declaring that Chrysogonus cannot, 'as so many worthless and

---

[60] *Att.* 6.2.1–2.

[61] *Att.* 12.10. A. Gabinius (cos. 58 BCE) appears to have had an equally close freed confidant. Cicero, *Att.* 4.18.4, mentions that as punishment for the acquittal of his patron in 54 the freedman was prosecuted for illegal usurpation of the citizenship.

[62] *Fam.* 16.4.3: 'domestica, forensia, urbana, provincialia, in re privata, in publica, in studiis, in litteris nostris'.

[63] *Fam.* 16.24; 16.11, 12.

[64] *Fam.* 16.26.2: 'valde enim mi semper et vera et dulcia tuis epistulis nuntiantur'; cf. 16.27.

[65] *Fam.* 7.25.2: 'secreto hoc audi, tecum habeto, ne Apellae quidem, liberto tuo, dixeris'.

wicked freedmen use to do', attempt to make his patron responsible.[66] Cicero tries to counter the assumption that a freedman normally acts on behalf of his patron – which in this case might get Cicero into trouble. A passage of Cicero's defence of Cluentius also implied that freedmen never acted without the knowledge of their patrons.[67]

These examples illustrate the freedman's complete integration into the *familia*. When the freedman took his place in the household as a quasi-son, his role was defined in reassuringly familiar terms, and his position in the domestic hierarchy clear-cut and unambiguous. Within this particular environment the conventional stigma of servitude appears to have played no part, which may be explained by the particular Roman 'construction' of the slave. As argued above, the slave was defined by his subjection to the will of another, a state which left him dishonoured and permanently marked, mentally and in many cases also physically. But the simple fact that any degradation he had suffered had been received at the hands of his former master made the stigma irrelevant within the *familia*; it only existed between the freedman and the outside world. Between patron and freedman there could be no shame, since it was the authority of the former that had made him who he was.[68]

Therefore, what might at first seem to be a curious split in the freedman's persona – between trusted confidant and stigmatised former slave – may be more apparent than real. And Treggiari's suggestion that Cicero's often expressed prejudices against freedmen were merely for public display (because privately he was on friendly terms with many *liberti*) misses the important point that a freedman's social persona to a great extent was contextual.[69] Cicero's – or any other Roman's – 'view of freedmen' would always have depended on the specific situation; not least because what was appropriate within the *familia* often would have been unacceptable outside of it.[70] The invention of the freedman as a pseudo-son created a unique

---

[66] *Rosc. Am.* 130: 'quem ad modum solent liberti nequam et improbi facere'.

[67] 61: 'libertus autem eius in maleficio deprehensus esset, illum expertem eius consilii fuisse non probabatur'.

[68] For that reason it could not be obliterated either. For example, a grant of *ius anulorum* and its fictional *ingenuitas* only altered the relationship between the freedman and the outside world; his patron could still claim *obsequium* and a share of the estate, D. 2.4.10.3 (Ulpian); 38.2.3 pr.; 40.10.5 (Paul); *Cod. Iust.* 9.21.1. The patron's consent was also needed for the grant, which merely 'cleansed' the freedman in the eyes of the public, D. 40.10.3 (Marcian), and could therefore be described as an *imago*, *Frg. Vat.* 226.

[69] It also overlooks Cicero's occasional positive public statements about freedmen.

[70] The emperor Claudius provides a vivid illustration of this split, since he was strict towards freedmen in general (cf. Levick (1990) 122) but indulgent towards his own, some of whom were allowed unprecedented influence and wealth. See also Poma (1982).

relationship between former master and slave, free of conventional stigma, and it was this particular aspect of manumission that made freedmen so uniquely useful. In principle, such closeness was acceptable only within the closed world of the *familia*. For example, one senses the social boundary Q. Cicero was crossing when he promised to kiss Tiro next time they met, 'even if I first catch sight of you in the middle of the forum'.[71]

In practice it was of course not feasible to keep the domestic and the public spheres entirely separate. The complexity of patrons' businesses and the growth of empire made it necessary for the elite to employ their freedmen also outside the *familia*. Most obviously they were used to carry messages between members of the elite. Cicero's letters document a wide range of people performing the function of *tabellarius*, including freeborn friends, freedmen, and slaves.[72] But freedmen appear to have held a distinct advantage, since the written message typically was accompanied by an oral communication delivered by the messenger himself.[73] In that case the letter carrier would provide a fuller exposition of points made in the letter or add confidential information too sensitive to commit to writing. Thus, Cicero writes back to Ap. Claudius Pulcher that Phanias (Appius' freedman who had returned with the letter) is so clever that he can explain everything, allowing Cicero to write briefly.[74] In letters to Atticus, Cicero might say that 'the letter carrier can tell you what happens here, I kept him fairly long', or answer a request for news by referring Atticus to his own freedman, whom Cicero had returned with the letter.[75] On another occasion Cicero complained about a freedman, in this case Philotimus, who handed over a letter from Ser. Sulpicius without comments, although Sulpicius had explained everything to him and therefore kept his letter short.[76]

The role of freedmen as go-betweens in the Roman elite meant that the rulers of the empire would spend considerable time in the company of former slaves and engage in serious political conversation with them. For example, when Cicero wanted to advise C. Furnius on his political career

---

[71] There were fine lines to negotiate when appearing with freedmen in public, and even more so if they were *liberti alieni*. Thus, Scipio Aemilianus was taken to task for campaigning for the censorship accompanied by two freedmen, only one of them being his own, Plut. *Aem.* 38.

[72] *Att.* 3.8.2; 3.17.1; 5.20.8; 6.1.21; 6.2.1; 6.3.1; 10.7.2; 11.6.7; 11.13.1; 11.20.1; 13.3.2; 14.9.1; 14.17.1; 16.4.1; *Fam.* 2.7.3; 3.9.1; 8.7.1; 8.8.10; *Q.fr.* 1.3.4. Cf. Benöhr (1998) 120–1. 'Libertum mitto' in elite parlance meant taking action, in this case providing a loan, *Att.* 1.12.1. Martial plays on this meaning, when he sends his freedman to perform his cliental duties for him: 'libertum sed tibi mitto meum', 3.46.2.

[73] Nikitinski (2001) has drawn attention to the combination of written and oral communication evidenced in Cicero's letters.

[74] *Fam.* 3.1.1.   [75] *Att.* 11.3.1; 11.4a; cf. 5.20.9; 16.13.3.   [76] *Fam.* 4.2.1.

he invited three of Furnius' best friends to his house, along with Furnius' freedman Dardanus, who would report back directly to his patron.[77] Likewise, Cicero mentions a discussion he had with Ap. Claudius' freedman Phanias, who is praised as a good source of information, being sensible and inquisitive, 'prudens' and 'curiosus'.[78] Pulcher also sent another freedman, Cilix, whom Cicero also came to like – 'in fact within a couple of days he has become my friend'.[79] Still, Cicero missed Phanias and asked Pulcher to reinstate him as their regular contact, and later he again refers to talks with Phanias.[80]

Perhaps less surprisingly, Cicero became intimate with the freedmen of his friend Atticus. Cicero called Atticus' freedman Eutychides 'meus amicus' and showed considerable interest in his manumission.[81] Cicero also mentions another freedman of Atticus, Nicanor, who was with Cicero in Cilicia and was treated handsomely, 'a me liberaliter tractatur'.[82] Elsewhere Cicero asked why Atticus' freedman Alexis did not write letters of his own to Cicero instead of merely adding his greetings to Atticus'. Cicero notes that 'his own Alexis' did not hesitate to do so, and we know that on occasion Atticus would also write to Tiro directly and even met up with him to discuss various matters.[83]

The freedman's confidential role gave him a pivotal position within the elite networks which also allowed him to pass on news and information to third parties. Thus, Cicero learned from Lentulus' freedman Pausanias, who was Cicero's *accensus* in Cilicia, that Ap. Claudius Pulcher had complained in conversation with Lentulus about Cicero's failure to come and meet him.[84] And Atticus expressed his concerns to Cicero in 58, having heard from Crassus' freedman that Cicero looked anxious and unwell, which provoked an angry response from Cicero.[85]

This level of intimacy with other people's freedmen implies a suspension of the 'servile' stigma in these contexts, which of course was highly convenient for the elite but nevertheless requires an explanation. What seems to have happened was that the freedman's own dishonoured person became subsumed into that of his patron – a mental process facilitated by their shared name and pseudo-filial relationship. Thus, Cicero could assure Tiro

---

[77] *Fam.* 10.25.3.
[78] *Fam.* 3.1.1. Cicero writes that Phanias will explain Cicero's views to Pulcher after their discussions.
[79] *Fam.* 3.1.2: 'biduo factus est mihi familiaris'.
[80] *Fam.* 3.5.3; cf. 3.6.1; 3.8.5, which mention a meeting with Phanias at Brundisium.
[81] *Att.* 5.9.1; 4.15.1; 4.16.9.   [82] *Att.* 5.20.9.
[83] *Att.* 5.20.9; 12.19.4; 12.48.2, 16.13.3; 16.16.1.   [84] *Fam.* 3.7.4–5.
[85] *Att.* 3.15.1–3. Cicero also reacted to information he had received about his brother from Diodotus, Lucullus' freedman, *Q.fr.* 1.2.12.

that 'nobody cares for me who does not care for you'.[86] The qualities of the patron as well as his social role would in a sense be transferred to a freedman acting on his behalf. When negotiating with a *libertus alienus*, a Roman senator was therefore dealing not so much with a dishonoured former slave as with a person who had no independent social identity. Thus, when Martial tried to flatter the powerful imperial servants, who are 'loved by all men', he claimed that their character was pleasant because their *mores* were not their own but those of their *dominus*.[87] The underlying assumption is that servants do not have a separate nature but acquire some of their master's. There were, in other words, situations in which the freedman could transcend his status and as a direct extension of his patron represent him outside the household and be his eyes, ears, and mouthpiece.[88]

With the increased scale and complexity of Roman society and indeed the growth of her power and territory, the advantages of manumission became ever more apparent. The institution allowed the Romans to 'reproduce' themselves through a legal act, which propagated their name, multiplied their social persona and created personally tied agents who could be put in positions of trust. Given the size of the empire and the wide dispersal of elite estates and economic and political interests, freedmen became invaluable tools of communication, not just delivering letters but contributing to negotiations by explaining their patron's views and position. Manumission enabled the Roman elite to negotiate and interact through low-born intermediaries who were accepted by third parties as extensions of their patrons, a leap of faith that would have been impossible had they still been slaves.

The 'freedman as son' model thus provided the answer to a number of practical and ideological problems raised by the integration of former slaves into Roman society. By defining them as subject to a semi-paternal authority, it also responded to the need for staff that could be put in positions of trust and used as go-betweens and confidants. The freedman was not just an employee but a member of the patron's *familia*, carried his

---

[86] *Fam.*16.4.4: 'neminem esse qui me amet quin idem te amet'.

[87] 9.79, 'Nemo suos . . . sed domini mores Caesarianus habet', 7–8. In his *consolatio* to the powerful imperial freedman Polybius, Seneca stresses that he wholly belongs to Caesar, 'totum te Caesari debes', *Cons. ad Pol.* 7.3. Analysing the *exempla* of loyal slaves, Parker (1998) noted that they take on the character of their noble masters.

[88] Another strategy when dealing closely with *liberti alieni* is illustrated by Cicero's recommendation of C. Rabirius Postumus' freedman C. Curtius Mithres (his patron was later adopted, hence the different *nomina*), at whose house at Ephesus Cicero had stayed. Cicero justified this familiarity with the freedman by stressing that Mithres had showed 'as much respect and attention to me as to his own patron', *Fam.* 13.69.1: 'me colit et observat aeque atque illum ipsum patronum suum', thereby blurring the – otherwise sharply drawn – line between *liberti alieni* and *liberti sui*.

name, and was tied to him by a life-long bond rooted in the patron's role as a pseudo-father, benefactor, and 'giver of life'.

CONTROLLING FREEDMEN: *OBSEQUIUM, PIETAS,* AND *FIDES*

This image of the patron as a paternal figure who would continue to guide and control the freedman after his release from slavery was in many respects merely an ideal which in the nature of things would often have been rather different from the reality. Thus, many patrons did not conform to the conventional image of the mature and authoritative *pater familias*, some being female while others were too young to exercise any patronal function. Moreover, some patrons were not even freeborn but were themselves freedmen or freedwomen. And patrons might not just fall short of the established norm; there was also the possibility that the freedman might disregard the patron's authority altogether and resist attempts at controlling him, in which case the ideal would be completely shattered.

When considering how the Romans reconciled the split between ideal and reality, ideologically and practically, one is struck by the remarkable degree to which the Romans managed to ignore the issue of inappropriate patrons. No action was ever taken to curtail the rights of female or freed owners to manumit their slaves. In those cases the Romans were apparently willing to accept the fiction that all patrons were equally suited to control their freedmen. The Augustan legislation did take steps to address some of the anomalies, barring the young and the insane from freeing slaves, but these measures were probably more concerned with the selection of slaves before manumission than with the owners' ability to provide suitable patronage afterwards. Thus, in the case of under-age slave owners, the law allowed them to free slaves if there was proper justification and formal advice had been taken from a *consilium*.

However, the most glaring departure from the ideal of patronal guidance and control was testamentary manumission, which removed the paternal element from the equation entirely. These particular freedmen were recognised as a category apart, so-called *orcini*, i.e. freedmen whose patron resided in the underworld.[89] They were not subject to the 'paternal' authority of the patron from whom they derived their name and identity. Even when the *ius patronatus* was passed on to a son, he would not have been personally responsible for the manumission, and in cases where the patronal role was transferred to external heirs the patron's moral authority would

---

[89] D. 26.4.3.3 (Ulpian); 33.4.1.10 (Ulpian); 40.5.4.12; 40.5.49 (Africanus); 40.8.5 (Marcianus).

have been much reduced, perhaps even eliminated. If the household was broken up and houses and slaves sold off, the freedmen might be left practically unattached. The phenomenon by no means was unique to slaves freed by testament, but the fact that they had never experienced 'proper' patronal supervision might have been a cause for concern at least on an ideological level. The provisions of the *lex Fufia Caninia* can therefore be seen as an attempt to rescue a particular ideal of the freedman–patron relationship. Above all it sought to eliminate the worst combination of factors – posthumous and indiscriminate – by forcing owners to make a choice and select the most 'deserving' of their slaves.

Caesar's efforts to reduce the population of Rome may be viewed in a similar ideological context, since they involved the foundation of overseas colonies for the urban plebs, at least one of which, Corinth, is recorded as having been dominated by freedmen.[90] This information is incidental, however, and we have no reason to believe that it was exceptional among Caesar's colonies. The foundation of new settlements for urban freedmen raises interesting questions. It seems inconceivable that the state could ship freedmen off to foreign colonies without the approval of their patrons, who are unlikely to have consented to this, given the many advantages they derived from freedmen and their labour. The colonists in question may therefore have been freed *ex testamento* and/or had lost their owners or patrons during the civil war.[91] Moreover, urban manumission may have been particularly frequent in the decade after Clodius introduced the free grain dole, which provided a strong incentive for owners to free their slaves.[92] For those reasons it is possible that an unusually large number of patronless freedmen emerged at this juncture, posing a challenge to the conventional Roman ideal of manumission.

The issue of the absent 'paternal' patron merely highlighted the fundamental problem how much control over freedmen was maintained in practice; for it was one thing to define the freedman as a son and subject him to the moral authority of a patron, quite another to make him accept

[90] Cf. Brunt (1971a) 256–7; Jehne (1987) 295–6. Urso was a colony 'urbanorum' and freedmen held local office at Carthage, Curubis, Clupea, and Corinth, cf. pp. 74–5. Brunt warned against a strict separation of Caesar's veteran and plebeian colonies. Spawforth (1996), however, minimises the veteran element among the settlers at Corinth.

[91] Fabre (1981) 141, thought Caesar's colonies resettled freedmen of poor patrons, but it seems unlikely that the poor would have had many freedmen or that they would have been more willing to give them up.

[92] Cf. Dio 39.24.1; Dion. Hal. 4.24.5. Augustus also tried to curb the practice of freeing slaves in order to entitle them to public handouts, *congiaria*, Suet. *Aug.* 42.2. The point was that manumission be seen to happen for the right reasons, i.e. personal merit.

this role. The question is therefore how patrons controlled their freedmen – assuming of course that they did. In the following pages we will look in some detail at the means by which patrons could make them conform, which may be divided into two categories: formally defined patronal rights and prerogatives and informal conventions which served the same purpose by acting as a form of social conditioning.

The Roman patron, it must be emphasised, did not hold any formal authority over his freedmen, nor did he enjoy any legally enshrined *potestas* over them.[93] He could administer 'levis coercitio' over those in his service, including freedmen, without the involvement of the courts. As the jurist Paul states: 'If a freedman or a client steal from the patron or a hired labourer from his employer, he commits theft but no action for theft arises'; he is dealt with domestically.[94] In those cases the patron had the right to chastise the freedman physically – within reason, since a freedman could sue his patron for serious injuries such as flogging – although this right was not specific to the patron–freedman relationship but covered all domestic subordinates.[95]

Although the patron had no defined powers over the freedman, he did enjoy certain rights and privileges. A freedman was not allowed to damage the patron in any way or attack his reputation, or use verbal abuse, let alone physical violence, nor was he generally entitled to sue the patrons or his children.[96] In that respect the rules were the same for patrons as for parents, although there were a few exceptions, e.g. when a patron had made his *liberti* swear on oath not to marry.[97] Freedmen's obligations also included a duty to support their patrons, especially in case of illness.[98] But that was, like several other duties, a reciprocal bond which worked both ways.

More generally the patron was entitled to *obsequium*, dutiful respect from his freedman. In practical terms it involved treating the patron and his family with consideration, and abstaining from any action which might harm them.[99] Complaints against *liberti ingrati* who failed to pay respect

---

[93] Watson (1975) 104–5; Gardner (1993) 24. Kaser (1938); (1971) 118–19, 298–301, and Fabre (1981) 222–3, thought the patron's authority included the right to kill the freedman, but see the sensible comments by Watson (1975) 105–6.

[94] D. 47.2.90; cf. 48.19.11.1 (Marcian) on 'furta domestica si viliora sunt'; Crook (1967a) 196.

[95] D. 2.4.10.12 (Ulpian); cf. 47.10.7.2 (Ulpian).

[96] E.g. D. 48.5.39.9 (Papinian). The *lex Iulia de vi* stated that no person freed by the accused or his father could give evidence against him, D. 22.5.3.5 (Callistratus).

[97] D. 2.4.4 (Ulpian); D. 2.4.8.2 (Ulpian).   [98] D. 1.12.1.2 (Ulpian).

[99] Waldstein (1986) 60–1; Masi Doria (1993a) 76–81. Gardner (1993) 23–5, noted that *pietas* was a key term used in the legal sources, which firmly locates the obligation within the familial sphere; cf. Saller (1994) 105–14.

had to go before the courts, which would consider each case on its merit. The Augustan *lex Aelia Sentia* introduced an *accusatio liberti ingrati*, but apart from the stipulation that the son could bring such a case but not more distant heirs, little is known about this part of the law.[100] Patrons could also sue for *iniuria*, considered aggravated if committed by freedmen.[101]

Ulpian described the duties of the urban prefect concerning complaints by patrons over their freedmen, 'for indeed freedmen often have to be punished'.[102] Offences included insolence, in which case the prefect could inquire and then administer punishment, reprimand, flog, or perhaps go even further. If the freedman had conspired against his patron he could even be sent to the mines.[103] According to the jurists it was also possible to send the offending freedman into exile for a period.[104] Tacitus mentions the right of patrons to relegate their freedmen beyond the hundredth milestone from Rome, which might refer to the exile that could be imposed on freedmen.[105] But while Tacitus seems to suggest this was a right the patron could freely exercise, Ulpian makes it clear that it was up to the courts. Most likely therefore Tacitus is either inaccurate or referring to a different measure.[106] A particular punishment was the imposition of a *societas Rutiliana*, named after P. Rutilius Rufus (pr. 118 BCE). The *societas* entitled the patron to 50 per cent of the freedman's income in addition to services, *operae*. The nature of this measure is much debated, but most likely it was, as Waldstein argued, 'a penalty for the freedman who did not show the proper respect for his patron'.[107]

There is no doubt that the law allowed for quite severe punishments to be meted out to *liberti ingrati*, depending on the gravity of their offences.[108]

---

[100] D. 50.16.70 (Paul); cf. Wilinski (1971); López Barja de Quiroga (1998) 140.

[101] D. 47.10.7.7–8 (Labeo *apud* Ulp.).

[102] D. 1.12.1.10 (Ulpian): 'Nam et puniendi plerumque sunt liberti.'

[103] D. 37.14.7.1 (Modestinus) noted that provincial governors hearing cases against freedmen 'are to exact penalties from freedmen according to the tort that has been committed', and the punishment meted out to these *liberti ingrati* might include confiscation of part of their property, being handed over to their patron, or beatings with sticks.

[104] D. 37.14.1.1 (Ulpian), on cases brought before proconsuls against *liberti ingrati* by their patrons. If a freedman is found to be 'inofficiosus', he should be reprimanded with admonition that more severe measures might follow. If he has abused his patron, he will be sent into temporary exile, and if he has used actual force he is condemned to the mines.

[105] *Ann.* 13.26.2.

[106] Treggiari (1969a) 73–4, and Fabre (1981) 77, believed Tacitus referred to the *lex Aelia Sentia*.

[107] D. 38.2.1.1 (Ulpian). Meissel (2004) 198–204, gives a survey of interpretations. Waldstein (1986) 131–41, 242; cf. Watson (1967) 228–9; Masi Doria (1989). *Pace* Fabre (1981) 296–9, who saw it as an improvement based on the assumption that freedmen were in a near-servile position with little or no control over their income.

[108] Further controls on freedmen were imposed under Trajan, who extended the *SC Silanianum* to freedmen, D. 29.5.10.1 (Paul).

One form of punishment remained controversial, however, which was re-enslavement. Patrons could not go to the courts to have their decision reversed, nor had they any right to do so on their own account. Thus, when Cicero wanted to retract the freedom of two of his freedmen, the library assistant Chrysippus and a 'labourer', whom he accused of having absconded while accompanying Cicero's son in Cilicia (as well as theft), he had to resort to a legal fudge.[109] Cicero had freed the two slaves under his own praetorian *imperium*, and following the example of Drusus (pr. 120–115) Cicero tried to make the – legally dubious – case that since there formally had been no master from whom the slave could be 'vindicated' the manumission was null and void. The fact that Cicero denied the legality of the manumission itself rather than trying to reverse it suggests that there was no mechanism for the re-enslavement of *liberti ingrati* under the republic.

Suetonius tells us that Claudius reduced to slavery the *liberti ingrati* about whom their patrons complained, but he may generalise from isolated incidents.[110] Claudius' penalty probably applied only to those freedmen who caused informers, *delatores*, to question their patrons' status.[111] Thus, Dio relates that Claudius condemned to the arena those who had conspired against their masters and patrons and maliciously informed against others during the reign of his predecessor.[112] Tacitus devotes considerable attention to the issue of re-enslavement, which apparently came to the fore during the reign of Nero.[113] A proposal had been made in the senate, 'de fraudibus libertorum', suggesting that patrons be given the right to annul the manumission of ungrateful freedmen. The consuls referred the proposal to the emperor, whose advisers disagreed on the measure. Some argued for the need to enforce obedience against 'notorious offenders', 'criminum manifestos'; others warned against singling out freedmen and making them all suffer collectively, noting their good services to society, while also reminding the emperor of the different types of manumission

---

[109] *Att.* 7.2.8. Cf. Watson (1967) 191–2, 229; Tondo (1967) 26–9; Treggiari (1969a) 73, 257–8; Fabre (1981) 54.

[110] *Claud.* 25.1: 'ingratos et de quibus patroni quererentur revocavit in servitutem advocatisque eorum negavit se adversus libertos ipsorum ius dicturum'.

[111] D. 37.14.5 pr. (Marcellus). Watson (1987) 17; Gardner (1993) 43–4. Claudius also punished a freedman who had appealed to the tribunes against his patron, Dio 60.28.1.

[112] Dio 60.13.2. Similar actions followed the fall of Domitian, Dio 68.13.

[113] *Ann.* 13.26–7. See the detailed commentary on this poorly transmitted passage in Koestermann (1963–68) 3.283–7. Manning (1986) 69, argued that Seneca's *Ben.* 3.6–17, might be seen in the context of this debate, which also reflected the Romans' 'almost obsessive concern' about the relationship between freedmen and patrons.

that allowed a patron to decide his freedmen's status. Eventually the latter argument won the day, and Nero wrote to the senate that no general restriction was needed and each case should be assessed individually.

The emperor's reluctance to allow patrons to reverse manumission may be explained by the formal inalienability of freedom and the extreme nature of the proposal as recorded by Tacitus. Enslavement was used as punishment only for the most serious crimes, while the proposal would allow private individuals to deprive Roman citizens of their freedom.[114] The courts could under certain circumstances order the re-enslavement of a *libertus ingratus*. Under Commodus it was decreed that, 'where it is proved that a patron has been violently attacked by his freedman or badly beaten or abandoned while suffering from the effects of poverty or illness, he must first be placed in his patron's power again and forced to serve him as a master. If he does not take this warning, he should be sold on the authority of the consul or the governor and the price given to the patron.'[115] Even in these severe cases the measure was first forced service, followed by sale and finally enslavement.

We may conclude from this survey that patrons had access to the courts but few statutory rights over their freedmen. It is therefore one of the many paradoxes of Roman manumission that, although the patron's pseudo-paternal role was seen as an essential pillar of the institution, it was only partly enshrined in law. His powers over the freedmen remained limited, not least when compared to those he exercised over relatives *in potestate*, which demonstrated that subjection to the authority of another was not per se incompatible with free status or citizenship. However, the point was precisely that a freedman was *not* comparable to a son-in-power since he had been released from his master's *manus*/power through the act of manumission. The closest equivalent to his status was therefore that of an emancipated son. As Isidor of Seville explained, children are called *liberi* to distinguish them from slaves: 'because just as a slave is in the power of his master, so a child is in the power of his father. Thus, "emancipation" occurs for the son, so that he is free from his father, just as "manumission"

---

[114] On a practical level it would also undermine the effectiveness of manumission as an incentive for slaves, an issue to which we will return below.

[115] D. 25.3.6.1 (Modestinus), cf. Watson (1987) 17–18. As late as 294 CE *ingratia* constituted no ground for *revocatio in servitutem*, *Cod.Iust.* 7.16.30. Not until Constantine was the re-enslavement of *ingrati* prescribed, *Cod.Th.* 4.10.1 = *Cod.Iust.* 6.7.2 (332 CE); even their children suffering this fate. Kaser (1971) 1.292–3, saw *revocatio* as post-classical, as also suggested by its absence from e.g. D. 1.16.9.3 (Ulpian); 37.14.1.

occurs for a slave, so that he is liberated from his master.'[116] Manumission and the emancipation of sons can be seen as direct parallels since in both instances the *dominus/pater familias* surrendered his formal control but not his entire authority.[117]

Manumission therefore provided the patron with relatively few means of coercing the freedman, whose duties were defined in vague terms of *obsequium*, *reverentia*, and *pietas*. Patronal sanctions were reduced to light chastisement, and although the patron could take legal action the law might often side with the freedman, unless the transgressions were serious and manifest. Re-enslavement, as the ultimate threat, was considered a step too far, probably because it challenged basic legal principles and undermined the whole institution of manumission.[118]

The patron's dilemma is illustrated by Cicero's difficulties with his freedman, Hilarus, whom he accused of undermining his standing in Asia. Having served as Atticus' accountant, Hilarus had joined the governor of Macedonia, Cicero's former consular colleague Antonius Hybrida, who was levying funds among the provincials, claiming part of it was for Cicero; Hilarus' presence suggested he had even sent a freedman to oversee the operation.[119] Cicero was upset and asked Atticus to investigate and, if possible, try to get the freedman out of the province. The letter gives the impression that Cicero could do very little to stop the freedman from participating in Antonius' scheme and – at least indirectly – damaging his patron's reputation. The courts were not an option since an open airing of Cicero's grievance would threaten his relationship with Antonius, apart from the difficulties involved in proving any manifest guilt.

Although the circumstances were highly specific, the problems Cicero faced when trying to bring his freedman to justice may not have been uncommon. Because of their trusted position, many freedmen would have

---

[116] 9.5.17: 'Filii autem ideo in legibus liberi appellantur, ut isto vocabulo secernantur a servis; quia sicut servus in potestate est domini, sic filius in potestate est patris. Inde etiam filio fit emancipatio, ut sit liber a patre, sicut fit servo manumissio, ut sit liberatus a domino.' Trans. Barney *et al.* (2006) 207. Maurin (1975) emphasised the similarities between the status of children and slaves in relation to their *pater familias* and *dominus*, and the parental construction of the latter relationship.

[117] On emancipation of sons see Gardner (1998) 10–15, who noted that emancipated sons were 'still socially and emotionally regarded as part of the "family"', 14. There were also important differences, particularly in respect of inheritance, cf. *ibid.* 20–4.

[118] Cicero, *Q.fr.* 1.1.13, declared that the ancestors had controlled freedmen very much like slaves, but the passage should not be taken literally (cf. Watson (1967) 228 n.3; *contra* Kaser (1971) 298; Fabre (1981) 222). The passage, nostalgically invoking the good old days, is closely linked to Cicero's stern advice to Quintus to rein in the influence of his favourite freedman Statius.

[119] *Att.* 1.12.2 (61 BCE). Fabre (1981) 256, thought Cicero was disingenuous and had actually sent Hilarus to collect his share of the provincial spoils, but that seems implausible; cf. Treggiari (1969a) 256–7.

been deeply involved in their patron's political, economic, and personal affairs, making a public prosecution very delicate. Most patrons would presumably also have balked at the negative publicity associated with such a trial, which in effect meant admitting a lack of control over one's *familia*.[120] The image of a patron unable to assert his authority was, as the example of the emperor Claudius illustrates, very similar to that of a hen-pecked husband.[121] The only effective remedy would have been to give patrons much wider powers, including the right to administer punishment in private without the involvement of courts and public authorities, but, as we saw, that was not considered a viable option in Rome.

However, given the ideological significance of patronal authority – and the many practical uses the elite made of freedmen – the limited legal sanctions increased the importance of informal regulation correspondingly. That puts the spotlight on the nature of the *obsequium* demanded of the freedman, which in many ways represented a compromise between his emancipated status and the patrons' claim to exercise continued authority. *Obsequium*, itself a non-technical term, did not invest the patron with any specific rights, essentially being an obligation imposed on the freedman to treat his patron with respect.[122] But if *obsequium* basically was a moral duty, a freedman could in theory choose to disregard it. For precisely that reason, Syrus' 'filius sine natura' was not just any freedman but the 'probus libertus', i.e. the one who acknowledged his debt and responsibility.

Ideally, freedmen would voluntarily accept the role society had defined for them and remain within the 'modus liberti'. This informal 'code of conduct' was communicated through an ongoing public discourse that encompasses all literary genres as well as legislation and legal writings.[123] If strong legal measures were inapplicable, the freedman had to be made to conform in other ways, and the normative discourse about the proper behaviour of freedmen therefore served a very specific social function. It can be seen as a means of conditioning freedmen and inculcating a distinct

---

[120] D. 1.16.9.3 (Ulpian) noted that among the matters a proconsul could dispose of out of court (*de plano*) was the correction of disrespectful freedmen 'aut verbis aut fustium castigatione'. However, the patron still had to appear before the governor and present his case in detail.

[121] E.g. Dio 60.28.2, who described Claudius as 'the slave of his wife and the freedmen'. For the perceived servility involved in male submission to women see e.g. Cic. *Par.Stoic.* 36; Propert. 2.23.

[122] D. 37.15. On *obsequium* see Watson (1967) 227–9; Gardner (1993) 23–5.

[123] Tac. *Ann.* 13.2, on Pallas, whose 'sullen arrogance transcended the limits of a freedman (*modum liberti*)'. Gellius, *NA* 6.3.8–55, took Tiro to task for daring to criticise a speech by the elder Cato, arguing that 'surely Tiro showed more presumption than can be tolerated or excused', 'profecto plus ausus est quam ut tolerari ignoscique possit', 9. Although Gellius accepts that Tiro was a man of taste and education, 8, it was unacceptable for a freedman to judge the style of a Roman statesman and paragon of ancient virtue.

set of values; incidentally this function means that excessive concern with freedmen's behaviour cannot be taken at face value as a reaction to actual problems caused by disrespectful *liberti*. The issue was further complicated by their ambiguous position as 'servile' citizens – equal but inferior – which required that a separate social identity be defined for them that to some extent denied their formal status. If former slaves were accepted on a par with freeborn citizens, both categories would lose their rationale, and the answer was to invent the freedman as distinct social type, different from both slaves and freeborn.

The public 'discourse' on freedmen defined their place in society by presenting two stereotypes, the 'good' and the 'bad' freedman, who recur with remarkable consistency throughout Roman literature.[124] The 'bad' freedman was the one who, as Tacitus' proponent of re-enslavement says, is not content to be equal before the law with his or her patron, but mocks his patience, and even uses physical force against him.[125] He shows ingratitude and disrespect, and fails to accept his lot – in relation to his patron and within society as a whole. The root sin of the 'bad' freedman was disobedience towards his patron, condemned as unbridled *licentia*. From this basic transgression flowed a host of other sins of character and behaviour, most flagrantly ambition and disregard for the limitations which his past imposed. The result was usurpation of status unbefitting for a freedman and arrogance towards his freeborn betters.[126] The stereotype was routinely held up to public condemnation and became so familiar that it could even be used metaphorically. Thus, Livy described the Thessalians who abused the indulgence of Rome in the same way as slaves who were unexpectedly freed and tried out 'their freedom of voice and tongue', 'licentiam vocis et linguae', and were 'making a show of themselves by attacking and insulting their masters'.[127]

Tacitus' debate on the *liberti ingrati* was part of this discourse on the proper conduct of freedmen.[128] The speeches for and against re-enslavement are probably fictional, as suggested by the anonymity of the interlocutors and the private setting within the emperor's *consilium*. The emperor's response to the senate is presumably authentic, however, and it may have been the survival of this document that inspired Tacitus to

---

[124] Fabre (1981) 232–41, explored the theme of the 'good' and the 'bad' freedman.
[125] *Ann.* 13.26.
[126] E.g. Tac. *Hist.* 2.57, describing Vitellius' freedman Asiaticus as 'foedum mancipium', 'a vile slave'.
[127] 39.26.8: 'iactare sese insectatione et conviciis dominorum'. In Plut. *Mor.* 66D, an insolent man is compared to 'a freedman of the comic stage, who thinks that abuse is a fair use of equal speech'.
[128] *Ann.* 13.26–7.

develop the episode into a set-piece debate. The sharp focus it put on the ungrateful freedman – as well as the emperor's inaction – fitted perfectly into Tacitus' vision of moral decline, a message also emphasised by the arguments ascribed to the opponents of re-enslavement which are so defeatist that they suggest a battle already lost.[129] This theme was a recurrent one in Tacitus' work. In the *Histories* he gives the main symptoms of a social disintegration as slaves corrupted against their masters and freedmen against their patrons.[130] Masters and patrons, he further claimed, lived in fear of their slaves and freedmen who abused them verbally and physically, escaping punishment by grasping an image of the emperor.[131] Elsewhere, in a story of libertine betrayal, he describes how the freedman dreamed of the rewards of wealth and power, while 'morality and the patron's safety and the freedom he had received' receded in his memory.[132]

The public condemnation of the 'bad' freedman contrasted with the praise awarded to the 'good' freedman. In Terence's *Andria*, the good freedman Sosia is acclaimed by his patron for his *fides* and *taciturnitas*. He was freed for his good services and remained grateful for the *beneficium*, making him an 'exemplary figure', as Rawson observed.[133] His character is contrasted with the 'bad' freedmen, who also appear regularly on the Roman stage. They are marked by their lack of deference to their patron. Thus, in a fragment of Plautus' *Faeneratrix*, a bad freedman says 'Go to hell!' to his *patrona*.[134] In Plautus' *Persa*, a character launches an attack on a certain type of freedman, claiming that, 'if they don't cross their patron, they don't think they are free enough or good enough or respectable enough, unless they've done this, unless they've been rude to him, unless they've proved themselves ungrateful to their benefactor'.[135] The reference to their wish to be *frugi* and *honestus* through disobedience is obviously a joke, since these virtues are part of the standard qualities ascribed to a good – i.e. compliant – freedman.

---

[129] The argument against re-enslavement is typically Tacitean in its cynicism and disillusion, implying that singling out freedmen would merely demonstrate how numerous they were and how prominent their descendants had become. It is also remarkably weak, since a patronal right to re-enslave *liberti ingrati* could not have had the claimed effect or publicly demonstrated the numbers of freedmen.
[130] 1.2.20.   [131] *Ann.* 3.36.
[132] *Ann.* 15.54: 'cessit fas et salus patroni et acceptae libertatis memoria'.
[133] *Andr.* 34. Rawson (1993) 220.
[134] 'Heus tu! In barbaria quod dixisse dicitur libertus suae patronae, id ego dico tibi: "Libertas salve! Vapula Papiria"'; cf. Rawson (1993) 220f.
[135] 838–40: 'Sed ita pars libertinorum est: nisi patrono qui adversatust, nec satis liber sibi videtur nec satis frugi nec sat honestus, ni id effecit, ni ei male dixit, ni grato ingratus repertust.' The whole passage is itself a jocular play on a commonplace, since the complaint is put in the mouth of a slave who is admonishing a slave girl he has just bought.

Praise of freedmen generally invoked a specific set of virtues.[136] Absolutely central was the devotion to their patron, whose approval distinguished the good freedman from the bad.[137] *Fides* was therefore the key virtue of a freedman, which ensured his patron's trust and a useful role in society.[138] The importance of *fides* is underlined by Q. Cicero's suggestion that *fidelitas* was Tiro's fundamental virtue, even taking precedence over his 'litteris et sermonibus humanitateque', which in a sense was quite logical, since *fides* provided the vital bond that allowed Cicero to benefit from Tiro's many other qualities. The inseparable nature of trust and skills is also implied in Cicero's comment that he sorely misses Tiro's 'opera et fidelitas'.[139]

There appears to have been a fairly well established format for the praise of freedmen, but in 50 when Tiro lay ill Cicero described him as 'an accomplished, conscientious young fellow as you know and, you are at liberty to add, an honest one'.[140] Cicero's formulation suggests he is trying to move beyond mere conventions, and this boundary was explicitly breached in his approval of Atticus' freedman Dionysius, who had worked as a teacher for Cicero's son. He was returned to his patron with the comment that he was not just 'doctum', 'learned', but also 'upright, serviceable, zealous moreover for my good name, an honest fellow, and in case that sounds too much like commending a freedman, a really fine man'.[141] Cicero first invoked the common stereotypes used to praise freedmen, and then went a step

---

[136] The parallel existence of a conventional 'good' slave is illustrated by Martial's comment, 12.30, about Aper, who is dry and sober – 'the way you recommend a slave'.
[137] Recommending the freedman L. Nostius Zoilus, Cicero, *Fam.* 13.46, mentions that he has inherited from his patron, which speaks for his character and makes him 'patroni iudicio ornatus'. Treggiari (1969a) 217, noted that: 'The patron's approval was the conventional guarantee of virtue in a freedman.'
[138] On *fides* see the detailed discussion in Fabre (1981) 226–32.   [139] *Fam.* 16.16.2; *Att.* 9.17.2.
[140] *Att.* 7.2.3: 'adulescentem [doctum et diligentem], ut nosti, et adde, si quid vis, probum'. In 7.5.2, Cicero told Atticus that Tiro was very useful to him but that he hoped for his recovery mostly because of his *humanitas* and *modestia*. In *Scaur.* 23, a good freedman who avenged wrongs done to his patron is described as 'litteratum ac facetum', 'cultured and witty'. In *Verr.* 2.1.123–4, a freedman who got himself into trouble for carrying out his patron's final wishes is counted among 'viros bonos et honestos'.
[141] *Att.* 7.4.1: 'sanctum, plenum offici, studiosum etiam meae laudis, frugi hominem, ac, ne libertinum laudare videar, plane virum bonum'. Atticus also characterised him as 'vir optimus', *Att.* 7.7.1, while Cicero describes Dionysius as 'homine mirifico' for his great learning, 4.11.1. He later became Cicero's and Atticus' 'joint' freedman with a composite name, M. Pomponius Dionysius, *Att.* 4.15.1. However, Dionysius also illustrates how easily a freedman could fall from grace and be reclassified as a stereotypically 'bad' freedman. As soon as Cicero sensed the slightest lack of gratitude the reaction was harsh, *Att.* 7.7.1, and when Cicero fled Rome in 49 and Dionysius refused to follow, the condemnation was fierce and unrelenting, Cicero dismissing him as a mere Greek, 7.18.3; cf. 8.4.1–2: 'nihil cognovi ingratius'; 8.5.1; 8.10: 'hominem ingratum'; 9.12.2: 'odi hominem et odero'; 9.15.5: 'ego autem illum male sanum semper putavi, nunc etiam impurum et sceleratum puto'.

further and included 'vir bonus', which implies a certain moral standing and integrity, normally associated with the propertied classes.[142]

Cicero wrote several recommendations for freedmen belonging either to his friends or to his own clientele. A comparison with other letters of recommendation suggests that freedmen are praised for a different set of qualities than Cicero's other clients. As noted above, *fides* was the pivotal virtue, to which came industry, modesty, and frugality.[143] In his letters of recommendation *probatus*, 'approved, pleasing', is applied only to freedmen. On the other hand, no freedman is ever credited with *virtus*, and, as we saw, the particular expression 'vir bonus' is used only in exceptional cases where established boundaries are explicitly crossed.[144]

Individual examples include his letter recommending L. Cossinius' freedman L. Cossinius Anchialus as 'a man very highly thought of by his patron and his patron's connections' as well as 'a very worthy, amiable and attentive person'.[145] Likewise, T. Ampius Menander, freedman of T. Ampius Balbus, appears as 'a worthy, modest person, of whom both his patron and I have an excellent opinion'.[146] Cicero recommended M. Aemilius Avianianus and his freed *procurator* C. Avianius Hammonius, who was praised for his 'exceptional conscientiousness and fidelity towards his patron'.[147] He also provided services to Cicero during the exile with 'as much loyalty and good will', 'fideliter benevoleque', as if Cicero had freed him himself. He was in short a 'modest and serviceable person', 'pudens' and 'officiosus'. A freedman of P. Crassus, Apollonius, was after his patron's death received into the *fides* and *amicitia* of Cicero, because, as Cicero put it in his recommendation, 'he felt it proper to pay respect and attention to those whom Crassus had loved and who had loved him in return'.[148] Apollonius had joined Cicero in Cilicia, with good *fides* and *prudentia*, and he also supported Caesar with 'studio et fidelitate'. Now he wished to join

[142] For *vir bonus* as a member of the *boni*, see Hellegouarc'h (1963) 485–93. As noted above, Cicero could count a dutiful freedman and victim of Verres among the 'bonos et honestos', but that was clearly exceptional, *Verr.* 2.1.123.

[143] Blänsdorf (2001) rejected the idea of a specific vocabulary for the praise of freedmen, claiming that their virtues were not exclusive to freedmen. However, it is important to look at the overall pattern and combinations as well as individual instances; cf. Fabre (1981) 229.

[144] Deniaux (1993) 180–3. McDonnell (2006) 159–60, accepting the untenable theory of Treggiari (1969a) 264–5, that freedmen were regarded as *servi*, suggests they could not acquire *virtus* for that reason; cf. Fabre (1981) 262.

[145] *Fam.* 13.23: 'homo et patrono et patroni necessariis... probatissimus', and 'summa probitate humanitate observantiaque'.

[146] *Fam.* 13.70: 'hominem frugi et modestum et patrono et nobis vehementer probatum'.

[147] *Fam.* 13.21: 'probatus quod est in patronum suum officio et fide singulari'.   [148] *Fam.* 13.16.2.

Caesar and write an account of his career in Greek.[149] Cicero also wrote a recommendation for C. Curtius Mithres, at whose house in Ephesus Cicero had stayed. He gave ample proof of his *benevolentia* and *fides*, and Cicero still made use of his 'opera et fide'. In some of his speeches Cicero used the same vocabulary to sing a freedman's praise. In *Pro Cluentio* the defence was used, which he claimed always had been considered 'honestissima' in freedmen's cases, namely 'patrono esse probatum', patronal approval being the proof of a good freedman.[150]

This language was not specific to Cicero but recurs in the works of other writers. When the younger Pliny recommended the imperial procurator Maximus, it was as 'probum et industrium et diligentem', and fully devoted to Trajan's interests. He also praised a freedman whom he sent to recover from illness at a friend's house as 'parcus et continens', 'abstemious and moderate', and distinguished by *frugalitas*.[151] Similarly Martial lauded the imperial freedmen for their gentle character, respectfulness, calm, and modesty.[152] Fronto recommended a freedman, Aridelus, to the emperor as 'frugi et sobrius et acer et diligens'.[153] Interestingly, when the senate offered unprecedented honours to Claudius' powerful freedman Pallas, the decree, cited by the younger Pliny, remained within conventions praising his 'outstanding loyalty and devotion to duty', and describing him as 'a self-denying and faithful custodian of the imperial finances'.[154]

The closest we get to full-blown panegyrics of freedmen in Latin litera-ture are Statius' *Silvae* 3.3 and 5.1.[155] The first poem is dedicated to Claudius Etruscus in commemoration of his (un-named) father who had been a high-ranking imperial freedman.[156] The praise is fulsome and unambiguous, but even here the words are carefully chosen to fit the limited range of virtues open to freedmen. His success was ascribed to 'ingens fortuna' (44–5),

---

[149] His freedom to move around and attach himself to various nobles probably reflected the fact that his patron had died at Carrhae; Deniaux (1993) 512.

[150] *Cluent.* 52. Likewise, in *Flacc.* 89, the reliability of a freedman is underscored by reference to his being 'probatissimum' in the eyes of his patron.

[151] *Ep.* 10.85; 5.19.9, further praised as 'homo probus officiosus litteratus', 3.

[152] 9.79.5–6: 'tam placidae mentes, tanta est reverentia nostri, tam pacata quies, tantus in ore pudor'.

[153] *Ad M. Caes.* 5.52.

[154] *Ep.* 8.6.6–7: 'singularis fidei singularis industriae', 'abstinentissimi fidelissimique custodis princi-palium opum'.

[155] *Silv.* 3.4, was also dedicated to an imperial freedman, the eunuch Flavius Earinus, but the sole focus of this poem was his beauty. In *Silv.* 2.1, Statius mourns the young freedman Glaucias, who had been the *alumnus* of Melior, by stressing his *modestia*, *probitas*, and *verecundia*, 39–40, 43, 136. The same freed *delicium* is commemorated by Martial, 6.28, as 'castus moribus, integer pudore, velox ingenio, decore felix', 'pure in manners, unblemished in modesty, nimble of mind, fortunate in good looks'.

[156] For a full discussion of his biography and career see Weaver (1972) 282–94.

while his own qualities are given as 'vigil idem animique sagacis', 'watchful and shrewd' (98).[157] Statius stresses the late freedman's hard work, modest lifestyle, and sobriety (106–7), before finally greeting him as 'mitisseme patrum', 'gentlest of fathers' (208). *Silvae* 5.1 was dedicated to the imperial *ab epistulis* Flavius Abascantus, who was mourning his wife. Again Statius describes how a benign fortune helped his career, noting 'the devoted young man's quiet diligence, his untainted loyalty, his mind alert for business, his watchful intelligence, his sober judgement fitted to unfold great matters as they arose'.[158]

The construction of specific libertine qualities reflected the notion that they realised their potential for virtue differently from freeborn male citizens; essentially it happened through fidelity and hard work rather than valour and independent action.[159] Modesty, discipline, and obedience were their fundamental qualities, and striving for those virtues that were reserved for freeborn, especially those related to war and politics, meant going beyond the natural limits entailed by their separate nature. Ironically, therefore, the praise of freedmen – as much as the criticism – served as a reminder of their innate deficiencies. In that respect there are interesting similarities between the position of freedmen and women, who were also lauded according to a limited – and limiting – set of qualities.

The social processes reflected in these sources were not unique to Rome or to Roman freedmen. Later European history provides many parallel cases of social conditioning which reinforced supposedly natural inequalities related to gender, status, class, etc., but the Roman 'discourse' on freedmen nevertheless had a different edge to it. Two factors gave it an added urgency. Firstly, the positions of trust in which many freedmen were placed made their loyalty and obedience a matter of critical importance. At the same time this also made them more difficult to discipline through conventional public channels, correspondingly increasing the need for effective informal controls. Secondly, the role allocated to the freedman was based on a fiction. Whereas the roles prescribed for women might be justified by reference

---

[157] Bernstein (2005), following Veyne (1961) 244, interprets 'ingens fortuna' as 'wealth', which seems too literal, cf. Leppin (1996) 77 n.47. No freedman was ever praised for the amount of wealth he possessed; indeed, doing so would undermine well-established notions of the relationship between status and wealth, cf. below. Shackleton Bailey's Loeb translation gives it as 'splendid career', but 'good fortune' may be more appropriate.

[158] 76–9: 'pii iuvenis navamque quietem intactamque fidem succinctaque pectora curis et vigiles sensus et digna evolvere tantas sobria corda vices'. As Leppin (1996) 84, noted, Statius invents a striking oxymoron, 'nava quies', to describe his dedication to work, 5.1.76.

[159] This archetype was invoked when Fronto compared the deference of one of his senatorial clients to that of 'liberti fideles et laboriosi', *Ad Verum* 2.6.2.

to biological difference and the stereotype of the lower classes by their external circumstances, e.g. lack of education and resources, 'the freedman' was a purely artificial construct. It denied the existence of his natural family, invited him to regard his former owner as his father, presented manumission as a 'birth' for which he must be eternally grateful, and invested in him a set of personal limitations, which were justified solely by past misfortune and had no foundation in either biology, education, culture, or resources.

The ongoing 'discourse' about the 'good' and the 'bad' freedman was therefore not simply a snobbish reaction to social mobility and privileges under siege; these concerns expressed themselves rather differently. The freedman as a former slave was defined as inherently different, and it was therefore crucial that he knew his place in society as a whole and within the *familia* in particular. This in turn raised other problems, for his place was to a great extent defined socially rather than legally. The formal status of freedmen as Roman citizens – albeit dishonoured – did not make this operation any easier. These issues will be explored in the next chapter, which also looks at the main Roman anxiety concerning freedmen – the spectre of former slaves wielding power over their masters.

CHAPTER 4

The power and status of freedmen

In the eyes of the Romans a freedman could never become equal to an *ingenuus*. The experience of slavery had destroyed his honour and irreversibly degraded his mind and body. Despite his legal transformation the freedman still possessed his 'servile ingenium', and he would always remain inferior to those untainted by servitude.[1] His natural place was therefore at the bottom of the hierarchy of status which formed the basis for Roman society. The stability and success of Rome was founded – at least from an elite perspective – on the maintenance of proper distinctions between people of different class and personal ability. The *gradus dignitatis* – or 'scale of honour' – remained the cornerstone of any free and just society, and Cicero stressed the fundamental inequality entailed by complete equality which ignored the natural differences that are bound to exist between people. He famously declared that: 'So-called equality is most inequitable; for when the same honour is accorded to the highest and the lowest (who must be present in every nation), equity itself is most unequal.'[2] The *gradus* was not just a question of formal rank; it defined who was allowed to exercise authority over whom, and as such reflected the given hierarchy by which the higher being dominates and controls the lower – in the interest of all parties. Disregard for this rule was therefore more than a social transgression; it was in effect a violation of the natural order.

Viewed against this background it might seem surprising that freedmen were fully enfranchised and granted a status which in principle was equal to that of any other citizen. 'Natural' differences were therefore not matched by corresponding civic distinctions. Already in antiquity contemporary Greek observers were puzzled by the Roman custom. Most famously, Philip V of Macedon in his letter to the city of Larisa (214 BCE) recommended a less

---

[1] As Tacitus was keen to stress on several occasions, e.g. *Ann.* 2.12.3, and *Hist.* 2.92.3.
[2] *Rep.* 1.53: 'eaque, quae appellatur aequabilitas, iniquissima est. Cum enim par habetur honos summis et infimis, qui sint in omni populo necesse est, ipsa aequitas iniquissima est.' A similar point was later made by Pliny, *Ep.* 9.5.3.

66

restrictive citizenship and used Rome as a – perhaps extreme – example of a state with a generous enfranchisement policy whose manpower resources swelled as a result.[3] The contrast between Roman and Greek practices was indeed striking. While it was possible for freedmen to obtain citizenship in the Greek world, it remained exceptional and was always granted on an individual basis.[4] Generally, former slaves received the lower status of metics, resident aliens, which barred them from political influence and authority. The Roman custom of enfranchising freedmen would therefore have seemed anomalous, as also illustrated by Dionysius of Halicarnassus' digression, which tried to explain the advantages of the Roman practice to a sceptical Greek audience. According to Dionysius, the main benefit lay in the steady contribution which the freedmen and their descendants made to the citizen body in general as well as to the *clientelae* of individual nobles.[5]

Modern scholars have typically followed in the footsteps of the ancient Greeks and regarded the Roman policy as remarkably generous in its treatment of an otherwise stigmatised social category.[6] Most explanations have focused on the ethnic background of the slaves and Roman citizenship policies in general. Sherwin-White traced its origins back to early Latium. Members of the Latin League who migrated to another Latin town may have had the right to local citizenship, and Sherwin-White suggested former slaves originating from these communities could have been covered by the rule and entitled to citizenship upon manumission if they stayed in Rome.[7] However, not all slaves in early Rome came from Latium, and more importantly it is not clear why former slaves, who must have lost their civic status and identity when enslaved, were treated as Latins after manumission. The same objection can be raised against Chantraine's model, which invoked Rome's policy of incorporating defeated neighbours into the Roman state. He argued that since most slaves in the early period would have come from Italy, it was logical to give, for example, a freed Volscian the same status as the other Volscians who had been incorporated. Again, we

---

[3] SIG³ 543. Masi Doria (1993c) 232; Klees (2002) 92–4; Weiler (2003) 173–80. The first decree of 219 concerned the local citizenship of metics of Larisa, which had been rescinded after just two years. The king wrote again in 214, this time also referring to the Romans who he claimed even enfranchised their freedmen and admitted them to public office – incorrectly, as we shall see. Philip's own decree did not go nearly that far.

[4] On Greek manumission see Garlan (1988) 73–84; Fisher (1993) 67–71; Weiler (2003) 180–9; Zelnick-Abramovitz (2005).

[5] 4.23.6. Meyer (1961) 186; Fraschetti (1982). Ste. Croix (1988) 25, argued that the Roman practice of enfranchising freedmen should be sought in the institution of *clientela*.

[6] E.g. Finley (1980) 97, found it an 'astonishing rule'.

[7] Sherwin-White (1973) 323–4; cf. Gardner (1993) 15.

must remember that enslavement wiped out the person's previous status. A freed slave of Italian origin was therefore profoundly different from a free citizen of a subjugated Italian community.[8]

The terms in which the historical problem has been couched will have to be reconsidered, especially the notion that enfranchisement represented Roman 'generosity' towards freedmen. While it may have appeared so to outsiders and later observers, that may not necessarily have been the case when the custom was first introduced. We have little concrete evidence for the origins of enfranchisement, but the Romans themselves assumed it went back to the earliest stages of their state. Dionysius ascribed the policy to Servius Tullius, while Livy explained the origins with the tale of Vindicius, set in the first year of the republic; a slave called Vindicius, who had saved the new republic, was freed as a reward and enfranchised by the method that later became known as 'vindicta'.[9] As a classic aetiological myth the story reflected the perceived antiquity of the practice, whose introduction probably predated surviving records. The earliest evidence comes from the Twelve Tables, which implies that the freedman already held full citizenship and could own and dispose of property by testament.[10] Some scholars have questioned whether all three forms of *iusta manumissio* – *vindicta, censu,* and *testamento* – originally conferred citizenship, as was the case in historical times. It has been suggested that the latter was a purely private act which initially conferred only informal freedom.[11] This must remain conjectural, however, and there is in any case no reason to doubt

---

[8] Chantraine (1972) further argued that broad cultural similarities would have facilitated the integration of freedmen into Roman society.

[9] 2.5.9–10. Schumacher (1982) 46–55, argued the myth could not be dismissed as 'unhistorisch', 47, and even used it to reconstruct early Roman manumission practices.

[10] V.8, *Roman Statutes* 646–8. According to Fabre (1981) 8–9, with reference to Mommsen (1887) 3.58–9, cf. Kaser (1938) 89–94, early manumission had no legal implications. It was even suggested that the position of freedmen originally differed little from that of slaves, with whom they shared the label *servi*, Mommsen (1887) 3.421 n.1, 428 n.1. Cf. Treggiari (1969a) 265–6; Fabre (1981) 222, 286–91; Andreau (1993) 184. The central evidence for this theory comes from Paul's conjecture that the 'servi' who were exempt from the *lex Cincia de donis et muneribus* (204 BCE) included freedmen, *Frg.Vat.* 307. But Stein (1985) 131–3, has convincingly refuted this idea; cf. *Roman Statutes* 741–4. Dumont (1981) 108, also examined the epigraphic material adduced in support of the theory and concluded that the notion of freedmen being *servi* is 'un mythe mommsénien'.

[11] Cf. Kaser (1971) 117–18, who described testamentary manumission as 'reiner Privatakt'. On the basis of Livy 9.46, he assumed that not until 312, with the reforms of Ap. Claudius Caecus, did slaves freed *ex testamento* become full citizens, but Masi Doria (1993c) 240–9, argued persuasively that Appius' reform concerned the tribal allocation of freedmen, along with other *humiles*, not their civic status. Others have argued that the practice can in fact be traced as far back as the Twelve Tables, 6.2, which has been seen as reference to *statuliberi*, slaves freed conditionally by testament. However, in *Roman Statutes* 658, it is suggested that the rule may have related to bondage slaves, *nexi*.

that the practice of enfranchising former slaves went back to early stages of Roman history.[12]

The procedures by which former slaves were enfranchised suggest an important difference between Rome and the world of the Greek poleis. It remains a striking fact that the Roman citizenship in effect was conferred by the owner of the slave. Although officials were present – a magistrate with *imperium* for *vindicta*, the censor at *manumissio censu* – they merely recognised and confirmed the change of status rather than actually effecting it.[13] A private citizen could in other words grant a political status with minimal involvement of state authorities. This stands in stark contrast to classical Greece, where access to citizenship was highly circumscribed and the exclusive prerogative of the supreme political bodies. In this context Linke has drawn attention to the decentralised nature of the early Roman state, where certain state functions were devolved to the heads of the households.[14] In his view, Roman society originally consisted of semi-autonomous family units governed by the unlimited powers of the male heads, whose authority was comparable to the magisterial *imperium* which it would overrule within a familial context. Thus, although manumission was overseen by the state, the powers of the *pater familias* remained in principle unlimited. It was in the nature of things a public act, since the slave's change of status had wider repercussions and had to be announced to the entire community.

We are therefore dealing with a process fundamentally different from that known from the Greek poleis, and viewing it from a Greek perspective, or through the eyes of later Roman observers, may not further our understanding of its original nature. Most importantly we may consider the notion of Roman citizenship as a distinct privilege. It could be argued that in earlier periods it was simply the status held by free members of the community. As such it was inextricably linked to place and soil, as indicated by the institutions of *postliminium* and *exilium*, which reflected the principle that citizenship was forfeited through change of domicile. It followed that defeated foreigners whose communities were incorporated into the Roman state would also receive the Roman citizenship.[15] From a legal perspective Volterra argued that *libertas* without *civitas* made no sense,

---

[12] Cf. Volterra (1954) 707–8, which remains fundamental.
[13] Sherwin-White (1973) 324, spoke of magisterial sanction as essential, but the evidence suggests that he merely oversaw the procedure. Gardner (1993) 9–10, speculated that *manumissio vindicta* originally might have been a collective operation.
[14] Linke (2005) 132–40.
[15] The existence of seemingly intermediate statuses, generally known under the (later?) label *civitas sine suffragio*, does not affect this model, since the people in question presumably were not regarded

since they effectively were identical.[16] A free person required a legal status in relation to the society of which he was a member, and in Rome free members of society were citizens. Accordingly, citizen status was, as Volterra rightly maintained, the direct and inevitable consequence of manumission.

The unique Roman construction of the relationship between the former slave and his owner as a pseudo-filial bond also lent the freedman's enfranchisement an added necessity. The freedman was created through the exclusive action of the master into whose *familia* he was 'reborn'. It was therefore entirely logical that he should hold the same civic status as the 'father' who had given him social existence. Volterra thus compared the manumission of freedmen to the birth of children, who automatically received the status of their parents, and noted that the Romans applied the same principle to provincial *Latini* and *peregrini*, always assuming that freed slaves were granted the *ius civitatis* of their patron.[17] It was therefore a cause for concern whenever discrepancies arose between the status of a patron and his freedmen, as might happen for example when provincials were enfranchised. When Pliny petitioned the emperor to enfranchise his doctor and his family, he also asked for *ius patronorum*, which would allow them to maintain control over their *liberti*. Apparently this right was in some way associated with the shared status of patron and freedmen.[18]

The enfranchisement of freedmen appears less anomalous when viewed in the historical context of early Rome, its citizenship, its familial and social structure, and perhaps also its unique conception of the *patronus–libertus* relationship. It is not given that it represented a particular favour towards freedmen and it may have been a simple mechanism by which outsiders were formally integrated into society. However, irrespective of the original motivation, the eventual outcome was a sub-category of citizens who were considered intrinsically inferior to other citizens. The freedman's lack of

---

as members of the Roman community. Rather these statuses reflect the complexity of the Roman hegemonic system in Italy; cf. Mouritsen (2007b).

[16] Volterra (1954) esp. 704–5; cf. Weiler (2003) 176.

[17] Volterra (1954) 715. According to Bleicken (1998) 506, the grant of citizenship was not particularly generous but reflected 'den Eigentümlichkeiten des römischen Familienrechts, wonach der Freigelassene unter die Hauskinder aufgenommen wurde'.

[18] *Ep.* 10.11.2. Similar problems arose when a patron was exiled, or a patron with Latin status gained citizenship *per magistratum*. The *lex Irnitana* 23, stated that whoever gains Roman citizenship 'is to have the same rights and the same position, as they would have if they had undergone no change of citizenship, over their own and their parents' freedmen and freedwomen, who have not acquired Roman citizenship, also over their goods and the obligations imposed in return for freedom', González and Crawford (1986) 183. The same rule applied where a freed person had acquired citizenship through the office holding of sons and husbands, *lex Irn.* 97.

honour made his participation in civic life problematic; above all it excluded them from any position of public authority.[19]

In the early republic, citizenship did not in itself confer much political influence.[20] At this time, access to public office was highly restricted, and the role of the assemblies to a great extent acclamatory. Little choice was put before them, and the format of assembly proceedings seems specifically designed to produce affirmative responses. As several scholars have noted, it was the ritualised nature of Roman politics – and the corresponding lack of direct political influence of most citizens – which allowed the Romans to extend their citizenship beyond the limits of their city and grant it to subjugated peoples far from Rome.[21] More importantly in this context, it meant that former slaves could be enfranchised without posing any risk to established political structures.

During the middle republic the situation gradually changed. Access to public office was broadened, and the assemblies assumed real elective functions. This presented a new challenge, since the Romans had to ensure that despite his citizenship the freedman was kept away from political power. The answer to this conundrum was provided by the timocratic character of Roman political institutions, which in turn reflected the inequalities of the Roman citizen body as a whole. The poor had always been politically marginalised, and the solution to the problem posed by the freedmen was to assimilate them to the lowest category of Roman citizens, the *proletarii*, and the urban poor in particular. This was essentially a legal fiction, ignoring the manifest reality of freedmen's property, but it allowed the de facto exclusion of proletarians from politics and warfare on the grounds of penury to be extended to the freedmen on grounds of 'servility'.

In the military sphere their assimilation to *proletarii* meant that freedmen generally did not serve in the legions.[22] Freedmen are documented in a military context but apparently they were used only very sparingly

---

[19] Quintilian, *Inst. Or.* 11.1.86–9, discussed situations in which the orator had to generalise about whole classes of people, e.g. soldiers, *publicani*, foreigners, or freedmen, and advised that criticism be tempered by the addition of positive features, the aim apparently being to dispel suspicions of prejudice. It is revealing that in the case of freedmen the standard accusation against them focused on their *auctoritas*, 'libertinis detrahenda est auctoritas', 88, that is, the simple fact that a freedman has *auctoritas* is deemed unacceptable, comparable to the notorious greed and insolence of soldiers.

[20] Cf. Meier (1997). See also Gauthier (1974), (1981); Whitehead (1991) 144ff, who all stress that the Roman citizenship, in contrast to the Greek, was defined in terms of *libertas* rather than active political participation.

[21] Bleicken (1995) 21, located the policy of enfranchising freedmen in the early period when the mass of (plebeian) citizens had little political influence; cf. Kaser (1941) 176–7; Meyer (1961) 186.

[22] Sherwin-White (1973) 324–5, suggested they were not barred from normal military service but simply too old to serve when they were freed. There is no evidence to support this theory.

and in functions which kept them away from direct combat. Generally freedmen were called up only when manpower resources were stretched to the absolute limit and all available forces had to be deployed. Thus, it is telling that when Dionysius of Halicarnassus outlined the benefits of enfranchising freedmen, he mentioned the military use that could be made of their sons rather than of the freedmen themselves.[23]

Most commonly, freedmen were employed as rowers in the fleet, where occasionally even slaves were used. Thus, during the second century there are five recorded instances of freedmen being called up for naval service.[24] In some instances they were also used for garrison duty, where they might carry arms but were not expected to engage with the enemy. It thus remains a striking fact that even during the most critical moments of the republic we have no evidence that freedmen were ever put in the front line.[25] The background for the exclusion of freedmen from active military service may be sought in concerns about their loyalty to the state as well as their fighting abilities, misgivings rooted in conventional prejudices against the 'slave nature'. There was a perceived incompatibility of servile origins and the moral authority that came from carrying arms and defending the state. Thus, their officers always appear to have been freeborn (so explicitly Livy 40.18.7), and in 217 only freedmen with children were called up, presumably because child rearing was seen as a sign of a 'responsible' citizen who made a contribution to society.[26] The taboo against armed freedmen persisted into the empire, albeit with a few notable exceptions. During the Pannonian revolt and after the Varian disaster, Augustus drafted freed slaves for the legions, but interestingly there was no general call-up of freedmen. Better-off slave owners were compelled to provide a freedman according to their census, but the procedure followed is not entirely clear.[27]

The ban on freedmen serving in the army had a number of knock-on effects. It automatically excluded them from the equestrian order, *equites*

---

[23] 4.23.5.

[24] 191 BCE, Livy 36.2.15; 181 BCE, Livy 40.18.7; 172 BCE, Livy 42.27.3; 171 BCE, Livy 42.31.7; 169 BCE, Livy 43.12.9. Cf. Welwei (1988) 28–44.

[25] Slaves had exceptionally been fielded during the second Punic War; Welwei (1988) 5–18. These *volones* were generally freed after their service. During the desperate military emergency caused by the allied revolt in 91 BCE the Livian epitomator reports that freedmen first began to serve in the army: 'Libertini tunc primum militare coeperunt', *per.* 74 (for the year 89). But as Appian, *BC* 1.6.49, indicates, even then they were only given garrison duties.

[26] Livy 22.11.8: 'Libertini etiam, quibus liberi essent et aetas militaris, in verba iuraverant.' Of this 'urbano exercitu', those under 35 were enrolled in the fleet, while the older freedmen were stationed in Rome for garrison duty.

[27] Vell. 2.111; Suet. *Aug.* 25.2; Dio 55.31.1. Cf. Welwei (1988) 18–22, who points out some inaccuracies in Dio's version. Augustus also set up a paramilitary fire-fighting force, the *vigiles*, manned by freedmen, Dio. 55.26.4f; cf. Sablayrolles (1996). Later they became predominantly freeborn.

equo publico, which in turn meant that they were barred also from law courts manned by *equites*. C. Gracchus explicitly excluded freedmen from the juries, specifying in the *lex repetundarum* that jurors had to give the name of their father.[28] The aim was to prevent former slaves from sitting in judgement of freeborn, which would have seemed an inversion of the natural order. For that reason freedmen could not become magistrates or public priests either, nor could they enter the senatorial order.[29] No exceptions are known to this rule before the upheavals of the triumviral period, and as far as we know it was never formally challenged. But it could be argued that these disabilities did not diminish the freedman's citizenship any more than they did that of other disadvantaged citizens, including the urban poor.[30]

At municipal level, freedmen may not have been formally barred from holding local *honores* until the reign of Tiberius, when the *lex Visellia* (24 CE) was passed, prohibiting 'persons of the condition of freedmen from daring to assume such honours and dignities as belong to those who are freeborn, or to usurp the office of decurion, unless they have been authorised to do so by having obtained the right from the emperor to wear gold rings'.[31] The penalties were severe, with usurpers of the decurionate becoming *infames*. The ban on freedmen in local office was also applied to non-citizen communities in the provinces, as shown by the Flavian charters for the Spanish towns with Latin status, which prescribed that magistrates should be appointed 'ex eo genere ingenuorum hominum'.[32]

It is not clear whether the *lex Visellia* merely restated an existing policy or changed current practice. Allowing freedmen to hold local office would have breached a fundamental taboo; most likely therefore the law was a largely symbolic gesture, which spelt out a basic principle that had already applied. Thus, there are no examples of freed local magistrates from the republican period.[33] Under the principate a few instances are known of

---

[28] *Lex rep.* 15. Treggiari (1969a) 63, 67.

[29] Treggiari (1969a) 54–5, 60–1. She rightly suggested that *De vir. ill.* 34.1 probably is a slip, 55.

[30] Taylor (1960) 132–49, 133, called them 'second-class citizens', which is not strictly correct. As Weber (1988) 257, noted, freedmen shared their disadvantages with most of the Roman population.

[31] *Cod. Iust.* 9.21.1: 'Lex Visellia libertinae condicionis homines persequitur, si ea quae ingenuorum sunt circa honores et dignitates ausi fuerint attemptare vel decurionatum adripere, nisi iure aureorum anulorum impetrato a principe sustentantur.'

[32] *Lex Malac.* 54; cf. González and Crawford (1986) 188. *CIL* 14.2807 refers to an imperial freedman, Crescens, who 'omnes honores municipi n(ostri) delatos sibi sincera fide gessit' at Gabii, but the *honores* were probably only those open to a freedman; *pace* Abramenko (1992) 99.

[33] Cf. Treggiari (1969a) 63. At Capua we find freed *magistri* acting as officials of *collegia* and *pagi* between 111 and 71 BCE. In the absence of normal civic institutions in that city, they took over functions

freedmen who entered the *ordo decurionum*, but no *libertus* is securely documented holding local office. Most unequivocally, C. Gabbius Messallae
l. Aequalis became 'adlecto in ordin(em) decurionum' at Larinum, presumably in the early first century.[34] At Castrimoenium, M. Iunius Silani
l. Monimus received official recognition in return for his benefactions in
a decree by the local *ordo* which mentions that 'he belongs to our [i.e. the
decurions'] order'.[35] These examples may indicate that membership of the
council was considered more acceptable than office holding, since it did
not confer any direct personal authority.[36]

Caesar's colonies represent an important exception which would appear
to prove the general rule. The charter for his colony at Urso states that: 'If
anyone shall say that any of the decurions is unworthy of his place or of the
order of the decurionate, except on the ground that he shall be a freedman,
and it shall be demanded of a IIvir that a trial be granted concerning the
matter the IIvir to whom approach shall have been made for a pre-trial
concerning the matter, is to administer justice and grant trials.'[37] As a
result of this clause we find freedmen holding office in Caesarian colonies.
Thus, both M. Caelius M.l. Phileros and L. Pomponius L.l. Malc[–] were
duoviri in Curubis in Africa, and the former also at Carthage.[38] It did not
represent a general change of policy, however, but specifically related to the
Caesarian colonies, as also indicated by the fact that although Phileros was
a prominent benefactor at Formiae he only received the title of *Augustalis*
in the Italian city.

The explicit permission for freedmen to hold office in Caesar's colonies
reflected the unusual composition of the settlers, many of whom appear
to have been drawn from this social category. Suetonius mentioned that

usually associated with magistrates but held no formal authority. *CIL* 1².672–91; cf. Heurgon (1939);
Frederiksen (1984) 264–5, 286; Solin (1990).
[34] *AE* (1966) 75.
[35] 14.2466 (31 BCE): 'ex ordine sit nostro'. Mommsen suggested he might just have held *ornamenta
decurionalia*. Garnsey (1975a) 169 n.5.
[36] A single instance from the Roman colony of Dion seems to break the pattern completely, since P.
Anthestius P.l. Amphio is recorded as 'aug(ur) aed(ilis) IIvir quinq(uennalis)', *AE* 1950 20; *AE* 1998
1209 = *SEG* 34 630; cf. Demaille (2008). A Severan date has been suggested, but no explanation of
this glaring anomaly.
[37] *Lex Urs.* 105: 'si quis quem decurion(em) indignum loci aut ordinis decurionatus esse dicet,
praeterquam quot libertinus erit, et ab IIvir(o) postulabitur, uti de ea re iudicium reddatur, IIvir
quo de ea re in ius aditum erit, ius dicito iudiciaque reddito', *Roman Statutes* 409–10, 428. The
commentary, 446, describes the passage as ambiguous, since it could be argued that the exclusion
of freedmen may have been so automatic that no trial was required. However, the extant examples
of freedmen holding office in Caesar's colonies suggest it allowed rather than banned them.
[38] *CIL* 10.6104; 8.977 with add. 12451, Luisi (1975); Gascou (1984); Jehne (1987) 296. M. Antonius
Hipparchus, Antony's freedman, became *duovir* at Corinth, *PIR²* A 838; cf. Treggiari (1996) 875.

Caesar had depleted the population of the city through the enrolment of 80,000 citizens in overseas colonies.[39] In the case of Corinth, Strabo noted that Caesar 'colonised it with people that belonged for the most part to the freedmen class, and the official name of Urso, *Colonia Genetiva Iulia Urbanorum*, reflected the urban origins of the settlers, many of whom would also have been freedmen.[40] It therefore made sense to allow freedmen access to public office in these particular settlements, despite the departure it marked from normal practice. Prior to the *lex Visellia*, freedmen were probably kept out of office by the standard requirement of social respectability, since the clause of the *lex Ursonensis*, quoted above, implies that if a freedman gained office, a legal complaint could be made on the grounds of *indignitas*.

While the direct exercise of public authority by freedmen was easily prevented, the enfranchisement of former slaves was still bound to cause concern in a system where the *populus Romanus* constituted the only source of political legitimacy. The people formally expressed its will in the assemblies, and as Roman citizens freedmen were fully entitled to take part in the proceedings. The libertine vote was therefore the most problematic aspect of their citizen rights and the subject of considerable controversy. But despite its sensitive nature the Romans never seriously considered depriving freedmen of their *ius suffragii*, probably because in the end there was no need for such radical measures. Firstly, the system of block voting allowed the weight of individual votes to be carefully graduated, in effect eliminating the political power of the lower classes, and secondly, the de facto assimilation of freedmen to the urban proletariat ensured that they remained at the bottom of this hierarchy.

In the *comitia centuriata*, formally the Roman people organised as an army, the exclusion of freedmen from the legions meant they were confined to a few unarmed centuries.[41] In the tribally structured assemblies the

---

[39] *Caes.* 42.1: 'Octoginta autem civium milibus in transmarinas colonias distribuis, ut exhaustae quoque urbis frequentia suppeteret.'

[40] Strabo 8.6.23 (381); Dio 43.50.3–5; Plut. *Caes.* 57.5; Diod. 32.27.3; Paus. 2.1.2; App. *Lib.* 136.646.

[41] Despite Taylor's more cautious stance (1960) 140, Treggiari (1969a) 51, Brunt (1971a) 24 and Dumont (1987) 63, argued that freedmen were inscribed in *classes*, partly on the grounds that the assembly's military character had faded and partly with reference to *Com.Pet.* 29 which mentions freedmen who were 'gratiosi navique in foro'. However, there are serious objections to be made against this theory. The *comitia centuriata* was still structured as a military assembly, e.g. dividing the citizens into *iuniores* and *seniores* and meeting outside the *pomerium*, and if its divisions had become purely financial, some freedmen would logically have been inscribed in equestrian centuries, which we know they were not. Admitting freedmen to the *classes* would have been politically inconceivable, not least because that would give them effective control over the urban centuries of the first class. Given the decisive influence of the *centuria praerogativa*, selected by lot among the first-class centuries, they

situation was different. *Tribus* were voting units based on territorial divisions of the *ager Romanus*, which reached a total of thirty-five in 241 BCE. A crucial distinction was drawn between the thirty-one rural and the four urban *tribus*, into which the urban masses were confined. Landowners, on the other hand, were generally inscribed in the rural tribes, even those who lived in the city. This principle was abandoned in the case of freedmen, who as a rule were inscribed in the urban *tribus* irrespective of domicile and land ownership. As Dionysius says, Servius Tullius 'distributed them among the four urban tribes, in which the body of freedmen, however numerous, continued to be ranked even to my day', and later Asconius could describe the rural *tribus* as 'propriae ingenuorum', the preserve of freeborn.[42]

While their restriction to the unarmed centuries was a logical consequence of their (perceived) inability to serve, their inscription in the urban *tribus* was essentially arbitrary. It breached the geographical principle underlying the *tribus* allocation, and whereas the restriction of the urban plebs to just four *tribus* was formally justified by their domicile, allocating the freedmen *en bloc* to the urban *tribus* – whether they lived there or not – was openly discriminatory. This anomaly ensured that their tribal inscription would remain a contentious issue throughout the Roman republic. The means by which freedmen were neutralised in the tribal assemblies was untidy and irregular, and therefore destined to attract the repeated attention of ambitious politicians with an eye on the untapped electoral resource which the freedmen represented.

The evidence does not allow us to reconstruct the history of the freedmen's tribal vote in full detail.[43] The issue first surfaces in the historical record in 312 when Ap. Claudius Caecus appears to have reallocated the urban population among all the thirty-five *tribus*.[44] According to Livy, he distributed the urban masses, 'urbanis humilibus', in all the *tribus*, which presumably also included the freedmen.[45] A few years later, in 304, the censors Q. Fabius Maximus Rullianus and P. Decius reversed the Claudian

would have had a good chance of choosing the consuls, cf. Mouritsen (2001) 99–102. The passage of the *Commentariolum* may be viewed in the context of Plut. *Aem.* 38.3, which mentions men 'who were of low birth and had lately been slaves, but who were frequenters of the forum and able to gather a mob and force all issues by means of solicitations and shouting'.

[42] 4.22.4; Asc. 52C.   [43] Fabre (1981) 136, provides a survey.

[44] According to Diod. 20.36.4, Ap. Claudius gave all citizens the right to be enrolled in any *tribus* they wished, but as Taylor (1960) 136, noted, that would hardly have been practically feasible.

[45] 9.46.11. Cf. Masi Doria (1993c) 240–9; Oakley (2005) 629–35, who interprets the reform as specifically concerned with freedmen rather than the urban plebs in general, and as a forerunner for later attempts at distributing freedmen in the rural *tribus*. Later sources claimed he had given freedmen the right to vote. Plut. *Publ.* 7.5, says that the legendary Vindicius became the first freedman to have the

reform and returned the city populace to the urban *tribus*.[46] At some point during the later third century this measure was also undone, since the Livian epitomator states that: 'Freedmen were returned to the four urban *tribus*, although they had earlier been spread among all of them.'[47]

During the second century, further changes were introduced which allowed freedmen with a son over 5 years old and those with a country estate worth more than 30,000 HS to be inscribed in the rural *tribus*.[48] The initiative is significant since it modified the policy of ignoring freedmen's property and also took account of their reproduction, regarded as an added qualification. However, the censors of 169–8, Ti. Sempronius Gracchus and C. Claudius Pulcher, after some debate, reversed the reform and confined all freedmen to just a single urban *tribus* which was to be chosen by lot.[49] The senate backed the censors, and its approval was later echoed in Cicero's hyperbolic claim that 'if Ti. Gracchus had not done that we would have lost the *res publica* long ago'.[50] The issue refused to go away, however, and we are told that M. Aemilius Scaurus (cos. 115) carried a law on luxury and on the libertine vote. Taylor reasonably suggested it must have improved their status, which could hardly have deteriorated further.[51]

During the tumultuous year of 88 BCE, the tribune P. Sulpicius passed a law distributing the newly enfranchised Italians and the freedmen in all *tribus*. Sulpicius' legislation was soon annulled, but in 84 Carbo passed another bill to the same effect, which was undoubtedly also rescinded by Sulla.[52] The question re-emerged in the 60s, when C. Cornelius suggested placing freedmen in the tribes of their patrons, and in 66 the tribune C. Manilius continued this policy but backed down in the face of senatorial opposition.[53] Clodius also seems to have embraced the issue. Allegedly he had prepared a law in the run up to the praetorian elections of 52, which

suffrage, while 'other freedmen received the right to vote in much later times from Appius who thus courted popularity'; cf. Fabre (1981) 135; Humm (2005) 229–66. This would seem unlikely given their status as Roman citizens.

46 Val. Max. 2.2.9.

47 Bk 20: 'libertini in quattuor tribus redacti sunt, cum antea dispersi per omnes fuissent'. The notice comes under the year 220, but covers the *lustra* between 234 and 219.

48 Livy 45.15.1.

49 Livy 45.15.1–7. That year it fell on the Esquilina, but as Taylor (1960) 140–1, suggested, this was probably not fixed but decided at each census. Masi Doria (1993c) 251–4.

50 Cic. *De Or.* 1.38; *De vir. ill.* 57.3; cf. Dumont (1987) 57–63.

51 *De vir. ill.* 72.5: 'legem de sumptibus et libertinorum suffragiis tulit'; Taylor (1960) 141–3.

52 Sulpicius: Liv. *Per.* 77; Asc. *Corn.* 64C. Carbo: Liv. *Per.* 84, 'Libertini in quinque et triginta tribus distributi sunt.'

53 Asc. *Corn.* 64cf; *Mil.* 45C; Dio 36.42.2. A corrupt passage of Cic. *Mur.* 47, may also allude to this law. Fabre (1981) 135, suggested that all these initiatives concerned the freedmen's inscriptions in their patrons' *tribus*, on the basis of a single comment in Dio, 36.25.

Cicero claimed would 'make us subjects to our own slaves'.[54] Asconius
later explained the bill as an attempt to redistribute the freedmen in all the
tribus; supposedly their new voting power would allow them to dominate
the assemblies and hence also their former masters.[55] Some modern scholars
have disputed this version and suggested that Clodius wanted to give
informally freed slaves a recognised legal status as freedmen. The idea is
based on Cicero's additional claim that the law would 'make our slaves his
[i.e. Clodius'] freedmen'.[56] Others have argued for two separate proposals,
one concerning the tribal inscription of freedmen and another dealing
with the status of informally freed slaves.[57] The hypothesis is ingenious but
faces the problem that the informally freed slaves would have to be fully
enfranchised in order to allow Clodius to exploit their votes. This would be
a very radical step, out of tune with Clodius' other measures which tended
to be less extreme than Cicero would like us to believe.[58] It also views
Clodius' law in light of the later Augustan reform, to which it becomes a
direct precursor. But not only was Augustus' law far more limited in its
implications (stopping well short of full enfranchisement); it also belonged
to a very specific historical context that did not obtain in the 50s BCE.
There was, on the other hand, a long tradition – going back 250 years – for
politicians tinkering with the tribal inscription of freedmen; most likely
therefore Clodius' proposal was yet another attempt at exploiting this issue
to his own advantage.

The attention paid to freedmen's votes reflected the basic anomaly of
their restriction to a few tribes. The focus on this issue may have become
stronger in the late republic, which saw a gradual breakdown of traditional
political patterns, increased elite competition, especially at elections, and
a growing mobilisation of the masses in Rome, perhaps also including
freedmen.[59] Cicero regularly accused Clodius of arming slaves, which has
often been interpreted as a derogative reference to freedmen. However,
there is little evidence to support this inference, and it is difficult to see
how freedmen could ever have constituted an independent force in Roman

[54] Cic. *Mil.* 87: 'incidebantur iam domi leges quae nos servis nostris addicerent'. Fragments of his
speech *De aere alieno Milonis* may also refer to this proposal, *Schol.Bob.* 173 Stangl; cf. Crawford
(1994) 275, 283–4.
[55] Asc. 52C.
[56] *Mil.* 89: 'lege nova quae est inventa apud eum cum reliquis legibus Clodianis, servos nostros libertos
suos fecisset'. Loposzko (1978–79), followed by Lehmann (1980). Tzounakas (2006) adds little new.
[57] Tatum (1999) 236–8.
[58] See e.g. Fezzi (1999). According to this theory, the state would effectively intervene in the relationship
between the former master and slave and enforce a formal manumission against the will of the patron.
[59] See Mouritsen (2001) 129–48.

politics.[60] The occasional attempts to mobilise their support through tribal redistribution attracted opposition and condemnation partly because of the potential threat it posed to political stability and partly because of the sensitive nature of libertine participation in public affairs.

To summarise, it has been suggested that, if viewed in the context of early Roman society and its familial structures, the citizenship the freedmen received appears less as a specific privilege than as a means of integrating them into free society. The problematic issue of political power was neutralised by their assimilation to *proletarii* who were naturally excluded from most public and military roles because of their lack of resources. As such they provided a template for a civic role that could accommodate the specific 'disabilities' which former slaves carried as 'citizens without honour'. Without pressing the case too hard, it is possible to point to certain shared characteristics between the two categories which both carried a stigma; whilst the poor were considered 'morally bankrupt', freedmen were disqualified because of their servile past. In the case of the freedmen it involved a disregard for their property, which was not allowed to endow the owners with the respectability that might compensate for their lack of ancestry. The strategy ensured that a freedman remained outside the normal property-based hierarchies; formally they could never become 'men of substance'.

As the republic waned, the question of freedmen's political power was transformed. The strength of their votes became irrelevant and a new issue emerged which concerned freedmen's *informal* influence on the leaders of state. This would come to dominate the 'discourse' under the empire, as we shall see in the third section. First, however, we will consider the

---

[60] Klees' claim (2002) 112, that they contributed 'nicht wenig' to the disruption of political life in the late republic, and Vanderbroeck's suggestion (1987) 81–92, that the politically active urban masses were 'independent freedmen' appear equally unfounded. The riot blamed on wealthy freedmen in 31 BCE, protesting against heavy taxation, is evidently exceptional, Dio 50.1.4–6; 51.3.3. Dumont (1987) 64, argued that the censorial actions of 169 represented an attempt to confront a real danger posed by freedmen, who threatened to dominate the *comitia*. There is no evidence to support that theory, apart from Cicero's transparent hyperbole in *De Or.* 1.38. Scipio Aemilianus famously denounced the crowd at a hostile *contio* as the stepchildren of Italy, who had been brought there in chains, but this hardly allows any conclusions to be drawn as to the composition of political crowds in general, Vell. 2.4.4; Val. Max. 6.2.3. The only ancient statement which points in that direction, App. *BC* 2.120, is tendentious. Neither can Cicero's allegations that Clodius used slaves in his gangs (*Att.* 4.3.2, 4; *Sen.* 33; *Dom.* 5–6, 53, 79, 89, 92, 111, 129; *Sest.* 34, 53, 75, 81, 95; *Cael.* 78; *Har.* 22, 24–6, 39; *Pis.* 9, 11, 23, 30; *Planc.* 35; *Mil.* 36–7, 59, 73) necessarily be taken as derogatory references to freedmen, as it has often been done; cf. Treggiari (1969a) 264; Brunt (1971b) 137; Achard (1981) 215–16. Interestingly, there is never any mention of freedmen being among Clodius' supporters. They appear only in Asconius' description of the crowd that passed C. Manilius' bill on the freedmen's tribal inscription, 45C.

Augustan reforms, which marked the most important change in policy towards freedmen and manumission.

THE AUGUSTAN REFORMS: AIMS AND BACKGROUND

The most comprehensive set of laws regulating manumission and the status of freedmen was passed during the reign of the first emperor, who established a legal framework that, with few modifications, was to endure throughout the imperial period. Some elements of the reform have already been touched upon, but this chapter will take a closer look at the legislation, its aims and purpose, and the social and political background. A study of the Augustan laws also casts a revealing light on modern approaches to the freedman in Roman society, since most scholars have perceived the reform as a response to specific social problems caused by a rise in manumission during the late republic. Supposedly, 'excessive' and 'indiscriminate' freeing of slaves had destabilised society, to which Augustus reacted by reducing the scale of manumission, preventing the freeing of unsuitable slaves, restricting the rights of freedmen, and generally imposing tighter controls on this category.

This interpretation has taken its cue from Suetonius, who stated that: 'Considering it also of great importance to keep the people pure and unsullied by any taint of foreign or servile blood, he [i.e. Augustus] was most chary of conferring Roman citizenship and set a limit to manumission.'[61] In line with this assessment, it has generally been assumed that a primary objective of the reform was to cut the overall scale of manumission and by implication also the number of freedmen in society.[62] As such, the initiatives were aimed at 'restoration and preservation of social stability'.[63] Indeed, to another scholar they addressed a general 'anomaly' in society, since the

---

[61] *Aug.* 40.3. 'Magni praeterea existimans sincerum atque ab omni colluvione peregrini ac servilis sanguinis incorruptum servare populum, et civitates Romanas parcissime dedit et manumittendi modum terminavit.'

[62] Nicolet (1984) 97, casually mentions Augustan 'laws or provisions to limit the numbers of manu-missions and the rights of freedmen'. Likewise, Martino (1954–72) 4.314, refers to 'misure limitatrici delle manumissioni emanate da Augusto'. Treggiari (1969a) 245, mentions Augustus' 'measures to check the rate of manumission'. Sherwin-White (1973) 327, said Augustus' legislation: 'sought to lessen the frequency of manumission'. Watson (1987) 29, argued that 'the point of the provision is to restrict their numbers [of freedmen]'. Welwei (1988) 21, referred to 'die aus der *Lex Fufia Caninia* und der *Lex Aelia Sentia* zu erschliessenden Bestrebungen des Augustus, die Zahl der Freilassungen zu vermindern'. Starace (2006) 67, 'fortemente limitative'. Contra Atkinson (1966); Alföldy (1986a) 290–6.

[63] Gardner (1993) 39, who also refers to the laws as attempts at restoring 'order and stability'.

influx of 'unsuitable' freedmen into the citizen body had contributed to the crisis of the republic.[64]

Each of the Augustan measures concerning freedmen has been placed within this framework and construed as a response to a specific social problem. Thus, the *lex Fufia Caninia* would have tackled the issue of large-scale testamentary manumission and the indiscriminate freeing of slaves who would lack proper supervision. These slaves manumitted by 'childless testators' posed problems of social control and integration, and to cut their numbers the law forced owners to make a choice and select the most deserving.[65] The risk posed by 'unsuitable' freedmen has been seen as the inspiration for the *lex Aelia Sentia* which prescribed basic qualifications for both manumitters and freedmen. Likewise, the strengthened patronal claim to freedmen's estates reflected a wish to curb the rise of the 'freedman class' in society.[66] Finally, the new legal remedy against *liberti ingrati* was explained as a response to growing problems caused by the 'ambitious parvenu' and the experience of libertine disloyalty during the civil wars.[67]

While there is broad consensus on the background and motives of the Augustan reforms, most attempts at explaining the actual harm caused by freedmen have remained vague.[68] Apart from the increased cost of the grain dole – which was solved by fixing the number of recipients – it is difficult to pinpoint any specific problems arising from manumission during the late republic. Therefore, when describing the 'freedman crisis' historians tend to fall back on conventional concerns about the 'dangerous' lower

---

[64] Klees (2002), 112–16, described it as a 'Missstand' (114) and saw it as an attempt to curb 'das ungeprüfte Eindringen Ungeeigneter in die Bürgerschaft' (113). Cogrossi (1979) 160, believed it was the answer to a host of concrete social problems caused by freedmen. Alföldy (1986a) 287, thought that 'die Massen der Freigelassenen für den Staat bereits als eine politische und soziale Gefahr erschienen'. According to Le Glay (1990) 622, social and economic problems forced Augustus to limit manumission. Rink (1993) 53, saw the reform as an attempt to stabilise the institution of slavery.

[65] Gardner (1993) 41.

[66] E.g. Schnurr (1992) 158, on Augustus' attempt to 'repress... the drive for upward mobility... especially that rich, independent, Trimalchio-type of freedmen'.

[67] Gardner (1993) 41–50, esp. 46, where she suggests that the law may have 'been thought necessary because of pressure of business arising from such complaints'. She also saw the law as a reaction to weakening 'deference', and claimed that 'the general standards of behaviour of freedmen towards patrons were perceived as having degenerated to the point where special legal remedy was needed', 49.

[68] There are notable exceptions. Carcopino (1941) 60, perceived the *lex Fufia Caninia* as a response to prodigality and indulgence rather than the danger of unsuitable freedmen, but his views on freedmen were generally atypical for his time. Likewise, Bradley (1984; 1987 edn) 90f, saw it as a measure against *luxuria*. To Buckland (1908) 546–7, the aim was to protect the interest of heirs, followed by Westermann (1955) 90; Atkinson (1966). Although not without plausibility the model does not explain why Augustus focused so strongly on this particular issue rather than other, presumably more common, forms of profligacy.

classes. In some instances the perspective comes close to that of the Roman slave owners, with frequent use of terms such as 'deserving' slaves and references to 'rash' and 'reckless' manumission of 'immoral slaves'.[69] As a result, the ancient distinction between 'good' and 'bad' slaves/freedmen has been incorporated into the modern debate, where we also find references to the 'quality' of freedmen, which supposedly deteriorated during the late republic when 'unworthy elements' gained freedom and citizenship.[70] The implication of this approach is that, for the sake of society, some slaves were better kept in servitude, a viewpoint that would be perfectly normal for a Roman *dominus* but perhaps more surprising to encounter among contemporary scholars.

Fears about 'irresponsible' manumission were undoubtedly real but any attempt to understand an issue such as the Augustan reform must distinguish between the anxieties of Roman slave owners and concrete social problems. Furthermore, it is important to bear in mind that freedmen as a category represented a challenge to the Roman 'construction' of slavery and freedom as such. The Roman institution of manumission rested on two central pillars – selection and patronal authority. In order to maintain the fiction that slaves were inherently inferior to all free, the transition between the two categories must have the appearance of discrimination, letting through only slaves of particularly good character, maturity, and treatment. If any slave could take his place in society as a free man alongside freeborn Romans, the given character of these categories would be questioned and their arbitrary nature revealed. Crucial too was the convention that a freedman never overcame his disabilities and always required the guidance of a patron.

These were essentially ideological concerns, however, which existed independently of actual manumission practices. Therefore, when Augustus set out to address them, he may not have responded to a specific crisis demanding his attention. Because the anxieties about freedmen were so fundamental, they could in principle only be fully assuaged by a ban on manumission,

[69] E.g. Sherwin-White (1973) 327–8, who believed Augustus' main concern was to limit manumission 'to the deserving', and prevent 'excessive manumission', 329; cf. Treggiari (1969a) 237.
[70] Kaser (1971) 297: 'unwürdige Elemente'; he also suggested that: 'In der ausgehenden Republik verschlechterte sich das Niveau [of freedmen]', 296. Warde Fowler (1908) 228, mentioned 'the enfranchisement of crowds of rascals', and noted that, 'Had manumission been held in check . . . there would have been more good than harm in it.' Barrow (1928) 179: 'Freedmen were threatening to outbid in number and wealth the free population; and it was not always the best type of slave that was freed', so 'The danger was indeed obvious'. Mette-Dittmann (1991) 193, spoke of keeping 'sozial unzuverlässige' freedmen out of the citizen body. Gardner (1991) 24, referred to the 'quality of the slaves manumitted' and distinguished between 'quantity' and 'quality'.

which no Roman could seriously contemplate. The ideological problems they posed were essentially insoluble and therefore destined to remain part and parcel of Roman manumission. Moreover, since they existed on an ideological plane it made little sense to address them through practical intervention. For that reason Augustus' legislation may be best understood as a statement of principle rather than a radical attempt to alter current practice. Thus, on closer inspection, the individual measures turn out to be curiously half-hearted; often it is far from evident what the original 'problem' might have been or how the law was supposed to address it.

For example, much emphasis has been placed on the 'criminal' slaves, whom Augustus gave the status of *peregrini dediticii* and relegated from the city of Rome, but we may doubt the practical impact of this provision.[71] Few owners would presumably have felt inclined to free slaves they had previously chained or punished, and unless the maltreatment had left visible marks, they could simply ignore the law, whose implementation relied entirely on their co-operation. The background for the little-known action against *liberti ingrati* is also a matter of conjecture. However, the common explanation – disloyalty of rising parvenus – is hardly convincing; even if that had been a growing problem – for which we have no evidence – there were already laws in place to deal with the issue. In this case we should not forget that the very notion of *liberti ingrati* offended basic Roman sensibilities, no matter how infrequently the problem may have occurred.

The *lex Fufia Caninia* introduced a sliding scale for the number of manumissions allowed in wills and many scholars believe it had a strong practical impact.[72] But the assumption that entire households routinely were freed by testament is hardly realistic, not least given the economic damage inflicted on the heirs.[73] The only support for this interpretation comes from Dionysius of Halicarnassus' tirade against excessive manumission, which insists that it did happen. Still, the scenario was clearly so exceptional that Dionysius felt compelled to assure his – presumably

---

[71] E.g. Klees (2002) 116.

[72] Gaius *Inst.* 2.224, 228. To Last (1934) 433, the law dammed 'one of the broadest channels by which foreign blood flowed into the community of Roman citizens'. Kaser (1971) 297: 'Die *lex Fufia Caninia* schränkt, um die in Testamenten besonders häufig und gefährlich auftretende Prahlsucht zu bekämpfen, die testamentarischen Freilassungen ein.' Mette-Dittmann (1991) 193, suggested an enormous quantity of manumissions by the elite was curbed by this law; cf. Fabre (1981) 33–4.

[73] Champlin (1991) 136–42, cf. below. The presence of *pilleati* in funerary processions is well documented, e.g. *Cod.Iust.* 7.6.5, but there is little evidence that this was a major incentive for manumission. Neither can we assume that all the freedmen in funerary processions necessarily had been freed by will.

sceptical – readers that he was not just reporting hearsay but personally knew of some instances.[74] Our remaining evidence for the freeing of entire households comes from Petronius' *Satyricon*, where Trimalchio makes such a promise (which he could never legally fulfil), and an equally unrealistic *declamatio* attributed to Quintilian.[75] Moreover, if the aim were to reduce large-scale freeing of slaves the *lex Fufia Caninia* would also have been quite ineffectual, since it limited only one particular type of manumission.[76] An owner wishing to free more slaves than the law permitted could still do so during his own lifetime.[77] And if that was too costly or inconvenient, he could in principle free all his slaves on his deathbed in the presence of witnesses, a procedure that would make them Latin freedmen.

The *lex Aelia Sentia* barred owners under 20 and the mentally ill from freeing slaves, both formally and informally. The practical impact of these limitations is dubious, however, since either category is unlikely to have freed many slaves in the first place, especially if it was considered socially unacceptable.[78] It would hardly have affected the overall number of slaves freed either, since in the case of young slave owners the ban was purely temporary; as soon as they turned 20 they could free as many slaves as they wished. It may have sent a signal about the necessary vetting of slaves, but in practical terms the measures would have been largely cosmetic, ignoring, for example, the problem of selection posed by owners who were themselves freed, criminal, or *infames*.

The Augustan measures emerge as peculiarly half-hearted and easily circumvented, and the mismatch between their supposed aims and actual content suggests they might be better understood as official declarations which emphasised the need for proper selection and 'quality' control in the manumission process.[79] As such they probably belong in the same

---

[74] 4.24.6: 'ἔγωγ' οὖν ἐπίσταμαί τινας ἅπασι τοῖς δούλοις συγκεχωρηκότας εἶναι ἐλευθέροις μετὰ τὰς ἑαυτῶν τελευτάς'.

[75] *Sat.* 71.1–3; *Decl.Min.* 311. Cf. *CIL* I².1703. See below p. 183 n.294.

[76] It is often overlooked, too, that even with the restrictions in place many owners could free the large majority of their urban households, since the rural slaves (rarely freed, as we shall see) would have counted towards the total.

[77] Gardner (1991) 30–1, discussed a passage of the Visigothic *Epitome* of Gaius, 1.2.3–4, which also curbed deathbed manumissions, but she noted that the provision is unlikely to go back to classical law where such limitations are unknown.

[78] *Contra* Duff (1928) 32, who mentioned 'young boys of immature judgement recklessly throwing liberty and citizenship among their slaves'. He also speculated that 'Clever Orientals, whose characters were sometimes of the criminal order, often gained such ascendancy over imprudent and weak-minded masters that they easily acquired their liberty though they were entirely unworthy of it.'

[79] Gardner (1991) 24, noted that while the *lex Fufia Caninia* insisted on selection, it did not specify on what criteria slaves should be selected for manumission. This was probably because the law

context as the Augustan laws concerning marriage and family, measures whose ideological character has generally been much better appreciated.[80] Only the most literal-minded historian would nowadays see Augustus' legislation on adultery as a direct response to rampant sexual dissolution that threatened to bring down society rather than a symbolic statement of moral restoration and the return to ancestral *mores*. Augustus' legislation on freedmen may not have differed in essence, since the issue of the freedman's *fides* and good behaviour was as sensitive as that of female chastity or matrimonial fidelity. Like these, they were perennial sources of anxiety, perceived to be under constant threat or even in terminal decline. Although in principle timeless, such concerns were naturally heightened during periods of social and political upheaval, and it is therefore not surprising to find them addressed by the first emperor, who had come to power after a series of devastating civil wars that left him badly in want of moral and political legitimacy.

Augustus' ambition to cut the number of freedmen has become a widely established 'fact', but the overall impact of his laws was probably modest. The limitations imposed on owners' rights to free their slaves were to a great extent symbolic and would have done little to reduce the scale of manumission.[81] Thus, even the most important new limitation, the minimum age of 30 required of the slave, did not have this effect. The age limit applied only to formal manumission and enfranchisement. It was still possible to free slaves informally, and for this particular category Augustus invented the new status of Latinus Iunianus. Informal manumission had not previously been recognised in Roman law.[82] According to Ulpian, those freed *inter amicos* had been protected by the praetor and allowed 'the mere form of freedom'. This meant they could live as free but died as slaves.[83] The Augustan *lex Iunia* for the first time enshrined their liberty in law, which put their legal position on a much firmer footing and gave them

---

was primarily concerned with the *appearance* of selection rather than with the selection process itself.

[80] *Lex Iulia de maritandis ordinibus*, 18 BCE; *lex Papia Poppaea* 9 CE; cf. Mette-Dittmann (1991). Cohen (1991) stressed the limited impact of the *lex Iulia de adulteriis coercendis*, whose real innovation lay in the state's intervention into the domestic sphere.

[81] For example, young owners under 20 could still free slaves, but were required to take advice from a *consilium*.

[82] Cf. e.g. Cic. *Top.* 2.10.

[83] *Reg.* 1.10; Gaius *Inst.* 1.22: 'olim servi viderentur esse'; 3.56: 'olim ex iure Quiritium servos fuisse, sed auxilio praetoris in libertatis forma servari solitos'; *Frg.Dosith.* 4–8: 'Hi autem, qui domini voluntate in libertate erant, manebant servi', 5. Fabre (1981) 55–9.

a recognised civic status.[84] The result was that, rather than limiting the number of freedmen, the Iunian law actually increased it.

The fact that the Augustan laws did not significantly reduce the 'freedman element' in society undermines attempts to see them as part of a broader cultural and 'ethnic' policy pursued by Augustus. Occasionally these theories have descended into xenophobia and even racism. Duff suggested that Augustus reacted against 'imprudent owners lightly and thoughtlessly lavishing enfranchisement on low-born Orientals'. The emperor therefore 'decided that this scum of the earth must be prevented from corrupting the time-honoured Italian character', which had to be 'preserved from their contagious taint'.[85] Even by the standards of his time Duff's views were extreme, but also Kaser, the eminent legal historian, could declare that Augustus had sought to keep the 'health', 'Gesundheit', of the Italian core population and maintain its majority and traditional strong morals.[86] More moderately, Klees argued that the increase in the number of freedmen, many of whom were unfamiliar with Roman culture and values, presented Augustus with a challenge.[87] Supposedly, their alien background impeded a full integration into Roman society.[88]

The posited clash of cultures, nations, or even races has little ancient support. Certainly it is difficult to reconcile to the fact that the Augustan measures would have increased the proportion of the population that could claim freedman descent and actively encouraged reproduction among

[84] Gaius *Inst.* 3.56, notes that the Latini Iuniani 'liberos esse coepisse', cf. 1.22; *Frg.Dosith.* 6: 'lex Iunia, quae libertatem eis dedit'. The date of the *lex Iunia* has long been disputed, but Balestri Fumagalli (1985) convincingly showed that it cannot as previously assumed have been Tiberian but must pre-date the *lex Aelia Sentia*; *pace* Venturini (1995–96). Treggiari (1991) 53, referred to the 'half-free class of Junian Latins', cf. Carroll (2006) 189, but their freedom was complete and guaranteed. Tac. *Ann.* 13.27, may have stated they were held 'vinclo servitutis', in chains of slavery, but there is no evidence to back this up. Most likely it is a rhetorical reference to the fact that their property was treated as *peculium*, with all the implications of dependency that created. In addition they were barred from receiving inheritances.

[85] Duff (1928) e.g. 30, 32. Later he described the reform as a check on 'the process of Orientalization', 34. Along similar lines Last (1934) 429, referred to Augustus' measures to 'preserve that material [i.e. Italian population] from uncontrolled contamination [from Greeks and Orientals]. Cf. Dench (2005) 229.

[86] Kaser (1971) 296–7. Similar language is even found in Treggiari (1969a) 231–2, who spoke of the 'infiltration of the Roman population by foreigners', and even mentioned their impact on the 'racial purity of Rome', 215.

[87] Klees (2002) 112, who also suggested that Augustus only allowed those who could adapt to Roman lifestyle and values to be integrated, 116. Likewise, Bradley (1994) 157, stated that citizenship was to be restricted to those properly qualified, 'proper qualification' being 'a demonstrated commitment on the part of the slave to Rome and Roman values'.

[88] Gardner (1991) 28–9, suggested that the problem caused by 'unattached' freedmen was the 'lack of a close bond' to 'a member of an existing *familia* which could assist his integration into society', but does not explain what kind of problems these 'un-integrated' freedmen actually caused.

freedmen as well as their intermarriage with freeborn. A central motivation behind many of the new provisions appears to have been population
growth, irrespective of ethnic background or legal status. Thus, the *lex
Aelia Sentia* offered Latini Iuniani an opportunity for enfranchisement via
procreation. Through the procedure of *anniculi probatio causa*, a child born
to married Latini Iuniani below the age of 30 entitled both parents and
child to full citizenship when it passed its first birthday.[89] In line with this
policy, the law also promoted intermarriage between patron and *liberta*,
and explicitly sanctioned unions between freed and freeborn. In addition,
it offered specific incentives for freedwomen, who obtained the coveted *ius
liberorum* when they had produced four children, one more than the three
required of freeborn women. The new regulations governing the freedman's estate also promoted child rearing, since the patron's share of large
estates was steadily reduced by each child the freedman produced, and he
was entirely excluded when the number reached three.[90] Finally, one of
the main consequences of the Iunian law was that children of informally
freed Latini Iuniani, who would previously have been slaves, now became
free.[91] Prior to the reform, informally freed *liberti* legally remained slaves,
which must imply that their offspring belonged to their master in the same
way as their estates did. After the reform, the property of a Latinus still
returned to his patron on his death but his children became Latins.

The fact that Augustus' laws reveal no concern about the social, cultural, or ethnic impact of manumission takes us back to Suetonius' claim
that Augustus, intent on keeping the people pure and unsullied by foreign
and servile blood, was reluctant to confer citizenship and limited manumission. The question is how we reconcile this statement to the recorded
measures which seem to have had the opposite effect. Thompson long ago
demonstrated the fallacy of racial or ethnic readings of Suetonius' text, and
suggested that his reference to the *populus* should be interpreted in strictly
legal terms as the citizen body, not the 'Roman people' in a cultural or biological sense.[92] This interpretation also helps us understand better a passage

---

[89] The *lex Aelia Sentia* gave Latini under 30 the opportunity to gain citizenship through reproduction.
This rule was later extended to Latini freed after the age of 30 by the *SC Pegasianum* passed under
Vespasian, probably in 75 CE, cf. *PIR²* P 512. Gaius *Inst.* 1.31; Ulp. *Reg.* 3.4; *Schol.Iuv.* 4.77. For a
detailed account of the procedure see Camodeca (2006a). Likewise, the *lex Iulia et Papia* exempted
freedmen with two children *in potestate* (or one 5-year-old) from providing the services to their
patron which had been promised in return for freedom, D. 38.1.37 (Paul).

[90] Astolfi (1999) 295, rightly saw this as a demographic measure, *contra* Masi Doria (1996) 178, who
identified it as a conscious attempt to stymie the development of 'famiglie libertine'.

[91] Cf. Fabre (1981) 56.

[92] Thompson (1981), cf. Brunt (1971a) 240; Dench (2005) 257–8.

of Dio, which prima facie might seem to point in the same direction. Dio records that among the advice Augustus passed on to his successor and the public was an injunction not to free many slaves, 'lest they should fill the city with a promiscuous rabble'.[93] However, since Augustus' laws made no concerted effort to limit manumission, the Severan historian may extrapolate from the second part of the emperor's advice, which warned against enrolling 'large numbers as citizens in order that there should be a marked difference between themselves and the subject nations'.[94]

On this interpretation the real focus and overriding concern of the Augustan legislation was the freedman's civic status rather than manumission as such; for what Augustus did limit – or at least regulate – was their access to Roman citizenship. As we saw, he invented two new statuses: freedmen who had suffered physical punishment and degradation became *dediticii*, while young and informally manumitted freedmen received the status of Latini Iuniani.[95] Together with Roman citizenship *optimo iure* this effectively constituted a three-tier structure, and this radical innovation triggered several of the other Augustan measures since the new hierarchy required that each freedman be placed at the appropriate level.

The highest status was to be granted only after careful vetting and selection. The responsibility rested on the slave owners who therefore had to meet some basic qualifications themselves, being of sound mind and maturity. The main requirement for the slaves was a minimum age set at 30. In addition, a system was devised by which Latini Iuniani could gain full citizenship, which included *iteratio*, i.e. repetition of the manumission process when the freedman was old enough to be formally freed, *probatio anniculi*, the production and rearing of children, and other services to society. While the concern with marriage, reproduction, and population growth may have been specifically Augustan, child rearing had long been

---

[93] 56.33.3–4: 'ὅπως μήτ' ἀπελευθερῶσι πολλούς, ἵνα μὴ παντοδαποῦ ὄχλου τὴν πόλιν πληρώσωσι.'

[94] 'μήτ' αὖ ἐς τὴν πολιτείαν συχνοὺς ἐσγράφωσιν, ἵνα πολὺ τὸ διάφορον αὐτοῖς πρὸς τοὺς ὑπηκόους ᾖ'. Suet. *Aug.* 40.4, observed that Augustus made it far more difficult for slaves to gain citizenship than freedom: 'Servos non contentus multis difficultatibus a libertate et multo pluribus a libertate iusta removisse.'

[95] The state may also have derived economic benefits from the reform, since the new Latin freedmen most likely would have become liable for the *vicisima libertatis*, which was a tax on manumission rather than citizenship; cf. Last (1934) 430, 432. Bradley (1984a) 197 and Albana (1987) assumed the tax applied only to formal manumission, but that is questioned by Petronius, *Sat.* 65.10–11, who refers to a deathbed manumission which in the nature of things must have been informal. In those cases payment of the tax would have fallen to the manumitter, since the entire estate of the deceased Latin freedman reverted to the patron. Last, *ibid.*, noted that prior to the reform informally freed slaves had probably not paid the tax.

regarded as the mark of a responsible freedman. As we saw, reproductive freedmen had received more favourable tribal allocations and occasionally also been recruited for army service, another mark of public trust.

The question that needs to be addressed is why the civic status of freedmen became a source of public concern under Augustus. Since we have no reason to believe that the freed citizens posed any real social or political problem – especially after the redundancy of the comitia and the disappearance of the controversial tribal issue – we may look for an explanation in the Roman citizenship itself. During the late republic and early principate it underwent profound changes, evolving from an essentially local, 'national' status into a universal, 'supra-national' status of privilege. Roman citizenship had, like the citizenship of most other ancient states, traditionally been the status held by free members of that community. As such it was intimately connected to the territory, to the extent that citizenship was forfeited when a Roman moved to another state. Therefore when offered to individual foreigners it normally involved surrendering the existing citizenship and taking up domicile in Roman territory. And on those occasions where it was presented as a reward, for example for bravery or successful litigation, it was typically linked to additional privileges such as *vacatio militaris*, *immunitas* from taxation, or eligibility for veteran settlement schemes. On its own, Roman citizenship would have been less attractive since it formally cut the person off from his local community.

The first collective demands for Roman citizenship were raised in the later second century BCE, probably by the descendants of 'disenfranchised' Roman settlers in 'Latin' colonies, and the request reflected their unique status as Roman 'satellite' communities, which had been separated from the mother state. There is little evidence that Roman citizenship had yet become a status widely coveted by non-Romans and, as I have argued elsewhere, the outbreak of the Social War may not have been driven by a unanimous Italian desire for Roman citizenship.[96] That version of events is perhaps better explained as a later projection of the eventual outcome onto the origins of the conflict, which led to the incorporation of the defeated Italians into the Roman state.

Despite the massive territorial expansion, Roman citizenship appears to have remained a 'normal' citizenship for some time after the Social War. Not until the triumviral period do we find the first grants to provincials who

---

[96] Mouritsen (1998a).

were allowed to maintain their local status alongside Roman citizenship.[97] An important step in the transformation of citizenship came with the introduction of the *ius civitatis per magistratum adipiscendae*, which offered citizenship to local magistrates in provincial communities with *ius Latii*.[98] The use of Roman citizenship as a reward for the provincial elite in return for – often costly – office holding demonstrates its value as a 'carrot', as well as its – newly conceded – compatibility with local statuses. This function is also apparent in the Augustan army reform which offered the Roman franchise as reward for auxiliary soldiers after completed service.

It follows that the imperial citizenship was fundamentally different from that of the republic. It had become a status on a different level from any local citizenship, thereby solving the old problem of double citizenship.[99] The traditional link between soil and citizenship was broken, and, as Dench noted, the Roman citizen body had developed into a virtual community.[100] It became part of a new, empire-wide system of statuses which were organised hierarchically and in some cases provided formalised opportunities for advancement. Ambitious provincials were invited to climb this ladder, and for those who reached the citizenship a number of personal and financial advantages awaited them. Augustus actively encouraged the process, using citizenship as a reward for loyalty to Rome, and to maintain and enhance its attraction he also made a point of 'protecting' the Roman citizenship against an influx of 'unworthy' provincials.[101] He also expressed public concerns about access to citizenship becoming too lax, insisting on proper checks before provincials were admitted.[102]

The changes to Roman citizenship cast Augustus' concerns about the freedman's citizenship in a different light. They meant that the age-old practice of enfranchising servants released from servitude had begun to

---

[97] Ferenczy (1982) 1048–9, noted that under the principate provincials could hold Roman citizenship without severing ties to their home community. This development was preceded by triumviral antecedents which gradually introduced compatibility; cf. Sherwin-White (1973) 296–9; Mouritsen (1998a) 91.

[98] This institution has been much debated but there is in my view no firm evidence for its existence before the middle of the first century BCE; cf. Mouritsen (1998a) 99–108, with previous literature. *Pace* Coskun (2009) 135–48.

[99] Nörr (1963) 578ff.   [100] Dench (2005) 134–5.

[101] Ferenczy (1982) 1053, on the systematic use of *ius Italicum* under Augustus, who granted it to provincial towns and overseas veteran colonies. Suet. *Aug.* 47, on Augustus' use of Latin and citizen rights as rewards for provincial cities which had offered services to Rome.

[102] Cf. Suet. *Aug.* 40.3–4. Stories circulated about the emperor's 'stinginess' in granting citizenship to provincials, even those sponsored by his relatives, and in one instance a provincial was stripped of his citizenship when it turned out he spoke no Latin, Dio. 60.17.3–4. Dench (2005) 138, noted that access to citizenship for provincials was tightened, at least on a symbolic level.

look increasingly anomalous; it raised the question how Rome could justify withholding from provincial leaders a privilege that was granted as a matter of course to any slave freed by a Roman citizen. The answer was to introduce a graded scale of statuses, which did not affect the freedmen's *status libertatis* but gave them a place in the imperial hierarchy more appropriate to their personal background. It ensured that, like provincials, freedmen were seen to meet certain requirements before entering the citizen body, for which reason the need for proper 'vetting' procedures was also re-emphasised.[103]

If Augustus' manumission laws were attempts to strengthen the privileged status of the Roman citizenship, that naturally situates them within the broader Augustan project which sought to 'bring Rome's house in order' by restoring traditional hierarchies and distinctions within the citizen body. *Discrimina ordinum* was a central plank of Augustan policy, as also illustrated by the attention paid to symbolic markers of status.[104] Thus, Augustus re-enacted the *lex Roscia theatralis* (67 BCE) and tightened the seating regulations in the theatre, imposing large fines in municipal charters for people who usurped status by sitting in the wrong seats.[105] He even disallowed legates from free or allied states to sit in the *orchestra*, generally reserved for senators, when he heard that freedmen were occasionally appointed as envoys.[106] As part of this policy Augustus also barred senators from marrying freedwomen (and actresses and daughters of actresses) through the *lex Iulia de maritandis ordinibus* which even extended the ban to three generations of senatorial descendants.[107] The *lex Iulia* may, as McGinn argued, have had little practical impact, since there probably always had been an expectation of marriage being between social equals; most likely the law simply prescribed what the current ideal was already.[108] As such it appears above all to be an ideological statement about the dignity of the senatorial order and the need to keep a proper distance between top and bottom of society.

---

[103] Like good provincials, freedmen could gain citizenship through a range of benefactions summarised in Ulp. *Reg.* 3.1, as 'beneficio principali, liberis, iteratione, militia, nave, aedificio, pistrino'.

[104] Respect for rank and standards: Suet. *Aug.* 35, 39, 41.1, 43.3.

[105] Suet. *Aug.* 44.1–2, on his division of the spectators at games according to rank. Rawson (1987); Schnurr (1992); Canobbio (2002) 11–41. In Shaw's reconstruction (2000) 389, freedmen and the poor are placed together at the back of the theatre. Claudius later extended this policy to the circus, Dio 60.73–4; Suet. *Claud.* 21.3; Tac. *Ann.* 15.32.

[106] Cf. Brunt (1961) 76–7.

[107] Dio 54.16.2; 56.7.2; D. 23.2.23, 44; Ulp. *Reg.* 13.1. A parallel ban on marriage between freeborn Roman citizens and adulteresses was also imposed.

[108] McGinn (2002), cf. Bouvrie (1984); *pace* Gardner (1993) 39, who suggested the law was a purely practical measure aimed at preventing senators from marrying women without family connections.

For a self-styled restorer of traditional political values, the standing of
the senate was destined to be a particular concern, not least because the
fall of the republic was widely perceived to be the result of the moral
collapse of the ruling class. Augustus had to draw a line under the chaos
and disruption of the triumviral period and present his rule as a fresh start
also in this respect. The dying years of the republic had seen freedmen
entering the senate and holding public office, usurping equestrian status,
and becoming army officers, even generals.[109] Dio relates that the triumvirs
in 39 BCE 'enrolled ever so many men in the senate, not only from among
the allies, or else soldiers, or sons of freedmen, but even slaves'. Among
the examples was one Maximus, who was about to become quaestor when
he was recognised by his master and detained. Another slave was detected
while actually holding the praetorship.[110] However isolated and few in
number, these instances were potent indicators of a world out of order,
and the outrage they caused is reflected in texts such as Horace's fourth
Epode.[111]

The upheaval of the triumviral period provided the immediate backdrop
for the Augustan 'restoration'.[112] The political crisis was accompanied by
a general sense of moral dissolution, and few transgressions symbolised
social anarchy more effectively than freedmen who ignored their natural
limitations and usurped rank, power, and status. It is telling that Dionysius
of Halicarnassus contrasted present ills with an idealised, rosy past, when
manumission was responsible and of great benefit to society. In sum,
Augustus' reform may be interpreted as a politically motivated response to
what was essentially a timeless ideological problem, which was felt more
acutely as the old political order disintegrated and society went through
a period of radical change. The measures were concerned with freedmen
only in so far as they constituted the most sensitive social category whose
status and behaviour were widely seen as an indicator of the overall health
of society.

[109] The period was generally characterised by social upheaval and the influx of large numbers of new
men into the Roman elite on the back of triumviral patronage. Osgood (2006) 250–97.
[110] 48.34.4–5; cf. Poma (1987). Freedmen are also documented as *tribuni militum* under the triumvirs,
Treggiari (1969a) 65, 187. P. Vedius Rufus may have been another freedman who prospered under
the triumvirs and entered the equestrian order as *tribunus militum*, cf. Kirbihler (2007). Sex.
Pompey's use of freed generals in this period became notorious.
[111] *Schol.Iuv.* 5.3, commenting on an episode during the triumviral period when a freedman of
Maecenas, Sarmentus, was tried for sitting in the first fourteen rows in the theatre, reserved for
knights, but acquitted because of his patron's influence. Osgood (2006) 263–4.
[112] Rawson (1987) 84, mentions Augustus' 'attempt to rebuild society after the chaos of the triumviral
period when, to Roman eyes, *discrimina ordinum* had been scandalously overridden'.

Potentia libertorum

Roman concerns about the power and status of freedmen did not vanish with the Augustan reforms but moved in a different direction and found a new focus – the emperor's own freedmen. This particular category came to dominate the public discourse on freedmen during the following centuries, and this section explores the nature of the problem as well as the Roman preoccupation with imperial freedmen. The Roman emperor had literally hundreds if not thousands of freedmen, and it was of course only a handful of them who ever came near the centre of power and only for what seems to be a relatively short period during the first century CE. The issue is nevertheless significant and deserves to be considered in some detail. Firstly, it highlights the underlying problem of manumission, which is the admission of a supposedly inferior category of people into society. Secondly, this particular discourse has contributed to the perception of manumission as an inherently problematic and disruptive social phenomenon. In this case the question is whether ancient critics reacted to a specific problem of governance or the attacks on powerful freedmen should be seen as part of a broader discourse about Roman society, above all the relationship between power, status, and liberty.

It has often been remarked that the imperial court grew out of the aristocratic household of the late republic.[113] The very limited size of the republican 'civil service' meant that the annual office holders would use their own staff, slaves and freedmen, to help them carry out public functions.[114] In this way a semi-'privatised' administration developed during the republic, which blurred the boundaries between the domestic and the public sphere, functionally as well as physically since there were no dedicated buildings for many public functions. Moreover, the domestic world was not 'private' in the modern sense, since the *domus* of an aristocrat formed part of his public persona.[115] Therefore, when a single ruler emerged out of the civil wars, the existing system of administration was naturally continued, not least because the principate presented itself as a republican restoration. The result was a monarchy where the rulers governed with the help of what was formally still their private household.

During the first century, the *familia Caesaris* gradually moved away from the republican template, and at the end of the Julio-Claudian period it had become a structure *sui generis*, as shown, for example, by the many freedmen

---

[113] As Rilinger noted (1997) 73: 'Aus dem aristokratischen Haus entwickelte sich der Kaiserhof.'
[114] Millar (1977) 59–61.   [115] See e.g. Wiseman (1987); Hesberg (2005).

who remained in post despite dynastic changes.[116] The internal make-up also evolved with the development of a complex system of titles and dedicated administrative tasks for individual freedmen. The grammatically odd titles, such as *a rationibus*, *ab epistulis*, and *a libellis*, emerged from the time of Augustus onwards, and others were added continuously, e.g. the *a studiis*, or patronage secretary. However, at no point are we dealing with administrative departments in the modern sense, with formalised career structures. It was in essence still an aristocratic household.[117] The 'domestic' framework within which the imperial administration was carried out gave the emperor's freedmen a unique opportunity to influence public affairs, since they would assist the emperor with his correspondence, accounts, etc., in very much the same way as Tiro had used to assist Cicero in all his affairs.

The emperor's freedmen, however, did not hold any formal power, nor was their influence due to any officially recognised 'public' position within the administration, despite the titles and functions, mentioned above. The slaves and freedmen who gained influence did so through their proximity to the emperor.[118] In her biography of Claudius, Levick suggested that the imperial court 'may be seen as a series of concentric circles of diminishing power, with their centre at the Emperor's bed and his bedroom; next his board and his dining room; then private offices and reception rooms. All who had access to them were sustained directly by their ties with the Emperor, indirectly by deploying the influence that the ties gave them.'[119]

The loose structure of the *familia Caesaris* blurred distinctions normally drawn in court societies between personal staff and public administrators. While some posts evidently offered far greater opportunities than others, there was no essential difference between the servants in charge of, for example, financial administration and those attached to his private chambers. Epictetus implies that even someone put in charge of the lavatory might suddenly become influential, as a slave cobbler apparently did who had been purchased by the imperial household.[120]

There was a disconcerting informality about their position, which enabled them to get dangerously close to the levers of power. The first

[116] Cf. Winterling (1999) 23–6, who also argued that the concept of *familia Caesaris* is unhistorical and inaccurate, 115–16. For the development of the *familia* see Schumacher (2001a). Examples of freedmen continuing in service under successive emperors in Panciera (2007); cf. e.g. Bruun (1989); Gregory (1995).
[117] Millar (1977) 73–8; cf. Burton (1977), who questions the model of Boulvert (1970), (1974).
[118] Saller (1982) 66, argued their influence was based not on official powers but on personal contact with the emperor. Cf. below p. 201, on the imperial *degustatores*.
[119] Levick (1990) 53; cf. Saller (1982) 66–7.   [120] *Diss.* 1.19.17–22; cf. Millar (1965) 144.

emperor showed some awareness of the offence this was bound to cause. Suetonius devotes a section to stories about Augustus and his freedmen, stressing his strictness as well as his humanity towards them.[121] The message was one of propriety, fairness, and control, and Augustus emerges as a 'model patron' who upheld natural hierarchies. There may be an element of special pleading here, since we know that some of his freedmen, e.g. Celadus, seem to have held substantial influence.[122] Even more prominent was the procurator Licinus, whom Augustus put in charge of tax collection in Gaul, a role that earned him a long-lasting reputation for avarice and fabulous wealth.[123]

Later emperors appear to have been even less concerned with keeping up appearances. Their reliance on freedmen became more openly acknowledged and a few emerged as powerful figures at court. Under Tiberius there is some evidence for rich and influential freedmen.[124] But it is not until Gaius that the first major figure appears, Helicon, an Egyptian slave who had been given to Tiberius and gained prominence under his successor. Serving as head *cubicularius*, he was accused of using his position to incite his patron against the Jews of Alexandria.[125] This was also the period when Callistus, later influential under Claudius, first emerged as a player, allegedly even conspiring against his patron when he felt his position was under threat.[126]

With the emperor Claudius, libertine influence reached a high point, and his reign has come to be defined largely by the power of freedmen.[127] The reasons for their unprecedented prominence may, as Levick suggested, partly be explained by Claudius' personal background and elevation against senatorial opposition, which would have increased his willingness to trust his freedmen more than the nobility.[128] Claudius also seems to have given his freedmen more public credit than his predecessors. The most prominent among them were Narcissus, Pallas, the favourite freedman of his mother Antonia, and Callistus, Gaius' freedman who had established good

---

[121] *Aug.* 67.

[122] *PIR²* c 616. Suet. *Aug.* 67.1; Joseph. *Ant.* 17.12.2 (332); *Bell.* 2.7.2 (106–9).

[123] *PIR²* l 381. He had originally belonged to Caesar. Suet. *Aug.* 67.1; Sen. *Ep.* 119.9; 120.19; *Apoc.* 6.1; Juv. 1.109; 14.306; Pers. 2.36; Sidon. Apoll. *Ep.* 5.7.2. Dio, 54.21.2–8, suggests he could run rings around Augustus to save himself from punishment. His magnificent tomb on the Via Salaria is mentioned in Mart. 8.3.6, and *Poet.Lat.Min.* IV p. 64–5, 43.24.

[124] Joseph. *Ant.* 18.6.1 (145); 18.6.4 (167); 18.6.8 (205); Plin. *NH* 13.93–4. Tac. *Ann.* 4.6.7, noted Tiberius' limited use of freedmen, cf. Levick (1976) 117.

[125] Philo *Leg. ad Gaium* 166–78.

[126] Joseph. *Ant.* 19.10 (64–9); Tac. *Ann.* 11.29; Dio 59.25.7–8.

[127] Cf. Suet. *Claud.* 25.5; 28–29.1; Dio 60.2.4; Sen. *Apoc.* 6.2. Levick (1990): Eck (1994).

[128] Levick (1990) 83.

relations with Claudius already before his accession.[129] But several other freedmen are also known to have enjoyed Claudius' favour, e.g. Felix, Pallas' brother, who became governor of Judaea, the *a studiis* Polybius, Harpocras, and the eunuch Posides.[130] Despite the evident bias of the sources there is sufficient evidence to put the political influence of these men beyond doubt. Tacitus, for example, stressed their role in the downfall of Messalina and held them responsible for his subsequent marriage to Agrippina, who would later entrench her own influence through these freedmen.[131] The power of the leading freedmen is further illustrated by their ability to exercise patronage. Vespasian allegedly gained his legionary legateship 'Narcissi gratia', and the consular and future emperor Vitellius placed golden images of Narcissus and Pallas among his household *lares*.[132] From his exile in 43 Seneca addressed a *consolatio* to Polybius, hoping to be restored through his intervention with the emperor. The wealth of Claudius' freedmen became proverbial and their fortunes were rumoured to run into hundreds of millions of sesterces.[133] The reactions to their wealth and power were virulent, and the historical tradition surrounding these individuals is exceptionally hostile. The elite harboured an intense dislike of Claudius' freedmen, and faced with this opposition his successor Nero promised to reform the use of freedmen. In practice, however, he largely continued the system. Thus, when Nero went to Greece, he left the freedman Helius in charge of Italy.[134] He also used freedmen as envoys, sending Polyclitus to Britannia.[135] Similarly, Vitellius is later presented as entirely dominated by his freedman Asiaticus.[136]

The first real change came with the Flavians, who made up for their lack of dynastic legitimacy by presenting themselves as the standard

---

[129] Narcissus: *PIR²* N 23, *ab epistulis*. Pallas: *PIR²* A 858. Joseph; *JA* 18.6.6 (181–2); Suet. *Claud.* 28; Dio 60/61.30.6b; Sidon. Apoll. 5.7.2; Callistus: *PIR²* I 229. Plin. *NH* 36.60: 'potentia notus'; *a libellis*, Dio 60/61.33.3a. His daughter became the mother of C. Nymphidius Sabinus, the praetorian prefect, Plut. *Galb.* 9.

[130] Felix: *Hist.* 5.9; *Ann.* 12.54; Suet. *Claud.* 28; *PIR²* I 695, with further refs. Polybius: Dio 60/61.29.3; Suet. *Claud.* 28; Sen. *Ad Polybium de consolatione*; Harpocras: Suet. *Claud.* 28: Posides: Suet. *Claud.* 28.

[131] *Ann.* 11.29; 12.1–3; Dio 60.8.4–6; 60/61.31.8, 32.2, 33.3a.   [132] Suet. *Vesp.* 4.1; *Vit.* 2.5.

[133] Plin. *NH* 36.60, on Callistus' wealth. Dio 60/61.34.4, mentions Narcissus' fortune of 400 million HS; Juv. 14.329–31. The wealth of Pallas, Narcissus, and Callistus became notorious, e.g. Plin. *NH* 33.134, implies that their fortunes exceeded 200 million HS. Tacitus, *Ann.* 12.53, attributes a fortune of 300 million HS. to Pallas, also suggesting that Nero poisoned him for his wealth, *Ann.* 14.65; cf. Dio 62.14.3.

[134] *PIR²* H 55. Dio 62.12.1–3, declared that the empire now was a slave to two emperors at once, Nero and Helius. According to Tacitus, *Ann.* 13.1, Helius poisoned Junius Silanus.

[135] Tac. *Ann.* 14.39. Dio 62.12.3, also claims Polyclitus enriched himself in Nero's absence in 67. Likewise, Phaon, the *a rationibus*, and Doryphorus, *a libellis*, Dio 61.5.4.

[136] Suet. *Vit.* 12.

bearers of traditional values. It was therefore decided to expand the use of *equites* as 'civil servants' in the imperial administrations, which had first been introduced under Vitellius.[137] In addition Suetonius reports stories of imperial firmness with servants and freedmen, which presumably reflected a deliberate change of tack.[138] However, we still find prominent freedmen, such as the well-documented father of Claudius Etruscus who had begun his distinguished career under Tiberius and served several other emperors until be became *a rationibus* under Vespasian.[139] He was granted equestrian status and even married the sister of a consul.[140] According to Suetonius, Domitian divided the main administrative posts between *liberti* and *equites*, but the continued prominence of some imperial freedmen is suggested by the flattering dedications they received from Martial and Statius.[141]

The introduction of equestrian administrators was a slow and grad-ual process, not fully completed until the reign of Hadrian. Eventually, however, all the main secretariats passed to *equites*, bringing an end to the long-running 'freedman problem' in the imperial household. It would resurface, however, in the later second century, when *cubicularii* and other personal attendants were accused of wielding undue influence, including Commodus' *cubicularius* Saoterus and Cleander, his *nutritor*, who was even made prefect and enrolled freedmen in the senate.[142] Later we are told that Heliogabalus, whose freedman Zoticus gained great influence, 'appointed freedmen as governors, legates, consuls and generals, and defiled every office with low-born profligates'.[143] As always, we may approach these claims with caution, not least since 'potentia libertorum' by that time had become a fixture of any critique of 'bad' emperors.[144]

The use of freed administrators eventually changed in the face of unre-lenting criticism from the Roman elite. Normally mild-mannered writers such as the younger Pliny launched into lengthy tirades when confronted with powerful freedmen such as Pallas, who is described as *caenum* and

---

[137] Millar (1977) 78–110; Levick (1999) 182; Jones (1992) 64; Schumacher (2001a) 344–5.

[138] *Vesp.* 23.   [139] Statius *Silv.* 3.3. Weaver (1972) ch. 22. *PIR*² c 860, *AE* 1972 574.

[140] Stat. *Silv.* 3.3.143–5; 111–18. Vespasian's freedman Hormus became a knight and seems to have been influential; Tacitus attacked him for depravity, *Hist.* 3.12.3, 28; 4.39.1. Vespasian's mistress, the freedwoman Antonia Caenis, also gained considerable influence, Dio 65.14.3–4.

[141] *Dom.* 7.2. On Domitian's freedmen see Jones (1992) 61–9. The dedicatees include Parthenius, *a cubiculo* (later executed by Nerva, *Epit. de Caes.* 12.8), Mart. 4.45; 5.6; Entellus, *a libellis*, Mart. 8.68; Flavius Earinus, imperial eunuch, Mart. 9.11, 12, 13, 16, 36; Stat. *Silv.* 3.4; Abascantus, *ab epistulis, Silv.* 5.1. Stat. *Silv.* 3.3; Mart. 6.83; 7.40, celebrated the anonymous *a rationibus* who was the father of Claudius Etruscus.

[142] Saoterus: SHA *Comm.* 3.6; 4.5; Dio 73.12.2. Cleander: Dio 73.12.3–13.1; SHA *Comm.* 6.3–7.1. Cf. Hekster (2002) 67–75.

[143] SHA *Hel.* 11.1; 10.2–3.   [144] Cf. Hekster (2002) 69.

sordes, 'dirt' and 'filth', and *furcifer*, 'yoke-bearer'.[145] Given the depth of hostility it is perhaps surprising how slowly the emperors reacted. Simple inertia may be part of the explanation, and the process may also have been hampered by elite reluctance to accept professional employment. But the main reason was probably the sheer usefulness of freedmen, which easily compensated for the public opprobrium they attracted.

Trust is the key issue for any ruler delegating tasks and responsibilities, and this was precisely where the use of freed administrators had its major advantage over freeborn and aristocrats. To the Romans nobody was considered trustworthier than a freedman, an assumption based on three factors.[146] Firstly, the pseudo-filial construction of the relationship between freedman and patron imposed strong moral obligations of *pietas* and *obsequium*. Secondly, the fact that freedmen had no other family connections and no patrimony made them wholly dependent on patronal support and goodwill. A freedman was his patron's 'creature', deprived of an independent political existence and interests distinct from his patron's, thereby eliminating any risk of split loyalties. Thirdly, because of their personal dishonour they could not themselves entertain political ambitions. Thus, it was their very disability as 'real' politicians that made them so valuable to the ruler. As Levick noted, they were only bettered by eunuchs – the ultimate example of a person without *virtus*.[147]

Ironically, it was precisely these factors which also made freedmen a liability for the imperial patrons who relied too heavily on their services. While the freedman's status gave him unique access to the ruler's confidence, it also made him uniquely unsuited to exercise any influence. There was a built-in tension in the 'construction' of the freedman, who was at the same time a trusted familial insider and a stigmatised outsider. His marginal status enabled him to get close to the levers of power – but he was never allowed to touch them.

The problem of influential freedmen was in some respects the age-old paradox of low-ranking domestic staff, wives, relatives, and 'unsuitable' friends being closer to the ruler than his official advisers and high-ranking

---

[145] *Ep.* 7.29.3; 8.6; cf. Roller (2001) 270–1.

[146] There were of course glaring exceptions, e.g. Menas/Menodorus, who betrayed his patron Sex. Pompey and was rewarded by Octavian, and Callistus, who conspired against Gaius, but the disloyal freedman was generally condemned as an abomination. Dio, 67.14.4, mentions Domitian's fear of his freedmen, which turned out to be justified.

[147] Levick (1990) 57, also observing that their 'political interests lay primarily in loyalty to their master', which made them 'safe to have as confidants'. Blackburn (1988) 275, noted Byzantine and ancient Chinese parallels of imperial administrators, who were the ruler's property. The use of eunuchs offered a 'double guarantee of kinlessness'; cf. Hopkins (1978) 172–96.

nobles. As such, the problem was not unique to ancient Rome but part of every court society. However, the personal background of these imperial administrators gave it a different twist in Rome. The fact that they carried a personal stigma which, in the eyes of society, made him incapable of exercising power meant that the *potentia* of freedmen was more than an embarrassment to the elite but seen as actively undermining society.[148] The point was that in terms of authority a freedman still counted as a slave – with all the moral deficiencies that entailed – which explains why ancient writers consistently describe powerful freedmen in those terms. For example, Tacitus stated that when Polyclitus was sent to Britain, the natives, unaccustomed to 'libertinorum potentia', were astonished that army and general had to obey 'a troop of slaves', 'servitiis'.[149] Likewise, when Claudius' freedman Narcissus arrived in Gaul before the invasion of Britain, the soldiers mocked him and shouted 'Io, Saturnalia', indicating a world turned upside down where the slaves give orders to their masters.[150] According to Tacitus, Pallas' brother Felix, whom Claudius had given control over Judaea, 'practised every kind of cruelty and lust, wielding the power of a king with all the instincts of a slave'.[151] In a similar vein Vitellius' freedman Asiaticus is described as a 'foedum mancipium', and after Vitellius' fall Asiaticus paid for his 'malam potentiam' by crucifixion, the servile form of punishment *par excellence*.[152] The elder Pliny called the freedmen who had usurped equestrian status 'servitia', while the younger Pliny expressed outrage at Pallas' praetorian honours and labelled him a slave.[153] The whole issue is neatly summarised in Tacitus' description of the African Mauri's fight against 'libertos regios et servilia imperia', 'regal freedmen and servile power'.[154]

The servility of freedmen is emphatically stressed when they assume authority over freeborn, the one area where their manumission apparently

---

[148] On *potentia* Levick (1990) 53; cf. Mehl (1974) 67. Tac. *Ann.* 11.28; Plin. *NH* 33.134–5, where Pallas, Narcissus, and Callistus are presented as sovereign rulers, 'rerum potiantur'.

[149] *Ann.* 14.39.2.   [150] Dio 60.19.3.

[151] *Hist.* 5.9: 'per omnem saevitiam ac libidinem ius regium servili ingenio exercuit'. The name of the freedman given as Antonius Felix by Tacitus may in fact have been Ti. Claudius Felix, Joseph. *AJ* 20.137, cf. Weaver (2005) 248, with further references.

[152] *Hist.* 2.57; 4.11.   [153] *NH* 33.33; *Ep.* 8.6.4.

[154] *Ann.* 4.23. Commenting on the negative influence of freedmen on Claudius, Dio declared that he was ruled by slaves, even using the verb δουλοκρᾰτέομαι, 60.2.4. Florus described Sex. Pompey's two powerful freedmen, Menas/Menodorus and Menecrates, as 'foeda servitia', 'base slaves', *Epit.* 2.18.2. Tacitus mentions an uprising in Pontus led by a 'barbarian slave', Anicetus of Polemo, who in fact turns out to be a freedman, *Hist.* 3.47. In a similar vein he explained Nero's disgust at Pallas by his unwillingness to bend to slaves, 'neque Neroni infra servos ingenium', *Ann.* 13.2.

counted for nothing and they consistently were referred to as slaves.[155] Their presumed inability to exercise power made them directly compara-ble to women, with whom they shared many attributes and characteristics as well as disabilities. The power of women was as unacceptable as that of freedmen, and fittingly Tacitus presented Pallas and Agrippina as partners in crime.[156] The influential freedmen did not just undermine the natural order; they also caused embarrassment to members of the elite who had to demean themselves before social inferiors.[157] This upside-down world is illustrated by Seneca's story about Callistus' former master who had sold him on the market; later he had to wait in line to see the power-ful freedman, only to be turned away.[158] Epictetus repeatedly noted the humiliation of having to beg a freedman for favours and patronage. He also taunted senatorial 'friends' of the emperor, telling them that, 'for the sake of these mighty and dignified offices and honours you kiss the hands of other men's slaves – and are thus the slaves of men who are not even free'.[159] Or as Pliny put it, Pallas' honours were granted 'by slaves to a slave'.[160]

While some of the senatorial outrage may be explained as a reaction to these experiences, the imperial freedman also acquired a wider political significance, since he came to epitomise the erosion of civic freedom in general. The connection between 'potentia libertorum' and *dominatio* runs through much of the surviving writings from the empire, and the corre-lation between the rise of freedmen and the decline of freedom becomes even clearer when we look at the history of the 'problem'.

The issue of the powerful freedman first emerged in the late repub-lic with the rise of the dynasts.[161] Each of the great leaders of the late

---

[155] It has been suggested that freedmen sometimes could be referred to as slaves without insult, e.g. Treggiari (1969a) 172, 265–6; Andreau (1993) 184. Rawson (1987) 88, claimed that freedmen were 'often rhetorically described as slaves'. The evidence is extremely weak, however, not least since Shackleton Bailey (1977) 1.466–7, demolished the theory that Cicero describes M. Tullius as his slave, *Fam.* 5.20.1. Most likely he was *ingenuus*. In Cic. *Fam.* 8.15.2, a freedman is called *verna*, but that usage also occurs in epitaphs, e.g. 14.943; 1427; 1520, to indicate the origins of former slaves within the *familia*, cf. Chantraine (1967) 171; Solin (1971) 124–7. When Cicero, *Verr.* 2.3.91, described Q. Apronius (freed and also called 'hominem vix liberum', 2.3.134) and P. Naevius Turpio (of unknown status) as 'servos homines' it was a deliberate insult and closely linked to the accusation of *potentia*; cf. e.g. 2.3.31.

[156] *Ann.* 13.2. Also the elder Pliny stressed the close link between Pallas' honours and Agrippina's influence, *NH* 35.201.

[157] In some cases the criticism of powerful freedmen may of course have been a reaction to actual abuse of power. Bribery seems to have been common, as suggested by the apparent wealth of many imperial freedmen, cf. Suet. *Claud.* 28. However, there is limited evidence for widespread misgovernment by freedmen.

[158] *Ep.* 47.9.   [159] Epict. *Diss.* 4.1.148–9; 3.7.31; 4.7.19–20; cf. Millar (1965) 145.

[160] *Ep.* 8.6.4.   [161] See in general Millar's exhaustive discussion in (1977) 69–83.

republic was associated with freed confidants who gained unseemly wealth and influence. The elder Pliny outlined the problem in a passage discussing a substance, 'cretaceous earth' also known as 'silversmiths' earth', which was used to mark the feet of imported slaves. Pliny first listed freed authors, 'literarum honore commendatos', all positively regarded, before turning to the powerful freedmen of the great leaders of the late republic. They included Sulla's Chrysogonus, Catulus' Amphion, Lucullus' Hector, Pompey's Demetrius and freedwoman Auge, Mark Antony's Hipparchus, and Sex. Pompey's Menas and Menecrates. Pliny complained that, having once arrived with marked feet, they enriched themselves during the proscriptions from the blood of Roman citizens: 'Such is the mark set on these herds of slaves for sale, and the disgrace attached to us by capricious fortune!'[162]

Several of these freedmen are well known from other sources.[163] Sulla's Chrysogonus occupies a special position, being the appointed villain of Cicero's *Pro Roscio Amerino*, where he is described as 'perhaps the most powerful young man in the state at the moment'.[164] Pompey's favourite freedman, Demetrius, was known for his *superbia*, which even his patron put up with, and he received great honours in the East, sometimes even overshadowing those of Roman senators. When the younger Cato arrived at Antioch accompanied by Demetrius, it was the latter who received the grand reception.[165] Relatively little is known about Caesar's freedmen, but their prominence may be suggested by the rumours which circulated in April 44 of a plot hatched by the late dictator's *liberti*.[166] Sex. Pompey, on the other hand, was notoriously reliant on his freedmen, including his two leading admirals, Menas (referred to as Menodorus in Appian) and Menecrates, whose status contributed to the common description of his fleet as mere pirates.[167] Plutarch tells us that Antony's freedman Hipparchus had 'the greatest influence over Antony and was the first of

---

[162] *NH* 35.199–201: 'Hoc est insigne venaliciis gregibus obprobriumque insolentis fortunae.'

[163] Treggiari (1969a) 182, presents additional evidence.

[164] 6: 'adulescens vel potentissimus hoc tempore nostrae civitatis'.

[165] Plut. *Pomp.* 40; *Cato Min.* 13. According to Josephus, *BJ* 1.7.7 (155), Pompey rebuilt Gadara in 63 to please Demetrius, who came from that town. His wealth was apparently substantial (4,000 talents, Plut. *Pomp.* 2.4; cf. Sen. *Tranquil. An.* 8). Dio, 39.38.6, says that it was Demetrius who built Pompey's theatre, but named it after his patron – to deflect criticism of his own fortune. Later he would run Cyprus for Mark Antony, Dio 48.40.6. P. Vedius Rufus appears to have been another rich freedman associated with Pompey, cf. Kirbihler (2007).

[166] Cic. *Att.* 14.5.1.

[167] App. *BC* 5.78.330–2. Treggiari (1969a) 188–9; Gowing (1992) 187; Watson (2002) 219. Menas-Menodorus: *RE* 15.1 774–5; Menecrates: *RE* 15.1 799–800. For Pompey's fleet as pirates and bandits see e.g. Hor. *Epod.* 4.19; Plut. *Ant.* 32.1; App. *BC* 5.80.341; Florus 2.19.1–2; Dio 48.31.1; Oros. 6.18.19.

Antony's freedmen to go over to Caesar [i.e. Octavian], and afterwards lived in Corinth.'[168]

These examples of powerful freedmen all belong to the last generations of the republic, which would suggest that, despite the extensive powers the Roman republic traditionally invested in the leading magistrates, the influence of their freedmen had not previously posed a problem. The most likely explanation is that the ruling class had been able to police its membership and enforce a common code of practice. We get an idea of how this worked in practice from Cicero's letters and speeches, and above all from the controversy caused by Statius, his brother Quintus' favourite freedman. Quintus' decision to free him in 59 had upset Cicero deeply; at the time, he wrote to Atticus that among all the concerns on his mind (and they were many in 59) none was more distressing than Statius' manumission.[169] Later he expressed indignation over Statius' involvement in his brother's divorce, claiming he had misrepresented Cicero's own position, and insisted that Quintus should never have written to a freedman on such important personal matters.[170] But Cicero's annoyance took on a new dimension when Quintus became governor of Asia. First he reminded him in a long letter outlining the duties and responsibilities of provincial governors that he ought to control his freedmen.[171] This does not seem to have had much effect, however, and soon Cicero again complained about Statius' unseemly influence over his patron. An outraged Cicero describes how he had been asked by people in Rome to recommend them to Statius (rather than Quintus). The damage done to Quintus' public standing alarmed Cicero; as he said, Statius may be loyal, but 'the look of the thing, a freedman or slave with so much influence, could not fail to be utterly undignified'.[172] He warned Quintus that people had started talking, and that Statius, especially after his manumission, was providing Quintus' critics with plenty of ammunition, fast becoming a political liability.

The episode illustrates the effectiveness of peer pressure in regulating the behaviour of the elite – which was the republican system of government in a nutshell. Although Quintus took some persuading before changing tack, the taboo of libertine influence was clearly a powerful weapon in the political game in Rome. The mere appearance of being under the

---

[168] Plut. *Ant.* 67.7; cf. *RE* 8.2 1664–5. At Corinth he later featured as *duovir* on local coins; as Pliny suggested (see note 162), his wealth may well have derived from triumviral proscriptions.
[169] *Att.* 2.18.4, and *Att.* 2.19.1, where he says 'sed mihi nihil est molestius quam Statium manu missum'.
[170] *Att.* 6.2.1–2.   [171] *Q.fr.* 1.1.13.
[172] *Q.fr.* 1.2.1–3: 'tamen species ipsa tam gratiosi liberti aut servi dignitatem habere nullam potest', cf. Roller (2001) 265–6.

influence of inferiors damaged one's public standing. It is therefore not surprising that Cicero made much capital out of Verres' closeness to his freedman Timarchides, who is described as a wicked *fugitivus* who ruled Sicily as a king and represented the guiding spirit behind his patron's crimes.[173]

The aversion to influential freedmen was so ingrained in the Roman elite that in his defence of Roscius Cicero could build a successful case against Chrysogonus largely by playing on this prejudice. To make his case, Cicero stressed Chrysogonus' wealth and power as well as his foreign appearance and effeminacy, the final outrage being that he – a freedman – has freeborn Roman citizens in his entourage.[174] This spectacle did not just offend Roman sensibilities but actively demeaned the *res publica*, 130ff, and Cicero therefore finished with a rhetorical question alluding to current politics, asking whether the nobility had regained its power under Sulla, only to see it pass to wicked freedmen and slaves.[175] The tactic was clearly effective and Cicero used it again in his defence of Flaccus, where he asked the jury if 'Asia was to be surrendered to the freedmen of powerful and influential men'.[176]

Such accusations only lost their force when some politicians became so powerful they could ignore public opinion. The rise of the powerful freedman therefore became a symptom of much deeper changes to Roman society. With power accumulating in the hands of a few, traditional means of enforcing elite cohesion weakened. Sulla's position not only undermined the republican system of collective government, it also put him beyond direct criticism; hence Cicero's somewhat disingenuous attempt to deflect blame from Sulla, stressing that Chrysogonus' patron knew nothing of his freedman's crimes. Still, it remained an uncomfortable fact that Chrysogonus owed his position to a patron so powerful he could no longer be held accountable.

The experiences of the late republic highlight the connection between the powerful freedman and the rise of autocracy, and under the principate they would become living reminders of the loss of *libertas*. Absolute power is by nature arbitrary, and in Rome nothing illustrated this problem more acutely than the imperial freedman, who, as Edwards put it, embodied

---

[173] *Verr.* 2.2.69, 134–6; 2.3.154–8; 2.5.81. Cf. Cels (1972). Likewise, in a private letter Cicero refers to a 'homo nequissimus' who had been perverted by the freedman Salvius, presumably Caesar's freedman. *Att.* 10.18.1. Shackleton Bailey (1965–70) 4.426.

[174] 135: 'per forum volitet cum magna caterva togatorum'.

[175] 141. Again, one notes that the power of Chrysogonus is described as 'servi nequissimi dominationem', reducing the freedman to the level of slave.

[176] *Flacc.* 88: 'hominum gratiosorum splendidorumque libertis fuit Asia tradenda?'

the ruler's power 'to raise individuals to position of enormous power from the lowest ranks of the "proper" social hierarchy (and, by implication, the power to cast others down as dramatically)'.[177] When the emperor promoted the unworthy above not just ordinary Roman citizens but also knights and senators, the precarious position of any rank became apparent. The powerful freedman brought home the painful realisation that the social order was no longer sustained by a system of shared government, but rested on the whim of a single individual.

Already during the triumviral period the anarchy caused by an unchecked executive had shocked the Roman public, and eager to distance himself from this turbulent stage of his career, the first *princeps* seems to have made a deliberate attempt to distance himself from freedmen and maintain decorum. Precisely because he had the power to subvert traditional hierarchies, it became crucial that he demonstrate his respect for them. In this way *dominatio* was – paradoxically – presented as the guarantor of *libertas*. Augustus' successors were less concerned with keeping up this appearance, and *potentia libertorum* soon became a byword for tyranny. As Epictetus observed, the senator who has to beg a freedman becomes lower than a slave.[178] And Tacitus claimed even barbarians enjoyed greater freedom, noting the Britons' incredulous response to Polyclitus giving orders to Roman soldiers.[179] In his pseudo-ethnographic treatise *Germania*, Tacitus spells out even more clearly the connection between the role of the freedman and the state of society in general. Among the northern tribes, Tacitus asserts in a programmatic statement, freedmen are not much above slaves, apart from those ruled by monarchs, where they are above freeborn and nobles. Among other Germanic peoples the subordination of freedmen is a mark of freedom.[180]

This ideological significance of the freedmen in imperial society may help us understand better Tacitus' debate on *liberti ingrati* mentioned above. An ungrateful freedman, who could freely abuse his patron without the emperor intervening, was in some respects comparable to the powerful freedman, who also subverted the natural order. Both types were symptomatic of a general loss of freedom and Tacitus makes this connection explicit when he then turns to the story of the freedman Paris who managed to have himself declared freeborn – to the discredit of the emperor, 'non sine infamia principis'.[181] In doing so, the emperor had violated natural hierarchies at a whim, and the damage done to society and indeed to *libertas* is stressed by Tacitus' opening line of the following paragraph, in which he recorded more uplifting events, noting that 'there remained nonetheless some shadow of the *res publica*'.[182] What had happened ideologically was that the concept of the free *res publica* had in effect been divorced from political power and now resided entirely in the hierarchical organisation of society. Control over his freedmen therefore became the hallmark of the good emperor – and a standard element of any imperial eulogy – while lack thereof conversely signalled weakness and despotism.[183] As Tacitus noted about Nero's freedman Crescens: 'in bad times even freedmen take part in the *res publica*'.[184]

In Dio's famous digression on the good *princeps*, Augustus is advised by Maecenas to keep his freedmen on tight reins since their conduct reflects on him.[185] Philostratus also advised Vespasian to keep his freedmen under control: 'Let us end extravagance in the slaves and freedmen that power gives you, but make them used to humbler behaviour, as befits a greater master.'[186] Later Pius was praised for controlling his *liberti*; not only was he willing to listen to complaints against his freed procurators, he also treated them with the greatest strictness.[187] We are also told that the 'good' emperor Pertinax kept the imperial freedmen in very tight reins.[188] But the fullest and most emphatic praise comes from the younger Pliny's panegyric of Trajan, which devotes a whole section to this issue.[189] The emperor is credited with maintaining firm control over his freedmen, but this laudable trait is not simply one of many imperial qualities; it emerges as *the* defining virtue of the perfect ruler. The passage thus marks the culmination of a long build-up which leads directly to the celebration of the title *pater patriae* in the following section.

---

[181] *Ann.* 13.27, cf. D. 12.4.3.5 (Ulpian). Paris was the freedman of Nero's aunt Domitia, and after the process which granted him *ingenuitas* he reclaimed the sum he had paid for his freedom.

[182] Tac. *Ann.* 13.27: 'manebat nihilo minus quaedam imago rei publicae'.

[183] For example, in the SHA *Verus* 9.3–6, Verus' indulgence of his powerful freedmen is used to distinguish him from his virtuous brother, who dismissed them after Verus' death. The criterion of virtue also applied to provincial governors. The issue had surfaced already under the republic, as illustrated by the examples of Verres and Q. Cicero, and Tacitus includes in his list of Agricola's many good qualities his refusal to transact public business through slaves or freedmen, *Agr.* 19.2.

[184] *Hist.* 1.76: 'Nam et hi [sc. liberti] in malis temporibus partem se rei publicae faciunt.' Interestingly, the complaints to Marcus Aurelius by the Athenians about the usurpation of status by Herodes Atticus' freedmen appear to have been framed as a discourse on tyranny; see Kennell (1997); cf. below p. 274.

[185] Dio 52.37.5–6. [186] *Vit.Apoll.* 5.36.4.

[187] SHA *Pius* 6.2; 11.1: 'libertis suis severissime usus est'.

[188] SHA *Pert.* 13.9: 'libertos aulicos vehementissime compressit'; cf. Dio 74.8.1. [189] *Pan.* 88.1–3.

Pliny stressed that Trajan respected his freedmen, but only as freedmen, that is, honouring them in accordance with their natural station, which is the essence of the *gradus dignitatis*. It was a question, therefore of keeping freedmen away not just from actual power but also from inappropriate insignia and symbols of status. In a world where real power was beyond the grasp even of most senators, the trappings of status naturally gained in importance. For that reason the issue of freedmen's usurpation of rank became a matter of considerable concern.[190] The greatest offence was caused by the honours presented to Claudius' freedman Pallas. In gratitude for the *Senatus Consultum Claudianum*, for which Pallas was credited, the senate – at the suggestion of a consul designate – offered him a cash gratuity of 15 million sesterces and the *ornamenta praetoria*, the freedman only accepting the latter. The senate also issued a flattering decree, suggesting descent from Arcadian kings.[191] Two generations later, the younger Pliny devoted two letters to the episode, deploring the general devaluation of honours entailed by this grant: 'People of good family could be found who were fired by ambition for distinctions which they saw granted to freedmen and promised to slaves.'[192] Thus, according to Pliny, the 'threat' posed by freedmen went right to the core of the Roman concept of *honores*, that is, the system of public distinctions for which the elite would compete and spend generously.

The case of Pallas illustrated a particularly insidious form of usurpation, since it was the senators themselves who subverted the *gradus dignitatis*. They did so because the freedmen's influence was real, and the logic of power is to translate itself into formal distinctions which confer legitimacy and social esteem. So although the honours of Pallas (and Narcissus) remained the exception (the senatorial outcry ensured that), they highlighted the fragility of social hierarchies under an autocratic system. Most emperors, even those heavily dependent on freedmen, therefore presented themselves as defenders of the existing social order. The most effective means of doing so was to pass measures against status usurpation.

---

[190] The obsession with rank is reflected in Martial's book five on shows. No fewer than eight epigrams deal with violations of the *lex Roscia*, mostly by freedmen and men carrying Greek names, 8, 25, 35, 38, 41; cf. Hor. *Epod.* 4.15–16. Tert. *Pallio* 4.8.4, reveals similar preoccupations in relation to dress.

[191] Plin. *NH* 35.201; Plin. *Ep.* 8.6; Tac. *Ann.* 12.53. Narcissus had also received *ornamenta quaestoria*, *Ann.* 11.38; Suet. *Claud.* 28. *Ornamenta* were a device by which honours could be bestowed on the unqualified by stripping the titles of any content. The suggestion of royal blood to raise the standing of freedmen or slaves seems to have been a topos in Rome; cf. Hor. *Odes* 2.4.15, on a favourite slave girl, and Suet. *Ner.* 28, on Nero's mistress Acte. In Petr. *Sat.* 57.4 the claim of regal descent is used as a joke by the freedman Hermeros.

[192] *Ep.* 8.6.16: 'Inveniebantur tamen honesto loco nati, qui peterent cuperentque quod dari liberto promitti servis videbant.'

Pliny tells us that under Tiberius a *senatus consultum* (22 CE) restricted the right to wear golden rings, the mark of equestrian rank, to men of free birth for three generations plus property qualifications of 400,000 sesterces.[193] Two years later the *lex Visellia* barred freedmen from holding *honores*, and threatened those who passed themselves off as freeborn with prosecution.[194] Later, Claudius confiscated the property of freedmen who pretended to be knights.[195] Alongside other disciplinary measures against *liberti*, Claudius also prosecuted 400 freedmen who had entered the equestrian order because, as Pliny put it, 'an order intended to distinguish the holder from other men of free birth has been shared with slaves'.[196]

The paradoxical relationship between rank, status, and imperial power is highlighted by a remarkable invention, which allowed freedmen to be 'cleansed' of their *macula servitutis* and qualify for honours otherwise beyond their reach. The *ius anulorum aureorum*, or right to wear golden rings, was an expedient which enabled emperors to elevate freedmen to the equestrian order.[197] Octavian first granted freeborn status to Sex. Pompey's freedman Menas/Menodorus, who had betrayed his patron and thereby given Octavian control over Corsica, Sardinia, sixty ships, and three legions.[198] Later, the freed physician Antonius Musa, credited with Augustus' recovery in 23 BCE, also received the right in addition to many other honours.[199] The new status was a legal fiction 'imago', which posited that while the recipient remained a freedman in relation to his patron he became an *ingenuus* in relation to all others. It enabled them to hold 'honores et dignitates' and perform public duties reserved for freeborn without the risk of prosecution.[200]

The *lex Visellia* for the first time gave emperors the right to confer *ius anulorum aureorum* and equestrian status, and the two seem to be directly linked under the empire. For example, Tacitus explained that Galba's freedman Icelus received *ius anulorum* and people called him Marcianus, 'an equestrian name', while Vitellius granted Asiaticus *ius anulorum*

---

[193] Plin. *NH* 33.32. This measure, if correctly recorded, is puzzling since the *ius anulorum* gave the freedmen an 'imago ingenuitatis'. Moreover, there are numerous examples of first-generation *ingenui* holding equestrian status; cf. Eck (1999).

[194] *Cod.Iust.* 9.21.1, 31.1.

[195] Levick (1990) 122. In general on Claudius and slaves/freedmen see Poma (1982).

[196] Plin. *NH* 33.33: 'Ita dum separatur ordo ab ingenuis, communicatus est cum servitiis.'

[197] Millar (1977) 488–90. The first recorded example of *ius anulorum* was Sulla's grant to the actor Sex. Roscius, who seems to have been freeborn, cf. Nicolet (1974) no. 300. Under the empire the privilege was granted only to freedmen, D. 40.10. Demougin (1988) 815; Sherwin-White (1973) 331; Duncan-Jones (2006) 215–16; Damon (2006) 246–50.

[198] Dio 48.45.7; App. *BC* 5.78.330–1; Plut. *Ant.* 32; Suet. *Aug.* 74: 'asserto in ingenuitatem'.

[199] Dio 53.30.3–6.   [200] *Cod.Iust.* 9.21.

and 'equestri dignitate'.[201] The *ius* illustrated how the ruler could overturn the social order, and it may seem surprising that it was Augustus, otherwise intent on maintaining a conservative image, who masterminded this invention.

The *ius anulorum aureorum* involved the miraculous suspension of the freedman's servile 'stain', but emperors would gradually introduce an even more subversive legal device, which transformed the freedman into a freeborn. Through the process of *restitutio natalium* emperors would 'restore' the free birth of favoured freedmen, granting them complete *ingenuitas*.[202] The procedure derived from real cases of restored free birth which could be claimed before the courts.[203] In the early empire it seems that some 'evidence' of free birth usually was produced, but later the process became entirely fictitious. As a result, a person's past could now be retrospectively altered by imperial fiat, and although such instances may have been rare, they nevertheless cast a revealing light on the emperor's ability to define his own reality.

To sum up, freedmen and empire became closely linked in the moral and political discourse of the principate. The standing of the emperor's own became indicative of his ability and willingness to uphold social hierarchies. The significance of the freedman also allowed emperors to advertise their respect for traditional values by taking general measures against this category. Our image of the freedmen in this period has been deeply influenced by these factors, which have contributed to a perception of them as a dangerous element that needed to be contained. But contrary to the ancient stereotype, the dominant role of freedmen in the imperial administration is better seen as indicative of their usefulness and competence. Emperors needed people they could trust and freedmen presented the obvious solution. There was nothing new in this arrangement. The imperial court had developed from the aristocratic household of the late republic where freedmen had assisted the leaders of the state in their performance of public functions. During most of the republic this situation had caused little concern, since the government had been collective and power shared between men of rank. This changed in the late republic with the rise of the great leaders whose freedmen started to attract public attention – and condemnation. The problem was therefore one of growing inequality within the Roman elite.

---

[201] *Hist.* 1.13; 2.57. It not clear whether the former conferred equestrian status or just the *ornamenta*. Sherwin-White (1973) 331 n.1; Duncan-Jones (2006) 216.
[202] D. 2.4.10.3 (Ulpian); *Cod.Iust.* 6.8.2. Duff (1928) 86–8; Millar (1977) 489.
[203] *De natalibus restituendis* D. 40.11.

The emergence of the 'freedman problem' reflected the move from a pluralistic political system based on formalised negotiation of power to one of personalised authority. Under the empire the influential freedman evolved into a symbol of tyranny. As *libertas* was redefined as respect for social hierarchies and distinctions, the powerful freedman emerged as the most glaring inversion of the existing order. Essentially this debate sprang from concerns about the precarious nature of rank and status under autocratic rule. The real problem was therefore not the imperial freedmen as such but the fact that their patron had eroded the foundations of traditional *libertas*. Despite the vitriol they attracted, the freedmen were merely a symptom of a wider malaise. The imperial freedman demonstrated more vividly than any other category the twin faces of Roman manumission: on the one hand, the great advantages it offered patrons as a source of personally dependent staff and, on the other hand, the anxieties raised by former slaves gaining any form of social prominence.

OPES LIBERTINAE: THE WEALTH AND VULGARITY OF ROMAN FREEDMEN

The debate about the power of freedmen and the threat it posed to established hierarchies – indeed to the 'freedom' of the Roman people – fed directly into a closely related concern about the wealth of freedmen, which dominated much of the moralising discourse under the empire. While the economic roles of freedmen are the subject of a later chapter, the ideological background for this debate will be considered in the following pages.

Freedmen could acquire wealth, occasionally even substantial wealth; generally they could operate economically without any specific constraints and those who were citizens were able to inherit on a par with other Romans. But although freedmen could accumulate riches by perfectly legitimate means, their wealth still posed an ideological problem since – in Rome as in most other societies – it was inextricably linked to power and status. During the republic the connection was enshrined in the political institutions, executive power being reserved for men of means, while the main elective assembly was organised timocratically to correlate influence with property. During the reign of the first emperor existing hierarchies of rank were redefined even more sharply to reflect economic distinctions.[204]

---

[204] As Reinhold (1971) 279, noted: 'The Augustan social structure was patently plutocratic.' Verboven's assertion (2007) 863, that 'wealth in itself doesn't generate social status' must be qualified, since it was the foundation for Roman social stratification and only unfree background affected its positive value.

As argued above, the Roman authorities kept freedmen away from the power and influence normally associated with wealth by ignoring their property and in effect treating them as *proletarii*. Later, Augustus and Tiberius partly clarified the situation by imposing a formal requirement of free birth for the higher ranks, in the case of the senatorial order even going back several generations. However, while the official insistence that freedmen's wealth did not count may have prevented their economic strength from translating into political power, it did not eliminate the underlying ideological problem.

Status and wealth appeared inseparable to the Romans, and the very existence of rich freedmen therefore posed a challenge to their collective relegation to the bottom of the hierarchy, below even the poorest freeborn.[205] The problem was given a further twist through the common association of property with respectability and morality. Ancient philosophers may have preached the irrelevance of wealth and poverty for the attainment of personal virtue, but the two remained closely connected in the Roman mind, at least as represented in elite discourse. The link between wealth and morality rested on the notion that a certain amount of property was required in order to live a virtuous life in accordance with higher principles. On this view, virtue depended on personal autonomy and freedom from external pressures, and land was therefore considered the ideal source of wealth, farming providing a stable income free of deceit.[206]

The poor, on the other hand, lived under the law of want which knows no morals, for as Publilius Syrus' dictum stated, 'necessity makes a poor man a liar'.[207] The morals of the urban poor were considered particularly weak, since they would do anything to survive and accept even the most demeaning jobs – without the option of the peasant's frugal simplicity.[208] Banausic occupations were seen as damaging both to body and mind. Thus, while wealth was routinely associated with respectability, poverty signalled depravity.[209] Accusations of indebtedness and insolvency had strong moral

---

[205] Interestingly, the freedmen appear to have been grouped together with the poor in the theatre as prescribed by the *lex Iulia theatralis*; cf. Shaw (2000) 388–90.

[206] The ideal of frugal simplicity was deeply rooted in Greek popular morality, cf. Vischer (1965), and later embraced by many Romans and may also have influenced Roman notions of domestic self-sufficiency.

[207] *Sent.* N31 (407): 'Necessitas egentem mendacem facit', and to Sallust the poor man 'considers anything honourable for which he receives pay', 'omnia cum pretio honesta videntur', *Iug.* 86.3. MacMullen (1974) III, on the general disdain for poverty, cf. 115–17; cf. Mouritsen (2001) 139–40.

[208] Dio. Chrys. *Eub.Or.* 7, illustrates the association of the urban rather than the rural poor with low morals; cf. Trapp (2007) 203–4.

[209] E.g. Cic. *Verr.* 2.5.154: 'homines locupletes atque honesti', cf. *Verr.* 2.2.28, 155, 175; 2.3.52, 108, 120; 2.4.46; 2.5.154. Also, the emperor Claudius referred to 'viri boni et locupletes', *CIL* 13.1668 II 5.

implications in Roman political discourse. The posited connection between property and morality was of course a transparent attempt to bolster the position of the ruling class, and we should not assume that all Romans necessarily subscribed to this view. Still, they would probably have recognised that a freedman with greater wealth than most freeborn posed a challenge to the *gradus dignitatis*.

The problem was not unique to Rome, but was a typical example of what in sociological terms is known as 'status dissonance', i.e. the clash between different parameters which naturally occur whenever hierarchies of status are based on more than one criterion.[210] In most traditional societies these hierarchies rest on the twin pillars of birth and wealth, which usually go hand in hand since fortunes are accumulated only slowly and then passed on to the next generation. But since this 'construction' of status is predicated on a fundamentally stable socio-economic structure new money becomes problematic. Examples of rapid social ascent have typically been met with the reassertion of birth as the primary source of esteem and a corresponding denigration of recently acquired fortunes. 'Rags to riches' stories generally have an element of ridicule to them, precisely because they serve to downgrade the importance of wealth at the expense of breeding.[211] The familiar stereotype of the *nouveau riche* can therefore be seen as a defence mechanism by which old elites assert their supremacy against newcomers and restore the hierarchical order.

In Rome similar processes can, for example, be traced in the snobbery which greeted new men such as Cicero, but the Roman ruling class otherwise seems to have been remarkably fluid and open to newcomers.[212] However, the case of the rich freedman differed in important respects from other forms of social mobility. Because of the unique – and irredeemable – stigma the freedman carried, he represented a far more fundamental form

Sall. *Cat.* 2.18: 'Horum hominum species est honestissima – sunt enim locupletes.' *Att.* 5.20.4. Cf. Hellegouarc'h (1963) 470–2. Riches – *divitiae* – also held a moral quality, cf. *ibid.* 235–6. 'Egens', 'poor/ needy', on the other hand, indicated depravity, e.g. Sall. *Cat.* 18.4, 37.8; Cic. *Dom.* 45, 58; *Cluent.* 70; *Flacc.* 52; *Att.* 1.19.5

[210] Hopkins (1965), who also noted that 'so long as an aristocracy depends on birth alone it can remain exclusive; when it admits complementary criteria of achievement, whether money or political skill, it opens the way to arrivistes', 17.

[211] As Bodel (1999b) 42, observed, Aristotle already 'sniffed that the newly rich generally had more and worse bad habits, owing to their "lack of education in wealth"', *Rhet.* 2.1391a. Other Roman examples include Horace's famous description of Nasidienus' dinner party, *Sat.* 2.8. Roman mime apparently had a stock character known as the 'repente dives', the *nouveau riche*, Cic. *Phil.* 2.65.

[212] For the snobbery Cicero encountered, Cic. *Att.* 1.16.10; Sall. *Cat.* 31.7; Ps-Sall. *In Tull.* 1–4; Dio 46.1–28, esp. 5. On the open structure of the Roman elite see Hopkins and Burton in Hopkins (1983) chs. 2–3.

of 'status dissonance' than other types of newcomers, who in principle could be integrated into the official elite.[213] As Veyne famously noted, Petronius' Trimalchio was not a parvenu because he had never arrived – and importantly he never *could*.[214]

As a concept, the rich freedman was profoundly troubling for conventional Roman notions of honour, status and property, which may explain some of the hostility with which he is treated in the literary sources. Some of these texts explicitly set out to clarify the relationship between birth and wealth, itself a typical reaction to social mobility. Juvenal's first satire describes a rich freedman who was born on the Euphrates but now owns five *tabernae* which bring in 400,000 HS, 1.102–6. Much to Juvenal's indignation, the freedman claims precedence over freeborn in the queue for handouts, even standing his ground when challenged by senators. Faced with such insolence Juvenal then reminds the reader of the fortunes of Pallas and Licinus, before sarcastically declaring: 'Let money rule supreme' – 'vincant divitiae'; 'The man who has just arrived in our city with whitened feet shouldn't have to give way to sacrosanct office.' In conclusion, 'we now revere money more than any god'. The same message is conveyed by Martial in an epigram where he confesses that although he is poor (at least relatively) he is still an *eques* and renowned for his literary works. By contrast Callistratus is rich, owning a large townhouse and estates in various parts of the empire. Martial concludes the comparison by stating: 'But what I am, you cannot be; what you are, any man in the street can be.'[215] Martial weighs up two different sources of status, birth and wealth, and concludes that only the former counts, while the latter is trivial.

As part of this attempt to give birth priority over wealth, the social 'value' of freedmen's wealth was also redefined. Martial famously describes Callistratus' fortune as 'libertinae opes' (6), and the meaning of this expression deserves closer consideration. Translating it simply as 'the wealth of a freedman' is not very illuminating. Neither does it make sense to see it as a reference to a particularly large fortune, since not every fortune owned by a freedman would by definition have been substantial. Rather, the designation of Callistratus' wealth as 'libertine' suggests that a freedman's fortune was considered to be of a different kind from that owned by freeborn because wealth was deemed incompatible with the freedman's character.

---

[213] There were, of course, other categories of Romans without honour, e.g. the poor, but not only was their dishonour relative rather than absolute; their chances of getting rich were generally so minimal that the issue therefore did not attract the same attention.

[214] Veyne (1961).

[215] Mart. 5.13.9–10: 'sed quod sum non potes esse: tu quod es e populo quilibet esse potest'.

It is not uncommon for new money to be described as different in nature from old wealth, less respectable and of more dubious origins, but in the case of Roman freedmen this line of argument was taken a step further. Seneca, for example, mentions a certain Calvisius Sabinus, a rich man endowed with 'the patrimony and the mind of a freedman', 'et patrimonium . . . libertini et ingenium', adding that his good fortune was an affront to decency.[216] The moral of the letter is that you cannot buy 'bona mens', 'a sound mind'. The expression 'patrimonium libertini' – itself a joke since freedmen had no parents – hints at the flawed nature of his wealth. Seneca's point is that although Calvisius was not himself freed, he deserved it as little as a freedman, because his character was as debased as that of a former slave. While the underlying argument is the disparity between the person and his fortune, Seneca wittily implies they are in perfect harmony – since they are both equally tainted. The comparison with a freedman, the standard example of the undeserving rich, therefore sums up, less the size of his fortune, as much as his unworthiness of it.[217] Moreover, the fact that the wealth of a freeborn Roman can be described as 'libertine' suggests that the concept was so established that it could be used metaphorically.[218]

When classifying freedmen's fortunes as belonging to a separate, inferior type of wealth, writers played on an inherent ambiguity in the Roman view of personal property. On the one hand, a minimum of wealth was deemed a necessary condition for an honourable life, while, on the other hand, it was also evident that wealth might be dangerous in the wrong hands. There was always a risk that riches would come to control the owner, leading to self-indulgence, greed, and materialism. The dangers of *luxuria*, the negative flipside of affluence, meant that to live honourably with great wealth required moral fibre, a quality acquired through generations of experience and good education. For that reason the *nouveaux riches* were considered particularly prone to *luxuria*.

This point is illustrated by Cicero's comments on Lucullus. Despite his proverbial lifestyle, Lucullus is criticised less for his own *luxuria* than for the bad example he set for those of lesser moral stature, Cicero explicitly

---

[216] *Ep.* 27.5: 'numquam vidi hominem beatum indecentius'.

[217] Again, the idea that *patrimonium libertini*, like *opes libertinae*, simply refers to the size of his fortune founders on the fact that not even the most biased Roman writer could claim that all wealth owned by freedmen was substantial.

[218] Edwards (1993) 153–5, rightly noted that what was considered luxurious (and hence morally dubious) depended on status, also observing that 'For Seneca, there was something "wrong" and "unnatural" about men who had money but no real status', 155.

mentioning his two neighbours, an *eques* and a freedman.[219] While Cicero
of course also tries to shield his friend from criticism, his distinction
between the wealth and lifestyle that was appropriate for a Roman general
and that suitable for people of lower rank is nevertheless significant and was
probably widely shared.[220] The reference to a freedman is not fortuitous, for
to live honourably with great wealth required character and self-control,
and that was precisely what the freedman according to the traditional
Roman stereotype did not possess.[221]

The idea that the fortune had to fit the man implied that the 'value' of
wealth as a social and moral good became relative rather than absolute. By
linking it to the owner's status and character a fortune could be turned from
a positive asset into a liability; in fact the larger the fortune the greater the
opprobrium it attracted, as the example of Chrysogonus well illustrates. As
noted above, Cicero's defence of Roscius was shaped as an attack on Sulla's
favourite freedman Chrysogonus, who is singled out as the true villain of
the piece. The wealth of Chrysogonus – and not just the insinuation of
its illegitimate origins – forms a central pillar of Cicero's demolition of his
character. He lists his properties on the Palatine and in the suburbs, his
many farms, and 'a house full of Delian and Corinthian vessels, among them
that self-cooker, which he recently bought at a price so high that passers-
by, hearing the auctioneer crying out the bids, thought that an estate was
being sold'.[222] Cicero goes on to list the silver, textiles, pictures, statues, and
marble, and the highly specialised staff in his vast household, before turning
to his lavish banquets and his luxurious lifestyle; his house was less a *domus*
than an 'officina nequitiae et deversorium flagitiorum omnium', 'a factory
of vice and an inn for all things disgraceful'. Only when he has finished
stripping Chrysogonus' possessions of their last dignity does Cicero turn
to the man himself, describing him in similar terms as over-groomed and
reeking of perfume.

The tactic allows the scale of Chrysogonus' wealth to become part of
Cicero's indictment of his character, and ironically his opulent lifestyle

---

[219] *Leg.* 3.30–1.

[220] The theme reappears in his invective against Piso, whose *luxuria* is not of the more refined kind
that was acceptable for 'ingenuo ac libero', *Pis.* 67. Tertullian, *Apol.* 6.3, mentions enormous pieces
of silverware which might be suitable for senators but not for freedmen or 'flagra rumpentium',
'whip-spoilers', i.e. slaves who had been whipped. Tacitus, *Ann.* 14.55, also has the young Nero
lamenting the fact that some freedmen flaunted greater wealth than Seneca without having his
virtue: 'Pudet referre libertinos, qui ditiores spectantur.'

[221] As a literary theme the morality of wealth could be used both to denigrate and to praise. Thus, in
Nepos' biography of Atticus his ability to live with great wealth without any excess or luxury forms
a central plank in his encomium, *Att.* 13–14.

[222] *Rosc.Am.* 133.

also provides the motive for his alleged murder of Roscius senior and appropriation of his estate. For the kind of *luxuria* which the orator evokes in such detail was by definition always insatiable, going hand in hand with the covetousness that leads to criminality.[223] By contrast, the defendant is presented as almost philosophically detached from the materialism that defines Chrysogonus. According to Cicero, Roscius is resigned to the loss of his patrimony and merely wishes to be cleared of a terrible accusation, 143f.

The disjunction between fortunes and their owners is a recurring theme in Roman literature, most extensively developed in Petronius' description of Trimalchio's banquet. In Petronius' tale the host's extravagant attempt to emulate the lifestyle of the elite is undermined by his lack of taste and breeding, which exposes his social pretensions. The lapses of good taste are more than embarrassing social *faux pas* but reveal his true nature. Trimalchio's vulgarity is integral to his identity as a freedman, and that in turn determines the character of his possessions. Trimalchio is merely the most fully developed example of a common literary stereotype, which also includes for example Juvenal's Crispinus, who used to be an Alexandrian fishmonger but now owns large mansions and spends huge sums on fancy fish.[224] Likewise, in the case of Martial's Syriscus there is a jarring contrast between his vast fortune and his unreconstructed plebeian tastes.[225] Thus, having inherited 10 million sesterces from his patron, he spent it all on food at *popinae* – simple inns where, as the poet reminds us, you do not even recline for dinner.[226] Suetonius' short biography of the freed grammarian Q. Remmius Palaemon focuses on his twin sins of depravity and profligacy, the latter illustrated by the fact that he bathed several times a day.[227] Thus, despite earning almost 800,000 HS annually, his expenses exceeded his income. Similarly, Seneca suggested that freedmen did not know how to spend their money, noting that they build luxurious baths and decorate them simply to spend money.[228]

In his fourth epode Horace goes one step further in his denunciation of the rich freedman and points out that despite his change of circumstances he remains a slave. Contrasting the vast estates of the anonymous freedman

---

[223] There is a lacuna in our manuscripts at paragraph 132, but according to the scholiast the missing section contained a suggestion that Chrysogonus' extravagance made him desperate for money.

[224] Juv. *Satire* 4.   [225] 5.70.

[226] Koortbojian (2002) discusses the status difference expressed in dining positions, reclining being reserved for free people, standing for unfree. Martial's point is therefore that Syriscus was in essence still a slave; cf. Roller (2006) 92–3. Similarly, Lucian's *How to write history* 20, refers to a 'newly-rich servant who has just inherited his master's fortune', and does not know how to live with his wealth.

[227] *Gramm.* 23: 'Luxuria ita indulsit, ut saepius in die lavaret.'   [228] *Ep.* 86.7.

with his humble background and disgraced body, Horace notes that he may
plough a thousand acres of Falernian land but still carries the scars on his
back and the marks of the shackles.[229] A very similar point is made by
Martial, who gives a lengthy description of one Rufus, sitting in the front
rows, expensively groomed, lavishly dressed and bejewelled. However, to
find out who Rufus really is the poet suggests that you remove his face
patch which presumably covered the branding marks or tattoos he had
received as a slave.[230]

The message is that despite his fortune a rich freedman had not
acquired any real nobility. For once, therefore, wealth did not confer social
respectability or imply any particular moral standing. An otherwise positive
attribute is thereby being turned into a mark of difference, even inferiority.
In making this point, Roman authors paradoxically separated wealth from
honour in order to maintain the integrity of both concepts as well as the
conventional link between them. Or put differently, wealth is essentially
good but will be corrupted when held by former slaves, who are themselves
further corrupted by their possessions. Ironically, the rich freedman who
made claims above his station merely vindicated the supremacy of virtue
over wealth by reminding the observer of his lack of true merit. Thus, one
author compared the ostentatious tomb of Licinus, Augustus' freedman,
with that of Cato, which was famously non-existent, declaring that 'stones
press Licinus down, fame raises Cato high'.[231]

Again the ideological concerns have important consequences for our
image of freedmen and their place in Roman society. In this case, the denigration of their wealth has led to an exaggeration of its scale. Thus, Petronius' hyperbolic description of Trimalchio's fortune served to highlight the
gap between the person and his circumstances.[232] By amplifying the mismatch between the rich freedman's personal and economic status it became
self-evident that they could never be reconciled. Moreover, since fortunes,
estates, and even objects would change character and become more overtly
luxurious if owned by a freedman rather than a senator, a freedman's
wealth automatically attracted a disproportionate amount of attention in

[229] *Epod.* 4.5–6, 11–16.
[230] 2.29. Juvenal also stressed in the first satire the foreign and decadent appearance of the rich freedman
     who was born on the Euphrates and had effeminate ear piercing, 1.102. Other examples include
     Martial's freedman who had inherited great wealth from his patron but used to be a simple cobbler,
     9.73, and the barber Cinnamus, who became a knight by a gift from his *domina*, 7.64. Another
     barber who had gained millions and a golden ring is pilloried by Juvenal, 1.24–5.
[231] *Poet.Lat.min.* (Baehrens) 4.24 64–5: 'saxa premunt Licinum, levat altum fama Catonem'.
[232] *Sat.* 71.12: he left 30 million sesterces; cf. 37–8, 47–8, 53.

the moralising discourse of the empire. For example, when Seneca discussed the connection between mirrors and luxury, he used the daughters of freedmen to illustrate modern manners, comparing them unfavourably with the modest daughters of republican generals.[233] Likewise, the elder Pliny repeatedly returned to the excesses of imperial freedmen, noting that the costly tables of Nomius were finer than those of his patron.[234] This interest in the possessions of freedmen reflects their particular significance as part of a moral discourse on *luxuria*. For as already noted by Edwards, when Pliny explicitly mentioned the fortunes of Callistus, Pallas, and Narcissus, it was 'not because they were the richest men in Rome, but because they were freedmen, whose wealth could not be justified by their ancestry or merit'.[235] The subtext is apparent also in Seneca's discussion of luxurious baths, where predictably the modesty of Scipio Africanus is compared with the extravagance of contemporary freedmen.[236]

This discourse has often been viewed as a response to the vulgar display of *nouveaux riches* or, alternatively, as examples of 'defensive' snobbery directed at upstarts who posed a threat to the establishment. Thus, Duff took the descriptions of rich freedmen at face value, arguing that, 'with this wealth went a certain amount of the boorish ignorance, vulgar ostentation and ridiculous lack of taste that are associated with the parvenu of modern times'.[237] Even Treggiari could refer to the 'materialistic values' of freedmen as a historical fact and accuse a freedman of being 'vulgar'.[238] But the stereotype was the product of a complex process of status differentiation. Assumptions of vulgarity were hard-wired into the Roman perception of freedmen's wealth, and this expectation would eventually become self-fulfilling since their lifestyle and preferred forms of display came to represent the current standard of poor taste.

There are of course echoes of this discourse in later descriptions of the parvenu, but the Roman attacks on rich freedmen were part of a far more profound debate about society in general. Its aim was to reassure the Roman public that the social order was intact, stable and founded on given

---

[233] *NQ* 1.17.9.

[234] *NH* 13.93–4. He also commented on the marble columns owned by Callistus, *NH* 36.60. The silver dishes commissioned by the imperial slave Drusillanus Rotundus, Claudius' *dispensator Hispaniae Citerioris*, receives detailed comment, *NH* 33.145.

[235] *NH* 33.134–5, also adding C. Caecilius Isidorus; cf. e.g. *Epit. de Caes.* 4.8. Edwards (1993) 154. Oost (1958) 128, had already noted the proverbial character of these fortunes.

[236] *Ep.* 86.6–7.

[237] Duff (1928) 126. Following this approach some archaeologists have taken the literary image of the freedman as a guide to identifying where they lived; supposedly their houses were distinguished by a particular garish taste; e.g. Maiuri (1942); Zanker (1998) 136–203.

[238] Treggiari (1969a) 239–40. See below p. 284.

and immutable categories. It also reminded the freedmen themselves that whatever fortune they might acquire did not alter their place in the hierarchy. As such it acted as a warning against usurpation of status by insisting that wealth did not count in their favour and in fact might be a liability if spent unwisely. On a more positive note it was suggested that simple living was a particular virtue for freedmen. Statius, for example, praised the *frugalitas* of Abascantus and his wife, as well as the modest lifestyle of Etruscus' father, and Seneca eulogised Polybius' 'antiqua frugalitas' and 'abstinentia'.[239] Ideally, these freedmen would not spend their fortunes on themselves but embrace the aristocratic ideology of euergetism, and, as we shall see, a number of public initiatives encouraged them to do precisely that.

The attention paid to rich freedmen in the literary sources reflected the ideological sensitivity of this category and we cannot therefore measure the actual scale of the phenomenon on the basis of texts which must be regarded less as social commentaries than as contributions to an ongoing debate about the ideal nature of Roman society.[240] Hopkins rightly noted that 'the wealth of ex-slaves became notorious', but that was not necessarily, as he suggested, because of its scale as much as the simple fact that it was 'libertine' and therefore in some way 'tainted'.[241] The issue appears to have gained a particular urgency under the empire, although that does not allow us to conclude that the 'problem' grew in scale. 'Opes libertinae' became part of a wider discussion about what it meant to be a Roman citizen in an unequal society with limited civic freedom. Thus, the rich freedman, along with the ungrateful and the powerful freedman, came to act as a lightning rod for more generalised anxieties about imperial society.

SUMMARY

These chapters have explored the ideological issues raised by the phenomenon of manumission, highlighting the problems caused by the admission of former slaves into free society. The suggestion is that literary and legal sources must be approached in light of these overriding concerns, which meant that no statement about freedmen could ever be plainly

---

[239] *Silv.* 5.1.76–9, 117–22; 3.3.106–8; *Cons. ad Pol.* 3.2–5; cf. Hardie (1983) 186; Leppin (1996) 78.

[240] A strikingly literal interpretation of the *Satyricon* is found in e.g. Ebersbach (1995), who sees the text as a 'Diagnose eines gesellschaftlichen Verfalls', i.e. as plainly descriptive in its vision of rich freedmen rising at the expense of freeborn Romans.

[241] Hopkins (1978) 117; cf. Samson (1989) 101: 'freedmen's wealth was something of a topos in Roman times'.

descriptive. The freedman evoked deep-seated anxieties and unease, which would feed directly into broader concerns about morality and virtue, the social order, and ultimately freedom and tyranny. The freedman therefore became emblematic for much wider concerns about Roman society, especially under the empire. As a result, it could never be a neutral topic; it carried with it a complex 'baggage', which has to be borne in mind when we try to reconstruct how manumission functioned in practice and how Roman freedmen lived their everyday lives, an issue to which we will turn in the following chapter.

CHAPTER 5

The practice of manumission at Rome

The previous chapters explored what might broadly be called the 'construction' of the freedman at Rome, i.e. the concepts used to define the process of manumission and the anxieties it gave rise to. These concerns formed part of the ideological backdrop against which we have to assess the practice of manumission, but they remain distinct and should ideally be kept separate analytically. The aim of this chapter is to establish how manumission actually worked and that means asking who was freed, how it happened, and what the underlying motivation was. The logical starting point for this inquiry is the question of scale, since a basic quantitative framework is crucial if we want to understand the practice of manumission.

THE SCALE OF MANUMISSION

Ancient history is notoriously short of reliable statistics and the study of slavery and manumission is little different in that respect. No extant source tells us how many freedmen were attached to any single patron, nor are there any figures for the number of freedmen at a given point in time in any Roman community. To complicate matters even further, there is little evidence on which even a vague estimate of the number of slaves might be based.[1] As Scheidel pointed out, the most common estimate of the number of slaves in Italy, Brunt's suggestion of 3 million slaves under the empire, is not based on any specific evidence.[2] This figure was reached by combining a number of – largely speculative – figures into a single equation for the total population of Italy. Scheidel has suggested lowering Brunt's figure to

---

[1] The few figures we have for the size of individual households, e.g. Tac. *Ann.* 14.45, are generally rhetorical, cf. Scheidel (1996).

[2] Brunt (1971a) 121–5; Scheidel (1999a), (2005a), (2008); cf. Weiler (2003) 69–70. The overall size of the Roman population is currently the subject of considerable debate, which has important implications for the question of manumission, since the number of slaves in Italy would be directly affected by the so-called 'high count', advocated most prominently by Lo Cascio (1994).

around 2 million slaves, mostly by reducing the scale of rural slavery in relation to urban, which illustrates the fundamental difficulties involved in any attempt at quantifying Roman manumission.[3]

Some estimates have nevertheless been ventured. The earliest focused on the income from the 5 per cent manumission tax, the *vicesima libertatis*, which according to Livy was introduced in 357 BCE.[4] Livy tells us that in 209 BCE 4,000 pounds of gold had been accumulated from the proceeds of this tax, which was then used for the war effort.[5] But as Brunt demonstrated, that does not allow us to make any estimates of the frequency of manumission in the intervening period. Not only is the price of slaves unknown but there is no certainty that the *aerarium sanctius* contained all the funds accumulated since 357.[6]

A more promising attempt at quantifying manumission used the recorded numbers of recipients of public grain in the late republic and early empire. According to Suetonius, Caesar reduced the number of recipients from 320,000 to 150,000. This limit was soon disregarded, however, since Augustus again brought the number down from 320,000 to just above 200,000 in 2 BCE, a figure later cut to 150,000 by Tiberius. Part of Caesar's reduction is assumed to have come from his resettlement of 80,000 members of the urban plebs in overseas colonies, including many *liberti*. Supposedly the remaining 90,000 were the result of a blanket exclusion of the remaining freedmen.[7] The same argument has been applied to Augustus' reform, since the figure of 200,000 was arrived at by removing all freedmen from the grain dole. The theory would therefore imply the existence of well over 100,000 freed adult males in and around the city of Rome, perhaps representing close to one third of all adult males.

---

[3] Anticipated by MacMullen (1987) 375, although his arguments were open to doubt; cf. Samson (1989). Along similar lines, Jongman (2003b) 113–14; De Ligt (2004) 746–7; Scheidel (2005a). The overall number of slaves as well as their share of the population may also not have been constant. Lo Cascio (2002) suggested a decline during the empire as external supplies became scarcer while natural reproduction was insufficient to maintain numbers.

[4] Livy 7.16.7; cf. Oakley (2005) 2.182–3. Albana (1987); Günther (2008) 95–126. As Dominic Rathbone has suggested to me, the manumission tax may not originally have been the 5 per cent tax later documented. The fact that it was paid in gold (before the introduction of a gold coinage) may imply it was a token gift of a gold item deposited in the *aerarium Saturni*.

[5] Livy 27.10.11–12. Frank (1933) 1.101–2.

[6] Brunt (1971a) 549–50; Bradley (1984b) 175–6; Dumont (1987) 48–51. Frank (1932) speculated on the basis of the funds appropriated by Caesar in 49 BCE that 500,000 slaves had been freed between 82 and 49 BCE. The argument was effectively demolished by Brunt, *ibid.*

[7] Suet. *Caes.* 41.3; Dio 55.10.1; cf. Aug. *RG* 15. Virlouvet (1991) 52–5; cf. Virlouvet (1995) 191–2, 216–41. Brunt (1971a) 377, had already suggested that M. Octavius reformed the Gracchan scheme by excluding freedmen. Supposedly, he could only have got a reduction through the tribal assembly by targeting a status group with limited voting power. He further argued that Caesar had excluded *liberti* who had been freed after a given cut-off date, 136.

The hypothesis rests on three pieces of evidence: Dionysius' claim of mass manumissions following Clodius' introduction of free grain distributions;[8] Dio's story that Pompey as *curator annonae* planned to take a census of freedmen, an initiative foiled by the burning of the Temple of the Nymphs where the records were kept; [9] and finally Suetonius' comment that Augustus took measures to prevent recently freed slaves from receiving public handouts, *congiaria*.[10] It has also been suggested that Clodius' scheme may have been the first to include freedmen, since we do not hear of slaves being freed for the purpose of the dole before 58; in that case the Caesarian and Augustan reforms would simply have marked a return to normal practice.[11] It seems unlikely, however, that such a radical change to the *annona* would have gone unmentioned, and the apparent rise in manumissions after 58 may plausibly be explained by the introduction of free grain, which presented slave owners with clear-cut financial benefits that outweighed any disadvantages, including the manumission tax.[12]

It would have been difficult to justify the *en bloc* exclusion of freedmen from the dole, since their citizenship in principle was equal to that of freeborn; as argued above, the civic disabilities they suffered were almost exclusively linked to the thorny issue of public authority to which the *annona* was unrelated.[13] Moreover, the recorded figures for the number of recipients are suspiciously round, all divisible by 50,000. Most plausibly therefore they were chosen as convenient and economically sustainable figures and the beneficiaries were probably a random selection of citizens chosen by lot, *sortitio*.[14] This procedure would automatically have prevented the freeing of slaves for this purpose alone, since there was no longer any certainty that the new freedman would get on the dole. This practical and equitable system, which may also have been applied to the public *congiaria*,

---

[8] Dion. Hal. 4.24.5; cf. Dio 39.24.1.
[9] Dio 39.24.1–3; cf. Cic. *Cael.* 78; *Mil.* 73. Garnsey (1988) 213, suggested it was Pompey's intention to reduce their participation in the scheme.
[10] Suet. *Aug.* 42.2. Garnsey (1988) 236, thinks it implies he did the same for the grain dole. Virlouvet (1991), (1995) 221–8; *contra* Lo Cascio (1997) 47.
[11] Freedmen's eligibility for *congiaria* is suggested by the *Sententiae Hadriani*, *Corp. Gloss. Lat.* III 31.45–32.12; 387.22–33. Brunt (1971a) 380–1, suggested that many of those freed for the dole and later excluded by Augustus might have been informally freed. However, it is inherently implausible that non-citizens would ever have been eligible for public grain, and until the passing of the *lex Iunia* these freedmen were legally still slaves.
[12] Cf. Millar's comments on Virlouvet (1991) 65.   [13] Cf. Suet. *Caes.* 41.3.
[14] As part of his policy to encourage 'responsible' manumission, which, as we saw, was supposed to reward 'undeserving' slaves rather than provide benefits to the owners, Augustus may have decided that newly freed slaves were not immediately allowed to join the lottery for public grain and handouts, although that remains conjectural.

meant there was no need for the overtly discriminatory measures envisaged by some scholars.[15]

The negative conclusion entails that we have no means of reconstructing the number of freedmen – in Rome or anywhere else.[16] But despite the absence of reliable figures most historians have agreed that freedmen, in the words of Brunt, constituted 'a very numerous class'.[17] He estimated that freedmen might have constituted half of the urban proletariat, while some scholars have gone even further, suggesting that the entire Roman plebs may have been made up of former slaves.[18] Apart from the well-known literary and anecdotal evidence, the basis for this radical hypothesis comes from inscriptions, and above all from the tens of thousands of epitaphs which have survived from antiquity. Studies of this material have suggested that the large majority of those commemorated were former slaves, and the criteria on which they have been identified as well as the overall representativity of this type of evidence therefore deserve closer scrutiny.

Despite the formulaic character of most Roman epitaphs, they often contain enough information to allow us to determine with some degree of certainty the status of the deceased and their relatives. The safest indicator is of course filiation and pseudo-filiation (libertinisation), but during the empire the use of these status markers declined, which leaves the status of the large majority of those commemorated uncertain. The missing status indicators increase the importance of onomastic criteria, and particularly

[15] Despite the absence of statistical evidence some scholars have nevertheless tried to quantify Roman manumission. Dumont's calculations (1987) 57–82, of the proportion of freedmen in relation to slaves as well as to the freeborn population, present a salutary warning against such attempts. Each of the figures used is purely conjectural. For example, he posits that 30 was the standard age of manumission and that two thirds of slaves in professions would be freed, 66. Since both suppositions lack evidential support, the end result is too speculative to be of any value. Likewise Nicolet (1994) 605, suggested a figure of around 200,000 freedmen in the city of Rome in the late republic, but see Harris (2007) 527. Scheidel (1997) 160, 166, (2008) presented some statistical experiments which tested the implications of different rates of manumission in order to explore 'the limits of the plausible'. The risk is that hypothetical figures are adopted as 'estimates' by other scholars. Thus, Temin (2004) 531–3, (2006) used Scheidel's figure of 10 per cent of slaves over 25 being freed every five-year period as an estimate of the actual rate and compared it to the rates known from other slave societies.

[16] Brunt (1971a) 122, cf. 69, 121–30, 377. Freedmen and the high frequency of manumission played a central role in Brunt's reconstruction of the demography of the Roman republic, where they accounted for almost the entire growth of the Roman citizen body during this period.

[17] Brunt (1971a) 377, 386–7, adding that 'most of the inhabitants of Rome were apparently of servile origin', 136; cf. Brunt (1971b) 136.

[18] Purcell (1996) 797, went even further and declared that 'The city population *was* in many ways the *plebs libertina*'; cf. Purcell (1994) 657–8; Jongman (2003a); *contra* Hopkins (1978) 115–16; Morley (2006) 31.

the *cognomen*, the third element of the Roman *tria nomina*, which was given individually (although there was a growing tendency to pass it on to the eldest son). There is much evidence to suggest that certain types of names, above all Greek and other foreign-sounding, 'barbaric' names, typically would be given to slaves.[19] Literary texts reveal an instinctive association of Greek names with a 'servile' background.[20] Famously Suetonius tells the story of L. Crassicius Pasicles who changed his name to Pansa, and Martial suggests the freedman Cinna was originally called Cinnamus.[21] Surveys of Roman naming practices have established that such names overwhelmingly were reserved for slaves, and that parents of freeborn children tended to avoid them. Thus, Solin's fundamental study of the Greek names in Rome revealed that among freeborn Romans documented in inscriptions only 11.4 per cent carried Greek or 'barbaric' names, the remaining 88.6 per cent Latin.[22] The result is confirmed by other samples. The freedmen and slaves mentioned in Cicero's letters almost all carry Greek names, 94 out of 106 (89 per cent), and there is also strong epigraphic support from other parts of Italy. Thus, a large fragmentary inscription from Herculaneum lists the names of freeborn and freed males in separate columns. Among the former we find 20 per cent Greek *cognomina* and 80 per cent Latin, while the *liberti* carried 56 per cent Greek *cognomina* and only 44 per cent Latin.[23] At Minturnae the republican *magistri* and *ministri* inscriptions record a large number of slaves and freedmen, only 15 per cent of whom carried Latin *cognomina*.[24] The *album* of the *magistri vicorum* from Rome, *CIL* 6.975 (136 CE), is also instructive, since it included both freeborn and freed *magistri*, explicitly indicating the status of each individual. Here we find 56 per cent Greek *cognomina* among the freedmen (129 out of 230), but only 26 per cent among the freeborn *magistri*, the latter, however, constituting a much

[19] The responsibility for the naming of slaves is not always clear, but e.g. D. 35.1.28.1 (Paul) mentions an owner who named a slave he had purchased. In other instances one suspects that slaves may have named their own offspring.
[20] Horace, *Sat.* 1.6.38, uses Syrus, Dama, Dionysius as shorthand for slaves, and Juvenal 3.120, Protogenes, Diphilus and Hermarchus. In the *Digest* the standard slave or freedman is called Stichus or Pamphilus.
[21] Suet. *Gramm.* 18; Mart. 6.17. Solin (1971) 134–5, rightly questions the extent of this practice, for which there is no documentary evidence. *Pace* Wiseman (1985) 189.
[22] Solin (1971) 124. See also Solin's monumental catalogue of slave names in Rome (1996). The critique by Huttunen (1974) 194–7, fails to convince, as does the unsupported claim by Allison (2001), followed by Flohr (2007), that Greek *cognomina* did not carry servile connotations outside Rome; cf. e.g. Camodeca (1993) 349; (2006c) 192–3.
[23] *CIL* 10.1403; cf. Mouritsen (2007a). Camodeca (2000) 67, estimated that 54 per cent of *liberti* at Herculaneum carried Greek *cognomina* compared to 17 per cent among *ingenui*. In Altinum 59.7 per cent of slaves and freedmen carried Greek *cognomina*, Zampieri (2000) 123–4.
[24] Johnson (1933) 109. Forty-eight out of 312 individuals had Latin names.

smaller sample (with a total of only 31). Similarly, among the dedicators and dedicatees of funerary inscriptions from Ostia, the proportion of Greek and Latin names among the *ingenui* is 21 per cent to 79, compared with 63 and 37 per cent among slaves and freedmen.[25] The figures which Solin presented for the naming of children in Rome and Ostia also showed a much lower incidence of Greek names in the second generation, indicating that Greek names gradually 'died out' among the free population, who tended to prefer Latin names.[26]

While these figures clearly demonstrate the 'servile' character of Greek *cognomina*, they were not exclusive to slaves and freedmen. Surprisingly, some freeborn Romans also received names that normally signalled slavery, but in these cases there is evidence to suggest that they usually were the descendants of freedmen. This relationship is often made explicit in the inscriptions, and the onomastic balance between parents and children also points in that direction. As Solin's figures showed, far more parents with Greek names gave their children 'servile' *cognomina* than parents with Latin names did. Their reasons for continuing the use of Greek names despite their 'servile' character will be considered in the final chapter.

Another implication is that most of the apparently freeborn Romans in the epigraphic material most likely were first-generation *ingenui*. This underlines the general dearth of sources for the freeborn population below the elite, whose naming practices are largely unknown. However, the onomastic patterns of the higher orders might give us a hint how the freeborn plebs may have named their children, assuming they took their inspiration from the elite. At the highest level of Roman society, Greek *cognomina* were as a rule not used. Senators hardly ever carried Greek *cognomina*, unless they

---

[25] Mouritsen (2004). At Puteoli, Camodeca (1996b) 98, found 80 per cent Latin names among *ingenui* and only 30 per cent among *liberti*.

[26] Solin (1971) 133, gave these figures for the naming of children in Ostia and Rome:

	Ostia		Rome	
	Greek	Latin	Greek	Latin
Both parents carrying Greek names	100	91	123	93
Father Greek/mother Latin	63	68	37	67
Father Latin/mother Greek	22	60	37	90
Both parents carrying Latin names	15	118	11	79

Rawson (1968) 157 n.4, reached very similar figures: both parents Greek *cognomina* – 40 per cent of children Latin; Father Greek/mother Latin – 56 per cent Latin; Father Latin/mother Greek – 72.5 per cent Latin; both parents Latin *cognomina* – 83.5 per cent Latin.

originated in the East.[27] A survey of the *equites* from the Julio-Claudian period confirms this pattern. A very small percentage carried Greek names, and they were virtually all freedmen granted *ingenuitas*, ethnic Greeks, or from the eastern Greek-speaking part of the empire.[28] A similar picture emerges from the extensive records of local magistrates and candidates in first-century Pompeii, where only seven out of 156 *cognomina*, 4 per cent, were Greek.[29] This pattern is fully in line with the evidence from Puteoli and Herculaneum.[30] Likewise, in an early imperial list of *pontifices* at Sutrium none of the thirty-one *cognomina* was Greek.[31] These figures might indicate that the incidence of Greek names among the freeborn population without close family ties to freedmen may have been much lower than some epigraphic samples would suggest.[32]

In conclusion, Greek *cognomina* seem to provide a fairly reliable yardstick for the composition of any given group of people. We must bear in mind, however, that it represents a statistical tool and that the status of any single individual cannot be ascertained solely on onomastic criteria. Also, among Latin *cognomina* some names appear to have been more popular for slaves than for freeborn, above all those denoting positive personal qualities and good luck.[33] But this tendency is less pronounced than the 'servile' connotations of Greek *cognomina*, which should be taken into account when analysing the material statistically. Other means of determining status include shared *nomen* by spouses, which suggests that at least the woman may have been freed (either by her husband or by a common master).

---

[27] Solin (1971) 138–45; *pace* Weaver (1964), (1972) 85. Notably, none of the thirty-one senatorial *patroni* in the *album* from Canusium, 223 CE, carried Greek *cognomina*, *CIL* 9.338.

[28] Cf. Demougin (1988) 821–47. Of the 553 *cognomina* only 7 per cent were Greek/Barbaric and the large majority of their carriers were either freed or Greek provincials, 550–1. According to Nicolet (1977) 56, only 2 per cent of republican *equites* carried Greek *cognomina* and 3 per cent of the centurions.

[29] Mouritsen (1988) 104–6, 109–12: Cilix, Chilo, Polybius, Ponticus, Grosphus *bis*, Lalus. Two of these were anomalous, since the Pompeii Grosphi belonged to a prominent equestrian family from Sicily. The Latin *cognomen* Syrticus, derived from Syrtis in North Africa, also occurs twice.

[30] For Puteoli see Camodeca (1996b) 98. In Herculaneum Camodeca (1996a) identified 35–40 likely members of the late *ordo*, of whom only one, C. Iulius Spendo, carried a Greek *cognomen*. The *album* from Canusium, *CIL* 9.338, reveals a much higher incidence of Greek *cognomina* in the local elite, which has been explained by bilingualism; cf. Hor. *Sat.* 1.10.30. Solin (1971) 138 n.2, is sceptical, however, and the overall epigraphic record from the town does not suggest widespread use of Greek; cf. Chelotti *et al.* (1985–90) who list only one Greek inscription, 2.257–8 no. 282. More likely it reflects a greater tendency in this period to pass on *cognomina*, even Greek ones, through several generations, cf. *ibid.* I.64.

[31] *CIL* 11.3254. Likewise, *AE* 1985 401 contains a long list of sailors from the fleet at Ravenna (sixty-one with *cognomen*), only one of whom carried a Greek *cognomen*.

[32] Solin (1971) 128, noted that freeborn children of freedmen stand out as a distinct onomastic category characterised by a much higher presence of Greek *cognomina*.

[33] See Kajanto (1965); Duthoy (1989); Solin (1996).

Finally we may note that the *tribus Palatina* seems to indicate descent from former slaves.[34]

By combining these criteria we find that around three-quarters of those commemorated in the epitaphs from Rome probably were freed, while most of the remainder presumably were closely related to freedmen.[35] A similar picture can be found at the imperial port of Ostia.[36] Although the samples from other Italian towns reveal slightly different percentages, the overall message remains the same, namely a solid majority of freedmen in funerary epigraphy.[37] When first discovered, this profile caused consternation among scholars who speculated about a possible 'Orientalisation' of the Roman people and the effects of 'race-mixture'.[38] Although the debate obviously has moved on, the freedmen's near-monopoly of funerary epigraphy is still central to modern discussions of Roman social structure.[39]

The important question to consider is whether the material reflects the actual composition of the Roman population. Most scholars now accept some degree of libertine over-representation. The most basic distortion derives from the simple fact that putting up inscriptions requires a minimum of wealth, which automatically excluded the poorest. Thus, Treggiari explained the virtual absence of freeborn by the penury of most plebeians, while also suggesting that the better off may have been buried in their Italian hometowns.[40] The notion that poverty prevented almost all *ingenui* from commemorating themselves and their relatives is hardly plausible, and the theory also ignores the important insight into funerary epigraphy which was first presented in Taylor's ground-breaking study of the urban epitaphs.[41] Taylor argued that the profile was fundamentally skewed for the simple reason that the motivation which led to the commissioning of inscribed monuments was not uniformly shared by all sections of the

[34] Cf. Garnsey (1975a); Eck (1999). Freedmen rarely included *tribus* in their name, but the appearance of the Palatina among sons may be used to determine the status of parents.
[35] Taylor (1961). Using slightly different methods, Solin (1971) 135, estimated around 70 per cent.
[36] Mouritsen (2004).
[37] At Puteoli D'Arms (1974) 112, estimated one in ten was freeborn; Canusium: 73 per cent freed, cf. Chelotti *et al.* (1985–90) I.256, Pompeii: 58 per cent freed.
[38] E.g. Frank (1916), (1927) 202–18; Duff (1928); cf. Solin (1971) 122–3; Mouritsen (2005) 39.
[39] Treggiari (1969a) 33, noted that: 'Taken at their face-value, they [i.e. the figures] suggest that freedmen far outnumbered native Romans in their own city', cf. e.g. Holliday (2005) 123.
[40] Treggiari (1969a) 33; followed by Purcell (1983) 161–7, esp. 166; (1994) 656. However, the evidence for widespread return to ancestral tombs outside Rome is too limited and ambiguous to explain the apparent absence of non-elite *ingenui* in Rome. In many cases those leaving Rome were in fact *liberti* rather than *ingenui*.
[41] Taylor (1961) 113–14. MacMullen (1987) 376, referred to freedmen's 'unbelievable prominence among surviving inscriptions', while Brunt (1971a) 121, 387, noted that inscriptions are imbalanced because freeborn did not commemorate their lives at all, whereas a freedman could be proud of his freedom.

population. Accordingly, because of their personal background, freedmen were keener on preserving their name and achievement (especially their citizenship) for posterity and therefore put up more epitaphs than other Romans did. This approach has paved the way for a new understanding of Roman epigraphy as a cultural practice, and there is now a much greater appreciation of the contingent nature of epigraphic practices, sometimes described as a 'habit'.[42]

The impression of near-universal epigraphic commemoration evoked by the sheer scale of the surviving material may be deceptive. Studies have shown that the use of inscriptions in the Roman world was concentrated in specific locations and periods. Even within individual communities we can detect distinct practices, and there are indications that large, often affluent sections of the population never commissioned epitaphs.[43] For example at Pompeii and Ostia (and probably also other Italian towns) the elites appear effectively to have withdrawn from funerary display during the first century CE.[44] There was also significant variation at local level. The epigraphic profile of north-western Italy does, for example, differ substantially from the rest of the peninsula. In this part of Italy far more sub-elite freeborn are documented in funerary inscriptions, which not only demonstrates the existence of this otherwise invisible class, but also serves as a reminder that their apparent absence elsewhere most likely is the result of specific epigraphic practices.[45] In fact, the absence of the freeborn population is in many places so complete that it paradoxically becomes an argument against the social representativity of the material. It demonstrates that far from being a universal practice funerary self-representation was in effect the preserve of one specific group in society, the freedmen. The few *ingenui* who do feature mostly seem to be close relatives of freedmen, or soldiers, who also developed an epigraphic 'habit'. And while the first-generation freeborn appear alongside their parents, their descendants soon vanish from the record and merge with the rest of the – invisible – freeborn population.

There are obvious implications for the value of inscriptions as a source on Roman social history and demography. The nature of the material means that the figures cannot simply be taken with a modest pinch of salt,

---

[42] MacMullen (1982) remains fundamental; cf. Mouritsen (2005) 38–9, with further literature.
[43] At Ostia a study of names listed in the *collegia* inscriptions point to the existence of a substantial class of freeborn citizens, of whom we find no trace in the funerary inscriptions; cf. Mouritsen (2005) 42–3.
[44] Mouritsen (2005). The main exception appears to be young decurions and those who did not reach the higher ranks of the *ordo*.
[45] Cf. e.g. Gallivan and Wilkins (1997) 248.

as many scholars have done: we must accept that they bear no meaningful relation to the composition of the population. This conclusion undermines any attempt to measure the scale of manumission epigraphically and hence also the notion that the entire Roman plebs consisted of freedmen. The material does of course confirm that manumission was common, as many other sources also suggest, but it cannot tell us how many freedmen there were or what their share of the population was.[46]

To that end we need evidence which is less directly linked to the freedmen's own epigraphic 'habit'. The *collegia* inscriptions from Ostia constitute one of the largest bodies of onomastic material, listing hundreds of members of these – mostly professional – associations.[47] While the average proportion of Greek names is lower than among slaves and ex-slaves, it still lies around 26–30 per cent, suggesting a substantial representation of freedmen in these bodies. The tablets of Iucundus and the Sulpicii record large numbers of individuals as buyers, sellers and, above all, witnesses, the majority of whom appear to be freedmen.[48] Altogether there is sufficient evidence to conclude that in these towns freedmen made up a sizeable section of the population, although the actual proportion escapes us.

Another important source on the number of freedmen comes from Herculaneum, where several fragments of a large marble inscription have been discovered, which contain the names of hundreds of people arranged in long columns, mostly with indication of status.[49] The individuals are organised in *centuriae*, one of which is given as 'freeborn', while another had the status of *adlecti*, co-opted members. The precise nature of these lists is not clear, but the old hypothesis that we are dealing with the *album Augustalium* can safely be discarded because of its size, the surviving fragments alone recording no fewer than 497 individuals. The original document must have been considerably larger and contained at least a thousand names and possibly

---

[46] There is also anecdotal evidence for the high frequency of manumission. For example, Philo, *Leg. ad Gaium* 23.155–7, with Hezser (2005) 228–9, commented that during the reign of Augustus the Roman neighbourhoods across the Tiber were inhabited by Jews, who had been brought to Rome as captives and set free by their masters. App. *BC* 1.100, 104, also implied large numbers of freedmen. On the other hand, when Tacitus decried the number of freedmen and the shortage of freeborn in his speech on the re-enslavement of *liberti ingrati*, *Ann.* 13.27: 'si separarentur libertini, manifestum fore penuriam ingenuorum', it should be seen in the context of the wider debate about status, hierarchy, and freedom, discussed above.

[47] For the *collegia* at Ostia see Meiggs (1973) 311–36. Ausbüttel (1982) 42–8, rightly noted that members would need to be financially comfortable to be able to take part in the social activities of the associations. For the composition of their membership see Mouritsen (2005) 42–3.

[48] Sulpicii: Camodeca (1999a) 28–9; Iucundus: Jongman (1988) 271, plausibly suggested that 77 per cent of the witnesses may have been freed.

[49] *CIL* 10.1403; *AE* 1978 119 a–d; cf. Guadagno (1977).

many more.[50] The names seem to be predominantly those of Herculanean citizens, with only a small contingent of outsiders,[51] and the lists were apparently compiled at a single moment in time since there are relatively few later additions (fifty-one or 10 per cent).[52] The size of Herculaneum's population is uncertain, but it was a relatively small town with perhaps no more than 5,000 inhabitants. The implication is that most of the male population is likely to have been represented in the document.[53] The surviving fragments contain 353 identifiable freedmen and 119 freeborn, and although this of course cannot be taken as a precise figure for the proportion of freedmen in the population, we are still left with the inescapable conclusion they must have been extremely numerous.[54] Further support for this conclusion comes from the wax tablets found in Herculaneum which derive from a number of different archives and may give a relatively reliable picture of at least the better-off section of the population. According to Camodeca's calculations, they contain the names of 370 different individuals, 41 per cent of whom carry Greek *cognomina*.[55]

The same implication emerges from a number of dedications from Misenum published by D'Arms, who also ventured some estimates as to number of *Augustales* in relation to the population as a whole.[56] The sums set aside for an annual distribution, along with the rates prescribed, indicated a body of *Augustales* that cannot have been much below 200, which may be compared with a total citizen population in the range of

---

[50] The document consisted of at least three separate inscriptions, which each consisted of several marble panels, as indicated by fragments 10.1403 a, d, and g, whose external frames show they belong to the right-hand side of the inscription. Fragment g gives us the full height of the inscription, which allows some rough estimates of the original number of names. If each of the three inscriptions consisted of two marble sections we reach a total of 1,080 names, and if they were made up of three separate panels, no fewer than 1,620 names.

[51] There is a marked dominance of important local families such as the Nonii, Marii, Mammii, and Volusii. Moreover, the large majority (81 per cent) of the freeborn belong to the local *tribus* Menenia. On the other hand, those specifically listed as *adlecti* appear to be outsiders, only 37 per cent belonging to the Menenia. They also seem far more 'isolated' than the other freeborn, whose *praenomina* and *gentilicia* frequently are represented elsewhere on the list, 23 per cent compared to 69 per cent.

[52] The three fragmentary inscriptions could in theory record the membership at different moments in time but the absence of recurring names would argue against that. Only one name appears twice, C. Petronius Stephanus in 1403b and *AE* 1978 119b (Guadagno G), but a homonymous father and son of that name are documented elsewhere in Herculaneum, t. 30.

[53] Pesando (2003) 337, suggested the list may have included almost all citizens in Herculaneum.

[54] This also includes the individuals without status indication from *AE* 1978 119b (Guadagno B), since their *cognomina* and the presence of the freedman L. Venidius Ennychys demonstrate their freed status. The names in fragment 1403d are almost certainly those of freeborn; cf. Mouritsen (2007a).

[55] Camodeca (2000) 67–8, who suggested they offer 'una solida base di partenza per ogni indagine sulla composizione sociale di Ercolano negli ultimi decenni prima della catastrofe'.

[56] D'Arms (2000) 133–4.

3,300–4,000.[57] Since the *Augustalitas* involved considerable expense its membership by definition represented a wealthy minority of the local freedmen, who must therefore have constituted a sizeable proportion of the inhabitants of Misenum.

We may consider the proportion of slaves who were freed. Given the state of our evidence, most scholars have remained cautious about the rate of manumission, merely suggesting that many slaves had a 'good chance', *vel sim.*[58] Among this prudent vagueness one radical theory stands out. In a famous study from 1972 Alföldy argued that virtually all slaves, at least in the cities, could expect to be freed. The only exceptions from this rule would have been in 'bestimmten harten Ausnahmefällen'.[59] There are wide implications of this theory, which in effect reduces slavery to a mere phase for large sections of the unfree population.[60] Not only does this transform the character of Roman slavery itself but it also changes the significance of manumission. Thus, the question of motivation becomes largely irrelevant if manumission were a routine procedure that did not require any specific justification. Freeing slaves would simply conform to a common pattern of behaviour.

Alföldy's thesis remains controversial, and it is not difficult to question it on grounds of general probability.[61] The sustainability of such a system raises obvious questions, since the model assumes that manumission was not just near universal, but also happened relatively early in the lives of most slaves, generally below the age of thirty. The implication is that many slaves would not have reproduced before being freed, increasing the need for outside replacements, presumably through imports, and undermining the long-term survival of the system.[62] We may also query the economic logic

---

[57] The *Augustales* at Misenum were divided into two sections, the *corporati* who apparently counted 100 and those outside the *corpus*, who D'Arms plausibly suggested could not be fewer than the inner core. The freed status of the *Augustales* is indicated by a reference to 'ingenui corporati', presumably members of *collegia*.

[58] Dumont's (1987) guesstimates present an exception. To Brunt (1971a) 121: 'skilled slaves could no doubt generally earn their freedom, if they lived long enough.' Similarly, according to Patterson (1991) 320, 'most had a realistic expectation of being manumitted within their lifetime'. Nicolet (1994) 605, suggested that the grant of freedom was 'a normal expectation for a high proportion of slaves, maybe up to a third', but does not provide any evidence.

[59] Alföldy (1986a) 319, 296. References are to the second edition of the paper which included addenda and responses to his critics.

[60] Horsmann (1986) 319, and Vittinghoff (1990) 188, called slavery a 'Durchgangsstadium'.

[61] E.g. Hopkins (1978) 141 n.18, 127 n.63; Ste. Croix (1982) 575 n.18; Wiedemann (1985); Garnsey (1981) 361; Weaver (1991) 181; cf. Harris (1980b) 118, 133–4, (2007) 527: 'the evidence for readily available manumission is insufficient'; *contra* Dumont (1987) 78; López Barja de Quiroga (1998) 152–5.

[62] Alföldy (1986a), 313–15, acknowledged this problem and suggested that self-purchase by slaves was a factor that might explain the economic rationality on a household level, but it does not solve the larger issues of slave supplies; for which see Scheidel (1997), (2005a); Harris (1999).

of comprehensive manumission. Alföldy explained the benefits in terms of greater productivity of slave labour, but if the rewards were virtually certain, slaves would have had little incentive to apply themselves.

While many scholars have expressed reservations about Alföldy's theory, there has been little direct engagement with the central epigraphic argument, and he could therefore restate his position in 1986 with few modifications.[63] At the core of his theory lies an analysis of a large sample of epitaphs from Rome, Italy, Spain, and the Danube region, comparing the age at death recorded for freedmen and slaves. Alföldy discovered a marked difference between the two groups, since among the freedmen in the city of Rome 18.3 per cent (132 of 722) were recorded with an age at death over 40, while the corresponding figure for slaves is only 0.6 per cent (2 of 340). In other regions similar patterns could be detected, albeit often less pronounced, e.g. in southern Italy where the figures are 24.7 per cent for freedmen and 11.5 per cent for slaves (of a much smaller sample), and in Spain the relations were 14 to 40.8 per cent. From this evidence Alföldy concluded that the apparent absence of old slaves from the funerary record reflected the simple fact that there *were* no old slaves; they had all been freed before reaching old, or even middle, age.[64] Alföldy further concluded that manumission took place relatively early, since out of the 1201 freedmen in his sample whose age at death was recorded, no fewer than 750 (or 62.4 per cent) were still under 30. In Italy itself it was more than half. He also noted that more *servae* than *servi* were freed below the age of 30, which he explained by marriage to their patron. Alföldy accepted only one major modification of his thesis, since he pointed out that it applied only in the cities.[65]

By coincidence two other studies of Roman manumission rates appeared the same year as Alföldy's article, reaching almost identical conclusions. Harper (1972) compared the average age of slaves and freedmen in the city of Rome, and found an average age at death of 17.2 for male slaves, 17.9 for female slaves, and 25.2 for freedmen. On that basis he concluded that

---

[63] Alföldy later accepted that manumission was not automatic but dependent on the slave's good behaviour, but it is not clear how manumission could be near-universal without being automatic. He also acknowledged that his original assumption of only a few years of service being required before manumission might be too optimistic, 329–30, but the evidence on which he based the idea still implied that the slaves were quite young when freed. Thus, the concessions merely weakened the overall coherence of his thesis.

[64] Alföldy (1986a) 302–3, 304–5.

[65] Some manumission in the countryside was recognised, Alföldy (1986a) 305–7. Alföldy also believed the rate of manumission declined in the later empire, partly because of lesser desire for freedom among slaves, 308.

if 'a city slave survived to maturity his chances of freedom must have been considerable'. Following the same approach, Weaver found that imperial freedmen appeared to be considerably older than the slaves of the emperor, which he saw as indication that most of them could expect to be freed, usually between the ages of 30 and 40. In that respect, he suggested, the imperial slaves were at a disadvantage compared to other urban slaves, who he assumed were freed even earlier.[66]

These studies were all based on the assumption that epigraphic samples can be treated as a demographic database and that the information on age and status offers a fairly reliable picture of the relative composition of different population groups, in this case slaves and freedmen. There are good reasons to doubt this premise.[67] Scholars have noted that the epigraphic medium invariably distorts reality simply because of the costs involved in putting up inscriptions.[68] This factor evidently must be taken into account, but more fundamentally the use of funerary epigraphy also constituted a distinct cultural practice that became the almost exclusive preserve of some social groups, above all freedmen and soldiers. And within these epigraphically active sections of the population we find patterns of usage which skew the overall profile even further.

It has long been noted that infants and women are seriously under-represented in the funerary material, but this distortion is not evenly applied. For example, the proportion of recorded children below the age of 14 varies between 42 and 16.5 per cent in different parts of Italy. Likewise the sex ratio in these samples covers a range from 111 to 198 (in favour of males).[69] In some cases this may reflect differences in the attitudes to children or gender, or perhaps to early death.[70] But most likely they are simply variations of epigraphic practice, as underlined, for example, by the culturally inexplicable differences in the frequency of families recording two boys or two girls; in different Italian regions these vary from 5:1 to 13:1, in favour of two boys.[71]

---

[66] Weaver (1972) 100–4. According to Weaver, half of the *servi Caesaris* were 28 or older when they died, one third were 35 or older, and one fifth 41 or older. By comparison, the imperial freedmen died much later – half were 42 or older, one third were 55 or older, and one fifth 65 or older. Only 24 per cent of the *Augusti liberti* died before the age of 30, suggesting to Weaver that their manumission took place quite late.

[67] The fact that the average freedman was older than the average slave is self-evident, since relatively few children would have been freed.

[68] Brunt (1971a) 132, 387; Harris (1980b); Wiedemann (1985).   [69] McWilliam (2001) 80.

[70] Shaw (1991) believed the concern for children was primarily an urban phenomenon, but the practice of funerary epigraphy was itself essentially urban.

[71] Gallivan and Wilkins (1997) 242.

Commemorative patterns also reveal the importance of local conventions. Thus, in general more children were commemorated by their parents than vice versa. In peninsular Italy parents commemorated children at a ratio of 68 to 32, but in the north the reverse was, for some reason, the case, 47 to 53.[72] These variations occurred even at the level of the individual burial site. For example, the two broadly contemporary *columbaria* of the Volusii and the Statilii both record large aristocratic *familiae* in the city of Rome but developed their own distinct epigraphic habits. Thus, among the Volusii the names of dedicating relatives were usually included in the inscription, while that rarely happened in Statilian epitaphs.[73] Such disparities are unlikely to reflect different family structures or attitudes to bereavement, but are essentially epigraphic.

The impact of culturally and locally specific epigraphic practices takes us back to the patterns of commemoration which led Alföldy to conclude that the apparent absence of older slaves from Roman epitaphs showed that they had all been freed. Two distinct but closely related issues are involved here: firstly, did old slaves receive epigraphic commemoration? And secondly, if they did, would their epitaphs have included information about their age? To reach an answer we will have to consider the question of age in inscriptions more broadly. It has long been recognised that Roman epitaphs do not present a believable demographic profile, infants being seriously under-recorded. The explanation may be a combination of lack of commemoration and absence of age indication, the former probably being the more significant factor, in turn reflecting Roman attitudes to newborn children. Older slaves may have suffered from similar under-commemoration, since children generally were less likely to commemorate parents than vice versa. They might have anticipated this by commissioning their own epitaphs, but these would in the nature of things not have included age at death.

The decision to include the age of the deceased was separate from the decision to put up an inscription, which potentially adds another layer of distortion to the overall profile. Stating the age reflected a wish to highlight this particular aspect of the deceased's identity. For that reason it appears only in a minority of epitaphs, some samples suggesting less than a quarter.[74] It was most common for older children and young adults,

---

[72] Gallivan and Wilkins (1997) 245.

[73] Volusii: 43 per cent – 147 dedicators/194 dedicatees (341 total). Statilii: 17 per cent – 78 dedicators/ 392 dedicatees (470 total); cf. Mouritsen (forthcoming).

[74] Hopkins (1987) 113, estimated 24 per cent of epitaphs in the western empire included age. McWilliam (2001) 75, suggested 20 per cent in the city of Rome.

suggesting that indicating the age may have been part of the response to *mors acerba*. Within this general pattern we find an almost infinite variation at local level – between different provinces, regions, towns, and even burial sites. For example, at Patavium the age was given for only 9 per cent, while at Pompeii the figure was three times higher, 29 per cent, the average ages recorded being 26 and 19 respectively.[75] Even within individual towns the picture is not consistent. In the familial burial site of the Epidii, just south of the Porta Stabiana in Pompeii, no less than 57 per cent contain information about age, compared with 23 per cent in the rest of the city. This disparity also affects the average age, which is much higher in the Epidian burial ground than outside.[76] The existence of such epigraphic 'micro-environments' highlights the contingent nature of the age profiles, and it is against this background the question of the 'missing' older slaves must be viewed.[77] To help us understand the commemoration of older people in Roman inscriptions Shaw has provided an invaluable survey of sexagenarians in different parts of the empire, organised according to status groups and periods.[78] His figures demonstrate a general under-representation of older people in Roman epitaphs, with the notable exception of North Africa and Spain, which have radically different age profiles. The lowest share of sexagenarians comes from the slave population of Rome, only 0.3 per cent, thus confirming Alföldy's figures.[79] Among the freedmen in Rome they made up 3 per cent, but that figure is still well below their proportion of 13.4 per cent in various African towns during the classical period. Weaver noted that older slaves of the emperor were far more common in the *columbaria* at Carthage than anywhere outside this province, concluding that all the old imperial slaves were freed in Rome but not in Africa.[80] More likely, this reflected different patterns of commemoration, for, as Shaw's figures show, the proportion of non-slave sexagenarians in

---

[75] The sample includes *CIL* 5 pp. 277–304.

[76] Twenty-four compared to sixteen outside the Epidian site; *NSc* (1893) 333–5; (1894) 382–5; (1897) 275–6; (1916) 302.

[77] Another example comes from Rome, where the *columbaria* of the Volusii and Statilii have different age distributions. Among the Statilii, 30 per cent were 10 or younger, while in the *familia* of the Volusii, the corresponding figure is only 16 per cent. On the other hand, children of one year or less make up 16 per cent among the Volusii, but only 1 per cent of the Statilii. On the other hand, none of the slaves of the Volusii was commemorated between ages 4 and 13, an age group which makes up no less than 31 per cent among the Statilii; cf. Mouritsen (forthcoming).

[78] Shaw (1991) 79.

[79] It is also noticeable that the figure for soldiers stationed in Rome is almost as low as that for slaves, just 1.2 per cent. In this specific case, however, it might be explained by their return to their home regions after completed service.

[80] Weaver (1972) 103.

Carthage, 6.7 per cent, is very close to that found among the slave population, 6.1 per cent, suggesting that age at death was included for much wider
age groups and social ranges than was common elsewhere in the empire.
Otherwise we would have to accept that Africans of all classes and statuses
lived longer than any other Romans.

A similar conclusion is offered by the fact that the second-lowest figure
for sexagenarians comes from Ostia, where the overall share of older people
was only marginally higher than for urban slaves, just 0.9 per cent. Taken at
face value this figure would indicate that older people virtually did not exist
in Ostia, but few scholars would probably accept this inference.[81] A simple
explanation is that they are absent from the Ostian records because the age
of older people was not normally included in their epitaphs. The existence
of such epigraphic quirks has implications for the thesis of Alföldy, Harper,
and Weaver, suggesting as it does that the disparity between the numbers of
older slaves compared to older freedmen may be explained by differences
in commemorative practice; as a rule, slaves were commemorated only
when they died young, or at least their age was stated only in the case of
premature death. In that respect they were not unique, but the tendency
to focus on the young may have been more pronounced in the case of
slaves.[82] It follows that these figures cannot throw any light on the rate of
manumission.

In addition to the epigraphic argument, Alföldy also adduced literary
and legal evidence in support of his theory, most prominently Dionysius of Halicarnassus' tirade against irresponsible owners who freed entire
households, including criminal slaves. However, Dionysius' critique of
these over-generous masters hardly suggests normal practice, and his moral
indignation would ring hollow if virtually all slaves could expect to be
freed anyway. Similarly, the stern condemnation of masters freeing slaves
on 'frivolous' grounds, e.g. with a view to qualifying them for the grain
dole, makes little sense in a context of near universal manumission, which
reduced the decision to free a slave to a question of timing.[83]

The *lex Fufia Caninia* has also been taken as indicative that masters
habitually liberated all remaining slaves in their wills. But as argued above,

---

[81] Ostia's population may have been relatively more transient given its mercantile character, but it can
hardly have been completely devoid of older people.

[82] Owners often seem to have invested emotionally in their slave children, as illustrated by the
concept of *delicia*. As they grew up their status in the household changed, as the case of Seneca's old
doorkeeper illustrates, *Ep.* 12.1–3. He had once been his *delicium* but had apparently since fallen from
favour and been left on a farm, where he had little chance of receiving epigraphic commemoration.

[83] Cic. *Balb.* 24, quoted by Alföldy (1986a) 286, does not refer to the frequency of manumission in
general but to exceptional cases where slaves were awarded their freedom by the state.

the limitations on testamentary manumission imposed by the law may also be interpreted as an ideological statement about the need for proper discrimination.[84] As such it reflected the Roman ideal that freedom be granted selectively in recognition of the slave's hard work and dedication. Alföldy's theory therefore implies a fundamental – and barely credible – gulf between the ideal of manumission and a reality in which most urban slaves were freed as a matter course. Thus, Roman writers took it for granted that freedmen gained their freedom through particular efforts, or *industria*, as Quintilian expressed it, and Seneca Maior noted that a master thought well of the slave before freeing him.[85] Likewise, in Roman comedy freedom is generally presented as the reward for good service and loyalty, long anticipated and certainly no trivial matter.

Against this consensus, one celebrated passage has been adduced as unequivocal proof of frequent manumission. In early 43 Cicero delivered his Eighth Philippic oration, asking his audience: 'Indeed, Conscript Fathers, now that after six years we have begun to entertain the hope of liberty, having endured servitude longer than enslaved war captives are wont to do if they are well behaved and conscientious, what vigils, what anxieties, what labours for the sake of the freedom of the Roman people should we shrink from?'[86] The statement has been taken as evidence that slaves could expect to be freed after just six years of service.[87] But it has also been pointed out that Cicero's *sexennium* was determined by the historical context of the speech, which traced the 'enslavement of the Roman people' back to the outbreak of the civil war in January 49 – precisely six years earlier.[88] Moreover, a closer reading further qualifies the statement, for, in line with the Roman ideal of selective manumission, the *captivi* who could expect their freedom were the 'frugi et diligentes', i.e. those who had earned it through hard work and dedication.

This passage must also be set beside a host of Ciceronian evidence, which suggests that manumission was never a step taken without careful consideration. Thus, in the case of Tiro, a seemingly obvious candidate for

---

[84] The statement of Gaius *Inst.* 1.44, that the *lex Fufia Caninia* did not prevent owners from freeing entire households, is hardly a strong argument that many owners actually did that; *contra* Alföldy (1986a) 292.

[85] Quint. *Inst. Or.* 11.1.88; Sen. Maior *Contr.* 4.8: 'bene de servo iudicasti: manu misisti'.

[86] *Phil.* 8.32: 'Etenim, patres conscripti, cum in spem libertatis sexennio post sumus ingressi diutiusque servitutem perpessi quam captivi servi frugi et diligentes solent, quas vigilias, quas sollicitudines, quos labores liberandi populi Romani causa recusare debemus?'

[87] Alföldy (1986a) 286–7; Horsmann (1986) 318; Watson (1987) 23; Dumont (1987) 78; Rink (1993) 46–7; Cohen (2000) 144.

[88] Cf. Wiedemann (1985) 165–6. Harris (1980b) 133–4, also noted that according to Dio 53.25.4, *captivi* might be freed after twenty years.

manumission, the reward was long anticipated and held out as a promise, and, when finally granted, was celebrated by the family as a significant event.[89] Tiro seems to have been educated by Cicero from boyhood, and already before becoming a freedman he was a trusted member of the household, on very familiar terms with the Cicerones.[90] But despite his privileged position he may have been around 30 when he was finally freed in 53.[91] Similarly Quintus' favourite slave, Statius, seems to have been freed after long consideration. Judging from the letters of Cicero, who bitterly opposed the grant, it was not a decision taken lightly, let alone routinely. Cicero also inquired about the manumission of Atticus' favourite slave Eutychides, telling his friend that he would like to know 'what you have done about Eutychides'.[92] Such instances give the impression that, while there was a strong sense that slaves like Tiro, Statius, and Eutychides deserved to be freed, it was far from certain this would actually happen.

Most revealing is the letter Cicero sent to his wife Terentia shortly before going into exile in 58. He tells her not to worry about freeing the slaves, stating that:

in the first place, the promise made to your people was that you would treat each case on its merits (Orpheus, in fact, is loyal so far, none of the others very noticeably so). The position of the other slaves is that if it turned out that my property was no longer mine, they would be my freedmen, provided they could make good their claim to the status; whereas, if I still had a hold on them, they would remain my slaves except for just a few.[93]

Cicero's advice to Terentia was to deal with the slaves as each of them deserved, only one of her slaves standing out, Orpheus. This seems to be standard practice, but if Cicero under these extraordinary circumstances should lose his entire estate, he is willing to free his household to prevent them being sold off on the open market – if they can make their claim, 'si

[89] *Fam.*16.10, 14, 16.
[90] Gell. *NA* 13.9.1, describes him as Cicero's *alumnus*. Tiro seems to have been a *verna* like many other intellectual slaves; cf. Treggiari (1969b) 202; Christes (1979a).
[91] Treggiari (1969a) 259–61, (1977), rightly rejects the implication of Jerome, *apud* Euseb. *Chron.Olympiad* 194, that Tiro was 50 when he received his freedom; cf. Christes (1979a) 118–21. In 50 BCE he was still described as *adulescens*, *Att.* 6.7.2; 7.2.3.
[92] *Att.* 4.16.9: 'de Eutychide quid egeris'. Later he again commented on Eutychides' manumission, *Att.* 4.15.1.
[93] *Fam.* 14.4: 'De familia liberata, nihil est quod te moveat. Primum tuis ita promissum est, te facturam esse ut quisque esset meritus; est autem in officio adhuc Orpheus, praeterea magno opere nemo. Ceterorum servorum ea causa est ut, si res a nobis abisset, liberti nostri essent, si obtinere potuissent; sin ad nos pertinerent, servirent, praeterquam oppido pauci', trans. Shackleton Bailey (Loeb). The slaves described as 'tuis' may have been part of Terentia's dowry; cf. Dixon (1986) 95–6, whose interpretation of the legal issues otherwise seems problematic.

obtinere potuissent' (which may be linked to the fact that he is now physically absent). Otherwise, normal practice prevails and only the deserving
will be freed.

Many other sources imply that manumission was considered neither
universal nor automatic. For example, Seneca tells the story how he met
his slave Felicio, the son of the bailiff and once Seneca's pet slave, *delicium*,
but now grown old. Despite his favoured position and early closeness to
the master he had never been freed and now worked as doorkeeper at the
country estate. To Seneca the encounter merely inspired a meditation on
old age and gave no cause for regret.[94]

The impression of selective manumission is reinforced when we turn to
what is probably the best evidence we have for the frequency of manumission in the Roman elite, the *columbaria* of the Volusii and the Statilii.
The material is particularly useful because of its scale, its secure prove-
nance, and the relatively short time span it covers. Uniquely it enables us
to identify slaves and freedmen of the same households, which the Roman
naming of slaves otherwise precludes. None of the two bodies of evidence
is complete, but there are good reasons for assuming that they represent a
realistic cross-section of these households, since access to commemoration
in the *columbaria* appears to have been available for even the humblest staff
members. The distortions that remain are those which can be found in
virtually all collections of Roman epitaphs, namely under-representation of
the youngest slaves and probably also of women. There are also variations
in the epigraphic profile of the two households, which may be explained
partly by differences in the excavation history of the two sites and partly by
differences in their epigraphic cultures.[95] Despite these caveats, the statistics produced by this material are illuminating. They indicate that between
a quarter and a third of the households may have been freed at any time.
The incidence of freedmen naturally increases among the more advanced
age groups, but even here it seems that more than half of the adults in the
households remained slaves.[96]

---

[94] *Ep.* 12.1–3. There was a general assumption that even urban *familiae* would include older slaves, e.g.
Mart. 11.70, where the poet pleads ironically with Tucca not to sell his expensively purchased pretty
slaves – sell anything else, old slaves, his father's slaves, etc. (cf. Mart. 9.87). Cicero's outrage at Piso
using *senes* to serve at table related to their function, not the fact that he owned old slaves, *Pis.* 67.

[95] The inscriptions from the Volusii are longer and more ornate, representing the upper echelons of
the household, while those from the Statilian tomb are more modest and give a broader coverage of
the *familia*.

[96] Slaves are identified on the basis of their single names. *A priori* it seems unlikely that freedmen would
be commemorated without proper indication of status, which could easily be done simply by adding
an 'l' to the name, as often happened; *pace* Weaver (2001) 104. Of the 565 slaves and freedmen in
the Statilian material 179 (31.7 per cent) were freed, while the corresponding figures for the Volusii
are 134/291 (46 per cent). The latter figure should probably be revised downward because of the

The conclusion to be drawn from this evidence is that manumission was both very common and very selective. A similar picture emerges from other quantitative sources, such as the stamps found on pottery. The interpretation of this evidence is much disputed, including the economic function of the stamps, the identity of those who feature in them, and their relationship with the owners of the potteries. However, what immediately becomes clear is the diversity of the material, since the stamps from different 'firms' vary greatly in content and structure.[97] Some of them give only a single *nomen*, others a wide range of different names. In some cases they are virtually all slaves; in others we find an intriguing combination of what appear to be slave names and *tria nomina*. Most of them are abbreviated and some scholars have dismissed any attempt to distinguish between slaves and freedmen. That may be overly pessimistic, however, for while there may be local variations in naming practices, we must *a priori* assume a general recognition of names as indicators of personal status.[98] Thus, two stamps carrying the names 'C. LAEK BAS/ FELIX SER' (C. Laekanii Bassi Felix servus) and 'C. LAEK FELIX' (C. Laekanius Felix – rather than C. Laekanii Felix, as read by some scholars) would logically refer to different stages in the life of the same Felix, before and after his manumission. Following that interpretation it would appear that manumission was quite common among the potters/managers whose names we find stamped on the products, although it of course may have affected only a minority of the slaves working on the sites.[99]

particular bias of the material. For detailed statistics see Mouritsen (forthcoming); cf. Westermann (1955) 88; Hasegawa (2005). The figures presented by Madden (1996) 109, are misleading. For the archaeological and epigraphic evidence see Buonocore (1984); Caldelli and Ricci (1999).

[97] Oxé (1968); Prachner (1980), Fülle (1997), Kenrick (2000).

[98] Based on Oxé's old hypothesis, Aubert (1993) 179, (1994) 222, 257–8, 275, 287–8, argued that it is 'impossible to determine the status of people on the basis of their name only, because the names of slaves and freedmen could be formed on the same pattern', 222. Supposedly a slave could be represented by the master's name (*nomen* or *praenomen* + *nomen*) in the genitive followed by the slave's name also in the genitive. In that case, however, the name would appear identical to the normal *tria nomina*. The fundamental point is that the Romans had an onomastic system which allowed people to identify a person's status by a quick glance at his or her name. It seems inconceivable that potters would adopt a practice which represented slave names in forms that to any outsider would seem to be those of free persons. None of Aubert's supporting examples, drawn from the household of the Umbricii Scauri, actually reads as *tria nomina*, 290. Aubert's suggestion, (1994) 287–90, that stamps normally were binominal is not entirely convincing either, since a full slave name (with indication of master) is technically still that of one person – just like *tria nomina* with filiation. He further doubts whether a name in the genitive found next to a slave name was the owner's, suggesting it could mean 'ex officina', which seems less plausible, 299. Helen (1975) 23, argues that *cognomen* alone could be used of free persons, since some of these individuals appear elsewhere with *gentilicium*. However, manumission always involved a change of name during the lifetime of a slave.

[99] *Contra* Aubert (1994) 258. For the relationship between slaves and freed see the tables in Fülle (1997).

In sum, despite the shortcomings of the documentation, which offers only impressionistic snapshots of individual locations, households, and industries, there seems to be sufficient evidence to conclude that manumission was very common, at least in some environments. Although it was by no means universal, even in elite urban households, it appears to have been more widespread in Rome than in any other slave society for which we have more detailed information.[100] Thus, even in societies where manumission was fairly accepted (which was not always the case) the frequency with which it happened remained well below that found in some parts of the Roman world. For example, for classical Athens most estimates of the rate of manumission have been very low.[101] Outside Athens there is evidence for more extensive manumission, but the overall impression is that of a society where freedmen were far less numerous than in Rome. A similar picture emerges from later slave societies which practised manumission. Eighteenth- and nineteenth-century Latin America provides the best-documented modern example of a high-frequency manumission regime. In the large cities the freeing of slaves was relatively normal, and in many places the slaves who could pay enjoyed some – formal or informal – right to freedom. Nevertheless, the overall scale remained relatively small, which leaves us with the question why manumission became so popular in Rome.[102] In the following chapter possible explanations of the Roman situation will be explored.

INCENTIVES AND REWARDS: A MODEL OF ROMAN MANUMISSION

Keith Hopkins once famously asked: 'Why did the Romans free so many slaves?' While the question put like this may seem deceptively simple, the answer will of course have to be far more complex. It is possible to envisage an almost infinite range of reasons for an owner to free a given slave. As

[100] *Pace* Patterson (1991) 235, who declared that: 'In comparative terms, there was actually nothing peculiar about the high manumission rate in Italy, especially Rome. *All* urban slave systems, both ancient and modern, exhibit high rates of manumission.' 'There is no known exception to this sociological law of slavery', because manumission was 'the only effective means of motivating slaves to perform complex tasks'.
[101] Klees (1998) 298–302, 320–1, with previous literature.
[102] In Rio between 1807 and 1831, 1,319 slaves received letters of liberty. In 1849, shortly before abolition, there were more than 10,000 freedpersons in Rio, out of a population of some 200,000, Karasch (1987) 341. According to Queirós Mattoso (1986) 147, freed slaves made up only 0.5 to 2.0 per cent of the population of cities like Rio, Salvador, and Paraty. Johnson (1979) 277, on Buenos Aires, in 1778 less than 0.4 per cent of the slaves were freed annually, rising to 1.3 per cent in 1810. Hünefeldt (1995) presents an exceptional scenario from nineteenth-century Lima of very high manumission rates, which eventually led to the decline in slavery. The reason for this anomaly lay in the wage-earning capacity of the slaves in Peru and their access to separate plots of land.

we know from other, better-documented slave societies, masters could free slaves for the purpose of marriage; young slaves, in some cases the master's own offspring, could be freed on grounds of personal affection; dying slaves could be given freedom as a last favour and consolation; and old or infirm slaves might be freed in order to avoid the cost of maintaining them. Manumission could be induced by outsiders offering payment, or payment could be offered by the slaves themselves. Manumission could be suspended until after the owner's death, or until certain conditions had been fulfilled. Finally it could be given freely as a reward for years of hard work and loyal service. This diversity of forms and motivations does not preclude attempts at understanding Roman manumission in structural terms as a distinct cultural and economic practice. No matter how personal, a decision to free a slave would not have been taken in isolation from prevailing social conventions and values or unaffected by existing economic and financial structures. It would inevitably have related to established patterns of behaviour, and we may therefore consider what these may have been.

Earlier generations of scholars often stressed the altruistic aspect of Roman manumission. Some saw the influence of Stoicism or Christianity in the generous manumission practices which supposedly formed part of a relatively 'humane' type of slavery.[103] While the apologetic aspect to this model is undeniable, we cannot dismiss a charitable element entirely. There is, for example, no point in doubting the importance of personal affection in the manumission of slaves like Tiro or Statius. But as a general explanation it falls short; in every slave society, owners have been fond of certain slaves, especially domestic servants, but nowhere has that led to manumission on the scale we encounter in Rome.

More rewarding have been the attempts to explain the practice in economically rational terms. The most comprehensive was made by the economist Fenoaltea, who formulated a model based on transaction costs, i.e. the associated costs of labour, with particular focus on the cost of supervision.[104] He perceived slavery and manumission as elements of an economic system that included both 'care intensive' and 'effort intensive' sectors which demanded different sets of performance-enhancing incentives. Fenoaltea argued that slavery without incentives is economically

---

[103] See above pp. 4–5. More recently scholars, led by Westermann (1955) 116, 120, have expressed doubt about the positive impact of Stoicism and Christianity, Finley (1980) 40–4; Boulvert and Morabito (1982) 98–182; Manning (1989); Bradley (1994) 145–53, (2008); Harrill (1995); Garnsey (1996); Glancy (2002); Wöhrle (2005). Herschbell (1995) 201, noted that despite his servile past Epictetus 'never denied that slavery was part of a providential plan according to which human beings were assigned different stations in life'.

[104] Fenoaltea (1984), building on Findlay (1975); cf. Temin (2004); Scheidel (2008).

viable only in certain forms of production, since it relies on coercion which is not always practicable or cost-efficient. Functions that require care, skills, and perhaps even independent initiative cannot be performed by simple application of force, which will often be counter-productive; for these roles positive incentives are required. In addition, there are work environments where systematic violence may be undesirable, e.g. in a domestic setting where incentives generally are preferred.[105]

In this model, manumission represents a primary motivation for slaves to work hard and diligently. High-frequency regimes, such as Rome's, are explained by the need for powerful, performance-enhancing incentives, particularly in the urban economy. Moreover, by embedding manumission firmly in the economic system, the model provides a structural explanation of the prevalence of manumission in the city and its apparent absence in the countryside. It is essentially an advanced version of the old 'stick and carrot' argument and, as such, self-evidently plausible; to make efficient use of unfree labour, a combination of coercion and incentives was obviously needed. However, Fenoaltea's is a universal model, in principle applicable to all societies using slave labour, while Rome stands out as a society that practised unusually frequent manumission. Other slave societies have also been economically complex and employed slaves in positions which required responsibility, care, and dedication, but without reaching the same level of manumission. Thus, while the model may explain Roman manumission in general economic terms, it does not answer the question of scale. To address this issue, other, non-economic factors must be taken into account.

Some scholars have drawn a broad distinction between 'open' and 'closed' slave societies, the latter operating with an unbridgeable barrier between free and unfree, often based on posited biological or ethnic differences, considered innate and immutable.[106] Such conventions naturally present an obstacle to large-scale manumission and distinguish these cultures from the so-called 'open' slave societies where the barriers are considered less

---

[105] As Scheidel (2008) pointed out, Fenoaltea's classification of all rural labour as 'effort intensive' is questionable, and at variance with his recognition that viticulture required mostly care and skills. The fact that it relied on care rather than effort affects his overall argument that slavery without the prospect of freedom was unsuited to these functions. Scheidel suggested that the advantage of slavery here may have been the owner's direct control over skilled labour, which reduced the 'turnover' costs that might be considerable in 'thin' labour markets like that of Rome. This explanation, on the other hand, implies a loss of labour following manumission which, as we shall see, is not given at Rome.

[106] The distinction was first formulated by Watson (1980) esp. 9–13; cf. Glancy (2002) 94–5; Weiler (2003); Temin (2004) 523–5; (2006) 142; Scheidel (2008).

fundamental and therefore more easily crossed. Rome evidently falls into the latter category, given its rejection of 'natural slavery' and ready acceptance of manumission, even enfranchising former slaves. By contrast Greece is classified as a relatively 'closed' slave society, with limited manumission and a marginalised freed population. The ultimate 'closed' system was the antebellum American South, where slavery was justified on strictly 'racial' grounds and manumission was either banned or extremely rare.[107] An intermediate position is occupied by Latin America, where – despite the racialist underpinning of slavery – manumission was accepted and practised on a considerable scale, at least in the cities.

The model is useful in highlighting the influence of non-economic factors on the rate of manumission, although the relationship between the 'open/closed' distinction and the scale of manumission is partly circular, since the former to a great extent is based on the latter.[108] Moreover, we may wonder whether Rome really was so 'open' as its manumission rate might suggest. While the notion of 'slaves by nature' may have been rejected, this did not, as we have seen, mean the absence of prejudices against slaves. The unfree population was still seen as a carrier of distinct, 'slavish' characteristics that triggered fears about servile 'contamination' of free society. The situation in Rome may therefore be too complex to fit into a simple model of economic rationalism and 'carefree' manumission. Not only were there ideological factors militating against widespread manumission, but the economic argument also needs to be qualified.

The effectiveness of manumission as a spur to good work was widely recognised in antiquity. The elder Pliny noted that work by chained slaves is poor, as is everything done by men without hope, 'desperantibus', and Cicero declared that 'it would be utterly intolerable for slaves if some hope of liberty were not held out to them'.[109] But even if manumission may represent the ultimate goal, the mere possibility of freedom would probably have sufficed to encourage many slaves. In Greece, where manumission

---

[107] On the strict limitations on manumission in the United States see Lewis (2004) 152, 165. In his foreword to Watson (1987) x–xi, A. L. Higginbotham noted that in the American South slaves were kept away from positions of responsibility and competence, which of course also would have reduced the need for manumission as an incentive. The two factors would therefore have been mutually reinforcing.

[108] In Watson's model (1980), the distinction went beyond the mere observation of different manumission practices, since he linked the absorption or non-absorption of slaves into society to differences in the role played by land and people/labour in the property regimes of these societies.

[109] *NH* 18.36. Cic. *Rab.Perd.* 15: 'servi, si libertatis spem propositam non haberent, ferre nullo modo possent'.

appears to have been much rarer than in Rome, Aristotle also recommended that all slaves be given the prospect of freedom.[110]

The importance of incentives is beyond dispute, but manumission was not the only means of encouraging slaves.[111] Modern scholarship has focused so strongly on the reward of freedom as the single most important incentive that it has come to define different types of slavery along the axes of 'effort' and 'care' and 'open' and 'closed'. But all systems of slave labour – perhaps apart from mining and other extreme forms of physical exploitation – would have relied on some combination of 'stick and carrot'. Freedom was obviously a very effective incentive, but in certain situations – or within some slave systems – where for various reasons (economic, practical, or ideological) this was not considered acceptable other ways of organising slave labour would have evolved. In Greece, for example, we find rich and privileged slaves living and working away from their master's home.[112]

Slaves could also be encouraged through a range of alternative incentives, including humane treatment and personal benefits, training, and education, which would lead to more responsible roles within the household. These in turn would be accompanied by the right to *peculium*, *vicarii*, and a better lifestyle. Some might be given more independent economic roles in charge of investments or production units. A central incentive was linked to marriage and child rearing, which required the master's permission. The agrarian writers advised landowners to treat their slaves with consideration, praise their good work, and give them individual benefits. The bailiff, *vilicus*, was to be particularly encouraged, but none of the writers considered the possibility of freeing him – or any other rural slave. Varro described the various rewards for slaves, including material favours, exemption from certain types of work, and permission to graze cattle of their own, i.e. hold a *peculium*. Columella discussed similar means of encouraging slaves but also noted that *vilici* should not be too young – recommending an age of 35 to 65 – again without mentioning the prospect of manumission.[113]

Manumission was therefore not the only form of incentive available, and it would be a mistake to assume that without this level of manumission the slave economy would have collapsed. In most slave societies manumission has been relatively limited simply because of its consequences. Release from

---

[110] *Pol.* 1330a 31–3; cf. Ps.-Arist. *Oecon.* 1.5.6 (1344b 15). Klees (1998) 317–18.

[111] Shaw (1998) 71 n.108, noted that the rational motives suggested by Hopkins 'ought also to have moved economically rational calculators in the Greek polis to manumit their slaves in the same way, which seems not to have been the case'.

[112] Cohen (2000) 130–54; Fisher (2008).   [113] Varro *Rust.* 1.17.5–7; Colum. *Rust.* 1.8.15, 18; 11.1.3.

servitude is in the nature of things the most radical type of reward. Therefore it naturally forms the conclusion to a process of gradual promotion, being the ultimate prize for a lifetime of toil. It was, moreover, essentially a financial transaction, for, as George observed, 'the act of freeing a slave meant giving away a piece of property'.[114] The question is therefore why so many Roman slave owners decided to do just that.

From a wider economic perspective manumission may appear perfectly rational, but it must have made sense also on an individual level. When deciding to part with some of their property, slave owners must have perceived a distinct personal advantage. There was no moral imperative urging owners to free their slaves and no condemnation of 'stingy' masters who refused. Nor was manumission so common that it can be regarded as a matter of routine. It was in each case a conscious choice, which had the effect of reducing the estate. Attempts to understand the reasoning that informed this decision must involve a consideration of the slave's role *after* manumission, since we can only begin to understand the motivation behind a given action when we have an idea of the anticipated consequences. And this is precisely where Roman manumission had unique features which compensated the owner for his loss.

The Romans insisted on a lasting formal bond between the former master and slave, which has few direct parallels in other slave societies and seems to reflect a distinctly Roman conceptualisation of the manumission process.[115] The root of this bond was the 'beneficium', which imposed a strong moral obligation on the recipient. As Publilius Syrus noted, 'to accept a favour is to sell one's freedom', and freedmen received the greatest favour of all, namely a whole new life as free persons with recognised personal rights.[116] The position of freedmen was therefore always regarded as one of dependency, the irony being that by accepting freedom they also

---

[114] George (2006) 19 n.3.

[115] Zelnick-Abramovitz (2005) argued at length that in Greece one type of freedmen, *apeleutheroi*, whom she distinguished sharply from *exeleutheroi*, remained tied to their former owner and were obliged to provide services long after their manumission. The theory has several weaknesses. The terminological argument is hardly credible since the two terms often seem to have been used interchangeably; cf. Kamen (2005). The continued services performed by many Greek freedmen may be best understood in terms of conditional freedom and *paramonê* contracts, which allowed Greek owners to circumscribe the slave's freedom very considerably. Certainly there seems to be no basis for assuming an enduring relationship between former owner and freedman comparable to that which existed in Rome. Cf. below pp. 168–9. As noted above, the closest parallels to the Roman system are probably to be found in the Islamic world; cf. Forand (1971) and Marmon (1999).

[116] *Sent.* B5 (48): 'Beneficium accipere libertatem est vendere.' The obligations imposed on a freedman could, hyperbolically, be described as 'servitudo', Ps.-Quint. *Decl.Min.* 388.23, who also observed 'vindictam magno redimere solent', 'they usually pay a heavy price for their freedom'.

surrendered a major part of it.[117] The very gift of *libertas* made them subject to the lasting authority of their benefactors.[118]

Manumission was for that reason an ambiguous symbol of freedom, as reflected in the metaphorical use of the freedom cap, the *pilleus libertatis*. On the one hand, it could represent emancipation and release from captivity.[119] Most famously the *pilleus* was employed in this sense when Brutus put it on his coins in 42.[120] And after Nero's death the plebs allegedly celebrated their freedom by donning *pillei*.[121] On the other hand, the *pilleus* was also a symbol of dependency, moral obligation, and even submission. We are told that Q. Terentius Culleo, freed from Punic captivity by Scipio Africanus, wore the *pilleus* at the triumph of his liberator as a sign of his eternal debt.[122] Likewise, Prusias, the client king of Bithynia, donned the *pilleus libertatis* and declared himself the freedman of Rome.[123]

The ties between freedman and patron were, as we have seen, conceived of in pseudo-familial terms. The former slave became a son 'sine natura', while the owner took the place of the (absent) father. There were far-reaching consequences of this construction, which gave the freedman a new role *within* the household. His new gentilicial name automatically defined him as part of the patron's wider family unit, which in principle he never left. Viewed from this perspective, the release from servitude merely entailed the transition from one familial role to another. The freedman's integration into the household is illustrated by the phrases used in funerary inscriptions, which routinely list freedmen, freedwomen, and their descendants among those entitled to use the burial site, and generally make no distinction between freedmen with different degrees of involvement with the patron, or between those who stayed and those who left the household. The

---

[117] The crucial role of the *beneficium* in the *patronus–libertus* relationship is illustrated by a declamation attributed to Quintilian, which describes the terrors of a shipwreck where everybody naturally thinks of himself first, even 'the freedman so bound by the manumitter's benefaction', 'libertus tam beneficio obligatus manumittentis', *Decl.Min.* 259.9; cf. Cic. *Verr.* 2.1.124.

[118] Similarly, when Seneca said that a freedman can be the only free person in a crowd of *ingenui*, he explored the paradoxical contrast between inner, true freedom and external circumstances, *Ep.* 44.6. The point is that although a freedman cannot be really free he may still obtain inner freedom, just like a slave.

[119] *Pilleus/pilleum* as metaphor for manumission: e.g. Sen. *Ep.* 47.18; Mart. 2.68.4; Livy 24.32.9; Suet. *Tib.* 4.2; Petr. *Sat.* 41.1,7; Val. Max. 8.6.2; *Cod.Iust.* 7.2.10. *Pilleati* as synonymous with *liberti*, e.g. *Cod.Iust.* 7.6.1.5; Livy 24.16.18; cf. Koortbojian (2002). *Pillei* are also shown on epitaphs in Gaul; cf. Carroll (2006) 238. The idea that they might indicate the number of slaves freed *ex testamento* is unlikely.

[120] Dio 47.25.3; Plut. *Brut.* 40. Crawford (1974) nr. 508.3.   [121] Suet. *Nero* 57.

[122] Livy 30.45.5; 38.55.2; Ps.-Quintilian *Decl.Mai.* 9.20; Plut. *Apophth.Scip.Mai.* 7 (*Mor.* 196E); Dio 17.86; cf. Val. Max. 5.2.6.

[123] Polybius 30.18.3–4; Diod. 31.15.2; Livy 45.44.19; Dio 20.69 (Zonar. 9.24.7); App. *Mithr.* 2.4–5.

freedmen appear to constitute a single category, and what defined them as members of the *familia* was the shared *nomen*, whose continuance is often stressed in epitaphs and recorded wills.[124]

As argued in the opening chapters, the Romans dealt with the wider ideological concerns raised by the slave's entry into free society by 'constructing' an ideal form of 'safe' manumission which focused on the need for careful selection and continued patronal control and supervision. These concerns may possibly explain the stress placed on the freedman's obedience and willing subjection to authority. But within this discourse the freedman's *fides*, *frugalitas*, and *industria* were as important as his *obsequium* and these were all virtues that imply a continuous working relationship with the patron. Thus, it would make little sense to elevate trust, reliability, and hard work as particular libertine qualities unless the patrons were able to profit from them.

This image of the dependent freedman was not restricted to moralising or normative sources. Roman writers apparently regarded their presence in the house – or entourage – of their patron as completely unremarkable. For example, noting that Hortensius had opened up his house to Verres, Cicero stated that 'this is the man your freedmen, slaves and slave girls are devoted to', including *liberti* among the standard components of the household.[125] Similarly, Plutarch comments that Scipio did not allow any of his slaves or freedmen to take part in the looting of Carthage, while Appian describes how Mithridates killed Roman traders in Asia along with their children and women, their freedmen and slaves.[126]

The correspondence of Cicero presents a world where freedmen as a matter of course remain intimately involved with their patrons, the only exceptions being freedmen who had lost their patrons or been expelled from their households. They typically appear as agents and middlemen for their patrons, as illustrated by the letters of recommendation in which Cicero routinely asks for support for his client's interests as well as the

[124] For example, the phrase 'libertis libertabus posterisque eorum' occurs in around 400 dedicatory *tituli* in Rome. Johnston (1988) 100–3, noted that it was much more common to provide burial for all freedmen than for named individuals. On the *nomen* see also Champlin (1991) 135, 179–80. Cf. above p. 39.

[125] *Verr.* 2.3.8.

[126] *Apophth.Scip.Min.* (*Mor.* 200B.7); cf. Polybius, 33.9.5, who describes Popilius Laenas' staff as consisting of slaves and freedmen. Zelnick-Abramovitz (2005) 110, suggests *apeleutheroi* here means clients rather than freedmen, which seems unparalleled and implausible; cf. Plutarch's similar description of Cato's entourage, *Cato Min.* 9.4. App. *Mithr.* 23.91. In *BC* 4.398, he gives the same listing of the household, consisting of wives, sons, freedmen, slaves. In Ps-Quintilian's *Declamationes Maiores* freedmen invariably appear in conjunction with *servi/servuli*, 7.11; 17.11, 17; 18.7, 13; 19.3.

freedmen who tend to them.[127] Therefore, when a freedman strayed, the patron was almost automatically implicated. As we have seen, when Cicero's freedman Hilarus joined Antonius Hybrida in Macedonia, people accepted the claim that he was raising funds on behalf of his patron. The episode thus sums up the position of the Roman freedman: while in principle he could go his own way, it was naturally assumed that he represented his patron.[128] This expectation recurs in speeches such as *Pro Cluentio* and *Pro Sulla* where the actions of the freedmen are seen as incriminating for their patrons.[129] The patron–freedman link was considered so strong that it put Cicero in a tight spot during the Roscius trial, forcing him to declare that Chrysogonus, unlike other freedmen, could not blame his patron as the one responsible.[130] Ironically, Chrysogonus thereby becomes the only 'independent freedman' known from the works of Cicero.

The involvement of freedmen with their patrons was economic as well as social. Thus, Seneca noted that Cn. Lentulus (cos. 14 BCE) possessed 400 million sesterces before his freedmen reduced him to poverty, and in the *Satyricon* we are told that a man was ruined by his freedmen, in neither case with any explanation as to how they got access to their patrons' funds.[131] Continued residence in the patron's house was apparently not considered unusual either, judging from the evidence of Martial and other writers.[132] When describing his Laurentine villa, the younger Pliny mentions in passing the section of the house used by his slaves and freedmen, and Tacitus' comments that Otho's 'intimi libertorum servorumque' had more licence than in private houses, implying that these were also full of freedmen.[133] Such evidence is largely incidental, however, and Roman writers rarely discuss where freedmen live. The issue only comes to the fore when relations become strained or break down entirely. According to Tacitus, the only

---

[127] E.g. *Fam.* 13.14, 21, 23, 33, 70.   [128] *Att.* 1.12.2. Treggiari (1969a) 256–7.

[129] *Cluent.* 61. In *Sulla* 55, P. Sulla's involvement in the Catilinarian conspiracy was apparently suggested by games given at Naples, of which his freedman had been in charge. Cf. *Cluent.* 49, where a conviction of the freedman Scamander is seen as implicating and endangering his patron C. Fabricius.

[130] *Rosc.Am.* 130.

[131] *Ben.* 2.27.1; *Sat.* 38.12: 'sed liberti scelerati, qui omnia ad se fecerunt'. Likewise Rawson (1993) 224, suggested that the pretend freedman in Plautus' *Curculio* acted 'in order to appear a loyal and reliable agent of his supposed master'.

[132] E.g. 7.62; 11.39. Tac. *Ann.* 2.31. Pliny, *Ep.* 7.27.12, mentions freedmen sleeping in his house. Quint. *Inst.Or.* 6.3.84, based on Cicero, also implied that a freedman lived with his patron. D. 7.8.2.1, 6 (Ulpian) notes that rights of habitation extend to one's close relatives, slaves, and freedmen. Fabre (1981) 132ff, argued that freedmen were legally required to stay with their patrons, at least under the republic. This is unlikely, however, and certainly under the empire there was no such obligation; cf. e.g. *Cod.Iust.* 6.3.13; Waldstein (1986) 84–6, and Watson (1987) 40.

[133] *Ep.* 2.17.9; *Hist.* 1.22.

remedy available for a patron suffering *liberti ingrati* was to send them away, the underlying assumption being that they lived under the patron's roof and could be punished by relegation.[134] In a similar vein, we learn from Pliny of Sabinianus, who had forgiven his errant but repentant freedman and taken him back into his house.[135] In a highly rhetorical passage Tacitus discussed what he claimed to be a new practice of avoiding arrest and punishment by grasping an object with the emperor's image.[136] Now, Tacitus declared, masters and patrons lived in fear of their slaves and freedmen, having to put up with abuse and violence. Again the implication is that the freedmen in question stayed in the patron's house where they traditionally would have been subject to his authority. The issue became most acute when the patron was killed in his own home. Thus, after the death – possibly murder – of the consul Afranius Dexter the senate discussed what to do with the freedmen. Should they be acquitted, banished, or executed?[137]

There is further evidence to support this interpretation of Roman manumission, historical as well as epigraphic. As we have seen, slaves were allegedly freed in order to entitle them to free grain and public *congiaria*. Irrespective of the actual scale on which it happened – 'a flood of manumissions', according to Brunt – the fact that it was considered rational to free slaves for that purpose is itself significant.[138] Since the aim was to let the state assume some of the cost of feeding the *familia*, the former slave must have been expected to remain in the household.[139]

The evidence for slaves being freed relatively early would also suggest continuity of service. Alföldy argued on epigraphic grounds that most of them were freed below the age of 30.[140] Age indications in epitaphs are, as noted, an unreliable guide to Roman demography, but even if the material is seriously skewed by culturally specific patterns of commemoration, we are still left with a very considerable number of young freedmen.[141] The evidence from the large familial *columbaria* is also important in this context,

---

[134] *Ann.* 13.26. In the *Digest* relegation also features as punishment of a freedman who as tutor of the patron's daughter married her off to his own son, 23.2.64 (Callistratus).

[135] *Ep.* 9.21, 24.   [136] *Ann.* 3.36.

[137] *Ep.* 8.14.12–26. Tacitus mentions a proposal to banish from Italy the freedmen who had lived in the house of the murdered Pedanius Secundus, *Ann.* 14.45. The question was eventually resolved by Trajan, who prescribed that also slaves freed during the master's lifetime should be examined under the *SC Silanianum*, D. 29.5.10.1 (Paul).

[138] Dion. Hal. 4.24.5; Dio 39.24.1; Suet. *Aug.* 42.2: on manumission for *congiaria*; Brunt (1971a) 380.

[139] It has been speculated that masters took the opportunity to off-load old and infirm slaves, but members of that category would probably have been abandoned rather than freed.

[140] Alföldy (1986a); followed by Weaver (1990).

[141] It could also be argued that Augustus' age for formal manumission at 30 would make little sense if it was exceptional for slaves to be freed below that age.

since it allows us to compare the ages of slaves and freedmen within the same households. There is no obvious reason why age indications should differ significantly between the two categories, although we might expect some over-representation of freed children and very young freedmen. The *Monumentum Statiliorum* provides the largest sample, and the figures suggest that relatively early manumission of slaves still in their twenties and thirties was not uncommon.[142] At that age the freedmen had a considerable portion of their lives before them, which would make manumission economically irrational unless continuity of service was implied. If it terminated their working relationship, we would logically expect a much older age profile. Moreover, the simple fact that so many freedmen are represented in the familial burial site shows that most of them never left the household, as indeed implied by the domestic job titles which many of them carried.

The widespread use of *vicarii*, 'under-slaves', is one of the most striking features of this material. A considerable proportion of the household appears to have been owned not by the aristocratic family but by other slaves, *ordinarii*, to whose *peculium* they belonged. This structure served as a means of delegating tasks and responsibilities, as well as providing an incentive for slaves to improve their position by acquiring slaves of their own, potentially including a spouse. The Statilian inscriptions show that even slaves with extensive holdings of *vicarii* would be freed while retaining their slaves. The familial context of the burial as well as their job titles also indicate that these former under-slaves stayed in the aristocratic household along with their owners. Again, the expectation of continuity seems to have been implicit in the process of manumission; the freeing of senior slaves with large holdings of *vicarii* would otherwise have entailed the loss not only of important staff members but also of the sizeable sections of the household they controlled.

It follows from these considerations that manumission in Rome may have had consequences that differed from those in most other slave societies, where a clean break generally could be envisaged, even if it was not

---

[142] Figures from the *Monumentum Statiliorum*:

Age	Slaves	Freed	%
11–20	18	7	28
21–30	10	8	44
31–40	8	7	46

always realised in practice.[143] As such this provides an important clue to understanding its remarkable popularity, since the loss of labour, normally associated with manumission, seems not to have occurred in Rome. If manumission merely converted slave labour into free labour, it became part of a different system of rewards – one where manumission did not mark the end of a process but represented a point on a broad continuum of incentives that covered the entire working life of the slave/freedman.

The apparent expectation of continuity raises the question how this was achieved in practice and puts the focus on the ties which bound the freedman to his patron. The employer's authority was based no longer on *dominica potestas* but on a much weaker patronal authority, and while the patron could punish certain misdemeanours such as theft he could not force a freedman to stay, let alone to work hard and diligently. The change in status therefore required new incentives and forms of control to enhance performance and ensure loyalty. At one level this issue was dealt with through the imposition of moral obligations and the creation of a distinct social role for freedmen, which stressed their twin duty of obedience and industry. But alongside these attempts at social conditioning we also find powerful economic and social factors that enabled patrons to retain and benefit from their services.

The most fundamental degree of dependency came from the fact that many relatives of freedmen, including spouses, parents, and children, would have remained in slavery. Since manumission was individual and selective, many freedmen, especially *vernae*, are likely to have had family members who were still enslaved.[144] The evidence from the aristocratic *columbaria* suggests that 40 per cent of marriages within the *familia* were between slaves and freed, while 45 per cent of freed parents had enslaved children.[145] Such disparities of status were not necessarily a transitional phenomenon, as indicated by the examples of freedmen inheriting their *contubernales* and children, which implied they had to wait until the owner died.[146] A

---

[143] See e.g. Karasch (1987) 263. In Rio freedmen were allowed to live independently and keep their earnings, as reflected in the existence of conditional manumission which obliged them to serve the patron until his or her death; cf. Queirós Mattoso (1986) 163. Some freed persons, however, would remain as dependent clients out of sheer necessity. Some freedwomen continued to work for their old masters, who could hire them out.

[144] Roth (2005) 282, suggested in the context of slaves freed for the dole, that they might have been expected to feed dependants still in slavery, which might have kept them attached to their patron's household.

[145] See Mouritsen (forthcoming). The epigraphic evidence studied by Rawson (1966) also suggested that 'mixed' families were very common.

[146] *Sat.* 71.2; D. 31.88.12; 32.37.7; 32.41.2; 34.1.20 pr. (Scaev.); cf. Bürge (1988) 324. D. 33.7.12.7 (Ulpian) refers to family units on farms.

freedman might try to buy the freedom of relatives but owners were under no obligation, moral or legal, to accept the offer; indeed they could threaten to sell family members of a freedman who caused trouble, thus providing a powerful incentive to conform.

In addition there was basic economic dependency. Epictetus famously described the plight of the newly freed slave, who had to fend for himself.[147] The passage is part of a Stoic argument about the futility of seeking true freedom outside oneself, but it nevertheless plays on the conventional view that without support a freedman's lot was precarious, a theme that also recurs in Roman comedy. For example, in Plautus' *Epidicus* a slave is reluctant to accept the offer of freedom, complaining that 'A new freedman needs something to eat'; in *Menaechmi* the former slave declares 'But I need a better start, so that I'll stay free forever'; and in *Rudens* the new freedman immediately asks for payment for his work.[148]

The misgivings about manumission attributed to Plautine slaves reflect the vulnerability of freedmen without *familia* or *patrimonium*.[149] As such, it was a timeless complaint which may go back to the Greek originals, but the support the freedman generally receives is likely to be a specifically Roman feature. Thus, Epidicus finally overcame his misgivings and accepted his freedom when his patron had promised to provide food. Similarly in *Menaechmi* the concerned Messenio becomes an auctioneer for his patron, and in Terence's *Adelphi* the freedman Syrus is loaned money to set up house.[150] Roman patrons tended to support those they had decided to free. Thus, while the uncertain life of the freed slave may be a familiar theme, we hardly ever hear of poor freedmen, and that was probably because they were rarely left to fend for themselves.[151] Patrons may have been legally obliged to

---

[147] *Diss.* 4.1.33–7.

[148] *Epidic.* 721–30, 726: 'novo liberto opus est quod pappet'; *Men.* 1149: 'Sed melior est opus auspicio, ut liber perpetuo siem'; *Rud.* 1218–22. Rawson (1993) 225, suggested that the *Menaechmi* might refer to the risk of falling into debt.

[149] Plaut. *Cas.* 293, the slave Chalinus rejects the offer of freedom with the words: 'Liber si sim, meo periclo vivam; nunc vivo tuo', 'If I were free, I should have to live at my own cost: as it is, I live at yours.' The passage has been taken as indicative of the precarious life of the freedman who might prefer to remain a slave, e.g. Brockmeyer (1979) 158. But the context is important since the master wanted to get rid of him in order to marry off a slave girl to another slave. It is therefore a highly anomalous situation, in which the freedman effectively will be cast out of the household. The slave's refusal is also determined by the prospect of giving up the woman he hopes to marry. Nevertheless, the excuse for rejecting freedom, which in this case meant relegation from the *familia*, was real enough.

[150] *Adelph.* 980–4.

[151] By contrast, the plight of the freedman is a recurring theme in descriptions of later slave societies, where manumission in effect could mean abandonment. Karasch (1987) 362–3, describes how most freedpersons in Rio faced poverty after manumission, many being so poor they turned to crime.

assist a freedman in need, but in practice it would often have been difficult to enforce, especially if the freedman was old, poor, or ill. The support the freedmen received would in effect have remained discretionary, and economic dependency – and the risk of abandonment – is therefore likely to have been a major factor binding a freedman to his patron's household.

Alongside these 'pain' incentives, the system also offered positive rewards for freedmen who kept up their good work. Thus, Roman manumission was probably unique in the way it opened up opportunities for further advancement and social promotion. The patron's support might take the form of financial investments and other immediate benefits, which will be discussed in greater detail in the next chapter. But it could also be deferred and held out as a promise of future support extending beyond the patron's lifetime. Legacies and (small) shares of the estate appear to have been far more common than sometimes assumed.[152] Indeed it could be argued that an obligation to take care of the freedman, also after the patron's death, may have been implicit in the Roman construction of manumission, which recognised the freedman's status as a dependent member of the extended *familia* for whom the *pater familias* assumed a personal responsibility.[153]

The most famous example remains the younger Pliny's testamentary bequest of close to 2 million sesterces in support of a hundred freedmen, presumably freed testamentarily.[154] The document is unique, although legal sources suggest that legacies of this kind may not have been uncommon.[155] The jurists present bequests to freedmen as entirely normal, often using them to illustrate legal issues unrelated to the status of the beneficiaries.[156] The nature and content of the legacies varied, but the underlying concern was to provide – basic – material security after the patron's death.[157] Thus we frequently find references to bequests of food, clothing, habitation,

---

[152] Veyne (1997) 86, rightly observed: 'Manumitted slaves were rarely turned out to face life without some resources.'

[153] The duty of care is implied in Plaut. *Curc.* 547–8, where someone is told that it is better not to have any freedmen at all rather than having them and not looking after them. Cf. the comment by Donatus on Terence, *Adelph.* 979, 5.9.22.2: 'Siquidem tu tuum officium facies. Hoc est patroni, ut libertum non deseras sed alas manumissum.'

[154] We know about Pliny's bequest to his freedmen only because of the unusual inscription, *CIL* 5.5262, which lists all his benefactions to the city of Comum (the provision for the *liberti* is included because the fund set aside for them eventually would pass to the community); Eck (2001). At Gytheion the rich local benefactress Faenia Aromation entrusted the future care of her domestic slaves and her freedmen and women to the city and the council; Rizakis (2005) 239.

[155] Boyer (1965) 342–55; Champlin (1991) 131–6.

[156] E.g. D. 32.35.2 (Scaevola), which is concerned with the location of a farm.

[157] A study of the sometimes modest sums legated led Frier (1993) 229, to conclude that 'the social norm was evidently to furnish former dependents with a decent moiety, enough to escape from abject poverty, but not so much that beneficiaries were tempted to aspire above their station'.

in short *alimenta*, i.e. what is needed to sustain life. The *Digest* contains an entire section on legacies of 'alimenta vel cibaria', almost all relating to freedmen.[158] The cases discussed often reveal concerns about lodging of freedmen and try to minimise the possible disruptions caused by the patron's death. Old and infirm freedmen could, for example, be allowed to stay in the places they now occupied.[159] The emphasis on continuity recurs in a case where the freedmen were left what they had been receiving in the testator's lifetime, including habitation for those who lived with the patron until he died.[160] Financial protection of freedmen could also be achieved through annuities, which are well documented in the *Digest*. Sometimes a sum of money was left as a bequest, but often a specific country estate was handed over to provide for the freedmen.[161] Urban real estate could also serve this function, as illustrated by the bequest of an *insula* to freedmen and freedwomen.[162]

The aim of these legacies was to ensure continuity and security for dependent staff who might otherwise find themselves in economic trouble when their patron died. What is striking about these examples is the fact that the freedmen are treated as a single body, all benefiting equally from the legacy. No differentiation is made between freedmen closely involved with the patron and those who had become 'independent'. In that respect they reflect the same 'generic' approach to the freedmen found in epigraphic references to tombs and burial rights. Moreover, what defined them as a collective seems again to have been the *nomen*, which embodied their common identity and background. For example, the *Digest* records a *domus*

---

[158] D. 34.1; cf. 35.3.3.4 (Ulpian): on *alimenta* and *vestiaria* to freedmen. Peachin (1994) discusses a complex dispute, D. 34.1.3 (Ulpian), involving *alimenta* for freedmen who had been divided between several different heirs, and the general policy of avoiding freedmen having to 'apply for small measures of aliment from individual heirs', 'ne a singulis heredibus minutatim alimenta petentes distringantur'.

[159] D. 33.2.33.2 (Scaevola); cf. 33.2.18 (Modestinus). The 'Testamentum Dasumii' also bequeathed land to support freedmen with no right to sell or pledge, *CIL* 6.10229 lines 93–5.

[160] D. 33.2.33.1 (Scaevola); 33.1.10.3 (Papinian): freedmen given what they received during testator's lifetime, including right of habitation; 33.2.34 pr. (Scaevola): bequest of farm to freedmen (where patron wished to be buried), together with right of habitation in *domus* (but not to be passed on and after their death the estate would go to the city); 32.41.1 (Scaevola): *domus* left to freedmen.

[161] E.g. D. 31.88.11 (Scaevola); 33.1.9 (Papinian): farm left as pledge for annual legacies to freedmen; 31.24 (Ulpian): bequest to freedmen; 31.29 pr. (Celsus): legacy to freedman; 31.77.13 (Papinian): *praedia* left to freedmen; 31.77.27: estate left to freedmen on condition it stays with *familia libertorum*; 31.79: bequest of land to freedmen; 31.87.2 (Paul): bequest of farm to freedmen; 31.88.9 (Scaevola): bequest of part of farm to freedmen, if natural heirs predecease the testator; 31.88.12: bequest of farm to freedmen freed in will; 31.89.6: legacies to freedmen; 32.93.2: bequest of land to freedmen.

[162] D. 31.88.14 (Scaevola). There are also epigraphic examples of this practice, e.g. *CIL* 6.9681, mentioning 'taberna et hortulum' left to freedmen.

left to the freedmen on condition that 'it does not leave the nomen', 'ne de nomine exeat', a phrase that recurs several times.[163]

Individual freedmen could also be provided with legacies, sometimes in addition to collective legacies benefiting all the freedmen. They come in a variety of different forms, including specific properties, sums of money, and annuities. In some cases named freedmen were given annuities or the income, usufruct, from a certain estate.[164] In other instances not just the income from a farm but the farm itself was bequeathed.[165] More complicated arrangements also occur, such as the case where a farm was left to the freedmen and their descendants, who had to pay an annual amount to the heir, or the farm which was legated to a freedman with a fideicommissary obligation to pay an annual amount.[166] Again, the importance of the shared *nomen* is occasionally stressed. For example, two freedmen became heirs on condition that the estate would not leave the *nomen*, and fifteen named *liberti* received a plot of land, *praediolum*, and a *taberna* as long as their shares were not passed on to outsiders.[167] The same result could be achieved by stipulating that a legacy to a freedman would later revert to the children of the testator.[168]

Economic aid for favoured freedmen appears to have been considered the norm, and it is therefore not surprising to find that Cicero junior apologised for not having assisted Tiro in purchasing his country house and assured him of future support.[169] The case illustrates how provisions for the freedman's future could be made already during the patron's lifetime, and we know that the younger Pliny donated a farm worth 100,000 HS to

---

[163] D. 35.1.108 (Scaevola); cf. 31.77.28 (Papinian); 31.88.6 (Scaevola).

[164] 33.1.21 pr. (Scaevola): legacy to freedman of 1/50 of the income from estates; 33.1.21.4: freed *alumnus* receiving a fixed sum, administered until he was 25; 33.2.32 pr.: bequest of usufruct of farm to a slave who also received freedom; 33.7.3 (Papinian): legacy of a *fundus instructus* to freedmen, which was to be passed on to survivors after their death; D. 35.2.25.1 (Scaevola): annual legacy to freedman; 35.3.3.4 (Ulpian): legacy of ten gold pieces per annum to freedwoman (separate from legacy of *alimenta* and *vestiaria* to the freedmen). Usufruct was also bequeathed in the Ostian inscription published by Calza (1939), cf. p. 222.

[165] D. 32.35.2 (Scaevola): bequest to named freedmen of two farms and a shop; 32.41.3: bequest of farm to two freedpersons; 33.2.35: bequest of farm to two freedmen after five years; 33.7.20.1: legacy of a farm to a freedman; 33.7.20.6: bequest of farm to freedwoman.

[166] D. 33.1.18 pr. (Scaevola); 33.1.21.1 (Scaevola). Cf. Plin. *Ep.* 4.10, on a slave freed testamentarily with legacy. Other legacies to freedmen appear in D. 34.3.31.1 (Scaevola); 34.4.26 (Paul); 35.1.33.2 (Marcian).

[167] D. 32.38.1 (Scaevola); 32.38.5; cf. 32.94 (Valens): bequest of farm to three of his freedmen, with instructions that it should not leave testator's name.

[168] D. 32.39 pr. (Scaevola).

[169] *Fam.* 16.21.7: 'me tum tibi defuisse aeque ac tu doleo, sed noli dubitare, mi Tiro, quin te sublevaturus sim'.

his *nutrix*.[170] Many of the recorded legacies or inheritances were attached
to testamentary manumission, however, the obvious reason being that an
orcinus otherwise would face a highly uncertain future.[171] For example, a
blacksmith's shop was left to Lucius Eutychus (most likely a freedman) and
Pamphilus, who was to be freed, 'so that they can carry on the business'.[172]
The comment reflects the fact that without further support manumission
would be a mixed blessing, especially if the household was broken up
between external heirs. While the slaves would be passed on to new owners,
the freedmen had to rely on the 'duty of care' of their former master.

The legal sources contain numerous examples of slaves freed in wills
who received additional support. Thus, in one case the freedman was
left a farm, and in another he was given the usufruct of a farm.[173] The
jurist Paul records a case of a beneficiary of testamentary manumission
who received a conditional legacy that also included his *contubernalis*, and
Ulpian mentions a woman freed testamentarily who received an inheritance
as well as her daughter with fideicommissary instructions to free her.[174]
Elsewhere a slave was freed with a bequest of land, plus his *peculium* and
the arrears from the tenants, while another will gave instructions to free a
slave after ten years and provide an annual legacy for him thereafter.[175]

These bequests were not always made out of pure altruism, some being
conditional on future services rendered to the testator's relatives. Thus, in
some cases they are made dependent on the freedman staying with the
patron's children. One will left a legacy of *alimenta* of 100 denarii each per

---

[170] *Ep.* 6.3. On a much grander scale, Nero gave his favourite Doryphorus 10 million sesterces, Dio 61.5.4.
[171] Freedmen feature as heirs far more rarely. A few are mentioned in the literary sources, usually as moral exempla, but there are also some casual references, e.g. Cicero's passing comment on a freed co-heir. Usually freedmen only became part-heirs, sometimes to small fractions of the estate. E.g. D. 34.4.30.1 (Scaevola): a freedwoman heir to a twelfth of estate; 33.7.27.3: freedman part-heir, receiving farm as *praelegatum* (i.e. in addition to his share of estate); 39.5.35 pr.: freedman left as heir to two-thirds of estate; 40.7.2.3–4 (Ulpian): *statuliber* as heir to half of the estate. Plin. *Ep.* 7.6.8–10: freedmen as co-heirs. Cf. below pp. 240–2.
[172] 31.88.3 (Scaevola). Likewise, in 33.7.7, a *taberna* with *cenaculum* was left to a slave freed by will together with merchandise, *instrumenta*, and furniture. In addition he received a fully equipped *horreum vinarium*, and 'the managers whom he had been accustomed to keep with him', which suggests he was already running the business.
[173] D. 34.3.28.7 (Scaevola); 33.2.36 pr. Buckland (1908) 470–4; Boyer (1965) 360–3; cf. 10.2.39.2 (Scaevola): testator orders 15-year-old slave to be freed when reaching 30 and to receive annuity for food and clothing; 31.11 pr. (Pomponius): manumission with legacy, cf. 31.14 pr. (Paul); 31.31 (Modestinus); 31.37 (Javolenus); 31.84 (Paul); 32.29.4 (Labeo): bequest of farm to slaves to be freed in will; 34.5.29 (Scaevola): testamentary manumission with legacy, suspended until they reach 30; 35.1.47 (Marcellus): testamentary manumission with legacy or inheritance; 35.1.82 (Callistratus): bequest of a *fundus*; 40.4.19 (Julian); 40.4.26 (Marcian): testamentary manumissions with bequests.
[174] D. 35.1.81 pr. (Paul); 36.1.11.2 (Ulpian). [175] D. 32.97 (Paul); 33.1.16.

month and clothing to named freedmen on condition that they stay with
the testator's son, while in another a monthly or annual legacy was left to
a freedman 'so long as he conducts the affairs of the patron's daughter'.[176]

The prospect of financial security, potentially even a windfall if the
freedman struck it lucky, must have offered a strong incentive for freedmen to remain in service and seek continued patronal favour. It also gave
the patrons a powerful instrument of control, allowing them to dispense
not just rewards but also punishment long after they had surrendered ownership. The *Digest* contains several examples of freedmen excluded from
earlier testamentary provisions. In one case it happened because he was
'pessimum', in another owing to *ingratia*.[177] Elsewhere a freedman was
deprived of a legacy on grounds of *indignitas*, having denounced his late
patron for criminality, and two freedpersons, originally appointed heirs,
one of whom 'deserved nothing of me', were later disinherited and left only
jars of wine.[178] The 'Testamentum Dasumii' specifically barred a certain
Hymnus, who was most undeserving, from testamentary manumission,
and it also instructed the heirs to keep Menecrates and Paederos in their
present work.[179]

In another case where money had been left for the maintenance of freedmen, it was not clear whether two freedmen whom the patron had dismissed
from his house and stopped providing food for were also included.[180] The
verdict was negative, but the case illustrates the importance of maintenance
and legacies in tying a freedman to the *familia*. What also emerges is the
underlying assumption that those who lived in their patron's house were the
favoured freedmen, while those sent away were dismissed as a punishment
– rather than given their 'independence'. This notion of punitive relegation
from the *familia* recurs in epitaphs, where some freedmen occasionally are
singled out and excluded from the familial burial site. At Ostia an inscription mentions as beneficiaries 'my other freedmen and freedwomen, apart
from those I will exclude in my will', and an epitaph from Portus bars those
'who leave me while I am alive'.[181]

---

[176] D. 35.1.84 (Paul); D. 35.1.101.4 (Papinian). D. 35.1.72: bequest to freedman on condition that
he does not desert the patron's children; 35.1.31 (Africanus): on testamentary manumission with
conditional legacy attached (depending on marriage); 35.1.86 (Maecian): conditional testamentary
manumission with legacy; 35.1.66 (Modestinus): a *statuliber* was left a trust conditionally; 40.7.21
(Pomponius): legacy to freedman freed conditionally.
[177] D. 34.4.13 (Marcian); 34.4.29 (Paul).   [178] D. 34.9.1 (Marcian); 32.37.2 (Scaevola).
[179] *CIL* 6.10229 lines 80–3, 92.   [180] D. 31.88.11 (Scaevola).
[181] *CIL* 14.1437: 'ceteris libertis libertabusque meis omnibus posterisque, praeter quos testamento meo
praeteriero'; Thylander (1952) A 168: 'preter eas que me vivam relinquerunt [*sic*]'; cf. A 222 (excluding
two named freedmen). Similarly, the unpublished inscription of C. Voltidius Felicissimus, which

While there evidently were powerful economic incentives for the freed-man to stay with his patron, we should not overlook the psychological and emotional ties that bound him to the *familia*. The household was also a place of belonging inhabited by relatives and sometimes life-long friends of the freedman. The notion of the *familia* as a *res publica*, a mini-community that provided a social identity for its members, was actively fostered by the owners, as illustrated by comments by Pliny and Seneca.[182] For many slaves and freedmen the household represented the world and the people they knew, and their concern to maintain the connection, even into the next generation, is reflected in the striking requests laid down in some recorded wills that daughters marry 'within the *familia*'.[183]

This complex web of economic and personal ties, along with strong moral pressure, made up for the patron's limited legal authority over the freedman, who received a new but equally well-defined role within the household. We may also envisage a degree of genuine paternalism in the *patronus–libertus* relationship, which seems to have been endowed with an element of reciprocity. The sources reveal a widespread expectation that continued loyal service would be repaid by economic support and future security. The unique bond between freedman and patron created by the gift of freedom thus emerges as one of the defining characteristics of Roman manumission and it is in this light we will now consider two aspects of Roman manumission which many historians have regarded as central to the institution: self-purchase and testamentary freeing.

PECULIUM AND THE PURCHASE OF FREEDOM

Payment in return for freedom is often seen as an essential feature of Roman manumission. The idea was most fully developed by Hopkins, who observed that 'Roman slaves, frequently, even customarily in my view, paid substantial sums for their freedom.' The fact that Roman slaves could accumulate funds was seen as key to the whole system. 'Slaves could save out of their earnings. And eventually they could use their savings to buy their freedom.' The result was that, 'For skilled slaves, chattel

---

stated that 'excepto Hilaro liberto meo abominando ne in hoc monimentum aditum habeat', Meiggs (1973) 223–4; *CIL* 6.11027: exclusion 'propter delicta sua'; 6.13732: 'excepta Secundina liberta impia adversus . . . patronum suum'. Cf. Gardner (1993) 32–3; Carroll (2006) 103.

[182] Plin. *Ep.* 8.16.2: 'nam servis res publica et quasi civitas domus est'; Sen. *Ep.* 47.14: 'domum pusillam rem publicam esse iudicaverunt'.

[183] D. 27.2.4 (Julian); 32.27 pr. (Paul); 32.41.7 (Scaevola); 33.5.21 (Scaevola); 35.1.15 (Ulpian); 40.5.41.16 (Scaevola); cf. Bürge (1988).

slavery was effectively transformed into a medium-term labour "contract".'
Manumission on this view was acceptable to slave owners, 'partly because
the slave's purchase of freedom recapitalised his value and enabled the
master to replace an older slave with a younger'.[184] The idea that slaves
routinely paid for their freedom has become a standard feature of modern
discussions. Thus, Watson stated that: 'It was common for a master to
allow his slave to buy his freedom when he had saved up enough money to
do so.'[185] And in many broader studies of Roman society it has gained the
status of fact. For instance, a discussion of Pompeian art asserted – without
any supporting evidence – that 'the owners of the House of the Vettii were
former slaves, and wealthy ones at that. A. Vettius Restitutus and A. Vettius
Conviva were brothers who had been able to buy their freedom.'[186]

In this way, payment has been interpreted as part of an economically
rational model of Roman manumission whose remarkable scale it also helps
to explain.[187] Not only was the slave's *peculium* accumulated through hard
work and increased productivity, it also helped to pay for a replacement,
presumably a younger slave. From a simple cost–benefit perspective the
theory thus makes good sense,[188] and comparison with other slave societies
where self-purchase appears to have been common would prima facie
seem to add further credibility to the model. In Hellenistic and early
Roman Greece a large number of manumission inscriptions amply testify
to the practice of slaves buying their freedom. The largest bodies come
from Delphi and Thessaly, but other parts of Greece have yielded similar
evidence. Almost all the inscriptions mention the price paid as well as
other conditions imposed on the freed person. Likewise, in the Spanish

---

[184] Hopkins (1978) 118, 126. He also argued that the *vicesima libertatis* makes best sense if the slave
carried a definite price, 129 n.67. However, since many slaves clearly were freed gratis, they must
have been taxed on a notional sum. Estimated values of slaves also occur frequently throughout
the legal sources, e.g. D. 35.2.36–9; 40.5.31–2.

[185] Watson (1987) 19. Frank (1927) 215: 'Frugal and ambitious slaves, particularly the quick-witted
Orientals, could save enough in a few years to buy their freedom.' Weaver (1972) 95, suggested
there was an increasing obligation to recognise the 'slave's right to his peculium or savings, with the
primary purpose of buying his manumission', while Fabre (1981) 272, headed a section 'La liberté,
un don le plus souvent payant.' Cf. e.g. Dumont (1987) 66–7; Klees (2002) 117; Horsley (1998)
50; Kleijwegt (2002); Andreau (2004) 117; Temin (2004) 523; Bang (2008) 278. Bradley (1984a) 107
n.103, expressed doubt whether payment was as important as Hopkins suggested, but suggested,
in (1994) 164, that 'Gratuitous manumission cannot have been the norm.' Only Badian (1982) 168,
noted the lack of strong supporting evidence.

[186] Clarke (2003) 99.

[187] E.g. Alföldy (1986a) 311, who used payment to underpin his theory of near universal manumission.

[188] Although Badian (1982) 168, observed that 'payment of a price is no explanation of the practice
of enfranchisement: it is, at best, part of the problem. For if the master had not allowed the
accumulation of a *peculium*, he could in due course have collected the same amount (or, probably,
more) for himself without freeing the slave.'

and Portuguese colonies in America detailed manumission records were kept which demonstrate the frequency of self-purchase.[189] In Rio freed slaves received a 'letter of liberty', which would be entered into public registers, allowing a statistical breakdown of different manumission types. The most common form (39 per cent) was purchased freedom, normally paid for by the slaves themselves.[190] Nevertheless, Brazilian slaves had no legal entitlement to freedom, even after money had been handed over, and in this respect Brazil differed from the Spanish colonies in Latin America, where slaves had an informal but widely recognised right to buy their freedom at market rate. The state would provide some protection for slaves who offered their price in return for freedom, even if it rarely intervened directly.[191] In Cuba the distinct system of *coartación* existed, which was a formalised process by which the slave gradually paid off a fixed amount. During that period the slave held a special status, which he/she would maintain even if passed on to another owner.[192] The frequency of self-purchase in the Spanish colonies is illustrated by the figures for Buenos Aires, were 1,394 manumissions were recorded between 1776 and 1810, 63.3 per cent of which were purchased.[193] It meant there was a direct link between the earnings of slaves and the rate of manumission. In 1776 less than 0.4 per cent of the slaves were freed annually, a figure that rose to 1.3 per cent in 1810. During the same period the proportion of purchased manumissions also increased, reflecting a rise in slave incomes. In Louisiana, during the period of Spanish rule 1725–1803, purchased freedom accounted for 41.7 per cent of manumission in New Orleans.[194]

This evidence would seem to corroborate the notion of payment as a key factor in maintaining a high-frequency manumission regime, which was rendered economically viable only through the continuous transfer of slave funds used to pay for replacements. However, despite the economic logic and the strong comparative evidence, the theory of common payment in Rome raises a number of questions. Most crucially we must consider its

---

[189] Johnson (1979) 262, summarised manumission patterns in South America, cf. Bergad *et al.* (1995) 141 fig. 6.3.

[190] Few plantation owners freed slaves, and being sent to the plantations in effect meant losing the prospect of freedom, Karasch (1987) 344–5; Chalhoub (1989) 65. Lewis (2004) 169, noted that in Guadeloupe 'carpenters and masons secured their freedom at a rate more than ten times that of farm workers'.

[191] Johnson (1979) 261; Cole (2005) 1012–14. This contrasts sharply with Roman practice where no right to self-purchase existed. As Watson (1987) 43, emphasised, masters were under no obligation to allow slaves to buy their freedom.

[192] Bergad *et al.* (1995) 122–42.   [193] Johnson (1979) 277–9.

[194] Cole (2005) 1014, 1017. Here too the phenomenon was overwhelmingly urban, 81 per cent of purchased manumissions taking place in the cities.

effect on the freedman–patron relationship. As argued above, Roman manumission rested on the premise that the freedman would remain a member
of his patron's extended *familia*, making it part of a far more complex organisation of dependent labour which involved economic incentives, personal
dependency, and social conditioning. The question is how payment would
fit into such an intricate system.

Hopkins conceded that 'the Roman evidence for frequent self-purchase
of manumission is only circumstantial', and in support of the theory he
adduced its frequent appearance in the law codes and passing references
in literary sources, as well as Greek epigraphic evidence for self-purchase,
above all from Delphi.[195] In the following we will examine these three
bodies of evidence, beginning with the literary sources.[196] The two most
frequently quoted passages derive from Seneca and Virgil. In one of his
epistles Seneca says that 'The money which slaves have saved up by robbing
their own stomachs, they hand over as the price of liberty.'[197] The comment
is part of a philosophical argument about true freedom attainable only
through inner peace. Searching for external freedom is therefore futile,
Seneca argues, using the example of the slaves, even the lowest 'mancipia
condicionis extremae', who strive to throw off slavery. They hand over the
peculium they have accumulated by cheating their stomachs, but Seneca's
advice is not to cast glances at the strongbox since freedom cannot be
bought. In order to make this point the author paints an extreme – and
possibly unrealistic – scenario of abused and exploited slaves seeking an
unattainable freedom by all possible means, even offering money in return.

In Virgil's first *Eclogue* the old shepherd Tityrus says freedom came late
to him, after his beard had gone grey; long he had no hope of freedom or
thought for *peculium*, 'nec spes libertatis erat, nec cura peculi' (1.32), and
he did not make money from the sale of meat and cheese. While freedom
and *peculium* may seem to be paired, there is no explicit indication that
the latter would pay for the former, and as argued below (p. 178) other
interpretations are also possible. Further literary evidence includes Tacitus'
comment that Pedanius Secundus might have been killed by a slave whom
he had refused to free despite having agreed a price.[198] The elder Pliny also

---

[195] Hopkins (1978) 128.

[196] Epigraphic evidence is largely absent apart from the celebrated inscription from Asisium which
records a doctor who paid 50,000 HS for his freedom (*CIL* 11.5400). In Duncan-Jones' list of slave
prices in Rome and Italy, (1974) 349–50, only three out of twenty-eight refer to self-purchase, the
two other cases being D. 12.4.3.5 (Ulpian) and Petr. *Sat.* 57.6, for which see below p. 198.

[197] *Ep.* 80.4: 'Peculium suum, quod conparaverunt ventre fraudato, pro capite numerant.'

[198] *Ann.* 14.42: 'seu negata libertate, cui pretium pepigerat'. In Petr. *Sat.* 57.6, the freedman Hermeros
says he paid 1,000 denarii 'pro capite', but as Ehlers (Müller and Ehlers (1965) 460) observed, this

mentioned that rich stage actors often paid fortunes for their freedom.[199] Martial referred to a slave who had bought his freedom with all he possessed, while Dionysius of Halicarnassus claimed some slaves gained the money required through crime and prostitution.[200]

Given the supposed ubiquity of self-purchase, the instances recorded in the literary sources remain few. Moreover, they must also be set against a vast amount of evidence which either ignores payment or indicates that freedom normally was gratuitous and granted for personal merit only. Thus, nowhere in the surviving corpus of Cicero's writings do we find any hint that payment might be part of the manumission process; the premise is always that slaves earn their freedom through loyalty, hard work, and sheer good luck, and these qualifications recur throughout the literary evidence. For example, Phaedrus tells a story about a slave about to run away, complaining that 'I have earned my freedom, but I still serve in my old age', 'emerui libertatem, canus servio'.[201] In this story there is no mention of money or payment; the slave clearly thought he deserved freedom because of his hard work.[202] This point is made explicit in Suetonius' comment on L. Voltacilius Plotus, who was freed 'ob ingenium ac studium litterarum',

must be a reference to the *vicesima libertatis*. Thus, in the following paragraph the same freedman berates the insolent slave boy Giton, asking 'when did you pay the *vicesima*?', 'Quando vicesimam numerasti?', 58.2, referring back to his own payment just mentioned. Moreover, as an indication of his market value the sum of 4,000 HS is rather unimpressive, e.g. compared to the 50,000 HS at which Scissa's 'servo misello' was rated, *Sat.* 65.10. Hermeros was an educated and successful freedman with a large household and public honours. His account of his life is generally boastful, e.g. claiming royal descent, and an inflated value of 80,000 HS would therefore not be out of character.

[199] *HN* 7.128; cf. Axer (1979). The *pantomimus* Paris belonging to Nero's aunt Domitia paid for his freedom and later recovered the sum when he was awarded *ingenuitas* in court, D. 12.4.3.5 (Ulpian); cf. Tac. *Ann.* 13.27. Duncan-Jones (1974) 349–50, gives the figure as 10,000 HS, but Ulpian simply says he paid 'ten', which may be illustrative rather than a corruption of 'ten thousand'.

[200] Mart. 2.68; Dion. Hal. 4.24.1–6. In Suet. *Gramm.* 15, we are told that as a boy Lenaeus was stolen from Athens, escaped and returned to Greece, where he gained an education and offered the price of his liberty to his master, but received freedom gratis 'ob ingenium atque doctrinam'. The context is therefore Greek rather than Roman where, as we shall see, the practice of manumission differed significantly. Yarrow (2006) 43, doubts the story altogether.

[201] A 18.10 (Teubner).

[202] In a fragment of Varro's *Synephebus*, Nonius Marc. 156–7 (Müller), a slave desperate to be freed is advised first to offer something in return, before taking flight: 'verere, ne manu non mittat, cum tot Romae mendicari honestos audissemus? Dare possis; mittet; quod si non mittet, fugies, si me audies. Cum tempus revocat, ea praecox est fuga.' The offer of payment here represents the last option before absconding, suggesting we are not dealing with a normal manumission procedure. A similar impression is given by the fragmentary inscription from Narbo, *CIL* 12.5026, which mentions that 'pretio [obtin]uit quod prec[e n]on valuit' as part of a longer lament about his difficulty gaining freedom. Tacitus' suggestion that Pedanius Secundus might have been killed when an agreement about payment was reneged upon might also indicate that this represented a final desperate attempt to obtain freedom.

and Tacitus' advocate of re-enslavement of *liberti ingrati* who argued that
the freedman should keep his freedom by the same obedience, *obsequium*,
by which he had earned it.[203]

Roman comedy, especially Plautus, provides more references to payment
than any other literary genre. In the prologue to Plautus' *Poenulus* the
playwright asks the audience to keep the slaves out of the theatre and make
space for the free; if not, let them pay 'pro capite', and if they cannot
send them away.[204] According to Rawson this passage proved, 'if proof
were needed, that purchase of freedom by slaves was common'.[205] The
suggestion that slaves would buy their freedom to get a seat in the theatre is
obviously a joke, and the offer of money should be seen as part of this absurd
scenario, which also implies – counterfactually – that slaves could effect
their own manumission. In another scene a slave asks whether someone
could be induced to make him a present of 'talentum magnum' to buy
himself with, and in *Poenulus* the *advocati* had paid for their freedom.[206]
Likewise, in Plautus' *Pseudolus*, 224–9, the evil pimp tells a slave she will
for ever be counting the money for her freedom, and unless her friends pay
for her, she will get a lashing tomorrow. In *Rudens*, the slave Gripus believes
he has discovered a hidden treasure and declares he will offer the master
money for his freedom.[207] In *Stichus* a slave about to spend his money
on sex indicates that he is abandoning his *peculium* – 'Vapulat peculium,
actum est' – to which another comments: 'There goes his freedom', 'Fugit
hoc libertas caput', 747. While these passages demonstrate familiarity with
the practice of self-purchase, others are more ambiguous, because of either
textual problems or difficulties of interpretation. Thus, in *Poenulus* a good
slave expresses dismay at fellow slaves bought at a high price, who return
to their masters without their *peculium*.[208] Elsewhere a slave declares that

---

[203] *Rhet.* 3. Terence was likewise freed quickly 'ob ingenium et formam', Suet. *Poet. Ter.* 1. Similarly,
Lutatius Daphnis was bought for 700,000 HS and soon set free with no mention of payment, Suet.
Gramm. 3. Tac. *Ann.* 13.26. Similarly Cicero insisted that Milo had not freed his slaves because he
was afraid of their testimony (if given under torture) but had rewarded them for being 'benevolis,
bonis, fidelibus', i.e. the standard reasons, *Mil.* 58.

[204] 24: 'vel aes pro capite dent'.   [205] Rawson (1993) 221.

[206] Plaut. *Aul.* 309–10; *Poen.* 518–19.

[207] *Rud.* 928–9, 'pauxillatim pollicitabor pro capite argentum, ut sim liber'. *Casina* 309–14, also alludes
to payment for freedom. *Asinaria* 541, refers to hope built on the *peculium*. Lucilius, 891–3 Marx
= Krenkel 868–70, seems to describe a Greek-style comedy scene where a woman pays the pimp
for freedom.

[208] *Poen.* 842–4. Slater (2004) 295–7, thought it meant they squandered the savings with which they
would buy their freedom, but to Maurach (1988) 134, it was simply a case of wasting their patron's
money. Slater argues categorically that the passage is purely Roman because of the reference to
peculium which he believes to be a specifically Roman concept. However, there is extensive evidence
for self-purchase in the Greek world which evidently presupposes separate funds held by the slave.

his sexual services to the master are not 'gratiis' and he is confident he will be freed. In this case we should not necessarily see it as payment in a literal sense, although some commentators have done so.[209]

The playwrights clearly expected their audiences to be familiar with the concept of self-purchase, but as the scenario of slaves trying to buy their freedom also carried great comic potential the frequency with which it occurs in their works may tell us little about its importance in real life. Moreover, the fact that self-purchase also seems to feature more frequently in this genre than in any other type of writing inevitably raises the long-standing issue of the social world represented in these texts. Roman comedy famously sits between two cultures. The Greek elements are never easily separable from the Roman and in this case the interpretation of individual passages is complicated by the fact that self-purchase was well established in the Greek world. For that reason we cannot exclude the possibility that many of the jokes had already appeared in the Greek originals.[210] The manumission practices encountered in Roman comedy often seem to reflect different traditions. Thus, alongside the payments we also find what seem to be more conventional Roman justifications of manumission based on long service and good behaviour.[211]

We may therefore be dealing with a mix of diverse cultural elements. Interestingly we also find two different types of freedman, distinguished by their form of manumission. In Roman comedy the self-purchased freedman stands out as a social oddity, separated from his patron, and often associated with truculence and aggressiveness. Thus, Dumont observed that while gratuitous manumission did not affect ties to the master in Roman comedy, payment seems to have led to a clean break.[212] In *Rudens* Gripus becomes a stranger to the house, and a similar pattern is found in *Poenulus* where the *advocati* paid for their freedom and showed great independence of

---

[209] Plaut. *Persa* 286. *Capt.* 120–1, may be an oblique reference to an offer of money for freedom, reproaching a slave for not having saved a *peculium* to buy freedom with. At 408 a son promises that his father will set the slave free 'gratiis' but the reading is uncertain (the Teubner edition prefers 'gratus'). At 948 the manumission takes place free of charge.

[210] Fabre (1981) 46, on Greek legal practices in Plautus, including a son 'in potestate' who frees a slave; cf. Buckland (1908) 459; Watson (1967) 198–9; Spranger (1961) 69, who doubted whether *peculium* was important in the Greek originals.

[211] At *Casina* 283–4, the assumption is that a slave is freed if he enjoys his master's favour and goodwill, being *probus* and *frugi*; cf. Ter. *Andr.*, 34–9. Likewise, there is no indication of payment in *Adelph.* 958–71.

[212] Dumont (1987) 430–2, who suggested we may be dealing with a *suis nummis* procedure; cf. below pp. 172–4. Rawson (1993) 215–20, also noted the existence of two sharply contrasting types of freedmen in Roman comedy.

mind.[213] On the other hand, Sosia in Terence's *Andria* was freed for his good services and is humble, grateful, and closely attached to his patron.[214] The assertive, self-purchased freedman can also be traced outside this genre. The only two characters in Latin literature who had explicitly bought their freedom are both presented in this fashion. In Martial the freedman who bought his freedom later greeted his former owner by his name and not as patron, asking him not to think him contumacious.[215] The self-purchased Domitius Paris was cast in a similar mould as a *libertus ingratus*, who managed to gain *ingenuitas* from the emperor and cast off his *patrona*, from whom he even demanded his money back.[216]

These examples would suggest that payment for freedom was seen as a departure from the norm, and it is not difficult to see why this might have been the case. The involvement of money would evidently influence the selection process, ideally based entirely on personal qualities. Thus, Dionysius of Halicarnassus stated that in the olden days most slaves received freedom as a gift for good conduct, and the *few* who paid for their freedom had earned the money through honest and respectable work.[217] This depiction of an idealised early Rome is contrasted with a contemporary world in which slaves buy their freedom with money obtained through crime and prostitution. Dionysius' vision of societal decline is too lurid to be taken seriously, but it is significant that he regards widespread self-purchase as a degeneration of proper manumission practice.

The underlying logic of payment is self-replacement, the slave reimbursing the master for his pecuniary loss and helping to fill the place in the household that becomes vacant with the slave's departure. It was this basic rationale which dictated the manumission practices we encounter in most ancient and modern slave societies, including Greece where a large number of manumission inscriptions give valuable insight into the functioning of self-purchase. The Delphic material is the fullest and comprises some 1,200 manumission documents covering the period from Hellenistic to early Roman times and all mentioning payment. Hopkins rightly noted that this practice enabled 'masters to recapitalise the value of older slaves and to replace them with younger ones', 'particularly if a slave bought full freedom'.[218] The last comment referred to another characteristic aspect to Greek manumission, the additional conditions masters often imposed,

---

[213] *Poen.* 515, 811. Barsby (2004) 101–2, suggests the *advocati* were Plautus' own invention or perhaps based on a single non-speaking character in the original play.
[214] *Andr.* 35–44.   [215] 2.68.
[216] Tac. *Ann.* 13.27; D. 12.4.3.5 (Ulpian).   [217] 4.24.4.
[218] Hopkins (1978) 134. In general see also Klees (1998) 325–8, with further literature.

above all the so-called *paramonê*. These clauses stipulated that despite payment the freed person must remain in service for a specified period, usually until the death of the master and mistress. According to Hopkins, 'a substantial minority', rising to 52 per cent in the first century BCE, were freed conditionally, although sometimes with a get-out clause involving further payment.[219]

The *paramonê* sought to prevent the discontinuation of service, which is otherwise the logical implication of purchased freedom. Indeed, the standard phrase used of unconditionally freed slaves is that they are free to go wherever they wish. Hopkins, however, argued that even where the full price had been paid the freed person would have continued to serve the former master. This seemingly counter-intuitive suggestion was based on a study of the sums handed over, which appeared to show relatively little difference between the price of full and conditional, i.e. suspended, freedom. Hopkins therefore concluded that in practice the additional clauses made little difference, since most freedmen remained in service anyway.[220] He also observed a steep rise in the price paid, especially by male slaves, during the Roman period, which was explained by their greater tendency to move away and start a new life elsewhere. The rise in manumission prices therefore reflected a combination of rising slave prices and increased discontinuity of service; in the Roman period supplies of slaves were supposedly diverted to Italy while at the same time the new imperial economy offered better opportunities for independent freedmen.

This reconstruction raises a number of questions, however. Hopkins argued that when the price rose, 'more slaves compromised and bought conditional release', which 'was all they could afford'. But the slaves may not necessarily have had a choice between full and conditional manumission, since there were no market forces at play in a process. It was entirely the owner's decision whether to free a slave, under what forms, and at what price. The prices may therefore not be a fair reflection of the difference between the two forms of manumission but determined by individual factors such as age, gender, and skills. Thus, later evidence from Spanish Louisiana shows that owners, unfettered by any regulations, happily would 'over-charge' slaves paying for their freedom and perhaps even impose further conditions.[221] The relatively minor difference in the price of full

---

[219] Hopkins (1978) 142.
[220] Hopkins (1978) 162. Followed by Zelnick-Abramovitz (2005). Duncan-Jones (1984) casts doubt on the posited steep rise in the price paid by male slaves for unconditional freedom.
[221] Cole (2005) 1019–24. Already Jones (1956) 191, observed that manumission prices may have been higher than the market rate.

and conditional manumission is therefore above all indicative of the strong desire for freedom felt by slaves who were willing to hand over large sums even if they had to wait many years before they could fully enjoy it. In this context the hope of bearing freeborn children may also have been a factor.

The sharp rise in the price paid by male slaves in the Roman period may – if genuine – reflect the simple fact that some slaves, active in trade and commerce, had started to accumulate greater funds, which their owners wished to appropriate as far as possible before releasing them. The increase in the price demanded for these slaves may therefore be explained by a rise in the profitability of certain slave occupations during the Roman period. The fact that the most successful slaves were also those most difficult to replace would naturally drive the manumission price up even further.[222] On the other hand, the conditionally freed slaves who stayed with the owner paid relatively less during this period, either because they were less well off, or because the owners accepted a lower price. Since they continued to benefit from the slave's business activities, it may have seemed counter-productive to confiscate their savings at this point.

The logic of payment was to compensate owners for losses incurred, now or in the future, and enable them to replace the slave with another of similar or better quality.[223] As such, Greek practices would appear to be part of a different construction of the freedman's role in the household and in society from that which prevailed in Rome. The overall picture of Greek manumission is highly heterogeneous, with a wide range of different forms, but generally the scale appears to have been modest.[224] Most importantly there was no institutionalised system of continuous relations between freedman and patron. On Athens, Cohen stated that, in contrast to Rome, 'the freedman did not differ at all in legal status from

[222] Jongman (2007) 601–2, uses the Delphic records to calculate slave prices, but these are manumission prices not market prices; cf. Duncan-Jones (1984) 208: 'manumission payments were not transactions in the open market'. The apparent rise in the late republic and early empire is therefore most likely a function of the increased earnings of some industrious slaves during this period.

[223] Hopkins accepted that: 'In most cases, presumably the grant of full freedom to a slave involved the owner in buying a new slave to replace the slave who had been freed', 160. This statement is difficult to reconcile to the theory that in practice there was little difference between full and conditional manumission. Did the freed slave remain in the house alongside the newly purchased replacement? Tucker (1982) 234, discusses a case where a woman had to purchase her own replacement if she wished to be released from the *paramonê*. Frequently freedwomen also had to leave children behind in slavery.

[224] Generally on Greece, Calderini (1908); Fisher (1993) 67–70; Garlan (1988) 73–84; Klees (1998) 297–333; Weiler (2003) 180–9; Zelnick-Abramovitz (2005).

the other free non-*politai*: the freedman, enrolled by the city as a *metic*, had no continuing legal relationship with his former master'.[225] Cohen therefore drew attention to the wealthy slaves at Athens who worked and lived independently. These so-called 'khôris oikountes' were not, as often assumed, freedmen, and Cohen suggested they occupied a role similar to that of dependent freedmen in Rome. But since Athenian manumission – unlike Roman – meant severance of most formal ties, they developed 'a similar symbiosis not involving manumission'.[226]

In Roman Egypt the evidence from papyri reveals a manumission regime which differed in several respects from that of Rome.[227] Manumission with payment took place in public before the *agoranomos*, and the procedures and formulas used seem to reflect Greek traditions and suggest continuity from the Ptolemaic period.[228] The formalised system of payment is likely to be part of this heritage. Greek-style *paramonê* clauses, on the other hand, appear to be uncommon in Egypt, where the freedmen could expect full freedom, as indicated by one recorded case that came before the prefect.[229] A freedman complained about the patron who had received money and promised full independence but then presented obligations. The verdict went against the freedman, but Alexandrian law which applied in this case may have granted particular rights to patrons that did not apply outside.[230] The sums paid generally seem to have been in line with the slave prices recorded in Egypt.[231]

The broad match between value and price reminds us that in most slave societies payment has implied replacement. For example, in Rio de Janeiro we even find examples of slaves who bought and trained newly imported slaves and traded them in for themselves.[232] The freed slave would typically leave the household, which meant that except for market women and skilled craftsmen many of them faced poverty. Some freedwomen would therefore remain as dependent clients out of sheer necessity, and continue

---

[225] Cohen (2000) 130–54, 150. Zelnick-Abramovitz (2005) argues for a distinction between *apeleutheroi* and *exeleutheroi*, the former being tied to their former master, but see p. 146 n.115. A degree of dependency can be traced in some parts of Greece but they were of a very different nature from the Roman system of institutionalised pseudo-familial bonds. When money had changed hands, no lasting ties can generally be demonstrated in Greece.

[226] Cohen (2000) 142. On this category see now Fisher (2008).

[227] For a survey Biezunska-Malowist (1966), (1977)   [228] Messeri Savorelli (1978) 279–81.

[229] Samuel (1965) 296–7, noted one example from Egypt, *PSI* vol. XII 1263, where a slave is freed testamentarily with the obligation to stay with a descendant as long as she lives.

[230] *P.Oxy.* vol. IV 706; 442; cf. Taubenschlag (1955) 101. Scholl (2001) notes that in a few documents the owner formally renounces his patronal rights and suggests that this may also have applied in others.

[231] Straus (1973); Scholl (2001).   [232] Karasch (1987) 358.

to work for their old masters, who could advertise their services for rent.[233] This was not the norm, however, and many owners therefore offered only conditional freedom, which usually required the slaves' service until the owner's death; in the intervening period they counted and were treated as slaves.[234]

Since payment acts as restitution for loss of slave labour, self-purchase belongs to a system where continuity is not expected. In Rome, however, the freedman was formally integrated into the *familia* of his former owner and placed in a semi-filial role where life-long *fides* and *officium* were demanded. The ability to create a unique type of free but dependent labour therefore emerges as a defining feature of Roman manumission, which is difficult to reconcile with the simple *quid pro quo* arrangement implied by the theory of self-purchase. In this light we may reconsider the remaining, mostly legal evidence for self-purchase, and above all the intriguing 'suis nummis emptio' procedure.

There are a number of legal references to payment for freedom. In many instances, however, the money is paid not by the slaves themselves but by outsiders, which changes the nature of the transaction entirely. In that case it becomes a relatively straightforward purchase of goods, and it was, for example, prescribed that after an agreed date had passed the buyer could sue.[235] Offering money seems to have been a relatively common way of inducing masters to free relatives, the most frequent scenario probably involving the freed parents of enslaved children.[236] One ruling stated that if freed parents have paid for a child's freedom, they can request the manumission, but if it turns out that the money comes from a slave's *peculium* there is no such right. In another case the owner took the money and promised to free both mother and child, but only freed the mother.[237]

Other references to payment appear in the context of fideicommissary manumission, where the payment serves as compensation for losses incurred by heirs. These cases, which will be discussed in greater detail

---

[233] Karasch (1987) 362–3. Their position was precarious since freedom, conditional or unconditional, could be revoked by owners complaining about disobedience.

[234] 22 per cent of manumissions conditional, cf. Karasch (1987) 353–4.

[235] D. 12.1.19 pr. (Julian); cf. 12.4.1 (Ulpian); 12.4.3.2–5; 12.5.2–4; 19.5.7 (Papinian); *Cod.Iust.* 7.6.8: on outsider paying for slave's freedom; *Cod.Iust.* 4.57.4: if payment is received from outsider, manumission can be enforced; *Cod.Iust.* 6.3.3: on money received from outsider to free a slave who is also asked to pay; cf. Buckland (1908) 642.

[236] Literary examples include e.g. Plaut. *Rud.* 44; Petr. *Sat.* 57.6.

[237] *Cod.Iust.* 4.6.9; cf. 7.16.8. A slave could not get somebody else to buy his freedom with funds from his *peculium*, since the master's permission was needed before the slave could alienate his *peculium*. D. 16.3.1.33 (Ulpian): on a situation where a slave gives money to a third party to buy his freedom; if done with the owner's knowledge it is legal, if not it is fraud.

below, differ fundamentally from the situations where money passed directly from the slave to a living master. This form of self-purchase is surprisingly sparsely documented in the legal sources, not least when one considers the amount of attention the jurists otherwise pay to freedmen.[238] For example, book forty of the *Digest*, entirely dedicated to manumission, devotes just a few paragraphs to this issue, again mostly relating to fideicommissary manumission.

The jurists make it clear that a slave could enter an agreement, *pactio*, with his owner concerning his manumission, but it was not binding for the master.[239] Sometimes it involved payment but just as often it did not.[240] One case describes a *pactio* involving payment, but before the manumission had taken place the master died and left the slave his *peculium*. The question was whether he could then keep it. There are also references to slaves who borrowed money to pay for freedom or obtain the money illegally.[241] Thus, we hear of an owner who received a stolen *vicaria* in return for his slave's freedom.[242]

There are signs that payment did raise concerns about its effect on the relationship between the former master and slave. Marcellus gives the opinion that even if a master has accepted money, 'accepto ab eo pretio', his son can still accuse the freedman of ingratitude, and it is stressed that those freed under an agreement with the master also owe their patron respect.[243] Although *obsequium* was still demanded, there were other legal implications that suggest the situation may have been regarded as anomalous. Thus,

---

[238] Gardner (1993) 36–8. Her confident statement that 'legal evidence indicates that it was not uncommon for slaves to secure manumission by paying a sum of money to their owners' (36), may need qualification.

[239] On *pactio* Kaser (1971) 287; Jacota (1966); Behrends (1980) 58ff; Nörr (1983) 187, with further references. *Cod.Iust.* 7.16.36, states that a master is not bound by an agreement with a slave, indicating that there was no right to self-purchase in Rome. Buckland (1908) 640–6, showed convincingly that the passages that might seem to point in that direction are later interpolations, 40.1.19 (Papinian); *Cod.Iust.* 4.57.4.

[240] D. 2.14.7.18 (Ulpian); 4.3.7.8; 16.1.13 pr. (Gaius); *Cod.Iust.* 2.4.13.2; 7.16.36.

[241] D. 15.1.11.1 (Ulpian): a slave assumes a liability in return for his freedom; 15.1.50.3 (Papinian); 15.3.2 (Javolenus); 15.3.3 pr. (Ulpian); 40.1.6 (Alfenus Varus).

[242] D. 41.4.9 (Julian); 45.1.104 (Javolenus); 41.4.2.14 (Paul); 29.2.71.2 (Ulpian): if someone had paid money to his master in order to be freed, 'I think assistance should be given to him in every case.' The context is inheritances and the preceding clause dealt with fideicommissary manumission; Buckland (1908) 642, noted the vagueness of the formulation. *Cod.Iust.* 7.16.33: even if manumitted after payment freedom cannot be revoked; 44.5.2.2 (Paul) and *Cod.Iust.* 4.14.3: a promise of money from a slave can be enforced after his manumission; *Cod.Iust.* 4.14.5: a *servus quasi colonus* uses *peculium* to buy freedom 'adempto peculio libertate donatus es'; D. 37.15.10 (Tryphoninus): children do not pay parents for freedom; 39.5.8 (Paul): payment by freedmen imposed in order to obtain freedom is not a gift since they get something in return.

[243] D. 37.15.3; *Cod.Iust.* 6.6.3.

the customary rights to inherit from the freedman and to impose *operae* were affected. Ulpian states that if the patron has received 'nummos ut manumitteret', he does not take *bonorum possessio* contrary to the terms of a will.[244] It is not clear whether the money came from the slave in this case.[245] Still, the underlying rationale seems to be that payment – from the slave or from outsiders – changed the patronal bond, presumably because it was no longer rooted in a unilaterally bestowed favour.[246]

The impact of payment on the *libertus–patronus* relationship brings us to the concept of the 'servus suis nummis emptus', 'the slave bought with his own money'. This unique institution involved a third party who would buy the slave with the slave's own money and then set him free. A ruling by Marcus and Verus further developed the procedure by making the manumission legally enforceable, suggesting that the *pro forma* buyer occasionally might abuse the situation and keep the slave rather than setting him free as agreed.[247] Most likely, therefore, the imperial ruling merely closed a loophole in the system.[248] Earlier evidence for the practice is limited, but Suetonius tells us that Staberius Eros, who earned an income from teaching, was bought from the sale platform with his own money, and immediately freed.[249]

The procedure of 'suis nummis emptio' has puzzled modern scholars. Gardner suggested it took place 'when a master refused manumission', but that presupposes a system similar to that in South America where owners were obliged – at least morally – to accept the offer of payment.[250]

---

[244] D. 38.2.3.4: 'Si quis nummos accepit, ut manumitteret, non habet contra tabulas bonorum possessionem'; cf. 38.1.32 (Modestinus). This also applied to 'donum, munus, operas', received in return for freedom, 38.2.37 (Ulpian). However, *Cod.Iust.* 6.4.1, explicitly states that even where an owner has received money in return for freeing a slave, the patron (or his son) keeps 'omnia iura patronatus', including the right to claim against the will.

[245] Crook (1967a) 54, argued that 'if as often, the slave had "paid" for his freedom by, in effect, renouncing some or all of his *peculium*, the patron could not then defeat his will and claim part-succession'.

[246] The right of the patron to a share of the estate was rooted in the moral bond between them, as suggested by 38.2.33 (Modestinus), which states that 'if a patron has not maintained his freedman', 'si patronus non aluerit libertum', he loses his claim on the estate.

[247] D. 2.4.10 pr (Ulpian); 40.1.4 (Ulpian); 40.1.5 (Marcian). Other attestations include: D. 5.1.53 (Hermogenian); 5.1.67 (Ulpian); 25.3.5.22 (Ulpian); 40.1.19 (Papinian); 48.19.38.4 (Paul).

[248] Horsmann (1986) 309–10, saw the *constitutio divorum fratrum* as a major advance in easing Roman slavery, giving the slave 'ein Klagerecht gegen den eigenen Herrn'. However, this right only applied against the *redemptor* not the owner, who of course had to agree to the transaction.

[249] *Gramm.* 13: 'suomet aere emptus de catasta'.

[250] Gardner (1993) 37; cf. Jacota (1966); Behrends (1980) 60–2; Boulvert and Morabito (1982) 122, also seem to assume the imperial ruling applied to payments in general. Andreau (2004) 117, suggests that the *suis nummis* procedure, from the second century onwards, forced masters to free immediately, but that ruling probably only applied to the *pro forma* buyer, not to the original master.

Brunt assumed the procedure was a means of overcoming practical problems occurring when 'it was impossible or inconvenient for a master' to free *vindicta*, in which case he would transfer the slave to someone who could.[251] Here the problem is that the owner simply could have handed the slave over to the new manumitter – why involve money, indeed the full value? And why did it have to be the slave's own? Brunt compared the practice to sales with instructions 'ut manumittatur', but these generally specify manumission at some point in the future, not immediately.[252] It also overlooks the most extraordinary aspect of the procedure, which is the fact that it produced a freedman who in effect had no patron; while the freedman became completely separated from his original owner, the new *pro forma* patron gained a limited authority over the freedman, who owed him only basic *obsequium*.[253]

The formal detachment from the original owner may be the key to understanding the procedure. The 'suis nummis emptio' procedure had the effect that the freedman neither became part of his *familia* nor carried his *nomen*. It meant there was no patronal claim on the estate, no obligation to *obsequium*, no pseudo-filial bond. This separation worked both ways, since the procedure would also prevent the freedman from benefiting from any provisions made for the *familia libertorum*. The result was, as Garnsey has rightly pointed out, an almost fully independent freedman, and this fictional process would seem to be an attempt to circumvent the traditional semi-filial 'construction' of the freedman.[254] A freedman who became a stranger to his old master would appear to violate one of the most fundamental principles on which Roman manumission rested. This breach could, however, be seen as a deliberate attempt to minimise the negative consequences of self-purchase. The contrived sale served to negotiate an anomalous and ideologically uncomfortable situation where a slave bought his freedom and provided full compensation. In other words, the third party was introduced to prevent the conventional bond between freedman and patron from being compromised.

In this interpretation the fictive 'suis nummis emptio' procedure was invented to create a different outcome from that which was considered the norm. By completely severing the link between the freedman and

---

[251] Brunt (1983a) 146.
[252] Buckland (1908) 628–36. In some cases the slave was to be freed instantaneously, which would in effect turn the procedure into a gift/sale of a freedman, including services or share of the estate.
[253] A *servus suis nummis emptus* did not have to support the *redemptor*, cf. D. 25.3.5.22 (Ulpian); cf. *Cod.Iust.* 6.4.1, noting that the *redemptor* has no claim to the freedman's estate contrary to the will.
[254] Garnsey (1981) 198.

his patron, it rescued the ideal of the *patronus–libertus* relationship which would be undermined if the 'beneficium' was reduced to a financial transaction. When the 'greatest favour' was in fact purchased by the slave himself, the moral obligation that formed the basis for the patron's authority would be diluted. In this situation a fully independent freedman was, at least from an ideological point of view, preferable to a semi-detached one. Thus, while the 'independent' freedman certainly was a possibility at Rome, the procedure by which he was produced suggests his status was also considered anomalous.

At the core of the theory of common self-purchase lie the *peculium* and its importance in Roman society and economy. The institution is widely discussed in the legal sources, and other evidence also indicates that it was common for slaves to have a set-aside. Thus, it has been observed that all the slaves in Plautus' comedies seem to have *peculia*, and Cicero implies that slaves in any position of responsibility were expected to hold one.[255] Most studies of Roman manumission have assumed that a primary function of the *peculium* was to pay for freedom as soon as the slave had accumulated sufficient funds to cover his or her market value.[256] But before accepting this hypothesis we should look more closely at the function of the *peculium* in Roman commerce.

Although it has been possible for slaves to hold separate funds in almost all slave societies, the *peculium* was nevertheless uniquely Roman. It was not specifically linked to the institution of slavery but reflected the exceptional powers of the *pater familias* and the notion that only those who were *sui iuris* could own property. It provided a mechanism through which the *pater familias* could enable those in his *potestas* – children, wives *in manu*, and slaves – to hold separate funds that were recognised in law. While formally part of the family property, these set-asides were treated as de facto separate from the estate. The *peculium* therefore played a different role in ancient Rome than it did in Greece, where a comparable concept did not exist.

The Roman *peculium* allowed household members *in potestate* to carry out economic transactions independently of the *pater familias*. A complex legal framework was developed detailing the liabilities a father/master might incur through the economic activities of those in his power. Some scholars have even argued that the *peculium* in effect came to act as an instrument of direct agency, a concept otherwise absent from Roman law.[257] In any case, the importance of the *peculium* goes well beyond a

[255] E.g. Ligt (2007), cf. (1999) 223f. Cic. *Verr.* 2.3.86.
[256] Buckland (1908) 640–6; Kirschenbaum (1987) 31–88; Andreau (2004).
[257] Kirschenbaum (1987) 90, saw the granting of a *peculium* as 'implied general authorization'.

simple accumulation of funds for self-purchase, and its role in the organisation of Roman commerce may easily explain the amount of attention
it receives in the legal sources. For purely commercial reasons it was often
useful for masters to allow their slaves a *peculium* of a given size. Under
certain circumstances that could limit his financial liabilities, and if he
announced to third parties that the transactions of his slave were based on
the *peculium*, e.g. by putting up signs indicating the terms under which
the slave acted, the master would be liable only up to the limit of the slave's
funds.[258] This does not necessarily entail that the *peculium* functioned as a
'working capital' allocated to the slave in order to enable him to do business
on the master's behalf.[259] But it does suggest that the *peculium* might be a
substantial fund held by the slave over longer periods and not simply up
to the moment where it enabled him to buy his freedom. Although the
peculium probably often exceeded the slave's value, the legal sources barely
hint at the possibility that it might be used for self-purchase. Thus, book
fifteen of the *Digest*, entirely dedicated to the *peculium*, mentions its use
as payment for freedom on only three occasions, all linked to situations
where a slave had borrowed money which was then offered to the master
in return for manumission.[260]

It is difficult to demonstrate a direct connection between *peculium* and
manumission. Many slaves appear to have held very substantial *peculia*,
as suggested by the examples of the slaves with numerous under-slaves,
vicarii, of their own, the most famous being the imperial slave Musicus

---

[258] Scholars have argued that it played a vital role in Roman commercial law, since it offered limited
financial liability as long as the slave acted independently of the master and the latter did not
derive any 'direct use or benefit form it', Kirschenbaum (1987) 71. If the profits of the *peculium*
entered directly into the account of the master, he could be made liable up to the extent he had
been enriched through the *actio de peculio et de in rem verso*. Johnston (1998) therefore stressed the
need for the owner to distance himself from the slave's commercial activities in order to limit his
liability; cf. Verboven (2002) 28; Zwalve (2002); *contra* Bang (2008) 277–8, 280.

[259] Ligt (2007) 13, suggests the master could adjust the extent of his liability by varying the size of the
peculia held by his dependants. That would mean allocating specific investment funds to slaves,
which would later be withdrawn. But as Andreau (2004) pointed out in an important paper, there
is little evidence for that practice. Andreau further questioned the importance of the *peculium* in
commercial enterprises, noting the apparent rarity of profits being transferred from the *peculium*
to the master. Comparing references in the *Digest* to slaves working with *peculium* and as *institores*,
he noted that, in the case of the former, sharing of income with the master hardly ever features. He
therefore concluded that *peculia* were not used as a financial instrument by masters. In this context
it is also worth noting that withdrawal of the *peculium* or parts of it from a slave was regarded
as exceptional by the legal writers, further questioning the notion of the *peculium* as a 'working
capital'.

[260] D. 15.1.50.3 (Papinian): a complex case, part of which involves the slave borrowing money to pay for
his freedom; 15.3.3 pr. (Ulpian): a slave freed with borrowed money implied that the sum normally
covers the slave's value; cf. 15.3.2 (Javolenus), which also refers to payment 'nummis acceptis', but
is not clear whether it was the slave's own.

Scurranus who was commemorated with sixteen *vicarii*.[261] Among the
Statilii almost half the slaves appear to have been owned by other staff
members, a form of household organisation which is difficult to square
with a world such as that presented in Roman comedy where slaves offer
their price as soon as they have saved enough. The simple correlation
between manumission and savings is also questioned by the profile of those
who were freed. For example, Dumont assumed manumission was rare
among domestic and country slaves, whose opportunities for accumulating
substantial *peculia* would have been more limited.[262] But as the *columbaria*
material demonstrates, this was clearly not the case. In the *familiae* of the
Volusii and the Statilii we find a very high rate of manumission among
domestic servants, most of whom were not directly active in the market
economy. Apparently those outside the commercial sector did not suffer
unduly, and neither did younger slaves who evidently had less time to
save up. Moreover, the fact that so many freedmen are represented in the
columbaria and evidently remained in the household is difficult to fit into
a model of saving–payment–replacement.

The role of the *peculium* may therefore have been more complex than
a simple savings account converted into freedom as soon as it reached the
slave's market value.[263] In this context it is important to remember that the
peculium was regarded as the de facto possession of the slave. Unjustified
withdrawal of the *peculium* by a master was frowned upon and normally
invited moral censure.[264] Even when slaves were sold, it was common to
let them take the *peculium* with them. For example, Ulpian refers to the
sale of a slave with his *peculium*, and Varro mentions that 'In the purchase
of slaves it is customary for the *peculium* to go with the slave, unless it is
expressly excepted.'[265] The new owner might in principle incur financial
liabilities through the purchase of a slave who came with a *peculium*.[266] It

[261] *CIL* 6.5197.
[262] Dumont (1987) 66–8. Following Hopkins (1978), he saw the *peculium* as the central factor in Roman manumission, 81.
[263] Roth (2005) drew attention to the importance of the *peculium* in maintaining, indeed acquiring, a slave family, which might often have formed part of the slave's set-aside.
[264] Buckland (1908) 189; Gardner (1991) 32 n.25; Roth (2005). Knoch (2005) 176ff, 182, argued that *ademptio peculii*, i.e. the master reducing or confiscating the *peculium*, was a purely theoretical possibility. Cf. Kirschenbaum (1987) 36, who noted that unjustified withdrawal of a *peculium* was strongly condemned. Watson (1987) 43, observed that he had never come across a case where the master simply confiscated the *peculium*.
[265] D. 4.3.7 pr.; Varro *Rust.* 2.10.5: 'In horum emptione solet accedere peculium aut excipi.' However, the *peculium* did not automatically follow the slave; if there were any doubt, it was regarded as retained by the seller, D. 21.2.3 (Paul).
[266] Kirschenbaum (1987) 50, 56. D. 40.7.3.7 (Ulpian): a *statuliber* was sold without his *peculium* making it difficult for him to meet the conditions imposed on him, suggesting the situation was considered anomalous.

is therefore not surprising to discover that the *peculium* was expected to remain with the slave when he or she was freed. The jurists stated that unless a *peculium* had explicitly been taken away from the freed slave, it should be treated as granted.[267] Later this principle was enshrined in law. The rule applied only to manumission *inter vivos*, however, since testamentary manumission required a separate legacy of the *peculium*. The disparity reflects the special nature of wills, where implied, non-written rules had to be made explicit in order to avoid uncertainty.[268] However, as Watson noted, it seems to have been common to leave the *peculium* as a legacy.[269] There are two implications of this practice. Firstly, it suggests that payment was not considered the norm, and secondly it provides further support for the idea that the freedman generally was expected to continue working for the patron. Otherwise the habitual surrender of funds which formally belonged to the master would mean letting go of both the employee and his savings. If, on the other hand, he was expected to remain in his patron's service, the funds would not leave the *familia* as defined in its broadest sense.

Andreau argued convincingly that the *peculium* should be seen as part of the intelligent management of slave labour, although that does not imply that it therefore served as payment for freedom.[270] When Varro described the incentives and rewards offered to the estate manager, the *vilicus*, he included the right to a *peculium*, but without any hint that its growth might eventually result in manumission.[271] As we have seen, the Romans motivated their slaves through a range of incentives, and within this system the role of the *peculium* may have been twofold. On the one hand, it helped ease the slave's workload (e.g. through *vicarii*) and improve his quality of life, and, on the other hand, it also acted as a tangible measure of the slave's skill and application. The accumulation of a *peculium* became the hallmark of a 'good' slave, as illustrated by references in Roman comedy to

---

[267] *Cod.Iust.* 7.23.1: 'concessum tacite peculium, si non adimatur'; 2.20.20; D. 15.1.53 (Paul); cf. the discussion in Wacke (1991), who observes that the practice of treating the *peculium* as granted must be older than its first legal attestations, 74.

[268] Cf. Wacke (1991) 90, who also noted that the jurists here applied the principle of *favor heredis*, 64, 89.

[269] Watson (1987) 97; cf. e.g. 15.1.57 (Thryphoninus); 23.3.39 pr. (Ulpian); 40.7.28 (Javolenus). For legacies of *peculium* see D. 33.8: 'De peculio legato'.

[270] Andreau (2004) 125: 'le pécule est une institution visant à donner quelques avantages et quelques espérances à l'esclave'.

[271] *Rust.* 1.2.17; 1.17.5–7; 1.19.3; 2.10.5. The evidence from the *columbarium* of the Statilii also suggests that the *peculium* was an integral part of the organisation of the household, serving to delegate tasks through *vicarii*; cf. Mouritsen (forthcoming). As Roth (2005) pointed out, many *vicarii* may also have been part of the slaves' families.

a slave who is *peculiosus* and *probus*, a sentiment repeated in the approving comments on a slave with a large *peculium*.[272] Conversely, one Plautine play refers to a worthless slave who has not saved up so much as a lead coin.[273] The fact that a slave without *peculium* generally was considered lazy may help explain Virgil's old shepherd who had no thought for freedom or *peculium* as a description of a slave without drive or aspirations.[274] Virgil tells us he was 'inertem', 27, and therefore had neither *peculium* nor hope of freedom, but there is no direct indication that the *peculium* would be used to buy freedom (and eventually it was bestowed by the *deus* in Rome – i.e. Octavian, 6–10). There was a close connection between *libertas* and *peculium* because the accumulation of savings became the mark of the ambitious, hard-working slave who might be considered for manumission.

The use of the *peculium* as a measure of the 'good slave' implies that masters actively encouraged slaves to save up, but those most likely to succeed were the skilled and enterprising ones, whom their masters presumably would have been least happy to let go of. A system of payment and replacement would therefore seem to make little economic or practical sense. The slaves selected for manumission were by definition those who had found favour with their owners, who were therefore unlikely to confiscate their hard-earned savings when granting them their greatest reward. The rationale of the system was to offer the slaves incentives which could be carried over into their new role as freedmen. For that reason the typical freedman probably resembled the one described by Apuleius as 'acceptissimo liberto suo et satis peculiato', that is, a favoured freedman with a substantial (retained) *peculium*.[275]

Payment for freedom undoubtedly happened, but we may wonder under which circumstances. A range of situations may be envisaged where owners might have decided to keep the *peculium* and part with the slave. One scenario might involve slaves who were heavily exploited and might abscond when freed, although the likelihood is that they would never receive freedom in the first place. In the case of older and infirm slaves, payment would allow the master to replace them with younger and stronger ones, and it is often assumed that payment financed a steady renewal of the slave

---

[272] *Rud.* 112: 'peculiosum esse addecet servom et probum'; cf. *Trin.* 433. In the *Asinaria* a slave makes excuses for his shabby appearance, claiming: 'I'm an honest man and my savings cannot be counted', 498: 'frugi tamen sum, nec potest peculium enumerari'. Spranger (1961) 67–8, noted that slaves were not just allowed but expected to accumulate a *peculium*: 'das peculium wird zum Ausweis eines guten Sklaven'; cf. Fabre (1981) 274.

[273] *Cas.* 257; cf. *Capt.* 1015.   [274] *Ecl.* 1.32.

[275] *Met.* 10.17. Papinian, *Frg.Vat.* 261, also implies that freedmen generally retained some capital after manumission.

population. The practice is well known from later slave societies, but in Rome manumission was generally associated with a duty of care. More realistically, therefore, these slaves would simply have been discarded by their masters, as implied by Claudius' edict granting freedom to sick slaves abandoned on the Tiber Island.[276]

Payment was probably most common in certain professions. If the slave had acquired specialist skills which enabled him to earn a good living independently of his patron and did not have to rely on investments or continuous support, it may have seemed reasonable to retain some or all of his *peculium*. That would for example have applied in the case of doctors, teachers, actors, and certain artisans and it is for these types of professions we have evidence of payment. Thus, Pliny's comment on actors paying handsomely for their freedom is the only explicit statement of regular payment by slaves in any specific trade.[277]

In exceptional cases payment may in fact have been little more than the transfer of funds between different accounts. Thus, according to the elder Pliny Nero's *dispensator* Tiridates made 13 million sesterces from the Armenian War with which he bought his freedom.[278] In this instance it seems to be a pure paper transaction, but there are signs that the situation within the imperial *familia* may have been somewhat different. The existence of a 'fiscus libertatis et peculiorum' in the *domus Augusta* may reflect a more regulated system of manumission in which payment was a regular feature.[279] Here the absence of a personal relationship with the master may, as we shall see, have played a part.

If payment – with all its implications for the patronal relationship – had been agreed in principle, the master had two options: either receiving the money directly from the slave, or allowing a 'suis nummis emptio' procedure to take place, which would sever all ties between them. We can only speculate why some masters would have agreed to the latter, but the sums offered would probably have influenced the decision, 'suis nummis emptio' presumably being more expensive than direct payment with retained *ius patronatus*.

Briefly summarising, we may conclude that payment for manumission in itself is a logical hypothesis – but only if we accept that a replacement

---

[276] Cf. Cato's advice to sell old and sickly slaves, *Agr.* 2.7. This is also the most common pattern in later slave societies. For example, in Buenos Aires they would generally be abandoned in the street – although the authorities tried to curb it – for hygienic reasons; Johnson (1979) 269; cf. Queirós Mattoso (1986) 164, on Rio.

[277] *NH* 7.128; cf. Paris the *pantomimus* and the doctor from Asisium.   [278] *NH* 7.129.

[279] Boulvert (1974) 132; Albana (1987) 60–3. Cf. below p. 201.

would be needed. The fundamental difference between Rome and other slave societies such as Greece and South America lay in the slave's unique status after manumission and the well-documented expectation of continuous links between patron and freedman. Self-purchase did occur, but the evidence suggests it was the exception rather than the rule and probably concentrated in certain professions. The *peculium* was a tool to increase the efficiency of slave labour by offering greater freedom of action and a better quality of life. To the master the growth of the *peculium* constituted tangible proof of the slave's hard work and suitability, and after manumission the retained *peculium* served as an added sweetener to the newly gained freedom, perhaps providing start-up capital for future businesses, often in collaboration with the patron. Given the overall logic of Roman manumission, it made little sense to confiscate the *peculium* for which the slave was being rewarded. It might have increased his economic dependency, but it would also undermine the social and moral bond that was supposed to form the basis for the patron–freedman relationship.[280]

TESTAMENTARY MANUMISSION

This conclusion naturally takes us to the practice of testamentary manumission, which typically has been approached from the same perspective as self-purchase, that is, with an emphasis on the direct financial advantages enjoyed by the master. Thus, Watson stated that most slaves would have been freed by testament, 'since that would not deprive the master of the slaves' services during his lifetime and he would have . . . grateful freedmen to attend his funeral'.[281] His view has been echoed by other scholars, who have seen it as the perfect reward for slaves which came to fruition only after the master's death.[282] As such it provided a powerful incentive for

---

[280] Slaves might also need their savings to pay the manumission tax, *vicesima libertatis*, which would have fallen to them unless the master was particularly generous. Bradley (1984a) 177, mentions the modern assumption that the tax was paid for by the slave if he purchased his freedom, and by the master if freedom was granted free of charge. This is largely speculative, however. Epict. *Diss.* 2.1.27, implies the manumitter might pay the tax, but the evidence of Petr. *Sat.* 58.2 (cf. 71.2), clearly points to the slaves being responsible. Similarly, the testamentary donation of the tax in the 'Testamentum Dasumii', *CIL* 6.10229 lines 53–5.

[281] Watson (1987) 29; cf. (1967) 194.

[282] E.g. Buckland (1908) 442, 460; Weaver (1990) 278: 'By far the commonest method of formal manumission was by will'; Gardner (1991) 38: 'a popular method, since it cost the owner himself nothing'; Masi Doria (1993c) 236; Horsley (1998) 52–3: 'Testamentary manumission was the most popular mode among the Romans because it retained the services of slaves to the very last moment in which their owner could use them'; Klees (2002) 114. More sceptical, Treggiari (1969a) 27–8.

the slaves without any cost to the master, who could even look forward to posthumous gratitude.

The logic may seem impeccable but it remains predicated on the assumption that manumission represented a loss for the owner and, as we saw, that was not necessarily the case in Rome. If manumission typically transformed slave labour into free, dependent labour, the advantages of testamentary freeing would be much reduced: the owner would have lost a slave but gained a freedman. In such a system there wase no compelling reason why manumission of otherwise 'deserving' slaves should be postponed beyond the owner's death.

The impact of testamentary provisions on the household may also have been more complex. If, as Champlin suggested, it was common to disclose the content of wills in advance, the prospect of freedom would clearly have encouraged some slaves.[283] But the selection of beneficiaries, from the time of Augustus enshrined in the *lex Fufia Caninia*, would have caused disappointment among the greater number who were not included, so much more so since their exclusion would seem to imply they had lost every prospect of freedom. As a means of encouraging staff, a public will might therefore have been counter-productive. Petronius' Trimalchio could declare his intention to free his entire *familia* 'so that my slaves may love me now as if I were dead', but that scenario belongs to fiction.[284] It might also raise disturbing psychological issues, since the notion of slaves eagerly anticipating their master's death cannot have been comfortable for Roman slave owners. At worst, prospective beneficiaries might try to hasten their reward, and although such cases were extremely rare, the story found in *Rhetorica ad Herennium* of a slave who killed his master to get his freedom, suggests the scenario was not unthinkable.[285] Alternatively, the will could be kept secret, but that would deprive the master of the personal satisfaction of the freedman's gratitude in anticipation.

Testamentary manumission may therefore have been less unambiguously attractive to masters, and there were also factors – moral as well as ideological – militating against the freeing of large numbers of slaves by will. Drawing up a will was the natural occasion to reward or punish,

---

[283] Champlin (1991) 23–4.

[284] *Sat.* 71.1–3. The passage is internally inconsistent, since Trimalchio, having declared his slaves to be free, also bequeathed to one of his slaves his *contubernalis*, who would logically have been included in 'omnes illos' mentioned 71.2.

[285] 1.24. In the *Digest* we occasionally find concerns about the 'split interests' of beneficiaries, e.g. 35.1.72.1 (Papinian).

treating dependants, friends, and relatives as each deserved, and there was an expectation that testators would dispense justice and fairness in their final wishes. In this situation testators would often have to negotiate competing interests between those whom they were 'judging'. And while the freeing of slaves meant rewarding service and loyalty, it also deprived the heirs of parts of the estate. Viewed from this perspective, the favour granted one beneficiary was made at the expense of another. A balance had to be struck, and that was typically done by making the manumission conditional and forcing the new freedman to provide compensation to the heir(s). This could take a variety of forms, either by postponing the manumission or by making it dependent on payment or other services.

It is therefore in the context of testamentary manumission that we most frequently hear of payment for freedom.[286] A particular arrangement was by *fideicommissum*, which instructed the heir to free a slave after a given period of service or when certain conditions had been fulfilled.[287] In some cases the slave became a so-called *statuliber* during the period when he was working off the condition, a category which posed intricate legal questions extensively discussed by the jurists.[288] To compensate heirs, freedmen could also be obliged to perform *operae*, days of work. For example, in one case a slave was freed by will on condition of promising forty days of *operae* to the testator's son.[289] A formalised system of compensation made sense also because the close bond normally envisaged between freedman and patron did not obtain in cases where the patron was not directly responsible for the manumission but had inherited this role. While maintaining his legal claim on the freedman's estate, he would probably make less informal use of the freedman with whom he had no personal relationship. In this situation payment and regulated services would have represented an equitable compromise between the interests of freedman and heir.

Many owners probably also realised that if the newly gained freedom was to be of real benefit it would logically have to come with guarantees of future support, and as we have seen, testamentary manumission often seems to be accompanied by legacies and other forms of economic assistance. Some examples have already been discussed, but there is further evidence, such

---

[286] D. 40.4: 'De manumissis testamento.'

[287] D. 40.5: 'De fideicomissariis libertatibus.' These arrangements also presuppose that the *peculium* remained intact after the master's death and under normal circumstances would not be touched by the heirs.

[288] D. 40.7: 'De statuliberis'; Buckland (1908) 286–91.

[289] E.g. D. 40.4.36 (Paul); 40.7.20.5 (Paul); 40.7.24 (Marcellus). Champlin (1991) 135. We might speculate whether this could be the origin of the institution of *operae*, which I shall argue were poorly suited to regulate the ties between a freedman and his living patron, below pp. 224–6.

as *CIL* 13.5708 from Gaul which records a legacy to freedmen, some freed by will and some during the testator's lifetime, and the so-called 'Will of Dasumius' also includes several manumissions with legacies.[290] These additional expenses would have made it more difficult to balance the interests of freedmen and heirs and perhaps testators less inclined to free generously.

Overall, these considerations suggest that testamentary manumission may have been fairly limited, as indeed it was in most other slave societies. Comparative studies indicate that it applied to a relatively small minority of slaves, even in societies with substantial manumission rates. Thus, in places such as Rio, Suriname, and Spanish Louisiana the proportion of freedmen freed by will was around 12–15 per cent, mostly benefiting domestic staff.[291] In Rome the share of testamentary manumissions may have been even lower; the evidence certainly suggests small numbers and a high degree of selection. As Champlin noted, 'well over two-thirds of our references in the *Digest* are to one or two slaves', and many owners appear to have freed no slaves at all.[292] Even the extremely wealthy 'Dasumius' freed only a dozen or so slaves in his long and detailed will.[293]

As already noted, the evidence for large-scale testamentary manumission is limited to Dionysius of Halicarnassus' invective against contemporary manumission and the *lex Fufia Caninia*. The former is highly rhetorical, and Dionysius' insistence that he had actually heard of such instances suggests it remained exceptional. His claim was part of a general tirade against indiscriminate manumission, and the limitations introduced by the *lex Fufia Caninia* may, as argued above, be seen as a politically motivated response to similar concerns about moral decline. The new regulations sought to enforce proper vetting and selection of slaves, and the fact they applied only to testamentary manumission may reflect the (entirely realistic) assumption that *liberti orcini* would be subject to a weaker patronal authority. The law therefore demonstrates the sensitive nature of testamentary manumission rather than its popularity; certainly it cannot be taken as proof that testators regularly freed large sections of their households.[294]

---

[290] 6.10229. Champlin (1991) 138–40; Gardner (1993) 32–3. A Roman veteran who died in Egypt in 194 CE freed three slave women in his will, also providing an inheritance, *FIRA* 3.50. They may, as Keenan (1994) thought, be his two concubines and a daughter.

[291] Karasch (1987) 353: 12 per cent; Brana-Shute (1989) 55: 15 per cent; Cole (2005) 1014: 15 per cent.

[292] Champlin (1991) 140–2, also observing that: 'Of the wills preserved on papyrus, only three troubled to liberate slaves', 141.

[293] *CIL* 6.10229. Cf. the *tabulae* from Egypt (142 CE) with testamentary provisions, including the freeing of one slave whose *vicesima* was also paid, *FIRA* 3.47 lines 31–7.

[294] A republican epitaph from Venusia uniquely states that the *unguentarius* Philargyrus freed 'familiam suam', *CIL* I².1703. All other evidence is fictional. For Petr. *Sat.* 71.1–3, see above. Ps.-Quintilian,

Petronius' *Satyricon*, 42.6, mentions a Chrysanthus who freed some slaves in his will to make for a good mourning party. The phenomenon is known also from other sources, and scholars have identified it as an important incentive to testamentary manumission.[295] The appearance of newly freed slaves in funerary processions became something of a topos, partly because of the inherent paradox of festive celebrations occasioned by death.[296] The extent of this practice is uncertain, however, not least because owners had to consider the interests of heirs as well as their own posthumous reputation. The passing of the *lex Fufia Caninia* suggests that manumission, especially on a larger scale, was considered problematic when the freedman did not become subject to the authority of a patron who had personally freed him. Ideological concerns thus dictated that masters use this method sparingly and consider the fact that the *libertus orcinus* differed from other freedmen. Most likely a certain opprobrium attached to the display of 'irresponsible' generosity in wills, not least if there were any suspicion of personal vanity. This may of course not have deterred all slave owners but it would probably have tempered the satisfaction gained from it; the will was after all the last opportunity to present oneself as a responsible citizen. It may have been customary to free a few slaves in the will, but the most obvious candidates for manumission had probably already received their freedom at that point. Those left to the final moment might often have been younger slaves whose relatives had already been freed.

In some situations, especially when the family line came to an end and there were no *sui heredes*, the testator may have felt that greater generosity was called for. In that case the household was likely to be broken up, and the slaves divided between different heirs or perhaps sold off on the open market.[297] The latter was recognised as a terrible fate, and faced with that prospect owners might have looked more favourably on some of

---

Decl.Min. 311, outlines a complex scenario where a man becomes the *addictus* of another until his debt is paid off. The 'master' dies and in his will he sets all his slaves free; the question is whether the *addictus* is included. In this case the whole 'plot' hinges on the master's wish to free 'all the slaves' – rather than just a few – and the fact that it violated the *lex Fufia Caninia* and never could be implemented further suggests we are dealing with a hypothetical scenario of limited historical relevance.

[295] The freedmen could be required to attend the funeral, Ulp. *Reg.* 22.4, 24.18. Bodel's reference (1999a) 262, to the 'custom of manumitting slaves en masse in order to guarantee a well-attended funeral', probably goes too far. Three mourning figures wearing *pillei* were represented in the Haterii monument, *ibid.* fig. 3.

[296] Varro, *Men.Sat.* 47, notes that the master's funeral becomes a celebration of freedom, while Persius 3.105–6, mentions newly made citizens wearing (freedom) caps and carrying a body.

[297] Champlin (1991) 143, noted that there was a 'strong tendency among some of the childless not to make one friend sole heir but to split up the patrimony once and for all among several'.

their slaves and decided they deserved freedom rather than being passed on to new owners.[298] Thus, Cicero's willingness to free large numbers of slaves before going into exile was a direct response to the risk that his entire *familia* might be sold off. Tacitus also tells a story suggesting that owners behaved differently in such situations. Thus, when Scaevinus was accused of plotting against Nero, the fact that he had recently reopened his will and freed his slaves was seen as incriminating.[299] He defended himself by saying that he bequeathed more 'pecunias et libertates servis' because of straitened circumstances and pressing creditors, i.e. he explained his generosity by fears that his will might be disregarded and the *familia* broken up.

In conclusion, we may note that testamentary manumission occupied a distinct and somewhat anomalous position in Rome as it involved a separation of the freedman from the person who granted him his freedom. As such it raised ideological issues of supervision and control as well as moral concerns about self-indulgence and the danger of large-scale, 'irresponsible' manumission.[300] The large majority of freedmen were probably freed by patrons who expected to benefit from their gratitude and continued labour and services. Some were undoubtedly freed by will, but those selected were probably favoured slaves still in the process of 'earning' their freedom. Since death could intervene at any point, a master could ensure that they would not suffer unduly by making appropriate testamentary provisions. If there was a risk that the household might be divided up after the owner's death, he probably included larger sections of the urban *familia*, partly out of humanitarian concern and partly because he felt less inclined to preserve the estate for external heirs. The testator's multiple obligations remained crucial, to his heirs as well as to his loyal servants, which may explain the apparent frequency of conditional or suspended manumissions.

---

[298] E.g. D. 40.5.10 pr. (Pomponius), where an owner prescribes in his will that certain slaves should not be sold; cf. 40.5.12 pr. (Modestinus); 40.5.21 (Papinian); 40.5.24.8 (Ulpian). For the degrading experience of the slave market and the stigma attached to it, see Bodel (2005).

[299] *Ann.* 15.55.

[300] Champlin (1991) 142, following Wiedemann (1985), refers to a Roman 'ideal of manumission', but while there may have been a vague expectation that well-behaved slaves ought to be freed, the decision rested entirely with the owner, and there is no sign of social pressures being applied to reluctant masters who refused. Certainly, the law made no attempt to encourage masters to free slaves. Indeed, Papinian, D. 38.2.41, notes in passing that no one should be compelled to free by will any slave they find unworthy ('forte de se male meritum'). For that reason Marcus Aurelius also banned manumission 'ex acclamatione populi', D. 40.9.17 pr. (Paul). Other texts emphasise the *voluntas manumittendi* as crucial, *Frg.Dosith.* 7; cf. D. 40.9.9 pr. (Marcian). In this context the so-called *favor libertatis* is probably a red herring, since it merely implied that in ambiguous cases freedom should generally be favoured; cf. Ankum (2005).

THE PRACTICE OF MANUMISSION: SELECTION AND SUSTAINABILITY

After this attempt to establish a structural framework we may now turn to the practice of manumission, which means asking who was selected for manumission, under what circumstances, and for what reasons. As we have seen, Roman manumission can be interpreted as 'rational' in the sense that it provided an incentive for slaves in more responsible roles where simple coercion did not suffice. In this model the freeing of slaves was a means of making more efficient use of unfree labour, and in Rome this particular 'carrot' could be used more extensively because of the 'open' nature of Roman slavery in general. The problem is of course that despite its logical consistency the model may not describe how Roman slave owners actually behaved. In fact, there is no firm evidence that manumission was employed systematically as a managerial tool.

In Fenoaltea's model it was assumed that freedom was awarded to slaves performing specific functions where incentives were more efficient than supervision and compulsion, and much of the evidence for Roman freedmen would indeed seem to fit this pattern. Thus, a large proportion of the recorded freedmen appear to have been skilled craftsmen, business managers, and administrators, i.e. those in positions of responsibility within the households or actively involved in the market economy. These were all functions where personal motivation mattered and the apparent role of the *peculium* as a practical measure of the slave's dedication points in the same direction. We might therefore conclude that manumission was indeed used to improve the efficiency of slave labour, but there are other features that may suggest a different interpretation, or at least a modification of the 'rational' model. They relate primarily to the age and gender of the slaves who benefited from manumission.

The age at which slaves were freed provides an important indicator of the nature of the manumission process, and, as we have seen, there is evidence that many slaves were released even before they even reached adulthood. Thus, Weaver argued on the basis of a sample of urban inscriptions that 70 per cent were freed under the age of 20, and that 'as many were freed under the age of ten as could have been freed over the age of 19'.[301] These figures, however, are unlikely to give an accurate picture of actual manumission practices. As a demographic profile of the freed population, the epigraphic age records have limited credibility since they leave out

---

[301] Weaver (1990) 286, 291. Shaw (1991) 74, table 4.2, indicates that 21.4 per cent of freedmen in Rome were commemorated below the age of 10.

those who died in middle or old age. These people may also have received more infrequent commemoration because of the prevalence of parental commemoration of children. Thus, according to the figures of Saller and Shaw, the frequency of parent-for-child commemoration in Rome was more than twice that of child-for-parent, 33 per cent compared to 14.[302] These culturally determined patterns automatically distort the proportion of freed children in the sample. Moreover, it is in the nature of the evidence that all the young freedmen died prematurely, and we cannot exclude the possibility that their early manumission may have been linked to this feature. Thus, if we look at the proportion of freedmen among the early age groups in Roman epitaphs we find no steady progression in their share.[303] The fact that the ratio of freed to slave children does not rise cumulatively suggests that many of them were freed precisely because they faced *mors immatura*. This practice is well documented from Roman literature, where Petronius mentions a certain Scissa who freed 'servo suo misello' on his deathbed. Martial freed his young scribe Demetrius under similar circumstances, and Pliny said he readily granted freedom to *iuvenes* so they could die as free men.[304] These were largely symbolic gestures, and apart from the emotional attachment which they imply, there may also have been an element of social ostentation to the act, demonstrating the humanity as well as the power and wealth of the owner, who would have to pay the manumission tax (that is, unless he simply reimbursed himself from the slave's *peculium*).[305]

Some young slaves were freed under happier circumstances, usually children found particularly attractive or precocious, but there is no evidence this was considered normal practice. For example, Statius' eulogy for the father of Claudius Etruscus, who was freed by Tiberius while still a youth,

---

[302] Saller and Shaw (1984) 147; cf. Huttunen (1974) 145.
[303] Freeborn, freed and slave in epitaphs from city of Rome, vol. 6. The figures include those given as (v. or vixit) annis and ann. v, x, and xv.

	Freed		slave		freeborn		total
Five-year-olds	24	16%	81	55%	42	29%	147
Ten-year-olds	4	12%	17	50%	13	38%	34
Fifteen-year-olds	10	15%	29	43%	28	42%	67

The figures seem to indicate a rise in freeborn at the expense of slaves, but that reflects the epigraphic convention which favoured the commemoration of younger slaves over older.
[304] *Sat.* 65.10–11; Mart. 1.101; *Ep.* 8.16.1.
[305] Perhaps to avoid this suspicion Pliny explicitly tells us that he allowed his slaves to pass on their *peculium* to other members of the *familia*, *Ep.* 8.16.2.

stresses his premature talents – 'gifted as you were much beyond your years' – thereby explaining his unusually early manumission.[306] Similarly, Martial wrote an epitaph for Glaucias, already a freedman despite being just 12 years old, noting he had been freed 'before he could appreciate it' for his exceptional *mores* and *forma*.[307]

Some of the young *liberti* may also be explained as a result of testamentary manumission and the master's wish to save them from the slave market. In some cases they may have been passed on to parents already freed, while in other instances their freedom may have been achieved through payment by relatives, whether freed or slaves.[308] Others may have been the *filii naturales* of their masters, although there is little evidence to suggest that blood relationship generally led to early manumission.[309] Therefore, despite their frequent appearance in epitaphs, freed children are likely to have been the exception. On the other hand, when it comes to slightly older age groups we seem to be on much firmer ground; for although the epigraphic evidence is defective in respect of older slaves/freedmen, it does indicate the existence of substantial numbers of young freedmen manumitted already in their late teens and, above all, in their twenties.[310] This is in itself hardly surprising since the Augustan threshold for enfranchisement logically would have been set higher than the age at which manumission normally happened.[311] If the new regulations merely formalised existing norms, they would have been redundant from both a practical and an ideological point of view.

[306] *Silv.* 3.3.68–9: 'annis multum super indole victis'.

[307] 6.28; 6.29; cf. Statius, *Silv.* 2.1. Likewise *Silv.* 2.6, written for Ursus' favourite slave, who was still young (cf. 44–5 and *Praef.* 2.20), gives no hint that he might have deserved his freedom.

[308] In Rio 13 per cent of freed people were children, often bought free by their mothers, Karasch (1987) 347–8.

[309] Scheidel (2009), following Betzig (1992) 330–7, argued they might have been a very common type, and Augustus explicitly exempted *filii naturales* from the manumission regulations, Gaius *Inst.* 1.19; cf. D. 40.2.11, 20.3 (Ulpian). However, they are largely absent from the epigraphic record. In *CIL* 6 only fourteen people are described as *filii naturales*, and only one as *filia naturalis idemque liberta*, 6.21458. Betzig's (1992) 339, radical suggestion that the Romans freed so many slaves because they were their own offspring is hardly plausible.

[310] Alföldy (1986a); Weaver (1990), contradicting his earlier views expressed in (1972) 98. The evidence from the *columbaria* also suggests that manumission below the age of 30 was not uncommon, cf. above p. 151.

[311] *Contra* Weaver (1972) 104, who referred to the 'the normal minimum prescribed by the lex Aelia Sentia', cf. 86, 98. Dumont (1987) 65–6, 81, assumed 30 was the standard age of manumission, arguing that Augustus by fixing that age for enfranchisement sought to return to a long-established norm. Augustus, however, was concerned with restricting access to citizenship – not manumission, and the figure may have been chosen fairly randomly as a reasonable age at which the freedman should have reached sufficient 'maturity' to merit Roman citizenship. Augustus also set other normative age limits, e.g. specifying the age at which it was acceptable to remain unmarried, 50 for women and 60 for men. Again this was an ideological statement and we cannot deduce from these prescriptions at what age men and women normally chose not to remarry.

Before exploring the wider implications of this pattern of manumission we may briefly consider the consequences for the freedmen's civic status. After the Augustan reforms, formal manumission with full citizenship was largely restricted to slaves over 30, and the relatively low age of manumission suggested above would imply that large numbers of freedmen were affected.[312] For some their Latin status would have been temporary, since they could 'upgrade' through child rearing, a right later extended to those freed after the age of 30 (probably in 75 CE). Latini Iuniani could also gain citizenship through *iteratio*, that is, if their patron agreed to formal manumission when they had reached the appropriate age. It is not given, however, that age was the main factor determining their status. Masters may often have preferred informal manumission, which gave them a stronger claim on the freedman's estate – and for that reason perhaps also more effective control. There were also practical obstacles to formal manumission. If, as it seems, the presence of a magistrate with *imperium* was required, it would have been very difficult to free formally outside the city of Rome.[313]

The apparent youth of many freedmen poses a challenge to the conventional model of 'rational' manumission, suggesting as it does that freedom was a favour that could be bestowed on almost any slave – irrespective of age – who had gained the owner's trust and sympathy. As such, it emerges as a 'promotion' granted in anticipation of loyal duty rather than as a reward for services already provided; or in other words, the freedman's gratitude appears to have been considered a spur for good work as effective as the slave's hope of freedom. Viewed from this perspective, early manumission modifies the 'rational' model of manumission rather than overturning it, but it might still have important economic implications; for while it did not entail any immediate loss of labour, the freeing of slaves who had not yet reproduced meant forgoing the next generation of *vernae*, which might put the long-term survival of the *familia* at risk. The sources of slaves,

---

[312] López Barja de Quiroga (1998); Weaver (1990), (1997); Camodeca (2006b) 200. Individual Latini Iuniani cannot be identified epigraphically, since they seem to carry 'normal' Roman nomenclature despite their lack of citizenship, cf. Mouritsen (2007a).

[313] The evidence of Pliny, *Ep.* 7.16.4, 32.1, demonstrates the need for a magistrate with *imperium*. In the provinces the local magistrates could apparently oversee formal manumission, which gave the freedman local citizenship, *lex Irn.* ch. 28, cf. Gardner (2001). See also Salsano (1998); Vitali (2005). Most modern discussions have focused on the question of age but the need to appear in front of a magistrate would probably have acted as a far greater obstacle to formal manumission. This would also have made *iteratio* difficult to carry out. However, *Frg.Dosith.* 14, indicates that *iteratio* could be done both *vindicta* and by will: 'postea iterum manumitti possit vindicta vel testamento et civis Romanus fit'. In the latter case full enfranchisement could be effected without recourse to a magistrate. Whether that necessarily made the procedure more common cannot be determined, since testamentary 'up-grading' of Latini would deprive heirs of their estates.

especially under the empire, have been much debated, but a consensus seems to be forming that reproduction must have been a vital factor in maintaining Roman slavery.[314] The impact of manumission on slave reproduction will have to remain a matter of speculation. In theory it could be entirely self-sustainable, that is, if all freedmen had already reproduced before manumission. Total sustainability is unrealistic, however, not least given the apparent frequency of early manumission.[315] Particularly important, of course, is the rate of manumission of *servae*, who held the key to the demographic sustainability of the household.

It is a common assumption that women were freed more frequently than men.[316] The hypothesis partly relies on epigraphic evidence but is also bolstered by comparative studies which suggest that in most slave societies manumission has been predominantly female.[317] Thus, the manumission records from Delphi show that women made up the majority, or 63 per cent, of those freed. The same ratio is encountered throughout Latin America, where women consistently outnumber men. In Rio two thirds were female and similar percentages are found elsewhere on the continent.[318] The pattern is so pronounced that one study concluded that 'manumission is largely a gender-related phenomenon'.[319] Given this degree of consistency, we might expect a similar preference in Rome, but we have to remember that in most societies there were specific factors promoting female rather than male manumission.

In Greece manumission generally involved payment, with the attendant implication of discontinuity and replacement. In this situation owners appear to have been more willing to part with female slave labour. Moreover, the lower market value of female slaves also made it relatively easier for women to buy their freedom. In Latin America the common practice of self-purchase offered surprising advantages to female slaves who did

---

[314] Scheidel (1997); Roth (2007); *contra* Harris (1999). 'Breeding' of slaves is referred to in only three sources, Colum. *Rust.* 1.8.19, and D. 40.7.3.16 (Julian); 1.5.15 (Thryphoninus). The much debated passage D. 5.3.27 pr. (Ulpian) does not, as it has been suggested, indicate that female slaves were bought for the purpose of breeding; cf. Treggiari (1979) 188.

[315] Brunt (1971a) 143–6, discussed the factors which may have limited the size of freedmen's families and their ability to produce freeborn children. Some hypothetical scenarios have been explored by Scheidel (2008).

[316] Weaver (1972) 70; Pomeroy (1975) 195; Treggiari (1975a); López Barja de Quiroga (1998) 153–4; Madden (1996) 118; Smadja (1999) 356, 361; Weiler (2001) 127–31; sceptical Brunt (1971a) 144.

[317] Cf. Patterson (1982).

[318] Karasch (1987) 345; Johnson (1979) 262–3; Klein and Luna (2000) 917; Libby and Paiva (2000) 102–3; Queirós Mattoso (1986) 165; Bergad *et al.* (1995) 141, fig. 6.3, summarise the manumission patterns in Latin America.

[319] Brana-Shute (1989) 58.

not just carry a lower price but also were more directly involved in the urban economy. Many female slaves worked as petty traders and were able to accumulate savings. On the other hand, when male slaves worked outside the household, often hired out as day labourers, the payment would go directly to the owners. Scholars have also pointed to a specific African tradition of female market trading, which they brought with them to the New World.[320] Another issue that must be taken into account is manumission for the purpose of marriage, which in some societies made up a substantial share of the total. There were, in other words, particular reasons why women dominated the manumission records in these societies, and it is not given that they also applied in Rome, where we have no evidence for specifically female trading patterns and payment may have been more limited.[321]

Attempts have been made to quantify female manumission but the available epigraphic evidence presents the usual obstacles. The inscriptions from the large familial *columbaria* may represent our best chance since they offer a detailed 'snapshot' of distinct epigraphic environments in which men and women and slaves and freed appear to have had relatively easy access to commemoration. Analysis of this material suggests that at least in aristocratic households the overall gender balance may have been skewed towards males.[322] But there are also indications that women had a slightly higher manumission rate than men, although that feature may be specific to this particular type of household for reasons we will return to below.[323] In any case, there is little evidence to support the idea of a substantially higher female manumission rate throughout Roman society, but neither are there any signs of masters being less willing to free women. This naturally draws attention to the age at which they received their freedom. Alföldy's figures showed that freedwomen generally were younger than freedmen, a

---

[320] Johnson (1979) 276; Karasch (1987) 347; Libby and Paiva (2000); Lewis (2004) 169–71. Interestingly, where payment is not a factor the gender balance tends to be more even; cf. Handler and Pohlmann (1984), who discuss the evidence from testamentary manumission in seventeenth-century Barbados.

[321] In Roman Egypt it has been suggested that virtually all female slaves had been freed before reaching middle age, at which point they seem to disappear from the census records, Bagnall and Frier (1994) 158; cf. Scheidel (1997) 162. If authentic, however, such a pattern of manumission would be quite unique among known slave societies.

[322] In the *columbaria* of the Statilii, Volusii and Arruntii women make up between 31 and 36 per cent, but some of this imbalance may be explained by patterns of commemoration and general under-representation of younger *servae*; cf. Mouritsen (forthcoming).

[323] Among the Statilii the ratio of freed to slave was 30/70 among males and 36/64 among females, while in the Volusian material the corresponding figures are 41/59 and 44/56. Marriages between *libertae* and *servi* were also more common than between *liberti* and *servae*, 22 to 6.

pattern he explained by marriage to the patron, which obviously favoured early rather than late manumission.[324] Augustus had exempted slaves freed *matrimonii causa* from the age requirements for formal manumission, but the epigraphic evidence for *patronus/liberta* unions is limited. Phrases such as 'vir et patronus' and 'coniunx et liberta' occur in a very small percentage of the total number of epigraphically recorded marriages from the city of Rome.[325] The age difference itself is also open to doubt since age at death was indicated only for the deceased, not for the dedicator, and far more husbands commemorated wives than vice versa.[326] Women probably had a higher mortality rate in early adulthood because of the risks of childbirth, in which case they were probably more likely to receive formal commemoration with an inscribed epitaph that included their age at death. It is also worth noting that the *columbaria* material does not suggest any substantial difference in the ages at which men and women were freed. We may conclude that *servae* were freed neither earlier nor more frequently than *servi*. This modifies some modern theories, but still leaves open the question of what impact manumission had on the Roman slave supply.

The freedmen's marriage patterns may cast further light on the extent of the demographic 'losses' involved. The crucial issue is the rate of reproduction prior to manumission, and an important clue to answering that question is the extent to which freed people married outside their *familia*. Weaver suggested that only a third of them did so, but epigraphic samples from Rome, Ostia, and other Italian cities all seem to indicate substantially higher proportions of 'mixed' marriages.[327] In Rome a random sample of

[324] Alföldy (1986a) 301, whose figures indicated 305 *liberti* and 443 *libertae* commemorated below the age of 30. Cf. Weaver (1972) 99. On this practice see Rawson (1989) 18; Wacke (2001).

[325] Weaver (1972) 181, suggested a much higher figure (26 per cent) but there are methodological flaws in his calculations. His analysis included couples where at least one partner could be identified as freed, normally on the basis of pseudo-filiation. The identification of *patronus–liberta* marriages, however, is usually based on the phrases 'coniunx et liberta' or 'vir et patronus', which refer to the relationship between the dedicator and the deceased. The information about *patronus–liberta* marriages and 'normal' marriages therefore derives from two different types of epigraphic data which make them statistically incomparable. Huttunen's (1974) 147, sample revealed only a minuscule number of this type of marriages.

[326] Dedications from husband to wife were double that of wife to husband. cf. Huttunen (1974) 56; the sample of Saller and Shaw (1984) 140, table c, suggests an even stronger predominance of husband-to-wife commemoration in Rome, with a ratio of five to one.

[327] Weaver (1972) 191–2; (1991) 179. The figures, listed in (1972) 180–1, are partly distorted by the inclusion of *patronus–liberta* marriages among securely documented freed couples which, as noted above, generally were recorded differently from normal libertinisation. The same applies to references to *colliberti*. It also counts couples where one partner was still a slave, which further distorts the picture, since they can be identified simply through their nomenclature. Weaver (1990) 302, also argued that only one third of the children of freedmen were freeborn, but again the statistics adduced in support do not allow this conclusion. However, if we isolate the figures for

374 couples which may be identified as freed with varying degrees of certainty shows 37 per cent carry the same *nomen* while the rest belonged to different *familiae*. In Ostia the corresponding figures are 24 and 76 (total 132), at Portus 32 and 68 (total 99), and in Beneventum 14 and 86 (total 104).[328] It could be argued that since these figures include both probable and certain freedmen they may be unreliable, but if we look at the latter in isolation the result is only a slight modification – based on much reduced samples.[329] Nevertheless there is marginally higher frequency of identical *nomina* among the 'certain' freedmen, which may reflect the presence in the larger sample of first-generation *ingenui*, some of whom carried Greek *cognomina* and married outside the *familia*.

The big question is whether this profile corresponds to the actual marriage patterns, and here the evidence from the *columbaria* may give us an indication, since it differs in important respects from the general body of funerary inscriptions, discussed above. This material suggests that only 14 per cent married outside the *familia*, although there is a possibility that some of those who did so also were buried outside the *columbarium*.[330] However, this factor is unlikely to account for the entire difference between the two samples. The nature of the *columbaria* may provide part of the explanation since they offered formal burial for the whole *familia*, including its more humble members, whereas the main body of *sepulchrales* mostly consists of dedicatory *tituli* placed on individual tombs commissioned by freedmen. Given the cost involved, it would not be surprising if they showed a different social profile, representing a more affluent section of the freed population than those in the *columbaria*. These successful freedmen were those who had enjoyed the greatest patronal favour, been freed early, and married outside the *familia*, from which they may have

---

epigraphically comparable freed couples we get the ratio 119/217 for identical and different *nomina*, which is broadly in line with the figures presented below. Taylor (1961) 124, estimated that 40 per cent of marriages were between partners with identical *nomen*.

[328] The Roman survey covers *CIL* 6.18491–796; 6.24321–706; 6.28298–707; 6.33422–704; 6.34029–624. In Ostia the sample is provided by the complete list of 'titulary' epitaphs in Mouritsen (2004), and for Portus the Thylander (1952) section A is the basis for the figures. At Beneventum the sample covers *CIL* 9.1567–2040. The criteria for identifying freedmen are pseudo-filiation and Greek cognonima. Marriages where one partner is a slave or a member of the imperial household and *patronus–liberta* unions are not considered.

[329] In Rome the balance shifts to 44/56 per cent (but on the basis of just 18 per cent of the original sample, or 68 couples); Ostia 27/73 (34 per cent of the full sample); Beneventum 20/80 (29 per cent of the sample). At Portus libertinisation is too rare to allow this comparison.

[330] Eleven marriages out of seventy-nine among the slaves and freedmen of the Statilii and Volusii involved outsiders. Of those who married within the *familia*, almost half of the freed couples (fifteen out of thirty-three) had children who were still slaves, itself a minimum figure since the free children of course might also have been slaves at some point; Mouritsen (forthcoming).

become increasingly detached, especially if their patron died. This category of freedmen was in other words those who had the greatest incentive and ability to put up their own monuments and inscriptions as well as the best opportunities to marry outside the *familia*.[331] Therefore we cannot conclude from this evidence that most freedmen formed marital unions only after their manumission, although the proportion that did so may have been considerably higher than often assumed.[332] There may also have been structural factors involved, for while most slaves could find partners within the large aristocratic *familiae*, which would explain their higher degree of 'self-sufficiency', it is probably unrealistic to expect all slaves to pair up into family units in smaller households. The result would have been a lower reproduction rate, unless we envisage cross-familial *contubernia* where masters allowed their slaves to form unions outside their *familia* for the purpose of reproduction.[333]

   While manumission did cause a shortfall in the internal slave supply, it must also be put in perspective; only a minority of slaves were ever freed and for that reason the overall impact may have been limited, although it still represented a disadvantage for individual slave owners. In some cases 'humanitarian' sentiments may have prevailed over strictly economic considerations, but most often these 'losses' would probably not have been subject to cost–benefit calculations. The Roman elite did not conceive of their households in purely rational terms, the *domus* functioning as an extension of the *pater familias'* public persona and embodying his status and position in society. As such it was a vital locus of consumption and competitive display, and the household staff, their numbers, quality, and specialisation, were essential components of this process. The point is well

---

[331] This conclusion also affects Weaver's theory, (1972) 179–95, that an unusually high proportion of imperial freedmen married outside the *familia*, which he explained by their greater prestige and attractiveness as marriage partners, even to *ingenuae*. The difference may in fact have been relatively small, and to the extent it existed it may simply have reflected a certain laissez-faire attitude in the imperial household, permitting slaves and freedmen to form families outside the *familia*. Such a policy might also have been dictated by purely practical concerns, since there probably were far more men serving in the imperial administration. Moreover, the emperor is unlikely to have been overly concerned with the supply of new slaves, given his position and the steady flow of inheritances he received. Weaver's hypothesis that the *senatus consultum Claudianum* was an attempt specifically to preserve *vernae* for the *domus Augusta* is therefore less plausible.

[332] For example, D'Arms (1981) 134, declared that more than 90 per cent of freed couples carried the same *nomen*.

[333] Tertullian, *Ad uxor*. 2.8.1, makes the interesting comment that some very strict masters forbid their slaves to form *contubernia* outside the household, 'foras nubere', suggesting that others allowed it. In Petr. *Sat*. 61.6–9, a slave is trying to form a relationship with a *serva* living next door, but without either master's permission; cf. Rawson (1966) 79; Weaver (1972) 191; Treggiari (1975a) 398; Bradley (1984a) 74.

illustrated by the section of Cicero's invective against Piso which focused
on his household. Cicero described it as unworthy of a man of Piso's status,
his slaves being unkempt and some of them even old. To make matters
worse, each of them carried out several tasks, cook and *atriensis* being the
same, and there was not even a baker in the house. Such economy of labour
was a definite sign of meanness.[334] As Treggiari demonstrated in her classic
study, the elite household was characterised by an extreme specialisation
of domestic tasks, which served no purpose beyond the demonstration
of wealth and status.[335] Many domestic slaves were therefore regarded
not as investments from which actual returns were expected so much as
luxury items on a par with other extravagant elements of the aristocratic
household.[336]

The internal divisions of labour and the wide range of specialised craftsmen may have reflected an aristocratic ideal of domestic self-sufficiency,
which paradoxically applied to the individual functions within the household but not to the overall supply of staff members. Thus, an entirely
self-sustainable household was incompatible with the elite's concern for
the 'quality' of their slaves. In that context Cicero's friend Atticus was
clearly unusual in his insistence on running his household entirely with
vernae; indeed his eulogising biographer, Cornelius Nepos, had to point
out that despite this policy he did not lack competent staff.[337] To many
masters, an entirely sustainable household would have been neither realistic nor desirable. Because the skills and qualities required were so refined
and the vacancies occurred so unpredictably, there would always be a need
for supplementing elite households with slaves from the market. Normally
the household would therefore be composed of a mix of *vernae* of all
ages and purchased slaves, often distinguished by specialist skills. The literary sources reveal a distinction between the 'homely' slaves born in the

---

[334] *Pis.* 67. Garland's claim (1992) that Cicero himself had a small and modest household is not convincing. In Petr. *Sat.* 68.8, the mean Habinnas praises a slave who can perform many different tasks, whereas Trimalchio himself had a larger number of specialised staff, although Baldwin (1978) suggested he too had to cut corners. See however Puglisi (1987).

[335] Treggiari (1975b).

[336] There are plenty of examples of 'ornamental' slaves and freedmen in the households of the Statilii and Volusii, e.g. *cantrix, citharoedus, nomenclator, silentiarius, comoedus, symphoniacus* (and the Statilii had no fewer than seven *unctores*), in addition to some highly specialised staff members, e.g. *specularius, vestipicus* (clothes folder), *lanipendus* (wool weigher), *fartor* (poulterer), *colorator*. The author of the 'Testamentum Dasumii' freed his *dropacator* (depilator), *CIL* 6.10229 lines 69–70.

[337] *Att.* 13.3–4. Nepos chose to present Atticus' domestic economy as a sign of modesty with the added implication of clean living, since attractive slaves (bought on the market) could be seen as an indicator of *luxuria* and indulgence. Moreover, *vernae* were typically seen as less degraded than those from the market.

household and the expensive 'luxury' slaves from the market.[338] In addition to these categories there was also another important source of slaves, namely those acquired though legacies and inheritances, which would often have provided a steady supply of new staff. For example, in Petronius a cook is asked whether he is bought or homeborn, to which the answer is that he is neither since he was left to Trimalchio in a will. The same tripartite origin recurs in Ps.-Quintilian, where slaves are defined as 'either born, left in an inheritance or bought'.[339]

The long-term sustainability of the household is therefore unlikely to have been a major concern for the elite. The losses involved in freeing young and fertile slaves may have been accepted as part of the regular cost of running the *familia*. The notion of 'profitable' manumission would have been out of tune with the ideology of the Roman elite, for whom the ability to make generous gestures with little concern for the economic consequences was a reflection of wealth and status. Taking such a high-minded approach may have been the privilege of a small but immensely wealthy elite, although we cannot discount the possibility that the aristocratic ideals may also have shaped behaviour further down the social scale. Most likely, however, less affluent owners would probably not have been able to afford such disregard for their future slave supply.

It follows that while manumission as an institution served a broadly rational purpose its application was not governed by any strict economic logic. The question is therefore which factors determined who was freed and who was not. When looking at the profile of freedmen in the large aristocratic households, it is difficult to identify a clear or consistent pattern. Certainly, no regulated career paths leading to manumission seem to have been in place. While most of those performing more responsible roles eventually would be freed, young and unskilled servants also appear to have benefited. Our picture remains incomplete, not least because freedmen were commemorated with their job titles less frequently than slaves, but the overall impression is that personal contact with the master and his family greatly increased the slave's chance of gaining freedom. For example, in the *columbarium* of the Statilii we find staff members of relatively high rank (as indicated by job titles and number of *vicarii*) who remained slaves,

---

[338] E.g. Martial 2.90.9; 12.70.1, 87.2; Hor. *Carm.* 1.4.19; *Epod.* 2.65. On the attraction of *vernae*, Treggiari (1979) 188–9.

[339] *Sat.* 47.12–13; *Decl.Min.* 311.7: 'aut natus aut relictus hereditate aut emptus'; cf. Quintilian, *Inst.Or.* 5.10.67, who lists the ways a slave might come into one's possession as birth, purchase, gift, bequest, or capture from enemy.

while others working more closely with the master's family were freed.[340] Similarly those freed in the 'Testamentum Dasumii' were almost all directly involved with the master.[341]

Simple proximity and the familiarity it naturally generates may have been major factors in the manumission process, especially in the large households where the number of slaves might run into hundreds. Pliny's moralising description of 'mancipiorum legiones', 'armies of slaves', may exaggerate only slightly, and his suggestion that a *nomenclator* was required also has a ring of truth to it.[342] This may explain why *servae* were freed so regularly in this environment, since female servants, despite their relatively humble status in the domestic hierarchy, often had close personal contact with the owner's family. At the same time, these households comprised many low-ranking male slaves such as bodyguards and litter-carriers who apparently were freed only rarely.

There appears to have been a 'subjective' aspect to the manumission process and in some instances perhaps even an element of spontaneity, as suggested by various anecdotes. For example, the fabulists tell a story of an imperial house-slave at Misenum. When Tiberius visited and took a stroll in the grounds, he tried to attract favourable attention by watering the ground before the emperor to lay the dust. His hopes of freedom were thwarted, however, when the emperor told him he had to work much harder to earn the 'slap on the shoulder'.[343] Claudius Etruscus' father was obviously luckier. As Statius stressed, early career opportunies emerged when he came close to the emperor: 'always were you privileged to walk close to the deity, always to attend Caesar's side', and manumission therefore followed quickly.[344] Other examples include the story about Cicero freeing a slave who happened to bring him good news, and Petronius' Trimalchio who

---

[340] To the former belong e.g. Chrestus Auctianus (three *vicarii*, 6.6228, 6385, 6398); Hipparchus (three *vicarii*, 6292, 6293, 6392; and Chrestus Tauri with two (6390, 6402). One also notes the slave status of Thyrsus *medicus* (6320). Among the latter we note e.g. T. Statilius Zabda, *paedagogus*, 6330; Statilia T.l. Tyranis, *paedagoga*, 6331; T. Statilius Tauri l. Spinther, *supra lecticarius*, i.e. in charge of the litter bearers, 6301; Phileros lib. *unctor*, 6381; T. Statilius Phileros, Corneliaes *cubicularius*, 6264; T. Statilius Dasius Tauri l. *ad vestem*, 6372; T. Statilius T.l. Hilar[–] Cor. *vest.*, 6373, and T. Statilius Malchio, *ad vestem*, 6374.

[341] CIL 6.10229. They include two *notarii* (40, 43), a *cocus* (42), a *vestiarius* (50), a *paedagogus* (51), a *cubicularius* (68), the afore-mentioned *dropacator* (69), a *sutor* (70), a *medicus* (73), a *cubicularius maior* (78), and an *actor* (86). The *nutrix* Dasumia Syche, possibly a freedwoman of the testator's mother, also features (35, 47); cf. Eck (1978) 281ff.

[342] NH 33.26: 'mancipiorum legiones, in domo turba externa ac iam servorum quoque causa nomen-clator adhibendus'; cf. Tac. *Ann.* 14.44, who also implies that households were made up of many nationalities: 'nationes in familiis habemus'.

[343] Phaedrus 2.5 (Perry 489); Aesop 593.

[344] Silv. 3.3.64–6: 'semperque gradus prope numina, semper Caesareum coluisse latus'.

freed several slaves during a single dinner.[345] Although the latter example is clearly exaggerated, the ease of manumission that it illustrates was real and undoubtedly facilitated by the existence of both formal and informal procedures.

Roman masters mostly seem to have freed the slaves they had come to know and trust through direct personal contact.[346] The importance of familiarity would also explain the predominantly urban character of manumission, for although some of the evidence is inconclusive, there are good reasons for assuming that most country slaves generally had little chance of gaining freedom.[347] Thus, despite their keen interest in keeping the workforce motivated, the agrarian writers never suggest that manumission be used as an incentive for rural slave labour, apart from the specific rewards for particularly fertile *servae*. Instead they recommend other forms of encouragement and rewards, e.g. the allocation of a *peculium*. Even the *vilici* were apparently not considered for manumission.[348] Rural manumission is also conspicuously absent from the legal sources. As Champlin noted, in Roman wills country slaves normally feature as part of the farm equipment passed on to heirs rather than as beneficiaries of *manumissio ex testamento*.[349] Rural freedmen are very difficult to trace epigraphically, in stark contrast to the ubiquitous urban freedmen who put up thousands of inscriptions. The 'epigraphic habit' was admittedly an overwhelmingly urban phenomenon, but since it was also to a very great extent driven and defined by freedmen, there are no compelling reasons why rural freedmen

---

[345] Plut. *Apophth.Cic.* 21 (*Mor.* 205E); *Sat.* 41.6–8; 54.5. This may also be the case in Apul. *Apol.* 17–23, where three slaves were freed in one day – to celebrate the master's marriage? In Propert. 3.6.41–2, a slave is promised freedom if the lover and the slave's mistress are reunited.

[346] Already Strack (1914) 8, observed that 'persönliche Bekanntschaft' usually was 'die Vorbedingung für die Freilassung'.

[347] Limited rural manumission: Bradley (1987) 103–4; Scheidel (1997) 165–6. Following Frier (1979) 216, Scheidel (1993) 195, discussed the possibility of freedmen as *coloni*, suggesting landowners would benefit from greater familiarity with the tenants and hence better control. But there is little evidence for this practice and the owners' familiarity with rural slaves may often have been limited. Segenni (1990) suggested that many freedmen were employed in agriculture, often as agents of absentee landowners.

[348] Cato *Agr.* 5.1–5; Varro *Rust.* 1.4–7; Colum. *Rust.* 1.8.1–14; cf. Plin. *NH* 18.36. The *vilicus* in Horace's *Epist.* 1.14, was also a slave. This impression is largely confirmed by epigraphic evidence for estate managers: Beare (1978) 398; Scheidel (1990) 592; Teitler (1993); Aubert (1994) 149–58; Carlsen (1995) 92–101. Certainly in Italy examples of freed *vilici* are extremely rare and often ambiguous, the clearest being *CIL* 10.5081 and *AE* 1980 229.

[349] Champlin (1991) 141f. An exception is D. 33.7.12.31 (Ulpian), dealing with slaves on a farm who were included in the *instrumentum* apart from those who were to be freed. In D. 33.2.33.2 (Scaevola), old and infirm freedmen were allowed to stay in the places they now occupied, which may have been farms, since the jurist refers to the 'fructus' of these.

should not have adopted the practice.[350] The concentration of freedmen in cities may appear 'natural', not least from a comparative perspective, manumission being predominantly urban in most slave societies. But we should not mistake this pattern for a universal 'law', since in each case there were culturally specific factors responsible for the distribution, above all the prevalence of payment.[351]

The apparent rarity of rural manumission adds a further complication to the 'rational' model of manumission, for although some basic functions of agricultural slavery may not have benefited much from this type of incentive, others clearly did. Most obviously, the role of the overseer was precisely one of those responsible functions for which masters normally used the 'carrot' rather than the 'stick'. Reluctance to free *vilici* may be rooted in concerns about control and the difficulty of supervision, but in other contexts the Roman elite were happy to entrust important business to freedmen who acted as *procuratores* outside the household. The concentration of manumission in cities might therefore suggest that subjective factors and personal acquaintance took precedence over strict managerial logic.[352] Masters would typically have been on more intimate terms with their urban domestic staff than with even the most trusted *vilicus*, let alone slaves working in the fields.[353]

There were other household functions which rarely seem to have led to manumission, particularly those of *actor* and *dispensator*, and this may be explained by the particular sensitivity of their tasks, handling their master's

---

[350] Possible exceptions include e.g. *CIL* 11.600, from Forum Livi (Forli), which is a funerary dedication by *liberti* to their patron, who is praised for his kindness, especially towards those 'qui agros bene et strenue colant'; cf. Waldstein (1986) 289. Given the unusual nature of the inscription, it may well reflect an atypical farm regime. Moreover, the inscription is fragmentary and the extant text largely the result of Bormann's extensive restoration. It has been suggested the freedmen in question were *coloni*; Frier (1979) 216; Los (1992a) 748–9; Scheidel (1993).

[351] *Pace* Patterson (1982) 269–70. In most societies manumission has been largely urban but that is generally because of the practice of self-purchase, which requires integration into the (urban) market economy, cf. pp. 159–80. If, as I have argued, payment was less important in Rome, this might in principle have reduced the urban bias.

[352] Interestingly, the only documented instance of manumission used as reward for achieving pre-defined goals relates to childbearing in the countryside, Colum. *Rust.* 1.8.19; D. 40.7.3.16 (Julian); 1.5.15 (Thryphoninus).

[353] It is striking that Cicero never mentions any slave or freedman outside of his urban *familia*, and here only those who were directly involved in his work and personal affairs. Quintus' *vilicus* Nicephorus is mentioned in the context of building works at his villa, *Q.fr.* 3.1.5; cf. Carlsen (1995) 99, and his slave Cillo was summoned for a similar purpose, *Q.fr.* 3.1.3. In Petr. *Sat.* 69.3, the 'biography' of Trimalchio includes a rural episode; suspected of having an affair with his mistress he was demoted from *dispensator* to *vilicus* on a country estate, but later regained his master's favour. In this story the exceptional promotion of a *vilicus* was explained by his previous close relationship with the master. Trimalchio himself implied that he did not even know the *vilicus* of a certain estate, *Sat.* 53.5.

money. When it came to financial administration and book keeping, the balance of trust and control appears to have tilted in favour of the latter. Masters would have found the ultimate penalty a useful deterrent, in addition to a variety of other physical sanctions which could be dispensed without recourse to the courts.[354]

Personal trust remained the key to manumission, since the owner had to be convinced that the freedman would not cause trouble in the future when his formal authority would be much reduced. An unfaithful freedman could create considerable difficulties for his patron, and a disaffected one might simply abscond – which may be the reason why slaves in very menial or exploitative positions rarely were freed. Ownership would be surrendered only when the patron had been assured of the slave's reliability and obedience, and a decision to free therefore amounted to a declaration of trust in the slave's character. For example, the plot of one of Ps.-Quintilian's minor declamations revolved around a freeborn but enslaved child, who was saved years later by a good freedman, a *dispensator* described as 'libertus notae probitatis', who had been freed in his master's will.[355] Against the testimony of the freedman, the mother denied that the son was hers. In support of the freedman's credibility the orator declared: 'frugi servos libertos facimus', 'we make freedmen of honest slaves', 22. He further impressed on the woman that 'He is the freedman of your husband, madam, of whose will you are so proud', the point being that her late husband had chosen to free him, which in itself vouched for his probity.[356] Not by chance was the capital sin of freedmen *ingratia*, since it not only betrayed the master's trust but also showed up his poor judgement.

When a slave had attained a certain level of responsibility in the household, manumission was probably fairly certain, but he had of course reached that position only through his master's personal trust, rather than any formal criteria relating, for example, to age, seniority, or skills. Paradoxically, the lack of regular patterns and 'career' structures may have been an added strength of manumission as a means of encouraging slave labour. If freedom could be offered on a whim to any slave in the household who caught the master's attention and sympathy, it meant that all had a chance and no one was formally beyond hope. In reality, most slaves in humble functions would never be freed, but the very possibility may have been sufficient to motivate them.[357]

---

[354] For example, D. 34.3.12 (Julian), on an accountant who was freed and kept in the same employment, suggests that *actores* theoretically might be free.

[355] *Decl.Min.* 388.6.   [356] 22: 'Libertus viri tui, mulier, cuius iudiciis gloriaris.'

[357] Cf. Bradley (1984a) 104, who also noted that the uncertainty of manumission made it 'an effective form of social manipulation', 112.

If the personal relationship was essential, we may wonder where that left the slaves who belonged to the largest and most unusual household of all, that of the emperor. The *domus Augusta* may present the exception that proves the rule that manumission generally was 'subjective' and based on personal trust. For purely practical reasons, the emperor cannot have taken the decision to free each individual slave in his household; presumably he merely issued general guidelines on the advice of his senior administrators. A higher degree of 'standardisation' in the procedures is therefore likely, which may explain the differences in age structure, since imperial freedmen generally seem to be older than most other *liberti*.[358] Some of them also seem to have moved away and retired elsewhere.[359] The existence of the 'fiscus libertatis et peculiorum', with the implication of regular payments for freedom, further highlights the character of the imperial household as a structure *sui generis*. The sheer scale of the *domus Augusta* set it apart and created a need for more formalised structures and procedures. Nevertheless, in terms of promotion and selection for high office it may not have differed in essence from other households. Here too the importance of personal acquaintance and trust seems indisputable, as illustrated by the *degustatores*, tasters, who were promoted to powerful imperial posts and procuratorships.[360]

The most highly regulated manumission procedures were probably found in the public administration, among the *servi publici* who were under the authority of local councillors and the annually changing *duoviri*. This particular type of slave generally enjoyed higher status and certain legal privileges, and it is not inconceivable that they also had easier and more structured access to manumission.[361] For example, at Ostia we have a list of the members of a *collegium* of the *familia publica* which includes twenty-one slaves and fifty-seven freedmen and one freedwoman.[362] For

---

[358] Weaver (1972) 97–104.

[359] This may be the background for the ruling of 265 CE, which prescribed that imperial freedmen could be obliged to stay, *Cod.Iust.* 7.38.1.

[360] Of the ten recorded *praegustatores* eight were freed, and most of them are known to have moved on to higher offices, three becoming procurators: Ti. Claudius Bucolas, *procurator Castrensis*, *CIL* 9.3612; Ti. Claudius Epinicus, *procurator* in Pisidia, *ILS* 9504; Ti. Claudius Halotus, Suet. *Galb.* 15.2; cf. Schumacher (2001a) 337–8.

[361] Cf. Weiss (2004) 166. Public slaves could dispose testamentarily over half of their *peculium*, and they also had a right to maintain it on manumission, cf. D. 40.3.3 (Papinian). It is in the context of public slaves we find the only epigraphic attestation of *operae*, *lex Irnitana* ch. 72, suggesting formalised services may have been more important in cases of 'impersonal' patrons.

[362] *CIL* 14.255. Cf. Weiss (2004) 160, who observed that the list is not complete. It also includes twenty-five free non-public freedmen. Leaving an empty space for the future *tria nomina* was not entirely unique; cf. *EE* 8 124–5, although in that case the reasons might be purely epigraphic and reflect a wish for a straight right-hand column.

each slave a blank space had been left for their future *tria nomina*, suggesting they could expect to be freed at some point.

SUMMARY

The Roman system of manumission gave owners considerable scope for rewarding slaves irrespective of their age, gender, and occupation. The result is a picture that does not conform to any narrow economic logic. The main 'losses' came from the freeing of younger women but apparently that did not disadvantage them. A range of factors would have influenced the decision to free a slave, and future reproduction does not seem to have been a serious consideration for many owners. Households were never stable, but grew and contracted over time; indeed many were broken up on the death of the owner. It is difficult to point to any essential difference between categories of slaves who were regularly freed and those who were not. There were roles in the rural as well as the urban household which required positive incentives but manumission only seems to have been widely used in the latter. The importance of personal contact and trust put the rural *familia* at a serious disadvantage, even the *vilicus* having less opportunity to develop a close working relationship with the master than most domestic slaves.

Ideologically, *obsequium* and *fidelitas* were integral to the Roman construction of the good freedman. In real life, however, these qualities could not be taken for granted but relied on masters selecting the slaves most likely to conform to the ideal. This 'subjective' aspect lent Roman manumission a certain randomness, which in a broader perspective may have been useful in encouraging not just the obvious candidates but all members of the urban household, irrespective of age, gender, and position. The fact that there was nothing given or automatic about the process may thus have been one of its main strengths.

It also created further disparities in the chances of manumission. For example, slaves who had been bought or inherited probably would have needed time to build up a degree of familiarity and trust that might qualify them for manumission. By contrast *vernae* may have held an advantage.[363] Viewed from this perspective, the sale or transfer of a slave could have been disastrous on more than one level, not just involving alienation from

---

[363] Pliny, *Ep.* 5.86, expressed concern about the honesty of some slaves he had bought on the market. In the new world home-born slaves often had a greater chance of manumission, which they also tended to receive earlier, Johnson (1979) 270; Karasch (1987) 348.

relatives, friends, and a familiar environment, but probably also reducing the likelihood of gaining freedom. It is partly in this light we may consider the practice of testamentary manumission which sought to spare some slaves from this bleak prospect.

The widespread use of manumission may have helped neutralise potential misgivings about the morality of slavery. It implied a tacit acceptance of the – otherwise problematic – notion that some slaves did not deserve their fate. Greek attempts to justify slavery by attributing general biological deficiencies to this class had been unsatisfactory and found little support in the Roman world. The Roman response to this problem was a practical one that implied that the slave's personal qualities and development were subject to a continuous assessment, which in principle ensured that those capable of living in freedom generally would do so. As such it presented a much stronger case for the morality of enslavement which was no longer random or indiscriminate. The Roman distinction between slaves worthy of freedom and slaves irredeemably 'servile' justified the servitude of the latter far more effectively than a purely legal approach could have done. Bradley has recently queried the absence of abolitionist voices in Rome, but they may have been silenced by the practice of manumission which acted as an ongoing, if highly selective, 'abolition' process.[364]

This construction of slavery as 'probationary' did not entail a recognition of the slave's right to freedom. The decision to free a slave lay entirely in the hands of the owner, and if he judged a slave to be 'deserving', society took no further interest in the matter. The Roman state neither promoted nor discouraged manumission; the main public concern evolved around owners' ability to distinguish between 'deserving' and 'undeserving' slaves. Slave owners acted as the 'gatekeepers' of free society and vouched for the morality and maturity of their freedmen – hence the Augustan attempts to ensure their formal capacity to perform this role. The master's judgement was always final, the legal principle of *favor libertatis* only applying in ambiguous cases.

There is no denying that the Romans freed large numbers of slaves, who were often treated handsomely. But what emerges from this interpretation

---

[364] Bradley speaking at a seminar at the University of Edinburgh September 2007. Garnsey (1996) 238, concluded that: 'The ancient world does not fit the model of a slave society (or societies) wherein slavery was simply accepted, in the sense that there was so little discomfort felt about the institution that no one saw the need to defend it.' However, this debate also seems to have been distinctly Greek or part of a Greek intellectual tradition, above all Stoicism, and the relative absence of Roman voices might perhaps be explained by the greater frequency of manumission and the 'probationary' character it gave Roman slavery.

of Roman manumission is not a 'humane' form of slavery. For the majority of slaves the implied selection process would have been profoundly
demoralising. Powerlessness has been the common characteristic of slavery
throughout history, but in Rome another level of uncertainty was added
to their condition. The possibility of freedom, often accompanied by pros-
perity and material security, must have been a tantalising prospect for a
slave for whom the stark alternative was continued dependency, possible
abuse, and perhaps even torture. The personalised nature of the manumission process, which the slave could facilitate through obedience and hard
work but never influence directly, left the slaves as players in a lottery with
enormously high stakes.

Those freed were the winners of this unpredictable game, and one
insidious consequence of the system must have been to make the lot of
the slaves who found no favour even harder to bear. As such, Roman
manumission was extremely divisive, and Petronius' story of Hermeros,
who managed to maintain his master's goodwill despite the machinations
of fellow slaves, has the ring of truth to it.[365] In a household inhabited by
grateful freedmen hoping for further support and slaves eager to attract
their master's attention, there was little risk of the dependants realising
their common interests, let alone questioning their lot.[366]

The frequency of manumission automatically militated against the formation of any 'class solidarity' among slaves, whose fate became a personal
predicament out of which each of them in theory could find his or her
way. The fact that former slaves as a matter of course would establish their
own slave households – which has contributed to their mixed reputation in
many quarters – was entirely logical in this context, since their own good
fortune demonstrated that the slave system recognised individual merit.[367]
This aspect would have eased their integration into free society, since they
carried with them no collective slave identity or at least a much weaker
one. Bradley painted a vivid picture of continuous, low-level obstruction
by slaves, but certainly in urban households the possibility of manumission may have provided an effective counter-weight to the resistance one
might otherwise have expected.[368] Moreover, the seemingly random and
relatively ubiquitous character of manumission would have made it even

---

[365] *Sat.* 57.10.
[366] As Bradley (1989) 44, rightly noted: 'Manumission was a divisive tool, a counterforce operating
against any notions of servile cohesion and solidarity.'
[367] This was in no way specific to Roman freedmen but a common pattern in all societies practising
manumission, cf. Patterson (1991) 321–2, who found it misplaced to expect freedmen to have been
less tolerant of slavery.
[368] Bradley (1994) 107–31. This model was recently queried by McKeown (2007) 77–96.

more effective as a disciplining tool, since no slave in principle was beyond hope.

The impact of manumission on the sustainability of slavery must have varied according to the size and nature of the slave holding. Rural manumission was probably negligible, while aristocratic houses freed with little concern for the economic consequences. Between these two extremes we must envisage households where early manumission, especially of girls and young women, may have been rarer. Manumission rates would logically have been lower in smaller households, where the slaves performed vital economic roles, e.g. in small commercial enterprises. There manumission would probably have appeared more risky in terms of its potential consequences, and there was also less incentive to perform 'ostentatious' manumission. The high rate of manumission which has been demonstrated in some – elite – households does not therefore in principle undermine the hypothesis that Roman slavery to a great extent could have sustained itself through reproduction, although complete self-sufficiency of course remains unrealistic.[369]

Finally, we may briefly consider whether there were any diachronic changes to the practice of manumission. It is often assumed that the second century BCE saw the 'rise of the freedman', reaching a peak during the turbulence of the late republic and triggering the Augustan intervention. In the following two centuries, manumission was supposedly maintained at a high level, making freedmen a dominant element of imperial society, before declining in late antiquity along with slavery in general.[370] Most of this picture is not based on any solid evidence, but merely integrates the institution into a conventional narrative of Rome's rise, crisis, recovery, and fall. While the number of freedmen inevitably correlated to the overall scale of slavery, especially urban, it is in my view not possible to trace any variations in the relative frequency of manumission in different periods.

---

[369] In this context we must also distinguish between the empire and external territories, as well as between Rome/Italy and the provinces. If the rate of manumission, as seems likely, was higher in Rome and Italy than, for example, in the Eastern provinces, internal movements of slaves might have compensated for the deficit.

[370] E.g. George (2005) 27, referring to the 'rising number of freedmen among the population'.

CHAPTER 6

The freedman in the Roman economy

After the section on the practice of manumission, its frequency, modalities, and patterns, we will now turn to the place of the freedman in the Roman economy and society. The first of these chapters is devoted to their role in the economy, which has attracted much scholarly attention. The reason is partly the sheer abundance of evidence for their participation in the economy, especially the urban commercial sector, which they seem to dominate completely, and partly the phenomenon of the rich freedman. This issue will be dealt with separately in the second part of the chapter, but a brief survey of some of the evidence for freedmen in urban trade and manufacture may be useful.

Not all the evidence that has been adduced in this context is equally compelling; for example, the many funerary inscriptions with job titles may not be representative, since this medium was used only sporadically outside the freedman community.[1] But many other types of sources were not the result of the freedmen's epigraphic 'habit'. Thus, amphorae and other types of containers carry inscriptions indicating the producers and recipients of the contents, and here the majority of the names appear to be those of freedmen and slaves.[2] Similarly, pottery was stamped with the names of the producers, who often seem to be 'servile'. At Pompeii a number of seal stamps have been found which were used to mark a variety of products, and at least two thirds of them may feature freedmen.[3] From a different perspective the archives of L. Caecilius Iucundus and the Sulpicii at Puteoli give detailed insight into the social composition of the local business milieu during the first century CE. The documents feature not just buyers and sellers but also large numbers of witnesses drawn from the same socio-economic environment. The tablets of the

---

[1] Cf. Gummerus (1916) 1496–1511; see also Joshel (1992).
[2] For a discussion of aspects of this material at Pompeii see Andreau (1974) 223–71.
[3] Della Corte (1965) 465–70, lists this material; 38 per cent carry non-Latin *cognomina*, but the remainder are mostly 'servile' Latin *cognomina*; cf. Andreau (1974) 273–9.

Sulpicii consist of 125 documents featuring 249 individuals, around 51 per cent of whom carried non-Latin *cognomina*, while most of the Latin names were distinctly 'servile'. The 153 tablets of Iucundus give the names of 370 individuals, with 42 per cent Greek names.[4] In addition we have the large *collegia* inscriptions from Ostia, which list hundreds of members of the professional associations, mostly representing the more affluent section of Ostian society. Again the proportion of freedmen, judging from the incidence of Greek names, appears to be very considerable.[5] This impression is confirmed by plenty of isolated sources, such as *CIL* 10.6494, from Ulubrae, which presents a list of names, described collectively as *pistores*, bakers, nine of whom were freed, while only one was freeborn.

The impression of former slaves dominating a whole section of the Roman economy has given rise to the widespread notion of freedmen as a separate commercial class, distinct from – and to a great extent independent of – the aristocracy.[6] Some historians have gone even further and identified them as a genuine 'middle class' or 'bourgeoisie' located between the elite and the masses.[7] This hypothesis has, for example, been used to interpret the history of communities such as Ostia and Pompeii, where freedmen are presented as part of a 'plutocracy' that forced its way into the preserves of the old elite, even causing a 'social revolution'.[8] The theory thus assumes that freedmen – or at least a core section of them – were distinct from the elite in terms of economic outlook and behaviour, which enabled

---

[4] Sulpicii: Camodeca (1999a) 28–30. Camodeca (1993) 348–50, observed that the witnesses in the Sulpicii tablets, drawn from the 'business community', were not representative of Puteoli's population as a whole. Iucundus: Andreau (1974) 150–1; Jongman (1988) 271. In this context it is worth noting that the witnesses in the Iucundus tablets fall into two distinct categories, members of the local elite and more modest traders and businessmen, most of whom appear to be freed.

[5] Cf. p. 129 above.

[6] To MacMullen (1974) 103, freedmen constituted 'to an extraordinary degree the element of vigor, thrust, and venture' in imperial society. D'Arms (1981) 121–48, saw wealthy freedmen as independent entrepreneurs. To Schleich (1984) 71, 'Freigelassene waren die Wirtschaftsbürger der Antike.' Alföldy (1986a) 287–8, saw them as 'die wirtschaftlich aktivste Schicht der römischen Gesellschaft'. Vittinghoff (1990) 187, stated that: 'In den römischen Freigelassenen (*liberti*) dokumentierte sich das am stärksten dynamische Element der ökonomischen und sozialen Entwicklung.' Pleket (1990) 124: 'unabhängige Unternehmer'. Clarke (1991) 25: a class of 'entrepreneurial freedmen'. Torelli (1994) 184: 'aristocrazia libertina del denaro'. Fabiani (2002) 101: 'una classe imprenditoriale di condizione libertina'. Bodel (2005) 190, thought that: 'The unabashed acquisitive vigour of a certain echelon of independent freedmen during the last part of the Republic and the Early empire is too well known to require discussion here.'

[7] E.g. Rostovtzeff (1957) 46; Mazzarino (1973) 215, 230–1; Pleket (1988) 267, (1990) 45, 54, 124; Abramenko (1993b); Los (1995) 1027; Casson (1998) 62; Tate (2005) 170; Rowe (2001) 231–2. Sceptical Andreau (1993) 183; Vittinghoff (1980) 49. This particular theory has in recent years been closely linked to the institution of the *Augustales*, dealt with in the next chapter.

[8] Castrén (1975) 124, who also envisaged the 'gradual replacement of the landed aristocracy by the plutocracy', 121; Meiggs (1973) 196–208; *contra* Mouritsen (1997).

them to prosper independently of the aristocracy. This scenario recalls later European conflicts between upwardly mobile, commercially based bourgeoisies and landowning, hereditary nobilities and as such displays strong anachronistic features. It is therefore not by chance that Roman society in this model has acquired a recognisably modern aspect; indeed, the commercial freedman has in many accounts become indicative of the open and fluid social structure as well as the dynamic nature of the Roman economy.[9]

The notion of the freedmen as a separate economic class is of course paradoxical, since they constituted a transient category exclusively defined by a personal status that could not be passed on: either the next generation was enslaved or they were freeborn, in which case they did not belong to their parents' class. In other words, it was a social 'class' that could not reproduce itself.[10] Financially their funds either passed to freeborn children who did not share their status, or were divided between patrons and freed children with whom they had no formal familial links. Consequently, there could be no continuity, no accumulation of resources over several generations, and no consolidation or expansion of their businesses.

The theory also remains predicated on a dichotomous separation of commerce and agriculture in the Roman world. Supposedly, the elite deliberately abstained from commercial activities for ideological reasons, leaving this sector for others to exploit. The freedmen, on the other hand, having no honour to defend, could engage freely in these 'sordid' trades; indeed, the fact that they had no landed patrimony left them with few other options. And with the expansion of empire and the economic boom that followed, the freedmen soon established themselves as *the* commercial class.[11]

There is no denying that the sources show an aristocratic disdain for trade and commerce in Rome, most famously expressed in Cicero's *De officiis*. Following Panaetius, Cicero presents a hierarchy of professions ranked according to their respectability. Trade is dismissed as morally tainted,

---

[9] For example, Wells (1984) 191, in a widely used textbook on the empire, stated that: 'Society was more mobile. Great fortunes could be made by ex-slaves, not only ... by the emperor's own freedmen like Pallas and Narcissus, but also by those who did well out of trade and commerce.'

[10] Andreau (1999) 70, argued that slaves and freedmen were not entrepreneurs, since they could not accumulate funds within the business or hand it over to the next generation, preventing any continuity.

[11] Thus explicitly Mrozek (1975) 312. Likewise, Verboven (2007) 872, distinguishes between civic elite and business elite, contrasting 'elite values' with 'the ethos and values of Roman businessmen', 888. The aristocracy, he argues, considered money-making 'sordid', 889. Bang (2008) 153 n.71, takes Trimalchio, 'the stereotypical freedman, vulgar and greedy beyond measure', as proof of elite disdain even for the wholesaler. However, Trimalchio was also a freedman who overstepped the boundaries and therefore a poor example of a typical Roman businessman.

although being more acceptable when practised on a grander scale.[12] This view is echoed in other writers who imply that the Roman elite was not expected to engage in commerce, from which they were in fact partly barred by the *lex Claudia*.[13] The question is of course to what extent the practice conformed to the ideal. A degree of hypocrisy in the senatorial elite has long been suspected, and D'Arms argued that many Roman aristocrats had a more diverse portfolio of economic interests, including trade and other non-agrarian investments.[14] There is ample evidence for elite involvement in urban property, as well as for their engagement in the distribution and sale of the produce from their estates, including bricks and tiles.[15] Money lending in the provinces (often at extortionate rates) was another highly lucrative source of income. What emerges with some clarity is that the Roman elite had a keen eye for economic opportunities and – frequently strapped for ready cash – was willing to reap the profits of a wide range of activities.

Nevertheless, there is little evidence that Cicero or his senatorial peers were directly involved in commercial businesses or engaged in trade. The senators, however, constituted only a small section of the propertied classes and others may have observed different standards. The highest order, asserting its superior rank and status, would logically have embraced a stricter code of conduct than the rest of society, and the *equites* were deeply entangled in the economic exploitation of the empire at all levels. Likewise, among the municipal elites we find few traces of the stigma Cicero attached to commerce. As the jurists confirmed, traders were always allowed to seek 'the decurionate or some magistracy in their city'.[16]

In some Italian cities the distinction between landed and non-landed income makes little sense, most obviously Ostia, where the entire elite presumably had commercial interests. Also, the extensive epigraphic and archaeological evidence from the Vesuvian cities suggests that aristocratic lifestyles and commercial activities were closely entwined. Even the grandest houses in Pompeii have *tabernae* facing the street, and in many cases we also find commercial production units integrated into the fabric of

---

[12] *Off.* 1.150–1. Interestingly, Cicero says there can be nothing *ingenuum* about an *officina*, workshop.
[13] 218 BCE, Livy. 21.63.3–4.
[14] D'Arms (1981); cf. Pavis D'Escurac (1977); Schleich (1983), (1984); Gutsfeld (1992); Morel (1996); Drexhage *et al.* (2002) 61–6; Rosenstein (2008).
[15] Garnsey (1976); Parkins (1997).
[16] D. 50.2.12 (Callistratus). MacMullen (1974) 99; Pleket (1990) 36, rightly noted that: 'Die Verachtung solcher Aktivitäten in den höchsten Kreisen der Reichsaristokratie ist durchaus unschwer vereinbar mit einer gewissen Respektabilität ebendieser Tätigkeit auf der niedrigeren Ebene regionaler oder städtischer Eliten.'

the dwellings themselves.[17] The grand Casa del Labirinto incorporates a substantial bakery that clearly served commercial rather than domestic needs. The Casa dei Postumii, probably occupied by the *duovir* Q. Postumius Modestus in the last period, was rebuilt after the earthquake of 62 CE, when new semi-industrial kitchen facilities were installed right at the centre of the aristocratic *domus*.[18] This *insula* also included a number of smaller commercial units, some of which were directly linked to the *domus* while others were not. However, recent studies of the layout and building history have revealed that also the separate units must have formed part of the urban estate of the Postumii. A similar conclusion is suggested by analysis of the Insula of the Menander, where commercial units like the fullery in 1.10.6 presumably belonged to the owners of the grand house next door.[19] On the basis of this type of evidence it has been estimated that around 40 per cent of bakeries and textile production units were directly integrated into elite houses or formed part of their urban property; no conclusions can of course be drawn about the ownership of the remaining workshops and commercial units.[20] Traditionally this phenomenon was explained away by positing a 'vulgarisation' of the Pompeian elite in the last generation of its existence.[21] But there is little evidence to support this thesis, and the presence of commercial units in noble houses can be traced much further back. For example, the palatial Casa del Fauno dating to the second century BCE displays a series of *tabernae* on either side of its grand entrance.

Non-agrarian income emerges as an integral part of the elite's economic foundations, to which no shame appears to have been attached. The magistrate Postumius happily redesigned his ornate peristyle to accommodate new commercial facilities, which were barely out of sight of visitors. Even

---

[17] Pirson (1999) 138–9, estimated that 69 per cent of *tabernae* in Pompeii were incorporated into *domus*, the large majority of which were substantial; cf. Garnsey (1976) 130.

[18] Pirson and Dickmann (2002).   [19] Ling (1997) 145, 250–1.

[20] Robinson (2005) 94, 98. Along with Flohr (2007), Robinson also claimed that if a production site was structurally independent of neighbouring *domus* so were those who worked and lived there. The argument is flawed since the archaeological evidence can indicate links between properties – and hence presumably socio-economic ties – but not independence. As already noted by Rostovtzeff (1957) 190, the absence of such features tells us nothing about ownership. Moreover, workshops with comfortable accommodation attached did not necessarily belong to 'independent' craftsmen, since there is no reason why freed tenants or dependent business partners would not have been allowed a reasonable degree of comfort.

[21] Maiuri (1942) 217, famously referred to the transformation of patrician houses into workshops, the intrusion of shops, inns inside and alongside noble houses, the splitting up of noble houses, the 'mutamento e pervertimento di gusto', 'all'invadenza insomma del ceto mercantile nella compagine del vecchio ceto patrizio romano e campano della città'; cf. Rostovtzeff (1957) 579 n.20; *contra* Mouritsen (1988), (1997); Wallace-Hadrill (1994) 118–42; Pirson (1999) 165–73.

more strikingly, the *garum*-producing family of the A. Umbricii Scauri, one of whom held the duovirate, chose to advertise the source of their wealth in a remarkable floor mosaic in the atrium. Guests entering the grand mansion of a local magistrate would therefore have been met with the proud display of fish sauce containers, each carrying the name of their host.[22]

At local level we find few signs of any dichotomy between trade and agriculture. The former appears to have been no bar to respectability and we sense little embarrassment in the way the elite embraced commercial pursuits. Not only did members of the elite derive – sometimes substantial – parts of their income from urban trades and property, but also there appears to have been no discernible attempt to 'camouflage' this part of their portfolio.[23] The archaeological evidence suggests that misgivings about urban trades in practice were confined to philosophical discourse and lofty senatorial ideals. This does not mean that the local elites were themselves 'commercial' classes – the vast majority of their wealth was undoubtedly invested in land – but it remained a natural and integral part of their economic basis.[24] For example, epigraphic evidence from amphorae and stamps indicates relatively widespread commercial involvement by the local elite in Pompeii.[25] Some may have been more fully engaged than others but they did not stand out from the rest.

Although this evidence is well known, not all historians have been willing to accept that the local elites were fully active players in the urban economy. Thus, a recent authoritative account of the Roman economy stated

---

[22] Curtis (1984). Los (2000) 262–4, made the curious claim that since the *duovir* was survived by his father, he had himself no involvement in the *garum* business. His statement that the Umbricii were 'certainement' *homines novi* also seems unfounded, 271–2.

[23] D'Arms (1981) 45, paradoxically saw freedmen as a 'front' for elite involvement, but given their general association with the affairs of their patrons they would have provided a rather poor disguise.

[24] MacMullen (1974) 99: 'Money was invested in all sorts of businesses by the wealthy – in tileries or potteries, in bakeries or fulleries.' Garnsey (1976) 130: 'We might be tempted to suppose that the higher an individual stood in the social hierarchy, the less deeply he was involved in commercial operations. This would probably be a mistaken assumption.' Verboven (2007) 887: speculated that professional associations enabled businessmen to 'transform their economic capital in social and symbolic capital, eventually allowing them or their children to join the ranks of the aristocracy', but there is no evidence that given sufficient wealth a trader would not be welcomed into the civic elite.

[25] Cf. Wallace-Hadrill (1994) 118–42; Nonnis (1999); Los (2000); (2001) 86. Much of the evidence might seem to fall into the category of 'indirect involvement' but that is irrelevant to the broader economic argument. Often it was the manager rather than the principal who signed amphorae and other containers. The tablets of Iucundus point in the same direction. A very substantial proportion of the witnesses, to a great extent drawn from the freed business community, carried the family names of elite families documented as magistrates or candidates. Thirty-five of the 320 individuals listed belonged to top elite, while 185 or 65 per cent of the remaining 285 carried the names of families holding office or running for office.

that 'fortunes could be made in commerce and manufacturing . . . but the chief beneficiaries of the opportunities that the Roman empire offered for generating wealth in these sectors were generally people of more modest social and economic status, from wealthy freedmen to independent artisans'. 'Upper class Romans tended to be involved in these activities only indirectly.'[26] Such an assessment is in many ways an uneasy compromise between different models. It accepts that fortunes could be made, but mostly by people of 'more modest social and economic status', including 'wealthy freedmen', which begs the question why their 'economic status' remained 'modest'. The elite, on the other hand, was 'only indirectly' involved, but even indirect involvement produces an income. Nevertheless, they were not among the 'chief beneficiaries' of these activities, which implies an implausible degree of economic irrationality – or incompetence.

There is abundant evidence to suggest that the local elites – and presumably the rest of the freeborn population – had few misgivings about urban trades, and that has implications for the freedman's place in the urban economy. If they had to compete with established families already active in these trades, it would have been much harder for them to become economically secure purely through their own work and application. Many of the professions in which freedmen were active also required considerable skill and experience. Most likely these had been acquired through training and education prior to manumission, implying that the owner had the necessary facilities and knowledge to provide that, as well as an interest in educating the slave in that particular trade. The logical inference is that their patrons were already involved in this type of business.[27] And that raises fundamental questions about the logic of manumission, for if the skilled freedmen set up their own businesses, the patron would not just lose his original investment but also gain a new competitor. A freedman could generally not be barred from conducting business in competition with his patron, as the legal sources make clear in their discussions of such scenarios.[28] In reality this situation may have been quite rare, however, since few slaves who were likely to become serious competitors probably would have been freed in the first place. And if it happened, patrons might

---

[26] Kehoe (2007) 550, adding that the elite 'were not directly involved in the production and marketing of manufactured goods'.

[27] As Meiggs (1973) 224, already noted: 'The natural expectation is that freedmen were following their patron's trade.'

[28] D. 37.15.11 (Papinian); 37.14.2 (Ulpian); 37.14.18 (Scaevola); 38.1.26 (Alfenus Varus); 38.1.45 (Scaevola). Wacke (1982b) 200–11; Waldstein (1986) 316; Aubert (1994) 36–7; *contra* Fabre (1981); Andreau (1993) 181.

not have allowed them to keep their *peculium*, without which their chances of economic success would be much reduced.

They might also have faced difficulties when trying to get access to commercial premises, which may not have been as easily available on the open rental market as often assumed. For example, the two famous letting notices from Pompeii, concerning the Insula Arriana Polliana and the Insula of Iulia Felix, list individual rental units, including *tabernae*, but the blocks were probably let out to a single contractor.[29] Thus, they advertise all the units for renewal at precisely the same time, and in the case of Iulia Felix the letting period was six years, which cannot possibly have applied to the humble single-room dwellings also included in the advertisement.[30] Presumably, therefore, the owners envisaged letting the entire complex to an entrepreneur (appearing in the singular as *conductor*), who would handle the economic exploitation of the property. Individual habitation units would probably be sublet on a short-term basis, but it is not inconceivable that he would install his own dependants, including freedmen, in the productive units. In return they might pay rent or a share of profit, or some other arrangement might apply, as described in the case from the *Sententia Hadriani* discussed below.

Despite these obstacles, it seems that many freedmen became well off or at least materially comfortable, and the question is how such a marginal and socially disadvantaged category was able to reach this level of prominence and relative economic success. But, as argued in the opening chapters, there was a twin aspect to the freedmen's role, which gave their otherwise bleak condition a silver lining. On the one hand, they were stigmatised former slaves denied honour, *auctoritas*, and real equality. On the other hand, Roman manumission also entailed a formalised integration into their patron's *familia*, which created a range of practical economic opportunities for the new freedman.

The trust and familiarity which had paved the way for manumission became valuable assets for both patron and freedman, and in all walks of

---

[29] *CIL* 4.138; 1136. The fact we have only two such notices suggests that small commercial premises normally were not let on an individual basis, certainly not with separate letting notices – a situation that would have produced far more epigraphic evidence. The notion of an open renting market for commercial premises is also questioned by the fact that the two *insulae* are themselves unique, being rare examples of proto-*insulae* of the Roman/Ostian type with many small dwellings and commercial units integrated into a larger complex. For the architecture, see Pirson (1999) 23–52. Single contractors of entire blocks are well documented, cf. Frier (1980) 30–1.

[30] These would probably have been let on much shorter terms. As Frier (1980) 40, observed, the jurists were concerned primarily with elite tenants and the long-term leases they record did not normally apply to the poor. Moreover, given the nature of these dwellings it seems unlikely that none would have been vacated before the end of the six-year period.

Roman life we find freedmen acting as agents and managers on behalf of their patrons. The practice is vividly illustrated by Cicero's letters, where we are confronted with a domestic world entirely dominated by freedmen, who were in charge of all aspects of their patrons' affairs, *domestica* and *forensia, privata* as well as *publica*.[31] As we saw, their own inferior persons were subsumed into that of their patrons, enabling freedmen like Tiro to act as the personal representatives of their senatorial patrons and deal with sensitive matters of state. It is not surprising, therefore, that senior freedmen also managed their patrons' day-to-day economic affairs, overseeing the slaves who kept accounts and handled the money. Sometimes they were given specific instructions to carry out businesses. For example, Cicero at some point complained that he had bought too many and too expensive artworks, blaming an (unnamed) freedman to whom he had otherwise given clear instructions.[32] But freed agents often enjoyed considerable freedom of action, and some high-ranking freedmen effectively had *carte blanche* to carry out business as they saw fit. Thus, Cicero issued a few general instructions to Tiro but otherwise left it to his discretion to decide how to handle debtors and creditors.[33] Likewise Philotimus, Terentia's senior freedman, apparently enjoyed great autonomy in his conduct of Cicero's financial affairs, also being in charge of his Roman properties.[34] There was nothing unusual in these arrangements; in fact most economic transactions within the late republican elite appear to have been handled by freedmen. Atticus' freedmen routinely organised money transfers, and Cicero could make passing references to trusted freedmen involved in claiming and collecting inheritances. Indeed the use of freedmen in that role was so common that reference to someone delaying payment was by saying 'libertum mitto'.[35]

Under the empire, the senatorial elite continued to use freedmen in this capacity, as illustrated by the well-known epitaph for M. Aurelius Zosimus, *accensus* and freedman of M. Aurelius Cotta Maximus, cos. 20 CE. The inscription records that his patron had entrusted all his economic affairs to him and that they prospered under his management.[36] A similar picture emerges from the correspondence of the younger Pliny. For example, we are told that his freedman Hermes had sold an estate, left to his patron, to Pliny's friend Corellia, apparently without being directly prompted to

---

[31] *Fam.* 16.4.3.   [32] *Fam.* 7.23.3; cf. e.g. 8.3.2.   [33] *Fam.* 16.24.1.
[34] Kirschenbaum (1987) 138–9, with refs.   [35] *Flacc.* 89; *Att.* 1.12.1.
[36] *CIL* 14.2298.10–11, 'quique suas commisit opes mihi semper'. Cf Aubert (1994) 24; Brunt (1975); D'Arms (1981) 103–4. Despite the use of the first-person singular the epitaph was composed by the patron himself; Eck and Heinrichs (1993) 215.

do so but in accordance with Pliny's general wishes.[37] Again the freedman appears to be able to act financially with considerable independence.

The pattern recurs in many other contexts, where freedmen managed the businesses of their patrons, sometimes as overseas agents. Thus the *Digest* refers to the common practice of conducting business overseas and in other distant parts of the world, 'per servos atque libertos'.[38] There are numerous echoes of this practice in Cicero's letters. For example, he asked M. Brutus to support a freedman of the *eques* L. Titius Strabo, who had been sent to settle a business and collect money in his province, and he warmly recommends three freedmen of another knight, Cn. Otacilius Naso, who looked after their patron's business interests in Sicily.[39] The role of freedmen in the provinces is also noted in a philosophical discourse on the various means of enrichment, where Cicero refers to the practice of dispatching freedmen to the provinces to plunder and exploit them through usury.[40] Their trusted position made freedmen the ideal financial agents, and already the elder Cato had allegedly used them as middlemen; Plutarch famously claims that he engaged in maritime loans through his *libertus* Quintio. Petronius' Trimalchio also declared that he had begun 'libertos faenerare', i.e. to finance the businesses of freedmen against the interest received.[41]

Many freedmen involved in urban manufacture and retail worked as managers running individual production units. A good example comes from the *garum* production of the A. Umbricii Scauri at Pompeii. Painted inscriptions on surviving containers indicate that the business was divided up into several different workshops, *officinae*, which were run by individual freedmen, while other freed members of the *familia* apparently were in charge of the distribution.[42] Another well-studied example is the Italian

---

[37] *Ep.* 7.11.

[38] 40.9.10 (Gaius): 'Quod frequenter accidit his, qui transmarinas negotiationes et aliis regionibus, quam in quibus ipsi morantur, per servos atque libertos exercent'; cf. e.g. 14.3.20 (Scaevola): a freedman put in charge of a money lending business; 34.2.4 (Paul): a freedman sent to Asia to buy purple; 3.5.30(31) pr. (Papinian): a freedman or friend given mandate to raise a loan, 'liberto vel amico mandavit pecuniam accipere mutuam'; cf. Aubert (1994) 109 n. 282.

[39] *Fam.* 13.14.2; 13.33; cf. 13.21.

[40] *Par.Stoic.* 46: 'dimissiones libertorum ad fenerandas diripiendasque provincias ...'.

[41] *Cato Mai.* 21.5–6. Petr. *Sat.* 76.9: 'sustuli me de negotiatione et coepi libertos faenerare'. D'Arms (1984) 103, preferred the reading 'per libertos faenerare', i.e. 'to lend money at interest through freedmen', but this emendation seems unnecessary, cf. Mart. 1.76.6. Boyce (1991) 96; Duthoy (1988) 152–3; Camodeca (1996b) 98 n. 19.

[42] Curtis (1988); Aubert (1994) 267–9. The *officinatores* included A. Umbricius Agathopus, 4.2580, 5690–1, 6910, 9403–5, 9418–19, A. Umbricius Abascantus, 4.5689, 5714, Umbricia Fortunata, 4.2573, 5661, 5674–5 (Umbricia: 2578, 5688, 5696–7, 5710, 5723). One slave is also recorded, Eutychus 4.2576. A number of other *officinatores* feature in fragmentary inscriptions, 4.2579, 5687, 5692–3, bringing

terra sigillata production, which also appears to have been divided into many smaller production units. Fülle suggested a structure consisting of multiple units which functioned independently while remaining part of a larger enterprise, as indicated by the fact that individual managers signed their own wares.[43] Such decentralisation was probably typical of Roman manufacture, which offered few economies of scale. Instead we find what MacMullen described as a distinctive 'atomized' pattern where trade and production were 'minutely subdivided into little shops and little agencies'.[44] This structure had the added benefit of reducing the risk of mismanagement and fraud.[45]

The extensive use of freedmen as managers of these units is probably best explained by simple continuity, the freedman performing tasks similar to those in which he had already been trained as a slave. For example, the banking firm of C. Sulpicius Faustus was operated by a combination of freedmen and slaves, the former including Cinnamus and Eutychus, who were assisted by at least four slaves.[46] From a legal point of view there were no real advantages to the use of freedmen rather than slaves or hired labour. While the Romans knew of no direct agency, they did allow mandated agents to purchase on behalf of the principal.[47] These *institores* were appointed by a *praepositio*, which defined their sphere of competence and the scope of their appointment. The appointment would be made public in order to inform third parties of the liability carried by the principal. As long as the *institor* remained within the terms of his *praepositio* the principal assumed full liability, but not if the *institor* went beyond or against the instructions. The principal could also issue a *iussum* which instructed the agent precisely what to do, sometimes concerning a single transaction.[48] There were no legal obstacles to outsiders becoming *institores*.[49] The role may originally have been reserved for agents *in potestate*, slaves and sons, but early on it was extended to free persons not subject to the principal's

the total up to seven different workshop managers. Further evidence in Giordano and Casale (1991) nos. 216, 224, 225, 273, 355.
[43] Fülle (1997).   [44] MacMullen (1974) 98–9.
[45] Harris (1980b) 140, also proposed that freedmen could be used as managers of independent branches of businesses covering wide geographical areas. He used the example of the lamp production which spread from Italy to Gaul, suggesting lamps were made locally by *institores* set up in business by their patrons, who provided the moulds.
[46] *TPSulp.* 87, 48; cf Verboven (2000) 164, who suggested a total workforce of around fifteen.
[47] D. 50.17.73.4 (Scaevola); cf. Aubert (1994) 41.   [48] Aubert (1994) 9–16.
[49] Aubert (1994) 93, rightly rejected the idea that the freedman's financial role was based on *officium* (cf. Visky (1980)), noting that 'the liability of the principal for his agent's transactions was independent from the type of legal relationship existing between them'; cf. D. 14.3.7.1 (Ulpian): 'It is immaterial whether the manager is male or female, free or slave, or, if a slave, one's own or someone else's.'

direct control, which in Aubert's words meant that 'freedmen, *servi alieni*, and freeborn, could step into the shoes of business agents'.[50] There was no reason why freed or freeborn outsiders might not assume these roles, since the status – and gender – of the person entering into the arrangement in principle was irrelevant. There is nevertheless a striking absence of evidence for outsiders being put in charge of businesses or employed as agents.[51] A closer look at the *procuratores* suggests that the preference for members of the *familia* was based on social and to some extent ideological concerns rather than legal factors.

The *procurator* filled essentially a legal role acting as the representative of an absent party, the *dominus*.[52] This might involve general representation while a military commander was away on campaign, or – more frequently and exclusively so under the empire – the representative was given a specific mandate defining the scope of his responsibilities. In this capacity the *procurator* could carry out economic transactions on behalf of the *dominus*, whom the procurator would also represent in court. For that reason the *procurator* always had to be a free person.[53] *Procuratores* covered a wide social spectrum and a variety of functions. At the pinnacle of society we find senators looking after the interests of their *amici* in the provinces and local notables performing similar roles. This was part of the aristocratic exchange of favours, and as such non-remunerated. They would mostly carry out specific administrative and financial tasks, rather than acting as general agents, and their relationship appears to have been governed by an elite code of honour rather than law.[54] At the other end of the scale we find salaried staff members who oversaw the *dominus'* estates and looked after his day-to-day business. In Italy these were almost invariably freedmen.[55]

The freed *procurator* held a managerial position at the top of the domestic hierarchy. Some were employed to oversee tenants and *vilici*, as illustrated

---

[50] Aubert (1994) 93, also arguing that the extension of the *actio institoria* to individuals outside the principal's authority reflected the greater use of freedmen and a rise in emancipation.

[51] Prachner's (1980) 182, examples of *ingenui* recorded on Arretine wares are mostly speculative, based entirely on *cognomina*. The overall profile of names conforms to that known of slaves in general. Fülle (1997) 144, mentions that *officinatores* could be 'free [presumably meaning 'freeborn'], freedmen or slaves'. But no matter how we interpret the stamps there is virtually no trace of freeborn personnel employed in positions where they would get their names on the products. According to Aubert (1994) 291, we cannot tell whether production was in the hands of slaves or freedmen, but he assumed it was based on the *familia*.

[52] Aubert (1994) 183–6; Schäfer (1998); Verboven (2002).   [53] Verboven (2002) 253–6.

[54] Atticus represents an exception to this pattern, since he looked after the economic interests of various senators over longer periods. Verboven (2002) stresses the aristocratic value system underlying these relations. Interestingly, Cicero, *Fam.* 13.14.2, declared that 'one is more respectably "honestius" concerned about a friend's money than about one's own'.

[55] Schäfer (1998) 181–93.

by Pliny's use of *procuratores* to supervise estates together with *actores*.[56] Others were involved in financial transactions. Thus, at Puteoli the banker Sulpicius Faustus had a freedman, Cinnamus, who sometimes acted as his procurator, and Cinnamus himself also had a *procurator*, Eutychus. The use of freed *procuratores* was so well established that the Augustan *lex Aelia Sentia* offered exemption from the normal manumission requirements for slaves who were freed in order to take up this position.[57]

There were essentially two types of *procuratores*, freedmen and 'friends' in the broadest sense.[58] But what characterised both of them was their personal relationship with the *dominus*, which suggests that *fides* was the central pillar of the Roman procuratorship.[59] Despite the legal framework supporting the institution, it was in essence a question of personal trust, and disputes were probably not expected to go to court. This gave the freedmen a crucial advantage over low-born outsiders and secured them what appears to have been a near monopoly on managerial procuratorships.[60]

What emerges with some clarity from the study of managerial structures is the *familia* character of Roman 'firms'. Schiller long ago described the family in the widest sense as 'the major type of business organization' in Rome.[61] A good example of the 'family firm' comes from the archive of the Sulpicii at Puteoli, which was run entirely by Sulpicii, some working in a hierarchy of personal authority. To outsiders it probably made sense that all employees of the 'firm' they were dealing with carried the same *nomen*, which indicated their identity, belonging, and ultimately authorisation. Outside parties would presumably have expected a principal to honour any obligation he incurred through 'familial' dependants.

---

[56] *Ep.* 3.19.2.

[57] Gai. *Inst.* 1.18; D. 40.2.13 (Ulpian); *Inst.* 1.6.5; Buckland (1908) 540. Schäfer (1998) 198–9, argued that there was a shift in the early empire from the use of freeborn to freed *procuratores*, but the apparent change would merely seem to reflect a change in the composition of the source material. Much of the republican evidence comes from Cicero and relates to his own social world, while the imperial evidence is predominantly epigraphic. Therefore the two periods give insight into two different types of *procuratores*. In republican times there is evidence to suggest that freed, low-ranking *procuratores* may have been as common as under the empire, as indeed is implied by the provisions of the *lex Aelia Sentia*.

[58] Verboven (2002) 253ff.

[59] Aubert (1994) 107, notes that a *procurator* normally was a freed slave, who 'had wider power of administration than the mandatory, because of his tie to the principal's household'. On the significance of *fides* in Roman business see Wiedemann (2003).

[60] There were some legal advantages to employing freedmen rather than freeborn, but they were limited. Thus, a freedman could not sue his patron in a civil case and his ability to bring a criminal case was also seriously restricted.

[61] Schiller (1971) 24. Schleich (1984) 69, spoke of 'domestizierte Wirtschaft'; Bürge (1987) 500–8; Temin (2004) 528; Jones (2006) 218–43.

The 'family business' suggests a reluctance among the Romans to put in positions of trust anyone over whom they had no personal authority or bond, be they *officium*, *familiaritas*, or *amicitia*. This automatically excluded most outsiders whose general absence from these roles may reflect a preference for personally tied labour rather than reluctance to work for wages.[62] The familial businesses offered further advantages since they answered the structural problem of finding qualified employees in an economy with an under-developed labour market.[63] Slaves would generally receive some degree of education and professional training suitable for their abilities and tailored to the needs of the household.[64] The slaves' status as property meant their value could be improved and most owners presumably realised the economic advantages involved in training their slaves, either for their own benefit or for later resale as skilled labour.[65]

While a familial business structure made good economic sense, freedmen were of course not the only option, and the question is why the Romans chose to rely on them rather than slaves. Apart from the role of *procurator*, slaves could legally perform all economic tasks on behalf of their masters. In some respects they might even be preferable, since they could acquire rights directly for their owner, being in his *potestas*. Some posts, such as *actor*, *dispensator*, and *vilicus*, also seem to have been filled mostly with slaves. Presumably these functions – handling money and accounts and running estates without direct supervision – were considered so vital that the full force of the *dominica potestas* was required to control them.[66] The

[62] According to Hopkins (1978) 124: 'Free men apparently felt that a permanent job restricted their freedom of choice, constrained them like slaves', but the disdain for wage labour was probably the preserve of those who could afford it. Most likely, as Veyne (1997) 86 put it: 'Roman nobles preferred their freedmen to their impoverished fellow citizens because . . . freedmen remained loyal to their former masters, who knew them personally.' Aubert (1994) 417, also suggested it was a 'deliberate choice . . . to select their trusted representatives among the members of their slave household'.

[63] Temin's (2004) claim of an integrated and developed labour market in Rome seems too modernising. The Roman labour market appears to have been dominated by short-term manual jobs, especially in the building industry and the ports. There is little evidence that more responsible or specialist functions were filled with hired labour. Bürge (1990) argued that *mercennarii* could even be slaves, but see also Möller (1993).

[64] In richer households, slaves regularly received a basic education, sometimes in the *domus* but also at the *ludi magister*; cf. Booth (1979). While not amounting to a liberal education, they would learn reading and writing and maths, later described as *litterae communes*. Certainly there is evidence for the literacy and numeracy of many slaves and freedmen, Harris (1989) 255–9. Petronius' Hermeros declares that it is – basic – education that made him what he has become, *Sat.* 58.7–8. On the use of writing in business transactions see Aubert (2004).

[65] Plut. *Cato Maior* 21.7, on the practice of lending money to slaves to buy slave boys to train them and sell them with a profit.

[66] As Harris (2007) 527, noted: 'The logic of this system is obvious: the owner has far more power over his slave subordinate than he could ever have over a fellow citizen.'

authority of a master was, after all, of a very different kind from that of a patron.

The preference for freedmen – despite the many advantages offered by slave labour – is probably best explained by the internal structure of the *familia* and the complex system of rewards and incentives by which slaves in domestic and 'care-intensive' roles were motivated. Its most important component was obviously manumission, which created a two-tier structure within the *familia*. As part of the process, some freedmen may have been 'promoted' to positions of greater responsibility. There seems to have been a sense that freedmen could assume roles which involved a higher degree of personal initiative. Thus, in the case against P. Sulla the prosecution alleged that his freedman had purchased gladiators, thereby incriminating his patron. Cicero responded by saying that the freedman had not been in charge but merely performed a 'munere servili', taking orders from Faustus Sulla's freedman.[67] In other words, to obey orders was considered 'servile' while taking initiatives on behalf of the patron was 'libertine'.[68] It is therefore not surprising that the legal and literary sources tend to assume that *institores*, generally considered the most humble agents, were slaves rather than free.[69]

While freedmen were often given greater freedom of action after their manumission, continuity nonetheless remains the key to understanding the freedman's role in the Roman economy. The freedman–patron relationship, with its unique combination of familiarity and trust, moral authority and control, allowed for a more flexible, non-contractual form of agency. As Kirschenbaum observed: 'These quasi-familial relations, even more than formal contract, governed the behaviour of patron and freedman as principal and agent.'[70] For example, looking at the case of Cicero and Tiro, there is no perceptible change in their relationship when Tiro was freed in 53, although his legal status was fundamentally altered and their business dealings in theory would have to be regulated differently. But as Kirschenbaum also noted, we do not find 'the slightest suggestion that the idea of possible recourse to legal action was being entertained should there be any irregularity in the actions of the freedman'. There is

---

[67] Cic. *Sull.* 55. Cf. Berry (1996) 244: 'Cicero's aim is to demonstrate that Sulla's freedman took no initiative in the matter, but was under orders from Faustus' freedman throughout.'
[68] In terms of social interaction with the patron's peers, free status was probably also regarded as a distinct advantage – there is no record of Cicero or other nobles ever engaging in negotiations with unfree go-betweens.
[69] Cf. Aubert (1994) 417, who noted that 'the overwhelming majority of business managers were slaves'.
[70] Kirschenbaum (1987) 128.

no sign that their employment has any formalised basis, contractual or mandatory.[71]

Financially and practically there was no standard format for organising the patron–freedman relationship, which was also a dynamic one likely to evolve over time. The degree of involvement between freedman and patron could probably vary considerably, according to a range of factors. Demonstrating such diversity is by its very nature difficult, not least because of the informal character of the arrangements. In many cases manumission seems to have made no perceptible difference to the former slave's employment. Thus, in the large *columbaria* we find hundreds of freedmen remaining in the household, apparently carrying out the same tasks as before. Many freedmen probably also continued as *institores* running small businesses on behalf of their patron after their manumission, and receiving a salary in return. For example, the jurist Papinian discusses the case of a slave 'agent for the sale of the master's goods or overseer for the collection of debts' who continues in this position after manumission.[72] Among the Sulpicii of Puteoli we may assume that freedmen like Cinnamus and Eutychus had already worked in similar roles before their manumission. A very close involvement between patron and freedman is recorded in the epitaph for the goldsmith M. Canuleius Zosimus, who died aged 28. His patron relates that: 'He never did anything without his patron's permission. He always had access to much gold and silver, but he never appropriated any of it.'[73] We can only speculate about the precise arrangement but it does suggest some measure of responsibility.

In other cases the situation may have been more complicated. Aubert argued that *officinatores* were at times tenants, contractors, or usufructuary or business managers.[74] He used the example of the Umbricii Scauri, whose *garum* containers carry labels suggesting a variety of arrangements. While many simply indicate the producer as Scaurus, others give the specific *officina*, most frequently those of his freedmen Agathopus, Abascantus, and

---

[71] Kirschenbaum (1987) 138; cf. 142: 'the Roman business world was often faced with the *de facto* situation of a manumitted slave, now a freedman, acting as an agent in maritime or commercial establishment with ties to his principal, which originally based on *potestas*, were now replaced by an implied contract'. The difficulty of pinpointing the precise legal relationship between patron and *libertus* is illustrated by Cic. *Caecin.* 57–8, where the freedman simply acts on the patron's behalf; cf. Aubert (1994) 94.

[72] D. 26.7.37.1: 'institor dominicae mercis vel praepositus debitis exigendis'. Similar continuity is found in 26.7.58 pr. (Scaevola), on businesses carried out through two former slaves; 14.3.19.1 (Papinian), on a bank managed by a slave who is then freed.

[73] *CIL* 6.9222: 'sine voluntate patroni nihil fecit, multum ponderis auri arg. penes eum semper fuit, concupiit ex eo nihil umquam'.

[74] Aubert (1994) 235, 267–9.

Fortunata, but also the *officina* of Scaurus himself. The latter presumably
refers to a production unit run differently from the others, although obviously not by Scaurus personally, a member of the local elite.[75] In the case of
the *terra sigillata* production Fülle proposed that relations between owners
and individual *officinatores* might have been regulated by contract, *locatio
conductio*.[76] Supposedly, potteries were leased out (to slaves and freedmen)
and production stamps were applied as a means of checking that individual
contractors had fulfilled their contracts. Such arrangements probably also
left scope for the freedmen to increase their own profits.

   We may envisage situations where *tabernae* or other production units
belonging to the patron were put at the freedman's disposal, together with
start-up capital against a share in the profits. For instance, at Pompeii, L.
Popidius L.l. Dionysius ran a small fullery at 1.1.26. His patron was L.
Popidius Secundus, a candidate for the aedileship, whose family appears to
have owned the large aristocratic house next door to the fullery, 1.1.5/25.[77]
The freedman was in other words put in charge of a small business located
in premises which had been carved out of his patron's urban estate. Again,
we can only speculate as to the precise legal framework, but there can
be little doubt that the patron, who provided the premises, would have
received income from the arrangement.[78] A similar scenario is implied in
the testamentary provisions of Iunia D.f. Libertas at Ostia, who left to her
liberti and *libertae* the 'usum fructumqu[e]' (but not the ownership) of
her *horti*, *aedificia*, and *tabernae*, which they probably had been running
already before her death.[79] We may also envisage situations where freedmen
ran joint businesses together with their patrons, who took a back seat. With
the *peculium* normally retained, the freedman could enter a partnership,
societas, with his patron. Thus, it has been plausibly suggested that Sulpicius
Cinnamus may have been the business partner of his patron Faustus in some
transactions.[80]

   The sharing of profits may have taken many different forms. The *Sententiae Hadriani* reports a case concerning the use of commercial premises

[75] Andreau (1974) 296–8, suggested Scaurus also employed 'independent' freedmen in his business on
   the basis of 4.9406: 'ex officina Scauri ab Martiale Aug. l.', and 5686: 'Scauri a Stlabor'. However,
   the reading of the former is highly uncertain, especially the last letters. This leaves us with just a
   single anomalous inscription which is hardly sufficient to sustain the theory of hired managers.
[76] Fülle (1997) 132.
[77] *CIL* 4.1041, 2944, 2974. For the patron and his house see Mouritsen (1988) 40–1, 146–7; *CIL* 4.2380,
   2381, 2383. It is clear from the layout that the space occupied by the fullery had previously been an
   integral part of the Popidian mansion.
[78] As noted, there is a possibility that some freedmen might have been *coloni*, i.e. rural tenants. Scheidel
   (1993).
[79] Calza (1939); cf. Meiggs (1973) 224.   [80] Verboven (2000) 162.

by some freedmen, whose patron complained that they had not paid him anything.[81] The precise financial arrangements are not clear. The Latin text says they traded 'suis pecuniis' while the Greek version gives it as 'ἐκ τῶν αὐτοῦ χρημάτων', implying either the freedmen's own or the patron's money. It might not be a simple question of unpaid rent, but could involve a share of the profits, since the freedmen assured him of their continued willingness to pay 'si eis permitteret negotiari', 'should he allow them to trade'. The patron does not seem to complain about a breach of formal agreement, perhaps suggesting a non-contractual arrangement of personal favours and unwritten obligations. Also, the emperor's final admonition that the patron show 'community sense' might indicate we are dealing with an internal 'family matter' which ideally should not have reached the courts.

The overall impression is of financial relationships which could vary considerably. Freedmen could be tenants, paying regular rent and allowed to keep remaining profits. There could be contractual relationships, which also came in different forms, *locatio conductio operarum*, *operis faciundi* or *rei*, each involving different degrees of patronal control and involvement. Finally they could enter partnerships, often just *unius rei*, perhaps alongside 'independent' activities in which the patron was not directly involved. An example of the latter comes from the case of Atticus' freedman Dionysius, who was the teacher of Cicero's son and in 49 refused to follow him abroad. As excuse he referred to his investments, which needed attending to, also mentioning his 'servulis' as a reason.[82] The precise nature of his businesses must remain a matter of speculation but the example shows that it was considered entirely normal that a freedman closely involved with his patron (who in this case had 'loaned' him to a friend) had economic affairs of his own.[83] The simple concepts of dependence and independence therefore

---

[81] *Hadr.Sent.* 8: 'Dicente quodam se circumventum esse a suis libertis, et habere suas tabernas, in quibus ipsi negotiantur de suis pecuniis, et nihil ab illis accipere: ergo advocatus libertorum respondit, multo tempore eos patrono suo unumquemque praestitisse denarium, et adhuc paratos esse praestare, si eis permitteret negotiari: Adrianus dixit: curate ergo, ne iterum queratur; sed et ipse sensum communem habeat', *Corp.Gloss.Lat.* III 33.37–34.5, 388.30–47; cf. G. Flaminini's Teubner edition (2004) lines 1814–27. Waldstein (1986) 318; Lewis (1991) 278.

[82] *Att.* 8.10: 'Respondit se quod in nummis haberet nescire quo loci esset; alios non solvere, aliorum diem nondum esse. Dixit etiam alia quaedam de servulis suis.' Later Dionysius again mentioned 'rebus suis', *Att.* 10.16.1, which presumably also refer to business affairs.

[83] Similarly, discussing the Sulpicii, Verboven (2000) 163, noted that: 'On a l'impression que Faustus et Cinnamus s'étaient associés pour quelques affaires, mais pas pour toutes'; on other occasions they may have set up a *societas unius negotii*. Camodeca (2003) 76, observed that Cinnamus acted both as agent and *procurator* of Faustus and independently. Eventually he seems to have succeeded his patron around 52 CE. Verboven (2008) 222, also suggested that the slaves might have been 'allowed to participate in the operations with their own *peculium* as well'.

seem inadequate to describe the relationships that might exist between patrons and their most favoured staff.

Allowing freedmen to make money for themselves and share in profits might seem uncharacteristically generous but it would often have made good economic sense. Not only did it involve sharing of risks as well as benefits, but, as importantly, the relative economic freedom accorded to freedmen would have provided a vital incentive for them to apply themselves and make their new life a material success. Few Romans would have been better motivated than the freedmen, and their energy could be profitably harnessed by patrons who allowed them to prosper.[84]

One particular way of organising the patron–freedman relationship has attracted much attention. The so-called *operae libertorum* were specified services which the freedman promised in advance of manumission and then confirmed immediately afterwards when he had become a legally recognised person. This form of involvement has been seen as a fundamental element of the patron's continued exploitation of his freedman. Waldstein, the author of an exhaustive study of the institution, declared that they 'undoubtedly must have played a great role in the social life of Rome'.[85] This conclusion was based on the extensive coverage *operae* receive in the legal sources; according to Waldstein, they are mentioned no fewer than 197 times in the *Digest* alone. The jurists discuss a wide range of aspects and complications raised by the performance of these services. However, outside the legal sources the institution is virtually absent, a situation which Waldstein found puzzling.[86] The only literary texts that mention *operae* are *controversiae*, pseudo-legal disputes that often deal with highly unrealistic scenarios. For example, in Seneca Maior a case revolves around a promise of *operae*, which the patron had waived after having been sheltered by the freedman during the proscriptions but later tried to reclaim.[87]

---

[84] Kehoe (2007) 563, observed that 'many of these slaves and freedmen [in the *terra sigillata* production] were probably socially dependent but economically independent artisans who leased workshops from their owners or patrons. The master artisan, then, would run his own workshop, but he could make additional money by training artisans who would eventually set out on their own, providing their owner or patron with some financial consideration for helping to establish them in business.' The phrase 'some financial consideration' suggests a minor by-product of a largely charitable arrangement, when in fact it may have represented a substantial source of income for the patron and been designed with precisely that purpose in mind.

[85] Waldstein (1986) 19: 'die *operae libertorum*, die zweifellos eine grosse Rolle im sozialen Leben Roms gespielt haben müssen'; cf. e.g. Wacke (1982b) 200; Rainer (1988) 750.

[86] Waldstein (1986) accepted that *operae* 'zwar in den juristischen Quellen überaus häufig vorkommen, in den literarischen und auch in Inschriften jedoch so gut wie gar nicht', 16. Fabre (1981) 317–31, read the performance of *operae* into numerous references to freedmen working for their patron.

[87] *Contr. Exc.* 4.8; Ps.-Quint. *Decl.Min.* 388.23; Waldstein (1986) 21ff.

We are therefore confronted with a classic problem concerning the relationship between legal texts and lived reality.[88] In this case we have to consider whether the legal intricacies of the institution may have attracted a degree of attention among the jurists that did not correspond to its practical importance in Roman society. Roman *iuris prudentes* often explored complex legal problems through highly hypothetical scenarios, and the *patronus–libertus* relationship offered rich pickings because of the inherent tension between the freedman's free status and his moral obligations. *Operae* by their very nature were bound to attract legal attention, since the potential for dispute was almost limitless – when could they be imposed, how were they defined, could they be altered, how and when were they to be performed?

There are good reasons to doubt that the prominence of *operae* in the legal sources was matched in everyday life, above all because they offered a highly inflexible means of regulating the patron–freedman relationship. *Operae* were legally defined as one day's work, and their precise number would have to be stipulated in advance. On the other hand, working relations would typically have continued in essentially the same way as before manumission. That would, for example, have been the case for most domestic staff, and looking at the *columbaria* it is hard to see how *operae* could ever have played a part in the organisation of these households. Likewise, the picture of the *patronus–libertus* relationship we gain from the works of Cicero does not seem compatible with a formalised system of service days. For those engaged in their master's business affairs as agents, managers, or tenants, it is equally difficult to see how *operae*, rigidly defined as a day's work, could have been applicable. *Institores* or *procuratores* could, for example, hardly have divided their time into days devoted to their own affairs and days reserved for their patron/employer.[89] In fact we do not know of a single 'real life' relationship, whether actual or fictional, which was organised along those lines.

The theory of widespread use of *operae* also implies a formalised relationship between freedman and patron regulated in advance of manumission, which is hard to reconcile to the standard image of the freedman as dependent labour. Patrons could probably have dictated the terms of the relationship on the basis of their social and economic superiority and for

---

[88] Epigraphically *operae* appear only in the *lex Irnitana* ch. 72, in the context of *servi publici*, which, according to Waldstein (1986) 31, demonstrated their general importance. However, public slaves were a category apart, not least because they had no patron. No *operae* are recorded in papyri.

[89] Aubert (1994) 102–3, questioned whether *operae* could serve as the basis for agency, given their definition as single workdays.

most of them it would have made little sense to accept such limitations to their future use of the freedman. Most likely, therefore, they belong in specific contexts where employment was discontinued, as might happen after testamentary manumission, especially if the household was broken up among several external heirs.[90] In that case the *operae* would be comparable to the economic compensation which *statuliberi* often were obliged to provide to the heirs. There might also be several different parties who could make a claim to the freedman's services, in which case it was practical to define them as single units of workdays that could be easily divided up.

Some freedmen had acquired specialised skills which enabled them to prosper without the financial and practical support of a patron. To this category belonged actors, artists, and doctors, and they are precisely the ones who appear in the cases discussed by the jurists.[91] Most likely, therefore, the performance of *operae* was linked to specific economic roles where the practitioner received – often substantial – fees and salaries for their services. As we saw, it is also in these particular professions we find most of the evidence for self-purchase, suggesting that *operae* may have served as an alternative to payment in those situations where the freedman could leave his patron's employment and make an independent living for himself.

The picture that emerges from this survey is a very distinct, indeed unique, role for the freedman in Roman society. Theirs was paradoxically a world full of economic opportunities which for the most part were not open to freeborn outsiders. It could therefore be argued that we find freed businessmen in such numbers not despite their humble origins but precisely because of their lowly background. It was the combination of trust and familial integration, education and skills, capital investments and general support from their patrons that gave the freedmen their particular advantage and prominence in the urban economy.

Freedmen have nevertheless often been described as 'self-made' men or 'entrepreneurs'.[92] But this image probably overestimates the potential

---

[90] Weiler (2003) 198, noted that Waldstein (1986) 84f, had discovered only one legal reference to freedmen staying with their patron as part of their performance of *operae*, D. 38.1.38.1 (Callistratus), but that case does not suggest permanent residence. Treggiari (1980) 54, could find 'no example in the *Digest* of *operae* in the patron's shop or workshop'.

[91] The chapter 'De operis libertorum', D. 38.1, includes the following professions: 7: *librarius, nomenculator, calculator*, 'histrio vel alterius voluptatis artifex'; 23: *faber, pictor*; 24: *faber, pictor*; 25: *pantomimus, archimimus, medicus*; 26: *medicus*; 27: *pantomimus, medicus*; 37: actors and gladiators who perform in animal fights. In 49 a *librarius* is asked to look after his patron's house.

[92] Rostovtzeff (1957) 104, declared that shop owners were, 'to a great extent, former slaves who succeeded in receiving or buying their liberty and in acquiring a considerable fortune'. 'Self-made' men, e.g. Gordon (1931) 67, 76; D'Ambra (1995) 672; Goodman (1997) 174; Casson (1998) 62: 'self-

for money-making in antiquity.[93] Although few would doubt that fortunes could be made in the ancient economy, some start-up capital would
always have been needed. For example, the elder Pliny describes industrious freedmen who became rich through the improvement of vineyards, but
that could only happen because the land in question had come into their
possession in the first place.[94] The possibility of simple inventions which
today can produce millionaires almost overnight obviously did not exist
in antiquity. The modern 'lottery' economy was largely confined to the
realm of fantasy, sudden windfalls coming from hidden treasure or unex-
pected inheritances. In the *Satyricon* it was speculated that a freedman who
had risen from nothing but now was worth 800,000 sesterces might have
found a treasure.[95] Even in fiction no one assumed that fortunes could be
made without initial capital. Thus, despite his fabulous wealth and lifestyle,
Trimalchio was not portrayed as a 'self-made' man, since he had early on
become a favourite of his master from whom he inherited a vast (senatorial)
fortune, 'patrimonium laticlavium'.[96] When he later went bankrupt not
everything was lost, since capital raised from his wife's jewellery allowed
him back into business.[97]

We have little evidence, literary, anecdotal, or otherwise, of fortunes
made from scratch, apart from exceptional cases of personal skills and
talents, especially actors, doctors, and teachers, who of course also relied on
prior education and training.[98] Certainly, it would not have been possible

made *nouveaux riches*. Zanker (1998) 201, spoke of freedmen who 'had a chance to try their luck
as independent craftsmen and merchants, unhampered by obligations to patrons', and Verboven
(2007) 862, mentions 'freedmen upstarts who had made their fortune through trade and usury'.

[93] Mrozek's assertion, (1975) 315; cf Zanker (1998) 201, that during the 'golden age of the freedmen', it
was possible to become a millionaire 'aus dem Nichts' is unrealistic. As Garnsey (1981) 370, noted:
'Whether substantial fortunes could be made without the initial capital that a large legacy might
provide must remain doubtful.'

[94] *NH* 18.41–3; 29.7–9; cf. Petr. *Sat.* 43.4, where we are told that the brother of Chrysanthus did well
out of his vineyards but what had first got him on his way financially was an inheritance.

[95] 38.7–8. In Plaut. *Rud.* 906–37, the slave Gripus, believing he has found treasure, starts dreaming of a
grand lifestyle. Favorinus of Arles, cf. Grassl (1981) 70, listed four ways of overcoming poverty: *dosis*,
gifts; *heurêsis*, discovery (of treasure); *ergasia*, work; *autarkia*, self-sufficiency. The topos of finding
treasure also appears in the *Life of Aesop*, 78–80.

[96] 76.2. On Trimalchio as his master's *delicium* see Pomeroy (1992).

[97] 76.7. *Pace* e.g. Mrozek (1975) 313; Bodel (1999b) 46; Harrison (2005) 216; Verboven (2007) 889.
Another fictional candidate for 'self-made' status might be Petronius' Hermeros, the wealthy
Augustalis who claimed he now fed twenty bellies, but a closer reading of his biography suggests he did not prosper entirely independently, 57.6. Not only does he sing his noble patron's
praise, 'genio illius gratias', 57.10 (indicating he was still alive), he also received a valuable education
and worked as an *actor*, which would have allowed him to accumulate wealth, *Sat.* 58.

[98] For example, the grammarian Q. Remmius Palaemon, Suet. *Gramm.* 23. Pliny *NH* 29.7–9, discusses
rich doctors, a type illustrated by the freedman doctor T. Flavius Galata Eutyches from Ariminum,

for a whole class of new men to rise collectively from humble beginnings.[99] Moreover, if the opportunities for enrichment were so abundant in the Roman world, we would expect people of all statuses, including poor freeborn, to exploit them to a greater extent than seems to have been the case. The prominent role of freedmen in the urban economy must therefore be explained by the particular advantages this category enjoyed over most freeborn. The freedman's economic role grew logically out of his servile past, and as Brunt rightly noted, 'the great part that freedmen plainly played in commerce and in the crafts seems inexplicable unless their initial capital came usually from their former masters'.[100] It has nevertheless been argued that the existence of rich freedmen presents incontrovertible evidence of a distinct type of 'independent' freedmen, who broke the mould and formed a separate commercial class. We will therefore look at this category in more detail.

THE RICH FREEDMAN

The rich freedman has typically been interpreted as an 'independent' freedman, on the rationale that no patron could have any interest in allowing his dependants to become more than moderately wealthy. In order for that to happen, the freedman must therefore have broken free from his patron's authority and made his own fortune. 'Wealthy' and 'independent' have in this model become synonymous. Before considering the logic of this argument, it may be useful first to look at the scale of the phenomenon.

Rich freedmen obviously existed in Rome. Many examples have already been mentioned, including those of emperors and republican dynasts. Much of the evidence for 'libertine wealth' is biased, however. As argued above, rich freedmen became a literary topos – the ultimate undeserving rich who undermined the link between wealth and virtue – and their iconic status inevitably led to distortions of their numbers and fortunes. Still, the moralists did not invent this social type, as a wide range of epigraphic,

---

cf. Ortalli (2007). Epaphroditos (Suda 2.334/2004 *Adl.*) was a slave teacher with a large library and two houses in Rome. A statue of him has survived inscribed 'M. Mettius Epaphroditus grammaticus Graecus', 6.9454; cf. Christes (1979a) 103–4. When Atticus' freedman Q. Caecilius Epirota was expelled for alleged misconduct, he set up a school, which was probably one of the best ways of earning a living without patronal support, Suet. *Gramm.* 16.

[99] Alföldy (1986b) 72 n. 5; Vittinghoff (1990) 161. MacMullen (1974) 99, cautiously concluded that 'people who started with some minor skill or minor sum of money could indeed rise to relative affluence', but also warned against overestimating social mobility in Italy, 101.

[100] Brunt (1983b) 314. Meiggs (1973) 224: 'Freedmen who started working as slaves for their masters in his trade were probably helped by him to rise in it when they were freed.'

archaeological and legal sources amply demonstrates. The phenomenon has often been illustrated by reference to cases such as the baker Eurysaces, whose eccentric funerary monument survives outside the Porta Praenestina in Rome (although his freed status is in fact not entirely certain).[101] But isolated instances of this kind do not allow any conclusions about the relative numbers or wealth of this category; here the various legal measures concerning affluent freedmen may carry greater weight.

According to Livy, freedmen with landed property worth more than 30,000 sesterces had been inscribed in the rural *tribus*.[102] In 32 BCE the triumvirs imposed a special tax on rich freedmen, forcing those worth more than 200,000 sesterces to contribute an eighth of their fortune to Octavian's campaign. A riot in 31 was blamed on these freedmen, although it may have enjoyed wider support from the starving plebs.[103] The Augustan *lex Papia Poppaea*, 9 CE, strengthened the patron's claim to the estates of freedmen who left fortunes of 100,000 sesterces or more.[104] Claudius offered citizenship to Latin freedmen who built ships holding at least 10,000 measures of grain and brought provisions to Rome for six years.[105] After the Fire of Rome Nero did the same for Latini Iuniani who possessed at least 200,000 sesterces and spent half of it on building a house in the capital. Similar favours were offered by Trajan to the Latini who operated a grain mill in Rome for three years, grinding at least a hundred measures a day.[106] All these initiatives presuppose a substantial number of wealthy freedmen in Roman society, although they cannot tell us anything about their share of the propertied classes let alone the population as a whole.

The epigraphic and archaeological material from well-preserved towns like Pompeii, Herculaneum, and Ostia may give us a clue. At Pompeii the rich freedman has often been seen as a dominant figure; indeed the social history of late Pompeii was long constructed around this character. However, most of the inscriptions adduced in support of the model were the result of the freedmen's own desire for commemoration. Funerary self-representation is never an objective source on social structure, and taken at face value the profile of Pompeian monuments suggests that the town effectively had been taken over by former slaves. This evidence is therefore

---

[101] Ciancio Rossetto (1973); Petersen (2006).   [102] 45.15.1–2.
[103] Dio 50.10.4, 20.3; 51.3.3. Plut. *Ant.* 58.1–2; cf. Osgood (2006) 369–70.   [104] Gaius *Inst.* 3.42.
[105] Sirks (1980) 293, argued that Claudius' promise of privileges to women who invested in ships for the grain trade was aimed at freedwomen, hinting at the existence of a group of freedwomen: 'wealthy, independent and sufficient in number, to be attractive as subjects of legal encouragement'.
[106] Gaius *Inst.* 1.32.b, 33, 34.

another reminder that funerary epigraphy was a culturally embedded practice, from which few viable statistics can be extracted. In this case the local
elite largely abandoned funerary ostentation and adopted more modest,
even anepigraphic, forms of funerary commemoration.[107] Some measure
of affluence was of course required to erect funerary monuments but the
fact that freedmen's priorities appear to have differed so radically from those
of other groups in society prevents any estimate of their relative wealth.
That problem also applies to civic/religious dedications, where minor public bodies feature disproportionately in the epigraphic record. Thus, the
ministri Augusti account for a large share of the dedicatory inscriptions
from Pompeii despite being a fairly low-ranking institution filled by slaves
and freedmen.

   There are a handful of unequivocal cases of rich freedmen from Pompeii,
including Popidius Ampliatus who rebuilt the temple of Isis in the name
of his 6-year-old son Celsinus, presumably because he was himself barred
from a public career.[108] Less spectacular donations were made by N. Festius
Ampliatus, who sponsored games and received *ornamenta decurionalia* in
return, and Munatius Faustus, who financed a distribution of grain and
gained a *bisellium*. The same honour was bestowed on the *Augustalis* C.
Calventius Quietus, probably also a local benefactor, who may be the father
of a homonymous magistrate.[109] In a few cases we can identify freedmen as
occupants of substantial houses. The two Vettii, Conviva and Restitutus,
appear to have lived in the house named after them, and Cornelius Tages
seems to have occupied the sprawling Casa del'Efebo. At Herculaneum,
C. Petronius Stephanus and Calatoria Themis may be identified as the
occupants of the Casa del Bicentenario on the basis of wax tablets found
there.[110]

   At Ostia, a community on a different scale and with a different socio-
economic structure, there is substantial evidence for wealthy freedmen and
their descendants.[111] For example, inscriptions record *curatores Augustalium* who paid 10,000 sesterces for the honour, and freedmen who set up

[107] Mouritsen (2005).
[108] *CIL* 10.846–8, 921. Alleius Nobilis, who adopted Cn. Alleius Nigidius Maius, the leading citizen of late Pompeii, may also have been a freedman, as suggested by his marriage to Pomponia Decharcis, cf. below pp. 275–6.
[109] *CIL* 10.1026. A Calventius Quietus stood for the duovirate, 4.7604.
[110] Weaver (1991) 169. In Herculaneum L. Venidius Ennychus has been seen as the owner of the grand Casa del Salone Nero, where his archive was found, but more likely he may have been a tenant in the house; cf. Camodeca (2002) 265. At Pompeii numerous houses have been identified as belonging to specific freedmen on the basis of Della Corte's methods, but see Mouritsen (1988) 13–23.
[111] D'Arms (1981) 129–33, lists examples.

foundations worth 40,000 and 50,000 sesterces. Another freedman, M. Licinius Privatus, donated 50,000 sesterces to the municipal treasury.[112] Outside these well-documented towns we have scattered evidence such as the *sevir Augustalis* who apparently donated a basilica at Puteoli, and M. Annius Phoebus who built a *macellum* at Saepinum 'for the honour of the Augustalitas and the bisellium'.[113] Similarly, at Concordia, M. Acutius M.l. Noetus bequeathed a fortune to pay for public games and dinners, while the *Augustalis* A. Ritius A.l. Tertius left 300,000 sesterces to be spent on road paving.[114] Although these examples are impressive reminders of the possible scale of libertine wealth, they are essentially anecdotal and produced by the freedmen themselves. To assess their overall place within the elite we must look for independent corroboration, unrelated to the freedmen's own self-promotion.

Land was a natural part of the portfolios of the propertied classes, not just because of the superior status associated with country estates, but because it was the safest investment available. Land ownership must therefore count as a fairly reliable measure of affluence in the Roman world. The fullest and most detailed picture of land holdings in imperial Italy comes from inscriptions associated with the *alimenta* schemes, where local landholders pledged parts of their estates and promised to pay an annual sum for the support of children. In return they received (non-repayable?) loans from the sponsoring emperor or aristocrat. The two surviving documents come from Ligures Baebiani near Beneventum and Veleia in the north.[115] In both cases the inscriptions list the persons involved in the scheme, the value of the estate(s) pledged, and the size of the loan and the repayments. They also describe the location of the estates, often by reference to adjoining properties, and in the Veleian inscription these *adfines* are frequently named.

The inscriptions generally do not indicate the person's status, but we may take the frequency of Greek *cognomina* as a broad indicator of the social profile. At Ligures Baebiani the list contains seventy-four named individuals: forty-four owners, twenty-four *adfines*, and six featuring in both categories. Nine of them (12.2 per cent) carry Greek *cognomina*.[116] They were unevenly distributed among the two types of landowners on the list. Among the contributing landowners we find eight out of fifty (16 per cent), but only one *adfinis* out of thirty (3 per cent). At Veleia a total

---

[112] *CIL* 14.367; 374; 431. Meiggs (1973) 218, 221–2; Laird (2002) 38.
[113] *CIL* 10.1838; 9.2475: 'ob hon. Aug. et biselli'.
[114] *CIL* 5.1897–1900; 5.1894. Christol (1992) presents similar examples from Gaul.
[115] *CIL* 9.1455; cf. Champlin (1981); 11.1146; cf. Criniti (1991).   [116] Champlin (1981) 251.

of 176 individual landowners are mentioned with *cognomen*, nineteen or (10.8 per cent) of whom carry Greek names. Of the fifty-two *domini* who pledged estates to the scheme, seven (13.4 per cent) carry Greek names. The average value of the estates in the scheme is much higher at Veleia than at Ligures Baebiani, and taking this disparity into account we find that those with Greek names generally contributed relatively modest estates. At Ligures Baebiani the largest of these estates were those of Octavius Lybicus and Antius Gamus, both valued at just 100,000 HS, most of the other estates being considerably smaller.[117] At Veleia one very large estate valued at 1,240,000 HS was pledged by M. Mommeius Persicus, but his *cognomen* is likely to indicate aristocratic rather than freed background.[118] The largest estates in this category therefore seem to be those of P. Afranius Apthorus, valued at 425,000 HS, and C. Volumnius Epaphroditus, worth 418,250 HS.[119] Judging from the frequency with which they appear on the list, none of the *adfines* with Greek *cognomina* seems to have been a major landowner.

The incidence of Greek names of course provides only a very rough measure of the social profile of the landowning classes in these two towns. Some carriers may not have been freedmen themselves, while some of those with Latin *cognomina* undoubtedly were. However, the correlation between the two samples is significant and reassuring. The results confirm, on the one hand, the existence of wealthy freedmen in these communities, while on the other hand they also suggest that they made up only a small minority of local landowners. Certainly there is no indication that more than a handful controlled larger estates.[120] As such, the results may offer a corrective to the conventional image of the freedmen's economic strength. On might conclude that, while the evidence from towns like Pompeii shows that freedmen played a dominant role in urban commerce

---

[117] 3.33–4, 35–6. Los (1992a) 744–7, reached far higher figures by including 'servile' Latin *cognomina*, but they are much less reliable as status indicators, especially when dealing with small samples such as these.

[118] Obl. 13, 50; cf. 1, 18, 31. According to Solin (1982) 620, the eleven Persici at Rome included a senator, an *eques*, three *ingenui*, four *incerti*, and two *liberti*.

[119] Obl. 6 and 22.

[120] Land ownership can also be approached through the study of tile stamps, *figlinae* being part of landed estates. Helen (1975) 22–3, 94, counted 150 *domini*, of whom fifty-four were senators, seven *equites*, forty-three women, one imperial slave; cf. Aubert (1994) 223. Helen had observed that '*domini* and *officinatores* formed two mutually exclusive groups, in the sense that *officinatores* rarely became domini' (Aubert (1994) 229), the only exception being Vismatius Successus, who is documented as both *officinator* and *dominus*, 27. Among the *domini* we find only 10.1 per cent Greek *cognomina*, but 46.3 among the *officinatores*.

and trade, relatively few of them would seem to have reached a level of affluence that allowed them to invest in landed property.[121]

The phenomenon of the rich freedmen must be put into perspective. Apparently they were relatively few in numbers and those who reached the absolute elite represented the rare exception.[122] Nevertheless, the very existence of wealthy ex-slaves is of course a paradox that invites further consideration. However, it is not evident that the phenomenon is best explained by positing a link between wealth and 'independence', as many scholars have done. Taken to its logical conclusion, the argument implies that freedmen who were left to fend for themselves were also the most successful. Or put differently, a situation which in other slave societies such as Brazil has generally been associated with poverty is considered a distinct advantage in Rome.[123]

The concept of the 'independent freedman' was most fully investigated by D'Arms, who focused particularly on the *Augustales* at Ostia.[124] He defined the 'independent freedman' as 'a freedman released from the restricting controls of a former master and his *familia*, and in a position both to accumulate wealth in commercial and manufacturing ventures where success depended upon his own capacities, contacts and initiative, and to establish and maintain social relationships which were largely of his own choosing'. On that basis he concluded that 'many Augustales, both individually and as an institution, were patronless', and that they therefore constituted 'a group apart from the city's governing class, rather than one subordinate to it'.[125] We may query whether the strict polarity between 'dependent' and 'independent' is really useful, but the reference to freedmen 'released from the restricting controls of the former master' also suggests a

[121] The attempt by Los (1992a) to demonstrate extensive freed presence on country estates around Pompeii is hampered by our inability to distinguish epigraphically between owners and managers. Pleket's (2001) 1106, claim that 'We now know that in various Italian cities well-to-do freedmen were as numerous as members of the urban elite', is also difficult to substantiate.

[122] Ste. Croix (1982) 177, questioned the scale of freedmen's wealth and believed it was reserved for those who inherited.

[123] Karasch (1987) 362–3.

[124] D'Arms' (1981) study of Roman commerce is paradoxical, since it devotes much energy to demonstrating the direct involvement of Roman aristocrats in supposedly 'vulgar' trades and generally identifies freedmen as agents who carried out the 'dirty' work. But he also regarded the rich freedman as a type apart, who demonstrated the commercial opportunities offered by the Roman economy. However, as Brunt (1983b) has observed, the strong presence of freedmen in commerce is a more decisive argument for his main thesis than the odd case of senators directly involved in trade. Indeed, the very existence of rich commercially based freedmen is probably the best evidence we have for that proposition.

[125] D'Arms (1981) 48, 146; (1990) 394f. Cf. Veyne (1961); Garnsey (1981); Vittinghoff (1990) 189; Christol (1992) 250. Los (1995) 1025, believed most *Augustales* owed their position to their own efforts.

very modern understanding of 'independence' as an indisputable benefit. Since the one advantage which the freedmen enjoyed was their familial background and patronal connection, an 'independent' freedman would generally have been a disadvantaged freedman.[126] Of course, when material security had been achieved the freedman might well have enjoyed a 'patronless' existence, but otherwise this would have been a predicament rather than a benefit.[127]

The question is therefore whether wealth necessarily indicates independence.[128] At the heart of the commercial 'middle class' model lies the assumption that libertine wealth and close patronal relations were incompatible. This argument, however, implies that the most energetic and gifted slaves were trained and set up in business, then freed and endowed with a substantial *peculium* with which they would amass fortunes matching those of their patrons. More realistically, we might try to explain the rich freedman *within* the context of patronal relationships, and there is in fact much evidence to suggest that patrons were not opposed to their freedmen acquiring moderate or even substantial wealth. Indeed, an alternative model might argue that the richest freedmen were precisely those who enjoyed the greatest support.[129]

The most striking examples of favoured freedmen were of course the fabulously rich *liberti* of emperors and dynasts, but many other wealthy freedmen also seem to have remained closely involved with their patrons despite the economic security and independence they enjoyed. Tiro, for example, bought a country villa while still working for Cicero, which he even intended to share with the Tullii.[130] In that respect he was hardly unique; according to Appian, Titus Vinius had a freedman, Philopoemen, with a splendid mansion, where the patron sought shelter during the proscriptions, suggesting both wealth and continued close relations.[131]

---

[126] D'Arms (1981) 147, argued that: 'In effect, socially and economically, the institution of the Augustales functioned for the independent *liberti* as did the institution of the *familia* for other less fortunate freedmen: it provided not only social solidarity, but also economic cohesion.' There is no concrete evidence, however, to support this interpretation.

[127] There were of course exceptions such as the highly skilled professionals, already discussed, who included doctors, teachers, artists, and actors.

[128] For example, Bodel (1999b) 42, saw the *Satyricon* as a 'representation of a contemporary social phenomenon, the successful independent freedman', which seems to imply a link between independence and success.

[129] Cf. Andreau (1992) 27–8, noting that freedmen were enriched through their patrons.

[130] *Fam.* 16.21.7.

[131] *BC* 4.44, calling the freedman Philemon. According to Suet. *Aug.* 27.2 and Dio 47.7.5, the freedman was later awarded with equestrian status. Plutarch, *Sulla* 1.4, tells the story of a freedman about to be executed for having sheltered a condemned man during the proscriptions. He lived in independent lodgings but the man sheltered was presumably his patron.

When Cicero travelled through the Pomptine region he stayed overnight at the house of M. Aemilius Philemo, a prominent freedman of Lepidus, the future triumvir.[132] Philemo was, in other words, in possession of estates grand enough to accommodate a consular with his entourage but still regarded as part of Lepidus' extended *familia* and obliged to provide hospitality for his peers. Cicero also stayed at an estate at Colophon belonging to C. Curtius Mithres, a rich freedman of Cicero's friend Rabirius Postumus.[133] M. Caelius M.l. Phileros was probably the freedman of Cicero's protégé M. Caelius, and after his patron's death in 48 he became *accensus* of T. Sextius, the civil war commander in Africa.[134] Later he would hold local magistracies and make generous donations in several provinces. In these and many other cases the precise source of the freedman's wealth is not known, but presumably it derived either directly from the patron or from business or patronage opportunities which their relationship offered. The former is illustrated by the case of M. Aurelius Zosimus, the trusted freedman of the consul M. Aurelius Cotta Maximus, who provided funds worth the equestrian census several times over, as well as dowries for his daughters.[135] Under the empire, several freedmen of leading aristocrats became very rich indeed. C. Stertinius Orpex, freedman of C. Stertinius Maximus (cos. suff. 23 CE), and *scriba librarius*, later settled in Ephesus with a large fortune, which he used to set up foundations in return for civic honours.[136] L. Licinius Sura (cos. II 102, III 107 CE) had several rich freedmen, including his favourite Philostorgus and his *accensus* L. Licinius Secundus, who became highly influential in Spain and received no fewer than twenty-one honorific inscriptions.[137]

Also at municipal level we find numerous cases of affluent freedmen who remained closely involved with their patrons. At Pompeii, Cn. Alleius Eros provides an interesting example. Although deceased at the early age of 22, he had – free of charge – become a member of the *Augustales*, who also paid

---

[132] *Fam.* 7.18.3; cf. Asc. 37C.

[133] *Fam.* 13.69; Deniaux (1993) 490–2. His wealth is also illustrated by the local honours he received in return for benefactions at Naxos.

[134] *CIL* 10.6104. Luisi (1975); Gascou (1984). Le Glay (1990) 623–6, suggested Phileros was involved in commercial activities, but these opportunities must have derived from his personal connections.

[135] *CIL* 14.2298: 'mihi saepe libens census donavit equestris', 'Cottanumque meum produxit honore tribuni'. Pliny presented his old nurse, *nutrix*, with a farm worth 100,000 HS, modestly describing it as a *munusculum*, *Ep.* 6.3. Horace, *Epist.* 1.7.78–82, mentions a patron who helps a freedman to a farm. Rawson (1976) 93–4, suggested many freedmen may have been pensioned off in this way.

[136] *Inschr. Eph.* 2.411, 3.720, 6.2113, 7.2.4123. Eck (1999) 15.

[137] Epict. *Diss.* 3.17.4–5; cf. Mratschek-Halfmann (1993) 92, 358–9, 362; Fabre (1976) 428; Schulze-Oben (1989) 126–9. At Lyons a prominent freedman indicated his patron as the consul D. Valerius Asiaticus, cos. suff. 35, cos. II 46, *CIL* 13.5012.

for his funeral together with the *Pagani*. He was a freedman of the powerful local figure Cn. Alleius Nigidius Maius, and despite his own prominent status he was buried alongside other members of the patron's family and household.[138] At Tibur the *magister Herculeus* M. Varenus (mulieris) et M. Lartidi l. Diphilus dedicated a shrine to Augustus and a *mensa ponderaria*, table of measures, thereby demonstrating his own considerable wealth. But he also erected statues of his *patronus* and *patrona*, which would suggest close ties and obligations that were publicly recognised.[139] Also, at Ostia, many *seviri Augustales* appear to have been associated with curial families.[140] The extraordinary riches of the freedmen of the late republican dynasts and later imperial freedmen may therefore have differed from those of other prosperous freedmen in scale rather than essence, marking the extreme end of a continuum of different forms of patronal support. There are, in fact, good reasons to believe that the most trusted aides of the elite were allowed, perhaps even encouraged, to accumulate substantial funds through their association with their patron.[141]

We get a fascinating glimpse into these practices through Cicero's letters. We have already noted the case of Dionysius, who had to tend to his businesses, but more detail is provided in the intriguing story of Philogenes, another freedman of Atticus, who was involved in organising a money transfer for Cicero. Shackleton Bailey explained the complicated matter as follows: 'In July 51 [Philogenes] had been concerned in the negotiation of a bill of exchange for Cicero at Ephesus (cf. 5.13.2). It would seem that Cicero found he did not require the money and had let Philogenes employ it (himself charging interest or participating in the proceeds?) *quoad liceret*, i.e. presumably until Cicero returned to Italy.'[142] The case suggests that freedmen handling the affairs of their patrons could do business with the funds that passed through their hands, which may explain how Tiro got the money to buy his villa. The apology of Marcus *iunior* for not having chipped in suggests the funds did not come directly from Cicero, and they may therefore have derived from business opportunities offered by his privileged position.

---

[138] D'Ambrosio and De Caro (1983) 13 OS no. 10.   [139] *Inscr. Ital.* 1.224–5. Giuliani (1970) 62–7.

[140] Laird (2002) 58–9. Tassaux (2000) 398f, noted that half of the *seviri* at Aquileia belonged to leading aristocratic families. The same applied to the large majority of the leading freedmen at Pompeii. Among the local *Augustales* (for a list see Castrén (1975) 275) only C. Munatius Faustus and Festius Ampliatus (the latter a likely rather than a certain *Augustalis*) did not come from curial families.

[141] In Apuleius' *Metamorphoses* Lucius was passed on to a rich freedman, who treated him well, 10.17. The freedman wished to ingratiate himself to his patron and was generously rewarded, 10.23.

[142] *Att.* 7.7.2. Shackleton Bailey (1965–70) 3.304. *Att.* 7.5.3, mentions a sum of 100,000 HS, but the text is corrupt.

Similar questions are frequently raised by the epigraphic evidence. For instance, T. Statilius Posidippus stands out as the most successful of the many freedmen in the household of the consular T. Statilii Tauri. He is recorded with a separate household of no fewer than twenty-one freedmen and slaves, some of whom had their own *vicarii*. With job titles including a *cocus*, two *cubicularii*, and four *dispensatores*, they probably worked for Posidippus' aristocratic patrons, in whose familial *columbarium* they were all buried.[143] We may wonder whether the slaves had been directly allocated to him, funds had been made available, or he had made his own money out of his position in the household. M. Lollius Alexander presents another interesting case. He is recorded as a *margaritarius*, who built a substantial monument for himself and his *familia*. It seems plausible he belonged to the *familia* of the senatorial Lollii, well known for their expensive jewellery.[144] In that case he would have profited personally from his patron's lavish lifestyle, and we might wonder whether it was tacitly accepted that slaves and freedmen in large households would 'cream off' a personal income for themselves.[145]

The imperial *familia* attracts particular interest in this context. The wealth of the emperor's favourite freedmen became notorious, and throughout Italy and the provinces we find affluent imperial freedmen and their descendants playing a prominent role in municipal life.[146] The source of their wealth must be sought in the particular opportunities for enrichment available to imperial administrators. In this respect they were probably not unique, although the scale of the household may have given them even greater freedom of action. For example, Andreau discusses a case of

---

[143] *CIL* 6.6246, 6261, 6262, 6274, 6277, 6278, 6279, 6410, 6415, 6415, 6426, 6475, 6476, 6479, 6493, 6498, 6525, 6535, 6574. One of these *dispensatores*, Eros, appears to have had several *vicarii* of his own, Faustus and Suavis, 6275, 6276. The link to Posidippus is not made explicitly but the Eros *dispensator*, who owned them, is most likely identical with 'Eros T. Statili Posidippi ser. disp.', 6274.

[144] *CIL* 6.9433; Plin. *NH* 9.117; cf. Mratschek-Halfmann (1993) 92–3. Kolb (1995) 473, argued that the patron of Q. Haterius (Tychicus: Cf. 6.607), whose ornate tomb illustrates his links to the building industry, might have been Q. Haterius Antoninus (cos. 53), also known from tile stamps. For the monument see Leach (2006). Weber (1988) 261–2, suggested C. Ateilius Serrani l. Euhodus 'margaritarius de Sacra Via' (*CIL* 1².1212) may have been connected with C. Atilius Serranus, cos. 106 BCE.

[145] This probably went through the entire household structure, from the freedmen suspected of selling leftovers from their patron's table, Apul. *Met.* 10.13–14, to the imperial freedmen who made money from selling information from the court, Dio 69.7.4. Even the slaves may have made money out of their connections. As Juvenal 3.188–9, complains: 'we clients are forced to pay taxes and to supplement the savings, *peculia*, of well-groomed slaves', referring to clients paying for access and cakes. Horace uses the phrase 'cura peculi' to describe lust for petty gain, *Ars Poet.* 330.

[146] A notable example is C. Iulius Zoilus from Aphrodisias, whose wealth and status are known only through epigraphic sources. Reynolds (1982) 156–64.

an imperial freedman who speculated in the food supply to Rome. As documented in the tablet of the Sulpicii, he received as security for loans grain and dried legumes for certain periods, thereby causing it to remain in Puteoli rather than being sent to Rome.[147] As such his actions were hardly in accordance with imperial policy, suggesting he was able to conduct his affairs fairly independently. It may have been common for imperial freedmen to use (public?) funds for their own ends in the same way as freedmen of senators made money on the side.[148] This may be the background for the special tax which Vitellius imposed on imperial freedmen based on the number of slaves they owned.[149] It probably applied only to those who still worked in – and profited from – the imperial household, since it would have been difficult to trace all those who had retired and settled elsewhere.

This partial 'recall' of the freedmen's accumulated funds raises the possibility that patronal support might be less than altruistic. Although patrons could not, like the emperor, confiscate some of their freedmen's funds, a very substantial part was in due course likely to fall to them or their family. Freedmen were expected to consider their patrons in their wills, and if they failed to do so and died without direct natural heirs, the patron could claim half the estate (from Augustus onwards).[150] Moreover, if the freedman was a Latinus, the entire estate would automatically revert to the patron as if it had been a *peculium*.[151] Given the likely numbers of Latini (suggested not least by the requirement that magistrates with *imperium* be involved in the manumission process), this must have been a major benefit for patrons, their children, and their extraneous heirs.[152] Certainly the patron's claim on the freedman's estate would have provided a strong incentive to invest in freedmen rather than outsiders.

Even in the elite this may not have been a trifling matter, as suggested by the recurring concerns about maintaining patronal rights when a change

---

[147] Andreau (1991) 383. *TPSulp* 45; Ti. Iulius Aug.l. Euenus organised the deal through his slave Hesychus, cf. 51–2; cf. Lintott (2002) 557.

[148] Rathbone and Temin (2008) 388, raise the possibility that 'they may have been temporarily diverting public and patrimonial resources which they were handling to make short-term private investments'; cf. Nero's *dispensator* Tiridates who accumulated a fortune of 13 million HS from his management of the Armenian War, Plin. *NH* 7.129.

[149] Tac. *Hist.* 2.94.

[150] Gaius 3.39–53; Ulp. *Reg.* 29; cf. the *Digest* section: 'De bonis libertorum', 38.2.

[151] Gaius 3.56; Salvian *Ad. eccl.* 3.33, on Latini who lived 'quasi ingenui' but died 'ut servi', which meant that their patrons denied them any possessions when they died, 'nolunt quidquam habere morientes'.

[152] Patronage over Latini Iuniani was an asset which could be passed on to *extranei*, Gaius *Inst.* 3.58, and Plin. *Ep.* 10.104, where the son is bypassed. Watson (1987) 35, 42, believed the greater claim to the freedman's estate explained why some masters might free informally.

of status occurred. The *lex Irnitana*, ch. 23, explicitly stated that newly enfranchised provincial magistrates retained their rights over *liberti*. Similarly a legal ruling preserved the rights of patronage over freedmen for those whose fathers had been condemned for treason.[153] The financial aspect of the patronal relationship is made explicit in Tacitus' account of the freedmen who hid their money with friends or powerful people when Vitellius restored the patronal rights of exiles.[154] The implication is that patrons naturally expected to benefit from their freedmen's estates, which were often large enough to be a real asset to them. Wealthy freedmen were a resource for the Roman elite, even at the highest levels. Thus, Appian describes how Octavian tried to hasten his formal adoption in the *comitia calata* in order to gain full patronal rights over Caesar's rich freedmen.[155]

What emerges from this discussion is an almost symbiotic economic relationship between freedmen and their patrons. On the one hand, we find a remarkable degree of economic freedom among freedmen who were allowed or perhaps even invited to exploit the opportunities their connections offered them. On the other hand, the patron might take a cut of the freedman's income or be content in the knowledge that much of the freedman's estate eventually would return to himself or his heirs. The freedman's deep involvement in the patron's economic affairs would often have made it difficult to separate sharply the funds of the two parties. And while this symbiosis in general would have been mutually beneficial, the blurring of economies also held obvious risks, since it presented ample opportunities for freedmen to abuse their privileged position.

There were many illicit means by which trusted freedmen could prosper financially, as highlighted by Cicero's concerns about Philotimus, Terentia's freedman who took care of his finances. When Cicero was away in the East in 50, he suspected him of fraud in relation to a purchase of property and to an inheritance which he warned Atticus to protect against the freedman.[156]

---

[153] D. 37.14.4 (Marcellus).

[154] *Hist.* 2.92. The *Digest* devoted a whole section, 38.5, to freedmen defrauding their patrons of their share of the estate. Hence also the importance attached to the restoration of patronal rights to returned exiles, Mart. 10.34. Likewise, D. 38.2.3.7 (Ulpian). Asking for citizenship for relatives of his doctor, Pliny added a further request for continued *ius patronorum*, *Ep.* 10.11.2. Sherwin-White (1966) 577, thought the main object was *obsequium* and *operae*, but inheritances may have been a more important concern.

[155] *BC* 3.94.390–1. This consideration may also explain the anecdote about the imperial freedman who changed his name from Cerylus to Laches and declared himself to be freeborn, Suet. *Vesp.* 23.1. Vespasian responded with a witty quotation which indicated that when he died he would be Cerylus again, referring to the emperor's claim to the freedman's estate. On Cerylus see Shaw (2007).

[156] *Att.* 6.4.3; 6.9.2.

Similarly, Cicero wrote to Cornificius, governor of Africa, asking him to ensure that Turius Eros, freedman of the *negotiator* Q. Turius, did not appropriate an estate after the death of his patron. A freedman of Caesar was also accused of taking possession of estates in Lucania.[157]

These examples further underscore the fact that the Roman elite were utterly dependent on staff they could trust. The conventional praise of *fides* as the freedman's highest virtue was not an empty phrase but reflected real concerns among the rulers of the empire. However, rather than simply demanding the freedman's obedience, they wished to be honoured like a father. *Pietas* and *obsequium* were attributes of familial relationships, and ultimately it is the personal nature of the freedman–patron bond that provides the key to understanding the freedman's economic roles in general. It also helps to explain what must have been one of the main sources of 'new fortunes', namely death and inheritances.[158]

As Lucian stated, new wealth was generally sent by Pluto, the god of the underworld.[159] As we have seen, it was common to provide legacies for loyal freedmen, and the most favoured retainers may also have become heirs. Cicero, for example, implied that – modest – inheritances for freedmen were neither rare nor particularly controversial.[160] Leaving larger shares, let alone the entire estate, to a freedman was far more contentious, as illustrated by the notorious case of Geganius Clesippus, who inherited a fortune from his *patrona*/lover.[161] Such a scenario was generally considered neither respectable nor edifying, Pliny's moral tale of P. Catienus Philotimus

---

[157] *Fam.* 12.26.2: 'hereditatem Turianam avertere'; Cic. *Phil.* 13.12. These anxieties were reinforced by stories of men who had been bankrupted by their freedmen: Petr. *Sat.* 38, on a freedman who once had a million but had been reduced to poverty by his freedmen, who had done everything to suit themselves; and Seneca, *Ben.* 2.27.1, on Cn. Lentulus (cos. 14 BCE) who had 400 million HS before his freedmen consigned him to a similar fate. Tac. *Ann.* 16.10, tells the story of L. Antistius Vetus who was betrayed by his freedman Fortunatus, who had embezzled him 'interversis patroni rebus'. Bradley (1990) 141, discusses cases where freedmen were suspected of stealing from the estates of their recently deceased owners.

[158] Cf. e.g. Fabre (1981) 278–82. Temin's (2004) 529 claim that the freedman 'was not the recipient of inherited wealth' is inaccurate.

[159] Lucian, *Timon* 20–1. New money was generally associated with inheritances, cf. e.g. Juv. *Sat.* 1.37, 67–8; 4.19. The newly rich in Lucian's *Gallus* 14, had inherited from his cousin. To Martial the perfect life required an inheritance, 10.47.3. Cf. MacMullen (1974) 101. On the significance of inheritances see also Pavis D'Escurac (1978).

[160] Most inheritances appear to have been relatively modest, such as the freedman M. Fulcinius who received a 1/36 of the estate, Cic. *Caecin.* 17, or Brinnius' freedmen who was left a quarter, *Att.* 13.13–14.4, cf. 13.12.4, 21a.3, 50.2. Other examples include Cicero's co-heir, L. Nostius Zoilus, *Fam.* 13.46. See also Verboven (2002) 193–4.

[161] Plin. *NH* 34.11–12, his epitaph is preserved *CIL* 1².1004 = 10.6488. *RE* 7.1 928, 3; Treggiari (1969a) 239. The controversial nature of larger inheritances is also implied in Cicero's defence of a freedman who inherited from a rich knight, Cic. *Verr.* 2.1.123–4.

being a rare exception; the freedman loved his patron so dearly that he threw himself on his funeral pyre despite having inherited the entire estate.[162] Still, most of the rich freedmen featuring in Roman satire had inherited from their patrons, Trimalchio merely being the most famous example. Others include Hister, who fraudulently left everything to a freedman he slept with, Syriscus, who inherited 10 million HS from his patron, but spent it all on food, and the barber Cinnamus, who became a knight by a gift from his *domina*.[163]

These stories are often tinged with a concern that freedmen might abuse their familiarity and insinuate themselves into their patron's will. Most evocatively this anxiety was expressed in Phaedrus' story of the freedman who maligned both the patron's wife and his son, with terrible consequences, in the hope of replacing them in his will.[164] Likewise, Horace mentions a crafty woman or freedman who sways the mind of an old senile.[165] Although these stories reflect both suspicion and opprobrium at such closeness, they nevertheless illustrate the fact that freedmen often were on very intimate terms with their patrons and hence were natural beneficiaries in the absence of direct heirs. Revealingly, Horace could mention a 'son or freedman heir' without any hint of anomaly.[166]

Jongman suggested that a very large proportion of the personal wealth in the Roman empire was concentrated in the hands of an elite which had problems reproducing itself, concluding that, 'by and large, rich Romans had inherited their wealth'. Most likely this applied also to the rich freedmen. Indeed, some of the largest libertine fortunes would be difficult to explain without taking this factor into account.[167] For example, according to Pliny, C. Caecilius C.l. Isidorus left in his will in 8 BCE, despite losses incurred during the civil war, 4,116 slaves, 3,600 oxen, 257,000 other types of cattle, and 60 million sesterces. In this case it has plausibly

---

[162] *NH* 7.122.

[163] Juv. 2.58–9; Mart. 5.70; 7.64. Mart. 9.73, also refers to a freedman who had inherited from his patron.

[164] 3.10.8–12: 'maritus quidam cum diligeret coniugem togamque puram iam pararet filio, seductus in secretum a liberto est suo, sperante heredem suffici se proximum'. Phaedrus' story gains a sharper edge if, as Champlin (2005) argues, the author was in fact an educated Roman member of the elite impersonating a humble freedman. Likewise, Publilius Syrus noted the opportunities the clever slave had of influencing his master, Q44 (544): 'Qui docte servit, partem dominatus tenet'; cf. Christes (1979b) 206–7, who thought it hinted at a battle of wills and minds.

[165] *Sat.* 2.5.70–1. Plin. *Ep.* 7.6.8: freedmen appointed as co-heirs.

[166] *Sat.* 2.3.122. Epigraphic examples of freed heirs in Schulze-Oben (1989) 82; Carroll (2006) 245.

[167] Jongman (2003a) 193. In Lucian's *Timon* 23, the newly rich who benefited from inheritances were former slaves, who 'still shudder at the irons', cf. *How To Write History* 20.

been suggested he may have inherited from the noble clan of the Caecilii Metelli.[168]

There was an ongoing redistribution of estates within the Roman elite, and as trusted confidants some freedmen would have been uniquely well placed to benefit from this process. Very few would have been as lucky as Isidorus or the fictional Trimalchio, but even a small share of a large fortune would have raised the freedman economically far above most freeborn. Inheritance reflected the privileged position of certain freedmen for whom it probably marked the end of a long process of gradual promotion. Although inheritances in reality may have been quite rare, certainly on a grander scale, they probably played an important symbolic role within the system of rewards and punishments which facilitated the exploitation of slaves and dependent labour. Such a windfall could transform the life of the beneficiary, and, despite the unease this ancient equivalent to modern 'lottery winners' generated among freeborn Romans, it was an effective reminder to both slaves and freedmen that loyalty and hard work might be richly rewarded.

For the freedman who inherited, wealth came with *de facto* independence, having lost his patron and benefactor in the process, and this situation confirms that the patron–freedman relationship was not static. The death of a patron changed the position of a freedman fundamentally, not least because the patronal bond was construed as uniquely personal, created by a single act of benefaction. Therefore, although patronal authority and supervision were hailed as the pillars of Roman manumission, the reality would often have been different. Life expectancy was low in the ancient world; according to the Princeton life-tables, males aged 30 and 40 had just a 55 and 41 per cent chance of surviving another twenty years.[169] If we assume that most owners were mature when freeing their slaves, who were themselves often quite young when it happened, a large number of freedmen would have lost their patron relatively soon after gaining their freedom.

---

[168] 'C. Caecilius C.l. Isidorus testamento suo edixit, quamvis multa bello civili perdidisset, tamen relinquere servorum 4116, iuga boum 3600, reliqui pecoris 257,000, in numerato 60 mill. HS, funerari se iussit 1,100,000 HS', Plin. *NH* 33.135. Cf. Treggiari (1969a) 109; Brunt (1975) 630–3, suggesting that he might have benefited from their generosity in the same way as Cotta's freedman M. Aurelius Zosimus. Verboven (2009) 137, simply states he was 'like Trimalchio a former businessman', thereby also missing the real source of the fictional freedman's wealth.

[169] Coale and Demeny (1983) 106 (Model West level 2). Woods (2007) has recently challenged the Princeton tables but his preferred model implies even higher mortality rates for adults aged between 15 and 49.

We can only speculate about the practical implications of these mortality patterns. When a patron died the freedman's loyalty would normally be transferred to his children and grandchildren, and patrons could allocate their freedmen to individual descendants through a procedure known as *assignatio libertorum*.[170] In that case those appointed would acquire sole patronal rights, just as if they had freed the slave themselves. The familial link may therefore not have been seriously affected, but the new patron bore no personal responsibility for the manumission and the paternal element to their relationship disappeared. A freedman took his name and identity from his former owner, not his new patron, and when the patron left no *sui heredes*, the freedmen would be divided up among the external heirs, who would assume both responsibilities and benefits. In reality these patrons probably played a lesser role in the lives of the freedmen. The break-up of households therefore seems a much more likely source of 'independent' freedmen than self-purchase.[171]

This situation may not always have been advantageous and some freedmen would probably have struggled economically unless they had received some additional financial support. The point was that a freedman was not per se employable in the eyes of a new patron, since his particular attractiveness partly derived from familiarity and trust, of which the new patron may have had little. But for others, already economically secure, the patron's death would create the classic 'independent freedman', and the question is how to understand his place in society. Firstly, we might note that this independence provides no support for the 'middle-class' model, since freedmen did not form an alternative to the elite out of which they had emerged. Similarly, the successful freedmen are poor examples of social mobility, for despite their inferior personal status they did not start at the bottom of society. They were privileged insiders whose – occasional – good fortune was inextricably linked to the structure of the elite households. Some wealthy freedmen, exemplified by Trimalchio, engaged in commerce, but so did many other rich Romans and their wealth was therefore not essentially different from that of other members of their class. Ultimately they too would have owed their position to patronal favour, and the rich freedman was more likely to be the 'favoured' freedman than the 'independent' one.

---

[170] D. 38.4: 'De adsignandis libertis'; 34.1.3 (Ulpian); cf. Peachin (1994). *P. Oxy.* 27 2474, records a case where a wife inherits patronal rights from her husband.
[171] According to Schiller (1971) 27, *liberti orcini* had 'actually no patron'. External heirs did, for example, have limited rights to the freedman's estate, Gaius *Inst.* 3.48. And *liberti* freed by *fideicommissum* became the freedmen of the *fideicommissarius*, D. 40.5.4.12, 5.12 (Ulpian); 40.5.49 (Africanus), who had lesser patronal rights.

He might eventually – or even immediately – have gained a position of de facto independence but that is immaterial to the question of his wealth, which is best seen as part of an ongoing redistribution of resources within the elite. The resulting mobility did not reflect the internal dynamics of the economy as much as the fluidity of the ruling class and its freedom to elevate some of their dependants to positions of considerable wealth.

Occasionally we are confronted with wealthy freedmen who seem to be detached from any patron. For example, in Pompeii the family of the *Augustalis* Munatius Faustus is not otherwise recorded in the town and his epitaph(s) mentions no patron.[172] Similarly, in Capua a well-appointed late republican house was discovered with first style wall painting and a mosaic inscription which recorded the *sagarius*, cloak merchant, P. Confuleius P.M.l. Sabbio.[173] And at Aquileia the epitaph for A. Mulvius A.l. Alexa, *pistor*, *CIL* 5.1036, raises similar questions. He was the patron of A. Mulvius A.l. Iucundus, who built the monument for himself, patron, and eight named freedmen of his own (or of Alexa). As in the other cases, the question is how Alexa got into this position.

D'Arms took freedmen like these to be independent, and in a purely material sense this is undoubtedly true. But as Brunt noted, the fact that we have no evidence for the freedmen's patron 'does not prove that they had none'.[174] Context is important and in most of these sources we would not expect to find the patron. If we had encountered Posidippus – with his twenty-one dependants – outside the context of the Statilian *columbarium*, we would have taken him for a rich – and hence independent – freedman. And had Tiro been known to us only in a local context as an absentee villa owner, he would also have fitted this profile and presented scholars with yet another example of the 'self-made' freedman. In Alexa's case, his patron may be absent from the epitaph, but the social pattern that emerges from the inscription is one of close involvement between patrons and freedmen. Most likely, therefore, this type of relationship stretched further back and included Alexa himself.

D'Arms further suggested that the marriage patterns of the *seviri Augustales* at Ostia and Puteoli could be used as a measure of their degree of

---

[172] Kockel (1983) 100ff; *CIL* 10.1030; D'Ambrosio and De Caro (1983) 9 es.

[173] 'P. Confuleius P.M.l. Sabbio sagarius domum hanc ab solo usque ad summum fecit', Pagano and Rougetet (1987), 756. Frederiksen (1984) 298, noted he came from a local family, cf. e.g. *AE* 1982 174.

[174] Brunt (1983b) 314. It was in the nature of Roman epigraphic practice that many families outside the *ordo* would be known only through their freedmen, who put up the vast majority of Latin epitaphs. Moreover, since freedmen as a rule were unlikely to be wealthier than their patrons, we may assume that these 'invisible' families probably were fairly affluent too.

'independence'.[175] Supposedly they married outside the *familia* more frequently than other freedmen, in turn demonstrating their greater freedom from patronal control. The marriage statistics presented are open to some doubt, but the argument is in itself peculiar, since we have no evidence that patrons took much interest in their freedmen's choice of spouse.[176] The suggested marriage pattern rather indicates that they were freed relatively early – before having formed *contubernia* – which in turn would imply they had been among the most favoured slaves.[177] Patronal support is also the most likely explanation for their later economic success, as demonstrated by the costly honours they received. Otherwise we would be confronted with a scenario of young slaves, freed and left to fend for themselves with little *peculium* or business experience, who nevertheless rose to become the most successful freedmen in the city.

This picture is hardly realistic and its shortcomings should be borne in mind when we approach 'isolated' freedmen such as the famous Sulpicii from Puteoli. Camodeca has emphatically denied the possibility that C. Sulpicius Faustus might be a mere agent, primarily because no other Sulpicii were prominent at Puteoli at the time.[178] While this may be true, it is of little help if we wish to understand his place in the economy and society of Puteoli. C. Sulpicius Faustus may not himself have been a freedman, but his father probably was.[179] C. Sulpicius Heraclida is known from an epitaph (*EE* 8.451) in which he commemorated his patron C. Sulpicius Hyginus, probably also a freedman. We do not know when the banking business was started, or by whom, but the fact that we are faced with a series of freedmen and freedmen's freedmen – Cinnamus and Eutychus continuing the line – is surely not accidental. At some point one of the Sulpicii must have got involved in this specialised line of work, acquired the necessary legal and financial skills, accumulated sufficient capital, and gained enough contacts and clients to make the business viable. None of these premises was freely available in the ancient world, and attempting to explain the process without taking the patron into account – just because he does not feature – would seem to raise as many questions as it solves.

---

[175] D'Arms (1981) 135, 147; followed by Bürge (1988) 319–21.

[176] The anecdotal evidence adduced by Bürge (1988) 319–21, does not allow any general conclusions.

[177] There is no indication that the wives of these *seviri Augustales* were freeborn; half of them carried Greek names and a third of the Latin *cognomina* were distinctly 'servile'.

[178] Camodeca (2003) 73. Cébeillac-Gervasoni (2000) 110–11, claimed it was almost certain that their links to patrons were tenuous and that the sums they handled were entirely under their control; cf. Rowe (2001) 231.

[179] C. Sulpicius Heraclida and his wife Sulpicia Harmonia were presumably *colliberti* and their four children, Hyginus, Faustus, Onirus and Heraclida, could therefore be freed too.

Sulpicius Faustus may have been personally independent (indeed he may have been freeborn), but this hardly explains the existence of his banking firm. The point is that the 'independent freedman' was not necessarily a 'self-made' man. A freedman might become de facto independent on the death of his patron, especially if he left no natural heirs, at which point the freedman might choose to move away and settle elsewhere. This could also have happened with the patron's blessing during his own lifetime; as we saw, there is evidence for absent wealthy freedmen who remained involved in their patrons' affairs.

The problem we face is partly one of categories, since rich freedmen have no modern equivalent. They were 'nouveaux riches' in the sense that they were not born to wealth, which of course invited ridicule and contempt, but that did not make them members of a separate class with its own distinct outlook, values, and behaviour. They were part of the world of the elite, to whom the large majority owed their success. Freedmen could, in other words, be both 'nouveaux riches' *and* insiders.[180] Their financial security and self-reliance did not make them members of a specific category of 'independent freedman'; indeed no ancient writer ever distinguishes between 'dependent' or 'independent' freedmen. This classification is unlikely to do justice to the complex range of relationships that might exist between patrons and *liberti*, and rather than a simple polarity we should envisage a broad continuum of possible degrees of involvement.

Finally, we may briefly consider the evolutionary model of Roman society that has been constructed around the figure of the freedman. Supposedly the freedmen thrived particularly in the two first centuries CE, when they feature prominently in documentary sources relating to the urban economy. The empire has therefore come to appear more dynamic and 'modern' than the republic. However, there is little hard evidence to back up this impression. Generally, we do not have enough republican sources

---

[180] Freedmen might also enter into the *clientelae* of other members of the elite. Cicero had passed his freedman Hilarus on to Atticus, whose 'ratiocinator et cliens' he became, Cic. *Att.* 1.12.2. The fact that freedmen could be counted among the clients (and employees) of *amici* suggests more complex ties of obligation and economic connections, which might explain the situation we encounter in Pompeii where likely freedmen (as indicated by Greek and 'servile' Latin *cognomina*) are given as the *clientes* of candidates with different *nomina*. For example, L. Betutius Placidus features as *cliens* of both L. Popidius Ampliatus and C. Iulius Polybius (*CIL* 4.7275, 7279), Lollius Synhodus as *cliens* of L. Popidius Secundus (4.7418) and Popidius Natalis *cliens* of C. Cuspius Pansa; the latter was L. Popidius Secundus' running mate for the aedileship (4.1011). In other cases we only know the *cognomen* of the *cliens*, but since a freedman cannot be the *cliens* of his manumitter he must be supporting a different kind of patron, e.g. 4.822, 2925, 7685. The freedman's integration into broader networks of patronage was probably facilitated by his or her patronal connections, since the former master in a sense vouched for character and reliability.

to make a meaningful comparison, and since there is no sign of structural changes to the use of freedmen, we would *a priori* assume their relative economic importance to have been largely similar in both periods. Thus, there are sufficient hints in the republican evidence to suggest that affluent freedmen may have been a common feature also during this period. For example, the *magistri* inscriptions from Capua along with other evidence from Campania indicate that many local freedmen were able to make substantial contributions to the local building projects.[181] Similarly, much of the evidence underpinning the image of the empire as a 'golden age' of the freedman is directly linked to the introduction – and activities – of the *seviri Augustales*. In the next chapter we will therefore take a closer look at this institution.

[181] Frederiksen (1984) 284–318; Johnson (1933).

CHAPTER 7

The freedman (and his son) in public life

Roman public life was – as a matter of course – dominated by men of means. The rich monopolised all positions of status and influence, and, as we have seen, some freedmen (a very small minority, no doubt) became not just comfortable but conspicuously well off. Their blanket exclusion from positions of authority therefore produced a glaring case of 'status dissonance', that is, a clash between different parameters of social standing, in this case wealth and personal background. The taboo against former slaves exercising public authority was absolute and non-negotiable, justified as it was by the natural order that dictated that higher beings govern the lower. As a result, freedmen were excluded from the entire honours system, including magistracies, priesthoods, the senate, the equestrian order, the law courts, and the local town councils.[1] The fact that the bar on freedmen in the *ordo decurionum* apparently was enshrined in law only in 24 CE is of little import in this context since the *lex Visellia* merely formalised an existing de facto exclusion. Although the ban on rich freedmen pursuing careers severed the normal association between wealth, rank, and power, certain aspects of the public honours system remained open to them. Thus, the *ornamenta*, i.e. the outer symbols of rank and office, were occasionally bestowed on particularly deserving freedmen as a means of negotiating the paradox of rich citizens without a matching status.

There were also plenty of opportunities for freedmen to engage in public – and semi-public – life within their communities. At local level, freedmen were fully involved in cultic associations, some of which were entirely dominated by slaves and freedmen. The *compitales*, the cult performed at crossroad shrines, were traditionally organised by freedmen belonging to the adjoining households.[2] In this sphere the lack of *auctoritas*

---

[1] Le Glay (1990) 629, noted that freedmen were effectively excluded also from the *Iuvenes* organisations – although not formally barred.
[2] Cf. Dion. Hal. 4.14.3–4; Horace, *Sat.* 2.3.281–6. They also organised the annual neighbourhood festival, the *Compitalia*; cf. *CIL* I².777; 2984a from Pompeii.

248

was no obstacle, as also illustrated by the cultic roles allocated to freed-women and even slaves.[3] While public priesthoods generally were off-limit, freedmen appear as *galli*, even *archigalli*, priests of Cybele, which may be linked to the exceptional character of this foreign priesthood.[4] We also find freedmen strongly represented in the various *magistri* organisations of republican Rome and Italy, whose functions included dedications to tute-lary deities, provision of games, and occasionally also larger expenditures on building projects.[5] None of these roles questioned their fundamental exclusion from positions of authority, since they remained under the super-vision of freeborn officials who held the formal religious/political power. Viewed from this perspective, the *collegia* might seem to represent a radical departure from the norm, since they allowed freedmen to hold prominent positions and outrank freeborn members.[6] But the authority derived from these roles was of course confined to these particular associations and had no wider civic implications.

Although well established before the advent of the principate, the freed-men's public role underwent a number of changes during the reign of the first emperor. Thus, the compital cult was reorganised and associated with the worship of the princeps, whose *lares* and probably also *genius* were included among the crossroad deities.[7] A variety of local bodies also sprang up throughout Italy and the provinces, dedicated to the worship of the emperor, at Pompeii exemplified by the *ministri Augusti* and the *ministri Fortunae Augustae*. The membership of these organisations was dominated by slaves and freedmen, who also made up the large majority of the *seviri Augustales*, another type of local association which has commonly been linked to the emperor and his worship.

Most historians have interpreted these reforms and innovations as delib-erate attempts by the new regime to win the support of freedmen, engage them directly in the propagation of its ideology, and generally exploit their

[3] Apparently freedmen and women were particularly involved in the cult of Feronia, Livy 22.1.18; Serv. *in Aen.* 8.564; cf. Macr. *Sat.* 1.6.13.
[4] Beard, North, and Price (1998) 261 n. 49. Freedmen could also perform many of the lower functions involved in religious rites, e.g. as musicians, haruspices, and attendants, *ibid.*
[5] At Minturnae the body consisted entirely of freed *magistri* and slave *ministri* who made dedications to Ceres, Spes, and Mercurius Felix. The expenditures at Minturnae were modest, although they some-times also included games, Johnson (1933) 118–23. At Capua the *magistri* included both freeborn and freed, which may have reflected the unique position of the city, still deprived of a civic administration, Heurgon (1939); Frederiksen (1984) 264–6, 281–4, 301–2. Solin (1990) 156–9, noted that the freed-men in question were mostly those of grand local families. Similar institutions are known at Delos, cf. Hasenohr (2002).
[6] Waltzing (1895–1900) 1.357–68, 379–425; Royden (1988) 228–34.
[7] Cf. Fraschetti (1990) 204–73; Gradel (2002) 115–30; Tarpin (2002) 137–64; Lott (2004).

ambitions within a new civic framework. The apparent success of this policy has also been widely recognised, and some scholars have suggested that freedmen became some of the most ardent supporters of the Augustan principate.[8] Some have gone further and assumed that in particular the office of the *Augustalitas* served to defuse looming unrest caused by frustrated freedmen who could find no outlet for their aspirations.[9] In this interpretation, maintaining the loyalty of wealthy freedmen was a high priority for the rulers of the empire, who actively courted their support in order to preserve social and political stability. There is a risk of over-interpretation, however. The posited attempts to attract the freedmen can also be viewed as part of a much wider strategy to consolidate the new order, which encouraged all social strata, including the lower ones, to pay tribute to the emperor, ideally in a spontaneous and unsolicited show of support. Thus, as I shall argue, the introduction of the *seviri Augustales* probably did not originate in a centralised initiative but may have been local responses to the new political reality. The epigraphic activities of the *vicomagistri* and other low-ranking officials may also have misrepresented their importance in the cult of the emperor. Their role was clearly secondary to the prestigious *sacerdotes* and *flamines*, all drawn from the elite, and the new institutions can be seen as public 'niches', where people of lower rank could make their – modest – contribution to the celebration of the new political order.

The appearance of the title *Augustalis* in the early empire has become a central focus of modern research into the public roles of freedmen. The *Augustales* – frequently combined with the numeric designation *seviri* – were supposedly a major Augustan innovation which offered wealthy freedmen a 'safe' outlet for their ambitions by directing their energy and resources into civic activities on behalf of the new regime. As such, the new institution has been seen as the formal recognition of the freedmen's social and economic importance and the first concerted effort to give them an official role and status in public life. Indeed, it has become common to describe them as an institutionalised 'middle class'.

The current view of these titles and offices is not easily summarised, which is due partly to the vagueness of many modern interpretations and

---

[8] Zanker (1975) 282; (1988) 316–20; cf. e.g. Behrends (1980) 86, who saw freedmen as 'eine wesentliche Stütze des neuen Regimes'.

[9] Ostrow (1985), (1990), followed by e.g. Fabiani (2002) 102. No evidence was adduced to support the hypothesis, apart from the freedmen's complaints against triumviral taxes in 31 BCE, Dio 50.10.4–6, and the popular riot in Puteoli (58 CE), in which no freed involvement is mentioned by our only source, Tac. *Ann.* 13.48.

partly to shifting emphases in recent scholarship that has moved from a 'cultic' to a predominantly 'social' interpretation. Traditionally, the *seviri Augustales* were regarded straightforwardly as priests in the cult of the emperor. This model was based primarily on the imperial allusion of their title, and on comments in late *scholia*.[10] There is little corroborative evidence for this theory and it has now been largely abandoned, although some historians continue to link the *Augustales* with the worship of the emperor in some form. The strongest argument for this connection remains their title, but there is also more specific evidence from Campania of – albeit indirect – involvement in the imperial cult.[11] As a result most scholars now favour a vague compromise which accepts some cultic associations and at the same time recognises their role as local benefactors and sponsors of public events; for like all members of prestigious civic bodies they had to pay fees, *summae honorariae*, in return for the honour.[12]

Although the priestly role has been downplayed, the institution is still seen as an Augustan attempt to bind freedmen to the regime by offering them an alternative *cursus honorum*.[13] In line with this 'civic' approach the *Augustales* are increasingly identified as members of a specific 'ordo', placed right below the decurions and well above the plebs. This understanding of the *Augustales* is explicitly moulded over the relationship between the two highest orders in Rome, the senate and the *equites*, a comparison first made by Gordon and since widely accepted. In the same way, new senators were drawn from the equestrian order, so the *ordo Augustalium* was perceived as

---

[10] The *scholia* on Horace, *Sat.* 2.3.281, Ps. Acron and Porphyrion, both describe them as *sacerdotes* and link them with the *compitales*. The confusion is evident and understandable considering the time of writing when the institution had long ceased to exist.

[11] At Misenum a building complex has been discovered which included a temple, referred to as 'templo Aug(usti) quod est Augustalium', i.e. 'the temple of Augustus that belongs to the Augustales', De Franciscis (1991); Camodeca (1996c) 161–8; D'Arms (2000) 141; Laird (2002) 90–5. At Liternum the *fasti Augustalium* mentions 'Augustales creati, ii qui in cultu domus divinae contul(erunt)', i.e. *Augustales* who contribute to the cult of the *domus divina*, Camodeca (2001). The insignia of *Augustales* include *fasces* of a type distinct from those of priestly lictors, cf. Schäfer (1989) 229ff.

[12] E.g. Rives (2007) 152: 'Augustales, a formal rank in some way connected with the worship of the emperor', cf. 128. Very circumspect is the assessment by Beard *et al.* (1998) 357–8, who argue *Augustales* were not particularly associated with the cult of the emperor, but could have some cultic functions. They also describe *Augustales* as 'possessors of a particular local status'.

[13] Frank (1940) 246 described the *Augustales* as 'Augustus' shrewd institution', which served partly 'to bind them in loyalty to the imperial house'; Rostovtzeff (1957) 104: 'as an influential class they [the freedmen] were given a place in municipal society . . . especially by the institution of the Augustales in the cult of the emperors'; Sherwin-White (1973) 327: 'a civic corporation, the *ordo Augustalium*, was created by Augustus for their dignification'; Vittinghoff (1990) 208: *ordo Augustalium* invented as 'Ersatzorganisation'.

the natural recruiting ground for the *ordo decurionum*, where the sons of *Augustales* often gained a seat.[14]

The notion of the *Augustales* as a 'middle class' has now become so commonplace that it forms a standard component of many local histories.[15] However, the most radical version of this model was presented by Abramenko, whose – highly influential – interpretation has wide implications for our understanding of Roman cities in general.[16] His point of departure was the indisputable fact that in some areas freeborn are documented as *seviri Augustales*, which he took as proof that the institution was not invented specifically for freedmen but remained open to all citizens. The freedmen's dominant position in most of these bodies therefore indicated to Abramenko that former slaves made up almost the entire economic stratum located between the decurions and the rest of the population. The introduction of the *Augustales* in other words represented a formal recognition of their de facto role as the Roman 'middle class', offering them status, insignia, and privileges commensurate with that position. On the basis of this argument it was further suggested that the relative economic strength of the freedman class in different parts of Italy could be measured by their share of the local *seviri Augustales*. For example, Abramenko argued for the existence of a stronger freeborn 'middle class' in northern Italy based on the greater frequency of *ingenui* among the *Augustales* in this region.[17]

Common to all modern studies has been the search for a single definition of the *seviri Augustales*. The basic premise has been that, allowing for some gradual changes over time, all our evidence relates to what was essentially a single, relatively uniform institution, which was conceived centrally and adopted locally. However, there seems to be a basic elusiveness to the phenomenon which makes it difficult to pin down the precise 'meaning' of these institutions. This partly reflects the nature of the evidence, since they are virtually absent from the literary record, featuring only in the *Satyricon*, where Trimalchio, Hermeros, and Habinnas all hold the title.[18] It follows that we have no ancient descriptions of their character or purpose. The

---

[14] Gordon (1931) 73. Duthoy (1978) 1273, 1289; Ostrow (1985) 272; Purcell (2000) 427; Laird (2002) 236; Clarke (2003) 143; Patterson (2006) 245. Weber (1993) 247, declared that the *Augustales* stood directly before the door to the Curia, which would be opened to their children, and as such function as a 'Rekrutierungsreservoir'. To Bérard (1999) 52, the Seviri Augustales were 'un véritable seconde ordre', while Buchi (2002) 75, declared they were 'il vero e autentico ceto intermedio delle varie realtà locali'.

[15] For example, Bertini (2004) 25–38, discussed the *Augustales* in Parma under the heading 'ceti intermedi'.

[16] Abramenko (1993b).

[17] Abramenko (1993b) 128–89, 279–310; followed by e.g. George (2005) 64–5.

[18] Petr. *Sat.* 30.2; 57.6; 65.5; 71.12.

epigraphic evidence may be plentiful (consisting of around 2,500 inscriptions) but this type of evidence is, needless to say, also highly problematic. The number of inscriptions recording *Augustales* is itself not a reliable measure of their significance, since much of the material was produced by the *Augustales* themselves, often for their own glorification. Moreover, any attempt to base a historical argument entirely on epigraphic sources faces a fundamental hermeneutic challenge, since the information they provide is by its very nature diffuse and kaleidoscopic. Our evidence consists of disparate inscriptions recording individual *Augustales* and/or some of their public activities, and there is a risk that we construct a 'standard' version of the *seviri Augustales*, which is little more than a combination of 'typical' features extrapolated from numerous poorly documented and potentially highly diverse local institutions. Thus, a closer look at the evidence reveals a striking degree of variation at local level, between different towns and regions, which undermines any attempt to piece together a single picture of the institution that captures its origins, function, and 'essence'.[19]

At the most basic level, the variation expressed itself in the titles carried by these officials. The titles *Augustalis*, *sevir Augustalis*, and *magister Augustalis* were very common but seem to have been used according to local taste. In addition we find a wide variety of combinations of *Augustalis* with the names of deities and emperors or the numbers of officials. Duthoy counted no fewer than forty different variations, and to deal with this unwieldy amount of titles he invented a shorthand term for all of them, the **Augustales*, thereby producing a more streamlined 'national' institution.[20] The issue is further complicated by the fact that the title *sevir* also appears without the epithet *Augustalis*, while exhibiting the same social and functional profile as those whose titles contain overt imperial references. This also applies to a number of other bodies which appear to be local variations of the *seviri Augustales*. They include, for example, the *seviri Victoriae* at Aquinum, the *Apollinares* at Regium Lepidum and Luceria, the *quinqueviri* at Interamnia Praetuttiorum, the *decemviri* at Ferentinum, and the *quattuorviri* at Trea. Many more examples could be given, and this diversity suggests the institutions were not designed according to a centrally devised blueprint, an impression further borne out by the multiplicity of institutions that sometimes existed within a single town. Thus, at Paestum we find not just *Augustales*, but also *seviri Augustales*, *magistri Augustales Mercuriales*, and *magistri Bonae Mentis Augustales*, each apparently representing a

---

[19] Beard *et al.* (1998) 358 n. 131, noted a 'modern tendency to lump together some rather diverse epigraphic evidence under the heading of *Augustales*'.

[20] Duthoy (1978) 1254, cf. e.g. Buonocore (1995).

separate body. The coexistence of these institutions is occasionally demonstrated by cases where a person held several of them during his career.[21]

If we turn to the structure of these institutions we find a similar diversity. The number of office holders could vary, and more importantly the very nature of the position – a short-term office or a life-long status – is not always clear. It has been widely assumed that the permanent bodies gradually developed out of what had originally been short-term offices. Supposedly, former office holders began to establish themselves as a distinct body. Against this theory Abramenko pointed to early examples of permanent organisations with internal officials and suggested they had been integral to the institution from the outset.[22] While these cases show that we are not dealing with a straightforward transition from annual offices to a permanent body, we should also be open to the possibility of localised developments. Thus, the recorded sizes of these bodies also show considerable variation, and at least in some towns it would not have been possible for every former office holder to gain a seat.[23]

In terms of function, we have already noted that in a few places, geographically close, we have evidence for more formalised involvement in the worship of the emperor. Elsewhere such evidence is missing, and while imperial dedications occur occasionally, the sponsorship of games, statues of civic benefactors, buildings, and roads are far more commonly attested. Overall the impression is one of considerable flexibility when assigning tasks to these officials, who as a rule were appointed and overseen by the *ordo decurionum*.

---

[21] Further examples are given in Mouritsen (2006) 239–41. Bandelli (2002) 18–19, noted the existence at Aquileia of three distinct bodies, the *sexviri Augustales*, the *Augustales*, and the *sexviri*, the latter going back to republican times. At Lyons the inscriptions from the amphitheatre imply that the *Augustales* were distinct from the *seviri Augustales*, *CIL* 13.1667c.

[22] Abramenko (1993a); against e.g. Duthoy (1978) 1284.

[23] At Liternum two membership registers, *alba*, from the second century list eighteen (later extended to thirty-five) and twenty-one plebs. These figures are in line with the arrangements for public dinners prescribed at Petelia and at Cures Sabini, where the *Augustales* were allocated two *triclinia*, allowing for eighteen diners (10.114 lines 15–16, 9.4971). An inscription from Trebula Suffenas allows for between thirty-five and fifty-five members (*AE* 1995 423). Elsewhere much higher figures have been calculated on the basis of *sportulae* provisions. Duncan-Jones (1974; 1982 edn) 285, estimated between 190 and 240 at Ostia. He also assumed that the membership at Spoletium was 'probably well over one hundred'. At Puteoli the *Augustales* were divided into at least three *centuriae*, the Cornelia, Petronia, and Antia, *EE* 8.369; *AE* 2005 337; *CIL* 10.1873–4, 8178. Camodeca's (1996c) 165, suggestion of 150 members at Misenum was queried by D'Arms (2000) 133–4, who argued on good grounds for at least 200. There the *Augustales* were divided into two categories the *corporati* and those 'qui in corpore non sunt', which, as D'Arms (2000) 131–2, suggested, may refer to a permanent body with a fixed membership, apparently counting 100 members, and those who had not (yet?) gained access to this inner core. The implication is that the social element to the institution may not have been universal.

Finally, the social profiles vary substantially between towns and regions, although this is also the area where we find the highest degree of uniformity. Thus, it is largely the strong presence of freedmen encountered throughout Italy and the provinces that defines the organisations as belonging to a specific type.[24] In some provinces and Italian regions the posts were held exclusively by freedmen while in others there was a certain mix, at least during some periods. Northern Italy differs in several respects from the peninsula, since freeborn made up a much larger proportion there. In addition, we also find intra-regional variation. At Placentia almost half of the *seviri Augustales* were freeborn, and the same applied to the *seviri* and *magistri Augustales* at Parma. In neighbouring Bononia, on the other hand, the large majority of known *seviri* were freed, and at Florentia we find just two *ingenui*.[25] At Hispellum seven out of ten recorded *seviri* were explicitly freeborn, in sharp contrast to nearby Asisium where that applied to just three out of twenty-three.[26]

What emerges from this brief survey is an essentially local institution, shaped according to local circumstances and needs. Presumably it was introduced when appropriate and then adapted to local conditions.[27] Needless to say, few cities completely reinvented the model, and we find broad regional patterns suggesting inspiration from neighbouring communities. But each town also appears to have developed its own social 'micro-climate', which determined how many of these organisations were created, how large they became, and who joined them.

The origins of the *seviri Augustales* remain a puzzle, and probably an insoluble one. Despite broad similarities, the variations and exceptions are too many to suggest a centralised initiative. Likewise, the connection with the emperor seems too tenuous to allow us to identify 'imperial worship/celebration' as the sole – or main – reason for the sudden proliferation of these institutions. The *magistri* associations, already well documented in the republic, may provide the strongest clue. As we have seen, these mixed bodies had a substantial freed element, and interestingly the *magistri Augustales* all belong to the early empire, perhaps representing an

---

[24] There are some notable exceptions such as the *Herculanei Augustales* at Tibur, who included many members of the curial elite.

[25] Placentia: *CIL* 11.1223, 1225, *AE* 1982 362; Parma: 11.1058, 1063, 1064; Florentia: 11.1616, *AE* 1930 119.

[26] Hispellum: *CIL* 3.8261, 11.5275, 5278, 5286, 5287, *AE* 1950 82, *AE* 1988 525; Asisium: 11.5424, 5426, *AE* 1989 290.

[27] At Pompeii the *Augustales* appear relatively late, probably because of the existence of the *magistri Pagi Suburbani Felicis Augusti* who seem to have played a very similar role as sponsors of local projects; cf. Tarpin (2002) 231; Mouritsen (2006) 243.

element of continuity.[28] In some instances we might envisage the honorific title *Augustalis* being added to existing bodies, while in other cases organi-sations were created *de novo*. Sometimes it may have been a gradual process, not dissimilar to the transformation of the Pompeian *ministri Maiae Mer-curii*, into *ministri Maiae Mercurii Augusti*, and finally *ministri Augusti* between 14 and 2 BCE.[29] The title *Augustalis* was sufficiently vague to allude to the emperor without indicating any specific function or relationship, and the evidence suggests there was no clearly defined cultic role. The title may have been linked to games in honour of the emperor, perhaps hinting at involvement in the financing of the *Augustalia*.[30] The extent to which the emperor influenced the spread of these bodies must remain conjectural, but there is no evidence for any decisive role in the process.[31]

This reconstruction casts doubt on the '*ordo* model', which saw the introduction of the *seviri Augustales* as a means of turning wealthy freedmen into a formalised 'middle class'. The degree of local diversity observed in the epigraphic sources seems difficult to reconcile to the notion of a new 'second order' conceived centrally as part of imperial policy. There is no evidence that the *seviri Augustales* constituted a permanent body in all towns or that all former office holders automatically became members. Moreover, in many places there was more than one institution of this type, which raises the question of which one of them embodied *the* middle class. For example, which of the bodies at Interamnia Praetuttiorum represented the real 'second order' – the *Augustales*, the *seviri*, or the *quinqueviri*?

Given the wide range of local arrangements, we might wonder why they were called an *ordo* at all, and here the simple answer is that they were not. The epigraphic evidence for this title is far more limited and ambiguous than often assumed. Firstly, the number of attestations is quite small, consisting of twenty-six inscriptions from nineteen towns in Italy.[32] Most of them are also quite late, almost all dating to the second century CE,

---

[28] Mouritsen (2006) 243. Fabiani (2002) 105, noted that at Pisa and Lucca the *Augustales* were preceded by *collegia* of *Mercuriales*. For the republican origins of the *sexviri* at Aquileia, cf. n.21 above. The connection between *magistri* and the *seviri* and *Augustales* was discussed by Kneissl (1980) 307–17.

[29] 10.885–90.

[30] Among the earliest attestations is M. Caelius M.l. Phileros, cf. Luisi (1975) 56; Gascou (1984) 115, who regarded him as contemporary with *CIL* 11.3200 (13–12 BCE), recording the first *Augustales* at Nepet. The festival of the *Augustalia*, for which these officials may have been responsible, was introduced in 19 BCE, and Dio, 54.34.1–2, states that in 11 BCE it was for the first time celebrated by senatorial decree. In that case the title might indeed have been derived from this particular task. *AE* 1933 152, refers to a donation 'pro ludis augustalib(us)', and the provision of games (*munera*) seems to have been a standard obligation; cf. Mouritsen (2006) nn. 37–8.

[31] Fabiani (2002) 100, thought the spread of the institutions was 'non direttamente sollecita, ma suggerita dal potere centrale'; *contra* Zanker (1988) 319.

[32] *CIL* 5.1968 (Opitergium); 9.3181 (Corfinium); 4067 (Carsioli); 4891 (Trebula Mutuesca); 10.4760 (Suessa); 10.1249 (Nola); 5796 (Verulae); 11.5752 (Sentinum); 11.6164, 6174 (Suasa); 14.421 (Ostia);

suggesting this designation was not part of the original concept of the *seviri Augustales*. They would therefore have 'grown' into *ordines*, as also envisaged in the 'evolutionary' model which assumed a gradual development from a semi-religious body into a civic order. How that happened in practice is not clear, but before speculating about the possible nature of the process we may consider the context in which this designation was applied. A survey of the attestations shows that it was used almost exclusively by the *seviri Augustales* themselves. The term is hardly ever applied by non-members and no official inscription commissioned by the local authorities refers to them as an *ordo*.[33] When the decurions mention the *seviri Augustales* in official documents it is as a *corpus*, which places them on the same footing as *collegia*.[34]

We might also note that the term *ordo* carried a wide range of meanings. Even on an official level it was not restricted to the three highest orders, since lower state officials, including clerks, scribes, and heralds, also constituted *ordines*.[35] More broadly it could be applied to any category of people in Roman society, from matrons to slaves and prostitutes. In certain contexts it did confer a certain dignity and could be used to flatter, as Cicero did when he mentioned the 'ordo libertinorum' in the Verrines.[36] When the *seviri Augustales* employed the term to describe themselves, it might simply be a form of self-aggrandisement, especially when juxtaposed with the *ordo decurionum*. Their organisations bore little resemblance to the *ordo decurionum* and were *ordines* only in the sense that their members occasionally liked to designate themselves as such. It follows that they did not enjoy any officially recognised status comparable to that of senators, *equites*, and decurions, a point also underlined by the fact that legal sources never mention the *seviri Augustales*. In fact membership did not confer any rank higher than that entailed by any other civic organisation such as the *iuvenes* or the prominent *collegia*.[37]

14.2410 (Bovillae); 2809, 2795 (Gabii); *AE* 1927 124, 128; 1962 312; 1996 384 (Formiae); *AE* 1972 154(?), 163 (Trebula Suffenas); *AE* 1978 261 (Velia); *NSc* 1921 189 (Falerio); *Inscr.It.* 4.115, cf. 14.3601 (Tibur); *Inscr.It.* 10.9 (Brixia); Alföldy (1984) no. 97 (Aquileia). Further details in Mouritsen (2006) n. 52.

[33] The only exceptions are 14.2410 and 14.2795, the latter recording a dedication by a husband and wife who both appear to be freed.

[34] *AE* 1999 453. Camodeca (1999a) 7 n. 18; *CIL* 10.1881; cf. 10.144 lines 37–8; 10.6677; 6682; De Franciscis (1991) 22. This also applied in the provinces, where they almost invariably feature as *corpora*, e.g. 12.700; 704; 1005, cf. *CIL* 12 p. 941. A rare exception comes from Timgad, *AE* 1902 145, but Witschel (1995) 294–5, noted their low profile in the city.

[35] Cohen (1984).   [36] *Verr.* 2.1.123–4.

[37] Langhammer (1973) 35–6, counted the *Augustales* to the *honestiores*, but there is no evidence for that and it is inherently unlikely that former slaves would be allowed to hold a formal rank above *ingenui*.

The theory of the *seviri Augustales* as a formalised 'middle class' thereby comes to rest entirely on the inscriptions, in which they feature alongside the decurions in the context of public feasts and distributions.[38] On these occasions they often dined together with the councillors, separate from the plebs, and when *sportulae* were distributed the *seviri Augustales* generally received higher amounts than the rest of the population, and frequently only marginally less than the decurions. This evidence might seem to reflect an underlying social stratification that found expression at public rituals and social events, but it is important to consider the context in which the ranking was made. Dinners and distributions were part of the celebrations whereby an honouree repaid the distinction, usually a statue, he had received from the community or from specific groups or bodies. On closer inspection it appears that the choice of recipients and their relative ranking did not correspond to an official hierarchy but were contingent on the particular dedication that was being celebrated.[39] For example, civic groups such as *collegiati*, *vicani*, etc. were sometimes singled out instead of the *seviri Augustales*, depending on who had paid for the original honour. These rituals thus had a strong element of *quid pro quo*, where benefactors were thanked for specific donations.[40]

In other cases no immediate correlation can be demonstrated, and here we may assume that the preferential treatment of the *seviri Augustales* was justified by their general role as public benefactors; for, irrespective of titles, numbers, and structures, what linked these bodies – and allows us to treat them as a single phenomenon – was their common association with public spending.[41] Their financial contributions towards the running of Roman towns represent the one constant that runs through all our evidence relating to these organisations, whose members paid substantial sums for a wide range of amenities, including games (apparently their primary obligation), buildings, roads, and statues of local benefactors, as well as the running costs of temples.[42] This consideration may have provided the fundamental rationale behind the creation of these bodies which have a strong euergetic aspect to them.[43]

---

[38] The evidence is presented in Duncan-Jones (1974) 138–44; Andreau (1977); Mrozek (1987) 87–90;
[39] *Pace* Pelletier (1999) 273, who thought it reflected 'un ordre sans doute officiel'.
[40] Cf. Mouritsen (2006); Laird (2006) 33, 43.
[41] For *summa honoraria* see Duncan-Jones (1974) 152–4.
[42] See fuller documentation in Mouritsen (2006) 244 n. 52.
[43] Like the *collegia*, these organisations often had a social element to them and some of their generosity was directed inwards towards their own membership, but, as the inscriptions from Misenum illustrate, the large majority of their outlays were aimed at the community as a whole. Thus, Q. Cominius Abascantus bequeathed 110,000 HS for distributions to the decurions and *populus*, and

The euergetic ideal – with its continuous exchange of private munificence and public esteem – permeated all aspects of Roman society. Within this culture the rich freedmen represented an anomaly, since their background excluded them from the established euergetic system that was closely linked to office holding and public honours, thereby leaving a significant financial resource untapped. The answer to this conundrum was to break the normal connection between private euergetism and civic authority, or in other words to establish a formalised structure where benefactions conferred no power, symbolic or actual, over fellow citizens. The *seviri Augustales* can thus be seen as an attempt to create a permanent framework for both outlays and symbolic returns, which any citizen irrespective of status could buy into. Therefore, when their members received preferential treatment on public occasions, including participation in public dinners, special seats, and other symbols of status, this was a direct response to their euergetic role and sponsorship of public amenities rather than a reflection of their 'middle-class' position; 'libertine' wealth generated public esteem only when spent on the common good.

It is not a given that these institutions were 'invented' specifically for freedmen, as little as the *vicomagistri* were, but they were logically most attractive to freedmen, otherwise excluded from public *honores*. Unsurprisingly, freedmen therefore came to dominate these bodies, with further consequences for their social profile. As soon as they became 'libertine' the attraction to the freeborn sub-elite began to wane – in accordance with normal patterns of status differentiation. Still, there remained considerable local variety, and in some regions and cities they maintained a mixed membership.

The overall impression given by the epigraphic evidence is of institutions which responded to local circumstances, social, economic, geographical, demographic. In some places, for example Misenum, they were clearly a substantial factor in society with resources to pay for a large building complex. The same appears to have been the case at Ostia, where they appear very prominently in the epigraphic evidence. Elsewhere they may have been a more humble body. For example, an inscription from Teate lists thirty-four members of a funerary association, including ten *seviri Augustales*, who do not appear to have held a particularly prominent status.[44] The

---

30,000 HS to the *Augustales* themselves, D'Arms (2000) 130–5. At Petelia a local aristocrat donated a vineyard to the *Augustales* in the hope that the recipients would be more willing to accept the 'honor Augustalitatis', suggesting that the social aspect was an added sweetener to compensate for the public expenses that formed the core of the institution; cf. Bossu (1982).

[44] *AE* 1980 368.

attempt by a local donor at Petelia to make the *Augustalitas* more attractive
does not suggest abundant riches either.[45] The standing and attraction of
these bodies must therefore have varied greatly between different towns.
An *Augustalis* was not per se 'rich', and neither were all rich freedmen
necessarily *Augustales*, as some instances from Ostia and Pompeii would
suggest.[46]

In conclusion, the Augustan institutions are unlikely to be a clever ploy
invented to keep freedmen away from real authority by offering them
purely symbolic honours. Rather, they offered wealthy freedmen a broader
and more direct route to public esteem while also integrating them more
deeply into municipal life. In most societies the taint associated with
new money has been addressed by public munificence, as illustrated by
the many charitable foundations set up by self-made entrepreneurs even
today. In Rome benefactions by freedmen were actively encouraged, and
presented as the way to transform their disreputable 'opes libertinae' into
a source of status and prestige. Channelling fortunes into good causes not
only helped sustain the urban culture of the empire but also militated
against unseemly display of wealth that might upset elite sensibilities. The
new institutions thus had a moral aspect to them, steering the freedmen
away from the self-indulgence and *luxuria* to which they were considered
particularly prone.

The many different bodies set up to accommodate the freedmen's desire
for recognition testify to a general willingness to pay for public status, even
among freedmen who were little more than 'comfortable'. In this context
we should not overlook the possibility that many of them may have been
prepared to spend generously on the public because they had no children to
whom they could pass on their estates. Thus, it may not be accidental that
the apparently childless *Augustalis* Munatius Faustus at Pompeii paid for
a distribution of grain, for which he was rewarded a *bisellium* in return.[47]
For others, parental concerns about their children's future may have been
a particular spur towards public generosity, as illustrated most famously by
Popidius Ampliatus, who rebuilt the Temple of Isis at Pompeii to further
the career of his young son. The prospect of the patron taking a substantial
cut of the estate must also have offered a strong incentive to spend lavishly

---

[45] *CIL* 10.114.

[46] Laird (2002) 54, noted that 'some of Ostia's most conspicuous freedmen are notably absent', e.g. P.
Claudius Abascantus, M. Licinius Privatus, and L. Valerius Threptus; cf. Herz (1989). At Pompeii N.
Popidius Ampliatus does not seem to have been an *Augustalis* despite the fortune which allowed him
to rebuild the Isis Temple, *CIL* 10.846–8. Likewise, surprisingly few of the rich imperial freedmen
appear among the Italian *seviri Augustales*, cf. Laird (2002) 56.

[47] *CIL* 10.1030. For the monument see Kockel (1983) 100ff.

during one's lifetime and enjoy the esteem that followed. Certainly in the case of the Latini Iuniani, whose entire estate reverted to their patron, there was no reason why they should hold back. Such factors might plausibly explain some of the large donations from freedmen we occasionally come across in the epigraphic sources, and it also takes us to the much-debated issue of the role of the freedman's son in Roman public life.

THE FREEDMAN'S SON IN ROMAN SOCIETY

Many sons of *seviri Augustales* entered the local councils, and their rise is often perceived as a reflection of the economic power as well as the overweening ambition of their parents. Some of them were indeed heavily promoted, as illustrated by an inscription from Suessa which records the generous donations and career of a freedman and his freeborn son.[48] The aim was clearly to ease their entry into the *ordo* and the investment often paid off handsomely, the 6-year-old decurion Popidius Celsinus from Pompeii again providing the classic example. This was by no means an isolated instance; for example, an epitaph from Nola commemorates the son of an *Augustalis* who died aged 20 but already *duumvir designatus*.[49]

 This aspect of Roman manumission has attracted much attention, since Gordon set the agenda in 1931 with the bold statement that 'one fifth of local aristocracy of Italy was descended from slaves', a proportion that rose even higher, perhaps to a quarter, during the empire. Their entry into the *ordo* was perceived as an 'invasion by foreigners of a ruling class jealous of its old tradition and proud of its Italian blood', and they succeeded by using their wealth to buy goodwill from the *populus* through donations of games and distributions, a practice condemned as 'bad and demoralising'.[50] Rostovtzeff envisaged a similar scenario of Italian cities where 'the native stock . . . gradually decreased', 'their place . . . taken by freedmen'.[51] Although the moralising tone that characterised much earlier

---

[48] *CIL* 10.4760.

[49] *CIL* 10.1268. Jacques (1984) 595f. Silvestrini (2000) gives a useful summary of descendants of *seviri* and *Augustales* reaching higher offices. For Ostia see Laird (2002) 59–64, e.g. *CIL* 14.352; 4642. The phenomenon of freedmen's sons in the *ordines* is encountered not just in Italy, e.g. in the Iberian peninsula: 2.4527; cf. 4497, 3708, 3715, 3717, 4229, 4231 = 4275, 4232. For Gaul see e.g. Rémy (1998).

[50] 70–1, 73–5. Cf. 77: 'invasion of the upper classes'.

[51] Rostovtzeff (1957) 583 n. 33. 'In the industrial and commercial cities, side by side with this aristocracy of landowners, a new class was gradually springing up and taking the leading part in civic life, a class of rich merchants and shopkeepers, who were partly freeborn but mostly freedmen and their descendants', 186. Ebersbach (1995) 201, claimed that the freeborn were 'zunehmend ins soziale Abseits geraten'. Likewise Torelli (1994) 184, who suggested the old curial elites collapsed and were replaced by an 'emergente nuova aristocrazia locale seviralicia di rango libertino'.

scholarship has gone, the issue remains a focus of modern studies of social mobility during the empire. Attempts have been made to measure the scale of their presence in the elite, some of them very sweeping; thus, Mac-Mullen estimated that at Pompeii freedmen and their descendants made up a third to half of the governing aristocracy.[52] Other studies have been more measured in their assessment.[53]

The only ancient text commenting on this 'intrusion' is Tacitus' statement that 'the origin of most knights and of many senators was drawn from no other source [than the freedmen]'.[54] The context is the (fictional?) debate in Nero's *consilium* on the proposal to allow re-enslavement of *liberti ingrati*, and the comment is made by the defeatist opponent who argued that it would merely highlight the 'paucity of freeborn', 'penuriam ingenuorum'. Given its transparent bias, the statement has often been dismissed as a gross exaggeration.[55] However, Eck suggested that Tacitus may not have been entirely wrong. The point is that our knowledge of senators and *equites* of freed parentage relies on chance events such as the killing of A. Larcius Macedo, whose freed background Pliny notes in passing.[56] Considering the exceptional context of the information, there may well have been similar cases which went unrecorded. Eck also listed other indicators, above all membership of the *tribus Palatina* and *Collina*, which point to a number of senators and *equites* potentially being of libertine descent. In many cases, however, their fathers were imperial freedmen.

At a municipal level we face similar difficulties. While some sons of freedmen in local *ordines* are well documented, for example through epitaphs recording their lineage, most have been identified on circumstantial evidence such as *tribus, cognomina*, and prosopographical indicators, the latter often being little more than conjecture. Another complication derives from variations in the 'epigraphic habit', since newcomers seem to have used forms of epigraphic self-display different from the traditional curial families. Thus, the profile of councillors recorded in funerary inscriptions suggests that high-ranking magistrates employed this form of commemoration much more sparingly than younger and less prestigious members

[52] MacMullen (1974) 103, cf. Weaver (1991) 173, who referred to 'the penetration of this status group in formidable numbers into the ranks of municipal elites in Italy and the western provinces'.
[53] For a good survey see Patterson (2006) 236–41. Meiggs (1973); D'Arms (1974); Castrén (1975); Garnsey (1975a); (1975b); Mouritsen (1988), (1997); Los (1992b); Camodeca (1996b); Biundo (2000).
[54] *Ann.* 13.27: 'et plurimis equitum, plerisque senatoribus non aliunde originem trahi'. Echoed in Juv. 8.45.
[55] E.g. Syme (1958) 612–13; Griffin (1976) 282; Gara (1991) 354 n. 100.
[56] Eck (1999). *Ep.* 3.14.1. Cf. Suetonius' story of Vitellius, 2.1, whose family was said to have been founded by a freedman, even a cobbler, who made a fortune out of confiscated estates and informing, and whose son became an *eques*.

of the elite. The phenomenon is most clearly illustrated by a comparison between the funerary record and the duoviral *fasti* from Ostia, which shows a marked difference in the proportion of Greek *cognomina*.[57] Likewise, at Pompeii most of the curial elite appear to have withdrawn from the urban necropolis in the later period, when only junior magistrates feature. Where we have independent documentary evidence for the composition of the local elites, the share of potential freedmen's sons drops markedly compared to the total aggregates which include funerary inscriptions and other forms of self-representation. The *Fasti Ostienses* have already been mentioned and we also find very few Greek *cognomina* among the magistrates recorded in the tablets from Herculaneum or the many Pompeian candidates and magistrates known through the electoral inscriptions and the tablets of Iucundus.[58] This evidence strongly indicates that the high figures sometimes suggested for the proportion of freedmen's sons in the *ordines* must be revised downwards. Certainly, the notion that between a quarter and a third came from a 'servile' background can no longer be sustained.[59]

Nevertheless there is sufficient evidence to conclude that the entry of freedmen's sons into the local *ordines* was in no way exceptional. Some of the most successful descendants of freedmen became *equites* and a few even entered the senate. The question is how we interpret the phenomenon, which has typically been perceived as an 'invasion', i.e. the result of a forced entry against the opposition of the old families. However, apart from Tacitus' rhetorical outburst, quoted above, which was concerned exclusively with the highest orders, we find no complaints about the sons of freedmen pursuing public careers. This may not be very surprising since the relevant sources are overwhelmingly epigraphic and therefore non-narrative. But it does mean that the posited conflict is not based on any specific ancient testimony, relying instead on the tacit assumption that the old elite naturally would resist the entry of people of 'servile' origins into their order.[60] This might prima facie seem a reasonable expectation,

---

[57] Mouritsen (1997); (2005) 43–4.

[58] Ostia and Pompeii: Mouritsen (1997); Herculaneum: Camodeca (1996a) 176. The early third-century *album* from Canusium presents the one clear exception to this picture since Greek *cognomina* in various forms make up 29 per cent of the decurions' names. However, this is unlikely to reflect an increase in freedmen's sons entering the *ordo* as much as changes in the onomastic culture, where names tended to be passed on to the next generation irrespective of any social stigma attached to them. Many of the carriers of Greek names on the list may therefore be relatively distant descendants of freedmen. The frequency of Greek *cognomina* is unlikely to reflect bilingualism in this part of Italy, cf. above p. 126 n.30.

[59] Gordon (1931); Garnsey (1975a) 178; Pleket (1990) 45.

[60] As Gordon (1931) 73, first observed, 'the older families among the local gentry were probably little disposed to co-opt "new men" into the council'.

but there are a number of issues to consider, the most important one being the 'stigma of slavery'. It is often held that descendants of freedmen merely carried a paler version of the dishonour associated with servitude. For example, Weaver commented that the stigma was attached to 'the next generation as well, even those fortunate enough to be freeborn'.[61] But while sons of freedmen undoubtedly faced prejudices, it is not given that they shared their parents' 'stigma of slavery'. From a legal point of view they were *ingenui* on a par with any other Roman born to free parents. Their citizenship was in principle equal to that of other Romans; and although the subject sometimes caused controversy, they were never officially barred from public office.

It has been suggested that sons of freedmen only received full citizenship in 189 BCE, when the *lex Terentia* supposedly lifted the last restrictions.[62] The evidence is weak, however, since Plutarch, our only source on this law, merely says that the censors 'accepted as citizens all who presented themselves for enrolment, provided they were born of free parents'.[63] Taken at face value this would imply that sons of freedmen had not held citizenship before, which cannot possibly be true since the freedmen themselves had long enjoyed this status. Some scholars have therefore speculated that the law may have been concerned with their tribal inscription, although this is not what Plutarch says. While the passage raises many questions, it will probably have to remain a crux; certainly it cannot carry the full weight of such a radical proposition.[64] Closely linked to this hypothesis is the notion that sons of freedmen bore the label 'libertini' until the middle republic. The idea is based on a single comment in Suetonius' *Life of Claudius*.[65] In order to justify his admission of a freedman's son to the senate, the emperor used the famous example of his ancestor Ap. Claudius Caecus who had done likewise; but Suetonius noted, probably on the basis of objections raised at

---

[61] Weaver (1991) 177; cf. Ferenczy (1988) 68–70; Horsley (1998) 52.
[62] Following Mommsen (1887) 3.72–3, 3.420ff, Taylor (1960) 123, believed the sons of freedmen were not originally proper *ingenui*. She also thought the *lex Terentia* removed them from the 'class of libertini', and gave them access to all tribes, *ibid.* 138, cf. Mommsen (1887) 3.436–7. Likewise, Treggiari (1969a) 68 n. 8, argued that the *lex Terentia* had made the children of freedmen *cives optimo iure*; cf. Fabre (1981) 125 n. 1. Haley (1986) believed that sons of freedmen only became 'full-fledged *ingenui*' in 217 BC, but see below note 69.
[63] *Flamin.* 18.1: 'προσεδέξαντο δὲ πολίτας ἀπογραφομένους πάντας, ὅσοι γονέων ἐλευθέρων ἦσαν'.
[64] The identity of the new citizens who were admitted on the condition of *ingenuitas* is an open question, one possibility being foreign immigrants to Rome, cf. Mouritsen (2007b), although that will have to remain speculation.
[65] 24.1. Taylor (1960) 123, believed it applied until the second century BCE; cf. e.g. Fabre (1981) 125 n.1; Rizzelli (2006) 203; *contra* Treggiari (1969a) 52–3; (1979) 57; Levick (1990) 100. The theory is closely tied to the notion that in the early republic freedmen were considered barely different from slaves, but see above p. 68 n.10.

the time, that in the fourth century 'libertinus' referred to freeborn sons of freedmen, making the new senators the grandsons rather than the sons of freedmen. Later this interpretation was repeated in *scholia* and glossaries, keen to retrieve 'lost' meanings of words.[66] It remains a fact, however, that no surviving text describes the son of a freedman as a 'libertinus'. The terms 'libertus' and 'libertinus' appear to be have been used interchangeably, and only about people who had once been slaves.[67] Moreover, the underlying premise that the slave identity could be 'inherited' by individuals who had no personal experience of servitude seems incompatible with Roman perceptions of slavery.[68]

There is, in short, no compelling evidence that they were ever singled out as a special category. Neither were there any other specific markers of status attached to those descended from freedmen. As *ingenui* they were entitled to all the formal and symbolic indicators of freeborn status, including the *bulla* and the *toga praetexta*.[69] We may therefore conclude that the 'freedman's son' as a distinct social category is essentially a modern invention. The sons of freedmen enjoyed *ingenuitas*, which was an absolute quality that could be neither gradated nor forfeited.

This impression is confirmed and refined by the evidence of Horace, the most famous son of a Roman freedman, who provides the fullest as well as the most disputed evidence for the social identity of this group. Two poems are particularly important in this context: the 'notorious' *Epode* 4,

---

[66] *Schol.Ter.Bemb.ad.* 898; *Schol.Ter.* 105, 31; Isid. *Orig.* 9.4.47.

[67] As demonstrated long ago by Crumley (1906), and Treggiari (1969a). *TLL* s.v. libertinus, 1319, noted that 'exempla non exstare videntur'. Therefore, Tacitus' expression 'libertini generis', *Ann.* 2.85.4, cannot, as it has frequently been interpreted, mean 'descendants of freedmen', e.g. Smallwood (1961) 234; Fuks (1985) 26; Noy (2000) 42. The 4,000 Jewish freedmen who, Tacitus tells us, were sent to Sardinia to suppress brigandage may be comparable to Augustus' drafting of freed slaves for the army or, as Purcell (1994) 655, suggested, part of a colonial foundation.

[68] Cels-Saint-Hilaire (1985) has suggested that 'libertinus' could mean an enfranchised *peregrinus*, followed by e.g. Humm (2005). The only hard evidence adduced in support of the theory comes from Livy's description of Carteia as a 'colonia libertinorum', 43.3. While the title of the colony (if indeed authentic, cf. Galsterer (1971) 8–9; Schulze-Oben (1989) 18–21) remains puzzling, the notion that illegitimate sons of Roman soldiers and indigenous women could somehow be regarded as 'manumitted' when enrolled in a Latin colony is implausible. Saumagne's emendation (1962) of 'manumissent' to 'manumisset' (followed by Humbert 1976), which makes the colonists the manumitted rather than manumitters, is therefore unnecessary; cf. e.g. Briscoe's recent Teubner edition.

[69] Macrobius' story about the sons of freedmen originally not being allowed to wear the *toga praetexta* and the *bulla* seems confused, *Sat.* 1.6.7–14, apparently mixing up *libertini* and *libertinorum filii*, which are used interchangeably. Palmer (1989) 27–40, showed that Macrobius must be mistaken, and the sons allowed to wear *bulla* were not freeborn but the freed sons of freedmen, which also undermines Haley's theory (1986) based on this text. Other sources make clear that the *bulla* simply was the preserve of *ingenui*, e.g. Ps.-Ascon. *Verr.* P. 199; *Schol.Iuv.* 5.164, who describe it as a *signum libertatis*, cf. Goette (1986) 136–7. For freedmen's sons carrying *bullae* see e.g. Rawson (2003) 29–30.

already mentioned, and *Satire* 1.6, an autobiographical sketch addressed to Maecenas, which comments on the relationship between birth, status, and public office, while also offering an affectionate portrait of his freedman father. The fourth *Epode*, as we saw, is a stinging attack on a rich and swaggering freedman who had become a *tribunus militum* and gained equestrian status. Horace compares their relationship to that of the wolf and the lamb, before concluding that it makes no sense to fight Sex. Pompey and his band of pirates and runaway slaves ('latrones atque servilem manum', 19) when former slaves hold office in Rome.

Modern scholars have wondered how the normally mild-mannered Horace could attack a freedman in such terms when he was himself the son of a freedman and had held precisely the same military tribunate for which he castigates his target. Two lines of argument have been pursued to solve this problem. The most radical has been to deny that Horace's father was actually a freedman. This attempt, however, runs counter to Horace's unambiguous statement that he was himself 'patre libertino natus'.[70] In order to overcome this obstacle, scholars have suggested that Horatius senior was not a 'real' freedman and that the taunts to which Horace reacted in *Satire* 1.6 therefore were factually unfounded. Supposedly his father was merely a Latin colonist from Venusia who found himself on the losing side in the Social War, which later led to allegations of enslavement. Slightly different versions of this scenario have been suggested, some involving brief periods of servitude after his capture.[71]

None of these attempts, however, solves the fundamental problem that the Romans did not operate with a concept of semi- or pseudo-freedmen. Enslavement was either legal or it was not, and a person could only become a *libertus* when released from *iusta servitus*.[72] If this was not the case, his freeborn status would be fully restored without any remaining blemish.[73]

---

[70] The phrase occurs thrice in *Sat.* 1.6.6, 45, 46 and later in a very different, non-polemical context in *Epist.* 1.20.20. Suetonius repeats it in his Horace biography: 'son of a freedman, as he says himself', 'patre ut ipse tradit libertino'.

[71] Williams (1995). Followed by Oliensis (1998) 31; Cels-Saint-Hilaire (1999). Half-accepted by Schlegel (2000) 108, although she concedes that the 'essential falsity' of the freedman label, claimed by Williams, has 'successfully fooled most of his readers', including Suetonius. Maurach (2001) 1–3, speculates that Horace senior may have become a *captivus*, but later was allowed to buy his freedom by his patron and move to Rome. Following Armstrong (1989) 9–10, Anderson (1995) 153, suggested that Horace's father might have been a freeborn Venusinus who 'was sold into slavery for a year or two, then freed in the subsequent amnesty and endowed with Roman citizenship'.

[72] Gaius *Inst.* 1.11: 'libertini, qui ex iusta servitute manumissi sunt', cf. 1.17 and D. 1.5.6.

[73] There is no evidence that the Romans distinguished between freedmen of Greek or Eastern origin and those of 'Italian stock'. Horace's claim to Italian ancestry is therefore not a strong argument against his father's freedman status, *pace* Williams (1995) 300–7.

On the other hand, if the enslavement was legal he would upon man-umission become a freedman like any other, no matter how brief the enslavement. Moreover, if the defeated Italian allies really were regarded as collectively 'enslaved', half the Roman citizen population would have had 'servile' ancestors, making Horace's decision to write a public apologia for himself and his father even more peculiar. Finally, it seems odd that Horace composed a lengthy response to what were essentially false accusations without ever hinting that they might be factually wrong; instead of refuting them, he repeats them several times over.

An alternative approach to the fourth *Epode* reads the poem as a form of self-defence. Some scholars have posited deep-seated personal anxieties behind Horace's invective and have seen his stress on natural differences as an attempt to deal with his own sense of insecurity. Thus, Oliensis calls the poem 'distasteful, even disgusting', suggesting 'he claws at the face of the ex-slave in an attempt to eradicate its resemblance to his own'. 'Less a member of a different species than his distorted twin, the ex-slave reflects Horace in the mirror of other people's blame.' As such, the poem reveals 'the nausea of the poet who is beginning to recognize himself in his victim'.[74] Likewise, Osgood thinks he is 'little better than the parvenu he attacks', and that the allusion to the fable 'makes him at best that near twin of the wolf, a dog'.[75] The anonymous freedman's military tribunate has been a source of particular unease, since it supposedly highlighted 'disturbing similarities between him and Horace'. The result was a 'disquieting convergence between Horace and his target', suggesting that 'Horace is here deliberately sailing close to the wind, deliberately courting a charge of hypocrisy.'[76]

The image of Horace as a tortured soul fighting his inner demons by attacking them in others lacks psychological plausibility, and it also seems to be a response to what is an essentially modern concern which few Romans would have recognised. The current discussion is founded on the assumption that the son was only slightly removed from the status of his father. But since the freedman's son had never been a slave, his body had never suffered physical abuse, and his character had never been debased by submission, he could not share the stigma of his parents. Therefore, Horace and his target did indeed differ in *genus* and the difference was rooted in the slave's personal degradation, which explains the emphasis Horace puts on the physical manifestations of slavery, the scars on his back and the marks of the chains. When Horace writes as if the conventional stigma was

---

[74] Oliensis (1998) 66, 68.   [75] Osgood (2006) 267.   [76] Watson (2003) 151–2.

irrelevant to his own life and career, it is most likely because he did not perceive himself as comparable to a freedman. Moreover, the similarities between Horace's own career and that of the anonymous freedman were superficial. Whereas the notion of a former slave commanding freeborn citizens would have been anathema to any right-thinking Roman, Horace's own military tribunate raised some critical eyebrows but hardly breached any principles.[77] Apparently it was not even that exceptional.[78]

The important conclusion to be drawn from this discussion is that the freedman differed in fundamental respects from his freeborn son. Whatever disadvantage the latter may have suffered, it was of a different nature from the stigma of slavery carried by the previous generation. Thus, Dupont rightly observed that 'the son of the freedman inherited nothing of his father's servile past, of his blemishes or of his submissions'.[79] There is no evidence that the Romans operated with the concept of 'servile blood' in the sense of later generations exhibiting any of the 'servile' traits of their unfree ancestors. The term 'servilis' is, for example, used only about people who have themselves been slaves or who act as slaves. It is never applied to people who happened to descend from slaves and there is never any assumption that they could inherit these features.

Isaac recently argued on the basis of Gellius that 'servility' could indeed be passed on.[80] The text relates Favorinus' advice to mothers to breastfeed their children, since it would be damaging to use a wet nurse 'aut serva aut servilis'. However, we have no reason to assume that 'servilis' here means anything other than a freed slave. The term is probably used instead of the more common *liberta* in order to emphasise the negative qualities she might impart. Just a single text hints that 'servile' qualities might be seen as transferable. Valerius Maximus tells the story of Helvius Mancia, the son of a freedman, who clashed with Pompey in a court case.[81] Having recounted Helvius' accusations, Valerius roundly condemns him for being 'unbridled in his temerity, intolerable in his presumption': a 'municipali homine', who 'smells of his father's slavery', 'servitutem paternam redolenti'. Still, despite the harsh rebuke, the alleged servility is only by association, not a part of his person.

---

[77] Cf. *Sat.* 1.6.48. The choice of target has puzzled scholars, but it may be explained by the military context of the poem which was the war against Sex. Pompey. The attack on the freedman allowed Horace to make the point that servile enemies abroad were matched by powerful 'slaves' at home.
[78] Other examples include *CIL* 14.3948 (40–30 BCE), which shows L. Appuleius L.f. *trib. mil.* flanked by his freed parents, cf. Zanker (1975) 304–5, and Aurelius Cottanus, 14.2298.
[79] Dupont (1992) 64. Cf. Zanker (1975) 290: 'An den Söhnen der Freigelassenen haftet nicht mehr der Makel des ehemaligen Sklaven.'
[80] *NA* 12.1.17. Isaac (2004) 192.   [81] 6.2.8.

There are many indications that the freeborn son was viewed as entirely different from the freed father. For example, Dio presented the emperor Pertinax in a positive light despite his freed background, describing him as an excellent and upright man.[82] In a section on people who gained popularity, Dio tells that C. Thoranius enhanced his reputation when, as popular tribune in 25 BCE, he invited his freedman father to sit next to him on the tribunes' bench in the theatre.[83] Again, the positive image of the pious son of a freedman holding high office stands in sharp contrast to Dio's typical condemnation of powerful *liberti*. Similarly, when faced with an opponent of freedman descent, Cicero does not suggest there was anything 'slavish' about him. In the *Pro Quinctio* his client was engaged in a property dispute with a certain Sex. Naevius, who was apparently the son of a freedman. Thus, we are told that his father left him nothing but his freedom, and there are also references to his birth and his status as 'inferior atque humilior' in relation to Quinctius.[84] Cicero repeatedly attacks Naevius' honour, character, and social standing, even calling him a *scurra*, but there is no accusation of 'servility'. The contrast to his portrayal of Chrysogonus in the *Pro Roscio Amerino* could hardly have been more pronounced. Naevius' humble origins marked him as a social upstart, but that was a very different kind of stigma from that carried by his father. Thus, even in the case of P. Vedius Pollio, who became notorious for his cruelty, no attempt was later made to associate it with his freed background, which only one source happens to mention.[85]

Horace's claim that the freedman belonged to a different *genus* from himself was fully in tune with the Roman construction of 'servility' as a uniquely personal stigma. But that still leaves open the question of his father, for it has seemed incomprehensible to a modern sensibility that Horace could attack a member of the same stigmatised group to which his father belonged. Such concerns may be misplaced, however, since Horace attacks the tribune not for being a freedman but for violating the rules, written and unwritten, which were there to regulate his behaviour.

---

[82] 74.1.1; cf. 72.22.1; 74.3.1. Also, in the *Historia Augusta* no particular opprobrium is attached to his background, the author simply observing that: 'pater libertinus Helvius Successus fuit', *Pert.* 1.1.
[83] 53.27.6.   [84] 11: 'pater nihil praeter libertatem reliquisset', cf. 55, 95.
[85] Sen. *Ira* 3.40.2–5; *Clem.* 1.18.2; Plin. *NH* 9.77; Dio 54.23.1–6. Interestingly, Pollio enjoyed the friendship of Augustus, who clearly differentiated sharply between freedmen and their sons, cf. Suet. *Aug.* 74, a point also suggested by his – albeit exceptional – permission for the daughters of freedmen to become Vestals, Dio 55.22.5. Pliny, *Ep.* 3.14.1, hints that the deceased senator Larcius Macedo, who treated his slaves harshly despite being a freedman's son, might have forgotten his father's background too easily but there is no suggestion that his cruelty was somehow inherited.

Horace's father is presented as the very model of a 'good' freedman.[86] He had no ambitions for himself, and those he held for his son were primarily focused on virtue rather than social aspirations beyond his station. Despite slender means, working a small *agellus*, he invested his hopes in his son, but would have been equally happy if he had not made a career. Much of this is of course special pleading, for, as Rudd noted, he was in reality not just wealthy but also 'absurdly ambitious'.[87] We also have to remember that the *Satire* ultimately is about Horace and not his father, who enters the argument only in order to reassure the reader that he gave his son a proper upbringing and education. The affectionate portrait served to dispel any suspicion of 'servile' corruption, for while 'servility' could not be inherited, the lesser morals of the former slave might be imparted through nurture. This prejudice was the main cloud hanging over the reputation of the son and Horace therefore depicts his father as the very exemplar of a modest and hard-working freedman.[88] His direct negation and counter-image was the tribune of the fourth *Epode*, who transgressed against all aspects of this code, showing arrogance and presumption and usurping both office and status. It was the fundamental distinction between the 'good' and the 'bad' freedman which allowed Horace to display such contempt for one freedman and affection for another.

All groups in Roman society, whether defined by gender, age, rank, or class, were subject to specific moral parameters, which laid down the range of attainable and appropriate virtues as well as their attendant vices. No category therefore carried a single moral 'value'; the Romans could at the same time condemn the immorality of a Clodia or an Agrippina and praise the virtue of a Lucretia. We should therefore not be surprised to find Horace attacking one freedman and defending another. Furthermore, in honouring his father he does not question the freedman's inferior status or challenge the rationale behind the disabilities he suffered – as little as praise of female chastity questioned the political exclusion of women. The modern debate has thus reflected a conception of the freedmen as an exploited and disadvantaged category whose collective plight would naturally evoke sympathy and solidarity among those similarly afflicted and their relatives. But while enslavement as personal misfortune might elicit sympathy, it usually did not lead to any serious questioning of the institution as such, even by those who had personal experience of it. We

---

[86] Sat. 1.6.71–92.   [87] Rudd (1966) 46.   [88] Further praise for his good sense in *Sat.* 1.4.105–29.

should therefore not expect Horace to find the freedman's lot unfair because of his family background.[89]

According to Horace, Maecenas did not think birth mattered, 'dum ingenuus', i.e. as long the person was freeborn, *Sat.* 1.6.8, a view echoed by Augustus' famous refusal to dine with freedmen.[90] On the other hand, Maecenas' disregard for ancestry – if not personal status – was, in Horace's, view justified by ancient examples from the time of Servius Tullius, when men of humble origins reached high honours.[91] Maecenas' willingness to extend his patronage to 'men of unknown birth' such as Horace marked a departure from the conventional snobbery that often made life difficult for the sons of freedmen. The sixth satire thus presents a response to those who had complained about his tribunate and now begrudged him his success in obtaining Maecenas' friendship.

The disadvantages experienced by the freedmen's sons were of a different kind from the stigma attached to their fathers, a point most clearly illustrated by their controversial bids to hold high office and enter the senate. The issue first surfaced in 312 BCE, when the censor Ap. Claudius Caecus, having admitted sons of freedmen into the senate, faced accusations of 'debasing' this institution, and the policy was soon reversed by Fabius Rullianus in 304.[92] Claudius' *scriba* Cn. Flavius Cn.f., the son of a freedman, was also allowed to become curule aedile in 304 and his election

---

[89] On slavery in Horace see Highnet (1973); Stenuit (1977).

[90] Suet. *Aug.* 74. Some scholars have argued that 'ingenuus' here means 'noble in nature', partly based on Ps.-Acron; cf. Agnati (2000); Maurach (2001) 78; Osgood (2006) 284; Taurino (2007) 156–7; *contra* Lejay (1911) 177; Rudd (1966) 37–8. The direct juxtaposition with 'me libertino patre natum' questions this idea, however, as does the fact that the two other occurrences of 'ingenuus' in the poem refer to status rather than character, 1.6.21, 91. The interpretation is based on the mistaken notion that '*ingenuus* = freeborn' would be incompatible with Horace's affection for his father and with Maecenas' supposed disregard for birth. But we must distinguish between birth, i.e. rank, which did not matter to Maecenas, and personal status, i.e. slave, freed, or freeborn, which remained crucially important.

[91] Harrison (1965) 113, detected a gentle correction of his patron and his 'dum ingenuus' principle; otherwise Horace would 'be manifestly turning his back on his father, since he has only just labeled him *libertinus*', *ibid.* The reference to Servius Tullius – 'a conventional symbol of the insignificance of birth' (Harrison (1965) 114 n. 5) – becomes a veiled reproach of Maecenas' stance on freedmen, since legend had it he came from humble, perhaps even slave origins; cf. Rudd (1966) 38; Brown (1993) 152. It is worth noting, however, that while Servius Tullius' mother is given as *captiva* and *serva*, the king himself is never explicitly described as a former slave, e.g. Livy 4.3.12; Cic. *Rep.* 2.37; *CIL* 13.1668. Livy's description of him as 'patre nullo, matre serva' might seem clear-cut, but if he had wished to indicate slave birth, the 'matre' would also have to be 'nulla'. The implication is therefore that he was born to a (former) slave and an unknown father. It follows that his name might not necessarily have signalled disapproval of Maecenas' entirely conventional views of freedmen as much as the primacy of merit over (low) birth.

[92] Liv. 9.29.7; 9.46.11: 'senatum primus libertinorum filiis lectis inquinaverat'; Diodorus 20.36.3; cf. Oakley (2005) 350–89, with further references.

caused considerable aristocratic outrage.[93] But it is worth noting that it
was his 'humilitas' which later writers saw as the main obstacle rather than
any 'servility'.[94] The issue reappeared in the later republic, when we are
told that P. Furius and L. Equitius (99 BCE) held the plebeian tribunate
despite their freed background.[95] In 70 BCE Popillius was expelled from
the senate on similar grounds, but Cicero noted that the censor allowed
him to keep his *ornamenta* and place at the games and 'freed him from all
ignominy'. These concessions would suggest that no fraud was involved in
his admission.[96] Apparently there were no clear rules on this issue, leaving
it up to the censors to decide in each case.[97]

The same conclusion is offered by the censorship of Ap. Claudius Pulcher, 50 BCE, which saw the expulsion of sons of freedmen.[98] His actions
were considered severe at the time – still vividly remembered by Horace –
and the men had presumably entered the senate entirely legitimately.[99] It
would seem therefore that while some censors were willing to admit them,
others could reverse the decision. No consensus was ever reached on this
issue during the republic, probably because there was no clear-cut principle
on which a consistent policy could be based.

Horace's personal response to the constitutional grey zone in which he
found himself is interesting and complex. As Rudd noted, the message conveyed in the sixth satire is mixed.[100] Two lines of argument are pursued:
the irrelevance of birth and the folly of ambition, each pulling in opposite
directions. But viewed in light of the above, the two strands appear to
be tied together by the particular logic that derived from the ambiguous
public role of the freedman's son. As an *ingenuus*, Horace suffered no personal disabilities, and he therefore refuses to acknowledge any flaws in his

93 Taylor (1960) 133–8; Oakley (2005) 600–45, esp. 607–8. Pliny, *NH* 33.18, and D. 1.2.2.7 (Pomponius)
      both say Flavius had previously been a tribune, but see the doubts of Oakley. Based on Cels-Saint-
      Hilaire, Humm (2005) 220–6, questions whether he was the son of a freedman, suggesting the
      libertini were new citizens, but see above p. 265 n.68.
94 Liv. 9.46.4; cf. Val. Max. 2.5.2; 9.3.3: 'humillimae sortis'.
95 Dio fr. 93.2 (*eques*). App. *BC* 1.147, son of a freedman. App. *BC* 1.32.1, 33.2; *De vir. ill.* 73; Cic.
      Rab.Perd. 20. App. *BC* 1.141. A. Gabinius (trib. 139 BCE) may have been an earlier example, since
      he is described by Cicero, *Leg.* 3.35, as 'homine ignoto et sordido'; cf. Livy 54, *Pap.Oxy.* vol. 4
      668 lines 193–4: 'A. Gabinius verna[e nepos rogationem tulit] suffragium per ta[bellam ferri]', with
      commentary 113. Malitz (1975) 74–5 n. 35, gives other possible sons of freedmen.
96 *Cluent.* 132: 'eum omni ignominia liberat'.
97 Cf. Treggiari (1969a) 52–64; Sherwin-White (1973) 325.
98 According to Dio 40.63.4, he drove from the senate all the freedmen, *apeleutheron* (which here
      must mean sons of freedmen) and many others, including Sallust.
99 Cic. *Fam.* 8.14.4 (Caelius); Horace, *Sat.* 1.6.19–21: 'Namque esto populus Laevino mallet honorem
      quam Decio mandare novo, censorque moveret Appius, ingenuo si non essem patre natus.'
100 Rudd (1966) 38–9.

character that should prevent him from holding high office. His flaws are few and moderate, 'vitiis mediocribus ac paucis', 65, and his character is sound, 'natura mendosa', and free of vices, 66–9. But he also recognises that the world has never been kind to new men, however talented. In a central passage Horace notes that the people reward fame and noble ancestry and that censors such as Ap. Claudius would have expelled him from the senate for lack of freeborn ancestry, adding 'quite rightly, for not having stayed quiet in my own skin', 'vel merito, quoniam in propria non pelle quiessem', 22. He is what he is – the son of a freedman – which means he is not made for a public career. Having already experienced people's envy at his military tribunate, Horace resigns himself to the fact that for him the prudent thing to do is to enjoy a quiet existence. Indeed, given the iniquities of the world, the simple life is much to be preferred to that of a low-ranking *nobilis* with all the social obligations and public scrutiny it entailed. He is therefore happy with his lot and would not have chosen differently had he had the chance. In this way his father's humble status has – somewhat paradoxically – ensured for his son an ideal life free of social burdens.

The prejudices experienced by the freedmen's sons were not specific to this group but applied in principle to all new men, as the example of Cicero illustrates. Still, first-generation *ingenui* were in the nature of things the 'newest' men of all, whose suitability for public office could be most easily challenged. During the republic, some of them became senators, but they remained the exception and usually it required more than one generation to make the ascent. However, as the old political order collapsed and normality was suspended, more sons of freedmen gained office and senatorial seats. This was possible because no law formally barred them from either.[101] The apparent decline in standards under the triumvirs – to which Horace himself responded in the fourth *Epode* – triggered a reaction from the princeps, who instituted what appears to have been the first blanket ban on sons and even grandsons of freedmen (which of course could be subverted by the conferring of fictional *ingenuitas*).[102] This unprecedented measure against a group of freeborn citizens was in essence a propagandist statement about the need to uphold traditional hierarchies and a show of respect for venerable republican institutions. After all, the rapid ascent from slave to senator in just two generations might seem to

---

[101] Dio 42.51.5; 43.47.3; 48.34.4; 52.42.1–4; Suet. *Aug.* 35.1: on Augustus clearing out the low-born rabble admitted to the senate after Caesar's death (and hence given the nickname *orcini*). Syme (1938) 12–18; Treggiari (1969a) 61–3; Armstrong (1986) 269–70.

[102] Suet. *Aug.* 35.1. He also banned intermarriage between members of senatorial families with freedwomen but allowed them to marry children of freedmen, Treggiari (1991) 62.

compromise the dignity of the highest order, even if the descendants of freedmen were not themselves 'servile'.

Some of Augustus' successors made similar gestures. Thus, Claudius went even further and promised not to admit to the senate anyone whose great-great-grandfather was not a Roman citizen – although he apparently did not keep his word and admitted at least one freedman's son who had been adopted by a knight.[103] Suetonius also relates that for a long time Nero did not admit freedmen's sons to the senate and refused office to those admitted by his predecessors, inadvertently showing that there were no fundamental legal obstacles to freedmen's sons entering the highest orders.[104] Individual emperors might decide against it, but there could in the nature of things be no general ban since it was largely a matter of taste.

Most likely the difficulties they encountered were rooted in concerns about social distance rather than personal stigma. As the senate lost its central role as the seat of power, upholding its formal dignity became more important, and that was done by keeping it free of any contact with slavery. Thus, the requirement of freeborn ancestry became a criterion for graduating the relative standing of different public bodies and orders in the Roman empire. The higher the status of the institution, the longer the line of freeborn ancestors demanded of its members. A good example of this practice comes from Marcus Aurelius' letter to the Athenians establishing rules of eligibility for the Areopagus, the Panhellenium, and the Boule; from the latter, only the freedmen themselves were excluded, while their sons and grandsons were barred from the two other bodies.[105] The regulations were clearly modelled on those of Italy, where *ingenuitas* sufficed for the *ordo decurionum*, but several generations of freeborn status were generally required for the senate.

Simply because of the social distance travelled, the entry of first-generation *ingenui* into the senate was always destined to cause controversy. Equestrian rank was apparently considered less contentious, judging from

---

[103] Suet. *Claud.* 24.1. Swan (1970); Griffin (1976) 283. Moreover, when arguing for the admission of senators from Gallia Comata, Claudius noted that contrary to common opinion the admission of freedmen's sons to magistracies was no novelty but a frequent occurrence in the past, and that no law barred them from the magistracies, Tac. *Ann.* 11.24.

[104] *Nero* 15.2; cf. Eck (1999) 18. Pliny, *NH* 33.32, says that a law of 22 CE restricted the *anuli aurei* to third-generation freeborn Romans worth 400,000 HS. But as Eck pointed out, the account is confused. If, as *Cod.Iust.* 9.21 states, the *anulus aureus* conferred an *imago ingenuitatis*, it would have made little sense to require applicants to demonstrate two generations of freeborn status before receiving it. The examples of freedmen's sons holding equestrian status show that they were not barred from this order.

[105] See the discussion in Kennell (1997) with further references.

the relative frequency with which they appear in the epigraphic sources.[106] At municipal level the evidence suggests it was perfectly normal for freedmen's sons to hold local office and curial rank. There was in principle no reason why the local elites should oppose their entry into their order since they bore no particular stigma, apart from their *novitas*, and that disadvantage might easily have been offset by the prestigious *nomina* many of them carried. As argued in the previous chapter, there was a broad correlation between powerful patrons and successful freedmen. For example, L. Licinius M.l. Tyrannus from Thugga was one of the most successful freedmen known from Africa, himself becoming *patronus pagi* and a local benefactor and his wife *flaminica*. But his success must be explained by the fact that his patron was the equestrian grandee from Carthage M. Licinius Rufus, who owned estates in the area.[107] Similar instances of social promotion can be found throughout the empire, and in this context the *apparitores* attract particular attention. These prestigious public offices, which included *scribae*, *praecones*, and *accensi*, were often filled by freedmen, and Purcell stressed the importance of patronage in this process, describing it as a 'licensed mechanism of social mobility'.[108] Logically this support would be carried over into the next generation, benefiting the freeborn sons who shared the patron's name and might be regarded as lateral extensions of the lineage.[109] Thus, the freeborn son of Aurelius Cotta's freedman Zosimus became a *tribunus militum* through the support of his father's patron.[110] The success of some sons of freedmen could therefore be seen as a natural continuation of the favours already bestowed on their fathers. Indeed, when we consider the obstacles facing freedmen trying to pass their estates on to their sons, it becomes even more likely that the most successful ones had the active support of their patron and his family. It is therefore an open question whether they are better classified as members of existing social hierarchies than as newcomers.

The case of Cn. Alleius Nigidius Maius, the most eminent citizen of late Pompeii, is instructive. He held the quinquennial duovirate, made

---

[106] See catalogue in Eck (1999).
[107] *AE* 1969–70 648, 650–2. Le Glay (1990) 628; Rives (1995) 107–8.
[108] Purcell (1983) 171. A prominent magistrate at Barcino, L. Caecilius Optatus, left a legacy for the town on condition that if his freedmen reached the sevirate they should be freed of any of the attendant burdens, 'ab omnibus muneribus seviratus excusati sint', *CIL* 2.4514; cf. Schulze-Oben (1989) 201–26, on patronal support. Likewise, in D. 32.35 pr. (Scaevola), a patron asked the heir to buy a freedman a place in a *tribus*, which would give him benefits and largesse.
[109] In the *album* from Canusium (9.338) several decurions with Greek *cognomina* seem to be the protégés of leading families and most likely the sons of favoured freedmen, e.g. L. Abuccius Euryalus, T. Aelius Nectareus, Q. Iunius Musogenes.
[110] *CIL* 14.2298.

dedications, sponsored games, and was hailed as 'princeps munerariorum', while his daughter was honoured with several public priesthoods.[111] His birth family, the Nigidii, was relatively inconspicuous, however, and his adoptive parents turn out to be Pomponia Decharcis and Alleius Nobilis. His mother's Greek *cognomen* suggests a freed background, and her husband is therefore unlikely to belong to the elite, probably being a freedman himself. Previously a prominent local family, the Alleii disappear from the record in the first half of the first century CE, and the rise of Nobilis and his son suggests they passed at least some of their fortune on to their most favoured freedman. Maius also seems to have come into possession of the estate of the wealthy Eumachii, since his (adoptive) mother and freedmen were buried inside Eumachia's monumental tomb.[112] Whether this happened through his adoptive father cannot be determined, but the secret of Alleius' success seems to lie in the support he received from several aristocratic families, who actively promoted the newcomer – despite the background of his (adoptive) parents.

Such instances cast doubts on the conventional image of social upstarts intruding into the preserves of the old aristocracy, and we have to consider also the practical mechanisms by which individuals gained office and curial rank. Under the republic and early empire, access to magistracies was still regulated by public elections, but the evidence from Pompeian electoral campaigns suggests they were essentially contests between elite families, which called up support from their dependants and allies.[113] Local elections may therefore have been poorly suited as vehicles of social change, offering few opportunities for outsiders to force their way into the *ordo* against the opposition of the established elite. At Ostia the epigraphic evidence indicates that elections had already been replaced by co-optation during the first century CE.[114] The new practice reversed the traditional sequence of events, since the *ordo* first admitted the new members who would then become eligible for public office, a decision formally ratified by the *populus*. It follows from this procedure that it was impossible for freedmen's sons and other newcomers to 'force' their way into the *ordo* without broad acceptance from its existing members.[115] Certainly, the presence of newcomers can no longer be taken as a sign of instability or social upheaval.

---

[111] Mouritsen (1988) 126, (1997).
[112] D'Ambrosio and De Caro (1983) 11 OS; cf. Mouritsen (1997). [113] Mouritsen (1988), (1999).
[114] Meiggs (1973) 183, and with different arguments Mouritsen (1998b) 250–4.
[115] As Vittinghoff (1980) 52, noted: 'Der Bürger, der in den ordo decurionum strebte, musste Beziehungen zu Dekurionen suchen, sich sozial im Gleichklang mit ihnen verhalten'. Already Lepore (1950) envisaged a process of controlled mobility in Pompeii.

The posited conflict between new and old families becomes even more unlikely when we take into account the naturally occurring turnover within the ruling class. No aristocracy can ever be entirely stable, as simple demographic factors invariably produce a degree of attrition. In ancient Rome the mortality rate meant that estates changed hands on a regular basis, and the practice of partible inheritance, giving all children a share of the estate, would often have caused families to fall below the property thresholds for public rank and office.[116] As a result, new members had to be continually co-opted into the elite, and in towns like Pompeii we find a considerable turnover of curial families. A measure of stability was still provided by an inner core of established families, who maintained a strong presence in the *ordo* over several generations. The vacancies were filled by members of rising new families, among them the descendants of the elite's favourite freedmen.[117] The system thus allowed a wider circle of families a – sometimes brief – taste of public honours through a controlled process of continuous renewal.[118] The benefits for the community were evident, especially if the newcomers were willing to spend generously for the honours they received. In Canusium the *ordo* even seems to have been expanded to provide a broader basis for the curial class as well as raising additional funds.

In many modern discussions the public careers of certain freedmen's sons have become emblematic of the fluid and competitive nature of Roman imperial society which supposedly reached exceptional levels of social mobility.[119] However, the relative success of some first-generation

---

[116] As first demonstrated by Hopkins and Burton, in Hopkins (1983), cf. Gara (1991) 340.

[117] Mouritsen (1988), (1997). A similar picture has been drawn for Timgad, Witschel (1995) 297–305. The level of turnover of families may have varied according to a number of factors such as the size of the community, the number of councillors in relation to the population, the economic structure, etc. *Prima facie* it seems likely that in large cities, where the 'inner core' of families was sufficiently numerous and wealthy to monopolise the *ordo*, newcomers were relatively rarer than in smaller towns. The same would apply in towns with small *ordines*. Cébeillac-Gervasoni (2000) 110–11, claimed the curial elite at Puteoli was exclusive, like at Ostia, and suggested – implausibly – that the popular revolt in 58 CE (Tac. *Ann.* 13.48) was caused by the excluded. On Puteoli see also Camodeca (1996b) 99f, who notes that the sons of freedmen were mostly from the imperial *familia*, a category also prominent in Pompeii. López Barja de Quiroga's theory explaining the entry of freedmen's sons (1995) is hardly convincing; cf. Eck (1999) 16 n. 51.

[118] Cf. Gara (1991) 357, who saw local social mobility as an instrument of social control.

[119] Cf. e.g. Woolf (1996) 34, who spoke of the fluid and unstable nature of Roman society, which represented 'a dynamic system in which the places of individuals were less fixed than before'. Actual rates of social mobility are considered immaterial, since it was clear from the Vesuvian towns and from 'élitist satire directed against arrivistes' that there were widespread anxieties about mobility, 35. Likewise, 'the fluidity and mobility of some Roman societies' were exceptional 'by ancient and pre-industrial standards', 38. Similarly, Wallace-Hadrill (1994) 61, referred to a 'highly mobile society'; Herrmann-Otto (2005) 76: 'einer höchst mobilen Gesellschaft'. More sceptical MacMullen (1974); Pleket (1988).

ingenui may be better understood in terms of what modern sociologists call 'sponsored mobility' as opposed to 'contest mobility'. In many cases the promising sons of freedmen were promoted by their patronal *familiae* and accepted into the ruling class as – perhaps marginal – members of these families. They were often allocated the seats at the lower end of the table, and frequently their more limited resources did not allow them to establish family continuity. In other cases their fathers inherited aristocratic fortunes which naturally entitled their sons to rank and influence. Neither scenario lends itself to a vision of open and unfettered social mobility driven by dynamic market forces.

CHAPTER 8

Being a Roman freedman
The identity and experiences of former slaves

In previous chapters dealing with the ideology and practice of manumission the freedman was – inevitably – approached as an object of ridicule, concern, trust, or promotion, which naturally brings us to the question of the freedman's own subjective experience, his views and outlook. However, any attempt to approach what might tentatively be called the 'identity' of freedmen faces a number of obstacles, the most obvious being the fact that the literary sources at our disposal operate with a set of simple but evocative stereotypes, which have had a strong impact on the image of the freedman right up until the present day. The ancient stereotypes came in a positive as well as a negative version, but the latter – more colourful and engaging – has been the more influential. Thus, most scholars addressing the issue of the 'freedman identity' have relied heavily on ancient complaints about 'bad' freedmen, which is ironic, since the 'good' ones in reality must have been the more common; otherwise the practice of manumission would presumably have declined.

The end result has been a Roman *libertus* barely distinguishable from the literary caricature, whose vulgarity and obsession with status have been readily accepted as typically freed characteristics. The image has been further entrenched by the common identification of the freedman with the archetypal figure of the social climber, which has been important in familiarising the ancient concept of the ex-slave to a modern audience. We are, however, confronted with a normative discourse which by its very nature is distinct from actual patterns of behaviour. But while few historians studying gender in the Roman world would regard, for example, Juvenal's misogynist sixth *Satire* as a realistic portrayal of women's lives under the empire, the equally biased stereotypes of the Roman freedman have continued to form the basis for many interpretations. In the past this might partly be explained by the convergence between the social prejudices of modern historians and those of ancient moralists on issues of class, mobility, and taste. It has also been heavily promoted by the chance survival of one particular text, Petronius' novel *Satyricon* and above all the central episode known as the *Cena Trimalchionis*. Despite its picaresque features, the supposed 'realism' of the novel has given it a far more profound impact on our image of the freedman than the many isolated attacks found in Martial, Juvenal, and other Roman moralists.

The fictional Trimalchio and his dinner guests have in many respects become *the* representation of the freedman against which other evidence has been judged. That also applies to the vast body of authentic, first-hand statements produced by former slaves in the form of inscriptions. This material might be expected to offer a corrective to the conventional stereotype, but more often the opposite has been the case. This is partly because of the 'lapidary' nature of the material, which contains relatively few biographical details. But as importantly, the material has typically been approached in light of existing stereotypes rather than as an independent source of information, which in effect reduces it to an illustration of known patterns. Scholars have, for example, conducted an extensive search for funerary monuments which match the one commissioned by Trimalchio, thereby confirming the 'realism' of this fictional character.[1] The hermeneutic circle intrinsic to many of these discussions was laid bare in Kloft's statement that 'without Petronius we would have had only a limited chance of getting to know the internal structure, the socio-psychological dimension of the life of rich freedmen'.[2] The direct correlation of literary and documentary evidence has in turn led to an even stronger focus on the single issue of status as the key to understanding virtually all aspects of the freedman's self-representation: funerary monuments and inscriptions, as well as specific features such as naming patterns and nomenclature.

---

[1] Comparisons with Trimalchio, e.g. Torelli (1966) 80–1; Compostella (1989); Whitehead (1993); Guidetti (2006), (2007); Leach (2006). In Purcell (1987) 25, the distinction between fact and fiction has, as Petersen (2006) 8, noted, become blurred.

[2] Kloft (1994) 131: 'Freilich: Ohne Petron hätten wir nur geringe Chance, die innere Struktur, die sozialpsychologische Dimension des Lebens von reichen Freigellassenen näher kennenzulernen.' Trimalchio has been key to interpreting larger bodies of archaeological material; cf. Maiuri (1945) 24–31, who saw late Pompeii as an illustration of the *Satyricon*; cf. Wells (1984) 193: 'As for Trimalchio himself, we find his real life counterparts a few years later buried under the ashes of Pompeii.' Frequently he has been regarded as representative of a whole class of freedmen, e.g. Mrozek (1975) 313: 'Als typischer Vertreter des reichen Selfmademan muss vor allem Trimalchio gelten'; Schnurr (1992) 158: 'rich, independent, Trimalchio-type of freedman'; Fabiani (2002) 103. Individual figures have also been approached through the lens of Trimalchio, e.g., Remmius Palaemon, Kolendo (1985) 183: member of a 'groupe des riches affranchis du début de l'empire, dont le symbole est devenue le Trimalchion du roman de Pétrone'. Likewise the Sulpicii at Puteoli, Rowe (2001) 226: 'a real-life Trimalchio'; the Umbricii Scauri at Pompeii, Curtis (1988) 36–7; Caecilius Isidorus, Verboven (2009) 137; the testator in the 'Will of Dasumius', Tate (2005) 169: a 'real-life counterpart to Petronius's Trimalchio'.

At the most basic level, concerns about status have been used to explain the extraordinary popularity of funerary epigraphy among freedmen who dominate the record from Rome and peninsular Italy as well as in many provinces. According to Taylor, they put up epitaphs in disproportionate numbers because they wished to demonstrate their new citizen status and economic success.[3] The freedmen's epigraphic habit was thus fuelled by the pride they took in their achievements and wish to leave a durable monument to their own accomplishments. On closer inspection, however, their commemorative practices turn out to be considerably more complex, not least because many inscriptions did not address the wider public but were put up in secluded settings such as *columbaria* and funerary enclosures. This aspect is often overlooked, and there is also a tendency to pay too much attention to ostentatious, Trimalchio-style monuments, which in fact remain the exception, most freedmen building relatively modest tombs for themselves and their relatives. A handful of notable monuments have therefore come to define the 'freedman's tomb'.[4]

We must also distinguish between two types of 'funerary inscription', the dedicatory or 'titulary' inscription and the actual epitaph. The former represented the public 'face' of the monument and therefore included names and titles of the dedicator and the dedicatee, as well as information about other beneficiaries of the tomb, and indeed the future of the tomb and its upkeep. The epitaphs, on the other hand, marked the urn or sarcophagus and they were often entirely private in nature and setting. The prominence of this type among the freedmen's inscriptions suggests that the assertion of status and wealth may not have been the sole motivating factor behind their epigraphic 'habit'.

Some types of monuments appear to have been the almost exclusive preserve of freedmen, including the distinctive late republican and early imperial monuments which feature rectangular 'windows' with portraits of the deceased arranged in a row.[5] The freedmen's adoption of this type has been seen as an assertion of citizenship, as well as a celebration of the *ingenuitas* enjoyed by the next generation, the former demonstrated by

---

[3] Taylor (1961), followed by e.g. Carroll (2006) 146.

[4] The 'standard' examples demonstrating a 'Trimalchian' mentality include the tomb of Lusius Storax from Teate, the Haterii monument, Anteros Asiaticus' from Brixia, Munatius Faustus' and Calventius Quietus' from Pompeii; cf. e.g. Clarke (2003) 145–52. Strangely, the tomb of the Pompeian aedile C. Vestorius Priscus has also been included among these illustrations of 'freedman taste', despite the absence of any libertine connections; e.g. Mols and Moormann (1993–94). For a timely critique see Petersen (2006); Stewart (2008) 62–70.

[5] Zanker (1975); Kleiner (1977); Frenz (1985); Kockel (1993); Lo Monaco (1998); Borg (2000). See also Eckert (1988) for the distinct monuments of the freedmen from Capua.

the wearing of togas and the latter by the *bullae* carried by their sons.[6] However, while the toga on one level may have signalled citizen status, it was also the obvious costume for a funerary portrait. Similarly, the *bullae* of the freeborn sons may seem prominent, but it would have been even more striking if they had been left out. There is a risk of over-interpreting these features, and the attempts to construe the realistic style of portraiture as a further claim to status and respectability, perhaps even emulating the elite's self-representation, may also overstate the case. The choice of a dignified, veristic style would seem entirely natural given the context and function of the sculptures.[7] An external, essentially literary agenda has been read into the primary source material.

In line with this approach, scholars have also suspected freedmen of 'covering up' their past, trying to pass themselves off as freeborn in their inscriptions. Thus, the decline in the use of pseudo-filiation during the empire has been interpreted as a result of the freedmen's reluctance to acknowledge openly their servile roots.[8] But the 'cover-up' theory makes little sense, if, as many scholars also assume, the freedmen embraced the epigraphic 'habit' so enthusiastically because they were keen to advertise the personal achievement their manumission represented. The two explanations would seem to be mutually incompatible, since the freedmen either took pride in their new status or tried to keep it secret.[9] The argument also assumes that Roman freedmen accepted the servile stigma which 'society' insisted they carried. However, our evidence suggests they saw themselves as successful individuals who had managed to make the all-important leap from slave to free in large part thanks to their own efforts.[10] Moreover, it was not just pseudo-filiation that declined in this period. Among the

---

[6] Cf. e.g. Zanker (1975) 300, who declared that: 'In ester Linie waren sie cives Romani, alles andere ist sekundär. Nichts darf von dieser Hauptaussage ablenken.'

[7] Zanker (1975) 312, noted that they wanted a realistic representation in order to be recognised and remembered, but also thought they expressed: 'Stolz und selbstzufriedenheit'. We cannot exclude the possibility that they simply conformed to current taste and commissioned portraits in the style the sculptors were familiar with.

[8] Taylor (1961) 118–19, noted the dramatic rise in the proportion of *incerti* from republic to empire, where they made up 80 per cent in the second century. She also stated that: 'The decline of the use of libertus in the freedman's name is undoubtedly a reflection of the freedman's unwillingness to declare his inferior status and his dependence on and obligation to his patron', 122. But she also explained their prominence in the epigraphic record by the pride they took in their new citizenship, 129–30.

[9] Pseudo-filiation was often omitted from the nomenclature of a freedman whose status was indicated by other features of the inscriptions, e.g. references to *colliberti* or to patrons.

[10] For example, Rosen (1995) 90, noted that Petronius presented the attitude of the freedmen at Trimalchio's dinner as one of unconcealed pride in their achievement rather than bitterness and exclusion, and thought it might be an authentic feature, although somewhat at variance with the 'shadow world' otherwise envisaged.

freeborn, filiation also became a rarity, and some freedmen even omitted this status marker when commemorating their freeborn children. A model that focuses entirely on the question of status is therefore unable to do justice to all aspects of freedmen's epigraphy.

Similar concerns about status have been invoked to explain freedmen's choice of names for their children, who were given predominantly 'respectable' Latin *cognomina*, presumably to eradicate any trace of servile ancestry.[11] But while the overall preference for Latin names is manifest, we also find a significant minority of freedmen – including some of the most successful – who gave their freeborn children Greek *cognomina* despite their servile connotations.[12] At Ostia, for example, Aurelius Hermes called his son, a future *patronus coloniae*, Hermogenes, and the *Augustalis* L. Valerius [Eutyches] named his son, who later entered the equestrian order, Eutyches *iunior*.[13] Instances such as these are difficult to reconcile to a universal preoccupation with status and attempting to 'cover their tracks'. They suggest a more complex motivation, and we cannot exclude the possibility that by using Latin names they may simply have conformed to the general pattern according to which freeborn Romans carried Latin names. After all, it was only logical that freeborn children would be given 'freeborn' names.

These observations do not imply the irrelevance of status to freedmen. It was of course vitally important to their identity and self-image, just as it was for the rest of the Romans who all had to negotiate intricate social hierarchies and subtle distinctions of rank and status. Because of their marginal position, former slaves would naturally set particular store by the attainment of the outer symbols of status and material success, the wealthiest among them embracing the ideal of the civic benefactor, the royal road to public esteem. Euergetic bodies such as the *Augustales* and *seviri* recruited extensively among freedmen, who were attracted to the respectability and trappings of status these posts conferred. Their achievements were widely advertised in durable materials, and one of the reasons why the *Augustales* loom so large in our picture of urban life is precisely the energy they put into commemorating themselves. Similar concerns informed many of the freedmen's ostentatious funerary monuments which came to dominate the

---

[11] Gordon (1931) 73, implies illicit covering up of their servile past which was 'concealed from detection by the respectable cognomina'. Similarly Reinhold (1971) 288: 'to extinguish the social stigma involved, freedmen gave their children Roman cognomina. Some also sought to alter their own names for this purpose.' There is only literary evidence for this practice, cf. Solin (1971) 134–5.
[12] Solin (1971), cf. above p. 124.   [13] *CIL* 14.5340; 4671.

local necropoleis, with the result that the elite eventually withdrew and concentrated on other, more prestigious forms of commemoration sponsored by the local community.[14]

The issue is therefore not whether status mattered to freedmen – that is a given – but whether it dominated their lives to the exclusion of all other concerns. *A priori* it seems reductive to construct a collective identity for a substantial section of the population around a single issue.[15] The reality must by necessity have been more complex, not least because the freedmen as a group were highly diverse, covering a vast social range from well-educated teachers, doctors, and private secretaries, to wealthy businessmen and trusted procurators, all the way down to craftsmen, petty traders, and low-ranking domestic staff. It makes little sense to ascribe to all freedmen, irrespective of their education, profession, gender, or wealth, a single set of characteristics, mostly derived from the stereotype of the vulgar *arriviste* which is itself part of a specific Roman discourse on the relationship between wealth, power, and status.[16]

We may therefore ask whether it is possible to make any generalisations about freedmen; the *libertus* was after all a legal concept invented to provide a 'buffer' between masters and their slaves and entrench the notion of innate differences between the two categories. Still, their status as former slaves meant that despite their social diversity they all had one crucial experience in common. What united them was their slave past and subsequent transformation into a free person. Their release from slavery was undoubtedly the single most important and formative event in their lives, and one which cannot be reduced to a simple question of status or economic opportunities. It went far beyond a mere 'upgrade' in legal status, and transformed the person, his circumstances, and future prospects. The practical as well as the psychological impact may have varied, for example according to the slave's background (captive or *verna*) and age at manumission, but in principle the fundamental benefit of freedom would have been felt by all freedmen, and at the core of this freedom lay an entirely new sense of personal security.

---

[14] For a full discussion see Mouritsen (2005).

[15] The freedmen's assumed obsession with their new status is somewhat undermined by the simple fact that they were so numerous that it in many ways became a 'normal' status.

[16] The notion of a specific – generally vulgar – 'freedman taste' has also informed many studies of Roman art and society, e.g. Zanker (1998) (although with some reservations, 222); Clarke (1991) 25, 165–6, 208 (on the 'nouveau-riche mentality' of the Vettii); Whitehead (1993) 318–19, regarding the freedmen's 'tendency to excess, garishness, overstatement' as a historical fact. Andreau (1993) 194, described the freedman as 'a curious hybrid of mimesis and bad taste'. Kloft (1994) 129, noted their 'Geschmacklosigkeit'. Veyne (1997) 85, commented on their 'lack of cultivation'. *Contra* Petersen (2006) 123–62.

Slavery entailed a complete lack of control over one's own body, life, and future. This fundamental aspect of slavery has been explored by Bradley, who points out that while many slaves lived in relative material comfort, their entire existence was nevertheless dominated by a fundamental uncertainty.[17] Even in the households of sensible, non-abusive owners their lives would still have been precarious. Thus, on the owner's death, the household might be broken up and they might find themselves in entirely different circumstances with new and potentially violent masters. Favoured slaves might fall from grace, while younger slaves were exposed to the risk of sexual abuse. Punishments included not just flogging and execution, but also sale (to the mines as a worst-case scenario) or relegation from the household, perhaps to remote country estates. The risk of public torture was ever present, since their testimony might be required in a wide range of court proceedings, including civil cases.[18] And if the master was killed in his own home the entire household was condemned. It takes little imagination to realise the effect of such insecurity and powerlessness and conversely the exhilarating experience of leaving this state behind and embarking on a new life as a free person. Most likely this was a life-altering experience, which left a lasting imprint on their outlook and identity. Indeed, it is this shared experience of newly gained freedom that may justify the use of concepts such as the 'freedman mentality'. But it also makes it very different from the simple enjoyment of higher status and social promotion.

This approach may help to explain some of the distinctive features of freedmen's self-expression, above all their extensive use of epigraphy; for Patterson was evidently right when he noted that their epitaphs 'celebrated the most important event in their life . . . the simple fact that they had been manumitted'.[19] But while many monuments clearly are self-celebratory, there is an important aspect which Patterson does not mention, which is the crucial role of the family to the freedman's identity. The precariousness which lay at the core of the slave's existence was not confined to the individual but extended to his family, including parents, children, and spouses, who could all be permanently separated, either deliberately or as a result of household break-up.[20] Further uncertainty must have been added by the slave's inability to protect close relatives from physical abuse

---

[17] Bradley (1984a) 51–64.   [18] Watson (1983).

[19] Patterson (1991) 236. But his statement that 'the single, all-important message of these inscriptions is that being freed, and experiencing personal freedom, is the most important thing in life', 245, verges on hyperbole.

[20] Rawson (1966) discussed the evidence for 'broken' slave families. As Bradley (1984a) 64–70, suggested, the slave *familia* would probably be divided up with little concern for the family units (cf. Herrmann-Otto (1997) 262–5). Legally, masters could freely decide to disregard family ties, cf.

or punishment. The opportunity to secure the family unit must therefore have been a major benefit offered by manumission. It is not by chance that the first request the newly freed slave Syrus in Terence's *Adelphi* makes is to ask for the freedom of his *contubernalis*.[21] Freedmen with existing slave families would have tried to effect the release of relatives left behind in servitude, and those still unmarried could look forward to forming new families secure under the law. Going as they do to the core of the slave's condition, these concerns appear to be a universal feature encountered in many slave societies. As Karasch noted in her study of Rio de Janeiro, the important advantage of manumission was 'the right to marry and form a family without fear of being separated. The search for family stability was probably the most powerful force behind a slave's quest for freedom.'[22]

For those reasons the immediate family is likely to have carried a different meaning for freedmen than it did for the rest of society which could take these rights for granted, and in their inscriptions we find a strong emphasis placed on family relations.[23] As noted, one particular type of funerary monument featuring portraits of the deceased was almost exclusively used by freedmen, and what is characteristic of this type is the practice of showing several members of the family units together, parents, married couples, couples with children, and occasionally also siblings.[24] Freeborn sons did of course carry the weight of their parents' aspirations, and Zanker commented on a monument: 'Here the first freeborn from a freed family is presented as *civis Romanus*.'[25] But the public display of the family unit conveyed a more complex message than mere social ascent. The representation

D. 33.5.21 and 33.7.20.4 (Scaevola), Buckland (1908) 77. Some jurists, D. 33.7.12.7 (Ulpian), cf. 33.7.12.33 (Celsus), seem to have regarded the splitting up of slave families as cruel, but the evidence is disputed. Solazzi (1949) argued for an interpolation; *contra* Treggiari (1979) 196–9. Measures were eventually taken to protect them, but not until Constantine did the principle of keeping families together become official policy (*Cod. Theod.* 2.25.1; *Cod. Iust.* 3.38.11). In classical times the law probably protected them primarily in ambiguous cases. Thus, in D. 33.7.12 (Ulpian) the issue was whether the *instrumentum* of the farm included the slaves together with their families or these could be sold off separately. Only in cases of *redhibitio*, the return of a purchased slave to the vendor on grounds of illness, etc., was the separation of relatives prohibited, D. 21.1.35 (Ulpian); 21.1.39 (Paul).

[21] *Adelph.* 973–4. In Plaut. *Rud.* 1218, the slave asks first for his own freedom, then for his wife's, and finally for payment for his work. As soon as Petronius' Hermeros had gained his freedom he redeemed his *contubernalis*: 'ne quis in [capillis] illius manus tergeret', 'so that no one dries their hands in her hair', *Sat.* 57.6. Cf. Treggiari (1991) 51–4.

[22] Karasch (1987) 365. Cf. Bradley (1984a) 77.

[23] Mouritsen (2005) 60–2; George (2005) 40–1; Corbier (2006). Leppin (1996) 80, noted the stress put on marriage in the image of the good freedman.

[24] Zanker (1975) 286ff; Witzmann (2003) 304. Examples of prominent *bullae*: D'Ambra (1995) 678 fig. 12; Rawson (1997) 212 fig. 9.1.

[25] Zanker (1975) 289: 'Hier wird der erste Freigeborene einer Libertinenfamilie als civis Romanus vorgestellt.'

of the – deceased – young man between his parents was at the same time a statement of social ambition, an illustration of close and enduring family relations, and a personal response to loss and bereavement. Seeing children simply as tools of social display overlooks their role as the embodiment of the new family's freedom and security.[26] Commemorating their premature death was a means of celebrating the family itself and coming to terms with a misfortune that may have seemed even crueller because it reversed their run of good luck and destroyed their hope of creating a 'proper' family.

The emphasis on family relations can also be traced in their naming patterns. As we have seen, a substantial minority of freedmen ignored the 'taint' attached to Greek *cognomina* and gave their children names that would signal their servile background. This feature is not easily explained within a simple status model but makes sense in the context of their family concerns. Common naming practices in Rome often involved integrating the person into the family through not just the *nomen* but also the *cognomen*. In the elite these soon became hereditary, but in many families we find *cognomina* derived from either the father or the mother.[27]

It was this particular practice which some freedmen chose to adopt.[28] For example, P. Vallius Alypus called his son P. Vallius P.f. Pal. Alypus, and Q. Volusius Q.l. Anthus named his son Q. Volusius Sp.f. Lem. Anthus.[29] A daughter could also inherit a form of her father's name, as did Vasidia Zosime, the daughter of C. Vasidius Zosimus (6.28370). A Greek name could also derive from the mother's name (14.5037). Families often combined different principles. Thus, at Ostia the *Augustalis* C. Cornelius C.l. Isochrysus and his wife Silia Tyrannis named their three children Isochrysianus, Silianus, and Faustus (14.339). In some cases the

---

[26] Shaw (1991) 87: 'By visually portraying their families, they proclaimed their normality, their status as citizens, and their social position as free Romans.' Rawson (2003) 31, commented on freedmen who sought 'ways to advertise their improving status and wealth', and 'memorialized their family relationships, often using children to represent the family's upward mobility'. Similarly, D'Ambra (1995) 672, suggested – somewhat reductively – that they presented themselves 'with their freeborn children to show that they had proudly accomplished their obligation as Roman citizens to form a family', elsewhere referring to their 'hunger for status', (2002) 230, cf. Leach (2006) 4; Huskinson (2007) 325. McWilliam (2001) 93, thought that 'marking the death of a child brought a chance of recognition'. To George (2006) 20–1, cf. (2005) 42–52, it showed they 'wanted to be represented as upholders of socially conservative values', echoing Fabre's comment that 'les affranchis entourent leur vie familiale d'un moralisme plutôt conservateur', (1981) 215.

[27] By contrast, in eighteenth-century Jamaica there was much less onomastic continuity between slave and freed, Burnand (2001). Masters reserved specific names for slaves, many of which were of African origins, although they did not indicate ethnicity, being more popular for creoles than for Africans. When freed, the former slaves would choose different types of names for their freeborn children.

[28] As already noted by Solin (1971) 128–9, with further examples.

[29] *CIL* 6.28308, 14.1804. Cf. e.g. 6.29303, 6.28463, 14.508, 14.818; Thylander (1952) A 173.

inspiration for the Greek name is not obvious. For example, L. Veratius Orestes and Busidia Merope called their son L. Veratius Phainus (6.28541), and A. Egrilius Chrysodorus and Aelia Anthusa named theirs A. Egrilius Agapetus (14.928). In many cases we may suspect that such names were derived from other family members not mentioned in the inscription, as happened in the case of Lucilia D.f. Melitine, the daughter of D. Lucilius Glyco and Lucilia Helpis, who was named after her father's sister, Lucilia Sp.f. Melitine.[30]

When naming their children, freedmen often found themselves in a dilemma: either they could give them Latin *cognomina*, befitting their freeborn status, or they could give them Greek names which connected them to the family line.[31] Both options conformed to Roman practice but emphasised different aspects, *ingenuitas* or familial bonds. In some cases the two could be reconciled – for example, L. Castricius Hamillus and Obellia Felix called their son L. Castricius Felix (14.4841) – and often we find a mix of the two practices, as illustrated by the five children of M. Suavius Geta and Aristia Fortunata, who were called Geta, Fortunatus, Eutalia, Fortunata, and Urbana (14.5132). As these examples show, the wish to demonstrate family continuity could take precedence over the assertion of status.[32] The two concerns were essentially inseparable and only rarely clashed – as in the choice of names – and they also shaped their epigraphic 'habit', which remains one of the most striking expressions of their collective identity.

Freedmen dominate the epigraphic record from Rome, Italy, and most of the provinces, and as noted earlier this remarkable feature cannot be

[30] *CIL* 6.21599. Similarly 14.1808 records Q. Volusius Q.l. Anthus and Silia (mulieris)l. Felicula, who had two freeborn children Q. Volusius Q.f. Anthus and Volusia Q.f. Nice. The daughter's name may relate to that of Silia (mulieris)l. Nice, most likely her mother's sister. The inscription also features a C. Silius Anthus, who may be a son born before the mother was freed.
[31] In some cases Latin endings were added to Greek names as a solution, cf. Solin (1971) 126–7, 132–3. Kunst (1999) 159, suggested these transformed their Greek names into Roman ones which resembled their own, thereby conforming to the traditional 'familiäres Bezugssystem'.
[32] Cf. Solin (1971) 128. There may have been an increased tendency to maintain Greek *cognomina* in the family in the higher empire. For example, in Ostia the decurion M. Cornelius M.f. Pal. Valerianus appears to have named his son M. Cornelius M.f. Valerianus Epagathianus in memory of his grandfather the *Augustalis* M. Cornelius Epagathus, cf. Tran (2006) 394. Similarly, in the *album* from Canusium (223 CE) we find 29 per cent of the decurions carrying Greek names, in several cases clearly passed on from freeborn parents, e.g. Ti. Claudius Onesimianus *pater et filius*. However, the Greek *cognomina* still carried a servile association, as indicated by the difference between the low-ranking *pedani* and the *praetextati*, young decurions-in-waiting; cf. Mouritsen (1998b): 31 per cent of the *pedani* carried Greek names against 16 per cent of the *praetextati*. The difference in status between the two groups is indicated by their relative degree of integration into the curial class, since 56 per cent of the *pedani* had no shared family names among former office holders, compared to just 24 per cent among the *praetextati*. Cf. Garnsey (1975a) 173.

reduced to a simple question of status display. Two aspects must be taken into account, which are their subjects and their audiences. Firstly, most of the epitaphs were not self-celebratory but commemorated close relatives, and secondly, a large proportion of them had no public audience since they were put up in private settings such as internal burial chambers or enclosures.[33] We are therefore confronted with an interesting social phenomenon, which is the socially specific response to the common experience of bereavement. Considering the universality of this occurrence we would expect broadly similar reactions within a given culture, but in Rome it was overwhelmingly freedmen who reacted to bereavement by erecting inscribed monuments. The practice may originally have emulated elite practices, but it soon developed independently into a distinct expression of the freedman identity. It celebrated personal freedom in the broadest sense and reflected the particular emotional and social 'capital' they invested in their immediate family. Putting up inscriptions became part of the shared rituals through which freedmen dealt with bereavement on a personal level, and through participation in this ritual their group identity and sense of belonging may also have been reinforced. Thus, burial sites were often combined with socialising for the living.[34]

These practices were rooted in the freedman's personal experiences, which in the nature of things were non-transferable, and this may explain why their descendants seem to disappear so rapidly from the funerary record. Those who had never undergone the transformation from slave to free took their personal freedom for granted and felt less inclined to celebrate the secure family unit epigraphically. The freedman therefore differed from his freeborn children, not just legally but also in outlook and identity.[35] In the same way the social stigma of servitude was unique to the former slave, so the experience of manumission could not be passed on to the next generation. The fact that manumission gave rise to distinct epigraphic practices takes us back to the question of their social integration and overall place in society. Do these patterns allow us to speak of a freedman community? And if so, what did it look like?

---

[33] For fuller discussion see Mouritsen (2005).   [34] Heinzelmann (2000) 63–72, on Ostia.
[35] In his study of the western idea of freedom Patterson (1991) allocated an important place to the Roman freedmen, who he claimed played a crucial role in shaping western notions of freedom, even labelling a central chapter 'The triumph of the Roman freedman', 227–57. He suggests that virtually the entire plebs became 'libertine' in their outlook, since the freedmen imbued the Roman people with their particular concerns about personal freedom. There is little evidence to support this theory (the example of Horace rather underlines the difference between the freedman and his son) and freeborn Romans would presumably have regarded their personal freedom as a given.

Freedmen shared no common ethnic or cultural background, and their education and professions would have differed as widely as their many roles within the *familia*. In terms of lifestyle there is no reason to assume they stood out from the rest of the population. Most of them would have been acculturated and integrated into Roman society before manumission. For example, the notion of freedmen speaking a particularly common Latin is unlikely, since many of them were brought up and educated in elite households, while those who had been imported presumably spoke vernaculars too diverse to produce a single 'freedman language'.[36]

Scholars have long scrutinised inscriptions and monuments for signs of assimilation or dissidence. Generally the search has yielded few concrete results, and there is in fact little evidence of freedmen espousing values different from those held among the wider population.[37] This is hardly surprising, since conformity was built into the Roman system of manumission with its emphasis on incentives, selection, and continuity.[38] A rebellious slave or a recent captive who might return to his homeland or join an immigrant sub-community – to the extent they existed – would have had little chance of freedom.[39] Modern concerns about the integration of immigrants into western societies may have influenced this debate, but the Roman freedmen – even those of foreign extraction – differed in fundamental respects from other types of migrants, not least because they entered society through a regulated process and remained subject to patronal authority.

However, even if the freedmen as a rule showed few common characteristics, the stigma of slavery was nevertheless real. It was enshrined in law, circumscribed their public roles, and pervaded much of Roman literature

[36] Daheim and Blänsdorf (2003) 107, concluded that Petronius' language of the freedmen to a great extent is a literary construct rather than a realistic use of popular idiom.

[37] Joshel (1992), followed by George (2006) 27, has drawn attention to the apparent pride which many freedmen took in their occupations, suggesting it might be seen as a conscious departure from the common elite disdain for manual work. However, while in itself entirely plausible, the absence of comparable material produced by the freeborn plebs makes it difficult to identify this feature as distinctly libertine.

[38] Witzmann (2003) 321, found it remarkable that freedmen did not form a counter-culture or return to their ethnic roots, but that is less surprising if, as he noted himself, it was precisely their assimilation and conformity which had ensured their manumission in the first place. Cf. George (2006) 21, who suggested they 'modeled their behavior on elite attitudes and *mores*'. Veyne (1997) 83, 85, on the one hand, argued that freedmen 'developed a culture of their own', while, on the other hand, also describing their existence as 'totally imitative'. Leach (2006) 2, spoke of the social isolation which made them 'band together and create their own alternative culture', and concluded hyperbolically that they turned their 'extra-societal status into a compensatory claim to immortality attainable outside the fabric of Roman society', 18.

[39] For 'ethnic' communities in Rome see Noy (2000).

and moral discourse. We may therefore ask to what extent it affected the daily lives of freedmen. Did people's prejudices leave them socially isolated and confined to a separate sub-community? The single most influential text suggesting this scenario is Petronius' *Cena Trimalchionis*, which has inspired the notion of an almost closed libertine world, shunned by a hostile society. As Veyne famously concluded, Trimalchio was not a parvenu, for despite his attempts to emulate the elite he was forever denied access and recognition.[40] As a result, the freedmen became even more obsessed with status, assertive and over-compensating, fuelling society's resentment and in turn their own isolation.

In the *Cena Trimalchionis* we are confronted with a social environment entirely populated by freedmen, to which the novel's central character, the freeborn Encolpius, becomes the accidental visitor. While the comic exaggeration is apparent, the basic 'realism' of Petronius' portrayal of the freedmen has been widely accepted.[41] What makes the world of Trimalchio even more striking is the absence of patrons. While several of the freed characters perform this role themselves, their own patrons are mentioned only in two instances, Hermeros and Trimalchio, and that of the latter had left him free of any bonds. Since the freedman–patron relationship generally was hailed as the foundations of Roman manumission, it is possible to see the *Cena* as a world turned upside down, a saturnalian scenario (dreamt up by a senator) where (former) slaves assume the roles of their masters. But despite – or perhaps rather because of – this excess of freedom, theirs was not a cheerful existence; in fact the *Cena* offers, as Bodel observed, a 'starkly bleak vision of a freedman's place in the world'.[42] The freedmen show a morbid interest in death, suggesting an unreal netherworld into which Encolpius and friends descend. The absence of patrons – and *ingenui* – is therefore an essential element of the 'libertine' shadow world conjured up by Petronius' imagination.[43]

---

[40] Veyne (1961). Boyce (1991) 95, spoke of 'independent freedmen on the margins of society'; while to D'Ambra (1995) 667, the world of the freedman was a 'status-hungry society at the margins of respectability'.

[41] Veyne (1961) 213, described it as 'un excellent document d'histoire'; Boyce (1991) 94–7, declared that 'critics are unanimous in regarding Trimalchio as typical', 97. Kloft (1994) 131, argued that 'eine Figur wie Trimalchio [erhält] verläßliche Konturen'. Los (1995) 1014, defined the *Cena* as a 'miroir déformant', which conveniently allowed him to accept some elements and reject others. Sceptical about the claimed 'realism', Dupont (1977); Conte (1996) 171–94; Andreau (2009) 124.

[42] Bodel (1999b) 47.

[43] Andreau (2009) 120, raised the possibility that most of the freedmen at the dinner had belonged to the same owner, based on the appearance of the term *collibertus/i*. But while one of the freedmen was, like Trimalchio, called Pompeius, the group also included a C. Iulius Proculus. More importantly, Hermeros is explicitly given as Trimalchio's *collibertus*, 58.3, 59.1, but his patron was clearly different

In his classic work *Mimesis*, Auerbach identified the vagaries of fortune as a central theme of the *Satyricon*, observing that: 'It is easy to understand that a society of businessmen of the humblest origins is particularly suitable material for a representation of this nature, for conveying this view of things. Such a society most clearly reflects the ups and downs of existence, because there is nothing to hold the balance for it; its members have neither inward tradition nor outer stability; they are nothing without money.'[44] It follows that a conventional representation of freedmen enjoying patronal support and material security would not have fitted the theme, which may explain why they all feature as 'independent', that is, cut off from their original *familiae*. Petronius seized on the – indisputable – existence of wealthy 'independent' freedmen in Roman society and created a fictional 'underworld' entirely inhabited by members of this particular sub-category. The effect was both 'realistic' and highly unreal.

The image evoked by Petronius of an isolated libertine community scorned by the rest of society thus emerges as a literary invention. The prejudices against freedmen were undoubtedly real but we must also take into account a degree of social differentiation. MacMullen suggested that the disdain for freedmen was confined to the aristocracy and not shared by 'ordinary folk'.[45] However, even elite attitudes may have been more nuanced, for despite the fact that the most overt hostility appears in discourses on rank and status, more positive views were also expressed by members of the ruling class, and even by the rulers themselves. Thus, certain emperors actively promoted manumission and welcomed freedmen and their children into the citizen body. For example, when Pliny asked Trajan to grant citizenship to some Latini Iuniani, over whom he had inherited patronal rights, the emperor was happy to oblige and commended Pliny's action.[46] Under imperial auspices the jurists introduced the principle of *favor libertatis*, and often delivered opinions which balanced evenly the interests of patrons and freedmen. Roman authors and orators paid tribute to freedmen in public speeches and court cases when it suited

---

from Trimalchio's; indeed Hermeros' praise of his *Genius* indicates he was still alive, 57.11, while Trimalchio's famously was deceased. *Collibertus* must therefore mean 'fellow freedman' in this context.

[44] Auerbach (1953) 29f.

[45] MacMullen (1974) 105; cf. 120. Andreau (1993) 195–6; Purcell (1994) 655, warning against taking the 'obligatory sneers' at face value.

[46] *Ep.* 10.104–5.

their argument.[47] In polite society, fair treatment of freedmen was a sign of good manners and civilised lifestyle.[48]

In a declamation attributed to Quintilian we are told that a master would free his slaves because 'he was pleased with their services and wanted to repay their obedience'. The orator could therefore ask rhetorically: 'Are we reluctant and sad to see them as part of the community?' – the implicit response being that no one could possibly object to good slaves being freed.[49] Even more evocatively, Pliny applauded the freeing of a large number of slaves, 'plurimos manumissos', by a relative in his native Comum, adding that: 'I am always anxious for the advancement of our native place, and above all through the increasing numbers of her citizens, for that is an attribute which sets a town on the surest of foundations.'[50] The manumission of slaves is presented as an unequivocally positive development for the city.

On a more personal level, we have already noted the patron's duty of care for his *liberti*, and many also showed affection for their favourite freedmen, seemingly without embarrassment.[51] For example, Pliny expressed great concern for an ill freedman, using terms such as *caritas* and even *amor*, and when he sought to persuade his friend Sabinianus to take an expelled freedman back into his household, he reminded him that he had once loved him.[52] Persius did not shy away from opening his fifth satire with a highly personal, even emotional dedication to his teacher, the freedman L. Annaeus Cornutus, extolling their close friendship and even likening him to a father, 5.1–51.

---

[47] E.g. *Cat.* 4.16; *Verr.* 2.1.123–4. Cicero even praised the freedmen's 'modestum ordinem', which maintained its restraint in the face of Verres' injustices, including his refusal to recognise the freedom of freedmen, 2.1.127. Pliny, *Ep.* 7.6.8–9, mentions his defence of two freedmen who were accused of having poisoned their patron and faked his will. The successful farmer, C. Furius Chresimus, who was accused of magically increasing his revenues, also won his case before the people, Plin. *NH* 18.41–3.

[48] Pliny, *Ep.* 2.6.2–4, disapproved of the gradation of wine and food at dinner parties, confirming that he served the same for all his guests. The letter incidentally also makes clear that a senator would only socialise with his own freedmen or those of his guests, describing the freedmen in question as 'suis nostrisque'. On the other hand, Eck (1999) 18 n. 58, noted prominent senators and *equites* married to freedwomen, which may have been less controversial because it conformed to the 'natural order'.

[49] Ps.-Quint. *Decl.Min.* 311.9: 'Servos cur manumiserit manifestum est: delectatus est officiis, referre voluit gratiam obsequio.' 'Num inviti eos tristesque in numero civitatis aspicimus?', 2.

[50] *Ep.* 7.32: 'Cupio enim patriam nostram omnibus quidem rebus augeri, maxime tamem civium numero: id enim oppidis firmissimum ornamentum.'

[51] The language of affection, e.g. *amare*, is also found in Cicero's recommendations for freedmen, as well as in his private letters.

[52] *Ep.* 5.19; 9.21.2: 'Amasti hominem et, spero, amabis.'

The hostility against freedmen belonged to specific contexts and discourses and coexisted with more positive views expressed in different situations. Ultimately the elite had few reasons to see freedmen as a threat; after all, they were directly responsible for creating most of them. Moreover, the competitive gestures of some freedmen, typically seen as challenges to the established elite, were probably often aimed at other freedmen. Tombs and dedications did of course send a message to the general public, but the contest itself was by necessity confined to their own status group, which could aspire only to a limited set of honours. At Ostia, for example, the freedmen continued to build sometimes quite substantial monuments long after the curial elite had largely given up on this form of competitive display, in effect leaving the necropoleis to the freed population.[53] A close-up of this contest is found in Pompeii, where the ostentatious tomb of Naevoleia Tyche and her husband the *Augustalis* Munatius Faustus, in one of the most celebrated instances of libertine assertiveness, was built right next to that of another *Augustalis*, Calventius Quietus, and displayed precisely the same honorary seat, *bisellium*, as the neighbouring monument.[54] The local elite could hardly have taken offence from these gestures; after all, the honours advertised had been granted by the *ordo* itself and the manner in which they were displayed conformed to conventional norms.

Among the lower classes, supposedly far more accepting than the elite, the situation may have been equally complex. Some animosity towards freedmen is likely also among the broader population, which may have resented their privileged economic position. The literary tirades against them are often written by authors impersonating 'the man in the street', who is ignored by patrons despite being of 'old Roman stock', as illustrated by Juvenal's outcry about a 'filius ingenuorum' who escorted a rich slave.[55] Despite its commonplace character, the image carries a certain plausibility given the well-documented promotion of freedmen by their patrons. The question is whether that justifies a generalised model of contempt and separation. There is plenty of evidence for the integration of freedmen within their local communities, where they would have been in close personal contact with the freeborn population in their daily lives. Many local associations had a mixed membership, and in the *collegia* freedmen frequently held positions of honour and responsibility, outranking ordinary

---

[53] Mouritsen (2004), (2005).
[54] Kockel (1983) 90ff; *CIL* 10.1026, 1030. Already Zanker (1975) 285, suggested freedmen's self-representation was aimed at their peers, not the elite.
[55] 3.131f. Similarly, his complaint that there is no place for Romans at Rome, 3.119, or his famous comment about the Orontes flowing into the Tiber, 3.62.

freeborn members. The posts did not of course confer any real authority, but symbolically the acceptance of freedmen as formal superiors is nevertheless significant.[56]

On the other hand, there were also organisations which were filled exclusively by freedmen – presumably because the freeborn were reluctant to join. Thus, the *seviri Augustales*, after the initial involvement by *ingenui*, became overwhelmingly libertine in most places. As soon as the balance tipped, their attraction to freeborn apparently faded. Likewise, in those towns where we continue to find a sizeable freeborn contingent, these were sometimes separated formally from the freedmen.[57] The apparent contrast to *collegia* may be explained by the different nature of the *seviri Augustales* whose main function was to confer public esteem, a factor less important in the *collegia*, which often had much wider social and convivial functions.

There are no simple answers to the question of integration and discrimination. The reality was probably a complex mix of everyday acceptance and generalised prejudices, which individuals might 'switch on and off' according to circumstances and convenience. Then as now, most people would have been able to hold seemingly contradictory positions in different contexts. There is, for example, anecdotal evidence for solidarity between freedmen (even slaves) and the rest of the plebs, such as the popular support for the innocent slaves executed after the murder of Pedanius Secundus.[58] Close association with freedmen could also be seen as a means of courting popularity by showing one's common touch. Thus, Cicero accused Gellius of having married a freedwoman, not for lust but to appear 'plebicola', and insinuated that Antony married the daughter of a freedman, Fadia, in an attempt to commend himself to the 'infimus ordo'.[59] The implication is that associating with freed people somehow gave popular clout, which in turn would suggest that the freeborn/freed divide may have been less important among the plebs than the literary and legal sources would indicate. Along similar lines, Crook argued that distinctions of status became 'blurred and ultimately annihilated by the fact that so many of the free had

---

[56] MacMullen (1974) 120; Ausbüttel (1982) 39, estimated that in the collegial *alba* from Rome a third carried non-Latin *cognomina* and in those from Italy a quarter. In Ostia the figures vary between 26 and 30 per cent, Mouritsen (2005) 43. Royden (1988) 224, 229–31, argued that large numbers of office holders were of unfree descent.

[57] In Mediolanum and possibly also Brixia the freeborn *seviri Augustales* (who did not belong to the curial elite) were designated *iuniores* and the freedmen *seniores*; cf. Garnsey (1975b); Mouritsen (2006) 248. Cantarelli (2002) 99–111, presents the evidence but her explanation of the phenomenon is hardly convincing.

[58] Tac. *Ann.* 14.42; cf. Finley (1998) 170–1.

[59] *Sest.* 110; *Phil.* 2.3; cf. 3.17, cf. Favory (1981) 104; Rizzelli (2006).

once been slaves, and replaced by the simple distinction between "haves" and "have-nots"'.[60] The identification of this process is undoubtedly correct, but the relevance of the 'haves' and 'have-nots' distinction is not clear, since it does not explain why the freeborn 'haves' would begin to disregard the difference between themselves and the freed 'haves'. Likewise, there is no evidence that freed ancestry made people more 'tolerant' of freedmen, as illustrated by the example of Horace who fully subscribed to conventional views.

There are signs, however, that the distinction between freeborn and freed may have become less important. One of the most intriguing features of imperial epigraphy is the decline in the use of explicit status markers, filiation and pseudo-filiation. The freedmen's tendency not to advertise their status has – unsurprisingly – been seen as attempts to 'pass as freeborn', but, as Duthoy noted, that does of course not explain the parallel decline in filiation among the *ingenui* – and indeed in the epitaphs freedmen put up for their own freeborn children.[61] The context must be taken into account, since in many cases the inscriptions were aimed at a small and restricted audience, but also in more public or 'titulary' epitaphs the dedicators – freeborn as well as freed – renounced status indicators. Most strikingly we find organisations with a mixed membership putting up large monumental *alba* which did not differentiate between freeborn and freed. For example, none of the *collegia* inscriptions from Ostia included filiation or pseudo-filiation, suggesting that their freeborn members accepted a semi-public document which did not clearly distinguish between freeborn and freed.[62]

The decline in the use of status markers raises complex issues of identity and the relationship between formal status and lived reality. It could be argued that the category of the freedman was essentially artificial, a legal and ideological construct which had little real bearing on the lives of ordinary people. In the real world there was only one crucial divide, that between free and unfree. Therefore, when manumitted, the slave crossed that all-important boundary and became a member of the free population,

---

[60] Crook (1967a) 50; cf. e.g. Behrends (1980) 87. Already Veyne (1961) 224, had observed that: 'Au bas de la société, la pression économique enlève toute réalité pratique aux différences de statut, esclaves et hommes libres se confondant dans une égale médiocrité.'

[61] Taylor (1960), above n. 8. Duthoy (1989) 204 n.39.

[62] There are of course variations in practice; in the *album* of the *corpus lenunculariorum tabulariorum* in Ostia, *CIL* 14.250, three homonymous T. Cornelii Felices are the only members designated by 'lib', but that was clearly to distinguish them from two apparently freeborn T. Cornelii Felices who appear without filiation. Also, the *album* of the *familia Silvani* at Trebula Mutuesca shows a mix of statuses and a clear distinction between *ingenui* and *liberti*, but only the former are indicated explicitly, Buonocore and Diliberto (2006). The *vicomagistri* inscriptions from Rome carefully stated the status of each magister, e.g. *CIL* 6.975.

irrespective of the personal status he received. The intermediate status of 'freed' was secondary to this fundamental distinction, and epigraphically the ability of the Latin name system to indicate unequivocally which of these two categories a person belonged to made additional status indicators redundant in the long run. It could therefore be argued that 'the freedman' had always been something of a fiction, and that epigraphic practice simply caught up with reality.[63]

It is not given that the specific role of 'the freedman' as defined in legal and literary texts had much practical relevance outside these particular discourses. And if the Romans in their daily lives did not find the distinction meaningful, the search for a freedman community obviously becomes futile. But there is one issue, entirely central to the lives of freedmen, which may suggest a distinctive freedman community, and that is their pattern of marriage. For if the distinction between freeborn and freed had faded, it is puzzling that we find so few examples of intermarriage between the two groups. The rich epigraphic evidence we have for the family patterns of Roman freedmen consistently indicates that very few of them married freeborn, leaving aside the *libertae* who married their patrons, a separate issue.[64] Not even the most successful freedmen, including the *seviri Augustales*, appear to have found freeborn wives, suggesting there were limits to their social integration.

Traditionally scholars assumed that freeborn Romans were reluctant to 'marry down', in effect forcing freedmen to find partners within their own status group.[65] Clearly, unions that crossed this boundary might attract opprobrium, as illustrated by Seneca Maior's *Controversia* 7.6, but we also find the freed father of Claudius Etruscus, who married the sister of a consul, hinting that financial advantage might overrule reservations about disparities in status.[66] The marriage patterns of the emperor's freedmen have long been used to underpin the idea of *ingenui* generally shunning unions with former slaves, because the *liberti Augusti*, with their unique wealth and prestige, apparently bucked the trend and predominantly (no less than two thirds) married freeborn. The theory, first formulated by

---

[63] As Rawson (1989) 21, rightly noted, the masses of Rome did not use full nomenclature, 'reflecting the comparative unimportance of formal status in their everyday lives'.

[64] This observation is unrelated to the many freed couples who share the same *nomen* and presumably had belonged to the same *familia* before manumission. As already noted by Treggiari (1969a) 210, and Fabre (1981) 166–9, also in cases where the *nomina* differ are both spouses overwhelmingly likely to be freed.

[65] This view is reflected in e.g. Flory (1978) 89, who spoke of 'upward mobility through marriage with freeborn women'. Los (1995) 1017, claimed that marriage to a freeborn was always 'un succès social'.

[66] Stat. *Silv.* 3.3.111–18.

Weaver, has gained widespread acceptance despite the absence of hard evidence to support it.[67] Very few wives of imperial freedmen are recorded as freeborn, and the idea is essentially based on the high proportion of imperial freedmen who married outside the *familia Caesaris*, combined with the assumption that slaves generally were freed quite late, certainly well past the typical age of marriage for women. This led to the conclusion that the women in question must have been *ingenuae*. However, as Weaver himself recognised in his later work, many slaves were freed relatively early, and a study of the wives' *cognomina* suggests that the majority were in fact *libertae*.[68] In this respect the imperial freedmen would therefore seem to conform to the normal pattern.

Given the material success of many freedmen, it seems inconceivable that they would have been unable to find freeborn spouses had this been a priority for them, hard economic realities often prevailing over concerns about personal status. We might therefore consider the possibility that their marriage patterns could be the result of a conscious choice, which may be explained by a wish to form bonds within the social circle in which they moved, or a preference for spouses who shared their status, background, and experience. The two concerns would in reality often have been complementary, and together with the commemorative and epigraphic habits noted above, they may suggest the vague outline of a distinct freedman community. This was, however, a freedman community very different from the caricature described in the *Satyricon*: one focused on the family bonds and the shared celebration of freedom and security. Slavery was in every sense a defining experience, leaving a stigma but also creating a bond between those who had escaped from it. This may perhaps explain the – probably deliberate – social segregation we encounter in some spheres of their lives.

Freedmen always found themselves placed in two partly overlapping worlds, that of their *familia* and that of the wider community of freedmen. The *familia* was the obvious fixture of their identity, dominated by the patron's authority, and many freedmen probably never left the

---

[67] Weaver (1972) 112–36; cf. (1991) 177, 190, (2001) 109. Followed by e.g. Hopkins (1978) 116–17; Flory (1978) 82; D'Arms (1990) 394; Gara (1991) 353; Los (1995) 1016–17; Leppin (1996) 80 n.68; Storchi Marino (1999) 395; Saller (2000) 831; Milailescu-Birliba (2006) 71. D'Arms (1975) 336f, noted its speculative nature but found it plausible. Weaver's later work, esp. (1990), undermined the foundation for the theory, but since this implication was never acknowledged it continues to feature in modern discussions.

[68] Epigraphic samples, drawn from Weaver's database, of free women married to imperial slaves and freedmen suggest that around half of these women carried Greek *cognomina*, while a substantial proportion of the Latin ones were distinctly 'servile'.

household, in some cases serving generations of the patron's family. But other freedmen, especially those who already lived outside the household before manumission, may have become increasingly separated from it afterwards as their economic security grew. At the same time freedmen were linked to their fellow *liberti* from other households by shared experiences and common social and political status. Throughout their free lives they moved between these two 'communities', and the death of the patron is likely to have marked an important caesura, especially if there was no direct continuation of the household. The personal identity of the freedman was therefore neither fixed nor constant but naturally evolving during his lifetime under the impact of social, economic, and demographic factors.

But irrespective of these fluctuations there remained a unique and non-transferable core to their identity which set them apart from their freeborn descendants. It follows that we have no grounds for assuming that their children formed a distinct social category, let alone an economic one. There may have been relatively few of them, and more importantly they were probably quite heterogeneous. Since the freedman's relative success was a function of his socio-economic integration into existing power structures, there may also have been a tendency for the next generation either to rise or to sink economically – largely depending on the level of support they received from their patronal family. While the most successful among them entered the lower end of the elite, the less fortunate probably joined the large underclass which has left behind few traces of their existence.

Bibliography

Abbreviations of journal titles follow the *Oxford Classical Dictionary* (3rd edn).

Abramenko, A. (1992), 'Liberti als Dekurionen. Einige Überlegungen zur lex Malacitana', *Laverna* 3: 94–103.

(1993a), 'Die innere Organisation der Augustalität. Jahresamt und Gesamtorganisation', *Athenaeum* 81: 13–37.

(1993b), *Die munizipale Mittelschicht im kaiserzeitlichen Italien. Zu einem neuen Verständnis von Sevirat und Augustalität* (Frankfurt a. M.).

Achard, G. (1981), *Pratique rhétorique et idéologie politique dans les discours 'optimates' de Cicéron* (Leiden).

Affolter, F. (1913), *Die Persönlichkeit des Herrenlosen Sklaven. Ein Stück aus dem römischen Sklavenrecht* (Leipzig).

Agnati, U. (2000), *Ingenuitas. Orazio, Petronio, Marziale e Gaio* (Chieti).

Albana, M. (1987), 'La *vicesima libertatis* in età imperiale', *Quaderni Catanesi di Studi Classici e Medievali* 9: 41–76.

Alföldy, G. (1984), *Römische Statuen in Venetia et Histria. Epigraphische Quellen* (Heidelberg).

(1986a), 'Die Freilassung von Sklaven und die Struktur der Sklaverei in der römischen Kaiserzeit', in *Die römische Gesellschaft. Ausgewählte Beiträge* (Stuttgart) 286–331. First published in *RSA* 2 (1972) 97–129.

(1986b), 'Die römische Gesellschaft: eine Nachbetrachtung über Struktur und Eigenart', in *Die römische Gesellschaft. Ausgewählte Beiträge* (Stuttgart) 69–81.

Allison, P. M. (2001), 'Placing individuals: Pompeian epigraphy in context', *Journal of Mediterranean Archaeology* 14: 54–75.

Anderson, W. S. (1995), '*Horatius liber*, child and freedman's free son', *Arethusa* 28: 151–64.

Andreau, J. (1974), *Les affaires de Monsieur Jucundus* (Coll. École Fr. Rome 387: Rome).

(1977), 'Fondations privées et rapports sociaux en Italie romaine (Ier – IIIe s. ap. J.-C.)', *Ktema* 2: 157–209.

(1987), *La vie financière dans le monde romain. Les métiers de manieurs d'argent (IVe siècle av. J.-C. – IIIe siècle ap. J.-C.)* (Rome).

(1991), 'Mercati e mercato', in *Storia di Roma* II.2 (Turin) 367–85.

(1992), 'Mobilité sociale et activités commerciales et financières', in *La mobilité sociale dans le monde romain* ed. E. Frézouls (Strasbourg) 21–32.

(1993), 'The freedman', in *The Romans* ed. A. Giardina (Chicago and London) 175–98.

(1999), *Banking and Business in the Roman World* (Cambridge).

(2004) 'Les esclaves "hommes d'affaires" et la gestion des ateliers et commerces', in *Mentalités et choix économique des Romains* eds. J. Andreau, J. France, and S. Pittia (Paris) 111–26.

(2009), 'Freedmen in the *Satyrica*', in *Petronius. A Handbook* ed. J. Prag and I. Repath (Oxford) 114–24.

Ankum, H. (2005), 'Der Ausdruck favor libertatis und das klassische römische Freilassungsrecht', in *Unfreie Arbeits- und Lebensverhältnisse von der Antike bis in die Gegenwart* ed. E. Herrmann-Otto (Hildesheim) 82–100.

Armstrong, D. (1986), 'Horatius *Eques et Scriba*: 1.6 and 2.7', *TAPhA* 116: 255–88.

(1989), *Horace* (New Haven and London).

Astolfi, R. (1999), 'Il libro di Masi Doria sulla successione nei beni dei liberti: nota di lettura', *SDHI* 65: 283–308.

Atkinson, K. M. T. (1966), 'The purpose of the manumission laws of Augustus', *The Irish Jurist* 1: 356–74.

Aubert, J.-J. (1993), 'Workshop managers', in *The Inscribed Economy. Production and Distribution in the Roman Empire in the Light of* instrumentum domesticum ed. W. V. Harris (JRA Suppl. 6: Ann Arbor) 171–81.

(1994), *Business Managers in Ancient Rome. A Social and Economic Study of Institores, 200 B.C. – A.D. 250* (Leiden, New York, and Cologne).

(2002), 'A double standard in Roman criminal law? The death penalty and social structure in late republican and early imperial Rome', in *Speculum Iuris. Roman Law as a Reflection of Social and Economic Life in Antiquity* ed. J.-J. Aubert and B. Sirks (Ann Arbor) 94–133.

(2004), 'De l'usage de l'écriture dans la gestion d'entreprise à l'époque romaine', in *Mentalités et choix économique des Romains* ed. J. Andreau, J. France, and S. Pittia (Paris) 127–47.

Auerbach, E. (1953), *Mimesis. The Representation of Reality in Western Literature* (Princeton).

Ausbüttel, F. M. (1982), *Untersuchungen zu den Vereinen im Westen des römischen Reiches* (Kallmünz).

Axer, J. (1979), 'I prezzi degli schiavi e le pagne degli attori nell'orazione di Cicerone pro Q. Roscio comoedo', in *Actes du colloque sur l'esclavage Nieborów 2–6 XII 1975*, ed. I. Biezunska-Malowist and J. Kolendo (Paris) 217–25.

Badian, E. (1982), 'Figuring out Roman slavery', *JRS* 72: 164–9.

Bagnall, R. S. and B. W. Frier (1994), *The Demography of Roman Egypt* (Cambridge).

Baldwin, B. (1978), 'Trimalchio's domestic staff', *Acta Classica* 21: 87–97.

Balestri Fumagalli, M. (1985), *Lex Iunia de manumissionibus* (Milan).

Bandelli, G. (2002), 'I ceti medi nell'epigrafia repubblicana della Gallia Cisalpina', in *I ceti medi in Cisalpina. Atti del Colloquio internazionale 14–16 settembre 2000 Milano* ed. A. Sartori and A. Valvo (Milan) 13–26.

Bang, P. F. (2008), *The Roman Bazaar. A Comparative Study of Trade and Markets in a Tributary Empire* (Cambridge).

Barghop, D. (1994), *Forum der Angst. Eine historisch-anthropologische Studie zu Verhaltensmustern von Senatoren im römischen Kaiserreich* (Frankfurt a. M.).

Barrett, A. (2005), 'Vespasian's wife', *Latomus* 64: 385–96.

Barrow, R. H. (1928), *Slavery in the Roman Empire* (London).

Barsby, J. (2004), 'Actors and act-divisions in *Poenulus* and its Greek original', in *Studien zu Plautus'* Poenulus ed. T. Baier (Tübingen) 93–111.

Beard, M., J. North and S. Price (1998), *Religions of Rome*, 1: *A History* (Cambridge).

Beare, R. (1978), 'Were bailiffs ever free born?', *CQ* 28: 398–401.

Behrends, O. (1980), 'Prinzipat und Sklavenrecht. Zu den geistigen Grundlagen der augusteischen Verfassungsschöpfung', in *Rechtswissenschaft und Rechtsentwicklung* ed. U. Immenga (Göttingen) 53–88.

Benöhr, H.-P. (1998), 'Der Brief. Korrespondenz, menchlich und rechtlich gesehen', *ZSSR* 115: 115–49.

Bérard, F. (1999), 'Organisation municipale et hiérarchies sociales dans les provinces gauloises et alpines d'après la documentation épigraphique', in *XI Congresso internazionale di epigrafia Greca e Latina* 2.39–54.

Bergad, L. W., F. I. García, and M. del Carmen Barcia (1995), *The Cuban Slave Market 1790–1880* (Cambridge).

Bernstein, N. W. (2005), 'Mourning the *puer delicatus*: status inconsistency and the ethical value of fostering in Statius, Silvae 2.1', *AJPh* 126: 257–80.

Berry, D. H. (1996), *Cicero. Pro P. Sulla oratio* (Cambridge).

Bertini, M. G. Arrigoni (2004), *Parma romana. Contributo alla storia della città* (Parma).

Betzig, L. (1992), 'Roman polygyny', *Ethnology and Sociobiology* 13: 309–49.

Biezunska-Malowist, I. (1966), 'Les affranchis dans les papyrus de l'époque ptolémaique et romaine', in *Atti dell'XI Congresso internazionale di papirologia Milano 2–8 Settembre 1965* (Milan) 433–43.

   (1977), *L'esclavage dans l'Égypte gréco-romaine. Seconde partie: période romain* (Wroclaw).

Biundo, R. (2000), 'Struttura della classe dirigente a Pompei e mobilità sociale. I rapporti con il centro', in *Les élites municipales de l'Italie péninsulaire de la mort de César à la mort de Domitien entre continuité et rupture. Classes sociales dirigeantes et pouvoir central* ed. M. Cébeillac-Gervasoni (Rome) 33–69.

Blackburn, R. (1988), 'Defining slavery – its special features and social role', in *Slavery and Other Forms of Unfree Labour* ed. L. J. Archer (London and New York) 262–79.

Blänsdorf, J. (2001), 'Zum Thema der Sklaverei in Ciceros Briefen', in *Fünfzig Jahre Forschungen zur antiken Sklaverei an der mainzer Akademie 1950–2000. Miscellanea zum Jubiläum* ed. H. Bellen and H. Heinen (Stuttgart) 447–56.

Bleicken, J. (1995), *Die Verfassung der römischen Republik* (Paderborn) (1st edn 1975).

   (1998), *Augustus. Eine Biographie* (Berlin).

Bloomer, W. M. (2006), 'The technology of child production: eugenics and eulogics in the *De liberis educandis*', *Arethusa* 39: 71–99.

Bodel, J. (1999a), 'Death on display: looking at Roman funerals', in *The Art of Ancient Spectacle* ed. B. Bergmann and C. Kondoleon (New Haven) 259–81.

(1999b), 'The cena Trimalchionis', in *Latin Fiction. The Latin Novel in Context* ed. H. Hofmann (London and New York) 38–51.

(2005), '*Caveat emptor*. Towards a study of Roman slave-traders', *JRA* 18: 181–95.

Booth, A. D. (1979), 'The schooling of slaves in first-century Rome', *TAPhA* 109: 11–19.

Borg, B. (2000), 'Das Gesicht der Aufsteiger: römische Freigelassene und die Ideologie der Elite', in *Moribus antiquis res stat Romana. Römische Werte und römische Literatur im 3. und 2. Jhr. v. Chr.* ed. M. Braun, A. Haltenhoff, and F.-H. Mutschler (Munich and Leipzig) 285–99.

Bossu, C. (1982), 'M' Megonius Leo from Petelia (regio iii): a private benefactor from the local aristocracy', *ZPE* 45: 155–65.

Boulvert, G. (1970), *Esclaves et affranchis impériaux sous le Haut-Empire romain. Rôle politique et administratif* (Naples).

(1974), *Domestique et fonctionnaire sous le Haut-Empire romain. La condition de l'affranchi et de l'esclave du prince* (Paris).

Boulvert, G. and M. Morabito (1982), 'Le droit de l'esclavage sous le Haut-Empire', *ANRW* II 14: 98–182.

Bouvrie, S. des (1984), 'Augustus' legislation on morals. Which morals and what aims?', *Symbolae Osloenses* 59: 93–113.

Boyce, B. (1991), *The Language of the Freedmen in Petronius' Cena Trimalchionis* (Leiden).

Boyer, L. (1965), 'La fonction sociale des legs d'après la jurisprudence classique', *RHDFE* 43: 333–408.

Bradley, K. R. (1984a), *Slaves and Masters in the Roman Empire. A Study in Social Control* (Brussels; 2nd edn Oxford, 1987).

(1984b), 'The *vicesima libertatis*. Its history and significance', *Klio* 66: 175–82.

(1989), *Slavery and Rebellion in the Roman World, 140 B.C.–70 B.C.* (London).

(1990), '*Servus onerosus*: Roman law and the troublesome slave', *Slavery and Abolition* 11: 135–57.

(1992), '"The regular, daily traffic in slaves": Roman history and contemporary history', *CJ* 87: 125–38.

(1994), *Slavery and Society at Rome* (Cambridge).

(2008), 'Seneca and slavery', in *Seneca. Oxford Readings in Classical Studies* ed. J. G. Fitch (Oxford) 334–47.

Brana-Shute, R. (1989), 'Approaching freedom: the manumission of slaves in Suriname, 1760–1828', *Slavery and Abolition* 10: 40–63.

Brockmeyer, N. (1979), *Antike Sklaverei* (Darmstadt).

Brown, P. M. (1993), *Horace. Satires* 1 (Warminster).

Bruggisser, P. (2005), 'Hadrien et le sang des esclaves', in *Historiae Augustae. Colloquium Barcinonense. Atti dei Convegni sulla Historia Augusta IX* ed. G. Bonamente and M. Mayer (Bari) 67–82.

Brunt, P. A. (1961), 'The Lex Valeria Cornelia', *JRS* 51: 71–83.

(1966), 'The Roman mob', *P&P* 35: 3–27, reprinted in *Studies in Ancient Society* ed. M. I. Finley (London, 1974) 74–102.

(1971a), *Italian Manpower (225 B.C. – A.D. 14)* (Oxford).

(1971b), *Social Conflicts in the Roman Republic* (London).

(1975), 'Two great Roman landowners', *Latomus* 34: 619–35.

(1980), 'Evidence given under torture in the Principate', *ZSSR* 97: 256–65.

(1983a), 'Marcus Aurelius and slavery', in *Modus Operandi. Essays in Honour of Geoffrey Rickman* ed. M. Austin, J. Harries, and C. Smith (London) 139–50.

(1983b), 'Review of D'Arms (1981)', *Journal of Economic History* 43: 314–15.

(1988) *The Fall of the Roman Republic* (Oxford).

Bruun, C. (1989), 'The name and possessions of Nero's freedman Phaon', *Arctos* 23: 41–53.

(1990), 'Some comments on the status of imperial freedmen (The case of Ti. Claudius Aug. lib. Classicus)', *ZPE* 82: 271–85.

Buchi, E. (2002), 'Il sevirato nella società della *regio X*', in *I ceti medi in Cisalpina. Atti del Colloquio internazionale 14–16 settembre 2000 Milano* ed. A. Sartori and A. Valvo (Milan) 67–78.

Buckland, W. W. (1908), *The Roman Law of Slavery* (Cambridge).

Buonocore, M. (1984), *Schiavi e liberti dei Volusii Saturnini. Le iscrizioni del colombario sulla via Appia antica* (Rome).

(1995), 'Per uno studio sulla diffusione degli *Augustales nel mondo romano: l'esempio della *regio IV* Augustea', *ZPE* 108: 123–39.

Buonocore, M. and O. Diliberto (2006), 'Approfondimenti sull'album e la lex familiae Silvani da Trebula Mutuesca', *Minima Epigraphica et Papyrologica* 11: 210–54.

Bürge, A. (1987), 'Fiktion und Wirklichkeit: soziale und rechtliche Strukturen des römischen Bankwesens', *ZSSR* 104: 465–558.

(1988), 'Cum in familia nubas: Zur wirtschaftlichen und sozialen Bedeutung der familia libertorum', *ZSSR* 105: 312–33.

(1990), 'Der mercennarius und die Lohnarbeit', *ZSSR* 107: 80–136.

Burnand, T. (2001), 'Slave naming patterns: onomastics and the taxonomy of race in eighteenth-century Jamaica', *Journal of Interdisciplinary History* 31: 325–46.

Burton, G. (1977), 'Slaves, freedmen and monarchy', *JRS* 67: 162–6.

Caldelli, M. L. and C. Ricci (1999), *Monumentum familiae Statiliorum* (Rome).

Calderini, A. (1908), *La manomissione e la condizione dei liberti in Grecia* (Milan).

Calza, G. (1939), 'Epigrafe sepolcrale contenente dispozioni testamentarie', *Epigraphica* 1: 160–2.

Cambiano, G. (1987), 'Aristotle and the anonymous opponents of slavery', in *Classical Slavery* ed. M. I. Finley (London) 22–41.

Camodeca, G. (1993), 'Archivi privati e storia sociale delle città Campane: Puteoli ed Herculaneum', in *Prosopographie und Sozialgeschichte. Studien zur Methodik und Erkenntnismöglichkeit der kaiserzeitlichen Prosopographie* ed. W. Eck (Cologne) 339–50.

(1996a), 'La ricostruzione dell'élite municipale ercolanese degli anni 50–70: problemi di metodo e risultati preliminari', *Cahiers Glotz* 7: 167–78.

(1996b), 'L'élite municipale di Puteoli fra la tarda repubblica e Nerone', in *Les élites municipales de l'Italie péninsulaire des Gracques à Néron* ed. M. Cébeillac-Gervasoni (Naples and Rome) 91–110.

(1996c), 'Inscrizioni nuove o riedite da Puteoli, Cumae, Misenum: decretum Augustalium da Misenum', *AIONArchStAnt* 3: 161–8.

(1999a), *Tabulae Pompeianae Sulpiciorum. Edizione critica dell'archivio puteolano dei Sulpicii* (Rome).

(1999b), 'Un nuovo decreto decurionale puteolano con concessione di *superficies* agli Augustali e le entrate cittadine da *solarium*', in *Il capitolo delle entrate nelle finanze municipali in occidente ed in oriente. Actes de la Xe rencontre franco-italienne sur l'épigraphie du monde romain* (Coll. d'École Fr. Rome 256: Rome) 1–23.

(2000), 'La società ercolanese', in *Gli antichi ercolanesi. Antropologia, società, economia* ed. M. Pagano (Naples) 67–70.

(2001), 'Albi degli Augustales di Liternum della seconda metà del II secolo', *Annali di Archaeologia e Storia Antica* 8: 163–82.

(2002), 'Per una riedizione dell'archivio ercolanese di L. Venidius Ennychus', *Cron.Erc.* 32: 257–80.

(2003), 'Il credito negli archivi campani: il caso di Puteoli e di Herculaneum', in *Credito e moneta nel mondo romano* ed. E. Lo Cascio (Bari) 69–98.

(2006a), 'Cittadinanza romana, *Latini Iuniani* e *lex Aelia Sentia*: alcuni nuovi dati dalla riedizione delle *Tabulae Herculanenses*', in *Tradizione romanistica e costituzione* ed. L. Labruna (Naples) 887–904.

(2006b), 'La società ercolanese alla luce della riedizione delle *Tabulae Herculanenses*. L'élite municipale fra Claudio e Vespasiano. 1: un'oligarchia ritrovata', *Ostraka* 15: 9–29.

(2006c), 'Per una riedizione dell'archivio ercolanese di L. Venidius Ennychus II', *Cron.Erc.* 36: 189–211.

Canobbio, A. (2002), La *lex Roscia Theatralis* e Marziale: il ciclo del libro v (Como).

Cantarelli, F. (2002), 'Le qualifiche di *sexviri iuniores* e *sexviri seniores* nelle attestazioni epigrafiche della Cisalpina: una nuova interpretazione storico-epigrafica', in *I ceti medi in Cisalpina. Atti del Colloquio internazionale 14–16 Settembre 2000 Milano* ed. A. Sartori and A. Valvo (Milan) 99–111.

Carcopino, J. (1941), *Daily Life in Ancient Rome* (London).

Carlsen, J. (1995), *Vilici and Roman Estate Managers until AD 284* (Rome).

Carroll, M. (2006), *Spirits of the Dead. Roman Funerary Commemoration in Western Europe* (Cambridge).

Casson, L. (1998), *Everyday Life in Ancient Rome* 2nd edn (Baltimore and London).

Castrén, P. (1975), *Ordo Populusque Pompeianus. Polity and Society in Roman Pompeii* (Rome).

Cébeillac-Gervasoni, M. (2000), 'Les enseignements fournis par les archives des *Sulpicii* pour une meilleure connaissance de certaines couches de la société de Puteoli', *Cahiers Glotz* 11: 107–11.

Cels, D. (1972), 'Les esclaves dans les "Verrines"', in *Actes du Colloque 1971 sur l'esclavage* (Paris) 175–92.

Cels-Saint-Hilaire, J. (1985), 'Les libertini: des mots et des choses', *DHA* 11: 331–79.

(1999), 'Horace, *libertino patre natus*', in *Construction, reproduction et représentation des patriciats urbains de l'antiquité au XXe siècle* ed. C. Petitfrère (Tours) 23–46.

(2001), 'Citoyens romains, esclaves et affranchis: problèmes de démographie', *REA* 103: 443–79.

Chalhoub, S. (1989), 'Slaves, freedmen and the politics of freedom in Brazil: the experience of blacks in the city of Rio', *Slavery and Abolition* 10: 64–84.

Champlin, E. (1981), 'Owners and neighbours at Ligures Baebiani', *Chiron* 11: 239–64.

(1991), *Final Judgments. Duty and Emotion in Roman Wills, 200 B.C.–A.D. 250* (Berkeley).

(2005), 'Phaedrus the fabulous', *JRS* 95: 97–123.

Chantraine, H. (1967), *Freigelassene und Sklaven im Dienst der römischen Kaiser. Studien zu ihrer Nomenklatur* (Wiesbaden).

(1972), 'Zur Entstehung der Freilassung mit Bürgerrechtserwerb in Rom', *ANRW* 1.2: 59–67.

Cheesman, C. (2009), 'Names in –por and slave naming in republican Rome', *CQ* 59: 511–31.

Chelotti, M., V. Morizio, and M. Silvestrini (1985–90), *Le epigrafi romane di Canosa* i–ii (Bari).

Christ, K. (1980), 'Grundfragen der römischen Sozialstruktur', in *Studien zur antiken Sozialgeschichte. Festschrift Friedrich Vittinghoff* ed. W. Eck, H. Galsterer, and H. Wolff (Cologne) 197–228.

Christes, J. (1979a), *Sklaven und Freigelassene als Grammatiker und Philologen im antiken Rom* (Wiesbaden).

(1979b), 'Reflexe erlebter Unfreiheit in den Sentenzen des Publilius Syrus und den Fabeln des Phaedrus. Zur Problematik ihrer Verifizierung', *Hermes* 107: 199–220.

Christol, M. (1992), 'Les ambitions d'un affranchi à Nimes sous le Haut-Empire: l'argent et la famille', *Cahiers Glotz* 3: 241–58.

Ciancio Rossetto, P. (1973), *Il sepolchro del fornaio Marco Virgilio Eurisace a Porta Maggiore* (Rome).

Clarke, J. R. (1991), *The Houses of Roman Italy 100 B.C.–A.D. 250. Ritual, Space, and Decoration* (Berkeley).

(2003), *Art in the Lives of Ordinary Romans. Visual Representation and Non-elite Viewers in Italy, 100 B.C.–A.D. 315* (Berkeley).

Coale, A. J. and P. Demeny (1983), *Regional Model Life Tables and Stable Populations* 2nd edn (New York).

Cogrossi, C. (1979), 'Preoccupazioni etniche nelle leggi di Augusto sulla "manumissio servorum"?', in *Conoscenze etniche e rapporti di convivenza nell'antichità* ed. M. Sordi (Milan) 158–77.

Cohen, B. (1984), 'Some neglected ordines: the apparitorial status-group', in *Des ordres à Rome* ed. C. Nicolet (Paris) 23–60.

Cohen, D. (1991), 'The Augustan law on adultery: the social and cultural context', in *The Family in Italy from Antiquity to the Present* ed. D. I. Kertzer and R. P. Saller (New Haven and London) 109–26.

Cohen, E. E. (2000), *The Athenian Nation* (Princeton).

Cole, S. (2005), 'Capitalism and freedom: manumissions and the slave market in Louisiana, 1725–1820', *Journal of Economic History* 65: 1008–27.

Compostella, C. (1989), 'Iconografia, ideologia e status a Brixia nel I secolo D.C.: la lastra sepolcrale del seviro Anteros Asiaticus', *RdA* 13: 59–75.

Conte, G. B. (1996), *The Hidden Author. An Interpretation of Petronius' Satyricon* (Berkeley).

Corbier, M. (2006), 'Famiglia e integrazione sociale: percorsi dei liberti', in *Hiberia-Italia. Italia-Hiberia. Convegno internazionale di epigrafia e storia antica Gargnano-Brescia (28–30 aprile 2005)* ed. A. Sartori and A. Valvo (Milan) 339–51.

Coskun, A. (2009), *Bürgerrechtsentzug oder Fremdenausweisung? Studien zu den Rechten von Latinern und weiteren Fremden sowie zum Bürgerrechtswechsel in der Römischen Republik (5. bis frühes 1.Jh.v.Chr.)* (Stuttgart).

Crawford, J. W. (1994), *M. Tullius Cicero. The Fragmentary Speeches* 2nd edn (Atlanta).

Crawford, M. H. (1974), *Roman Republican Coinage* (Cambridge).

Criniti, N. (1991), *La tabula alimentaria di Veleia* (Parma).

Crook, J. A. (1967a), *Law and Life of Rome* (Ithaca).

(1967b), 'Gaius, *Institutes*, i. 84–86', *CR* 17: 7–8.

Crumley, J. J. (1906), *On the Social Standing of Freedmen as Indicated in the Latin Writers* (Baltimore).

Curtis, R. I. (1984), 'A personalized floor mosaic from Pompeii', *AJA* 88: 557–66.

(1988), 'A. Umbricius Scaurus of Pompeii', in *Studia Pompeiana et Classica in Honor of Wilhelmina F. Jashemski* (New Rochelle, NY) 19–49.

Daheim, J. and J. Blänsdorf (2003), 'Petron und die Inschriften', in *Petroniana. Gedenkschrift für Hubert Petersmann* ed. J. Herman and H. Rosén (Heidelberg) 95–107.

D'Ambra, E. (1995), 'Mourning and the making of ancestors in the Testamentum Relief', *AJA* 99: 667–81.

(2002), 'Acquiring an ancestor: the importance of funerary statuary among the non-elite orders of Rome', in *Images of Ancestors* ed. J. Munk Højte (Aarhus) 223–46.

D'Ambrosio, A. and S. De Caro (1983), *Un impegno per Pompei. Fotopiano e documentazione della necropoli di Porta Nocera* (Milan).

Damon, C. (2006), '*Potior utroque Vespasianus*: Vespasian and his predecessors in Tacitus' *Histories*', *Arethusa* 39: 245–79.

D'Arms, J. H. (1974), 'Puteoli in the second century of the Roman Empire: a social and economic study', *JRS* 64: 104–24.

(1975), 'Review of Weaver (1972)', *AJPh* 96: 335–9.

(1981), *Commerce and Social Standing in Ancient Rome* (Cambridge, MA).

(1984), 'Review of Fabre (1981)', *CPh* 79: 170–4.

(1990), 'Italien', in *Europäische Wirtschafts- und Sozialgeschichte in der römischen Kaiserzeit* ed. F. Vittinghoff (Stuttgart) 375–426.

(2000), 'Memory, money and status at Misenum: three new inscriptions from the *collegium* of the Augustales', *JRS* 90: 126–44.

Daube, D. (1946), 'Two early patterns of manumission', *JRS* 36: 57–75.

Davis, D. B. (1966), *The Problem of Slavery in Western Culture* (Ithaca).

De Franciscis, A. (1991), *Il sacello degli Augustali a Miseno* (Naples).

Della Corte, M. (1965), *Case ed abitanti di Pompei* 3rd edn (Naples).

Demaille, J. (2008), 'Les P. Anthestii: une famille d'affranchis dans l'élite munici-pale de la colonie romaine de Dion', in *La fin du statut servile? Affranchisse-ment, libération, abolition* ed. A. Gonzales (Besançon) 185–202.

Demougin, S. (1984), 'De l'esclavage à l'anneau d'or du chevalier', in *Des ordres à Rome* ed. C. Nicolet (Paris) 217–41.

(1988), *L'ordre équestre sous les Julio-Claudiens* (Coll. École Fr. Rome 108: Rome and Paris).

Dench, E. (2005), *Romulus' Asylum. Roman Identities from the Age of Alexander to the Age of Hadrian* (Oxford).

Deniaux, É. (1993), *Clientèles et pouvoir à l'époque de Cicéron* (Coll. École Fr. Rome 182: Rome and Paris).

Dixon, S. (1986), 'Family finances: Terentia and Tullia', in *The Family in Ancient Rome: New Perspectives* ed. B. Rawson (London) 93–120.

Drexhage, H.-J., H. Konen, and K. Ruffing (2002), 'Die Wirtschaft der römischen Kaiserzeit in der modernen Deutung: einige Überlegungen', in *Die Ökonomie des Imperium Romanum. Strukturen, Modelle und Wertungen im Spannungs-feld von Modernismus und Neoprimitivismus* ed. K. Strobel (St. Katharinen) 1–66.

Duff, A. M. (1928), *Freedmen in the Early Roman Empire* (Oxford).

Dumont, J. C. (1981), 'Le gentilice: nom de citoyen ou d'esclave?', *Ktema* 6: 105–14.

(1987), *Servus. Rome et l'esclavage sous la république* (Rome).

(1990), 'L'*imperium* du *pater familias*', in *Parenté et stratégies familiales dans l'antiquité romaine* ed. J. Andreau and H. Bruhns (Rome) 475–94.

Duncan-Jones, R. P. (1974), *The Economy of the Roman Empire. Quantitative Studies* (Cambridge; 2nd edn 1982).

(1984), 'Problems in the Delphic manumission payments 200–1 B.C.', *ZPE* 57: 203–9.

(2006), 'Who were the *Equites*?', in *Studies in Latin Literature and Roman History* XIII ed. C. Deroux (Coll. Latomus 301: Brussels) 183–223.

Dupont, F. (1977), *Le plaisir et la loi: du banquet de Platon au Satyricon* (Paris).

(1992), *Daily Life in Ancient Rome* (Oxford; 1st edn 1989).

Duthoy, R. (1976), 'Recherches sur la répartition géographique et chronologique des termes sevir Augustalis, Augustalis et sevir dans l'Empire romain', *Epigraphische Studien* 11: 143–214.

(1978), 'Les *Augustales*', *ANRW* ii. 16.2: 1254–1309.

(1988), 'Trimalchiopolis: cité campanienne?', *Euphrosyne* 16: 139–54.

(1989), '*Cognomen est omen?* Quelques jalons pour une anthroponymie sociale du monde romain', in *Mélanges P. Lévêque* ii (Paris) 183–205.

Ebersbach, V. (1995), 'Die "humanitas" des Petronius oder Diagnose eines gesellschaftlichen Verfalls', in *Prinzipat und Kultur im 1. und 2. Jahrhundert* ed. B. Kühnert, V. Riedel, and R. Gordesiani (Bonn) 192–202.

Eck, W. (1978), 'Zum neuen Fragment des sogenannten *Testamentum Dasumii*', *ZPE* 30: 277–95.

—— (1994), 'Die Bedeutung der claudischen Regierungszeit für die administrative Entwicklung des römischen Reiches', in *Die Regierungszeit des Kaisers Claudius (41–54 n.Chr.). Umbruch oder Episode?* ed. V. M. Strocka (Mainz) 23–34.

—— (1999), '*Ordo equitum romanorum, ordo libertorum.* Freigelassene und ihre Nachkommen im römischen Ritterstand', in *L'ordre équestre. Histoire d'une aristocratie (IIe siècle av. J.-C. – IIIe siècle ap. J.-C.)* ed. S. Demougin, H. Devijver, and M.-T. Raepsaet-Charlier (Rome) 5–29.

—— (2001), 'Die grosse Pliniusinschrift aus Comum: Funktion und Monument', in *Varia epigraphica. Atti del colloquio internazionale di epigrafia Bertinoro, 8–10 giugno 2000* ed. G. Angeli Bertinelli and A. Donati (Faenza) 225–35.

Eck, W. and J. Heinrichs (1993), *Sklaven und Freigelassene in der Gesellschaft der römischen Kaiserzeit* (Darmstadt).

Eckert, M. (1988), *Capuanische Grabsteine: Untersuchungen zu den Grabsteinen römischer Freigelassener aus Capua*, BAR int. ser. 417 (Oxford).

Edwards, C. (1993), *The Politics of Immorality in Ancient Rome* (Cambridge).

Evans-Grubbs, J. (1993), '"Marriage more shameful than adultery": slave–mistress relationships, "mixed marriages" and late Roman law', *Phoenix* 47: 125–54.

—— (1995), *Law and Family in Late Antiquity. The Emperor Constantine's Marriage Legislation* (Oxford).

Fabiani, F. (2002), 'L'augustalità nell'Etruria nord-occidentale: i casi di Luni, Lucca e Pisa', *Ostraka* 11: 99–112.

Fabre, G. (1976), 'Les affranchis et la vie municipale dans la péninsule ibérique sous le Haut-Empire romain: quelques remarques', in *Actes du colloque 1973 sur l'esclavage* (Paris) 417–57.

—— (1981), *Libertus. Recherches sur les rapports patron–affranchi à la fin de la république romaine* (Rome).

Faro, S. (1996), *La libertas ex divi Claudii edicto. Schiavitù e valori morali nel I secolo d.C.* (Catania).

Favory, F. (1981), 'L'intervention de l'esclave dans le discours polémique cicéronien: étude du corpus des "Philippiques"', *Index* 10: 82–172.

Fenoaltea, S. (1984), 'Slavery and supervision in comparative perspective: a model', *Journal of Economic History* 44: 635–68.

Ferenczy, E. (1982), 'Rechtshistorische Bemerkungen zur Ausdehnung des römischen Bürgerrechts und zum *ius Italicum* unter dem Prinzipat', *ANRW* ii.14: 1017–58.

(1988), 'Die Freigelassenen und ihre Nachkommen im öffentlichen Leben des republikanischen Rom', *Klio* 70: 468–76.

Fezzi, L. (1999), 'La legislazione tribunizia di Publio Clodio Pulcro (58 a.C.) e la ricerca del consenso a Roma', *SCO* 47: 245–341.

Findlay, R. (1975), 'Slavery, incentives and manumission: a theoretical model', *Journal of Political Economy* 83: 923–34.

Finley, M. I. (1998), *Ancient Slavery and Modern Ideology* (1st edn 1980) (Princeton).

Fisher, N. R. E. (1993), *Slavery in Classical Greece* (Bristol).

(2008), '"Independent" slaves in classical Athens and the ideology of slavery', in *From Captivity to Freedom. Themes in Ancient and Modern Slavery* ed. C. Katsari and E. Dal Lago (Leicester) 121–46.

Fitzgerald, W. (2000), *Slavery and the Roman Literary Imagination* (Cambridge).

Flohr, M. (2007), '*Nec quicquam ingenuum habere potest officina?* Spatial contexts of urban production at Pompeii, AD 79', *BABesch* 82: 129–48.

Flory, M. B. (1978), 'Family in *familia*: kinship and community in slavery', *AJAH* 3: 78–95.

Forand, P. G. (1971), 'The relation of the slave and the client to the master or patron in medieval Islam', *International Journal of Middle East Studies* 2: 59–66.

Frank, T. (1916), 'Race mixture in the Roman Empire', *American Historical Review* 21: 689–708.

(1927), *An Economic History of Rome* 2nd edn (London).

(1932), 'The sacred treasury and the rate of manumission', *AJPh* 53: 360–3.

(1933), *An Economic Survey of Ancient Rome* i (Baltimore).

(1940), *An Economic Survey of Ancient Rome* v (Baltimore).

Fraschetti, A. (1982), 'A proposito di ex-schiavi e della loro integrazione in ambito cittadino a Roma', *Opus* 1: 97–103.

(1990), *Roma e il principe* (Rome and Bari).

Frederiksen, M. (1984), *Campania* (London).

Frenz, H. G. (1985), *Römische Grabreliefs in Mittel- und Süditalien* (Rome).

Frier, B. W. (1979), 'Law, technology and social change: the equipping of Italian farm tenancies', *ZSSR* 96: 204–28.

(1980), *Landlords and Tenants in Imperial Rome* (Princeton).

(1993), 'Subsistence annuities and per capita income in the early Roman Empire', *CPh* 88: 222–30.

Fuks, G. (1985), 'Where have all the freedmen gone? On an anomaly in the Jewish grave-inscriptions from Rome', *Journal of Jewish Studies* 36: 25–32.

Fülle, G. (1997), 'The internal organization of the Arretine *terra sigillata* industry: problems of evidence and interpretation', *JRS* 87: 111–55.

Gager, J. G. (1992), *Curse Tablets and Binding Spells from the Ancient World* (Oxford).

Galinsky, G. K. (1981), 'Augustus' legislation on morals and marriage', *Philologus* 125: 126–44.

Gallivan, P. and P. Wilkins (1997), 'Familial structures in Roman Italy: a regional approach', in *The Roman Family in Italy. Status, Sentiment, Space* ed. B. Rawson and P. Weaver (Oxford) 239–79.

Galsterer, H. (1971), *Untersuchungen zum römischen Städtewesen auf der iberischen Halbinsel* (Berlin)

Gamauf, R. (2001), 'Zur Frage "Sklaverei und Humanität" anhand von Quellen des römischen Rechts', in *Fünfzig Jahre Forschungen zur antiken Sklaverei an der mainzer Akademie 1950–2000. Miscellanea zum Jubiläum* ed. H. Bellen and H. Heinen (Stuttgart) 51–72.

    (2007), 'Cum aliter nulla domus tuta esse possit . . . : fear of slaves and Roman law', in *Fear of Slaves – Fear of Enslavement in the Ancient Mediterranean* ed. A. Serghidou (Besançon) 145–64.

Gara, A. (1991), 'La mobilità sociale nell'Impero', *Athenaeum* 79: 335–58.

Gardner, J. F. (1986), *Women in Roman Law and Society* (London).

    (1989), 'The adoption of Roman freedmen', *Phoenix* 43: 236–57.

    (1991), 'The purpose of the *Lex Fufia Caninia*', *EMC/Classical Views* 35: 21–39.

    (1993), *Being a Roman Citizen* (London and New York).

    (1998), *Family and Familia in Roman Law and Life* (Oxford).

    (2001), 'Making citizens: the operation of the *Lex Irnitana*', in *Administration, Prosopography and Appointment Policies in the Roman Empire* ed. L. de Blois (Amsterdam) 215–29.

Garlan, Y. (1988), *Slavery in Ancient Greece* (Ithaca and London), 1st edn (1982).

Garland, A. (1992), 'Cicero's *familia urbana*', *G & R* 39: 163–72.

Garnsey, P. (1970), *Social Status and Legal Privilege in the Roman Empire* (Oxford).

    (1975a), 'Descendants of freedmen in local politics: some criteria', in *The Ancient Historian and his Materials. Essays in Honour of C. E. Stevens* ed. B. Levick (Farnborough) 167–80.

    (1975b), 'Economy and society of Mediolanum under the Principate', *PBSR* 44: 13–27.

    (1976), 'Urban property investment', in *Studies in Roman Property* ed. M. I. Finley (Cambridge) 123–36.

    (1981), 'Independent freedmen and the economy of Roman Italy under the Principate', *Klio* 63: 359–71.

    (1988), *Famine and Food Supply in the Graeco-Roman World* (Cambridge).

    (1996), *Ideas of Slavery from Aristotle to Augustine* (Cambridge).

Gascou, J. (1984), 'La carrière de Marcus Caelius Phileros', *Ant.Afr.* 20: 105–20.

Gauthier, P. (1974), '"Générosité" romaine et "avarice" greque: sur l'octroi du droit de cité', in *Mélanges W. Seston* (Paris) 207–16.

    (1981), 'La citoyenneté en Grèce et à Rome: participation et intégration', *Ktema* 6: 167–79.

George, M. (2002), 'Slave disguise in ancient Rome', *Slavery and Abolition* 23: 41–54.

    (2005), 'Family imagery and family values in Roman Italy', in *The Roman Family in the Empire. Rome, Italy and Beyond* ed. M. George (Oxford) 37–66.

    (2006), 'Social identity and the dignity of work in freedmen's reliefs', in *The Art of Citizens, Soldiers and Freedmen in the Roman World* ed. E. D'Ambra and G. P. R. Métraux (BAR int. ser. 1526: Oxford) 19–29.

Giménez-Candela, T. (1996), 'Bemerkungen über Freilassungen in consilio', *ZSSR* 113: 64–87.

Giordano, C. and A. Casale (1991), 'Iscrizioni pompeiane inedite scoperte tra gli anni 1954–1978', *Atti Acc. Pont.* 39: 273–8.

Giuliani, C. F. (1970), *Tibur*, vol. 1: *Forma Italiae reg. 1. no. 7* (Rome).

Glancy, J. A. (2002), *Slavery in Early Christianity* (Cambridge).

Goette, H. R. (1986), 'Die Bulla', *BJ* 186: 133–64.

Golden, M. (1985), 'Pais, "child" and "slave"', *AC* 54: 91–104.

González, J. and M. H. Crawford (1986), 'The lex Irnitana: a new copy of the Flavian municipal law', *JRS* 76: 147–243.

Goodman, M. (1997), *The Roman World 44 BC–AD 180* (London and New York).

Gordon, M. L. (1927), 'The *ordo* of Pompeii', *JRS* 17: 165–83.
   (1931), 'The freedman's son in municipal life', *JRS* 21: 65–77.

Gordon, W. M. and O. F. Robinson (1988), *The Institutes of Gaius* (Ithaca and London).

Gowing, A. M. (1992), *The Triumviral Narratives of Appian and Cassius Dio* (Ann Arbor).

Gradel, I. (2002), *Emperor Worship and Roman Religion* (Oxford).

Grassl, H. (1981), *Sozialökonomische Vorstellungen in der kaiserzeitlichen griechischen Literatur (1.–3. Jh. n. Chr.)* (Wiesbaden).

Gregory, A. P. (1995), 'A study in survival. The case of the freedman L. Domitius Phaon', *Athenaeum* 83: 401–10.

Griffin, M. (1976), *Seneca. A Philosopher in Politics* (Oxford).

Guadagno, G. (1977), 'Frammenti inediti di albi degli Augustali', *Cron.Erc.* 7: 114–23.

Guidetti, F. (2006), 'Note sull'iconografia di un rilievo funerario da *Amiternum*: modelli e scelte figurative di un liberto municipale', *Archeologia Classica* 57: 387–403.
   (2007), 'La tomba di Trimalchione. Saggio di commento archeologico al *Satyricon*', in *Lo sguardo archeologico. I normalisti per Paul Zanker* ed. F. De Angelis (Pisa) 77–95.

Gummerus, H. (1916), 'Industrie und Handel', *RE* 9: 1381–1535.

Günther, S. (2008), *'Vectigalia nervos esse rei publicae'. Die indirekten Steuern in der Römischen Kaiserzeit von Augustus bis Diokletian* (Wiesbaden).

Gutsfeld, A. (1992), 'Zur Wirtschaftsmentalität nichtsenatorischer provinzialer Oberschichten: Aemilia Pudentilla und ihre Verwandten', *Klio* 74: 250–68.

Haley, E. W. (1986), 'Suetonius *Claudius* 24,1 and the sons of freedmen', *Historia* 35: 115–21.

Handler, J. S. and J. Jacoby (1996), 'Slave names and naming in Barbados 1650–1830', *William and Mary Quarterly* 53: 685–728.

Handler, J. S. and J. T. Pohlmann (1984), 'Slave manumissions and freedmen in seventeenth-century Barbados', *William and Mary Quarterly* 41: 390–408.

Hardie, A. (1983), *Statius and the Silvae. Poets, Patrons and Epideixis in the Graeco-Roman World* (Liverpool).

Harper, J. (1972), 'Slaves and freedmen in Imperial Rome', *AJPh* 93: 341–2.

Harrill, J. A. (1995), *The Manumission of Slaves in Early Christianity* (Tübingen).
Harris, W. V. (1979), *War and Imperialism in Republican Rome 327–70 B.C.* (Oxford).
(1980a), 'Roman terracotta lamps: the organisation of an industry', *JRS* 70: 126–45.
(1980b), 'Towards a study of the Roman slave trade', in *The Seaborne Commerce of Ancient Rome. Studies in Archaeology and History* ed. J. H. D'Arms and E. C. Kopff (MAAR 36: Rome) 117–40.
(1986), 'The Roman father's power of life and death', in *Studies in Roman Law in Memory of A. Arthur Schiller* ed. R. S. Bagnall and W. V. Harris (Leiden) 81–95.
(1989), *Ancient Literacy* (Cambridge, MA).
(1999), 'Demography, geography and the sources of Roman slaves', *JRS* 89: 62–75.
(2000), 'Trade', in *CAH* xi 2nd edn ed. A. K. Bowman, P. Garnsey, and D. Rathbone (Cambridge) 710–40.
(2007), 'The late republic', in *Cambridge Economic History of the Greco-Roman World* ed. W. Scheidel, I. Morris, and R. Saller (Cambridge) 511–39.
Harrison, E. L. (1965), 'Horace's tribute to his father', *CPh* 60: 111–14.
Harrison, S. (2005), 'The novel', in *A Companion to Latin Literature* ed. S. Harrison (Oxford) 213–22.
Hasegawa, K. (2005), *The Familia Urbana during the Early Empire. A Study of Columbaria Inscriptions* (BAR int. ser. 1440: Oxford).
Hasenohr, C. (2002), 'Les collèges de magistri et la communauté italienne de Délos', in *Les Italiens dans le monde grec* ed. C. Müller and C. Hasenohr (BCH Suppl. 41: Paris) 67–76.
Heinzelmann, M. (2000), *Die Nekropolen von Ostia: Untersuchungen zu den Gräberstrassen vor der Porta Romana und an der Via Laurentina* (Munich).
Hekster, O. (2002), *Commodus. An Emperor at the Crossroads* (Amsterdam).
Helen, T. (1975), *Organization of Roman Brick Production in the First and Second Centuries A.D.* (Helsinki).
Hellegouarc'h, J. (1963), *Le vocabulaire latin des relations et des partis politiques sous la république* (Paris).
Herrmann-Otto, E. (1997), *Ex Ancilla Natus. Untersuchungen zu den 'Hausgeborenen' Sklaven und Sklavinnen im Westen des römischen Kaiserreiches* (Stuttgart).
(2001), 'Soziale Mobilität in der römischen Gesellschaft: Persönliche Freiheit im Spiegel von Statusprozessen', in *Fünfzig Jahre Forschungen zur antiken Sklaverei an der mainzer Akademie 1950–2000. Miscellanea zum Jubiläum* ed. H. Bellen and H. Heinen (Stuttgart) 171–83.
(2005), 'Die Bedeutung der antiken Sklaverei für die Menschenrechte', in *Unfreie Arbeits- und Lebensverhältnisse von der Antike bis in die Gegenwart* ed. E. Herrmann-Otto (Hildesheim) 56–81.
Herschbell, J. P. (1995), 'Epictetus: a freedman on slavery', *Anc. Soc.* 26: 185–204.
Herz, P. (1989), 'Claudius Abascantus aus Ostia. Die Nomenklatur eines libertus und sein sozialer Aufstieg', *ZPE* 76: 167–74.

Hesberg, H. von (2005), 'Die Häuser der Senatores in Rom: gesellschaftliche und politische Funktion', in *Senatores populi romani. Realität und mediale Präsentation einer Führungsschicht* ed. W. Eck and M. Heil (Stuttgart) 19–52.

Heurgon, J. (1939), 'Les magistri des collèges et le relèvement de Capoue de III a 71 avant J.-C.', *MEFRA* 56: 5–27.

Hezser, C. (2005), *Jewish Slavery in Antiquity* (Oxford).

Higgins, K. J. (1997), 'Gender and manumission of slaves in colonial Brazil: the prospect of freedom in Sabará, Minas Gerais, 1710–1809', *Slavery and Abolition* 18.2: 1–29.

Highet, G. (1973), 'Libertino patre natus', *AJPh* 94: 268–81.

Holliday, P. J. (2005), 'The rhetoric of *romanitas*: the "tomb of the Statilii" frescoes reconsidered', *MAAR* 50: 89–129.

Hopkins, K. (1965), 'Élite mobility in the Roman Empire', *P & P* 32: 12–26. Reprinted in *Studies in Ancient Society* ed. M. I. Finley (London, 1974) 103–20.

(1978), *Conquerors and Slaves* (Cambridge).

(1983), *Death and Renewal* (Cambridge).

(1987), 'Graveyards for historians', in *La Mort, les morts, et l'au-delà dans le monde romain* ed. F. Hinard (Caen) 113–26.

(1993), 'Novel evidence for Roman slavery', *P & P* 138: 3–27.

Horsley, R. A. (1998), 'The slave systems of classical antiquity and their reluctant recognition by modern scholars', in *Slavery in Text and Interpretation* ed. A. D. Callahan, R. A. Horsley, and A. Smith (Semeia 83/84: Atlanta) 19–66.

Horsmann, G. (1986), 'Die divi fratres und die redemptio servi suis nummis (Zu den Motiven der epistula ad Urbium Maximum, Dig. 40,1,4)', *Historia* 35: 308–21.

Hünefeldt, C. (1995), *Paying the Price of Freedom. Family and Labor among Lima's Slaves 1800–1854* (Berkeley).

Humbert, M. (1976), 'Libertas id est civitas: autour d'un conflit négatif de citoyennetés au IIe siècle avant J.-C.', *MEFRA* 88: 221–42.

Humm, M. (2005), *Appius Claudius Caecus. La république accomplie* (Rome).

Huskinson, J. (2007), 'Constructing childhood on Roman funerary memorials', in *Constructions of Childhood in Ancient Greece and Italy* ed. A. Cohen and J. B. Rutter (Hesperia Supplement 41: Princeton) 323–38.

Huttunen, P. (1974), *The Social Strata in the Imperial City of Rome* (Oulu).

Isaac, B. (2004), *The Invention of Racism in Classical Antiquity* (Princeton).

Jacota, M. (1966), 'Les pactes de l'esclave en son nom propre', *RIDA* 13: 205–30.

Jacques, F. (1984), *Le privilège de liberté. Politique impériale et autonomie municipale dans les cités de l'Occident romain (161–244)* (Coll. École Fr. Rome 76: Rome).

Jehne, M. (1987), *Der Staat des Dictators Caesar* (Cologne).

Jens, W. (1956), 'Libertas bei Tacitus', *Hermes* 84: 331–52.

Johnson, J. (1933), *Excavations at Minturnae* II *Inscriptions* (Philadelphia).

Johnson, L. L. (1979), 'Manumission in colonial Buenos Aires, 1776–1810', *Hispanic American Historical Review* 59: 258–79.

Johnston, D. (1985), 'Prohibitions and perpetuities: family settlements in Roman law', *ZSSR* 102: 220–90.

(1988), *The Roman Law of Trusts* (Oxford).

(1998), 'Law and commercial life of Rome', *PCPhS* 43: 53–65.

(1999), *Roman Law in Context* (Cambridge).

Jones, A. H. M. (1956), 'Slavery in the ancient world', *Economic History Review* 9: 185–99.

(1970), *Augustus* (London).

Jones, B. W. (1992), *The Emperor Domitian* (London and New York).

Jones, C. P. (1987), 'Stigma: tattooing and branding in Graeco-Roman antiquity', *JRS* 77: 139–55.

Jones, D. (2006), *The Bankers of Puteoli. Finance, Trade and Industry in the Roman World* (Stroud).

Jongman, W. (1988), *The Economy and Society of Pompeii* (Amsterdam).

(2003a), 'A golden age. Death, money supply and social succession in the Roman empire', in *Credito e moneta nel mondo romano* ed. E. Lo Cascio (Bari) 181–96.

(2003b), 'Slavery and the growth of Rome. The transformation of Italy in the second and first centuries BCE', in *Rome the Cosmopolis* ed. C. Edwards and G. Woolf (Cambridge) 100–22.

(2007), 'The early Roman empire: consumption', in *The Cambridge Economic History of the Greco-Roman World* ed. W. Scheidel, I. Morris, and R. P. Saller (Cambridge) 592–618.

Joshel, S. R. (1992), *Work, Identity and Legal Status at Rome. A Study of the Occupational Inscriptions* (Norman).

Kajanto, I. (1965), *The Latin Cognomina* (Helsinki).

Kamen, D. (2005) 'Review of Zelnick-Abramovitz (2005)', *BMCR* 2005.11.21.

(2009), 'Servile invective in classical Athens', *SCI* 28: 43–56.

Karasch, M. C. (1987), *Slave Life in Rio de Janeiro, 1808–1850* (Princeton).

Kaser, M. (1938), 'Die Geschichte der Patronatsgewalt über Freigelassene', *ZSSR* 58: 88–135.

(1941), 'Die Anfänge der manumissio und des fiduziarisch gebundenen Eigentum', *ZSSR* 61: 153–86.

(1971), *Das römische Privatrecht* I (Munich).

Keenan, J. G. (1994), 'The will of Gaius Longinus Castor', *BASP* 31: 101–7.

Kehoe, D. P. (2007), 'The early Roman empire: production', in *The Cambridge Economic History of the Greco-Roman World* ed. W. Scheidel, I. Morris, and R. Saller (Cambridge) 543–69.

Kennell, N. M. (1997), 'Herodes Atticus and the rhetoric of tyranny', *CPh* 92: 346–62.

Kenrick, P. (2000), *Corpus Vasorum Arretinorum* 2nd edn (Bonn).

Kirbihler, F. (2007), 'P. Vedius Rufus, père de P. Vedius Pollio', *ZPE* 160: 261–71.

Kirschenbaum, A. (1987), *Sons, Slaves and Freedmen in Roman Commerce* (Jerusalem and Washington).

Klees, H. (1998), *Sklavenleben im klassischen Griechenland* (Stuttgart).

(2002), 'Die römische Einbürgerung der Freigelassenen und ihre naturrechtliche Begründung bei Dionysios von Halikarnassos', *Laverna* 13: 91–117.

Kleijwegt, M. (2002), 'Cum vicensimariis magnam mantissam habet (Petronius *Satyricon* 65.10)', *AJPh* 123: 275–86.

Klein, H. S. and C. A. Paiva (1996), 'Freedmen in a slave economy: Minas Gerais in 1831', *Journal of Social History* 29: 933–62.

Klein, H. S. and F. Vidal Luna (2000), 'Free coloured in a slave society: São Paulo and Minas Gerais in the early nineteenth century', *Hispanic American Historical Review* 80: 913–41.

Kleiner, D. E. E. (1977), *Roman Group Portraiture. The Funerary Reliefs of the Late Republic and Early Empire* (New York).

Kloft, H. (1994), 'Trimalchio als Ökonom. Bemerkungen zur Rolle der Wirtschaft in Petrons Satyricon', in *E fontibus haurire. Beiträge zur römischen Geschichte und zu ihren Hilfswissenschaften* ed. R. Günther and S. Rebenich (Paderborn) 117–31.

Kneissl, P. (1980) 'Entstehung und Bedeutung der Augustalität. Zur Inschrift der ara Narbonensis (CIL XII 4333)', *Chiron* 10: 291–326.

Knoch, S. (2005), *Sklavenfürsorge im römischen Reich. Formen und Motive* (Hildesheim).

Kockel, V. (1983), *Die Grabbauten vor dem Herkulaner Tor in Pompeji* (Mainz).

(1993), *Porträtreliefs stadtrömischer Grabbauten. Ein Beitrag zur Geschichte und zum Verständnis des spätrepublikanisch-frühkaiserzeitlichen Privatporträts* (Mainz).

Koestermann, E. (1963–68), *Cornelius Tacitus. Annalen* I–IV (Heidelberg).

Kolb, F. (1995), *Rom. Die Geschichte der Stadt in der Antike* (Munich).

Kolendo, J. (1985), 'Eléments courants et exceptionnels de la carrière d'un affranchi: le grammairien Q. Remmius Palémon', *Index* 13: 177–87.

(1989), 'Les réalités romaines dans la "Germanie" de Tacite: le cas des esclaves et des affranchis', *Index* 17: 231–9.

Koortbojian, M. (2002), 'A painted exemplum at Rome's Temple of Liberty', *JRS* 92: 33–48.

Kudlien, F. (1991), *Sklaven-Mentalität im Spiegel antiker Wahrsagerei* (Stuttgart).

Kunkel, W. (1966), 'Das Konsilium im Hausgericht', *ZSSR* 83: 219–51.

Kunst, C. (1999), 'Identität und Unsterblichkeit: Zur Bedeutung des römischen Personennamens', *Klio* 81: 156–79.

Laird, M. L. (2002), '*Evidence in context. The public and funerary monuments of the Seviri Augustales at Ostia*' (Diss. Princeton).

(2006), 'Private memory and public interest: municipal identity in imperial Italy', in *The Art of Citizens, Soldiers and Freedmen in the Roman World* ed. E. D'Ambra and G. P. R. Métraux (BAR int. ser. 1526: Oxford) 31–43.

Langhammer, W. (1973), *Die rechtliche und soziale Stellung der* Magistratus Municipales *und der* Decuriones *in der Übergangsphase der Städte von sich selbstverwaltenden Gemeinden zu Vollzugsorganen des spätantiken Zwangsstaates (2.–4. Jahrhundert der römischen Kaiserzeit* (Wiesbaden).

Last, H. (1934), 'The social policy of Augustus', *CAH* vol. X ed. S. A. Cook, F. E. Adcock and M. P. Charlesworth (Cambridge) 424–64.

Leach, E. W. (2006), 'Freedmen and immortality in the tomb of the Haterii', in *The Art of Citizens, Soldiers and Freedmen in the Roman World* ed. E. D'Ambra and G. P. R. Métraux (BAR int. ser. 1526: Oxford) 1–17.

Le Glay, M. (1990), 'La place des affranchis dans la vie municipale et dans la vie religieuse', *MEFRA* 102: 621–38.

Lehmann, H. (1980), 'Ein Gesetzentwurf des P. Clodius zur Rechtsstellung der Freigelassenen', *BIDR* 83: 254–61.

Leigh, M. (2004), *Comedy and the Rise of Rome* (Oxford).

Lejay, P. (1911), *Œuvres d'Horace* (Paris).

Lepore, E. (1950), 'Orientamenti per la storia sociale di Pompei', in *Pompeiana. Raccolta di studi per il secondo centenario degli scavi di Pompei*, (Naples) 144–66.

Leppin, H. (1996), 'Totum te Caesari debes: Selbstdarstellung und Mentalität einflussreicher kaiserlicher Freigelassener im frühen Principat', *Laverna* 7: 67–91.

Levick, B. (1976), *Tiberius the Politician* (London and New York).
　(1990), *Claudius* (London).
　(1999), *Vespasian* (London and New York).

Lewis, F. D. (2004), 'The transition from slavery to freedom through manumission: a life-cycle approach applied to the United States and Guadeloupe', in *Slavery in the Development of the Americas* ed. D. Eltis, F. D. Lewis, and K. L. Sokoloff (Cambridge).

Lewis, N. (1991), 'Hadriani sententiae', *GRBS* 32: 267–80.

Libby, D. C. and C. A. Paiva (2000), 'Manumission practices in a late eighteenth-century Brazilian slave parish: Sao José d'El Rey in 1795', *Slavery and Abolition* 21: 96–127.

Ligt, L. de (1999), 'Legal history and economic history: the case of the *actiones adiecticiae qualitatis*', *Tijdschrift voor Rechtsgeschiedenis* 67: 205–26.
　(2002), 'Restraining the rich, protecting the poor: symbolic aspects of Roman legislation', in *After the Past. Essays in Ancient History in Honour of H. W. Pleket* ed. W. Jongman and M. Kleijwegt (Leiden) 1–45.
　(2004), 'Poverty and demography: the case of the Gracchan land reforms', *Mnemosyne* 57: 725–57.
　(2007), 'Roman law and the Roman economy: three case studies', *Latomus* 66: 10–25.

Lindsay, H. (2009), *Adoption in the Roman World* (Cambridge).

Ling, R. (1996), *The Insula of the Menander at Pompeii* 1: *The Structures* (Oxford).

Linke, B. (2005), 'Bürger ohne Staat? Die Integration der Landbevölkerung in der römischen Republik', in *Nicht-normative Steuerung in dezentralen Systemen* ed. J. Oebbecke (Stuttgart) 121–50.

Lintott, A. W. (2002), 'Freedmen and slaves in the light of legal documents from first-century A.D. Campania', *CQ* 52: 555–65.

Lo Cascio, E. (1994), 'The size of the Roman population: Beloch and the meaning of the Augustan census figures', *JRS* 84: 23–40.

———— (1997), 'Le procedure di recensus dalla tarda repubblica al tardo antico e il calcolo della popolazione di Roma', in *La Rome impériale. Démographie et logistique* (Rome) 3–76.

———— (2002), 'Considerazioni sul numero e sulle fonti di approvvigionamento degli schiavi in età imperiale', *Antiquitas* 26: 51–65.

Lo Monaco, A. (1998), 'L'*ordo libertinus*, la tomba, l'immagine: una nota sulla nascita del busto ritratto', *Bullettino Comunale* 99: 85–100.

López Barja de Quiroga, P. (1995), 'Freedmen social mobility in Roman Italy', *Historia* 44: 326–48.

———— (1998), 'Junian Latins: status and number', *Athenaeum* 86: 133–63.

Loposzko, T. (1978–79), 'Gesetzentwürfe betreffs der Sklaven im Jahre 53 v.u.Z.', *Index* 8: 154–66.

Los, A. (1992a), 'Les intérêts des affranchis dans l'agriculture italienne', *MEFRA* 104: 709–53.

———— (1992b), '*Quibus patet curia municipalis.* Remarques sur la structure de la classe dirigeante de Pompéi', *Cahiers Glotz* 3: 259–97.

———— (1995), 'La condition sociale des affranchis privés au Iᵉʳ siècle aprés J.-C.', *Annales HSS* 50: 1011–43.

———— (2000), 'Les affaires "industrielles" des élites campaniennes sous les Julio-Claudiens et les Flaviens', *MEFRA* 112: 243–77.

———— (2001), 'Les affaires commerciales des notables municipaux en Campanie sous les Julio-Claudiens et Flaviens', *Antiquitas* 25: 77–102.

Lotmar, P. (1912), 'Marc Aurels Erlass über die Freilassungsauflage', *ZSSR* 33: 304–82.

Lott, J. B. (2004), *The Neighborhoods of Augustan Rome* (Cambridge).

Luisi, A. (1975), 'Il liberto Marco Celio Filerote, magistro municipale', *Atene e Roma* 20: 44–56.

McCarthy, K. (2000), *Slaves, Masters, and the Art of Authority in Plautine Comedy* (Princeton).

McDermott, W. C. (1972), 'M. Cicero and M. Tiro', *Historia* 21: 259–86.

McDonnell, M. (2006), *Roman Manliness. Virtus and the Roman Republic* (Cambridge).

McGinn, T. A. J. (1991), 'Concubinage and the Lex Iulia on adultery', *TAPhA* 121: 335–75.

———— (2002), 'The Augustan marriage legislation and social practice: elite endogamy versus male "marrying down"', in *Speculum Iuris. Roman Law as a Reflection of Social and Economic Life in Antiquity*, ed. J.-J. Aubert and B. Sirks (Ann Arbor) 46–93.

———— (2004), 'Missing females? Augustus' encouragement of marriage between freeborn males and freedwomen', *Historia* 53: 200–8.

McKeown, N. (2007), *The Invention of Ancient Slavery?* (London).

MacMullen, R. (1974), *Roman Social Relations 50 B.C. to A.D. 284* (New Haven).

———— (1982), 'The epigraphic habit of the Roman Empire', *AJPh* 103: 233–46.

(1987), 'Late Roman slavery', *Historia* 36: 359–82.

McWilliam, J. (2001), 'Children among the dead. The influence of urban life on the commemoration of children on tombstone inscriptions', in *Childhood, Class and Kin in the Roman World* ed. S. Dixon (London and New York) 74–98.

Madden, J. (1996), 'Slavery in the Roman Empire: numbers and origins', *Classics Ireland* 3: 109–28.

Maiuri, A. (1942), *L'ultima fase edilizia di Pompei* (Rome).

(1945), *La cena di Trimalchione di Petronio Arbitro* (Naples).

Major, A. (1994), 'Claudius' edict on sick slaves', *Scholia* 3: 84–90.

Malitz, J. (1975), *Ambitio mala. Studien zur politischen Biographie des Sallust* (Bonn).

Manning, C. E. (1986), '"Actio ingrati" (Seneca, De Benef. 3, 6–17: a contribution to contemporary debate?)', *SDHI* 52: 61–72.

(1989), 'Stoicism and slavery in the Roman Empire', *ANRW* II.36.3: 1518–43.

Marmon, S. E. (1999), 'Domestic slavery in the Mamluk empire: a preliminary sketch', in *Slavery in the Islamic Middle East* ed. S. E. Marmon (Princeton) 1–23.

Martino, F. de (1954–72), *Storia della costituzione romana* I–VI (Naples).

Masi Doria, C. (1989), 'Die Societas Rutiliana und die Ursprünge der prätorischen Erbfolge der Freigelassenen', *ZSSR* 106: 358–403.

(1993a), *Civitas Operae Obsequium. Tre studi sulla condizione giuridica dei liberti* (Naples).

(1993b), 'Inpudicitia, officium e operae libertorum', *ZSSR* 110: 77–102.

(1993c), 'Zum Bürgerrecht der Freigelassenen', in *Ars boni et aequi. Festschrift für Wolfgang Waldstein zum 65. Geburtstag* ed. M. J. Schermaier and Z. Végh (Stuttgart) 231–60.

(1996), *Bona libertorum. Regimi giuridici e realtà sociali* (Naples).

Maurach, G. (1988), *Der Poenulus des Plautus* (Heidelberg).

(2001), *Horaz. Werk und Leben* (Heidelberg).

Maurin, J. (1975), 'Remarques sur la notion de "puer" à l'époque classique', *Bulletin de l'Association Guillaume Budé* 14: 221–30.

Mazzarino, S. (1973), *L'Impero romano* (Bari).

Mehl, A. (1974), *Tacitus über Kaiser Claudius. Die Ereignisse am Hof.* (Munich).

Meier, C. (1997), 'Der griechische und der römische Bürger. Gemeinsamkeiten und Unterschiede im Ensemble gesellschaftlicher Bedingungen', in *Griechenland und Rom. Vergleichende Untersuchungen zu Entwicklungstendenzen und -höhepunkten der antiken Geschichte, Kunst und Literatur* ed. E. G. Schmidt (Erlangen and Jena) 41–66.

Meiggs, R. (1973), *Roman Ostia* 2nd edn (Oxford).

Meissel, F.-S. (2004), *Societas. Struktur und Typenvielfalt des römischen Gesellschaftsvertrages* (Frankfurt a. M.).

Merola, F. R. (1990), *Servo Parere* (Camerino).

Messeri Savorelli, G. (1978), 'Note sugli atti di affrancamento di tipo Greco nei papyri (in appendice PSI Inv. 1433)', *Riv.Ital.Fil.Class.* 50: 270–84.

Mette-Dittmann, A. (1991), *Die Ehegesetze des Augustus. Eine Untersuchung im Rahmen der Gesellschaftspolitik des Princeps* (Historia Einzelschriften 67: Stuttgart).

Meyer, E. (1913), *Der Emporkömmling. Ein Beitrag zur antiken Ethologie* (Diss. Giessen).

Meyer, E. (1924), 'Die Sklaverei im Altertum', in *Kleine Schriften* I, 2nd edn (Halle) 169–212.

Meyer, E. (1961), *Römischer Staat und Staatsgedanke* 2nd ed. (Zurich).

Milailescu-Birliba, L. (2006), *Les affranchis dans les provinces romaines de l'Illyricum* (Wiesbaden).

Millar, F. G. B. (1965), 'Epictetus and the imperial court', *JRS* 55: 141–8.

(1977), *The Emperor in the Roman World (31 BC – AD 337)* (London).

(1984), 'Condemnation to hard labour in the Roman Empire, from the Julio-Claudians to Constantine', *PBSR* 52: 124–47.

Möller, C. (1993), 'Die mercennarii in der römischen Arbeitswelt', *ZSSR* 110: 296–330.

Mols, S. and E. M. Moormann (1993–94), '*Ex parvo crevit*. Proposta per una lettura iconografica della Tomba di Vestorius Priscus fuori Porta Vesuvio a Pompei', *Rivista di Studi Pompeiani* 6: 15–52.

Mommsen, T. (1875) *Römische Geschichte* I–III (Leipzig) (1st edn 1854–6).

(1887), *Römisches Staatsrecht* (Leipzig).

Morabito, M. (1981), *Les réalités de l'esclavage d'après le Digeste* (Paris).

(1985), 'Les esclaves privilégiés à travers le Digeste témoins et acteurs d'une société en crise', *Index* 13: 477–90.

Morel, J.-P. (1996), 'Élites municipales et manufacture en Italie', in *Les élites municipales de l'Italie péninsulaire des Gracques à Néron* ed. M. Cébeillac-Gervasoni (Naples and Rome) 181–98.

Morley, N. (2006), 'The poor in the city of Rome', in *Poverty in the Roman World* ed. M. Atkins and R. Osborne (Cambridge) 21–39.

Mouritsen, H. (1988) *Elections, Magistrates and Municipal Elite. Studies in Pompeian Epigraphy* (Rome).

(1996), 'Order and disorder in late Pompeian politics', in *Les élites municipales de l'Italie péninsulaire des Gracques à Néron* ed. M. Cébeillac-Gervasoni (Naples and Rome) 139–44.

(1997), 'Mobility and social change in Italian towns during the principate', in *Roman Urbanism. Beyond the Consumer City*, ed. H. M. Parkins (London and New York) 59–82.

(1998a), *Italian Unification. A Study in Ancient and Modern Historiography* (London).

(1998b), 'The *album* of Canusium and the town councils of Roman Italy', *Chiron* 28: 229–54.

(1999), 'Electoral campaigning in Pompeii: a reconsideration', *Athenaeum* 87: 515–23.

(2001), *Plebs and Politics in the Late Roman Republic* (Cambridge)

(2004), 'Freedmen and freeborn in the necropolis of Imperial Ostia', *ZPE* 150: 281–304.

(2005), 'Freedmen and decurions. Epitaphs and social history in Imperial Italy', *JRS* 95: 38–63.

(2006), '*Honores libertini*: Augustales and seviri in Italy', in *Zwischen Kult und Gesellschaft. Kosmopolitische Zentren des antiken Mittelmeerraumes als Aktionsraum von Kultvereinen und Religionsgemeinschaften* ed. I. Nielsen (Augsburg) 237–48.

(2007a) '*CIL* x 1403: the *album* from Herculaneum and the nomenclature of the Latini Iuniani', *ZPE* 161: 288–90.

(2007b), 'The *civitas sine suffragio*: ancient concepts and modern ideology', *Historia* 56: 142–58.

(forthcoming), 'Slavery and manumission in the Roman elite: a study of the *columbaria* of the Volusii Saturnini and the Statilii Tauri', in *Ancient Slavery and Material Culture* ed. M. George.

Mratschek-Halfmann, S. (1993), *Divites et praepotentes. Reichtum und soziale Stellung in der Literatur der Prinzipatszeit* (Historia Einzelschriften 70: Stuttgart).

Mrozek, S. (1975), 'Wirtschaftliche Grundlagen des Aufstiegs der Freigelassenen im römischen Reich', *Chiron* 5: 311–16.

(1987), *Les distributions d'argent et de nourriture dans les villes italiennes du Haut-Empire romain* (Collection Latomus 198: Brussels).

Müller, K. and W. Ehlers (1965), *Petronius Satyrica* (Munich).

Nicolet, C. (1974), *L'ordre équestre à l'époque républicaine (312–43 av. J.C.)*, vol. II: *Prosopographie des chevaliers romains* (Paris).

(1977), 'L'onomastique des groupes dirigeants sous la république', in *Onomastique Latine* ed. N. Duval (Paris) 45–58.

(1984), 'Augustus, government and the propertied classes', in *Caesar Augustus. Seven Aspects* ed. F. Millar and E. Segal (Oxford) 89–128.

(1994), 'Economy and society, 133–43 B.C.', in *CAH* IX 2nd edn ed. J. A. Crook, A. Lintott, and E. Rawson (Cambridge) 599–643.

Nikitinski, O. (2001), 'Die (mündliche) Rolle von Briefboten bei Cicero', in *ScriptOralia Romana. Die Römische Literatur zwischen Mündlichkeit und Schriftlichkeit* ed. L. Benz (Tübingen) 229–47.

Nishida, M. (1993), 'Manumission and ethnicity in urban slavery: Salvador, Brazil, 1808–1888', *Hispanic American Historical Review* 73: 361–91.

Nonnis, D. (1999), 'Attività imprenditoriali e classi dirigenti nell'età repubblicana. Tre città campione', *Cahiers Glotz* 10: 71–109.

Nörr, D. (1963), 'Origo. Studien zur Orts-, Stadt- und Rechtszugehörigkeit in der Antike', *Tijdschrift voor Rechtsgeschiedenis* 31: 525–600.

(1983), 'C. Cassius Longinus: Der Jurist als Rhetor (Bemerkungen zu Tac. Ann. 14, 42–45)', in *Althistorische Studien. Hermann Bengtson zum 70. Geburtstag dargebracht von Kollegen und Schülern* ed. H. Heinen (Historia Einzelschriften 40: Wiesbaden) 187–222.

Noy, D. (1988), 'A misunderstanding about Roman divorce law: the meaning of "praeter" in Digest 24.2.9', *CQ* 38: 572–6.

(2000), *Foreigners at Rome. Citizens and Strangers* (London).

Oakley, S. P. (2005), *A Commentary on Livy Books VI–X*, III: *Book IX* (Oxford).

Oliensis, E. (1998), *Horace and the Rhetoric of Authority* (Cambridge).

Oost, S. I. (1958), 'The career of M. Antonius Pallas', *AJPh* 79: 113–39.

Ortalli, J. (2007), 'Il medicus di Ariminum: una contestualizzazione archeologica dalla domus "del chirurgo"', *RSA* 37: 101–18.

Osgood, J. (2006), *Caesar's Legacy. Civil War and the Emergence of the Roman Empire* (Cambridge).

Ostrow, S. E. (1985), '*Augustales* along the Bay of Naples: a case for their early growth', *Historia* 34: 64–101.

(1990), 'The *Augustales* in the Augustan scheme', in *Between Republic and Empire. Interpretations of Augustus and His Principate* ed. K. Raaflaub and M. Toher (Berkeley) 364–79.

Oxé, A. (1968), *Corpus Vasorum Arretinorum* (Bonn).

Pack, E. (1980), 'Manumissio in circo? Zum sog. Freilassungsrelief in Mariemont', in *Studien zur antiken Sozialgeschichte. Festschrift Friedrich Vittinghoff* ed. W. Eck, H. Galsterer, and H. Wolff (Cologne) 179–95.

Pagano, M. and J. Rougeet (1987), 'La casa del liberto P. Confuleius Sabbio a Capua e i suoi mosaici', *MEFRA* 99: 753–65.

Palmer, R. E. A. (1989), 'Bullae insignia ingenuitatis', *AJAH* 14: 1–69.

Panciera, S. ed. (2004), *Libitina e dintorni. Libitina e i luci sepolcrali. Le leges libitinariae campane. Iura sepulcrorum: vecchie e nuove iscrizioni* (Rome).

(2007), 'Servire a Palazzo. Nuove testimonianze di *officiales Augustorum* da Roma', in *Herrschen und Verwalten. Der Altag der römischen Administration in der Hohen Kaiserzeit* ed. R. Haensch and J. Heinrichs (Cologne) 60–79.

Papadis, D. (2001), 'Das Problem des "Sklaven von Natur" bei Aristoteles', *Gymnasium* 108: 345–65.

Parker, H. (1998), 'Loyal slaves and loyal wives. The crisis of the outsider-within and Roman exemplum literature', in *Women and Slaves in Greco-Roman Culture. Differential Equations* ed. S. R. Joshel and S. Murnaghan (London and New York) 152–73.

Parkins, H. (1997), 'The "consumer city" domesticated? The Roman city in élite economic strategies', in *Roman Urbanism. Beyond the Consumer City* ed. H. Parkins (London) 83–111.

Patterson, J. R. (2006), *Landscapes and Cities. Rural Settlement and Civic Transformation in Early Imperial Italy* (Oxford).

Patterson, O. (1982), *Slavery and Social Death. A Comparative Study* (Cambridge, MA).

(1991), *Freedom I: Freedom in the Making of Western Culture* (London).

Pavis D'Escurac, H. (1977), 'Aristocratie sénatoriale et profits commerciaux', *Ktema* 2: 339–55.

(1978), 'Pline le Jeune et la transmission des patrimonies', *Ktema* 3: 275–88.

(1981), 'Affranchis et citoyenneté: les effets juridiques de l'affranchissement sous le Haut-Empire', *Ktema* 6: 181–92.

Peachin, M. (1994), 'The case of the heiress Camilia Pia', *HSCPh* 96: 301–41.

Pelletier, A. (1999), 'Les bourgeoisies gallo-romaines sous le haut-empire', in *XI Congresso internazionale di epigrafia Greca e Latina II* (Rome) 2. 263–73.

Pérez, C. (1981), 'L'esclave/l'affranchi "médiateur" dans les relations d' "amicitia" dans la correspondance de Cicéron', *Index* 10: 173–233.

Perl, G. (1977), 'Zu Varros Instrumentum vocale', *Klio* 59: 423–9.

Pesando, F. (2003), 'Appunti sulla cosidetta basilica di Ercolano', *Cron.Erc.* 33: 331–7.

Petersen, L. H. (2006), *The Freedman in Roman Art and Art History* (Cambridge).

Pirson, F. (1999), *Mietwohnungen in Pompeji und Herkulaneum. Untersuchungen zur Architektur, zum Wohnen und zur Sozial- und Wirtschaftsgeschichte der Vesuvstädte* (Munich).

Pirson, F. and J.-A. Dickmann (2002), 'Die Casa dei Postumii in Pompeji und ihre Insula', *MDAI(R)* 109: 242–316.

Pittenger, M. R. Pelikan (2008), *Contested Triumphs: Politics, Pageantry, and Performance in Livy's Republican Rome* (Berkeley).

Pleket, H. W. (1988), 'Labor and unemployment in the Roman Empire: some preliminary remarks', in *Soziale Randgruppen und Aussenseiter im Altertum* ed. I. Weiler (Graz) 267–76.

(1990), 'Wirtschaft', in *Europäische Wirtschafts- und Sozialgeschichte in der römischen Kaiserzeit* ed. F. Vittinghoff (Stuttgart) 25–160.

(2001), 'Review of Andreau (1999)', *Journal of Economic History* 61: 1105–6.

Pollini, J. (2003), 'Slave-boys for sexual and religious service: images of pleasure and devotion', in *Flavian Rome. Culture, Image, Text* ed. A. J. Boyle and W. J. Dominik (Leiden) 149–66.

Poma, G. (1982), 'Provvedimenti legislativi e attività censoria di Claudio verso gli schiavi e i liberti', *RSA* 12: 143–74.

(1987), '"Servi fugitivi" e schiavi magistrati in età triumvirale', *Index* 15: 149–74.

Pomeroy, A. J. (1991), 'Status and status concern in the Greco-Roman dream-books', *Anc. Soc.* 22: 51–74.

(1992), 'Trimalchio as *deliciae*', *Phoenix* 46: 45–53.

Pomeroy, S. B. (1975), *Goddesses, Whores, Wives, and Slaves: Women in Classical Antiquity* (New York).

Prachner, G. (1980), *Die Sklaven und Freigelassenen im arretinischen Sigillatagewerbe* (Wiesbaden).

Puglisi, G. (1987), 'Il microcosmo di C. Pompeius Trimalchio Maecenatianus. Schiavi e liberti nella casa di un mercante romano (Petr. 27–78)', *Index* 15: 207–26.

Purcell, N. (1983), 'The *apparitores*: a study in social mobility', *PBSR* 51: 125–73.

(1987), 'Tomb and suburb', in *Römische Gräberstrassen. Selbstdarstellung – Status – Standard* ed. H. von Hesberg and P. Zanker (Munich) 25–41.

(1994), 'The city of Rome and the *plebs urbana* in the late republic', in *CAH* 2nd edn, IX, ed. J. A. Crook, A. W. Lintott, and E. Rawson (Cambridge) 644–88.

(1996), 'Rome and its development under Augustus and his successors', in *CAH* 2nd edn, X, ed. A. K. Bowman, E. Champlin, and A. W. Lintott (Cambridge) 782–811.

(2000), 'Rome and Italy', in *CAH* 2nd ed. XI, ed. A. K. Bowman, P. Garnsey, and D. Rathbone (Cambridge) 405–43.

Queirós Mattoso, K. M. de (1986), *To Be a Slave in Brazil, 1550–1888* (New Brunswick; 1st edn 1979).

Rainer, J. M. (1988), 'Humanität und Arbeit im römischen Recht', *ZSSR* 105: 745–70.

Ramin, J. and P. Veyne (1981), 'Droit romain et sociéte. Les hommes libres qui passent pour esclaves et l'esclavage volontaire', *Historia* 30: 472–97.

Rathbone, D. and P. Temin (2008), 'Financial intermediation in first-century AD Rome and eighteenth-century England', in *Pistoi dia tèn technèn. Bankers, Loans and Archives in the Ancient World. Studies in Honour of Raymond Bogaert* ed. K. Verboven, K. Vandorpe, and V. Chankowski (Leuven) 371–419.

Rawson, B. (1966), 'Family life among the lower classes at Rome in the first two centuries of the Empire', *CPh* 61: 70–83.

(1968), Review of Kajanto (1965), *CPh* 63: 154–9.

(1989), '*Spurii* and the Roman view of illegitimacy', *Antichthon* 23: 10–41.

(1997), 'The iconography of Roman childhood', in *The Roman Family in Italy. Status, Sentiment, Space* ed. B. Rawson and P. Weaver (Oxford) 205–38.

(2003), *Children and Childhood in Roman Italy* (Oxford).

Rawson, E. (1976), 'The Ciceronian aristocracy and its properties', in *Studies in Roman Property* ed. M. I. Finley (Cambridge) 85–102.

(1987), '*Discrimina Ordinum*: the Lex Julia Theatralis', *PBSR* 55: 83–114.

(1993), 'Freedmen in Roman comedy', in *Theater and Society in the Classical World* ed. R. Scodel (Ann Arbor) 215–33.

Reinhold, M. (1971), 'Usurpation of status and status symbols in the Roman Empire', *Historia* 20: 275–302.

Rémy, B. (1998), 'Les élites locales et municipales de la colonie de Vienne au Haut-Empire', *AC* 67: 77–120.

Reynolds, J. (1982), *Aphrodisias and Rome* (London).

Rilinger, R. (1997), '*Domus* und *res publica*. Die politisch-soziale Bedeutung des aristokratischen "Hauses" in der späten römischen Republik', in *Zwischen 'Haus' und 'Staat'. Antike Höfe im Vergleich* ed. A. Winterling (HZ Beiheft 23: Munich) 73–90.

Rink, B. (1993), 'Sklavenfreilassungen in der späten römischen Republik als Beispiel für soziale Mobilität', *Laverna* 4: 45–54.

Rives, J. B. (1995), *Religion and Authority in Roman Carthage from Augustus to Constantine* (Oxford).

(2007), *Religion in the Roman Empire* (Oxford).

Rix, H. (1994), *Die Termini der Unfreiheit in den Sprachen Alt-Italiens* (Stuttgart).

Rizakis, A. D. (2005), 'Les affranchi(e)s sous l'Empire: richesse, évergétisme et promotion sociale. Le cas d'une affranchie de Gytheion (Laconie)', in *Esclavage antique et discrimination socio-culturelles* ed. V. I. Anastasiadis and P. N. Doukellis (Berne) 233–41.

Rizzelli, G. (2006), 'Antonio e Fadia', in *Studi sull'età di Marco Antonio, Rudiae* 18: 200–20.

Robinson, D. (2005), 'Re-thinking the social organisation of trade and industry in first century AD Pompeii', in *Roman Working Lives and Urban Living* ed. A. MacMahon and J. Price (Oxford) 88–105.

Roller, M. B. (2001), *Constructing Autocracy. Aristocrats and Emperors in Julio-Claudian Rome* (Princeton and Oxford).

(2006), *Dining Posture in Ancient Rome. Bodies, Values, and Status* (Princeton).

Rosen, K. (1995), 'Römische Freigelassene als Aufsteiger und Petrons Cena Trimalchionis', *Gymnasium* 102: 79–92.

Rosenstein, N. (2008), 'Aristocrats and agriculture in the middle and late republic', *JRS* 98: 1–26.

Rostovtzeff, M. (1957), *The Social and Economic History of the Roman Empire* 2nd edn (Oxford).

Roth, U. (2005), 'To have and to be: food, status, and the peculium of agricultural slaves', *JRA* 18: 278–92.

(2007), *Thinking Tools. Agricultural Slavery between Evidence and Models* (London).

Rowe, G. (2001), 'Trimalchio's world', *SCI* 20: 225–45.

Royden, H. L. (1988), *The Magistrates of the Roman Professional Collegia in Italy from the First to the Third Century A.D.* (Pisa).

Rudd, N. (1966), *The Satires of Horace* (Cambridge).

Sablayrolles, R. (1996), *Libertinus miles. Les cohortes de vigiles* (Coll. École Fr. Rome 224: Rome).

Saller, R. P. (1982), *Personal Patronage under the Early Empire* (Cambridge).

(1991), 'Corporal punishment, authority, and obedience in the Roman household', in *Marriage, Divorce, and Children in Ancient Rome* ed. B. Rawson (Oxford) 144–65.

(1994), *Patriarchy, Property and Death in the Roman Family* (Cambridge).

(1996), 'The hierarchical household in Roman society: a study of domestic slavery', in *Serfdom and Slavery. Studies in Legal Bondage* ed. M. L. Bush (London and New York) 112–29.

(2000), 'Status and patronage', in *CAH* 2nd edn, XI, ed. A. K. Bowman, P. Garnsey, and D. Rathbone (Cambridge) 817–54.

Saller, R. P. and B. D. Shaw (1984), 'Tombstones and Roman family relations in the principate: civilians, soldiers and slaves', *JRS* 74: 124–56.

Salomies, O. (1987), *Römische Vornamen. Studien zur römischen Namengebung* (Helsinki).

Salsano, D. (1998), 'Manumissio vindicta in ambiente provinciale: problemi e proposte', *Chiron* 28: 179–85.

Samson, R. (1989), 'Rural slavery, inscriptions, archaeology and Marx', *Historia* 38: 99–110.

Samuel, A. E. (1965), 'The role of *paramone* clauses in ancient documents', *JJP* 15: 221–311.

Saumagne, C. (1962), 'Une colonie latine d'affranchis, Carteia (Tite-Live, H.R. 43.3)', *RHD* 40: 135–52.

Schäfer, C. (1998), *Spitzenmanagement in Republik und Kaiserzeit. Die Prokuratoren von Privatpersonen im Imperium Romanum vom 2. Jh. v. Chr. bis zum 3. Jh. n. Chr.* (St. Katharinen).

Schäfer, T. (1989), *Imperii insignia. Sella Curulis and Fasces. Zur Repräsentation römischer Magistrate* (Mainz).

Scheidel, W. (1990), 'Free-born and manumitted bailiffs in the Graeco-Roman world', *CQ* 40: 591–3.

(1993), 'Sklaven und Freigelassene als Pächter und ihre ökonomische Funktion in der römischen Landwirtschaft (Colonus-Studien III)', in *De agricultura. In memoriam Pieter Willem De Neeve (1945–1990)* ed. H. Sancisi-Weerdenburg, R. J. Van Der Spek, H. C. Teitler, and H. T. Wallinga (Amsterdam) 182–96.

(1996), 'Finances, figures and fiction', *CQ* 46: 222–38.

(1997), 'Quantifying the sources of slaves in the early Roman empire', *JRS* 87: 156–69.

(1999a), 'The slave population of Roman Italy: speculation and constraints', *Topoi* 9: 129–44.

(1999b), 'The demography of Roman slavery and manumission', in *La démographie historique antique* ed. M. Bellancourt-Valdher and J.-N. Corvisier (Arras) 107–15.

(2005a), 'Human mobility in Roman Italy, II: the slave population', *JRS* 95: 64–79.

(2005b), 'Real slave prices and the relative cost of slave labor in the Graeco-Roman world', *Anc. Soc.* 35: 1–17.

(2008), 'The comparative economics of slavery in the Greco-Roman world', in *Slave Systems, Ancient and Modern* ed. E. Dal Lago and C. Katsari (Cambridge) 105–26.

(2009), 'Sex and empire: a Darwinian perspective', in *The Dynamics of Ancient Empires. State Power from Assyria to Byzantium* ed. I. Morris and W. Scheidel (Oxford and New York) 255–324.

Schiller, A. A. (1971), 'The business relations of patron and freedman in Classical Roman law', in *An American Experience of Roman Law* (Göttingen) 24–40. First published in *Legal Essays in Tribute to O. K. Murray* (1935).

Schlaifer, R. (1960), 'Greek theories of slavery from Homer to Aristotle', *HSCPh* 47 (1936) 165–204, reprinted in *Slavery in Classical Antiquity* ed. M. I. Finley (Cambridge) 93–132.

Schlange-Schöningen, H. (2003), *Die römische Gesellschaft bei Galen. Biographie und Sozialgeschichte* (Berlin and New York).

Schlegel, C. (2000), 'Horace and his fathers: satires 1.4 and 1.6', *AJPh* 121: 93–119.

Schleich, T. (1983), 'Überlegungen zum Problem senatorischer Handelsaktivitäten. Teil ɪ', *MBAH* 2: 65–90.

(1984), 'Überlegungen zum Problem senatorischer Handelsaktivitäten. Teil ɪɪ', *MBAH* 3: 37–76.

Schnurr, C. (1992), 'The *lex Julia theatralis* of Augustus: some remarks on seating problems in theatre, amphitheatre and circus', *LCM* 17: 147–60.

Scholl, R. (2001), '"Freilassung unter Freunden" im römischen Ägypten', in *Fünfzig Jahre Forschungen zur antiken Sklaverei an der mainzer Akademie 1950–2000. Miscellanea zum Jubiläum* ed. H. Bellen and H. Heinen (Stuttgart) 159–69.

Schulze-Oben, H. (1989), *Freigelassene in den Städten des römischen Hispanien. Juristische, wirtschaftliche und soziale Stellung nach dem Zeugnis der Inschriften* (Bonn).

Schumacher, L. (1982), *Servus Index. Sklavenverhör und Sklavenanzeige im republikanischen und kaiserzeitlichen Rom* (Wiesbaden).

(2001a), 'Hausgesinde – Hofgesinde. Terminologische Überlegungen zur Funktion der *familia Caesaris* im 1. Jh. n. Chr.', in *Fünfzig Jahre Forschungen zur antiken Sklaverei an der mainzer Akademie 1950–2000. Miscellanea zum Jubiläum* ed. H. Bellen and H. Heinen (Stuttgart) 331–52.

(2001b), *Sklaverei in der Antike. Alltag und Schicksal der Unfreien* (Munich).

Segenni, S. (1990), *I liberti ad Amiternum. Ricerche di onomastica* (Pisa).

Shackleton Bailey, D. R. (1965–70), *Cicero's Letters to Atticus* ɪ–vɪɪ (Cambridge).

(1977), *Cicero: Epistulae ad familiares* ɪ–ɪɪ (Cambridge).

Shaw, B. D. (1991), 'The cultural meaning of death: age and gender in the Roman family', in *The Family in Italy from Antiquity to the Present* ed. D. I. Kertzer and R. P. Saller (New Haven and London) 66–90.

(1998), '"A wolf by the ears": M. I. Finley's *Ancient Slavery and Modern Ideology* in historical context', in M. I. Finley, *Ancient Slavery and Modern Ideology* ed. B. D. Shaw (Princeton) 3–74.

(2000), 'Rebels and outsiders', in *CAH* 2nd edn, xɪ ed. A. K. Bowman, P. Garnsey, D. Rathbone (Cambridge) 361–403.

(2007), 'Sabinus the muleteer', *CQ* 57: 132–8.

Sherwin-White, A. N. (1966), *The Letters of Pliny. A Historical and Social Commentary* (Oxford).

(1973), *The Roman Citizenship* 2nd edn (Oxford).

Silvestrini, M. (2000), 'L'ascesa sociale delle famiglie degli *augustali*', in *Les élites municipales de l'Italie péninsulaire de la mort de César à la mort de Domitien entre continuité et rupture. Classes sociales dirigeantes et pouvoir central* ed. M. Cébeillac-Gervasoni (Rome) 431–55.

Sirks, A. J. B. (1980), 'A favour to rich freed women (libertinae) in 51 A.D. On Sue. *Cl.* 19 and the Lex Papia', *RIDA* 27: 283–93.

(1981), 'Informal manumission and the *lex Iunia*', *RIDA* 28: 247–76.

(1983), 'The *lex Iunia* and the effects of informal manumission and iteration', *RIDA* 30: 211–92.

(1994), 'Ad senatus consultum Claudianum', *ZSSR* ɪɪɪ: 436–7.

(2002), 'Conclusion: some reflections', in *Speculum Iuris. Roman Law as a Reflection of Social and Economic Life in Antiquity* ed. J.-J. Aubert and B. Sirks (Ann Arbor) 169–81.

(2005), 'Der Zweck des Senatus Consultum Claudianum von 52 n. Chr.', *ZSSR* 122: 138–49.

Slater, N. W. (2004), 'Slavery, authority, and loyalty: the case of Syncerastus', in *Studien zu Plautus' Poenulus* ed. T. Baier (Tübingen) 291–8.

Smadja, E. (1999), 'L'affranchissement des femmes esclaves à Rome', in *Femmes-esclaves. Modèles d'interprétation anthropologique, économique, juridique* ed. F. Reduzzi Merola and A. Storchi Marino (Naples) 355–68.

Smallwood, E. M. (1961) *Philonis Alexandrini Legatio ad Gaium* (Leiden).

Smith, C. J. (2006), *The Roman Clan. The Gens from Ancient Ideology to Modern Anthropology* (Cambridge).

Solazzi, S. (1949), 'Il rispetto per la famiglia dello schiavo', *SDHI* 15: 187–92.

Solin, H. (1971), *Beiträge zur Kenntnis der griechischen Personennamen in Rom* (Helsinki).

(1982), *Die Griechischen Personennamen in Rom: ein Namenbuch* (Berlin and New York).

(1990), 'Republican Capua', in *Roman Eastern Policy and Other Studies in Roman History* ed. H. Solin and M. Kajava (Helsinki) 151–62.

(1996), *Die stadtrömischen Sklavennamen. Ein Namenbuch* (Stuttgart).

Söllner, A. (2000), *Irrtümlich als Sklaven gehaltene freie Menschen und Sklaven in unsicheren Eigentumsverhältnissen* – homines liberi et servi alieni bona fide servientes (Corpus der römischen Rechtsquellen zur antiken Sklaverei 9: Stuttgart).

Spawforth, A. J. S. (1996), 'Roman Corinth: the formation of a colonial elite', in *Roman Onomastics in the Greek East. Social and Political Aspects* ed. A. D. Rizakis (Athens) 167–82.

Spranger, P. P. (1961), *Historische Untersuchungen zu den Sklavenfiguren des Plautus und Terenz* (Mainz).

Starace, P. (2006), *Lo statuliber e l'adempimento fittizio della condizione. Uno studio sul favor libertatis fra tarda repubblica ed età antonina* (Bari).

Ste. Croix, G. E. M. de (1982), *The Class Struggle in the Ancient World. From the Archaic Age to the Arab Conquests* (London).

(1988), 'Slavery and other forms of unfree labour', in *Slavery and Other Forms of Unfree Labour* ed. L. J. Archer (London and New York) 19–32.

Stein, P. (1985), 'Lex Cincia', *Athenaeum* 73: 145–53.

Stenuit, B. (1977), 'Les parents d'Horace', *LEC* 45: 125–44.

Stewart, P. (2008), *The Social History of Roman Art* (Cambridge).

Storchi Marino, A. (1999), 'Restaurazione dei *mores* e controllo della mobilità sociale a Roma nel I sec. d.C.: il *Senatusconsultum Claudianum de poena feminarum quae servis coniungerentur*', in *Femmes-esclaves. Modèles d'interprétation anthropologique, économique, juridique* ed. F. Reduzzi Merola and A. Storchi Marino (Naples) 391–426.

Strack, M. L. (1914), 'Die Freigelassenen in ihrer Bedeutung für die Gesellschaft der Alten', *HZ* 112: 1–28.

Straus, J. A. (1973), 'Deux notes sur l'affranchissement dans les papyrus de l'Égypte romaine', *ZPE* 11: 143–6.

Swan, M. (1970), 'Josephus, *A.J.* xix, 251–252: Opposition to Gaius and Claudius', *AJPh* 91: 149–64.

Syme, R. (1938), 'Caesar, the senate and Italy', *PBSR* 14: 1–31.

(1958), *Tacitus* (Oxford).

(1961), 'Who was Vedius Pollio?', *JRS* 51: 23–30.

Tarpin, M. (2002), *Vici et pagi dans l'occident romain* (Rome).

Tassaux, F. (2000), 'Sévirat et promotion sociale en Italie nord-orientale', in *Les élites municipales de l'Italie péninsulaire de la mort de César à la mort de Domitien entre continuité et rupture. Classes sociales dirigeantes et pouvoir central* ed. M. Cébeillac-Gervasoni (Rome) 373–415.

Tate, J. C. (2005), 'New thoughts on the "Will of Dasumius"', *ZSSR* 122: 166–71.

Tatum, W. J. (1999), *The Patrician Tribune. Publius Clodius Pulcher* (Chapel Hill and London).

Taubenschlag, R. (1955), *The Law of Greco-Roman Egypt in the Light of the Papyri 332 B.C. – 640 A.D.* 2nd edn (Warsaw).

Taurino, C. (2007), 'Evoluzione di un "*libertino patre natus*": dalla *Sat.* 1,6 alla *Sat.* 2,6', *Rudiae* 19: 153–202.

Taylor, L. R. (1960), *The Voting Districts of the Roman Republic* (Rome).

(1961), 'Freedmen and freeborn in the epitaphs of Imperial Rome', *AJPh* 82: 113–32.

Teitler, H. C. (1993), 'Free-born estate managers in the Graeco-Roman world', in *De Agricultura. In Memoriam Pieter Willem de Neeve (1945–1990)* ed. H. Sancisi-Weerdenburg, R. J. Van der Spek, H. C. Teitler, and H. T. Wallinga (Amsterdam) 206–13.

Temin, P. (2004), 'The labor market of the early Roman Empire', *Journal of Interdisciplinary History* 34: 513–38.

(2006), 'The economy of the early Roman Empire', *Journal of Economic Perspectives* 20: 133–51.

Texier, J. G. (1979), 'Les esclaves et l'esclavage dans l'œuvre de Polybe', in *Schiavitù, manomissione e classi dipendenti nel mondo antico* ed. M. Capozza (Rome) 115–42.

Thebert, Y. (1993), 'The slave', in *The Romans* ed. A. Giardina (Chicago and London) 138–74.

Thomas, Y. (1984), '*Vitae necisque potestas*. Le père, la cité, la mort', in *Du châtiment dans la cité. Supplices corporels et peine de mort dans le monde antique* (Rome) 499–548.

(1990), 'Remarques sur la jurisdiction domestique à Rome', in *Parenté et stratégies familiales dans l'antiquité romaine* ed. J. Andreau and H. Bruhns (Rome) 450–74.

Thompson, L. A. (1981), 'The concept of purity of blood in Suetonius' Life of Augustus', *Museum Africum* 7: 35–46.

Thylander, H. (1952), *Inscriptions du Port d'Ostie* (Lund).

Tondo, S. (1967), *Aspetti simbolici e magici nella struttura giuridica della manumissio vindicta* (Milan).

Torelli, M. (1966), 'Il frontone', in *Sculture municipali dell'area sabellica tra l'età di Cesare e quella di Nerone* (Studi Miscellanei 10: 1963–1964) 72–84.

(1994), 'Per un'eziologia del cambiamento in epoca Claudia. Vicende vicine e vicende lontane', in *Die Regierungszeit des Kaisers Claudius (41–54 n. Chr.). Umbruch oder Episode?* ed. V. M. Strocka (Mainz) 177–90.

Tran, N. (2006), 'Les affranchis dans les collèges professionnels du Haut-Empire romain: l'encadrement civique de la mobilité sociale', in *Les régulations sociales dans l'antiquité* ed. M. Molin (Rennes) 389–402.

Trapp, M. (2007), *Philosophy in the Roman Empire. Ethics, Politics and Society* (Aldershot).

Treggiari, S. (1969a), *Roman Freedmen during the Late Republic* (Oxford).

(1969b), 'The freedmen of Cicero', *G & R* 16: 195–204.

(1975a), 'Family life among the staff of the Volusii', *TAPhA* 105: 393–401.

(1975b), 'Jobs in the household of Livia', *PBSR* 43: 48–77.

(1977), 'The manumission of Tiro', *LCM* 2: 67–72.

(1979), 'Questions on women domestics in the Roman West', in *Schiavitù, manomissione e classi dipendenti nel mondo antico* ed. M. Capozza (Rome) 185–201.

(1980), 'Urban labour in Rome: *mercennarii* and *tabernarii*', in *Non-slave Labour in the Greco-Roman World* ed. P. Garnsey (Cambridge) 48–64.

(1981), '*Contubernales* in *CIL* 6', *Phoenix* 35: 42–69.

(1991), *Roman Marriage. Iusti Coniuges from the Time of Cicero to the Time of Ulpian* (Oxford).

(1996), 'Social status and social legislation', in *CAH* 2nd edn, x, ed. A. K. Bowman, E. Champlin, and A. W. Lintott (Cambridge) 873–904.

Tucker, C. W. (1982), 'Women in the manumission inscriptions at Delphi', *TAPhA* 112: 225–36.

Tzounakas, S. (2006), 'Clodius' projected manumission of slaves in Cicero's Pro Milone', *Arctos* 40: 167–74.

Vanderbroeck, P. J. J. (1987), *Popular Leadership and Collective Behavior in the Late Roman Republic (ca. 80–50 B.C.)* (Amsterdam).

Venturini, C. (1995–96), '"Latini facti", "peregrini" e "civitas": note sulla normativa adrianea', *BIDR* 37–38: 219–42.

Verboven, K. (2000), 'L'organisation des affaires financières des C. Sulpicii de Pouzzoles (Tabulae Pompeianae Sulpiciorum)', *Cahiers Glotz* 11: 161–71.

(2002), *The Economy of Friends. Economic Aspects of Amicitia and Patronage in the Late Republic* (Coll. Latomus 269: Brussels).

(2007), 'The associative order: status and ethos among Roman businessmen in the late Republic and early Empire', *Athenaeum* 95: 861–93.

(2008), '*Faeneratores, negotiatores* and financial intermediation in the Roman world', in *Pistoi dia tèn technèn. Bankers, Loans and Archives in the Ancient World. Studies in Honour of Raymond Bogaert* ed. K. Verboven, K. Vandorpe, and V. Chankowski (Leuven) 211–29.

(2009), 'A funny thing happened on my way to the market. Reading Petronius to write economic history', in *Petronius. A Handbook* ed. J. Prag and I. Repath (Oxford) 125–39.

Veyne, P. (1961), 'Vie de Trimalchio', *Annales ESC* 16: 213–47.

(1997), *The Roman Empire* (Cambridge, MA and London) (1st edn 1985).

(2000), 'La "plèbe moyenne" sous le Haut-Empire romain', *Annales HSS* 55: 1169–99.

Ville, G. (1963), 'Le relief R14(26) de Mariemont ne figure pas un affranchissement par la vindicte mais une scène de cirque', *Latomus* 22: 14–30.

Virlouvet, C. (1991), 'La plèbe frumentaire à l'époque d'Auguste. Une tentative de définition', in *Nourrir la plebe. Actes du colloque tenu à Genève les 28 et 29. IX. 1989 en homage à Denis van Berchem* ed. A. Giovannini (Basel and Kassel) 43–62.

(1995), *Tessera frumentaria. Les procédures de distribution du blé public à Rome à la fin de la république et au début de l'empire* (Rome).

Vischer, R. (1965), *Das einfache Leben* (Göttingen).

Visky, K. (1980), 'L'affranchi comme *institor*', *BIDR* 83: 207–20.

Vitali, C. (2005), '". . . manumissus liber((um))ve iussus erit . . . ": sul capitolo 28 della "lex Irnitana"', *Index* 33: 389–431.

Vittinghoff, F. (1980), 'Soziale Struktur und politisches System der hohen römischen Kaiserzeit', *HZ* 230: 31–55.

(1990), 'Gesellschaft', in *Europäische Wirtschafts- und Sozialgeschichte in der römischen Kaiserzeit* ed. F. Vittinghoff (Stuttgart) 161–369.

Vogt, J. (1975), *Ancient Slavery and the Ideal of Man* (Oxford).

Volterra, E. (1955), 'Manomissione e cittadinanza', in *Studi in onore di U. E. Paoli* (Florence) 695–716.

Wacke, A. (1982a), 'Das Relief-Fragment Nr.26 aus Mariemont: Zirkus-Szene oder manumissio vindicta?', in *Studi in onore di Arnaldo Biscardi* 1 (Milan) 117–45.

(1982b), 'Wettbewerbsfreiheit und Konkurrenzverbotsklauseln im antiken und modernen Recht', *ZSSR* 99: 188–215.

(1991), 'Peculium non adeptum videtur tacite donatum. Zum Schicksal des Sonderguts nach der Gewaltentlassung', *Iura* 42: 43–95.

(2001), 'Manumissio matrimonii causa. Die Freilassung zwecks Heirat nach den Ehegesetzen des Augustus', in *Fünfzig Jahre Forschungen zur antiken Sklaverei an der mainzer Akademie 1950–2000. Miscellanea zum Jubiläum* ed. H. Bellen and H. Heinen (Stuttgart) 133–58.

Waldstein, W. (1986), *Operae Libertorum. Untersuchungen zur Dienstpflicht freigelassener Sklaven* (Stuttgart).

(2001), 'Zum Menschsein von Sklaven', in *Fünfzig Jahre Forschungen zur antiken Sklaverei an der mainzer Akademie 1950–2000. Miscellanea zum Jubiläum* ed. H. Bellen and H. Heinen (Stuttgart) 31–49.

Wallace-Hadrill, A. (1994), *Houses and Society in Pompeii and Herculaneum* (Princeton).

Wallon, H. (1847), *Histoire de l'esclavage dans l'antiquité* (Paris).

Waltzing, J.-P. (1895–1900), *Étude historique sur les corporations professionnelles chez les Romains depuis les origines jusqu'à la chute de l'Empire d'Occident* (Brussels and Louvain).

Warde Fowler, W. (1908), *Social Life at Rome in the Age of Cicero* (London).

Watson, A. (1967), *The Law of Persons in the Later Roman Republic* (Oxford).

(1975), *Rome of the XII Tables. Persons and Property* (Princeton).

(1983), 'Roman slave law and romanist ideology', *Phoenix* 37: 53–65.

(1987), *Roman Slave Law* (Baltimore and London).

(1995), *The Spirit of Roman Law* (Athens, GA).

Watson, J. L. (1980), 'Slavery as an institution: open and closed systems', in *Asian and African Systems of Slavery* ed. J. L. Watson (Berkeley) 1–15.

Watson, L. C. (2002), 'Horace and the pirates', in *Sextus Pompeius* ed. A. Powell and K. Welch (London) 213–28.

(2003), *A Commentary on Horace's Epodes* (Oxford).

Weaver, P. R. C. (1964), '*Cognomina ingenua*: a note', *CQ* 14: 311–15.

(1972), *Familia Caesaris. A Social Study of the Emperor's Freedmen and Slaves* (Cambridge).

(1986), 'The status of children in mixed marriages', in *The Family in Ancient Rome. New Perspectives* ed. B. Rawson (London) 145–69.

(1990), 'Where have all the Junian Latins gone? Nomenclature and status in the early Empire', *Chiron* 20: 275–305.

(1991), 'Children of freedmen (and freedwomen)', in *Marriage, Divorce, and Children in Ancient Rome* ed. B. Rawson (Oxford) 166–90.

(1997), 'Children of Junian Latins', in *The Roman Family in Italy. Status, Sentiment, Space* ed. B. Rawson and P. Weaver (Oxford) 55–72.

(2001), 'Reconstructing lower-class Roman families', in *Childhood, Class and Kin in the Roman World* ed. S. Dixon (London and New York) 101–14.

(2005), 'Phaon, freedman of Nero', *ZPE* 151: 243–52.

Weber, E. (1988), 'Freigelassene – eine diskriminierte Randgruppe?', in *Soziale Randgruppen und Aussenseiter im Altertum: Referate vom Symposion 'Soziale Randgruppen und antike Sozialpolitik' in Graz (21 bis 23 September 1987)* ed. I. Weiler (Graz) 257–65.

(2008), '*Libertus et coniunx*', in *Antike Lebenswelten. Konstanz – Wandel – Wirkungsmacht. Festschrift für Ingomar Weiler zum 70. Geburtstag* ed. P. Mauritsch *et al.* (Wiesbaden) 367–79.

Weber, V. (1993), 'Die Munizipalaristokratie', in *Gesellschaft und Wirtschaft des römischen Reiches im 3. Jahrhundert* ed. K.-P. Johne (Berlin) 245–317.

Weiler, I. (2001), 'Eine Sklavin wird frei. Zur Rolle des Geschlechts bei der Freilassung', in *Fünfzig Jahre Forschungen zur antiken Sklaverei an der mainzer Akademie 1950–2000. Miscellanea zum Jubiläum* ed. H. Bellen and H. Heinen (Stuttgart) 113–32.

(2002), 'Inverted Kalokagathia', *Slavery and Abolition* 23: 11–28.

(2003), *Die Beendigung des Sklavenstatus im Altertum. Ein Beitrag zur vergleichenden Sozialgeschichte* (Stuttgart).

Weiss, A. (2004) *Sklave der Stadt. Untersuchungen zur öffentlichen Sklaverei in den Städten des römischen Reiches* (Historia Einzelschriften 173: Stuttgart).

Wells, C. (1984), *The Roman Empire* (London).

Welwei, K.-W. (1988), *Unfreie im antiken Kriegsdienst* III (Stuttgart).

Wenger, L. (1941), 'Vinctus', *ZSSR* 61: 355–78.

Wesener, G. (1958), 'Vicesima manumissionum', *RE* 8A2: 2477–9.

Westermann, W. L. (1955), *The Slave Systems of Greek and Roman Antiquity* (Philadelphia).

Whitehead, D. (1991), 'Norms of citizenship in ancient Greece', in *City States in Classical Antiquity and Medieval Italy*, ed. A. Molho, K. Raaflaub, and J. Emlen (Ann Arbor and Stuttgart) 135–54.

Whitehead, J. (1993), 'The *Cena Trimalchionis* and biographical narration in Roman middle-class art', in *Narrative and Event in Ancient Art* ed. P. J. Holliday (Cambridge) 299–325.

Wiedemann, T. E. J. (1985), 'The regularity of manumission at Rome', *CQ* 35: 162–75.

(1989), *Adults and Children in the Roman Empire* (London).

(2003), 'The patron as banker', in '*Bread and Circuses*'. *Euergetism and municipal patronage in Roman Italy* ed. K. Lomas and T. Cornell (London and New York) 12–27.

Wieling, H. (1999), *Die Begründung des Sklavenstatus nach ius gentium und ius civile* (Corpus der römischen Rechtsquellen zur antiken Sklaverei 1: Stuttgart).

Williams, C. (1999), *Roman Homosexuality. Ideologies of Masculinity in Classical Antiquity* (Oxford).

Williams, G. (1995), 'Libertino patre natus: true or false?', in *Homage to Horace. A Bimillenary Celebration* ed. S. J. Harrison (Oxford) 296–313.

Wilinski, A. (1971), 'Intorno all'"accusatio" e "revocatio in servitutem" del liberto ingrato', in *Studi in onore di Edoardo Volterra* (Milan) II 559–69.

(1974–75) 'Ricerche sull'alienazione degli schiavi nel diritto romano. Vendita dello schiavo con la clausola "ne manumittatur"', *Index* 5: 321–30.

Winterling, A. (1997), 'Hof ohne "Staat". Die *aula Caesaris* im 1. und 2. Jahrhundert n. Chr.', in *Zwischen 'Haus' und 'Staat'. Antike Höfe im Vergleich* ed. A. Winterling (HZ Beiheft 23: Munich) 91–112.

(1999), *Aula Caesaris. Studien zur Institutionalisierung des römischen Kaiserhofes in der Zeit von Augustus bis Commodus (31 v.Chr.–192 n.Chr.)* (Munich).

Wiseman, T. P. (1985), 'Who was Crassicius Pansa?', *TAPhA* 115: 187–96; reprinted in *Historiography and Imagination* (Exeter, 1994).

(1987), '*Conspicui postes tectaque digna deo*: the public image of aristocratic and imperial houses in the late republic and early empire', in *L'Urbs. Espace urbain et histoire* ed. C. Pietri (Rome) 393–413.

Witschel, C. (1995), 'Die Entwicklung der Gesellschaft von Timgad im 2. bis 4. Jh. n. Chr.', *Klio* 77: 266–331.

Witzmann, P. (2003), 'Integrations- und Identifikationsprozesse römischer Freigelassener nach Auskunft der Inschriften (1. Jh. v. Chr.)', in *O Tempora, o mores! Römische Werte und römische Literatur in den letzten Jahrzehnten der*

Republik ed. A. Haltenhoff, A. Heil, and F.-H. Mutschler (Munich and Leipzig) 289–321.

Wöhrle, G. (2005), 'Der "freie" Sklave. Antike Sklaverei und das Konzept der "inneren" Freiheit', in *Unfreie Arbeits- und Lebensverhältnisse von der Antike bis in die Gegenwart* ed. E. Herrmann-Otto (Hildesheim) 35–55.

Woods, R. (2007), 'Ancient and early modern mortality: experience and understanding', *Economic History Review* 60: 373–99.

Woolf, G. (1996), 'Monumental writing and the expansion of Roman society in the early empire', *JRS* 86: 22–39.

Yarrow, L. M. (2006), *Historiography at the End of the Republic. Provincial Perspectives on Roman Rule* (Oxford).

Zampieri, E. (2000), *Presenza servile e mobilità sociale in area altinate* (Portogruaro).

Zanker, P. (1975), 'Grabreliefs römischer Freigelassener', *JDAI* 90: 267–315.

(1988), *The Power of Images in the Age of Augustus* (Ann Arbor).

(1998), *Pompeii. Public and Private Life* (Cambridge, MA; 1st edn 1995).

Zelnick-Abramovitz, R. (2005), *Not Wholly Free. The Concept of Manumission and the Status of Manumitted Slaves in the Ancient Greek World* (Leiden).

Zulueta, F. De (1946), *The Institutes of Gaius* (Oxford).

Zwalve, W. J. (2002), 'Callistus' case. Some legal aspects of Roman business activities', in *The Transformation of Economic Life under the Roman Empire* ed. L. de Blois and J. Rich (Amsterdam) 116–27.

Index

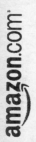

amazon.com

6221

SDRgkxmZMN

Returns Are Easy!
Visit http://www.amazon.com/returns to return any item - including gifts - if unopened, if original condition within 30 days for a full refund (other restrictions apply). Please have your order ID ready.

Purchase Order #: 36413
Your order of March 9, 2012 (Order ID 002-6873849-6010650)

Qty.	Item	Item Price	Total
1	The Civil War: The Second Year Told By Those Who Lived It (Library of America) Hardcover (** P-3-C58B103 **) 1598531441	$25.31	$25.31
1	The Freedman in the Roman World Hardcover (** P-3-F9D28 **) 0521856132	$91.49	$91.49

We've sent this part of your order to ensure quicker service.
The other items will ship separately.

Have feedback on how we packaged your order? Tell us at
www.amazon.com/packaging

Subtotal	$116.80
Shipping & Handling	$4.96
Tax Collected	$10.81
Shipment Total	$132.59
Paid via credit/debit	$132.59
Balance due	$0.00

A1

22/DRgkxmZMN/ 2 of 2 //CPS/std n us/7042442/0311-09 30/0309 22:20/sp0790906221/1 1

amazon.com

SDRgkxmZMN

Returns Are Easy!
Visit http://www.amazon.com/returns to return any item - including gifts - in unopened or original condition within 30 days for a full refund (other restrictions apply). Please have your order ID ready.

Purchase Order #: 36413
Your order of March 9, 2012 (Order ID 002-6873849-6010650)

Qty.	Item	Item Price	Total
1	**The Civil War: The Second Year Told By Those Who Lived It (Library of America)** Hardcover (** P-3-C58B103 **) 1598531441	$25.31	$25.31
1	**The Freedman in the Roman World** Hardcover (** P-3-F9D28 **) 0521856132	$91.49	$91.49

Subtotal	$116.80
Shipping & Handling	$4.98
Tax Collected	$10.81
Shipment Total	$132.59
Paid via credit/debit	$132.59
Balance due	$0.00

We've sent this part of your order to ensure quicker service.
The other items will ship separately.

Have feedback on how we packaged your order? Tell us at www.amazon.com/packaging.

22/DRgkxmZMN/-2 of 2-//CPS/std-n-us/7042442/0311-09:00/0309-22:14

A1